AF703011

THE SCOPE AND INTENSITY OF SUBSTANTIVE REVIEW

Inspired by the work of Professor Michael Taggart, this collection of essays from across the common law world is concerned with two separate but related themes. First, to what extent and by what means should review on substantive grounds such as unreasonableness be expanded and intensified? Jowell, Elliott and Varuhas all agree with Taggart that proportionality should not 'sweep the rainbow', but propose different schemes for organising and conceptualising substantive review. Groves and Weeks, and Hoexter evaluate the state of substantive review in Australia and South Africa respectively.

The second theme concerns the broader (Canadian) sense of substantive review including the illegality grounds, and whether deference should extend to these grounds. Cane and Aronson consider the relevance and impact of different constitutional and doctrinal settings. Wilberg and Daly address questions concerning when and how deference is to operate once it is accepted as appropriate in principle.

Rights-based review is discussed in a separate third part because it raises both of the above questions. Geiringer, Sales and Walters examine the choices to be made in settling the approach in this area, each focusing on a different dichotomy.

Taggart's work is notable for treating these various aspects of substantive review as parts of a broader whole, and for his search for an appropriate balance between judicial scrutiny and administrative autonomy across this entire area. By bringing together essays on all these topics, this volume seeks to build on that approach.

Volume 8 in the series Hart Studies in Comparative Public Law

Hart Studies in Comparative Public Law
Recent titles in this series:

Parliaments and Human Rights
Redressing the Democratic Deficit
Edited by Murray Hunt, Hayley Hooper and Paul Yowell

The Right to Freedom of Assembly
A Comparative Study
Orsolya Salát

An Inquiry into the Existence of Global Values
Through the Lens of Comparative Constitutional Law
Edited by Dennis Davis, Alan Richter and Cheryl Saunders

The Scope and Intensity of Substantive Review
Traversing Taggart's Rainbow
Edited by Hanna Wilberg and Mark Elliott

Entick v Carrington
250 Years of the Rule of Law
Edited by Adam Tomkins and Paul Scott

Administrative Law and Judicial Deference
Matthew Lewans

Soft Law and Public Authorities
Remedies and Reform
Greg Weeks

Legitimate Expectations in the Common Law World
Edited by Matthew Groves and Greg Weeks

The Dynamics of Exclusionary Constitutionalism
Mazen Masri

Constitutional Courts, Gay Rights and Sexual Orientation Equality
Angioletta Sperti

Principled Reasoning in Human Rights Adjudication
Se-Shauna Wheatle

Human Rights and Judicial Review in Australia and Canada
Janina Boughey

The Foundations and Traditions of Constitutional Amendment
Edited by Richard Albert, Xenophon Contiades and Alkmene Fotiadou

The Scope and Intensity of Substantive Review

Traversing Taggart's Rainbow

Edited by
Hanna Wilberg and Mark Elliott

•HART•
PUBLISHING
OXFORD AND PORTLAND, OREGON
2017

Hart Publishing
An imprint of Bloomsbury Publishing Plc

Hart Publishing Ltd
Kemp House
Chawley Park
Cumnor Hill
Oxford OX2 9PH
UK

Bloomsbury Publishing Plc
50 Bedford Square
London
WC1B 3DP
UK

www.hartpub.co.uk
www.bloomsbury.com

Published in North America (US and Canada) by
Hart Publishing
c/o International Specialized Book Services
920 NE 58th Avenue, Suite 300
Portland, OR 97213-3786
USA

www.isbs.com

HART PUBLISHING, the Hart/Stag logo, BLOOMSBURY and the Diana logo are trademarks of Bloomsbury Publishing Plc

First published in hardback, 2015
Paperback edition, 2017

© The Editors and Contributors, severally 2015

The Editors and Contributors have asserted their right under the Copyright, Designs and Patents Act 1988 to be identified as the Authors of this work.

All rights reserved. No part of this publication may be reproduced or transmitted in any form or by any means, electronic or mechanical, including photocopying, recording, or any information storage or retrieval system, without prior permission in writing from the publishers.

While every care has been taken to ensure the accuracy of this work, no responsibility for loss or damage occasioned to any person acting or refraining from action as a result of any statement in it can be accepted by the authors, editors or publishers.

All UK Government legislation and other public sector information used in the work is Crown Copyright ©. All House of Lords and House of Commons information used in the work is Parliamentary Copyright ©. This information is reused under the terms of the Open Government Licence v3.0 (http://www.nationalarchives. gov.uk/doc/open-government-licence/version/3) except where otherwise stated.

All Eur-lex material used in the work is © European Union, http://eur-lex.europa.eu/, 1998–2017.

British Library Cataloguing-in-Publication Data
A catalogue record for this book is available from the British Library.

ISBN: PB: 978-1-50991-704-4
HB: 978-1-84946-468-0

Typeset by Compuscript Ltd, Shannon
Printed and bound in Great Britain by
Lightning Source UK Ltd

To find out more about our authors and books visit www.hartpublishing.co.uk. Here you will find extracts, author information, details of forthcoming events and the option to sign up for our newsletters.

Foreword

When Michael Taggart died prematurely in 2009, the world of legal scholarship suffered a double loss. For many of us, the loss was that of a personal friend, for Mike had an unusual talent for friendship and even those of us who knew him for a comparatively short time felt the opening of a gap that would be hard to fill. This sense of loss was represented at the time in the number of obituaries and festschrifts that quickly followed. Equally, however, there was a diminishment in the wider world of legal scholarship because Mike was himself a considerable and innovative legal scholar with an unusually broad set of interests. He wrote as well on legal history as on modern judicial review and tackled uncommon subjects, ranging from an in-depth study of the purely domestic and private law topic of the nineteenth-century nuisance case of *Bradford v Pickles* to the impact of apartheid and globalisation on administrative law.

But this collection of essays is emphatically not a further festschrift. Its aim is something very different. It adopts a determinedly forward-looking perspective on Mike's achievements and uses the questions he was never tired of asking as a starting-point for further questions about the way the law is developing. In the Editors' own words, the impetus for the collection has been 'a desire to engage with and build on Taggart's work'. In so doing, they have wisely decided to concentrate on a narrow segment of Mike's wide interests, homing in on his work on judicial review. On this he wrote several provocative essays, challenging the formalist and revisionist character of Australian judicial review but also questioning and critiquing the often flabby reasoning of rights-based judicial review as it emerged in Canada and the UK. This collection concentrates on two particular themes: the development of reasonableness review into something deeper and more intensive than the classical *Wednesbury* formula would seem to allow and the relationship between courts and legislature as formulated in the doctrine of judicial deference.

This collection also represents two further concerns dear to Mike's heart. Mike was a comparative lawyer of a particular kind, interested in and concerned for the development of the common law throughout the Commonwealth and anxious to stimulate dialogue throughout the common law world, an enterprise in which he was remarkably successful. Mike had a particular gift for initiating such encounters and would undoubtedly have welcomed, participated in and seized upon the possibilities of the recent conference held under the aegis of the Cambridge Centre for Public Law and attended by visitors from throughout the Commonwealth.

On a smaller scale, this collection too strongly reflects the dialogue theme with contributions from Australia, Canada, South Africa and the United Kingdom, as well as Mike's own country of New Zealand.

Mike was an inspiring and devoted teacher, dedicated to developing the young and his interest in youth and the ideas of the young is also represented in this collection. Many of the contributors were longstanding friends of Mike's and, like Mark Aronson, Cora Hoexter, Jeffrey Jowell and Peter Cane, are well-established in their professional careers, as was Mike himself. It is pleasant, however, to see a younger generation of rising legal scholars, some of them his students or colleagues, engaging with Mike's work and helping to carry it forward. In this way it will stand as a benchmark for future scholarship and token of friendship across the common law world in which we all work and believe.

Carol Harlow
January 2015

Preface and Acknowledgements

The concept for this book was suggested to us by our reading of Professor Mike Taggart's work—a debt which we have sought to acknowledge in the book's subtitle. We are similarly indebted to our wonderful contributors for agreeing to join us in this project; for their varied and thought-provoking contributions to this book; for reviewing other contributions; and for their advice and support along the way.

We are grateful to Richard Hart for agreeing to our proposal and for his advice. The public law community has been so very fortunate in having had Richard as a publisher, and he will be sadly missed following his well-earned retirement from this endeavour. We also thank Rachel Turner of Hart Publishing for all her help in shepherding the book from the proposal through to publication—she has been a joy to work with.

During 2014, Hanna was on research leave first at the University of Cambridge and then at the University of Toronto, when most of the work on this book was completed. Her thanks go to Mark Elliott for being a wonderful host in Cambridge; the Cambridge and Toronto law faculties and Clare Hall, Cambridge, for providing such a conducive working environment; Herbert Smith Freehills for funding the faculty's visitor scheme at Cambridge; the University of Auckland for granting her leave; and her colleagues at the Auckland law faculty for shouldering her usual teaching and administration duties.

Mark's involvement in this project came about as a result of his being the New Zealand Legal Research Foundation Visiting Scholar in 2011, in which capacity he was based at the University of Auckland. He is grateful to the Legal Research Foundation for funding his visit to New Zealand; to Hanna Wilberg for being instrumental in the organisation of his visit and for being an outstanding host; and for the many opportunities afforded by the Faculty of Law in Auckland to discuss ideas relevant to his own chapter in this book and to the wider project that subsequently developed into this co-edited volume.

Hanna Wilberg
Mark Elliott
November 2014

Table of Contents

List of Contributors

Mark Aronson is Emeritus Professor of Law at the University of New South Wales.

Peter Cane is Distinguished Professor of Law at the Australian National University.

Paul Daly is an Assistant Professor of Law at the University of Montreal.

Mark Elliott is a Reader in Public Law at the University of Cambridge and a Fellow of St Catharine's College, Cambridge.

Claudia Geiringer is Professor of Public Law at the Victoria University of Wellington and Director of the New Zealand Centre of Public Law.

Matthew Groves is a Professor of Law at Monash University, Melbourne.

Cora Hoexter is Professor of Law at the University of the Witwatersrand, Johannesburg.

Jeffrey Jowell is Director of the Bingham Centre for the Rule of Law, a practising barrister and Professor Emeritus of Public Law at University College London.

Philip Sales is a Lord Justice of Appeal of the Court of Appeal in England and Wales.

Jason NE Varuhas is a Senior Lecturer at the Faculty of Law, University of New South Wales and a Fellow of Christ's College, University of Cambridge.

Mark D Walters is a Professor of Law at Queen's University, Ontario.

Greg Weeks is a Lecturer in Law at the University of New South Wales.

Hanna Wilberg is a Senior Lecturer in Law at the University of Auckland.

1

Introduction

MARK ELLIOTT AND HANNA WILBERG

I. THE NATURE AND PURPOSE OF THIS EDITED COLLECTION

THIS BOOK IS concerned with pursuing two separate but related central themes that we see in Professor Mike Taggart's scholarship on substantive grounds of judicial review. The first theme is addressed in part A of the book. It concerns the extent to which review of the merits, traditionally limited to *Wednesbury* unreasonableness, should be expanded into more intensive reasonableness review, or new substantive grounds of review, or both. In Taggart's final article on substantive review, entitled 'Proportionality, Deference, *Wednesbury*',[1] the headline point was his surprising and controversial conversion to the 'bifurcation' of judicial review into 'rights cases' and 'public wrongs' cases.[2] However, the article was by no means confined to that point. It was also Taggart's final contribution on a much wider range of issues concerning substantive grounds of review. A desire to engage with and build on Taggart's work on this wider range of issues forms the backdrop to and impetus for this collection. The aim, however, is not to revisit already well-trodden ground, but to provide an opportunity for scholars from across the common-law world to take forward aspects of the debate concerning substantive judicial review.

The second theme is addressed in part B. It concerns the extent to which deference is appropriate on questions of law—a question which Taggart raised most prominently in his essay on 'The Contribution of Lord Cooke to Scope of Review Doctrine in Administrative Law'.[3] Both themes are

[1] M Taggart, 'Proportionality, Deference, *Wednesbury*' [2008] *New Zealand Law Review* 423.

[2] This is the focus of the 2010 special issue of the *New Zealand Law Review* responding to Taggart's article; and also of M Hunt, 'Against Bifurcation' in D Dyzenhaus, M Hunt and G Huscroft (eds), *A Simple Common Lawyer: Essays in Honour of Michael Taggart* (Oxford, Hart Publishing, 2009) 99.

[3] M Taggart, 'The Contribution of Lord Cooke to Scope of Review Doctrine in Administrative Law: A Comparative Common Law Perspective' in P Rishworth (ed), *The Struggle for Simplicity in the Law: Essays in Honour of Lord Cooke of Thorndon* (Wellington, Butterworths, 1997) 189.

concerned with substantive review, but in two different senses of that phrase. The first, in part A, is the narrower sense in which the phrase is most commonly used in the United Kingdom, Australia and New Zealand—relating to judicial examination of the substantive merits of a decision. The second sense in which substantive review is considered in part B is the broader sense in which the phrase is commonly used in Canada—embracing questions of legality as well as merits questions. The question in relation to this broader sense of substantive review is the opposite of that in part A: not whether such review should be expanded, but whether its intensity should be reduced in some contexts by introducing deference.

Why review for legality should be treated as a species of substantive review is most obvious, even from the first perspective, in cases where judicial determination of the legal scope of a power serves to restrict the range of substantive decisions that are open to the decision-maker. The classification of legality issues as substantive is more contentious in cases involving legal process review that serves only (albeit importantly) to regulate the reasoning process and in that sense how, not what, decisions are made.

On each of these two themes, in addition to inviting fresh contributions to the debate, we have also taken the opportunity to present an attempt at an overview of the existing state of the debate—necessarily a personal and contestable exercise, but hopefully no less valid or useful for that. We have re-read Taggart's main contributions to the debates in order to identify what, in our view, are the main themes in that body of work, as well as to grapple with some puzzles. And we have identified some central themes in the wider existing literature and some notable existing contributions to those themes. The first chapter in each of parts A and B is devoted to these surveys.

Part C of the book deals with rights-based review, including in that category both rights that are protected by statute or by a written constitution, and fundamental common-law rights. As explained further in the introduction to this part below, we devote a separate part of the book to this topic because it potentially raises both of the questions addressed in the first two parts.

The varied and stimulating contributions to this book on these three topics come from several common-law jurisdictions. The contributors include both leading authorities in the field and members of the new generation of administrative law scholars. The inclusion of the latter seemed particularly appropriate in a book inspired by Mike Taggart, who never missed an opportunity to foster and encourage the work of younger colleagues. The ready willingness of all these scholars to contribute is further testament to the high regard in which Taggart was held around the common-law world, as well as to the continuing relevance of the questions about substantive review to which he devoted much of his work.

II. PART A: MODERN EXTENSIONS OF SUBSTANTIVE REVIEW

Throughout the common-law world, whether—and, if so, how far—judicial review should entail scrutiny of the merits is a vexed question. In orthodoxy, at least in the UK, Australia, New Zealand and South Africa, only very limited judicial incursion into that realm of substance is countenanced, its extent being severely circumscribed by such devices as the *Wednesbury* doctrine—which, in the words of Lord Greene MR, permits curial intervention only when the impugned administrative measure is 'so unreasonable that no reasonable authority could ever have come to it'.[4] This self-denying judicial ordinance is the doctrinal bedrock upon which the hallowed distinction between 'appeal' and 'review' is built, thus ensuring that—as Laws LJ has put it—the court 'does not ask itself the question, "Is this decision right or wrong?"', and so underlining the fact that (on this view, at least) 'judicial review has nothing to do with the question, "Which view is the better one?"'[5]

However, the adequacy of judicial oversight thus confined is increasingly questioned. This is so not least (but not only) as a result of growing emphasis in many common-law systems upon fundamental rights as entitlements that deserve to be guarded more jealously by courts than bare *Wednesbury* scrutiny would permit. Meanwhile, such normative concerns are accompanied by taxonomic doubts about whether 'process', 'legality' and 'substance' are meaningfully distinct categories separated by dividing lines capable of bearing the weight placed on them by mainstream administrative law theory.

Against the background of such considerations, part A of the book is concerned with several interlocking questions about the contemporary nature of substantive judicial review in common-law jurisdictions. It commences with our contribution in which we take the opportunity to present our understanding of what Taggart stood for in this area, followed by a survey of the existing wider literature on the subject.

One of the questions that arises in this area and which is considered in part A concerns whether substantive review should be confined by reference to the *Wednesbury* test or some variant of it—although as several contributions to this volume show, that question is really only a manifestation of underlying issues of doctrinal and constitutional structure. That substantive review should not *always* be thus limited is now readily accepted in most, if not all, common-law jurisdictions. However, while the proposition that substantive review should extend beyond *Wednesbury* may attract a

[4] *Associated Provincial Picture Houses Ltd v Wednesbury Corporation* [1948] 1 KB 223, 230 (CA).

[5] *R v Somerset County Council, ex p Fewings* [1995] 1 All ER 513, 515 (QBD).

reasonable degree of consensus, there is far less by way of agreement when it comes to deciding precisely *when* a more exacting approach ought to be adopted. In particular, there is disagreement about whether *Wednesbury* should be jettisoned altogether, or whether it should be eclipsed by a more demanding standard in only certain contexts.

Some scholars, notably Paul Craig, have argued in favour of the former approach (although Craig contends that appropriate invocation of deference means that replacing *Wednesbury* with proportionality would not necessarily result in a uniformly more intensive standard of review).[6] However, in their contributions to this volume, Jeffrey Jowell and Jason Varuhas adopt a different view, arguing that the *Wednesbury* test should not be entirely dispensed with. Jowell revisits the subject matter of his seminal 1987 article, written with Anthony Lester, in which reliance upon *Wednesbury* was criticised and the development of individuated, substantive principles of judicial review was urged.[7] In his chapter in this book, Jowell maintains, in line with the 1987 paper, that many cases of substantive judicial review disclose—whether explicitly or otherwise—the protection of values more precise than anything implied by a bald test of reasonableness. He also argues that the proportionality test, as distinct from any modified form of rationality test,[8] is the appropriate vehicle for judicial scrutiny of administrative action that impinges upon fundamental rights (whether statutory or common-law rights). Nevertheless, Jowell contends that proportionality 'cannot occupy the entire space of substantive review', and concludes that a residual role for the reasonableness test remains.

Varuhas also considers whether *Wednesbury* should be retained alongside proportionality, but he approaches this question by way of consideration of underlying issues concerning the structure of judicial review. In particular, he considers whether the law of judicial review should be conceptualised in unified terms or in terms that are bifurcated by reference to a distinction between cases that are and are not concerned with human rights. Varuhas argues that there are fundamental differences between substantive review as it pertains to human rights and substantive review as it operates in other contexts. In the UK context, argues Varuhas, common-law substantive review and review under the Human Rights Act 1998 (HRA) are functionally distinct. He advances this claim by reference to a number of different matters, including standing, remedies and matters of procedure, and argues that, at root, the purposes of the law in these two areas are distinct. The primary function of review under the HRA is the protection and vindication of individuals' fundamental rights, whereas the primary function of

[6] P Craig, *Administrative Law*, 7th edn (London, Sweet & Maxwell, 2012) 669.

[7] J Jowell and A Lester, 'Beyond *Wednesbury*: Substantive Principles of Administrative Law' [1987] *Public Law* 368.

[8] Such as the 'anxious scrutiny' test. See, eg *Bugdaycay v Secretary of State for the Home Department* [1987] 1 AC 514.

common-law review is to ensure that public power is exercised properly and in the public interest. To the extent that this entails the protection of individual rights, such protection is *incidental* to common-law review's main purpose. Against this background, Varuhas argues that public law in the UK has not been and should not be unified.

If, contrary to the 'unification' theory, an approach more demanding than *Wednesbury* is warranted only in certain contexts, a further question arises as to what exactly those contexts are. One way of drawing the line is by reference to the rights/non-rights distinction that is at the heart of the school of thought that supports bifurcation. In his chapter in this volume, Mark Elliott, while joining with writers like Taggart and Varuhas in resisting the notion of unification, questions whether the rights/non-rights distinction is an adequate way of mapping the terrain of substantive review. Elliott argues that it may be preferable to adopt a more flexible approach to determining the standard of substantive review that acknowledges more explicitly the variable normative purchase of different rights and other values. Elliott contends that such an approach is facilitated by distinguishing between two different senses of deference—'intrinsic' and 'adjudicative' deference—and that these can be used to determine the intensity of substantive review that is appropriate in any given case.

Matthew Groves and Greg Weeks are also concerned in their chapter with questions about the circumstances in which an approach to substantive review more demanding than *Wednesbury* might obtain. Their focus is on Australia, which, they point out, is exceptional in the common-law world by virtue of lacking an enumeration of fundamental rights.[9] Groves and Weeks argue that a more demanding approach is only possible if some 'anchor point'—in the form of a set of values whose infraction triggers something more than *Wednesbury* review—can be identified. They advance this argument on both normative and methodological grounds. However, they resist the suggestion that in the absence of a bill of rights or equivalent text there cannot be any anchor point upon which more demanding review might fasten. To the contrary, they argue that while the identification of fundamental values in the absence of a relevant legislative text is not without difficulty, an anchor point may already be immanent within the common law in the form of the principle of legality and the particular constitutional values associated with that principle.

Groves and Weeks's chapter serves as an important reminder that questions about substantive review are highly sensitive to matters of constitutional context. This point is underscored by Cora Hoexter's contribution to this book. She is concerned with substantive judicial review as it exists in the very different context of the new South African constitutional system. Hoexter notes that under the new constitutional dispensation in South

[9] Certain states have adopted bills of rights, but there is no federal bill of rights.

Africa, a somewhat bifurcated approach to judicial review was initially discernible, with more and less intensive approaches applying, depending upon whether the constitutional right to just administrative action is engaged. However, she goes on to argue that the distinction between the two approaches to review has been largely eroded, and that the earlier 'twin track' approach has largely been eclipsed. In this way, Hoexter's analysis intersects with questions relating both to the unification/bifurcation debate—albeit within the very particular circumstances of the South African Constitution—and the relevance to substantive judicial review of the sort of constitutional anchor point that Groves and Weeks refer to in their chapter concerning Australia.

III. PART B: DEFERENCE ON QUESTIONS OF LAW?

It will be recalled that part B of this book concerns the extent to which deference is appropriate on questions of law. To put it more concretely: 'Whose interpretation of statute law should prevail—that of the Judge or that of the administrative decision-maker?'[10]

For Canadian readers, this question naturally belongs in a book on substantive review: as noted earlier, the phrase 'substantive review' is most commonly used in Canada in a broad sense, embracing questions of legality as well as merits questions. Following the Canadians, that was also, we think, the way Taggart thought about the subject.

In the UK, Australia and New Zealand, in contrast, this broader sense of substantive review is more likely to be seen as challenging orthodoxy. In these jurisdictions, questions of legality tend to be seen as part of 'process' in a broader sense. Like process, legality is usually understood—and orthodox theory constructed—by reference to the distinction between it and the merits.[11] But it is not difficult to see that at least some legality questions can also be characterised as falling on the 'substance' side of the line between process and substance.[12] This is so most obviously when a judicial determination as to the legal scope of a power limits the range of substantive options that are open to the decision-maker. The effect of such legality review is quite different from the effect of process-oriented review, and, if a process–substance distinction is to be adhered to, can be accommodated much more readily on the 'substance' side of the line.

In Canada, indeed, the line between legality and merits has increasingly been questioned, and this is part of the background and reasons for the acceptance in that jurisdiction of deference on questions of law as well

[10] Taggart, 'Proportionality' (n 1) 195.

[11] See *Chief Constable of North Wales Police v Evans* [1982] 1 WLR 1155.

[12] The classification of some other legality issues is more open to argument, as noted earlier.

as on the merits. This is again a point on which Taggart adopted a more Canadian perspective. In his work, support for expansion of substantive grounds of review was always counterbalanced by his recognition of the need for judicial restraint or deference in appropriate contexts. The latter took the form both of his ultimate opposition to proportionality as a ground for review in non-rights cases (discussed in part A), and of his support for deference on questions of law.

In the United States and in Canada, there is a large literature and case law on this question of deference on questions of law and statutory interpretation. In Canada, the usual standard of review on issues of statutory interpretation is now 'reasonableness'—only a few special categories of case are said to attract a 'correctness' standard that involves the court substituting its own view.[13] A detailed account of this approach—and of the extent to which it is adhered to in practice—may be found in Paul Daly's essay in this part. Similarly, as outlined in Peter Cane's essay, in the United States in certain types of cases a reasonableness standard applies to review of administrative interpretations of statutes unless Congress is held to have spoken directly to the issue.[14]

In stark contrast, the topic is rarely even mentioned in the UK, New Zealand or Australia.[15] Courts there take it as a fundamental constitutional principle, largely without any questioning, that questions of law are questions for courts. In New Zealand, *Bulk Gas* established a strong, all but irrebuttable presumption that Parliament does not intend to empower administrative decision-makers to determine questions of law conclusively.[16] In doing so, it followed dicta of Lord Diplock in *Racal*[17] and *O'Reilly*[18] that further developed the House of Lords' landmark decision in *Anisminic*.[19] It anticipated *Page*, where the House of Lords confirmed the same position for the UK.[20] The rationale was that 'it is the constitutional role of the superior Courts to interpret the laws enacted by Parliament'.[21] Courts therefore 'have the function of interpreting Acts of Parliament

[13] *Dunsmuir v New Brunswick* 2008 SCC 9, [2008] 1 SCR 190; *Alberta (Information and Privacy Commissioner) v Alberta Teachers' Association* 2011 SCC 61, [2011] 3 SCR 654, [34].

[14] *Chevron USA Inc v NRDC* (1984) 467 US 837; and see the qualifications introduced in *United States v Mead Corp* (2001) 533 US 218.

[15] But see, for examples of the question at least being asked in passing, H Woolf and others, *De Smith's Judicial Review*, 7th edn (London, Sweet & Maxwell, 2013) 251; M Elliott, *Beatson, Matthews and Elliott's Administrative Law: Text and Materials*, 4th edn (Oxford, Oxford University Press, 2011) ch 2.

[16] *Bulk Gas Users Group v Attorney-General* [1983] NZLR 129 (CA), 133, 136; Taggart, 'Scope of Review' (n 3) 195.

[17] *Re Racal Communications Ltd* [1981] AC 374 (HL).

[18] *O'Reilly v Mackman* [1983] 2 AC 237 (HL).

[19] *Anisminic Ltd v Foreign Compensation Commission* [1969] 2 AC 147 (HL).

[20] *R v Hull University Visitor, ex p Page* [1993] AC 682 (HL).

[21] Taggart, 'Scope of Review' (n 3) 192.

and the duty to correct any errors of law made'.[22] Much the same view is confirmed for Australia by the High Court's dicta in the leading *Enfield* case: the Constitution allocates interpretive power exclusively to the judiciary.[23]

Paul Craig was the leading commentator in the UK who drew attention to the alternative approach observable in the United States, and suggested that this at least raised questions about the appropriateness of the English approach.[24] In New Zealand, the task of opening up this perspective was taken up by Taggart, whose focus was on the Canadian version of the North American deference approach and on the arguments developed there in support of that approach.[25]

The contributions to this volume pursue three lines of enquiry concerning deference on questions of law: first, the nature of the questions arising and the range of views on them; secondly, the extent to which different answers to these questions reflect different substantive commitments and priorities; and thirdly, questions remaining even once it is agreed that there should be deference on questions of law.

A. The Nature of the Questions Arising

The debate about deference on questions of law may be said to be centrally and fundamentally about reserving some autonomy to primary decision-makers by placing some limits on the extent to which reviewing courts will substitute their views. However, it must be immediately acknowledged that both sides agree on the need for *some* such autonomy: at a minimum, all agree that review on the merits and review of findings of fact cannot be on a correctness standard. That would entirely collapse the distinction between appeal and review, and amount to judicial usurpation of power allocated by legislation to the primary decision-makers.

What the debate is really about, then, is the types of questions to which this autonomy should apply—specifically, whether it should apply to questions of law as well as to factual findings and the merits. This turns broadly on two types of question. The first type are conceptual questions. Is it conceptually possible to draw a line between questions of law and other questions (facts and merits)? And if so, are questions of law capable of having more than one valid answer, or at least of indeterminacy as to what the best answer is? The second type are constitutional questions. If a line can

[22] Ibid, 195, referring to *Bulk Gas* (n 16) 133 and Lord Diplock in *Re Racal* (n 17) 382–83.

[23] *City of Enfield v Development Assessment Commission* (2000) 199 CLR 135 (HCA).

[24] P Craig, 'Jurisdiction, Judicial Control, and Agency Autonomy' in I Loveland (ed), *A Special Relationship? American Influences on Public Law in the UK* (Oxford, Oxford University Press, 1995) 173; P Craig, *Administrative Law* (n 6) ch 14.

[25] Taggart, 'Scope of Review' (n 3).

be drawn around questions of law, what is its constitutional significance as far as the power and responsibility of reviewing courts are concerned: what is the meaning and import of the rule of law, the separation of powers, and respect for Parliament's allocation of authority in this context? Do these principles demand correctness review on questions of law, or do they require deference on such questions in at least some contexts? There is fundamental disagreement on all of these questions, as outlined in this part in our survey of Taggart's contribution and of themes in the wider existing literature on this topic.

B. Possible Explanations for Different Answers

However, it should not be assumed that different answers to the constitutional questions must necessarily reflect different constitutional values and priorities. In the first instance, different answers to the constitutional questions may flow from different conceptual underpinnings. In addition, different answers may also flow in part from different *structures* of constitutional or doctrinal analysis and organisation—different ways of skinning the same proverbial cat. Two of the contributions to this part pursue this latter line of thought.

First, the same ultimate goals of controlling public power and protecting those subject to it may be served by a variety of different constitutional structures, within which courts play correspondingly different roles. This is the idea presented and pursued in Peter Cane's contribution to this volume in relation to Australia and the United States. He outlines and compares the relevant historical and constitutional setting in the two jurisdictions, suggesting reasons why a deferential approach developed in the United States but not in Australia. In particular, he points to the different versions of the separation of powers that are embodied in the two constitutions, which entail very different models of the judicial function and of the nature of judicial power. He also points out, however, that the difference does reflect opposite answers to the conceptual question whether there can be more than one correct interpretation of a provision.

Secondly, a focus on the deference question alone may give a very misleading impression as to the degree of autonomy reserved for primary decision-makers in different jurisdictions. Mark Aronson's contribution to this volume reminds us that there is a range of other doctrinal devices that may be, and are, used to carve out such autonomy. Resort to such alternative devices may be denigrated as manipulation and lacking transparency, and Taggart was inclined to see it that way.[26] But even where such devices

[26] Ibid.

are used in an explicitly pragmatic and functional fashion, this may also be seen more positively as a way of accommodating the universal need for an adequate measure of administrative autonomy within the variety of different constitutional and doctrinal contexts of different jurisdictions. That is the view advanced in Aronson's chapter, in which he surveys five common-law jurisdictions, identifying the devices used to carve out administrative autonomy in each jurisdiction and locating these devices within the constitutional and doctrinal contexts of those jurisdictions. Aside from the devices used, the differences he notes also include that autonomy is accorded to different types of bodies and for different reasons.

C. Questions Remaining Once Deference on Questions of Law is Accepted

Finally, even if the possibility of deference on questions of law is accepted in principle, many further questions remain. Two of the contributions to this part concern such questions.

One set of questions concerns what deference on questions of law means more concretely, and exactly when it should apply. Hanna Wilberg's contribution concerns the latter question. Her focus is on a particular group of grounds: the grounds of irrelevant considerations, failure to consider mandatory considerations, and improper purpose. She considers how these grounds should be categorised (which leads her into the conceptual question whether questions of law can be distinguished from other questions), and how they fit into both deferential and non-deferential approaches.

Another question is whether and how deference on questions of law can be made to work in practice. Both of the North American jurisdictions that have adopted deference on questions of law have experienced anything but plain sailing in this area since then. Paul Daly's contribution to this volume focuses on Canada and traces this voyage in detail. The persistent theme he identifies is the continuing challenge of maintaining a judicial commitment to deference on questions of law. This ties in with the earlier point about different structures of analysis leading to different answers: Daly notes that the move to deference on questions of law in Canada involved a paradigm shift, and points to the lingering influence of the old paradigm as a destabilising influence.

Taken in combination, the chapters that form part B of this volume demonstrate that although every system of administrative law must grapple with questions about deference on issues of law, the pervasiveness of such questions is not matched by any uniformity in the answers that are adopted. In this way, the contributions to this part of the book show that the extent and appropriateness of deference in this area are, at least to some extent, functions of institutional design and constitutional structure and history that inevitably vary from system to system. Even though this means that great caution must be exercised before concluding that a given common-law jurisdiction might profitably borrow from another's approach in this area, it does not undermine the utility of comparative work in this area. Far from it: understanding how and why things might be done differently elsewhere allows us to examine our own jurisdiction with fresh eyes, and to adopt a suitably critical approach to assessing the adequacy of its response to the complex questions that arise in this area.

IV. PART C: RIGHTS-BASED REVIEW

As noted, the third and final part of the book deals with rights-based review, including in that category both rights that are protected by statute or by a written constitution and fundamental common-law rights. While rights also feature frequently in part A, that is by way of considering the extent to which approaches that are established and appropriate in rights cases may be extended to other types of cases. This part, on the other hand, concerns the approach that should be taken to rights cases.

We devote a separate part of the book to this topic because it potentially raises both of the questions addressed in the first two parts. Rights claims are often seen as matters of law, and so it is often thought that they are among the areas that are most obviously the domain of the courts. Yet at the same time, it is also widely appreciated that issues about justification for limits on rights are a type of question that concerns the substantive merits, on which courts have traditionally accorded very substantial deference to decision-makers.

The tension between those two aspects of the topic indeed accounts for much of the unsettled nature of the law in this area.[27] The picture is also complicated by further distinctions, including those between rights enshrined in statute and common-law rights, and between administrative law and constitutional law. In the different contexts of the various common-law jurisdictions, these several fault-lines throw up different sets of issues. The contributions to this volume concern aspects of three such sets of issues: whether and what type of deference is appropriate in applying the proportionality test that applies in the context of statutory rights guarantees; the appropriate methodology for administrative law protection of common-law rights; and the appropriate methodology for administrative law protection of constitutional rights guarantees.

[27] See P Rishworth and others, *The New Zealand Bill of Rights* (Auckland, Oxford University Press, 2003) ch 5.8 (by G Huscroft); DR Knight, 'Mapping the Rainbow of Review: Recognising Variable Intensity' [2010] *New Zealand Law Review* 393, 427–29.

A. Statutory Rights: Deference in Relation to Proportionality?

In jurisdictions with a statutory bill of rights, the structure of the inquiry in cases invoking those rights is fairly well established (albeit that the precise details turn upon the particular bill of rights in question): it is necessary to ask whether a right is engaged on its proper interpretation, whether the infringement of the right can be justified, often by reference to a proportionality test, and whether an unjustified limit is nevertheless authorised by the empowering statute or whether that statute can be read so as not to authorise such unjustified limits.[28] However, it remains a highly unsettled question, thanks at least in part to the conceptual tension mentioned above, whether and to what extent deference may be due in disposing of rights-based challenges, and in particular in applying the proportionality test. In the UK, most commentators agree that there must be some room for deference,[29] and many cases follow this approach.[30] However, many judges and some commentators have attacked deference as constitutionally improper.[31] In New Zealand, it has recently been pointed out that in administrative law cases, courts may be engaging in an extreme form of deference in tacitly forbearing from carrying out a proportionality enquiry at all.[32]

Claudia Geiringer's essay in this part explores another possible version of tacit deference, according to which courts might adopt partly process- rather than purely results-oriented review when dealing with rights claims. Process-based review means review of primary decision-makers' reasoning processes, the effect of which is to impose a duty on those decision-makers to apply a proportionality test—or at least engage to some extent with the issues raised by that test—before reaching decisions that limit

[28] See, eg *R (Aguilar Quila) v Secretary of State for the Home Department* [2011] UKSC 45, [2012] 1 AC 621; *R v Hansen* [2007] NZSC 7, [2007] 3 NZLR 1.

[29] See, eg J McLean, P Rishworth and M Taggart, 'The Impact of the New Zealand Bill of Rights on Administrative Law' in *The New Zealand Bill of Rights Act 1990* (Auckland, Legal Research Foundation, 1992) 62, 78–79, 87 and 96; M Elliott, 'Proportionality and Deference: The Importance of a Structured Approach' in C Forsyth and others (eds), *Effective Judicial Review: A Cornerstone of Good Governance* (Oxford, Oxford University Press, 2010) 264; J Rivers 'Proportionality and Variable Intensity of Review' (2006) 65 *Cambridge Law Journal* 174; A Kavanagh, 'Defending Deference in Public Law and Constitutional Theory' (2010) 126 *Law Quarterly Review* 222.

[30] See, eg *R (Daly) v Secretary of State for the Home Department* [2001] UKHL 26, [2001] 2 AC 532, [28]; *R (SB) v Governors of Denbigh High School* [2006] UKHL 15, [2007] 1 AC 100; *Aguilar Quila* (n 28), [46], but cf [61]; *Ministry of Health v Atkinson* [2012] NZCA 184, [2012] 3 NZLR 456.

[31] See, eg *Huang v Secretary of State for the Home Department* [2007] 2 AC 167 (HL) [16] (Lord Bingham); *R (ProLife Alliance) v British Broadcasting Corporation* [2003] UKHL 33, [2004] 1 AC 185 (HL) [75]–[77] (Lord Hoffmann); T Allan, 'Human Rights and Judicial Review: A Critique of "Due Deference"' [2006] *Cambridge Law Journal* 671.

[32] C Geiringer, 'Sources of Resistance to Proportionality Review of Administrative Power Under the New Zealand Bill of Rights Act' (2013) 11 *New Zealand Journal of Public and International Law* 123; cf H Wilberg, 'The Bill of Rights in Administrative Law Cases: Taking Stock and Suggesting Some Reassessment' (2013) 25 *New Zealand Universities Law Review* 866.

statutory or constitutional rights. Where this is preferred to results-oriented rights-review, that could be seen as a form of deference: a court may desist from substituting its view of what the right requires, provided that the decision-maker has properly addressed that question. Whether this form of review is really less intrusive is, however, very much a contentious question, and Geiringer joins other commentators who have cast doubt on that idea. She also outlines several other policy arguments for and against such an approach, and traces the fortunes of those arguments in the different contexts of the English, Australian, Canadian and New Zealand human rights instruments.

B. Common-Law Rights: Protected via Legality or Rationality?

Both the UK and New Zealand retain, alongside their statutory human rights instruments, an active strand of case law concerning fundamental common-law rights.[33] There remains considerable uncertainty, however, as to the choice of doctrinal means by which such rights are to be protected, and consequently also as to the applicable standard or intensity of review. Courts have variously used one of two distinct options, largely without ever acknowledging that there is a choice, let alone discussing how the choice should be made.[34]

One option is to apply an interpretive presumption of consistency with fundamental common-law rights to empowering provisions—sometimes in the form of the so-called 'principle of legality' according to which general words do not abrogate fundamental rights.[35] Since the impact of the right on this approach is on the *vires*—the legal scope of the power, there is not usually any whiff of deference to be detected when this approach is used. The alternative option is to invoke the fact that a fundamental right is affected as a reason for increasing the intensity of review on the traditional unreasonableness ground—this is known as 'heightened scrutiny' or by various similar expressions.[36] Even with the rights-motivated increase in scrutiny, however, this approach still necessarily involves a degree of deference: the court reviews the rationality of the decision, not its legal correctness. By way of extension of this alternative approach, many consider that a proportionality test should be adopted instead of the heightened scrutiny unreasonableness test; but so far, case law remains equivocal on this further

[33] See, eg *Osborn v Parole Board* [2013] UKSC 61, [2013] 3 WLR 1020; *Cropp v Judicial Committee* [2008] NZSC 46, [2008] 3 NZLR 774 (SC).

[34] See, generally, M Elliott, *Constitutional Foundations of Judicial Review* (Oxford, Hart Publishing, 2001) 209–18; M Fordham and T de la Mare, 'Anxious scrutiny, the principle of legality and the Human Rights Act' [2000] *Judicial Review* 40.

[35] *R v Lord Chancellor, ex p Witham* [1998] QB 575.

[36] *R v Ministry of Defence, ex p Smith* [1996] QB 517 (CA). *Wolf v Minister of Immigration* [2004] NZAR 414 (HC).

step.[37] However, even if this further extension were unequivocally adopted, it would still likely involve at least the same degree of deference as that which is attracted when infractions of statutory human rights are alleged.

It is possible, and arguably attractive, to integrate the two approaches—respectively involving an interpretative presumption and scrutiny of the decision-maker's justification—into one composite approach that corresponds to the established approach to statutory rights. This was one of Michael Taggart's less widely noted suggestions.[38] Courts could first use heightened scrutiny or proportionality to decide whether a rights infringement could be justified. If the limit was not justified, they would then use the principle of legality, declaring the rights-infringing decision to be unlawful unless it was clearly authorised by the empowering provision. However, while such a composite approach can be seen in some cases,[39] it has not attracted much attention, let alone widespread acceptance.

Philip Sales's essay in this part addresses the choice between these two distinct approaches in the particular context of the Crown's 'third source' or common-law powers. Against the background of a wide-ranging discussion of the nature and limits of such powers, he rejects the notion that these powers are subject to fundamental common-law rights by virtue of the principle of legality just like statutory powers are, as well as the possibility that the two approaches might be integrated in this context. Instead, he argues that variable intensity rationality review provides the appropriate means for protecting fundamental common-law rights in this context. Also briefly addressed by Sales is the impact of statutory rights on common-law powers.

C. Constitutional Rights: Protected via Administrative Law or Constitutional Law?

In Canada, one might expect the tension between legality and substance in rights claims to be largely absent, given that Canadian administrative law has adopted the same standard of review analysis both for issues of legality and for review of discretion. Yet the correct approach to rights-based review there has been similarly contested, thanks to the fact that in Canada it straddles one of the other divides: that between administrative law and constitutional law (the latter involving the Canadian Charter of Rights

[37] See, eg the judgments of Lords Mance, Toulson and Carnwath in *Kennedy v Charity Commission* [2014] UKSC 20, [2014] 2 WLR 808.

[38] D Dyzenhaus, M Hunt and M Taggart, 'The Principle of Legality in Administrative Law: Internationalisation as Constitutionalisation' (2001) 1 *Oxford University Common Law Journal* 5, 22–23; see also, Taggart, 'Proportionality' (n 1) 431.

[39] Eg *R v Secretary of State for the Home Department, ex p Simms* [2000] 2 AC 115 (HL); the judgment of Lord Bingham in *Daly* (n 30).

and Freedoms).[40] Early case law applied the constitutional proportionality methodology even in challenges to exercises of administrative discretion,[41] but that was contentious from the start.[42] Recently, the Supreme Court finally accepted the validity of those doubts, and adopted instead the administrative law test of unreasonableness for assessing the justification for such administrative rights-infringements, albeit the application of that test is to be informed by constitutional concerns.[43]

Mark Walters in his essay in this part criticises this recent Canadian move away from a constitutional proportionality analysis in challenges to exercises of administrative discretion, as well as the Canadian courts' unwillingness to contemplate a proportionality analysis outside the sphere of constitutional rights. Indeed, he rejects the divide that has developed in Canada between administrative and constitutional law, and between the distinctive and apparently incompatible approaches or 'ethics' adopted by the courts in these two areas. He argues for a return to the 'unity of public law'.[44]

V. UNTO THE BREACH ONCE MORE

Returning to the overall set of questions concerning the appropriate scope and intensity of substantive review, it will be recalled that Taggart, while coming down in favour of 'bifurcation' in the end, maintained his view that there should be a unity of methodology across all cases involving rights, from whatever source.[45] The contributions to this book demonstrate that debate continues on this rights/wrongs divide and on many other divides that may be used either to organise substantive review or to delineate its boundaries—divides between: substance and process; outcome and procedure; merits and legality; law, fact and discretion or policy; unreasonableness and proportionality; administrative and constitutional law; administrative and human rights law; and almost countless others. All of these divides remain contested as to their validity, as to their relevance to the task at hand, and as to where they should be drawn if they are relevant. The 'unity of public law', declared by David Dyzenhaus, Michael Taggart and other contributors to the volume with that title,[46] remains elusive

[40] A feature which is also discussed in Claudia Geiringer's essay.

[41] *Slaight Communications Inc v Davidson* [1989] 1 SCR 1038 (SCC).

[42] Ibid; and much more recently, see *Multani v Commission Scolaire Marguerite-Bourgeoys* 2006 SCC 6, [2006] 1 SCR 256.

[43] *Doré v Québec (Tribunal des professions)* 2012 SCC 12, [2012] 1 SCR 395.

[44] A reference to D Dyzenhaus (ed), *The Unity of Public Law* (Oxford, Hart Publishing, 2004).

[45] Taggart, 'Proportionality' (n 1).

[46] Dyzenhaus (n 44).

in many respects. It may indeed be an illusory goal, but that would be a contentious claim in its own right.

However, even if distinctions such as those between legality and merits or between rights and other cases are valid and significant, it is still important and useful to see the issues on both sides of these divides as interrelated parts of a broader whole. Inspired by Taggart's work and by the Canadian perspective on which he drew, that is the approach we have sought to foster by combining exploration of issues concerning all of these versions of substantive review in this collection.

Part A

Modern Extensions of Substantive Review

2

Modern Extensions of Substantive Review: A Survey of Themes in Taggart's Work and in the Wider Literature

MARK ELLIOTT AND HANNA WILBERG

I. THE NATURE AND PURPOSE OF THIS SURVEY

THIS COLLECTION OF essays engaging with Professor Michael Taggart's work on substantive review, and building on that work, seems a good opportunity to attempt an overview of Taggart's work in this area and of the existing state of the debate. That is what we do in this chapter and in chapter eight, each chapter focusing on one of the two themes pursued in this book. In this chapter, the overview concerns the first of these themes: the debate about modern extensions of substantive review in the sense of review engaging the merits.

An overview of Taggart's work on each of the two themes may be useful in our view, given that for many years he filled roles both as the first and foremost authority on New Zealand administrative law, and as a contributor of robust and spirited contributions to debates about administrative law across the common-law world; and given the sadly abrupt end to his contributions in both roles. We have re-read much of Taggart's work in this area in order to identify what, in our view, are some central themes in that body of work, as well as to grapple with some puzzles. In surveying the wider literature for further context, we have identified some central themes and some notable existing contributions to those themes.

The purpose of this chapter and of chapter eight is not to evaluate or to endorse the work we discuss, but rather simply to explore it and present our personal best understanding of it, as part of the relevant background to further debate on each of the two themes.

II. SOME CENTRAL THEMES IN TAGGART'S WORK ON SUBSTANTIVE REVIEW

Responses to Taggart's final 'Proportionality' article[1] have tended, unsurprisingly, to focus on his controversial and characteristically provocative conversion to 'bifurcation' of judicial review into 'rights' cases and what he called 'public wrongs' cases—and that includes the next three of the contributions to this volume. In this survey, however, we examine Taggart's work on substantive review as a whole, and present our understanding of some central themes in his work in this area. Among other things, this allows the effect and extent of Taggart's 'conversion' to be appreciated in a broader context.

Two main points emerge from this survey, concerning the effect and extent of the bifurcation Taggart proposed. First, his category of 'public wrongs' cases in which proportionality review should not apply does not include everything other than Human Rights Act cases: rights from *any* source are included in his category of rights cases. Secondly, his proposed approach to 'public wrongs' cases does not involve confining substantive review to traditional *Wednesbury* unreasonableness alone: the specific modern substantive grounds would also remain available, as would modern improvement to procedural and adjectival rules. Whether Taggart is right on all of these points, is another matter. In this chapter, we are concerned only to present what we consider to be the best reading.

A. Constitutionalisation in Rights Cases

In this book, we devote a separate part C to essays discussing rights-based review. However, in outlining Taggart's work on substantive review, it is necessary to start by outlining his views on cases involving rights, so as to put his views on other cases, expressed in his late 'Proportionality' article, into context. A significant portion of Taggart's work was devoted to the impact of rights on administrative law. From this work, several strong and consistent themes emerge.

The first and overarching theme concerns a new 'constitutional' methodology for human rights cases. With the limited exception of *Wednesbury* unreasonableness, review on the traditional administrative law model was largely confined to scrutinising the decision-making process: even where rights were engaged, scrutiny was limited to the considerations taken into account and purposes pursued. The 'revolutionary' departure from that model in human rights cases, in the account given by Taggart and his co-authors, was that rights were not simply to be taken into account. Where a

[1] M Taggart, 'Proportionality, Deference, *Wednesbury*' [2008] *New Zealand Law Review* 423.

human right was infringed by a decision, that right was the 'starting point'. It was necessary to ask whether the limit could be justified—involving a proportionality test—and if not, whether it was nevertheless unequivocally authorised by the empowering legislation. If the rights challenge did not falter at one of those hurdles, then the right functioned as a 'trump'—as a 'valid constitutional impediment' to the challenged outcome.[2]

This account was both prescriptive and, at least in part, descriptive;[3] and Taggart with his co-authors argued that it was applicable to human rights sourced not only in constitutions or statutes[4] but also in the common law and international law.[5] In the area of constitutions or constitutional statutes, it described the approach that was then established in Canada for administrative law cases invoking Charter rights,[6] and subsequently spread to other common-law jurisdictions with statutory bills of rights.[7] In relation to common-law rights, in an essay co-authored with David Dyzenhaus and Murray Hunt, Taggart argued that the same approach could be seen in the way that the House of Lords in *Simms*[8] combined two previously distinct approaches: the so-called 'principle of legality'[9] and *Smith*[10] 'heightened

[2] J McLean, P Rishworth and M Taggart, 'The Impact of the New Zealand Bill of Rights on Administrative Law' in *The New Zealand Bill of Rights Act 1990* (Auckland, Legal Research Foundation, 1992) 62 (MRT essay) 67–69; M Taggart, 'Reinventing Administrative Law' in N Bamforth and P Leyland (eds), *Public Law in a Multi-Layered Constitution* (Oxford, Hart Publishing, 2003) 311, 324–27; Taggart, 'Proportionality' (n 1) 440.

[3] Insufficient attention is often paid to that distinction in this area, as pointed out in J Varuhas, 'Against Unification' (ch 5 in this volume).

[4] That was the subject of the MRT essay (n 2).

[5] D Dyzenhaus, M Hunt and M Taggart, 'The Principle of Legality in Administrative Law: Internationalisation as Constitutionalisation' (2001) 1 *Oxford University Commonwealth Law Journal* 5 (DHT essay).

[6] *Slaight Communications Inc v Davidson* [1989] 1 SCR 1038 (SCC); but see now *Doré v Québec (Tribunal des professions)* 2012 SCC 12, [2012] 1 SCR 395, discussed in part C of this book in M Walters, 'Respecting Deference as Respect: Rights, Reasonableness and Proportionality in Canadian Administrative Law' (ch 15 in this volume) and C Geiringer, 'Process and Outcome in Judicial Review of Public Authority Compatibility with Human Rights: A Comparative Perspective' (ch 13 in this volume).

[7] See *R (Daly) v Secretary of State for the Home Department* [2001] UKHL 26, [2001] 2 AC 532. The MRT essay (n 2) proposed this approach for the New Zealand Bill of Rights Act 1990, and in his subsequent writing Taggart took the view that it had been adopted.

[8] *R v Secretary of State for the Home Department, ex p Simms* [2000] 2 AC 115 (HL).

[9] Previously seen, for instance, in *R v Lord Chancellor, ex p Witham* [1998] QB 575 and *R v Secretary of State for the Home Department, ex p Pierson* [1998] AC 539 (HL). Taggart also liked to instance the dissenting judgment of Browne-Wilkinson LJ in the Court of Appeal in *Wheeler v Leicester City Council* [1985] 1 AC 1054 (CA, HL) as effectively a forerunner of this principle, and as much preferable to the unstructured basis on which the House of Lords in that case reached the same conclusion: M Taggart, 'The Impact of Apartheid on Commonwealth Administrative Law' [2006] *Acta Juridica* 158, 180–83; M Taggart, 'Globalization, "Local" Foreign Policy, and Administrative Law' in G Huscroft and M Taggart (eds), *Inside and Outside Canadian Administrative Law* (Toronto, University of Toronto Press, 2006) 259, 266–67.

[10] *R v Ministry of Defence, ex p Smith* [1996] QB 517 (CA).

scrutiny' unreasonableness review.[11] The essay approved of this approach,[12] and further argued that the same approach ought to be applied to international law rights, in preference to more limited administrative law approaches to giving effect to international law:[13] judicial protection of rights from both sources by means of the new 'constitutional' methodology was argued to be consistent with the common-law tradition of subjecting exercises of public power to values recognised by the common law as fundamental.[14]

Several aspects of the constitutional methodology require some further elaboration. These also represent important themes in Taggart's work in their own right, in that their relevance and application extended beyond cases engaging the new constitutional methodology.

i. Breakdown of Law/Discretion Divide

The 'principle of legality' faced the objection in *Brind*,[15] that broadly expressed discretionary powers were not ambiguous and hence not amenable to interpretive presumptions of consistency. Taggart consistently argued that this law/discretion divide needed to be broken down. The scope of discretionary powers had always been a matter of statutory interpretation, such as by divining permissible purposes or relevant considerations. In just the same way, such powers could be read down pursuant to interpretive presumptions so as to render them consistent with statutory, common law or international law rights.[16]

ii. Reasons and the Culture of Justification

Taggart had long been an advocate of a duty to give reasons.[17] In his later work, he adopted the idea of a culture of justification first developed by Etienne Mureinik and by Dyzenhaus,[18] and pointed out that this formed an integral part of the new 'constitutional' methodology: a crucial part of this methodology was that the proportionality test imposed a burden of

[11] DHT essay (n 5) 23.

[12] Ibid, 6, 23–34.

[13] These weaker administrative law approaches included the pure mandatory relevant considerations approach adopted in *Puli'uvea v Removal Review Authority* (1996) 2 HRNZ 510 (CA); or the legitimate expectations approach adopted in *Minister of Immigration and Ethnic Affairs v Teoh* (1995) 128 ALR 353 (HCA): DHT essay (n 5) 8–16 and 31.

[14] DHT essay (n 5) 23–34.

[15] *R v Secretary of State for the Home Department, ex p Brind* [1991] 1 AC 696.

[16] DHT essay (n 5) 20, 25–27.

[17] M Taggart, 'Should Canadian Judges Be Legally Required to Give Reasoned Decisions in Civil Cases' (1983) 33 *University of Toronto Law Journal* 1; M Taggart, 'Osmond in the High Court of Australia: Missed Opportunity' in M Taggart (ed), *Judicial Review of Administrative Action in the 1980s* (Auckland, Oxford University Press, 1986) 53.

[18] D Dyzenhaus, 'Law as Justification: Etienne Mureinik's Conception of Legal Culture' (1998) 14 *South African Journal on Human Rights* 11.

justification and persuasion on the public authority.[19] Requiring reasons alone was not enough to ensure accountability: judges also had to accept an obligation to scrutinise those reasons to ensure they were cogent in the particular context.[20]

Moreover, the merits of this approach were not confined to cases involving human rights. For instance, in charting the emergence of substantive legitimate expectation as a ground of review, Taggart welcomed the decision in *Bibi*[21] for imposing a requirement of justification for disappointing such expectations.[22]

Recognition of the substantive scrutiny that could be achieved through the culture of justification also entailed discarding any 'hard-and-fast distinction between process and substance'.[23]

iii. Due Deference and the Limits of Judicial Review

On the other hand, the culture of justification also allowed judges to afford protection to fundamental values without 'squeezing out' the space for the exercise of administrative discretion that had been delegated by Parliament: 'deference as respect', another Dyzenhaus concept,[24] was the flipside of the culture of justification.[25] Rather than judging for themselves whether a decision was justified, judges could focus on the reasons given by the decision-maker, and on whether these were capable of justifying the decision as being either in conformance with the fundamental value or a reasonable limit on it.[26]

The concept of deference had more generally been of interest to Taggart for some time.[27] The full scope and nature of its operation is further considered in part B of this book. Taggart's interest in deference was of a piece with his more general concern not only to ensure adequate scrutiny of exercises of public power, but conversely also to maintain appropriate

[19] Taggart, 'Reinventing' (n 2) 328–29, 332–33.

[20] DHT essay (n 5) 29.

[21] *R (Bibi) v Newham London Borough Council* [2001] EWCA Civ 607, [2002] 1 WLR 237.

[22] M Taggart, 'Administrative Law' [2003] *New Zealand Law Review* 99 at 106–107. More generally on the topic, see also M Taggart, 'Administrative Law' [2000] *New Zealand Law Review* 439, 446–50.

[23] DHT essay (n 5) 32.

[24] D Dyzenhaus, 'The Politics of Deference: Judicial Review and Democracy' in M Taggart (ed), *The Province of Administrative Law* (Oxford, Hart Publishing, 1997) 279.

[25] DHT essay (n 5), 28; Taggart, 'Reinventing' (n 2) 332, 334; Taggart, 'Proportionality' (n 1) 456–57, 458, 460, 461 and 463.

[26] DHT essay (n 5) 6, 34.

[27] See especially, M Taggart, 'The Contribution of Lord Cooke to Scope of Review Doctrine in Administrative Law: A Comparative Common Law Perspective' in P Rishworth (ed), *The Struggle for Simplicity in the Law: Essays in Honour of Lord Cooke of Thorndon* (Wellington, Butterworths, 1997) 189.

limits on judicial review and judicial discretion. He was fond of reminding us not to neglect the question of 'who guards the guardians?'[28]—unchecked judicial discretion was not necessarily to be preferred to unchecked executive discretion. And he always appeared to harbour sympathy for writers who resist the Diceyan judge-centred understanding of the rule of law that tends to deny the legitimacy and expertise of the administrative state and to undermine its ability to pursue legitimate collectivist goals.[29]

iv. 'Reinventing Administrative Law'—All of it?

To Taggart, these various developments all added up to such fundamental change from the traditional model of administrative law that one could talk of 'reinventing' administrative law.[30] The 'righting' of the subject[31]—the advent of human rights claims and of the new 'constitutional' methodology required for them—was only part of the process, though it was also an important catalyst for the more general development and spread of a culture of justification and transparency in administrative law. That general development extended to significant changes in the procedural grounds and adjectival rules of judicial review, as well as to the reconceptualisation and extension of substantive grounds.[32]

But did that 'reinventing' entail abandoning traditional administrative law methodology entirely? In most of his work, Taggart considered the 'thought of an administrative law rump, isolated from the rights-based developments … unappealing'.[33] But at that stage he did not really explore how the 'constitutional' methodology as such might work if it were extended beyond rights cases, and at least in some of his work he expressly left the question open.[34] That question was squarely addressed only in his 'Proportionality' article—his 'last word' on the subject.[35]

B. Taggart's 'Last Word' on Proportionality and Bifurcation

In his article entitled 'Proportionality, Deference, *Wednesbury*',[36] Taggart controversially abandoned his earlier doubts about a 'bifurcation' of public

[28] DHT essay (n 5) 27; Taggart, 'Reinventing' (n 2) 334.

[29] See H Wilberg and M Elliott, 'Deference on Questions of Law: A Survey of Taggart's Contribution and Themes in the Wider Literature' (ch 8 in this volume).

[30] Taggart, 'Reinventing' (n 2). This view is challenged in Varuhas (n 3) as relying on developments in only a few isolated areas; see also JNE Varuhas, 'The Reformation of English Administrative Law? "Rights", Rhetoric and Reality' (2013) 72 *Cambridge Law Journal* 369.

[31] Ibid, 323.

[32] Ibid, 328–30, 332–33.

[33] DHT essay (n 5) 31; also Taggart, 'Reinventing' (n 2) 334 fn 144.

[34] Taggart, 'Reinventing' (n 2) 334 fn 144.

[35] Taggart, 'Proportionality' (n 1) 423.

[36] Ibid.

law into 'constitutional' review in rights cases and administrative law review in cases not involving rights.[37] He now argued that the constitutional methodology of proportionality should apply only in rights cases. In other cases, which he labelled 'public wrongs' cases, courts should limit themselves to traditional *Wednesbury* unreasonableness, eschewing proportionality or even variable intensity reasonableness review.[38]

While this did represent a departure from Taggart's previous inclinations, it remained true to his commitment to striking a balance between proper scrutiny of exercises of public power on the one hand and avoiding judicial usurpation of such power on the other. This can be seen by exploring the various strands of his argument—some of which seek to constrain judicial review while others seek to expand it.

i. Established Categories Rather than One Overarching Methodology

One strand is an argument in favour of 'line-drawing'[39]—a 'mapping project'[40]—and this is a review-constraining strand. It involved rejecting proposals of one single methodology, whether proportionality or variable intensity reasonableness review, for all cases of substantive review.[41] Instead, Taggart favoured retention of established categories of substantive review. These included proportionality, reserved for rights cases, and also other modern expanded grounds of substantive review, on which more below. Requiring judges to fit their rulings into those categories, Taggart argued, serves to constrain judicial discretion to some degree,[42] and forces counsel and judges to articulate their reasons.[43] Discarding those categories would result in too much being left to judicial discretion: 'There is too much unrestrained judicial discretion in administrative law already.'[44]

Nor could proportionality be allowed to be available in all cases *alongside* those established categories. For one thing, proportionality was not suited to all cases, a point to which we will return. But for present purposes the point is that its availability across the board would in practice inevitably undermine the use of the established categories. That was because—in contrast with *Wednesbury* unreasonableness[45]—proportionality is not

[37] He acknowledged that this represented a change of mind: ibid, 478 fn 255, citing M Taggart, 'The Tub of Public Law' in D Dyzenhaus (ed), *The Unity of Public Law* (Oxford, Hart Publishing, 2004) 455 (see, eg 467) for his earlier view.
[38] Taggart, 'Proportionality' (n 1) 469–80.
[39] Ibid, 469.
[40] Ibid, 453.
[41] Another part of the 'mapping project' also seemed to involve calibration of intensity or deference ('signposts on the review rainbow') *within* proportionality: 'Proportionality' (n 1) 450, 460.
[42] Taggart, 'Proportionality' (n 1) 453–54, 478.
[43] Ibid, 470, 479.
[44] Ibid, 478.
[45] On which, see ibid, 427–29.

a residual safety net. Where it is available, it is much more likely to be litigants' first port of call, rendering all other grounds of review obsolescent: why 'wander the "maze" of administrative law when the constitutional "motorway" (*autobahn*) beckons?'[46] And the same concern applied to variable intensity reasonableness review.[47]

ii. Proportionality Analysis also for Fundamental Common-law Rights

A further strand, however, is a review-expanding strand. On the current state of the law in both the UK and New Zealand, both then and still, proportionality is not firmly established as the test for rights infringements other than those involving the Human Rights Act 1998 or the New Zealand Bill of Rights Act 1990.[48] Along with many other commentators and some judges, Taggart had already called for adoption of that test in cases also involving fundamental common-law rights.[49] Some cases may even be read as implicitly adopting that approach.[50] However, although there is increasing recognition, at least in the UK, that—as Sedley LJ put it—proportionality now 'has a life of its own in public law',[51] there is nevertheless a degree of equivocation as to the extent to which it is applicable beyond the confines of statutorily-recognised rights.[52]

Taggart, in the 'Proportionality' article, clearly endorsed the view that fundamental common-law rights should be protected by the same method as statutory rights—namely, by the constitutional methodology of proportionality review.[53] Indeed, he also seemed to take the view that there was no longer anything new about this: case law clearly established variable intensity unreasonableness review for cases engaging fundamental common-law rights, and that was in truth proportionality by another name.[54] On this last point, though, there is a little uncertainty, for elsewhere in the article he says that the two are the same *except* for the 'critical difference' that the

[46] Ibid, 438–39.

[47] Ibid, 479.

[48] For the approach in cases involving those statutes, see *Daly* (n 7); *R v Hansen* [2007] NZSC 7, [2007] 3 NZLR 1. Whether proportionality is the established test in New Zealand for administrative law cases even when they involve the Bill of Rights turns out to be much less certain than it has widely been assumed to be: C Geiringer, 'Sources of Resistance to Proportionality Review of Administrative Power Under the New Zealand Bill of Rights Act' (2013) 11 *New Zealand Journal of Public and International Law* 123; H Wilberg, 'The Bill of Rights in Administrative Law Cases: Taking Stock and Suggesting Some Reassessment' (2013) 25 *New Zealand Universities Law Review* 866.

[49] DHT essay (n 5).

[50] For instance, see *Daly* (n 7) per Lord Bingham; *Simms* (n 8).

[51] *R (Quila) v Secretary of State for the Home Department* [2010] EWCA Civ 1482, [2011] HRLR 11, [36].

[52] See, eg the judgments of Lords Mance, Toulson and Carnwath in *Kennedy v Charity Commission* [2014] UKSC 20, [2014] 2 WLR 808.

[53] Taggart, 'Proportionality' (n 1) 465–70.

[54] Ibid, 433–35, 448–49 and 466; also 471–72.

burden of justification shifts to the Crown under proportionality.[55] Either way, what is clear is that he favoured extension of proportionality review to cases involving fundamental common-law rights.

iii. 'Not a Retreat': Other Substantive Grounds Remain Available

Finally, the question is whether, or to what extent, the rejection of proportionality for 'public wrongs' cases represents a review-constraining strand. We have already noted that the insistence of separate categories does represent a constraining strand. But what are the categories Taggart would provide for 'public wrongs' cases, and how limited would review in these cases be, according to those categories? Taggart expressly insisted that what he advocated was 'not a retreat'.[56] But how can that be so, when he rejected not only proportionality (which is not so far established in the law for such cases), but also variable intensity review (which is at the very least potentially available as the law then stood and still stands), in favour of nothing more than old-fashioned *Wednesbury* review in 'public wrongs' cases? The answer, we suggest, is that this position must be read in context, in at least two respects.

First, Taggart was not arguing that proportionality for rights cases and *Wednesbury* unreasonableness for 'public wrongs' cases should be the *only* categories of substantive review available. That division was merely his answer to the '"proportionality versus *Wednesbury* unreasonableness" debate'.[57] He expressly relied on the availability of other substantive grounds in arguing that it was appropriate to exclude both proportionality and variable intensity reasonableness review in 'public wrongs' cases: the 'appropriate advances have already been made in the expansion and refinement of the specific substantive grounds of review', and as a result the traditional 'safety net' of *Wednesbury* unreasonableness would only very rarely be needed.[58]

There is no further detail here on what other substantive grounds Taggart had in mind; but the same point about *Wednesbury* unreasonableness as a safety net and the decreasing need for it is also made earlier in the article, and at that point the other substantive grounds are listed. The traditional list of specific grounds includes the various types of illegality and abuse of discretion.[59] The modern changes include the demise of the distinction between jurisdictional and non-jurisdictional error of law; and the emergence of first procedural and then substantive legitimate expectations, and

55 Ibid, 465; also 438–39.
56 Ibid, 479.
57 That is his introductory statement of his topic: ibid, 425.
58 Ibid, 479; see also under 'Conclusion' 480.
59 Ibid, 427.

of factual and evidential review.[60] Recall also that he had in earlier work welcomed the imposition of a justificatory burden as a means of protecting substantive legitimate expectations.[61] Resort to *Wednesbury* unreasonableness would be necessary only if none of these grounds availed. What Taggart was rejecting for 'public wrongs' cases, then, was only the '*methodology*' of either variable intensity unreasonableness or proportionality.

Secondly, it is necessary to understand how in Taggart's view proportionality review relates to what are usually thought of as procedural grounds and adjectival rules of judicial review. As we have seen, for him a main strength of proportionality was that—in stark contrast to *Wednesbury*—it put the burden of justification on the decision-maker,[62] thus promoting a 'culture of justification'.[63] At the same time, however, he resisted proportionality review encroaching unduly on the decision-maker's discretion: deference as an appropriate degree of respect for the justification advanced by the decision-maker was for him the quid pro quo of the requirement of justification.[64] Paired with variable deference in this fashion, proportionality review effectively becomes an implied duty to give reasons (at least to the reviewing court, if not at the time of decision), together with more or less deferential rationality review of those reasons.

While Taggart saw the lack of such a justification requirement as a characteristic feature of the *Wednesbury* unreasonableness ground, and while he advocated retention of that ground in 'public wrongs' cases, he nevertheless thought that the crucial 'culture of justification' should and would extend to that side of his divide.[65] In part, that was ensured by the point noted already, namely the expansion and refinement of 'specific grounds of substantive review' that are also available in 'public wrongs' cases, at least some of which also involve a burden of justification. Beyond that, it was also ensured by developments of a more procedural or adjectival nature: by the developing right to reasons as a ground of review in its own right; and by recent advances towards greater transparency in judicial review procedure, such as the more ready availability of discovery and cross-examination and even something approaching a duty to file affidavits.[66]

In conclusion, then, Taggart was not advocating a retreat. He was not proposing that *Wednesbury* unreasonableness should be the only substantive ground of review available in 'public wrongs' cases, nor that the 'culture of justification' should not extend to such cases.

[60] Ibid, 429.

[61] Taggart (n 22) and accompanying text.

[62] Ibid, 439–40. On the contrasting nature of *Wednesbury* unreasonableness and the associated traditional model of judicial review, see ibid, 427–29.

[63] Ibid, 461–62.

[64] Ibid, 450, 456–58; also 463.

[65] Ibid, 457, 477.

[66] Ibid, 462–65, 477, 480.

iv. Why No Proportionality for 'Public Wrongs' Cases?

Even so, however, his rejection of proportionality review for 'public wrongs' cases is a review-constraining strand in his argument—albeit merely re-affirming an existing limit. It remains to consider Taggart's reasons for affirming this limit. Some of the most important reasons have already been touched on. He considered that replacing the established categories of substantive review with one single overarching methodology would result in too much judicial discretion. He further thought that proportionality, wherever it is available even alongside the established categories, is likely to render those established categories and grounds of review obsolete, thus sacrificing their power to constrain judicial discretion.

Beyond that, Taggart also considered the proportionality methodology unsuited to cases that lack a rights 'anchor'.[67] Its proponents argue that proportionality is more structured and transparent,[68] yet Taggart considered that without rights as the starting point, 'the proportionality methodology loses many of its touted advantages as a transparent and visible tool for ensuring reasonable or proportionate decision-making'.[69]

Unfortunately, he did not spell out in any further detail why and how the methodology is unsuited.[70] However, his other work on substantive review suggests a likely answer. To Taggart, proportionality was integrally bound up with what he had long considered to be a new 'constitutional' methodology in rights cases. On this methodology, representing a radical departure from traditional administrative law methodology, rights are not merely matters to be taken into account: they are the starting point and, unless defeated by reasonable justification or unequivocal statutory authorisation, they operate as trumps.[71]

Against this background, his 'bifurcation' argument amounts to rejecting the idea that this 'righting' of administrative law should sweep the entire field of substantive review. Where there is no right invoked by the applicant, the starting and end points of the 'constitutional' methodology are missing, making that methodology unsuitable in normative terms. Indeed that is part of the explicit argument in the 'Proportionality' article.[72] Placing the burden on the applicant in such cases 'respects the institutional, functional, and pragmatic limitations on judicial review'. The traditional

[67] Ibid, 477; see also 440.

[68] Ibid, 473.

[69] Ibid, 477; see also 479.

[70] Varuhas (n 3) also considers the proportionality methodology unsuited in the absence of interference with a right or other protected value—for the very persuasive reason that its very function is to test the justification for such an interference. However, it does not seem that Taggart had quite the same argument in mind.

[71] MRT essay (n 2); Taggart, 'Reinventing' (n 2); Taggart, 'Proportionality' (n 1) 438–40, 461.

[72] Taggart, 'Proportionality' (n 1) 472, 477, 478–79.

deferential *Wednesbury* standard furthermore continues to strike the right balance between private and collective interests in such cases,[73] and helps guard against 'unduly privileging individualism ... at the expense of effective government'.[74]

We may object that the proportionality test can be adjusted accordingly in cases not involving rights. However, then it becomes nothing more than a requirement to balance the affected individual interest against the competing public interest. That may explain Taggart's point about structure: such a simple balancing test is open to his objection that it no longer has any great claim to structure and transparency.

III. THE WIDER DEBATE

The debate about substantive review to which Mike Taggart so prominently contributed is one that has engaged, and continues to engage, common-law scholars around the globe. It is a debate that raises fundamental questions about the intersection of judicial, administrative and—given the provenance of most administrative competence—legislative authority. Yet for all that such questions are pervasive, they fall to be answered within the framework of individual constitutional systems. As a result, the debate that plays out at the macro level is the product of a series of local debates concerning the extent of, and the relationships between, constitutional actors' powers. It is for that reason, among others, that the contributors to this part of the book are drawn from and examine the position in a range of common-law jurisdictions. What, then, is the nature of the existing debate that forms the backdrop to the contributions to this part of the book? The extent of that debate rules out any attempt to provide a comprehensive summary, but three key strands may be identified.

A. Beyond *Wednesbury*? And, if so, When?

The first strand is concerned with the circumstances in which something more demanding than *Wednesbury* may be appropriate. Here, there has been a major shift in the terms of the debate over the last 30 or so years. From a contemporary vantage point, it is easy to forget just how controversial—until relatively recently—was any suggestion that the line in the sand drawn by the *Wednesbury* doctrine could or should be breached. As recently as the early 1990s, the House of Lords exhibited strong opposition to the possibility of more intensive review generally—and to the proportionality doctrine

[73] Ibid, 477.
[74] Ibid, 478.

in particular. Perhaps the high-water mark of such scepticism is found in *Brind*, in which Lord Lowry referred with approval to Lord Greene MR's statement in *Wednesbury* to the effect that courts should, on substantive grounds, disturb a decision only if it is 'so absurd that no sensible person could ever dream that it lay within the powers of the authority'.[75] Limiting substantive review in this way, said Lord Lowry, was imperative if the supervisory, as distinct from appellate, character of review was to be preserved.[76]

It was against this background that writers such as Sir Jeffrey Jowell and Lord Lester made seminal—and, at that time, radical—contributions to the debate, arguing in favour of an approach to judicial review going beyond *Wednesbury*.[77] They contended that this would not necessarily lead the courts into constitutionally forbidden territory, and that, contrary to the view that proportionality was an exclusively 'European concept', the values it embraced were already immanent within the common law, even if the language and structure of proportionality remained more exotic.[78] The earliest days of the debate were thus concerned not with questions about when it would be appropriate for courts to apply a standard more exacting than *Wednesbury*, but whether it would *ever* be appropriate to do so.

Today, in contrast, it is generally accepted that substantive review will and should sometimes transcend a bare check for extreme unreasonableness—but precisely when a more demanding approach is warranted remains a matter of some contention. It is important to recognise that this issue is distinct from the question—to which we turn below—whether the proportionality test should supplant *Wednesbury*. That question is centrally about the doctrinal tools via which substantive review should be undertaken; a distinct (albeit related) question is concerned with the circumstances in which judicial scrutiny should be more demanding than traditional *Wednesbury* review, irrespective of the particular doctrinal vehicle through which more intensive review should be dispensed. As to when the standard of review ought to exceed that which is usually associated with *Wednesbury*, several positions may be, and are, taken by courts and commentators; four will be briefly sketched.

The most modest position holds that courts can and should adopt a more demanding approach when assessing justifications for alleged infractions of values that have been accorded presumptive priority through legislative

[75] *Wednesbury* (n 1) 229, cited with approval by Lord Lowry in *Brind* (n 15) 764.

[76] *Brind* (n 15) 765.

[77] J Jowell and A Lester, 'Proportionality: Neither Novel nor Dangerous' in J Jowell and D Oliver (eds), *New Directions in Judicial Review* (London, Stevens, 1988) 51; A Lester and J Jowell, 'Beyond *Wednesbury*: Substantive Principles of Administrative Law' [1987] *Public Law* 368.

[78] The stock example being *R v Barnsley Metropolitan Borough Council, ex p Hook* [1976] 1 WLR 1052 (CA).

intervention. The obvious example of such a situation is furnished by judicial review pursuant to a statutory or constitutional bill of rights, where the court has to decide not only whether one of the protected rights is engaged (a legal question), but also whether the infringement can be justified (a more substantive question).[79] On this view, conventional objections—based in the separation of powers and the importance of maintaining the appeal/review distinction—yield *only* in the face of a catalogue of rights with whose protection the judiciary is legislatively charged. A limited constitutional licence is thus conferred upon the judiciary to break free of the constraining forces that would otherwise operate. Such a position is advocated by Sir Philip Sales, who argues, in the UK context, that 'Parliament has promulgated legislation on the footing that it is the *Wednesbury*/rationality standard which applies', such that any move beyond *Wednesbury*—save in circumstances in which such a move has been statutorily permitted, such as by means of the Human Rights Act 1998—would be constitutionally improper.[80] This argument rests on a particular, and somewhat narrow, view of the ultra vires doctrine, a broader reading of which might be thought to facilitate review more intensive than *Wednesbury* to the extent that such review is consistent with application of contemporary rule of law principles.[81]

More generally, however, the issue Sales highlights is an aspect of what Tom Hickman refers to as the 'problem of legitimacy'.[82] Any move away from the standard of review inherent in *Wednesbury* implies an alteration of the balance of power between court and administrator: as such, the imposition of a (greater) burden of justification must be legitimated (as Hickman puts it) by 'some particularly good substantive reason'.[83] The question then becomes what might constitute such a reason. Whereas Sales's response is based upon legislative permission, others—including, as noted above, Taggart—favour an approach based upon the normative worth of the value at stake. On this view—which represents the second point on our spectrum—a more demanding approach to substantive review may be legitimate where sufficiently fundamental values or rights are at stake, irrespective of whether there is a constitutional or statutory bill of rights, and irrespective of whether the particular value in question features

[79] As noted at the beginning of this introduction, questions of legality may themselves be considered, in some senses, to be substantive in nature, but we use the term 'substantive' here in the narrower and more conventional sense in which that term is used throughout the introduction to this part of the book.

[80] P Sales, 'Rationality, Proportionality and the Development of the Law' (2013) 129 *Law Quarterly Review* 223, 231.

[81] M Elliott, *The Constitutional Foundations of Judicial Review* (Oxford, Hart Publishing, 2000) ch 4.

[82] T Hickman, 'Problems for Proportionality' [2010] *New Zealand Law Review* 303, 314.

[83] Ibid, 314.

in any such text as might exist. This approach is captured by Lord Cooke's view that the existence (or absence) of a textual statement of rights is relatively unimportant. '[S]ome rights,' he said, 'are inherent and fundamental to democratic civilised society. Conventions, constitutions, bills of rights and the like respond by recognising rather than creating them.'[84]

This raises the further possibility that fundamental *values*—whether or not they constitute *rights*—might be protected by a form of substantive review more demanding than *Wednesbury*. This view—the third point on our spectrum—is reflected in Jeff King's 'halfway house' model. While resisting Paul Craig's contention[85] (of which more below) that proportionality should sweep the board, King argues that a higher-than-*Wednesbury* standard of review is warranted in some non-rights cases. King includes in this category substantive legitimate expectation cases, on the ground that there is a 'special demand' in such cases 'for additional protection of the interest at stake'; indeed, King argues, in some circumstances the interest that accrues to the holder of a legitimate expectation is 'tantamount' to a 'weak right'.[86]

The fourth, and most radical, point on the spectrum—often associated, but not to be conflated, with the argument that proportionality should sweep the board—holds that the standard of review supplied by conventional *Wednesbury* is *invariably* inadequate; substantive review should *always* be more demanding. Lord Cooke, of course, was a prominent proponent of this view. The leading member of the New Zealand 'simplicity' school, he argued in favour of an overarching obligation to act reasonably.[87] Crucially, however, this was a more demanding requirement—implying a commensurately greater degree of judicial scrutiny—than the *Wednesbury* injunction *not* to act *unreasonably*. For Lord Cooke, *Wednesbury* was an 'unfortunately retrogressive decision', not least because it is unlikely that 'the law can [ever] be satisfied in any administrative field merely by a finding that the decision under review is not capricious or absurd'.[88] Although it might be pointed out that, in criticising *Wednesbury* in this way, Lord Cooke was attacking a straw man—given the possibility of understanding *Wednesbury* in more subtle and demanding terms—the burden of Cooke's argument is normative rather than doctrinal, and is to the effect that the standard of review should never be as low as the conventional understanding (or caricature) of *Wednesbury* permits.

[84] *Daly* (n 7) [30].

[85] See, eg P Craig, 'Proportionality, Rationality and Review' [2010] *New Zealand Law Review* 265.

[86] J King, 'Proportionality: A Halfway House' [2010] *New Zealand Law Review* 327, 363.

[87] R Cooke, 'The Struggle for Simplicity in Administrative Law' in M Taggart (ed), *Judicial Review of Administrative Action in the 1980s: Problems and Prospects* (Oxford, Oxford University Press, 1988) 1.

[88] *Daly* (n 7) [32].

B. Doctrine

Accepting—as most now do—that substantive review should not *always* be as deferential as (a conventional understanding of) *Wednesbury* implies invites the obvious question: through what doctrinal vehicle or vehicles should more demanding review be supplied? It is here that the '*Wednesbury* versus proportionality' debate rears its head most directly, although—as noted above—that debate is sometimes merely a proxy for disagreement about the underlying question, addressed in the previous section, as to what the *standard* or *intensity* of review should be.

There is, however, a danger in treating '*Wednesbury*' and 'proportionality' as synonymous with 'low-intensity' and 'high-intensity' review. The possibility that *Wednesbury* may prove more demanding than Lord Greene's formulation would suggest is illustrated by the emergence in the UK of the pre-Human Rights Act 'sub-*Wednesbury*' concept,[89] as well as by the emergence in New Zealand of the variable intensity approach.[90] Meanwhile, proportionality is not a uniformly demanding standard: indeed, one of the principal defences offered by those who advocate its universal adoption is that the intensity of review supplied by proportionality is malleable. Craig, for instance, points out that proportionality can apply 'with varying degrees of intensity in different types of case', and that courts would 'fashion lower intensity proportionality review' in 'non-rights cases'.[91]

Indeed, Craig challenges the notion that *Wednesbury* and proportionality map onto a low/high intensity distinction not only by pointing out that proportionality can be applied in a less demanding way, but by arguing that *Wednesbury* may—indeed, *does*—involve judicial scrutiny of precisely the questions of 'weight' and 'balance' that are also the subject matter of proportionality review.[92] This is particularly so when *Wednesbury* is conceived of in terms more demanding than its minimalistic, red-haired teacher formulation. To the extent that a more demanding view of *Wednesbury* is adopted, there can, says Craig, be 'no ground for … arguing that low intensity proportionality review is illegitimate, either in terms of process or substance'.[93] This, in turn, suggests that the bright lines that animate the '*Wednesbury* versus proportionality' debate begin, on closer inspection, to dim—at least when the distinction is viewed in terms of the intensity of review.

If, then, the argument between those who propose and resist a wholesale switch to proportionality is not straightforwardly about standards, might

[89] See J Laws, '*Wednesbury*' in C Forsyth and I Hare (eds), *The Golden Metwand and the Crooked Cord: Essays in Honour of Sir William Wade* (Oxford, Clarendon Press, 1998).

[90] D Knight, 'Mapping the Rainbow of Review: Recognising Variable Intensity' [2010] *New Zealand Law Review* 393.

[91] Craig (n 85) 290–91.

[92] P Craig, 'The Nature of Reasonableness Review' (2013) 66 *Current Legal Problems* 131.

[93] Ibid, 162.

it instead be about structure? Contrasting the relatively structured nature of proportionality and the relatively unstructured nature of *Wednesbury* clearly represents a potential line of demarcation,[94] but, even here, the picture is complex. Whilst in its most characteristic form the *Wednesbury* test is relatively shapeless, it is clear that the test can be understood—or at least reimagined—in more structured terms. Perhaps the leading exponent of this view is Paul Daly.[95] Challenging the assertion of Lester and Jowell that *Wednesbury* is (necessarily) 'confusing',[96] 'tautologous'[97] and 'vague',[98] Daly contends that *Wednesbury* can be 'cast in a new light'.[99] On this view, there exist several 'indicia of unreasonableness'[100]—including illogicality and differential treatment—the existence of which triggers a burden of justification obligating the administrator to establish the reasonableness of the impugned decision.[101] This analysis, if accepted, somewhat closes the gap between *Wednesbury* and proportionality, in that the former, like the latter, assumes a structured form, albeit that the structures respectively exhibited by the two tests remain distinct.

Just as *Wednesbury* may be conceived of in terms whose structured nature renders it less distinct from proportionality than is usually assumed, so can proportionality be understood and applied in terms that are less structured than is often claimed. Although proportionality is capable of being conceived of in highly structured terms,[102] it is not invariably applied by courts in a structured fashion.[103] In particular, the distinct stages of the proportionality test are sometimes conflated, for instance by bluntly asking whether a 'fair balance' has been struck between the right and the conflicting public purpose that are in play.[104] At the same time, however, it is arguable that proportionality can be *too* structured for some contexts. Tom Hickman, for instance, suggests that if proportionality were to be adopted across the piece, many types of decisions would have to be 'shoehorned into a proportionality review by distorting the nature of that review'.[105] This

[94] Craig (n 85) 272–73.

[95] P Daly, '*Wednesbury*'s reason and structure' [2011] *Public Law* 238. See also P Daly, *A Theory of Deference in Administrative Law: Basis, Application and Scope* (Cambridge, Cambridge University Press, 2012) ch 4.

[96] Lester and Jowell, 'Beyond *Wednesbury*' (n 77) 372.

[97] Daly, '*Wednesbury*'s reason and structure' (n 95) 372.

[98] Ibid, 381.

[99] Daly, '*Wednesbury*'s reason and structure' (n 95) 238.

[100] Ibid, 242–47.

[101] Ibid, 247–54.

[102] See, eg P Craig, *Administrative Law* (London, Sweet & Maxwell, 2012) 668–69.

[103] M Elliott, 'Proportionality and Deference: The Importance of a Structured Approach' in C Forsyth, M Elliott, S Jhaveri and others (eds), *Effective Judicial Review: A Cornerstone of Good Governance* (Oxford, Oxford University Press, 2010) 264.

[104] See, eg *R (Baiai) v Secretary of State for the Home Department* [2007] EWCA Civ 478, [2008] QB 143, [37]. See also J Jowell, 'Substantive Judicial Review, Unreasonableness and Proportionality: Merger or Takeover?' (ch 3 in this volume).

[105] T Hickman, *Public Law after the Human Rights Act* (Oxford, Hart Publishing, 2010) 285.

view is echoed in the judgment of Stewart J in *R (Rotherham Metropolitan Borough Council) v Secretary of State for Business*, who held that proportionality is useful only when there is in play 'a specific legal standard and a decision by a public body which derogates from that standard'.[106] Absent such a decisional framework, 'the principle of proportionality does not add anything to a rationality challenge'.[107]

C. Deference

It has been said that few legal terms have been invested with 'so many shades of meaning' as 'jurisdiction'.[108] 'Deference', however, may be one of them. But for all that the language of deference may be problematic—not least because it has been imbued with such a broad range of meanings—the ideas that underpin it remain highly pertinent. When the perimeter of substantive review was set by *Wednesbury*, talk of deference was rarely, if ever, encountered. This is not due to a lack of concern for deference, but to the fact that deference is hard-wired into the *Wednesbury* test: indeed, it would be hard to conceive of a standard of review more inherently deferential than *Wednesbury*. However, once more intensive approaches—whether by way of proportionality or otherwise—are contemplated, questions of deference assume a more pressing character. In one sense, this is paradoxical, since it implies the taking away with one hand that which has been granted with the other. In another sense, however, it is inevitable: concerns about courts overstepping the mark become real only if standards of review are first in play that raise a serious risk of judicial overreach. Viewed in this way, deference is a means by which an approach to substantive review that is *potentially* more intrusive in abstract or general terms can be rendered less intrusive when this is warranted by the particularities of the given case.

Perhaps the deepest fault-line within the debate about deference concerns the distinction between what Murray Hunt calls 'spatial' deference and more nuanced versions of the concept.[109] 'Spatial' deference is difficult—perhaps impossible—to distinguish from non-justiciability, in that it reduces to treating particular areas of decision-making as off-limits to judicial review. This approach derives a degree of support from some UK cases decided around the time of the entry into force of the Human Rights

[106] *R (Rotherham Metropolitan Borough Council) v Secretary of State for Business* [2014] EWHC 232 (Admin) [69].

[107] Ibid, [70].

[108] *Re McC* [1985] AC 528, 536 (Lord Bridge) (HL).

[109] M Hunt, 'Sovereignty's Blight: Why Contemporary Public Law Needs the Concept of "Due Deference"' in N Bamforth and P Leylands (eds), *Public Law in a Multi-layered Constitution* (Oxford, Hart Publishing, 2003) 337, 344–49.

Act 1998.[110] However, as Hunt points out, it falters not least because administrative measures rarely fall neatly within one area of decision-making: a decision that is 'about' national security may *also* be 'about' human rights. In such circumstances, conflicting forces pull in opposing directions, and spatial deference, as an essentially binary concept, proves to be of limited utility. In the light of such concerns, there is stronger support for a more sophisticated approach to deference, often termed 'due' deference.[111]

The key distinction between spatial and due deference is that the latter, unlike the former, does not seek to set a global standard of review for the case depending upon its subject matter. Rather, due deference allows the standard of review to vary within the confines of an individual case, in the light of the several questions that may arise for adjudication. Understood in this way, deference—unlike non-justiciability—does not imply a judicial refusal to engage with the issue; rather, it implies a judicial willingness to ascribe varying degrees of weight to the public body defendant's view. As David Dyzenhaus puts it, deference, thus conceived, involves 'respect' as distinct from 'submission'.[112] However, even in this more modest guise, the notion of deference excites disagreement, in two areas in particular.

First, and most fundamentally, there is disagreement about whether deference is appropriate at all. Trevor Allan is highly critical of any suggestion that there should be a 'doctrine' of deference, which, he argues, is nothing other than 'nonjusticiability dressed in pastel colours'.[113] The court's job, says Allan, is to determine whether the impugned administrative act is unlawful: a function it ought to discharge by reference to the quality of arguments advanced in support, not the characteristics of the defendant who advances those arguments. Allan does not dispute that (for example) a decision-maker's superior institutional competence may be relevant: but its relevance extends no further than its capacity to enable the decision-maker to produce more defensible decisions.[114] What courts must *not* do, says Allan, is to ascribe independent weight to such factors as democratic legitimacy or expertise.[115] Others have strongly criticised this view—including Taggart, who said it was 'extreme' and 'utterly implausible'.[116] Aileen Kavanagh, meanwhile, argues that Allan's position overlooks the fact that

[110] See, eg *R v Director of Public Prosecutions, ex p Kebilene* [2000] 2 AC 328 (HL) 380 (Lord Hope); *International Transport Roth GmbH v Secretary of State for the Home Department* [2002] EWCA Civ 158, [2003] QB 728, [77] (Laws LJ).

[111] See, eg Hunt (n 109); J Jowell, 'Judicial deference: servility, civility or institutional capacity?' [2003] *Public Law* 592.

[112] Dyzenhaus (n 24) 286.

[113] TRS Allan, 'Human Rights and Judicial Review: A Critique of "Due Deference"' [2006] *Cambridge Law Journal* 671, 689.

[114] TRS Allan, 'Deference, Defiance, and Doctrine: Defining the Limits of Judicial Review' (2010) 60 *University of Toronto Law Journal* 41, 51–52.

[115] Ibid.

[116] Taggart, Proportionality' (n 1) 456.

in substantive review cases, courts are faced with a duality of issues: they must not only consider the 'merits of the substantive legal issue before them', but must also reflect on the 'constitutional and pragmatic limits of their role'.[117]

Second, even those who accept that some form of deference is appropriate disagree about the grounds on which an administrative measure—or, more precisely, the arguments advanced in support of such a measure—may be deserving of respect. Many writers are willing to accept that there is some mileage in the argument that the decision-maker may possess superior institutional competence, and may therefore be in a stronger position than the court to determine, for instance, whether a legitimate public policy goal could be achieved in some other way that would be less restrictive of the right or value in question.[118] Where the administrative authority possesses such expertise that is relevant and has been brought to bear upon the question, it will, on this view, be appropriate for the court to ascribe particular weight to the position advocated by the decision-maker. The same may be true where, even in the absence of any realistic claim to superior expertise, the decision-maker has formed its view following an especially rigorous decision-making procedure.[119] (Whether it follows from this that decision-makers should *have to* follow a rigorous procedure if their decision is to withstand scrutiny is a different, and contestable, question.)[120]

However, while there is a reasonable degree of consensus that institutional and decisional factors may warrant a degree of deference (as 'respect'), there is far less agreement about the extent, if any, to which the decision-maker's democratic credentials may operate so as to blunt judicial review.[121] On the one hand, it is argued that to give in to decision-makers' claims to democratic superiority is to overlook the countermajoritarian impulse that drives the legal protection of human rights—in which field recourse to more demanding standards of review tends to be concentrated.[122] On the other hand, it is contended that at least some of the questions that fall for

[117] A Kavanagh, 'Defending Deference in Public Law and Constitutional Theory' (2010) 126 *Law Quarterly Review* 222.

[118] See, eg Hunt (n 109); Jowell (n 111); Hickman (n 105) 145–49; A Young, 'In Defence of Due Deference' (2009) 72 *Modern Law Review* 554.

[119] See, eg *R (SB) v Governors of Denbigh High School* [2006] UKHL 15, [2007] 1 AC 100; see further Hickman (n 105) 149–50.

[120] See D Mead, 'Outcomes Aren't All: Defending Process-Based Review of Public Authority Decisions under the Human Rights Act' [2012] *Public Law* 61; A Kavanagh, 'Reasoning about Proportionality under the Human Rights Act 1998: Outcomes, Substance and Process' (2014) 130 *Law Quarterly Review* 235; C Geiringer, 'Process and Outcome in Judicial Review of Public Authority Compatibility with Human Rights: A Comparative Perspective' (ch 13 in this volume).

[121] For instance, compare the judgments of Lords Kerr and Sumption in *R (Lord Carlile) v Secretary of State for the Home Department* [2014] UKSC 60.

[122] See, eg Jowell (n 111).

determination in substantive review cases reduce to value judgements, in relation to which elected and accountable political institutions enjoy greater legitimacy than independent courts.[123] This disagreement is emblematic of much of what is at stake in the wider debate about substantive review. At root, that debate is about the proper relationship between judicial and administrative authority, and makes sense only when situated within the context of specific constitutional and institutional arrangements. The questions may be pervasive, but the responses to them must, at least to some extent, be sensitive to context as the remaining chapters in this part of the book, concerned as they are with substantive review in three common-law jurisdictions, demonstrate.

[123] See, eg J Waldron, 'The Core of the Case Against Judicial Review' (2006) 115 *Yale Law Journal* 1346, 1389–95; Hunt (n 109) 350–51.

3

Proportionality and Unreasonableness: Neither Merger nor Takeover

JEFFREY JOWELL*

I. INTRODUCTION

THIS CHAPTER WILL consider the extent to which substantive judicial review has taken hold in British case law. Despite the various attempts to soften the definition of unreasonableness as defined in the *Wednesbury* case,[1] has its application significantly altered? Does the 'sliding scale' of review assist its coherent application? What is its relationship to review on the ground of breach of Convention and constitutional rights? To what extent is substantive review co-extensive with the principle of proportionality? What are the specific ingredients of substantive review? Should the general standard of unreasonableness be wholly abandoned?

This is a somewhat personal account, which draws on my attempts for almost 30 years, with others, to narrow down the *Wednesbury* standard into more specific criteria and principles, one of which is proportionality. It will contain a summary of those efforts and (hitherto unpublished) judicial and other responses to them. Any account of this subject needs to be grounded in its constitutional and institutional context, so passing reference will also be made to the extent to which judges must accord respect or deference to other branches of government and the extent to which some issues are not amenable to decision in courts of law.

This exercise has, unexpectedly, led me to conclusions sometimes different from those that I have even recently advocated but I am still of

* Director of the Bingham Centre for the Rule of Law, a practising barrister and Professor Emeritus of Public Law at University College London.

[1] *Associated Provincial Picture Houses v Wednesbury Corporation* [1948] 1 KB 223.

the view that in the interests of integrity and accountability the standard of unreasonableness should where possible be clarified by more precise categories, criteria and principles to guide and govern all official decisions.

II. THE CONSTITUTIONAL AND INSTITUTIONAL CONTEXT OF SUBSTANTIVE REVIEW

We must begin with the obvious: that any consideration of substantive review must be set in the constitutional context of public decision-making. In the United Kingdom, albeit in the absence of a single authoritative constitutional text, the primary guiding constitutional principle is generally (though not universally) accepted to be parliamentary sovereignty, which situates ultimate decision-making authority in a representative legislature. For most of the twentieth century a strong version of parliamentary sovereignty prevailed, so that when parliament conferred broad discretionary power upon the executive or any other person exercising public functions, the courts were reluctant to limit the exercise of that power. A power providing that a minister 'may so decide' could not mean 'must so decide'. Authority to act 'as the minister thinks fit' could not be read down so as to read in what the courts thought fit.

As is well known, from the mid 1960s, a weaker version of parliamentary sovereignty came into play.[2] Even the broadest discretionary power was held not to confer 'unfettered' power on the decision-maker.[3] Literal interpretation was eschewed in favour of a purposive approach, under which the courts would insist that the decision-maker abide by the 'policy and objects' of the governing statute. Artifices that the courts had devised to restrict fair hearings were replaced by the presumption of a general duty of procedural fairness. Later, where the terms of a statute were held to be ambiguous, the exercise of the power was interpreted consistently with other constitutional principles, especially the rule of law, described sometimes as 'legality'.[4]

The question as to why this major shift took place invites one of the most interesting case studies about the nature of judicial reasoning under our common-law system. Surprisingly, however, the constitutional route for arriving at that changed culture was barely justified or explained at the

[2] I have further discussed the history of administrative law in the twentieth century in J Jowell, 'Administrative Law' in V Bognador (ed), *The British Constitution in the Twentieth Century* (Oxford, Oxford University Press, 2003) 373. See also S Sedley, 'The Long Sleep' in M Adenas and D Fairgrieve (eds), *Tom Bingham and the Transformation of the Law* (Oxford, Oxford University Press, 2009) 183.

[3] *Padfield v Minister of Agriculture, Fisheries and Food* [1968] AC 997, 1060 (Lord Upjohn).

[4] *R v Secretary of State for the Home Department, ex p Leech (No 2)* [1994] QB 198; *R v Secretary of State for the Home Department, ex p Simms* [2000] 2 AC 115.

time it happened. Much later on a lively debate emerged as to whether the constitutional justification rested on a notion of ultra vires, 'qualified' ultra vires, or the inherent quality of the common law under which the courts are charged with articulating constitutional boundaries.[5]

The one area which was unaffected by the new approach was substantive review. During the 'activist' period of judicial review there was little challenge to the notion that the courts could only interfere with a decision's substance if it was 'manifestly' unreasonable, described in the famous *Wednesbury* case by Lord Greene MR as 'a conclusion so unreasonable that no reasonable authority could ever have come to it'.[6] By retaining that restraint on intervention in the area of substantive review, the intervention of the courts on the other grounds of review, such as breach of procedural fairness, was perhaps rendered more acceptable. Judges, after all, possess unique expertise in matters procedural; it is their metier. They therefore frequently emphasised that when interpreting the scope of a discretionary power they were entitled only to interfere with the procedures or process by which it was exercised; how it was reached rather than what it decided.[7] Even after the *Wednesbury* formula was softened to a 'decision not within the range of reasonable responses',[8] the constitutional principle of the separation of powers is still invoked to assert that judges, when carrying out judicial review (rather than conducting an appeal *de novo*), do and may not interfere with official decisions on the ground that they (the judges) would have come to a different conclusion on the merits of the issue under dispute.

Before we can properly examine the extent to which courts do or should possess the authority to regulate the substance of official decisions, we must briefly note that in order to do so courts must possess both institutional and constitutional capacity.[9] In respect of institutional capacity, the courts must possess the expertise to assess the matter in question and the issue must be 'justiciable'—that is, amenable to decision in the context of an adversarial setting.[10] In respect of constitutional capacity, judges may pronounce on a

[5] A number of articles on the subject are collected in C Forsyth (ed), *Judicial Review and the Constitution* (Cambridge, Cambridge University Press, 2000).

[6] *Wednesbury* (n 1) 243.

[7] See, eg Lord Brightman in *R v Chief Commissioner of North Wales Police, ex p Evans* [1982] 1 WLR 1155, 1173F: 'Judicial review is not concerned with the decision but with the decision-making process'.

[8] Eg *R (Razgar) v Secretary of State for the Home Department (No 2)* [2003] EWCA Civ 840, [40]–[41] (Dyson LJ). See also *AXA General Insurance Ltd v Lord Advocate* [2011] UKSC 46, [2012] 1 AC 868, [43] (Lord Reed), defining 'irrationality' as involving 'whether a given decision lies within the range of decisions which are open to a rational decision-maker proceeding upon a proper understanding of the purposes for which the power in question may be exercised and the issues which are relevant to its exercise'.

[9] The distinction between constitutional and institutional capacity is sketched in H Woolf, and others, *De Smith's Judicial Review*, 7th edn (London, Sweet & Maxwell, 2013) [1-032] ff.

[10] See J Jowell, 'What Decisions Should Judges Not Take?' in M Andenas and D Fairgrieve (eds), *Tom Bingham and the Transformation of the Law* (Oxford, Oxford University Press, 2009) 129.

matter of principle but not policy (which involves the utilitarian calculation of the public good, which is the constitutional function of the other branches of government).[11] It must also be remembered that the sovereignty of parliament is not the only constitutional principle that may be engaged in this issue. Another such principle is the rule of law. Whether or not the rule of law is subordinate to parliamentary sovereignty, it has a significant role in the interpretation of public powers. This is because it contains within its requirements that decisions not be arbitrary, that there be access to justice, and that laws be relatively predictable and equally applied.[12]

III. THE APPLICATION OF A GENERAL STANDARD

Subject to those background constitutional and institutional requirements, does unreasonableness (*Wednesbury* or no) provide a standard that is both sound and practical?

It is by no means impossible for law to guide by means of general standards, such as 'reasonableness', 'fairness', 'abuse of power', or 'natural justice'. There are advantages to the flexibility which a general standard may achieve by permitting adjustment to changing norms and expectations. After all, the standard of the reasonable person in tort law has famously permitted just such incremental development to changing circumstances. As has very recently been pointed out, these standards in private law are often referred to in terms of the standards of a fictional person, such as 'the reasonable man' (aboard the Clapham omnibus). In *Healthcare at Home v Common Services Agency* Lord Reed identified other such fictional persons, for example[13]

> the right-thinking member of society, familiar from the law of defamation, the officious bystander, the reasonable parent, the reasonable landlord, and the fair-minded and informed observer, all of whom have had season tickets [on the Clapham omnibus] for many years …
>
> As Lord Radcliffe observed in *Davis Contractors Ltd v Fareham Urban District Council* [1956] AC 696, 728: 'The spokesman of the fair and reasonable man, who represents after all no more than the anthropomorphic conception of justice, is and must be the court itself.'

[11] See the application of Dworkin's distinction between principle and policy (in R Dworkin, *Taking Rights Seriously* (Cambridge MA, Harvard University Press, 1978) 22ff) by Lord Hoffmann in *R v Secretary of State for the Environment, Transport and the Regions, ex p Holdings and Barnes plc* [2001] UKHL 23, [69]–[70]. See more recently, *Bank Mellat v HM Treasury* [2013] UKSC 39, [12], where Lord Sumption agreed with Lord Reed that 'the making of government and legislative policy cannot be turned into a judicial process' (but nevertheless held that the relevant Order in Council, though involving matters of foreign policy and national security, was neither rational nor proportionate).

[12] See T Bingham, *The Rule of Law* (London, Penguin, 2010) and the discussion below.

[13] *Healthcare at Home v Common Services Agency* [2014] UKSC 49, [1]–[3]. The case concerned the European Union concept of the 'well-informed and normally diligent tenderer'.

> It follows from the nature of the reasonable man, as a means of describing a standard applied by the court, that it would be misconceived for a party to seek to lead evidence from actual passengers on the Clapham omnibus as to how they would have acted in a given situation or what they would have foreseen, in order to establish how the reasonable man would have acted or what he would have foreseen. Even if the party offered to prove that his witnesses were reasonable men, the evidence would be beside the point. The behaviour of the reasonable man is not established by the evidence of witnesses, but by the application of a legal standard by the court.

The standard of unreasonableness in public law provides no reference to the mindset of a hypothetical public official. Yet, as Lords Radcliffe and Reed observed, it is the judge who is required to assess the decision. Under the *Wednesbury* test there is the added barrier that the decision must be not only unreasonable in itself but also *manifestly* unreasonable.

Why are judges equipped to decide matters of substance when they involve extremes but not otherwise? Put another way: What justifies an exemption from the prohibition against judicial interference on the ground of unreasonableness only when the decision is overwhelmingly so? One answer is that the *Wednesbury* definition implies that the burden of proof is against the claimant in respect of matters of substance in public law cases. However, as will be shown below, there are categories of substantive review where the courts do not place the burden of proof upon the claimant nor accord any margin of appreciation or area of discretionary judgement to the respondent. And how sound, practical, or predictable can a theory of institutional role be that rests on a matter of degree rather than kind? In any event, should not public law resist tests that lack precision in the interests of the rule of law values of legal certainty and predictability?

IV. BEYOND *WEDNESBURY*

Troubled by some of these and other aspects of the *Wednesbury* doctrine, in 1987 Anthony Lester and I wrote an article criticising the approach to substantive review as set out under the *Wednesbury* formula.[14] We argued that its pragmatic approach should be replaced by principles which 'would satisfy the need in a fast growing area of law for clarity and coherence'. We regarded the contorted *Wednesbury* definition as tautologous and therefore unhelpful as a guide. We asked for better explanation as to why an act is unreasonable.

Shortly before our article was written, Lord Diplock had redefined the *Wednesbury* test. In a case where he famously summarised the three

[14] J Jowell and A Lester, 'Beyond *Wednesbury*: Substantive Principles of Administrative Law' [1987] *Public Law* 368.

'grounds' of judicial review as 'illegality', 'procedural propriety' and 'irrationality' (rather than unreasonableness—with the tantalising reference to the future possibility of the ground of 'proportionality'), he defined irrationality in a similar, but more expansive way to the *Wednesbury* formulation. An irrational decision, he said, was one which 'is so outrageous in its defiance of logic or accepted moral standards that no sensible person who had applied his mind to the question to be decided could have arrived at it'.[15] This definition is more specific than the *Wednesbury* test, by directing attention to two particular aspects of unreasonableness, namely, defiance of logic and 'accepted moral standards' (whatever they may be). However, like *Wednesbury*, it still requires a high degree of irrationality in the form of an 'outrageous decision' before the courts may intervene.

We suggested more specific categories and principles to articulate why a decision was unreasonable. These were, first, decisions that were irrational in the accepted sense—lacking logic or that were simply arbitrary; secondly, decisions violating standards of administrative probity, namely, fraudulent decisions or those taken in bad faith; thirdly, decisions contrary to standards of good administration and fourthly, violations of human rights.

Under decisions violating principles of good administration, we proposed three such principles, echoing the three 'general principles of law' of the European Community of the time. These included proportionality (articulated more fully in a further contribution),[16] equality (in the sense of equal application of the law, or consistency), and legal certainty.

Although fundamental rights were not at that time incorporated into our law, we proposed that when rights were engaged—either as rights included in the European Convention on Human Rights as a treaty obligation, or as rights inhering in the common law—the courts in reviewing discretionary powers should, as they were then beginning to do, impose 'heightened scrutiny' upon decisions which violated those rights.[17]

V. REACTIONS TO THE ARTICLE

We sent a draft of our article to a number of judges and scholars for comment and assistance. Twenty-seven years on, a selection of the responses seem now worth summarising briefly, as an indication of the approaches to substantive judicial review of that time.

The reader will make his or her own assessment of how much discount to accord to politeness on the part of those who professed to agree

[15] *Council of Civil Service Unions v Minister for the Civil Service* [1985] AC 374, 410–11.

[16] J Jowell and A Lester, 'Proportionality: Neither Novel Nor Dangerous' in J Jowell and D Oliver (eds), *New Directions in Judicial Review* (London, Stevens, 1988).

[17] See, eg *Bugdaycay v Secretary of State for the Home Department* [1987] AC 514, 531 (Lord Bridge speaking of the right to life in deportation cases).

with our argument (those who disagreed were less inhibited by such a constraint). They included Lord Scarman, who believed (and claimed to know from personal contact) that Lord Diplock's rephrasing, in *GCHQ*,[18] of unreasonableness into irrationality was 'not intended to be creative' but was a mere summary of the *Wednesbury* test. He approved of the search for principles (citing Dworkin's *Law's Empire*[19] as 'superb on this front') which he thought would prevent judges trespassing 'into land too soft for judicial hooves'. Sir Thomas Bingham (as he then was) was also 'much attracted by the argument' and thought that 'there is a current moving in your direction'.

Lord Bridge said:

> I cordially endorse your view that the underlying principles of administrative law ought to be more clearly articulated in the judgments we deliver. The difficulty, of course, is to find the appropriate occasion, when deciding individual cases, to articulate a particular principle.

A similar view was expressed by Professor Sir William Wade, who began by agreeing that 'it would be a help to clarity if unreasonableness could be anatomised'. He also agreed that 'the *Wednesbury* test is far too stringently formulated, and most of the cases can be fitted more suitably under other heads'. However, he thought that 'there will always be a category of "pure abuse" for which the residual pigeon-hole will be needed', concluding as follows:

> I doubt also if the judges will ever be persuaded to classify methodically. Since so many of the component parts of unreasonableness overlap, there is usually more than one of them available in any case, and the judge will naturally throw in everything that helps him.

Lord Justice Woolf (as he then was) regarded 'discretion as a vital part of [the court's] jurisdiction', but 'I do feel that it makes it much more desirable that the principles for intervention should be clearly and appropriately defined'. He agreed that many of them are already being applied without this being appreciated. However, he said 'I suspect the process of recognition may be patchy and drawn out not least because for some common law lawyers their European ingredients will not be to their liking'.

Mr Justice Webster (as he then was) was in general sympathetic to the notion that

> an otherwise apparently reasonable decision could, or possibly could, be struck down if it conflicts with certain specified principles such as those you mention.... But I think it is necessary to retain the general principle of unreasonableness for two reasons: first in the interest of flexibility, so that further principles may emerge

[18] *Council of Civil Service Unions v Minister for the Civil Service* ('*GCHQ*') [1983] AC 374.

[19] R Dworkin, *Law's Empire* (Cambridge MA, Harvard University Press, 1986).

and be identified; and secondly so that a decision can still be struck down if it cannot be justified by any valid reason or line of reasoning ... [This is because] many decisions are not reasoned and only very rarely does the way in which the decision making body directed itself appear.

Professor David Edward (later Justice of the European Court of Justice) felt that our suggested principles of substantive law were really 'tests of the application of the substantive law'. He agreed, however, that a more clearly defined set of principles 'help to show what it is that the judge is doing' and would therefore be:

(a) useful as tools for interpretation of the substantive law and for judgments as to the propriety of its application and (b) be in truth a safeguard against intrusion of the judiciary into the province of legislation since they would more clearly articulate the nature of the judicial function.

Critical views were expressed by Lord Justice Ormrod, who felt that the British way was to be flexible rather than prescriptive, and Mr Justice Millett (as he then was), who did not like the term 'irrationality' and preferred 'perverse'. Commenting from the perspective of a Chancery lawyer, he felt that the notion of unreasonableness was a universal one where a discretion was vested in the primary decision-maker rather than the court. Thus the court could only interfere for 'perversity' in decisions about breach of trust, or breach of fiduciary duty, 'even where there was a difference of fact and degree'. Similarly,

where minority shareholders complain that the Board of Directors are paying themselves extravagantly high salaries, the ... shareholders are entitled to be generous, even unreasonably generous. But there comes a point where ... no reasonable body of shareholders ... could possibly have thought that the remuneration on this level was justified.

Thriftlessness? Proportionality? I don't think it matters—the principle's the thing.

Lord Justice (Michael) Kerr was even less impressed. Having read the draft three times, he regarded it as 'extremely feeble', and thought it 'goes nowhere'. He said that 'it seems to be advocating the replacement/modification of the *Wednesbury* doctrine, which is of course essentially negative in character, by something positive [such as justification on the ground of human rights or proportionality]'. By calling for more positive policy reasons to provide a basis for the correctness of the administrative decision which is under attack, and yet not seeking to abolish the *Wednesbury* test altogether and to permit merits review, the draft is

not (rightly) afraid to strike, but it is also (rightly) unwilling to wound. It is no more than a pious hope ... [What you are advocating] would not merely muddy the waters with half-baked judicial statements on complex policy matters where there is no obvious 'right' or 'wrong' [and would] merely provoke controversy and perhaps justified dissention ... [The *Wednesbury* test] provides a far better basis for maintaining the necessary degree of non-involvement, and the consequent (relative?) independence of the courts, than the sort of half-way house which you appear to be advocating, as between the present system and the American approach of virtually full control of administrative policy by the court. In effect, what you are saying is vague and at present quite unconvincing.

VI. WHAT IS SUBSTANTIVE REVIEW?

A few years after those two articles appeared, Harry Woolf and I began to prepare the fifth edition of de Smith's *Judicial Review of Administrative Action.*[20] Stanley de Smith's pioneering work had considered the ground of unreasonableness only briefly. He regarded it as an unusual ground of review, which required something which was, in Lord Greene's words in *Wednesbury*, 'overwhelming'. He said (at page 219 of the first edition, published in 1959):

> It is easier to give hypothetical examples of preposterous conduct—the most familiar is that of the local authority which dismisses a woman teacher because she has red hair [*Short v Poole Corporation* [1926] Ch 66, 91 (Warrington LJ)]—than to point to actual cases in the law reports.

We proceeded to trawl through the case law and found a surprisingly large number of cases where the substance of the decision was assessed. Sometimes the standard of unreasonableness was employed, but more often reference was made to a more specific principle but without confessing that any aspect of substantive review had been engaged. The analysis confirmed that Lester and I were correct in our speculation in the 'Beyond *Wednesbury*' article when we said that[21]

> just as Molière's Monsieur Jourdain had been speaking prose for more than 40 years without knowing it,[22] the existing case law shows that for many years English judges have been stating principles of substantive review of administration without knowing or, more likely, admitting it.

An important reason for the judicial reluctance to admit to substantive review is that it is too often conflated with the notion of 'correctness review', where judges second-guess the primary decision-maker on the merits of the case, in the way of appeal rather than review (such as when courts may disagree with a planning authority about whether a proposal is out of character with the area by impeding an historic view). In *De Smith*, we contended for principles of substantive review short of correctness

[20] Published in 1995 as S de Smith, H Woolf and J Jowell, *Judicial Review of Administrative Action*, 5th edn (London, Sweet & Maxwell). For the current (7th) edition, see n 9.
[21] Jowell and Lester (n 14) 374.
[22] Molière, *Le Bourgeois Gentilhomme*, Act II, Scene 4.

review. And we noted different categories into which those principles could be divided.[23] Reflecting on these categories for the purpose of this chapter, I now believe that they can be summarised more succinctly into three: the first category involves review of the *quality of the decision* itself, the second involves review of the *justification* of the decision and the third, review of the *impact* of the decision. The kinds of decisions which fall under each category are, briefly summarised, the following:

A. Review of the *Quality* of the Decision Itself

Under this category, the court assesses the decision itself and asks whether it passes muster. The court readily invalidates decisions which are uncertain, incomprehensible, or inconsistent; or where the decision is fettered by such as a rule, contract or policy.

i. Uncertain or Incomprehensible Decisions

It is well established that courts have the power to render a decision void for uncertainty.[24] A byelaw or statutory instrument may be pronounced invalid for uncertainty where it fails adequately to indicate what it is prohibiting; so too a condition attached to a planning permission when its meaning is unclear or confusing. Sometimes the decision is struck down because it is simply incomprehensible, or has the impression of being entirely arbitrary.

ii. Inconsistent Decisions

In this case the decision is assessed in relation to previous decisions or actions of the decision-maker. Like cases need to be treated alike and courts often seek justification as to why law is not equally applied. Increasingly, the principle of consistency is being urged as a 'free-standing principle of administrative law'.[25]

[23] See Chapter 11 of the 5th to 7th editions of *De Smith* (nn 9 and 19). The latest edition divides the categories into (1) unreasonable process, (2) violation of common law or constitutional rights, and (3) oppressive decisions. A fourth category is considered separately, namely, violation of Convention rights under the Human Rights Act 1998.

[24] See, eg *McEldowney v Forde* [1971] AC 632 and further in *de Smith* 7th edn (n 9) [11-040].

[25] See, eg R Clayton, 'Legitimate Expectations, Policy and the Principle of Consistency' [2003] *Cambridge Law Journal* 93; M Elliott, 'Legitimate Expectations, Consistency and the Abuse of Power: The Rashid Case' [2005] *Judicial Review* 281 (referring to *R (Rashid) v Secretary of State for the Home Department* [2005] EWCA Civ 744). See further *De Smith*, 7th edn (n 9) [11-062] ff.

iii. Where the Decision is Fettered by a Predetermined Rule or Policy

The notion of fettering of discretion can fall into different grounds of judicial review. In one sense, the fettering of a discretion falls under the ground of illegality, as the decision-maker has failed to exercise his authorised discretion and has instead constrained it by an inflexible rule. In another sense, fettering can be seen as a breach of procedural fairness in that the decision-maker failed to listen to someone who had something new to say. It can also, however, be seen as an example of an unreasonable exercise of power. This is because it binds the decision-maker to a rule or policy irrespective of whether it may reasonably be waived or adjusted in the light of the circumstances of the particular case.[26]

B. Review of the *Justification* for the Decision

Under this category, the assessment of the court focuses upon the quality of the reasoning or evidence underlying or supporting the decision, or the quality of its reasoning.

i. Irrational Decisions stricto sensu

The law reports contain a number of cases of decisions invalidated on the ground that the decision does not 'add up—in which, in other words, there is an error of reasoning which robs the decision of logic'.[27] Such cases give the impression of arbitrariness, perhaps 'by spinning a coin or consulting an astrologer'.[28] This happens where the given reasons are simply inadequate, unintelligible or self-contradictory. Sometimes decisions have been invalidated because the result is so out of line as to raise a presumption of lack of reasoning.[29] In other cases the question is whether the reasoning bears a 'rational connection' to the measures designed to further a policy objective.[30]

ii. Decisions Supported by No or Inadequate Evidence or Made on the Basis of Mistake of an Established and Material Fact

Courts, under judicial review, rather than appeal, will not normally interfere with a public's authority's assessment of the evidence or facts of a case.

[26] As applied in, eg *British Oxygen Co Ltd v Board of Trade* [1971] AC 610. See further *de Smith*, 7th edn (n 9) ch 9.

[27] *R v Parliamentary Commissioner, ex p Balchin* [1998] 1 PLR 1, 13.

[28] *R v Deputy Industrial Injuries Commissioner, ex p Moore* [1965] 1 QB 456, 488 (Lord Diplock).

[29] *R v Civil Service Appeal Board, ex p Cunningham* [1991] 4 All ER 310.

[30] See, eg *R v Minister of Defence, ex p Walker* [2000] 1 WLR 806, 812 (Lord Slynn). For further examples, see *de Smith*, 7th edn (n 9) [11-036].

However, interference has been permitted where the decision is unsupported by substantial evidence, sometimes simply called a 'perverse' decision.[31] Recently the courts have been prepared also to intervene where there has been a misdirection, disregard or mistake of a material fact.[32]

C. Review of the Decision's *Impact*

Under this category the court's assessment focuses on the effect of the decision on the individual who is affected by it. These include breach of a legitimate (substantive) expectation, a decision where undue weight has been accorded to a particular relevant consideration, and unduly oppressive decisions.

i. Decisions Which Disappoint a Legitimate Expectation

The notion of the legitimate expectation entered our law as a procedural concept. If an expectation of a benefit induced by a promise or practice had been disappointed, the person was entitled to a hearing on the matter.[33] Later, it was held that the person could also be entitled to the substantive benefit itself (provided that the representation was clear, unambiguous and unqualified).[34] Thus a prisoner could challenge the decision of the Home Secretary on the ground of its impact in dashing his legitimate expectation of parole after a given period.[35]

ii. Decisions Where Undue Weight has been Accorded to a Relevant Consideration

The law reports contain countless examples of such cases, where decision-makers have weighed up considerations that are relevant to the exercise of the power, but where too much or too little weight has been placed on one

[31] See, eg *Pulhofer v Hillingdon LBC* [1986] AC 484, 518 (Lord Brightman).

[32] *E v Secretary of State for the Home Department* [2004] EWCA Civ 49, [2004] QB 1044. See P Craig, 'Judicial Review, Appeal and Factual Error' [2004] *Public Law* 788. See further *de Smith*, 7th edn (n 9) [11-041].

[33] *R v Liverpool Corporation, ex p Liverpool Taxi Fleet Operator's Association* [1972] 2 QB 299.

[34] *E v IRC, ex p MFK Underwriting Agencies Ltd* [1990] 1 WLR 1545, 1570 (Bingham LJ). In *R (on the application of Reprotech Ltd v East Sussex CC* [2002] UKHL 8, [35], Lord Hoffmann said that: 'Public law has ... absorbed whatever is useful from the moral values which underlie the private law concept of estoppel and the time has come for it to stand on its own two feet.'

[35] *R v Secretary of State for the Home Department, ex p Pierson* [1998] AC 539, 590–91 (Lord Steyn, linking the legitimate expectation to substantive rule of law). See further *de Smith*, 7th edn (n 9) ch 12.

of the considerations. Such a case does not engage the ground of illegality, as there is no claim that the consideration in question strayed outside the objects or purpose of the power. For example, when the police, in the face of disruptive protests, withdrew some protection from demonstrators in order overall to protect others elsewhere in their jurisdiction, the courts have considered whether these (both relevant) considerations have been fairly balanced.[36]

iii. Decisions Which are Unduly Onerous or Oppressive

The courts have on countless occasions held a decision to be unreasonable, irrational or perverse where the claimant has endured excessive hardship or unnecessary infringement on his rights or interests. Planning conditions which require the developer in effect to dedicate his land to public use fall into this category. Excessively low compensation, excessive penalties or unacceptable delays also fall into this class of case,[37] as do cases where human rights are limited (under the common law or Convention rights under the Human Rights Act).

VII. SLIDING SCALES AND VARIABLE INTENSITY REVIEW

In recent years the notion of unreasonableness has been made more sophisticated by distinguishing different levels of scrutiny to fit different kinds of decision. It is generally assumed that there is a sliding scale of substantive review, and that the more interference with human rights the more the court would require by way of justification under the unreasonableness test.[38] Conversely, the greater the policy element in the decision, the lower the degree of scrutiny of the decision is required.[39]

It is notable, however, that a number of the principles for intervention described above require the courts to afford no deference or margin of appreciation to the decision-maker. Nothing 'manifest' is needed. The decision is either, in the courts' view, uncertain or it is not; inconsistent or not; involved in a fettering of discretion or not; strictly irrational or not; supported by adequate evidence or mistake of material fact or not. Similarly, where a legitimate expectation is in issue, the question is again not influenced by any degree of deference or sliding scale.

[36] *R v Chief Constable of Sussex, ex p International Trader's Ferry Ltd* [1999] 2 AC 418; cf *R v Coventry City Council, ex p Phoenix Aviation* [1995] 3 All ER 37. See further *de Smith*, 7th edn (n 9) [11-033].

[37] For these and other examples, see *de Smith*, 7th edn (n 9) [11-070].

[38] *R v Ministry of Defence, ex p Smith* [1996] QB 517.

[39] See Laws LJ in *R v Department of Education, ex p Begbie* [2000] 1 WLR 111, 130.

Outside of those areas, even where a degree of deference or discretionary area of judgement is required, the notion of sliding scale is not satisfactory. As Lord Carnwath has recently said:[40]

> Sliding scales only work if one has measurable standards to which they can be applied; otherwise it is a matter less of sliding scales than of 'slithering about in grey areas' (to quote Professor le Sueur).

VIII. PROPORTIONALITY

Two of the principles mentioned above involve proportionality, both in cases where the impact of the decision is in issue. First are decisions where undue weight has been placed upon a relevant consideration and second, where the decision's impact is unduly onerous or oppressive. We should note, however, that proportionality can be employed in two different ways, first, as a test of fair balance and second, as a structured test of necessity.

A. Proportionality as a Test of Fair Balance

In this sense of proportionality, the courts will evaluate whether manifestly disproportionate weight has been attached to one or more considerations relevant to the decision, or whether its impact is unduly oppressive. Here the burden of proof of disproportionality is with the claimant as the courts will bear in mind their institutional and constitutional limitations. There is no structured test but a mere balancing exercise.[41] As O'Regan J said in a South African case involving fishing allocations:[42]

> A decision that requires an equilibrium to be struck between a range of competing interests or considerations and which is to be taken by a person or institution with specific expertise in that area must be shown respect by the Courts.

B. Proportionality as a Structured Test of Necessity

Proportionality in this sense is more than a mere balancing exercise. It arises when a fundamental norm has been ignored or violated, and when

[40] Lord Carnwath, 'From Judicial Outrage to Sliding Scales', ALBA Annual Lecture 2013; citing Andrew le Sueur, 'The Rise and Ruin of Unreasonableness' [2005] *Judicial Review* 32. Lord Sumption agrees: see 'Anxious Scrutiny', ALBA Annual lecture 2014, where he describes anxious scrutiny as an approach which invokes 'the image of nail-biting anxiety as judges crouched in the road observe the oncoming headlights of a fundamental right'. Craig disagrees, see P Craig 'Judicial Review and Anxious Scrutiny' [2015] *Public Law* 60.

[41] Craig refers to this sense of proportionality as 'proportionality *stricto sensu*': P Craig, *EU Administrative Law*, 2nd edn (Oxford, Oxford University Press, 2012) 657.

[42] *Bato Star Fishing Ltd v The Chief Director: Marine and Coastal Management* 2004 (4) SA 490 (CC) 48.

the burden of proof shifts from the claimant to the official decision-maker to justify that violation.[43] We are familiar with the structured test under European Union law, where a set of questions is asked of the decision-maker: Is the measure which is being challenged legitimate? Is it suitable to attain the ends in view? Is there a rational connection between the means and ends? Is the measure necessary? Could it be achieved by a less onerous measure?

In respect of rights under the European Convention on Human Rights, as applied by the European Court of Human Rights and in the United Kingdom under the Human Rights Act, a similar structured test is imposed, especially to assess the extent to which the 'qualified' rights may be limited. It is for the authority to justify the departure from the right in question and to show that the measures are 'prescribed by the law', that they pursue a legitimate end or an end specified in the relevant Article of the Convention (ends such as national security or public safety); that the means are rationally connected to that end; that no less restrictive alternative could have been adopted and that the limitation is necessary (and not merely desirable).[44]

In respect of common-law rights, it seems time to abandon the sliding scale and 'heightened scrutiny' unreasonable test. There is no reason to favour convention rights over rights that have been tested and established in the common law. The unreasonableness test should therefore be softened beyond even heightened scrutiny. The burden of proof should therefore be on the decision-maker to justify violations of all fundamental and constitutional rights through the strictures of structured proportionality.[45]

IX. CONSTITUTIONAL JUSTIFICATIONS OF SUBSTANTIVE REVIEW

Returning now to the constitutional justification of substantive review, the constitutional principle that is most engaged is that of the *rule of law*. Although the rule of law is sometimes said to be a contested concept and unduly vague, Tom Bingham's recent book on that subject[46] shows that its ingredients are, if not completely cut and dried, relatively specific. Summarising Bingham, the rule of law consists of the following six

[43] The former President of the Israeli Supreme Court and scholar Aharon Barak has described this kind of proportionality as a 'legal construction' or 'methodological tool' to justify the limitation of constitutional rights: A Barak, *Proportionality: Constitutional Rights and their Limitations* (Cambridge, Cambridge University Press, 2012).

[44] See Lord Steyn in *R v Secretary of State for the Home Department, ex p Daly* [2001] UKHL 26, [2001] 2 AC 532, applying the Privy Council case of *de Freitas v Permanent Secretary of Ministry of Agriculture and Fisheries, Land and Housing* [1999] 1 AC 69, 80 (Lord Clyde). See also J Jowell, 'Beyond the Rule of Law: Towards Constitutional Judicial Review' [2000] *Public Law* 671; M Elliott, 'The HRA 1998 and the Standard of Substantive Judicial Review' (2001) 60 *Cambridge Law Journal* 301.

[45] As Lord Bingham suggested in *Daly* (n 44) [21].

[46] Bingham (n 12).

principal 'ingredients': (a) legality (that power should be authorised and not exercised in an arbitrary fashion); (b) legal certainty (that fair warning be given of change in the law, that law not be retrospectively applied and be comprehensible and accessible); (c) equality (that the law be equally applied to rich and poor, the powerful and the marginalised); (d) access to justice (including the opportunity to challenge decisions made about one's rights or interests); (e) that, when a challenge is made, there be a fair trial; and (f) that such trial be before an independent and impartial court or tribunal.[47]

It is clear that many of the substantive principles outlined above fall under the rule of law's requirements. Arbitrariness is the antithesis of the rule of law as it does not rely upon or provide reference to any rational justification. The rule of law's strictures against arbitrariness and in favour of legal certainty capture the prohibition on decisions that are unduly vague, irrational *stricto sensu*, or lacking an adequate evidentiary base. Upholding a legitimate expectation has explicitly been referred to as an example of the application of the rule of law in its substantive sense.[48] Inconsistent decisions offend the rule of law's core requirement of the equal application of the law.[49] The rule of law as a constitutional principle has been independently invoked to read down discretion so as to forbid the curtailing of access to the courts.[50]

What is the constitutional justification for the prohibition of a disproportionate decision? Although often seen as European in origin, proportionality has an impeccable English origin by way of Magna Carta, Article 20 of which provides that:

> For a trivial offence, a man will be fined only in proportion to the degree of his offence, and for a serious offence correspondingly, but not so heavily as to deprive him of his livelihood.

When structured proportionality is engaged, proportionality is simply a tool to restrain the unnecessary violation of a fundamental norm. When applied in the sense of fair balance, such as to constrain unduly oppressive decisions, proportionality supports and interacts with another constitutional principle, and one that is at the heart of the English legal

[47] Bingham also suggested that the rule of law included compliance by the state with its obligation in international as in national law.

[48] Lord Steyn in *Pierson* (n 34) 591, citing J Jowell, 'The Rule of Law' in J Jowell and D Oliver (eds), *The Changing Constitution*, 3rd edn (Oxford, Oxford University Press, 1994) 57, 74–77.

[49] I have argued elsewhere that equality qualifies as another constitutional principle in its own right: J Jowell, 'Is Equality a Constitutional Principle?' (1994) 47 *Current Legal Problems* (Part 2) 1; see also R Singh, 'Equality: The Neglected Virtue' [2004] *European Human Rights Law Review* 141; TRS Allan, *Law, Liberty and Justice: The Legal Foundations of British Constitutionalism* (Oxford, Clarendon Press, 1994). Baroness Hale has observed in *Ghaidan v Godin-Mendoza* [2004] UKHL 30, [132] that: 'Democracy is founded on the principle that each individual has equal value. Treating some as automatically have less value than others ... violates his dignity as a human being.'

[50] *R v Lord Chancellor, ex p Witham* [1998] QB 575.

system, namely, the *presumption of liberty*. Yes, the state may interfere with liberty when authorised to do so, but such authorisation, since *Entick v Carrington*[51] must be clear, and does not permit licence to impose onerous and unnecessary burdens. Similarly, criminal offences are interpreted and applied narrowly by the courts,[52] as are police and public order powers.[53] The principle of proportionality is thus a device to ensure that incursions on freedoms and liberties are not unnecessarily imposed.

When structured proportionality is engaged, it is simply a tool to restrain the unnecessary violation of a fundamental norm. When assessing whether a particular Convention right, or European Treaty provision is breached and can be justified by a stated limitation, the role of the court is one of assessing the legality, rather than the reasonableness, of the decision. In that sense the exercise is, as Lord Sumption has said, one of merits review.[54] The question is simply whether the decision-maker has sufficiently demonstrated that the departure from the right was proportionate to its legitimate aim, which is a stipulated exception to the right. There is no question but that the court possesses the constitutional authority to carry out that review, but it may nevertheless defer on the ground that the decision-maker is institutionally better equipped to make the decision.

X. WHERE ARE WE TODAY?

As we discovered in our exercise of research for the fifth edition of *De Smith*, there are many more cases in which unreasonableness had been successfully pleaded than was commonly supposed to be the case. In 2004 Professor le Sueur found that of a sample of 41 judicial review cases challenged for unreasonableness from January 2000 to July 2003, 18 were successful; a high success rate by any standard.

There can be little doubt that the courts are articulating more and more specific standards of substantive review. In particular, they are increasingly utilising the standard of proportionality in both its senses.

[51] *Entick v Carrington* (1765) 19 St Tr 1029.

[52] For a recent example of this, see *R v Zafar* [2008] EWCA Crim 184, [2008] QB 810, where the Court of Appeal adopted a restrictive interpretation of the provisions of s 57 of the Terrorism Act 2000, which prohibited the possession of material for a 'purpose connected with the commission, preparation or instigation of an act of terrorism'.

[53] See the recent decision of the House of Lords in *R (on the application of Laporte) v Chief Constable of Gloucestershire* [2006] UKHL 55, [2007] 2 AC 105 where police intervention in the interest of maintaining public order to prevent anti-war protesters picketing an air force base was held to be unlawful on the basis that the relevant public order legislation could not be interpreted widely so as to authorise the action taken against the protestors.

[54] See Sumption (n 40) and Lord Sumption's recent judgment in *R (Carlile) v Secretary of State for the Home Department* [2014] UKSC 60, [2014] 3 WLR 1404. For recent accounts of proportionality's reasoning and justification, see G Huscroft, B Miller and G Webber (eds), *Proportionality and the Rule of Law* (Cambridge, Cambridge University Press, 2014), especially chapters by TRS Allan, D Dyzenhaus, S Gardbaum and T Endicott.

In 2002, Lord Cooke thought that the day would come when *Wednesbury* would be regarded as an 'unfortunately retrogressive decision in English administrative law',[55] and in 2003 Dyson LJ had 'difficulty in seeing what justification there is now for retaining the *Wednesbury* test'.[56] However, he said too that it was for the House of Lords, rather than his Court of Appeal, to perform its 'burial rites'.[57]

Our new Supreme Court has still not pronounced firmly on the matter. However, in a recent case Lord Mance said that[58]

> the right approach is now surely … as de Smith … suggests, that it is inappropriate to treat all cases of judicial review together under a general but vague principle of reasonableness, and preferable to look for the underlying tenet or principle which indicates the basis on which the court should approach any administrative law challenge in a particular situation.

In his 2013 ALBA lecture, another Supreme Court Justice, Lord Carnwath said this:[59]

> The important question is not whether the decision is beyond the range of reasonable responses, but why? The reason must be found either in the statute, expressly or by implication, or in some other general but separately identifiable principle of the common law … [This approach] accords with my experience over the 45 years or so of my professional career. The judges are like sculptors chipping away at the relatively formless block bequeathed to them by Lord Greene, in order to carve out some more practical and specific tenets of the law such as can be applied to real cases … I think the time has come to abandon judicial outrage and sliding scales. We may also have to abandon the search for residual principles, whether of reasonableness or rationality.

XI. CONCLUSIONS

Although proportionality is, like unreasonableness, a general standard, is it in any way more precise and less vague than unreasonableness? We should note too that in some cases a decision is required to be 'manifestly' disproportionate before the court will intervene.[60] However, as Lord Mance has said:[61]

> The advantage of the terminology of proportionality is that it introduces an element of structure into the exercise, by directing attention to factors such as

55 *Daly* (n 44) [32].

56 *R (Association of British Civilian Internees (Far East Region)) v Secretary of State for Defence* [2003] EWCA Civ 473, [2003] QB 1397, [34].

57 Ibid, [35].

58 *Kennedy v Charity Commission* [2014] UKSC 20, [2014] 2 WLR 808, [55].

59 ALBA Annual Lecture 2013 (n 40).

60 *R (Sinclair Collis Ltd) v Secretary of State for Health* [2011] EWCA Civ 437, [2012] QB 394 (Lord Neuberger). But see Lady Justice Arden and, dissenting, Lord Justice Laws.

61 *Kennedy* (n 58) [54].

> suitability or appropriateness, necessity and the balance or imbalance of benefits and disadvantages....

Proportionality in its structured sense therefore, like the more specific standards of substantive review referred to above, does introduce a more explicit justification than mere 'unreasonableness' allows. Such a clearer articulation of standards promotes what Mureinik called a 'culture of justification' in place of a 'culture of authority'.[62] Proportionality cannot, however, occupy the entire space of substantive review.[63] This is because its role is in relation to specific situations only and it can provide little assistance to the assessment of those decisions or justifications which need to be guided by quite different requirements of lawful administration, such as those mentioned above.

Our judges have indeed been 'chipping away' at the block of *Wednesbury* unreasonableness, as they had earlier at the notion of strong parliamentary sovereignty. This exercise has brought into view, and has been supported by, other constitutional principles that properly support the fabric of our democracy. These include the rule of law, the presumption of liberty, and equality.

The exercise has not, however, completely whittled away the need for unreasonableness to remain what Sir William Wade, in his letter quoted above, called a 'residual pigeon-hole', so as to allow for the regulation of new or unusual cases. Outside of structured proportionality, the various principles of substantive review do not amount to an appeal on the facts and merits of a case. They still permit due deference in appropriate situations. Proportionality is a ground that is more specific and structured than unreasonableness but it too cannot wholly usurp the entire terrain of substantive review.

As in many areas of law, general standards may be required in the interest of flexibility and fairness in the individual case. However, more precise articulation of the specific principles underlying a relevant standard, whether unreasonableness or irrationality or proportionality, will surely assist the decision-maker, affected persons and their advisers to know the boundaries of administrative propriety. This will promote integrity and legal certainty. It will also assist judges to tread a more certain line between the hard ground of *Wednesbury* and ground that is, in the words of Lord Scarman's letter, 'too soft for judicial hooves'.

[62] E Mureinik, 'A Bridge to Where? Introducing the Interim Bill of Rights' (1994) 10 *South African Journal on Human Rights* 31, 32. See, eg the approach of Lord Sumption in *Bank Mellat* (n 11) where he (for the majority of the Supreme Court) held the relevant Order in Council to be neither rational nor proportionate, albeit that the matter would not normally be held amenable to the judicial process.

[63] I fully agree here with M Taggart, 'Proportionality, Deference, *Wednesbury*' [2008] *New Zealand Law Review* 423; cf P Craig, 'Proportionality, Rationality and Review' [2010] *New Zealand Law Review* 265.

4

From Bifurcation to Calibration: Twin-Track Deference and the Culture of Justification

MARK ELLIOTT*

I. INTRODUCTION

QUESTIONS ABOUT SUBSTANTIVE judicial review—its legitimacy, its appropriate intensity, its proper limits—often appear to be as intractable as they are beguiling. The appeal—but also the complexity—of the debate lies, at least in part, in the fact that it is animated by disagreement about underlying constitutional matters, including the rule of law, the separation of powers, and the nature, status, extent, legitimacy and interaction of legislative, administrative and judicial authority. In this chapter, I am concerned with substantive review in the narrower of the two senses in which the term is used in this book: that is, review of the decision itself, as distinct from the process by which the decision was taken, on grounds involving some degree of scrutiny of the merits. More particularly, the aim is to explore the relationship between the constitutional matters mentioned above and the front-line doctrinal tools, such as the *Wednesbury* and proportionality tests, that are associated with substantive review. I will advocate an approach that, while acknowledging the valuable role that doctrinal tools are capable of playing in the structuring of law and legal reasoning, insists upon such tools' subservience to the underlying concerns that ought to be in

* Reader in Public Law, Faculty of Law, University of Cambridge; Fellow, St Catharine's College, Cambridge. I had the benefit of presenting, at an early stage, some of the ideas contained in this chapter at a seminar at The University of Auckland in March 2011. It was a particular honour to have an opportunity to discuss Michael Taggart's work in that forum, and I am grateful to those who attended the seminar for the valuable feedback they gave me. I also wish to record my thanks to Trevor Allan, Cora Chan, Paul Daly, Bruce Harris, Cora Hoexter, Sarah Nason, Ted Thomas, Jason Varuhas, Hanna Wilberg and Jack Williams for their very helpful comments on earlier drafts of this chapter. Responsibility for the views contained in it, and for any errors, is mine alone.

the driving seat. I will also argue against approaches that promise neat, bright-line distinctions but which do so by masking underlying normative or constitutional complexity through the application of a formalist doctrinal veneer.

The purpose is not to suggest that administrative law generally, or substantive review in particular, should become a doctrine-free zone. Far from it. Rather, the aim is to argue in favour of an approach to doctrine which better acknowledges that it is a legal superstructure with deep normative roots. Proportionality, reasonableness and their several variants ought not to be airbrushed away in favour of a vague contextualism. However, front-line doctrinal tools need to be appreciated for what they are: namely, secondary—albeit crucial—manifestations of the primary constitutional, institutional and normative factors that form the bedrock of public law. The argument, therefore, is for a bottom-up approach to the construction of the doctrinal tools that operate at the sharp end of substantive judicial review.

In advocating such an approach, I will challenge aspects of the doctrinally-bifurcated vision of substantive judicial review that Michael Taggart advanced—although I will also endorse much of the sentiment that underpinned that vision.[1] In place of a bifurcated approach, I will set out and defend a framework within which the nature and intensity of substantive review is calibrated by reference to the notion of justification and to two distinct but complementary conceptions of deference, which can be used to inform and modulate the process whereby courts determine whether administrative (or legislative) measures are justified.

II. DOCTRINE

It is paradoxical that while the debate about substantive review is in fact a manifestation of deeper institutional and normative disputation, much of it consists of disagreements that are (at least superficially) doctrinal in nature. Take, for instance, early discussion in English law about whether it would be acceptable for courts, in certain circumstances, to rely upon the proportionality rather than the *Wednesbury* reasonableness test[2] when called upon to scrutinise the substance of an administrative measure. In cases such as *Brind* in which this question was canvassed, the focus—perhaps inevitably—was upon the differences between the two techniques at a doctrinal level.[3] This is not to suggest that underlying considerations, for

[1] M Taggart, 'Proportionality, Deference, *Wednesbury*' [2008] *New Zealand Law Review* 423.

[2] *Associated Provincial Picture Houses Ltd v Wednesbury Corporation* [1948] 1 KB 223 (CA).

[3] *R v Secretary of State for the Home Department, ex p Brind* [1991] 1 AC 696.

instance about institutional competence or democratic legitimacy, were not in play: but occupying the centre stage were questions about the doctrinal evolution of administrative law.

In recent years—largely as a result of changes wrought by the Human Rights Act 1998—disagreement about whether proportionality should play any role in the English courts has given way to controversy about precisely what role it should play, and in what circumstances. Yet here, too, the focus has often been on doctrinal matters. Considerable attention, for instance, has been paid to the content of the proportionality test: that is, to its internal structure, and to how its constituent elements might and ought to relate to one another.[4] The reasonableness doctrine itself has received similar attention, notable recent contributions in this area including Paul Daly's argument that the doctrine possesses a degree of 'reason and structure' in excess of that which its critics presuppose,[5] and Paul Craig's *Current Legal Problems* lecture, in which he examines the doctrinal nature of reasonableness review.[6] Meanwhile, considerable attention has been given to the question whether (as Aileen Kavanagh,[7] Murray Hunt[8] and Alison Young,[9] among others, have contended) deference should be conceptualised as a doctrine in its own right, or whether (as Trevor Allan has argued)[10] deference, or at least the thinking that animates it, is better conceived of as something that, at most, influences and internally shapes the application of the proportionality doctrine itself. Doctrinal questions about reasonableness and proportionality, and allied notions such as deference, are far from unimportant: indeed, I have considered them in detail elsewhere, arguing, for instance, that due appreciation of proportionality's structure is key to realising its potential as a tool of substantive review and to developing a sufficiently nuanced conception of deference.[11] There is, however, a risk of doctrine assuming the status of the tail that wags the dog: that is, of taking doctrine as a given and then attempting, as best as is possible, to gloss it so as to secure a reconciliation with underlying concerns, whether normative, institutional or constitutional.

[4] J Rivers, 'Proportionality and Variable Intensity Review' (2006) 65 *Cambridge Law Journal* 174.

[5] P Daly, '*Wednesbury*'s Reason and Structure' [2011] *Public Law* 238.

[6] P Craig, 'The Nature of Reasonableness Review' (2013) 66 *Current Legal Problems* 1.

[7] A Kavanagh, 'Defending Deference in Public Law and Constitutional Theory' (2010) 126 *Law Quarterly Review* 222.

[8] M Hunt, 'Sovereignty's Blight: Why Contemporary Public Law needs the Concept of "Due Deference"' in N Bamforth and P Leyland (eds), *Public Law in a Multi-Layered Constitution* (Oxford, Hart Publishing, 2003).

[9] A Young, 'In Defence of Due Deference' (2009) 72 *Modern Law Review* 554.

[10] T Allan, 'Human Rights and Judicial Review: A Critique of "Due Deference"' (2006) 65 *Cambridge Law Journal* 671.

[11] M Elliott, 'Proportionality and Deference: The Importance of a Structured Approach' in C Forsyth and others (eds), *Effective Judicial Review: A Cornerstone of Good Governance* (Oxford, Oxford University Press, 2010).

Perhaps the best example, however, of the way in which doctrinal controversy has tended to overshadow debate in this area is furnished by the strongly opposing views that have been expressed about the relationship between the reasonableness and proportionality doctrines. On the one hand, there are those, such as Paul Craig[12] and Murray Hunt,[13] who argue that proportionality can and should operate as a general head of judicial review, and that it should replace reasonableness. In sympathy with that view, the Court of Appeal of England and Wales concluded, as long ago as 2003, that—on grounds pertaining to proportionality's 'more precise and sophisticated' structure—it should be embraced across the board.[14] Indeed, it went as far as to say that *Wednesbury*'s 'burial rites' should performed:[15] a step that the UK Supreme Court shows no inclination to take.[16] On the other hand, there are those—including Paul Daly,[17] Tom Hickman,[18] Jeff King[19] and Jason Varuhas[20]—who resist the suggestion that proportionality should sweep the board, arguing that (some form of) the reasonableness test should remain within the courts' substantive-review toolbox.[21] And, as noted above, Michael Taggart became a prominent proponent of that view in his 2008 contribution to the *New Zealand Law Review*, in which he argued in favour of a 'rainbow of review' within which proportionality would apply to 'rights' cases, and reasonableness to cases concerning 'public wrongs'.[22]

The debates about substantive-review doctrine have been, and continue to be, valuable. Doctrinal lucidity is highly desirable, and debate that serves to clarify doctrine is therefore to be welcomed. There is, however, a risk that an undue focus upon doctrine may ultimately prove to be a distraction, with the doctrinal trees serving to obscure the normative wood. A related risk is that over-emphasising doctrine may yield a legal architecture whose

[12] P Craig, 'Proportionality, Rationality and Review' [2010] *New Zealand Law Review* 265.

[13] M Hunt, 'Against Bifurcation' in D Dyzenhaus, M Hunt and G Huscroft (eds), *A Simple Common Lawyer: Essays in Honour of Michael Taggart* (Oxford, Hart Publishing, 2009).

[14] *R (Association of British Civilian Internees (Far East Region)) v Secretary of State for Defence* [2003] EWCA Civ 473, [2003] QB 1397, [35].

[15] Ibid, [35].

[16] For a recent example of the UK Supreme Court's continuing willingness to apply a reasonableness, or rationality, test, see *R (McDonald) v Kensington and Chelsea Royal London Borough Council* [2011] UKSC 33, [2011] PTSR 1266. See also on this point J Varuhas, 'Against Unification' (ch 5 in this volume).

[17] Daly, '*Wednesbury*'s Reason and Structure' (n 5) and *A Theory of Deference in Administrative Law* (Cambridge, Cambridge University Press, 2012).

[18] T Hickman, 'Problems for Proportionality' [2010] *New Zealand Law Review* 303.

[19] J King, 'Proportionality: A Halfway House' [2010] *New Zealand Law Review* 327.

[20] Varuhas (n 16).

[21] I have also argued that reasonableness should be retained alongside proportionality. See M Elliott, 'The Human Rights Act 1998 and the Standard of Substantive Review' (2001) 60 *Cambridge Law Journal* 301.

[22] Taggart (n 1).

rigidity is unwarranted. Taggart's bifurcation thesis is arguably a case in point. It envisages a bright-line distinction between two realms of public law which are respectively the doctrinal preserves of proportionality and reasonableness. The former (on this scheme) is concerned with the protection of individual rights, the latter with the identification of public wrongs. The former is a structured form of review, whilst the latter is unstructured. The former constitutes an intensive form of review, the latter a relaxed one. And the former safeguards norms that are taken to be important in a way, or to a degree, that those in play in the latter context are taken not to be. It would be going too far to suggest that there is nothing in these distinctions, or that those, like Taggart, who support the bifurcation thesis fail to recognise that they may exist other than as bright lines. The difficulty, however, is that such distinctions map onto the normative terrain of public law only in a highly approximate way. They capture something of what is going on, but the bluntness of such tools diminishes their usefulness.

III. JUSTIFICATION

My intention in this chapter is not to seek to diminish the importance of doctrine (or of the debate referred to above). However, I do wish to suggest that the front-line doctrinal instruments that are deployed in substantive-review cases are specific manifestations of underlying considerations. The normative status of the value infringed by the impugned measure, the constitutional status of the measure, and the respective institutional positions of the reviewing body and the decision-maker are examples of factors that will—or should—affect the shape of substantive review within the confines of the particular case. On this view, front-line doctrinal tools such as reasonableness, proportionality and deference (and the many different variants which each of those meta-doctrinal concepts comprise) are merely the tip of the iceberg. Present, but sometimes beneath the waterline, is a network of deeper considerations that determine what doctrinal instruments should be brought to bear in the circumstances of the case, and precisely what form those instruments should take given the particularities of context.[23] For instance, the traditional view that substantive review should be confined

[23] I have no difficulty with the argument that some of those underlying considerations may themselves be characterised as doctrinal. However, there is, I think, a difference between front-line doctrinal tools such as reasonableness and proportionality, and underlying considerations—such as democratic legitimacy, the appeal/review distinction, relative institutional capacity, and so on—that may inform whether and if so how such tools are deployed. In any event, the fact that the distinction I seek to draw may not coincide with a line separating matters doctrinal from some other category is unimportant, not least because I am seeking not to attack the use of doctrine, but to argue for a clearer—and more clearly articulated—relationship between front-line doctrinal tools and the substrata of normative, institutional and constitutional considerations that (should) inform their application.

to determining whether the impugned measure is manifestly unreasonable reflects a conclusion drawn from a set of underlying and interlocking considerations concerning the way in which judicial and administrative authority should be divided, and the proper extent of curial supervision of the executive. At the same time, the willingness of English courts to engage—in pre-Human Rights Act cases that were concerned with rights—in a somewhat more demanding form of reasonableness review shows that what is normatively at stake may serve to reshape the front-line doctrinal instruments applied by the court. This, in turn, acknowledges the reduced purchase in some (for example, rights) contexts of democratic and institutional arguments that, other things being equal, would point towards a relatively limited judicial role.

The connection between doctrine (in the sense of front-line doctrinal tools such as reasonableness and proportionality) and underlying normative, institutional and constitutional considerations is important, and is one which—I will argue in this chapter—needs to be articulated more clearly. However, the way in which those two sets of factors relate—and ought to relate—to one another can be understood only within the context of an overarching conception of the nature and purpose of substantive judicial review itself. The way in which we conceive of substantive review at this level will necessarily influence our sense of the form that it should take, and of the extent to which different normative, institutional and constitutional factors enjoy traction when it comes to determining the role of the reviewing court and (hence) the nature and incisiveness of the doctrinal tools it ought to apply.

My preferred approach to this overarching issue draws upon understandings of the nature and purpose of public law advanced by Etienne Mureinik and later endorsed by Taggart. Mureinik, writing in the early 1990s against the backdrop of South Africa's transition to a new constitution, contrasted apartheid South Africa's 'culture of authority' with the 'culture of justification' promised by its new constitutional arrangements: 'a culture in which every exercise of power is expected to be justified'.[24] Taggart later argued that English administrative law was being 'constitutionalised' as it moved 'towards a culture of justification', the emergence of a duty to give reasons—and the associated erosion of the 'hoary general rule that reasons need not be given'—evidencing such a development.[25]

Taggart's claim about the emergence of a culture of justification appeared, to some extent, to be tied up with the somewhat fashionable view that administrative law is being 'righted'. That view holds that—thanks, at least

[24] E Mureinik, 'A Bridge to Where? Introducing the Interim Bill of Rights' (1994) 10 *South African Journal of Human Rights* 31, 32. See, further, D Dyzenhaus, 'Law as justification: Etienne Mureinik's Conception of Legal Culture' (1998) 14 *South African Journal of Human Rights* 11.

[25] M Taggart, 'Reinventing Administrative Law' in N Bamforth and P Leyland (eds), *Public Law in a Multi-Layered Constitution* (Oxford, Hart Publishing, 2003) 311, 332–34.

in part, to legislation such as the New Zealand Bill of Rights Act 1990[26] and the United Kingdom's Human Rights Act 1998[27]—administrative law is increasingly oriented towards the protection of rights, the implication being that the subject will, at some point, evolve so as to be capable of being viewed exclusively through a rights lens.[28] However, Taggart later stepped back from this position by acknowledging, in arguing for bifurcation, that some substantive-review cases are about 'public wrongs' rather than 'rights'.[29] Others, however, have exhibited more fulsome support for a rights-centric conception of administrative law.[30] Thomas Poole, for instance, goes as far as to suggest that the emergence of such a conception of administrative law constitutes nothing less than the 'reformation' of the discipline.[31] As Jason Varuhas has shown, such claims are highly problematic, not least because they are shot through with ambiguity and are insufficiently sensitive to the necessary doctrinal complexity of administrative law.[32] Too little doctrine—which the 'righting' thesis risks—is at least as problematic as too much. It is therefore important to make clear that my reliance upon the notion of a culture of justification, in order to avoid an unduly doctrinal approach to substantive review, does not amount to an endorsement of the unduly adoctrinal 'righting' thesis. The excesses of that thesis are avoided by my own, not least because I am concerned primarily with substantive-review cases (and so with only a subset of administrative-law cases). I am not, therefore, suggesting that *the whole of administrative law* (or, more precisely, the law of judicial review) can be understood in terms of the protection of rights. I am not even arguing that *the whole of substantive review* can be understood in those terms. And nor do I seek to deny that the nature and function of non-rights judicial review differs in very significant respects from judicial review that is undertaken in the service of human rights.[33]

[26] M Taggart, 'Tugging on Superman's cape: Lessons from Experience with the New Zealand Bill of Rights Act 1990' [1998] *Public Law* 266.

[27] Taggart (n 25).

[28] As J Varuhas, 'The Reformation of English Administrative Law? "Rights", Rhetoric and Reality' (2013) 72 *Cambridge Law Journal* 369, 375, fn 23, has noted, there is a degree of ambiguity in Taggart's position. In his paper on 'Reinventing Administrative Law' (n 25), Taggart (by means of a footnote) limits his contention to 'administrative law cases involving alleged infringements of rights'. This might be taken to suggest that his concern was only to show that rights cases can increasingly be acknowledged as such, rather than being approached through the prism of 'traditional' administrative-law doctrine. See also, on this point, Hunt (n 13) 104.

[29] Taggart (n 1).

[30] See, eg S Elias, 'Righting Administrative Law' in D Dyzenhaus, M Hunt and G Huscroft (eds), *A Simple Common Lawyer: Essays in Honour of Michael Taggart* (Oxford, Hart Publishing, 2009) 55; T Poole, 'The Reformation of English Administrative Law' (2009) 68 *Cambridge Law Journal* 142.

[31] Poole, ibid.

[32] Varuhas (n 28).

[33] See further Varuhas (n 16).

Subject, however, to those caveats, I argue that the notion of justification is a useful lens through which to approach substantive review. Talk about the *emergence* of a culture of justification notwithstanding, administrative law has, to an extent, *always* been about justification. That much is apparent from the rule-of-law bedrock upon which the edifice of modern administrative law is built. This chapter is not the place in which to revisit what Taggart, with characteristic bluntness, called the 'interminable' debate[34] concerning the constitutional foundations of judicial review in which public lawyers in England, and elsewhere, energetically engaged over a decade ago[35] (notwithstanding Philip Sales's suggestion[36] that the ultra vires doctrine may make it improper for courts to engage in proportionality, as distinct from reasonableness, review except in circumstances where the former is statutorily licensed).[37] But whatever might remain contentious about the foundations of judicial review (at least in the UK context), it is relatively uncontroversial that there is *something* in the ultra vires doctrine: that it is part, if not the whole, of the story. This is so because the doctrine serves to institutionalise the justificatory demands of the rule-of-law principle of legality, the general requirement[38] being that lawful executive action (unlike action undertaken by individuals) must be capable of justification by reference to positive legal authority.[39] It is, for instance, difficult to deny that the court is enforcing the statute—in line with ultra vires thinking—when it strikes down a decision on the ground that the decision-maker has exerted authority over a matter that is not warranted by the plain words of the legislation. Such a decision clearly breaches the principle of legality in the sense that the statute furnishes no legal basis—no legal *justification*—for the assertion of state authority.

What has changed, however, is that the set of criteria by reference to which governmental action must be justified—and so restrictions read, at

[34] Taggart (n 1) 426.

[35] See, generally, C Forsyth (ed), *Judicial Review and the Constitution* (Oxford, Hart Publishing, 2000).

[36] P Sales, 'Rationality, Proportionality and the Development of the Law' (2013) 129 *Law Quarterly Review* 223. That claim is based on the notion that Parliament has legislated on the assumption that discretion will be bounded only by the reasonableness, as opposed to the more demanding proportionality, doctrine. Space precludes detailed evaluation of that claim. Suffice it to say that I reject Sales's claim, on the ground that makes specific assumptions about Parliament's intention rather than the more defensible assumption that Parliament is to be taken to intend the powers it creates to be exercised compatibly with prevailing rule-of-law principles. See further M Elliott, *The Constitutional Foundations of Judicial Review* (Oxford, Hart Publishing, 2000).

[37] As, for example, it is by the UK's Human Rights Act 1998.

[38] This qualification is necessary in order to accommodate the 'third source' of authority. See B Harris, 'The "Third Source" of Authority for Government Action' (1992) 108 *Law Quarterly Review* 626; *R (New London College Ltd) v Secretary of State for the Home Department* [2013] UKSC 51, [2013] 1 WLR 2358.

[39] See, eg *R v Somerset County Council, ex p Fewings* [1995] 1 All ER 513 (QBD), 524 (Laws J).

least on an ultra vires analysis, into the authorising statute—has become richer. It is no longer (if it ever was) sufficient that executive action respects only those boundaries that can be traced in any direct way to the legislative text. To withstand judicial scrutiny, it must also conform, for instance, to the demands of the legitimate-expectation principle and fundamental rights—and so to the requirements of the proportionality doctrine through which infractions of rights and expectations increasingly fall to be assessed.[40] These changes, in turn, track the transition from 'thinner' to 'thicker' conceptions of the rule of law as it is understood in the administrative-law context; and they help to explain why conventional accounts of the ultra vires doctrine were increasingly found to be wanting. The constant in all of this is the requirement that exercises of administrative power be justifiable by reference to relevant legal standards: but those standards have become increasingly demanding.[41]

Understanding what a 'culture of justification' might boil down to thus requires consideration of the legal standards by reference to which courts may assess whether a given administrative measure is justified. To ask whether a given administrative measure is 'justified' is meaningful only if justification falls to be determined *by reference to* some benchmark or other. Failure to identify what those benchmarks might be lies at the core of many critiques of the *Wednesbury* reasonableness doctrine, whose superficially tautological and unstructured nature has caused many commentators to give up on it entirely. Yet, as Paul Daly has shown, articulating with greater precision the standards that are protectable via the reasonableness doctrine is capable of breathing new life into it—precisely because it turns the doctrine into a vehicle for the meaningful evaluation of the justifiability of administrative measures.[42]

However, knowing what the relevant benchmark is in any given case only gets us so far. Take, for instance, the *Coughlan* case, in which the defendant health authority sought to derogate from an undertaking to the effect that the claimant would be permitted to remain in a particular care facility 'for life'.[43] The operative benchmark was the substantive legitimate expectation generated by the promise, by reference to which the justifiability of the decision to close the facility—necessarily entailing breach of

[40] See, eg *R (Daly) v Secretary of State for the Home Department* [2001] UKHL 26, [2001] 2 AC 532 and *Paponette v Attorney General of Trinidad and Tobago* [2010] UKPC 32, [2012] 1 AC 1 on proportionality in human rights and legitimate expectation cases respectively.

[41] I recognise that the modern, more extensive sense of justification differs in important respects from the original, more limited justification-as-bare-legality notion, not least because the former involves judicial assessment of the justificatory potential of relatively open-ended reasons for action. This point of distinction notwithstanding, the different justificatory requirements embodied within contemporary administrative law can meaningfully be placed in relationship with one another on a continuum.

[42] Daly, '*Wednesbury*'s Reason and Structure' (n 5).

[43] *R v North and East Devon Health Authority, ex p Coughlan* [2001] QB 213 (CA).

the expectation—fell to be assessed. In other words, the decision had to be supported by reasons capable of overcoming the prima facie wrongfulness of overriding the expectation. That much is implicit in the very existence of the substantive-legitimate-expectation principle, the existence of which is a doctrinal manifestation of particular underlying norms—including legal certainty, trust and fairness—that are considered deserving of legal protection.[44] But to call for such a decision to be justified tells us nothing about what exactly will *count* as adequate justification for the purpose of surviving judicial scrutiny.

The notion of justification must, then, be specified in more concrete terms. And this requires us to engage with two further matters. First, when we say that an administrative measure must be justified by reference to a given benchmark, this will normally import a requirement other (and lesser) than that the reviewing court *agrees* with the measure, in the sense of being satisfied that it would have done the same thing had it been standing in the administrator's shoes. But ruling out this approach—which, if adopted, would cause the distinction between appeal and review to collapse—leaves open a range of possibilities. The court might, for instance, insist that the measure be shown to be strictly necessary and proportionate, or reasonable, or not flagrantly unreasonable, or that it satisfies some other different or interstitial standard. Viewed through the prism of justification, choosing between competing potential standards of review amounts to determining the extent of the *burden of justification* under which the defendant is to be placed, and by reference to which a decision that is 'suspect' falls to be evaluated.[45] This, in turn, raises questions about how courts should go about determining whether—and, if so, to what extent—a decision is 'suspect' and how, in the light of that, the extent of the justificatory burden should be determined. I will argue, in the next section, that this part of the substantive-review process should be driven principally by considerations relating to the normative significance of the value that is placed at risk by the impugned decision.

Once the extent of the justificatory burden has been determined, a second issue inevitably arises. Having decided *how heavy* the burden is, the court must decide whether it has been *discharged*. (For example, if the court decides, at the first stage, that the measure *must be shown* to be strictly necessary, it will have to determine, at the second stage, whether the decision *has been shown* to be necessary.) These two matters do not, of course,

[44] See, generally, S Schønberg, *Legitimate Expectations in Administrative Law* (Oxford, Oxford University Press, 2001) ch 1.

[45] As Daly, '*Wednesbury*'s Reason and Structure' (n 5) has observed, even *Wednesbury* review can be understood in terms of the imposition of a burden of justification, the presence of an 'indicium of unreasonableness' obliging the decision-maker (if it wishes to establish the lawfulness of the decision) to show that the decision is reasonable notwithstanding the existence of the indicium.

exist wholly in isolation from one another: the types of things a court may have to do in order to decide whether the burden has been discharged will necessarily be influenced by (among other things) what the burden is. But the fact that questions about the scale and discharge of the justificatory burden are related does not license their wholesale elision. Questions of the latter type are distinctive in that they entail deciding not on the *standard* to which the administrative body should be held, but whether that standard *has been met*. And that, in turn, involves assessing the quality of the justification actually offered rather than determining, in abstract terms, the characteristics that define what will be taken, in the circumstances, to constitute an adequate justification. Thus, a court might determine that a decision-maker is to be placed under a heavy justificatory burden (by, say, requiring that the measure adopted be shown to be strictly necessary rather than merely reasonable), but might simultaneously consider it appropriate to exhibit some degree of deference when evaluating the quality of the justifications offered so as to decide whether the burden has been discharged.

In the remainder of this chapter, I will argue that the interaction of these two dimensions of the justificatory process contain the seeds of a mature approach to substantive judicial review. This requires us to move beyond a doctrinal focus which results (depending on one's preferences) either in a bifurcated approach or one wedded to a specific doctrine (such as proportionality), and to concentrate instead on calibrating substantive review by reference to the normative, institutional and constitutional considerations that ought properly to shape it. The ambition of this chapter is not to produce that calibration, but, more modestly, to articulate a framework within which that task might be undertaken. The intention, in doing so, is to set out an approach to substantive review that is shaped from the bottom up by the underlying considerations of which doctrine should be a servant.

IV. DEFERENCE: SOME PRELIMINARIES

The two senses of justification sketched above imply two corresponding types of 'deference'. I will call these *intrinsic deference* and *adjudicative deference*, which relate respectively to the burden-allocation and burden-discharge aspects of the substantive-review process. The nature of, and the differences between, those two types of deference are considered below. I should begin, however, by acknowledging that the appropriateness and meaning of the term 'deference' are contested matters. One reason for this is that, within the substantive-review debate, the notion of deference has taken on a chameleonic character: it might be a doctrine in its own right,[46]

[46] As Kavanagh (n 7), Hunt (n 8) and Young (n 9), among others, argue.

or it might not;[47] it might imply (inappropriate) 'servility',[48] or merely the ascription of appropriate weight to particular factors;[49] it might be a function of relative institutional competence[50] or (more controversially) reflect constitutional or democratic concerns about the proper extent of the judicial role;[51] it might concern the asking of a less demanding question[52] or the less demanding policing of a given standard[53] (or both).[54] The deeply ambiguous nature of deference—an ambiguity that is compounded by its multifaceted nature—has become an obstacle to understanding. For this reason, it might be thought best to avoid the language, if not the idea, of deference entirely. I disagree, and consider deference to be a concept which is potentially useful to the mapping of the terrain of substantive review, provided that it is articulated and understood with sufficient clarity.

I have argued elsewhere that an adequately structured approach to proportionality review demands disaggregation not only of that doctrine's several elements but also of the distinct bases—most notably institutional competence and democratic legitimacy—on which deference may be appropriate.[55] It is, however, necessary to go further, by recognising not only the different grounds upon which deference might be warranted, but also the different ways in which it might interact with the idea of justification. This calls for the distinction sketched above between two different notions of justification—that is, determining the scale of the justificatory burden and determining whether that burden has been discharged—which are relevant in substantive-review cases, and for an accurate appreciation of how deference might be relevant, in different ways, to each of those matters. Approaching the issue in this way lends shape and structure to the idea(s) of deference, resolving many of the ambiguities identified above—if only, in some instances, by establishing by reference to intelligible criteria

[47] As Allan (n 10) argues.

[48] As Lord Hoffmann suggested in *R (ProLife Alliance) v British Broadcasting Corporation* [2003] UKHL 23, [2004] 1 AC 185, [75].

[49] See, eg Hunt (nn 8 and 13); *R (Nicklinson) v Ministry of Justice* [2014] UKSC 38, [296] (Lord Reed).

[50] See, eg *R (SB) v Governors of Denbigh High School* [2006] UKHL 15, [2007] 1 AC 100; *Belfast City Council v Miss Behavin' Ltd* [2007] UKHL 19, [2007] 1 WLR 1420.

[51] See, eg *R (Rotherham Metropolitan Borough Council) v Secretary of State for Business, Innovation and Skills* [2014] EWHC 232 (Admin); *Miranda v Secretary of State for the Home Department* [2014] EWHC 255 (Admin); *R (SG) v Secretary of State for Work and Pensions* [2014] EWCA Civ 156.

[52] Eg by asking whether a given measure is 'reasonably necessary' rather than 'necessary' or 'strictly necessary', as in *R (Clays Lane Housing Co-operative Ltd) v The Housing Corporation* [2004] EWCA Civ 1658, [2005] 1 WLR 2229.

[53] Eg by ascribing respect, or weight, to the view of the decision-maker in relation to some pertinent matter, as in *Denbigh* (n 50).

[54] These two techniques, which respectively amount to the lightening of the justificatory burden and the relaxation of the burden-discharge analysis, often appear to go hand in hand. See, eg *R (MA) v Secretary of State for Work and Pensions* [2014] EWCA Civ 13.

[55] Elliott (n 11).

that deference might mean *more* than one thing—and so helping to recast deference as a useful analytical device.

Finally, I acknowledge at the outset that burden-setting and burden-discharge aspects of substantive review are not hermetically sealed from one another, and that, as a result, neither are the corresponding notions of intrinsic and adjudicative deference. This point is developed towards the end of the chapter, where I suggest that the two forms of deference may be best characterised as different but overlapping lenses, both of which must be applied if a complete understanding of the court's role is to be produced. However, any overlap notwithstanding, the differences between the two notions of deference remain sufficient to make the distinction between them viable and analytically useful, not least because the full picture can be appreciated only if it is viewed through both lenses.

V. INTRINSIC DEFERENCE AND THE BURDEN OF JUSTIFICATION

Current administrative-law doctrine clearly acknowledges, at least implicitly, that the extent of the justificatory burden under which decision-makers are placed can vary substantially. In English law, this phenomenon is illustrated most graphically by the fact that certain decisions fall to be justified by reference to the reasonableness doctrine, whilst others are scrutinised by reference to proportionality.[56] As Lord Bingham observed in *Daly*, 'the intensity of review is somewhat greater under the proportionality approach' because (inter alia) it may require the court to assess 'the balance which the decision maker has struck' and 'the relative weight accorded to interests and considerations'.[57] And so, an 'overlap' between reasonableness and proportionality notwithstanding,[58] they represent different approaches to substantive review.

The nature of that difference is often presented in primarily structural terms—proportionality being, it is generally said, far more structured than reasonableness—although that view is questionable for two reasons. First, it is possible (but perhaps not desirable) to apply proportionality in a relatively unstructured way,[59] whilst reasonableness may be applied in a relatively structured way:[60] the two tests are, in other words, not *necessarily* as structurally distinct as their paradigm characterisations may

[56] Nor should it be assumed that reasonableness and proportionality are exhaustive of the possibilities: as Hickman, 'Problems for Proportionality' (n 18) 318–20, points out, there is a 'range of different standards of legality' the entirety of which is not adequately captured by rationality or proportionality or even the two taken together.

[57] *R (Daly) v Secretary of State for the Home Department* (n 40) [27] (Lord Bingham).

[58] Ibid.

[59] See Elliott (n 11).

[60] See Daly, '*Wednesbury*'s reason and structure' (n 5).

imply. And, second, whatever structural differences there might be between reasonableness and proportionality are largely functions of—and in any event subsidiary to—a more fundamental distinction concerning the extent of the justificatory burdens that they respectively impose. The ways in which the reasonableness and proportionality doctrines are structured—in terms of precisely what it is they call upon the reviewing court to assess—are, or at least ought to be, matters that flow from, and are determined by, the nature and scale of the burden of justification that each of them seeks in the first place to impose.

The *fundamental* question, then, is about what ought to count as justification in the particular circumstances of the case. How this should be translated into specific doctrinal terms—via requirements such as reasonableness, proportionality and necessity, and what the structural nature of those concepts ought to be—is a crucial, but ultimately *subsidiary*, question.

Approaching matters in this way enables us to contextualise the diversity evident within the contemporary substantive-review landscape. Indeed, the crude distinction between reasonableness and proportionality merely clothes a deeper level of complexity evidenced by significant differences *within* those broad categories. In English law,[61] for instance, multiple strands can be detected with the reasonableness doctrine,[62] including (as well as 'regular' *Wednesbury*) the 'super-*Wednesbury*' test,[63] the 'sub-*Wednesbury*' test[64] and the 'cogent reasons' test.[65] Moreover, as Taggart put it, 'Despite appearances to the contrary, proportionality ... is no more monolithic than (*Wednesbury*) unreasonableness.'[66] For instance, proportionality can be understood as calling for (inter alia) a 'fair balance' (which term is sometimes used to describe a *particular stage* within the proportionality test,[67] but is sometimes used as a synonym for what proportionality *globally* requires),[68] the adoption of the least-restrictive way of achieving a legitimate objective,[69] or the adoption of measures that are

[61] Other common-law systems are less receptive to variegated, or variable-intensity, reasonableness: eg on the position on New Zealand, see D Knight, 'Mapping the Rainbow of Review: Recognising Variable Intensity' [2010] *New Zealand Law Review* 393.

[62] See, generally, J Laws, '*Wednesbury*' in C Forsyth and I Hare (eds), *The Golden Metwand and the Crooked Cord: Essays on Public Law in Honour of Sir William Wade* (Oxford, Clarendon Press, 1998).

[63] See, eg *Nottinghamshire County Council v Secretary of State for the Environment* [1986] AC 240.

[64] See, eg *R v Ministry of Defence, ex p Smith* [1996] QB 517.

[65] See, eg *R (Bradley) v Secretary of State for Work and Pensions* [2008] EWCA Civ 36, [2009] QB 114.

[66] Taggart (n 1) 465.

[67] See, eg *R (Razgar) v Secretary of State for the Home Department* [2004] UKHL 27, [2004] 2 AC 368.

[68] See, eg *Kay v Lambeth London Borough Council* [2006] UKHL 10, [2006] 2 AC 465.

[69] See, eg *A v Secretary of State for the Home Department* [2004] UKHL 56, [2005] 2 AC 68.

reasonably, as opposed to strictly, necessary.[70] Indeed, in certain contexts, proportionality may be defined or applied in a way that makes it difficult to distinguish from a reasonableness test.[71] For example, the European Court of Human Rights has said that in discrimination cases concerning 'general measures of economic or social strategy' a measure will be considered to be unjustified only if it is 'manifestly without *reasonable* foundation'.[72] The Court of Appeal of England and Wales has taken this to amount to a requirement of a 'serious flaw' causing 'an *unreasonable* discriminatory effect'.[73] Equally, in European Union law, the proportionality test may, in a case engaging questions of high policy and macroeconomic judgement, become indistinguishable from a reasonableness test.[74]

These ostensibly structural differences between various formulations of the reasonableness and proportionality tests reflect—or mask—more profound differences pertaining to the nature and scale of the operative burden of justification. Labels—whether at a macro-level (for example, 'reasonableness', 'proportionality') or a micro-level (for example, 'strictly necessary', 'necessary', 'reasonably necessary')—may be helpful as a kind of shorthand. However, they can (or at least should) do no more than reflect prior choices about what justification should mean in the particular circumstances. Viewed thus, there is nothing *wrong* with such labels, but their role must be confined to a second order of importance. Otherwise, the risk is that they serve to obscure more than they illuminate, by overshadowing the underlying considerations that ought to determine what should be required by way of justification in the given factual matrix.

A potential difficulty with this approach is that it risks the collapse of the law in this area into a multiplicity of single instances, thereby depriving the law of any tangible structure or predictability. There is, then, a need—which arises in other areas of administrative law, too, including perhaps most obviously the doctrine of procedural fairness[75]—to temper an open-textured approach that is appropriately sensitive to underlying concerns with one that recognises the practical need to avoid reducing the field to a state of unhelpful shapelessess. The solution, however, lies not in a retreat into rigid categorisation—far less bifurcation—but in an attempt at

[70] See, eg *R (Clays Lane Housing Co-operative Ltd) v The Housing Corporation* (n 52).

[71] For criticism of cases that deviate from what she refers to as the requisite 'baseline intensity' of proportionality-review in human rights cases, see C Chan, 'Proportionality and Invariable Baseline Intensity of Review' (2013) 33 *Legal Studies* 1.

[72] *Stec v UK* (2006) 43 EHRR 47, [52] (emphasis added). See also *Humphrys v Revenue and Customs Commissioners* [2012] UKSC 18, [2012] 1 WLR 1545.

[73] *R (MA) v Secretary of State for Work and Pensions* (n 54) (emphasis added).

[74] See, eg *R (Rotherham Metropolitan Borough Council) v Secretary of State for Business, Innovation and Skills* (n 51).

[75] On the tension between prescriptiveness and flexibility in relation to procedural fairness, see Beatson LJ's judgment in *(L) v West London Mental Health NHS Trust* [2014] EWCA Civ 47.

calibration which exposes and harnesses the relationship between underlying normative factors and administrative law's doctrinal superstructure.

Central to that endeavour is an appreciation that the operative burden of justification ought to be informed by the normative significance of the value impacted by the impugned decision. This simple, but crucial, point was acknowledged in *Bugdaycay* by Lord Bridge, who said that[76]

> the court must, I think, be entitled to subject an administrative decision to the more rigorous examination, to ensure that it is in no way flawed, according to the gravity of the issue which the decision determines. The most fundamental of all human rights is the individual's right to life and when an administrative decision under challenge is said to be one which may put the applicant's life at risk, the basis of the decision must surely call for the most anxious scrutiny.

What is required, then, is an ordering of norms by reference to which the standard of justification falls to be set—the general principle being that the more important the norm threatened by a decision, the greater should be the onus upon the decision-maker to justify it. This, in turn, reflects an appropriately nuanced view of the relationship between judicial and administrative authority, the case for close judicial supervision of the executive branch turning, at least in part, upon the fundamentality of the values potentially compromised by the impugned measure. To some extent, an ordering of values is at least implicit in Taggart's bifurcation thesis, 'rights' cases attracting scrutiny by reference to the more demanding proportionality test, whilst 'wrongs' cases remain the preserve of the less demanding reasonableness doctrine. For the reasons sketched above, however, this kind of ordering is insufficiently granular.

For instance, not all rights cases exert, or ought to exert, the same degree of normative pull, some rights—including some manifestations of a single right—being more normatively compelling than others. At the most obvious level, this is apparent from the distinction between absolute and qualified rights, the normative importance of the former being such as to foreclose upon the possibility of justified infringement.[77] But the normative ordering of rights operates in more subtle ways, too. For instance, under the European Convention on Human Rights, less normative weight is ascribed to the right to peaceful enjoyment of possessions, infractions of which are judged by reference to a reasonable-necessity test, than to certain

[76] *R v Secretary of State for the Home Department, ex p Bugdaycay* [1987] AC 514, 531.

[77] It must, however, be acknowledged that the distinction between absolute and qualified rights is somewhat eroded by the fact that considerations that may found to be justifications for infringing qualified rights are sometimes internalised with the definition of the scope of an absolute right. For discussion, see T Hickman, *Public Law after the Human Rights Act* (Oxford, Hart Publishing, 2010) 116–23; N Mavronicola, 'What is an "Absolute Right"? Deciphering Absoluteness in the Context of Article 3 of the European Convention on Human Rights' (2012) 12 *Human Rights Law Review* 723.

other qualified rights, in relation to which the necessity requirement is not caveated by any notion of reasonableness.[78] The presence or absence of that caveat necessarily affects the scale of the burden of justification under which the defendant finds itself, reasonable necessity being a lighter burden than unqualified necessity.

Equally, a given qualified right may, depending on the context, be ascribed more or less normative weight by manipulating the scale of the justificatory burden under which the decision-maker is placed. For example, as Lord Hoffmann observed in *Miss Behavin'*, '[t]he right to vend pornography is not the most important right of free expression in a democratic society'.[79] In the light of this, a local authority entrusted with a power to licence sex shops acts lawfully provided that it 'exercises that power rationally and in accordance with the purposes of the statute', such that 'it would require very unusual facts for it to amount to a disproportionate restriction on Convention rights'.[80] On this approach, the normative pull of the right to freedom of expression is weakened by the context in which it is asserted, Lord Hoffmann's invocation of the language of rationality signifying a corresponding lightening of the justificatory burden. This may be contrasted with circumstances in which the same right is asserted in circumstances that invest it with greater normative pull, the obvious example being expression undertaken for political purposes. Here, requirements such as necessity and proportionality, as opposed to mere rationality, secure the imposition of a more demanding burden of justification.[81] A similar approach can be discerned within Convention jurisprudence on discrimination, the normative value attached to the status in question being a consideration that determines what the requirement to justify differential treatment reduces to in the particular case. For instance, differential treatment on grounds based exclusively on sex will normally be justified only if 'very weighty reasons' are supplied,[82] whereas a scheme that indirectly discriminates on grounds of sex but in direct reliance upon a distinction between some other—lesser—status may attract a lighter justificatory burden.[83]

Just as normative ordering is necessary—and evident—in rights cases, so it is appropriate outwith that context. The first point to note here is that rights are not the only norms whose prima facie infringement may call for justification. As Paul Daly has noted, lurking beneath conventional

[78] See, eg *R (Clays Lane Housing Co-operative Ltd) v The Housing Corporation* (n 52).
[79] *Belfast City Council v Miss Behavin'* (n 50) [16].
[80] Ibid.
[81] See, eg *Lingens v Austria* (1986) 8 EHRR 407.
[82] *Stec v UK* (n 72).
[83] Eg in *Humphrys v Revenue and Customs Commissioners* (n 72), such an approach was applied in circumstances where the primary distinction (albeit one that differentially impacted upon mothers and fathers) was between parents with majority and minority responsibility for the care of their children.

caricatures of *Wednesbury* we often find that review on that ground serves to demand justification because the impugned measure exhibits an 'indicium of unreasonableness', such as differential treatment or illogicality.[84] Another way of looking at this is to say that judicial review—beyond what would usually be regarded as the rights context—may nevertheless serve to protect substantive values of good administration,[85] examples of which may, says Murray Hunt, include consistency of treatment, non-retrospectivity and access to court.[86]

The norms implicated in non-rights decisions are not all equally important (or unimportant); nor does it follow that they are necessarily inferior to the norms implicated in rights cases simply because they fall outside the rights category. Take, for instance, situations in which an individual is given a clear and unequivocal undertaking that generates a substantive legitimate expectation. In *Coughlan*, it was held that, in such circumstances, the lawfulness of any departure from such an expectation should be tested by reference not to the reasonableness test but by asking whether the departure can be justified by reference to an 'overriding public interest'.[87] As Philip Sales and Karen Steyn have pointed out, the court was right to reject a bare rationality test, since this would have 'undermine[d] the court's finding that the individual has an important interest, founded on the constitutional ideal of the rule of law, which requires a high degree of predictability as to the behaviour of a public authority'.[88] The justificatory burden in non-rights cases has been adjusted in other contexts too, for instance to ensure an appropriate degree of respect as between different institutional actors. Thus, for instance, it was held in *Bradley* that the executive may not lawfully dismiss the findings of the Parliamentary Ombudsman unless it is able to demonstrate 'cogent reasons' for doing so, thereby placing

[84] Daly, '*Wednesbury*'s reason and structure' (n 5). Admittedly, *Wednesbury* is not universally understood in this way: for instance, Taggart (n 1) 438–40, characterised the reasonableness standard as one that placed the decision-maker under no burden of justification, but rather as one 'placing the burden of showing something unreasonable on the applicant'. However, Daly's redefinition of *Wednesbury*—which casts the distinction between it and proportionality in terms of the scale rather than location of the justification burden—is strongly to be preferred, not least because it lends reasonableness review a logic and structure that renders it defensible against the sometimes-unwarranted criticisms that are frequently levelled at it.

[85] J Jowell and A Lester, 'Beyond *Wednesbury*: Towards Substantive Principles of Administrative Law' [1987] *Public Law* 386.

[86] Hunt (n 13). At least some of these values might—and sometimes are—expressed as rights. This, however, merely serves to underline my point that what is important is casting judicial review in a form that secures appropriate protection for the value, rather than the insertion of an artificial distinction between rights and other cases.

[87] *Coughlan* (n 43) 242.

[88] P Sales and K Steyn, 'Legitimate Expectations in English Public Law: an Analysis' [2004] *Public Law* 564, 589. The appropriate scale of the burden of justification is one thing; a separate matter is to what extent, if any, the reviewing court should defer when assessing whether the burden has been discharged. On the latter point, it is arguable that the court got it wrong in *Coughlan*, as Sales and Steyn go on to argue at 590–91.

the decision-maker under a justificatory burden heavier than that which would obtain were a bare-rationality test to be applied.[89] On this approach, the constitutional status of the office of Ombudsman renders executive dismissal of its findings prima facie suspect, and so calls for justification beyond that which would be required on bald *Wednesbury* grounds.

It is not my purpose in this chapter to attempt exhaustively to engage in the process of normative ordering, examples of which are given above. Rather, the aim of this part of the chapter has been the more modest one of arguing that once the notion of justification is placed centre stage, such an ordering becomes imperative if the nature and scale of the burden of justification is to be set in an intelligible, coherent and principled fashion. It is evident from the examples given above that, on the current approach, such normative ordering is not wholly absent: it is at least implicit in much of what already happens. My argument, however, is that because such ordering ought to inform what the notion of justification concretely reduces to within the confines of a given case, it is necessary to acknowledge its role more explicitly. It should, in other words, be the starting point when any question about substantive review arises.

VI. DISTINGUISHING INTRINSIC DEFERENCE AND ADJUDICATIVE DEFERENCE

This leads on to a further point—or, more accurately, an alternative way of making the same point. There is a relationship between determining what the operative burden of justification is and the notion of deference. However, as noted above, a difficulty with the idea, or at least the language, of deference is that the imprecise way in which it is often used has begun to rob it of utility. The rehabilitation of deference as a useful and viable concept requires a distinction to be drawn between the two forms that it can take.[90]

The first of those forms can be thought of as *intrinsic deference*. This is an established phenomenon, even if the *language* of deference is less familiar in this context. Indeed, the notion is hard-wired into the traditional, doctrine-led approach to substantive review. Asking whether a decision is

[89] *R (Bradley) v Secretary of State for Work and Pensions* (n 65) [72].

[90] I do not rule out the possibility of other forms of deference. An obvious third possible form of deference is remedial deference. On such an approach, a court might, for instance, decide to withhold—or dilute—relief even though it has concluded that the impugned measure is unlawful. The efficacy of such deference is closely linked with questions about the status of unlawful administrative and legislative acts, one argument being that if such acts are necessarily void, the withholding of relief may have little (other than an obfuscatory) effect: *Ahmed v HM Treasury (No 2)* [2010] UKSC 5, [2010] 2 AC 534. The position may be different, however, where the relief sought is merely declaratory: *R (Nicklinson) v Ministry of Justice* [2014] UKSC 38.

Wednesbury reasonable in the normal sense is less demanding—or more deferential—than asking whether there are cogent reasons for it; asking whether a decision is reasonable is less demanding than asking whether it is proportionate; asking whether a decision is reasonably necessary is less demanding than asking whether it is strictly necessary; and asking whether a decision is manifestly lacking a reasonable justification is less demanding than asking whether it is accompanied by very weighty reasons. Some instruments within the substantive-review toolbox are, in other words, *intrinsically* deferential because, in the first place, they involve imposing upon the decision-maker a slighter burden of justification. Viewed in this way, setting the burden of justification and setting the level of intrinsic deference are merely two sides of one coin.

That type of deference needs to be distinguished from what might be called *adjudicative deference*. In this guise, deference may call for the ascription of respect to the decision-maker's view when the reviewing court assesses whether the burden of justification should be taken to have been discharged. The court might, for instance, be willing to attach greater weight to the view of the decision-maker when deciding whether imposing a particular restriction upon a right was necessary, on account of the fact that the decision-maker was peculiarly institutionally well placed to form such a view and deployed its expertise in doing so.[91] Or a reviewing court might ascribe a degree of respect to the view of the decision-maker when deciding whether the restriction placed by the impugned measure upon the relevant right (or other value) is justified by a public policy gain, such that the measure can be considered to have struck a 'fair balance', or to be proportionate in the 'strict' or 'narrow' sense.[92] I have argued elsewhere that adjudicative deference is appropriate in such circumstances,[93] and it is not the purpose of this chapter to rehearse that argument. The thrust of the present argument is not that adjudicative deference is *appropriate*—which, for the purpose of this chapter, I take to be a given—but that it is *distinct* from intrinsic deference, and that there is merit in acknowledging and making explicit that point of distinction.[94]

There are several reasons for doing so. One such reason—and perhaps the most obvious and straightforward—is that these two forms of deference map onto two tasks that reviewing courts have to perform: tasks which,

[91] See, eg *R (SB) v Governors of Denbigh High School* (n 50); *Belfast City Council v Miss Behavin* (n 50).

[92] See, eg *R (ProLife Alliance) v British Broadcasting Corporation* (n 48); *R (Farrakhan) v Secretary of State for the Home Department* [2002] EWCA Civ 606, [2002] QB 1391; *R (Animal Defenders International) v Secretary of State for Culture, Media and Sport* [2008] UKHL 15, [2008] 1 AC 1312; *Miranda v Secretary of State for the Home Department* (n 51).

[93] Elliott (n 11).

[94] As noted above, and for reasons elaborated below, the distinction is not watertight; but such overlap as there is between the two categories does not undermine the utility of distinguishing between them.

even if they are not invariably distinguished, are nevertheless distinct. The task being undertaken when adjudicative deference may be relevant—namely, determining whether the operative burden of justification has been discharged—is distinct from the task being performed—namely, deciding what the operative burden *is*—when intrinsic deference may be relevant. Burden-setting is informed, as argued above, by considerations pertaining to the significance of the norm compromised by the relevant administrative measure. As such, the process the court goes (or ought to go) through when engaging with questions of intrinsic deference have two (related) characteristics that serve to distinguish them from the considerations relevant to adjudicative deference.

First, the decision about intrinsic deference is relatively *abstract* in nature. It is unconcerned with the sort of issues that may arise—and which may call for or tell against adjudicative deference—when the burden-discharge analysis is undertaken, such as the interaction of the compromised norm and the impugned measure, or the relative competencies of court and administrator.[95] Second, the abstract nature of the burden-setting aspect of substantive review reflects the fact that it is concerned with the form that review should take on an all-other-things-being-equal basis. That is, it determines the level of judicial scrutiny that should *ideally* obtain without reference to factors, particular to the more specific features of the case, that may blunt such scrutiny. For example, the reviewing court might conclude that the norm at stake—such as freedom of political speech—calls for the administrator whose measure compromises that value to be placed under a heavy justificatory burden. Yet the same court might conclude, in the course of determining whether that burden has been discharged, that adjudicative deference is warranted on account (for example) of the decision-maker's superior institutional competence or democratic legitimacy. Adjudicative deference can, then, be thought of as the pragmatic counterpart to intrinsic deference: as something which shapes the on-the-ground assessment of whether the normatively warranted burden of justification

[95] The abstract nature of the burden-setting phase is uncompromised by the fact that the extent of the interference with, as distinct from the importance of, the norm in question is relevant to the review process. It is clear that a more extensive interference with a given norm will, all other things being equal, be harder to justify than a less extensive interference with it. However, it is the importance of the norm that determines how the justificatory burden is to be characterised; the extent of the interference, in contrast, goes to the ease or difficulty with which the burden can be discharged. Eg an extensive interference with political speech will be harder to justify than a lesser interference; but the characterisation of the burden will be determined by the fact that the value at stake in each case is political speech. In both cases, the decision-maker's burden will be to show that the restriction is strictly necessary and proportionate—albeit that how difficult it is to discharge that burden will be a function not only of its characterisation but also of the scale of the interference whose justification falls to be established. Another way of expressing this point is to say that the importance of the norm determines the abstract characterisation of the justificatory burden; the scale of the interference informs what that burden amounts to in practice.

has been discharged. Viewed thus, the nature and intensity of substantive review in any given case is a function of the interoperation of the notions of intrinsic and adjudicative deference, rather than something that can be adequately captured through the preconceived contours of the *Wednesbury* or proportionality (or any other doctrinal) concept.

VII. THE RELATIONSHIP BETWEEN INTRINSIC AND ADJUDICATIVE DEFERENCE

So far, I have implied that the two strands of deference are wholly separate from one another. The position is, however, more complex. There are a number of senses in which adjudicative and intrinsic deference relate to, or feed into or off, one another. However, whilst it is important to acknowledge, and understand the implications of, these points of contact, their existence does not detract from the desirability of distinguishing the two forms of deference (and of distinguishing between the burden-setting and burden-discharge aspects of substantive review to which they respectively relate).

A relationship between the two concepts—and between the two corresponding aspects of substantive review—can be discerned most readily from the fact that the way in which the reviewing court sets the justificatory burden will necessarily have implications for the nature of the burden-discharge stage of review. This, in turn, may have implications for the extent, if any, to which adjudicative deference may be warranted. Although I have argued that reviewing courts should begin not by asking which doctrine (for example, *Wednesbury* or proportionality) to apply, but by asking what justification ought to mean in the light of the norm that is at stake, the burden-setting process has a necessarily doctrinal outcome. That is, the burden will (quite properly) be expressed through the articulation of particular justificatory requirements—such as insistence upon reasonableness, cogent reasons, necessity, fair balance, and so on—which bring doctrine into play. In turn, the nature and extent of the burden, expressed in terms of the doctrinal tools which the court will go on to deploy in order to ascertain whether the burden has been discharged, will shape the extent to which adjudicative deference might be warranted.

Generally speaking, the heavier the burden—and, hence, the sharper the doctrinal instruments by reference to which its discharge falls to be assessed—the greater the potential scope for adjudicative deference. It is for precisely this reason that when, in English law, substantive review did not extend beyond reasonableness, (adjudicative) deference was rarely, if ever, spoken of. The intrinsic deference hard-wired into the *Wednesbury* test obviated the need for any other form of deference. It follows that when the burden under which the decision-maker is placed is especially light, adjudicative deference will have little, if any, role to play, since in such circumstances the adjudicative task of the reviewing court involves the making of determinations that are unlikely to take it close to the limits of institutional competence or constitutional appropriateness. However, as the justificatory burden becomes heavier, questions pertaining to its discharge fall to be engaged with through the deployment of necessarily more incisive doctrinal instruments. As a result, there is a heightened possibility that the burden-discharge analysis may raise concerns relating to the relative institutional or constitutional competence of the court. It follows that circumstances may—and do—arise in which an intrusive form of review, whilst normatively warranted, may be moderated in the light of concerns relating to the proper role of the court and its relationship with the decision-maker.

This reflects the fact that although intrinsic and adjudicative deference are relevant to different aspects of the substantive-review process, they are underpinned by common concerns. The whole deference project is animated by the perceived importance of maintaining a distinction between 'appeal' and 'review', by ensuring that judicial review—as distinct from statutory appeal—pertains to questions of legality rather than to full-blown determination of the merits.[96] As noted above, the need for a discrete doctrine of adjudicative deference was limited—if not absent—when the burden-discharge analysis had nothing more demanding upon which to bite than the *Wednesbury* concept.[97] In contrast, the case for adjudicative deference becomes more compelling once the burden-discharge analysis involves the asking of more demanding questions. Such questions might be technically difficult for the reviewing court to answer, and may therefore invite deference on competence grounds. Or they might present the court with questions with which it is constitutionally ill-equipped to engage, calling for deference on democratic grounds—a difficulty that arises particularly acutely in relation to the fair-balance element of the proportionality test.[98] Against this background, maintenance of the appeal-review distinction is accomplished through the combined effect of the two forms of deference, the adjudicative form potentially offsetting, at least to some extent, the implications of ascribing to the decision-maker a heavier justificatory burden. In this way, risks that used to be obviated by means of a globally-high level of intrinsic deference, which found expression through the *Wednesbury* doctrine, may

[96] For a defence of the appeal–review distinction, see D Irvine, 'Judges and Decision-Makers: The Theory and Practice of *Wednesbury* Review' [1996] *Public Law* 59.

[97] Assuming that the justificatory burden inherent in the traditional reasonableness test really is as undemanding as the rubric of the test suggests. It is arguable that the test—without formal departure from the traditional rubric—has sometimes assumed a more demanding character in substance: C Forsyth and W Wade, *Administrative Law*, 10th edn (Oxford, Oxford University Press, 2009) 304.

[98] This point was acknowledged with refreshing frankness by Laws LJ, with whom Ouseley and Openshaw JJ agreed, in *Miranda v Secretary of State for the Home Department* (n 51).

now be addressed instead via adjudicative deference. However, the underlying concerns—that courts should not undertake review functions for which they are institutionally or constitutionally ill-suited—remain constant.

This perhaps begs the question whether distinguishing between two forms of deference is merely a more complicated way of getting us to the place at which we would anyway arrive if the two forms of deference were collapsed into one global notion. That is not, however, the case. Separating out intrinsic and adjudicative deference is helpful because it acknowledges the distinction between, on the one hand, the level of review that is normatively warranted and, on the other hand, the level of review that can appropriately be supplied given the particularities of the individual case. Some situations disclose no disjunction between these two sets of considerations: this will be so, for instance, when the circumstances of the case are not such as to cast doubt upon the institutional or constitutional capacity of the reviewing court to determine whether a heavy justificatory burden has been discharged. At the same time, however, there will be circumstances in which concerns about judicial capacity rightly have the effect of blunting what would otherwise—thanks to the ascription of a heavy burden of justification—been a relatively sharp form of review. In this way, the distinction between intrinsic and adjudicative deference supplies a form of analytical (as well as descriptive) granularity that is helpful, in that it enables the concerns that animate calls for deference to be invested with degrees of relevance and weight that reflect the full range of issues—normative, constitutional and institutional—that are in play.

This, in turn, avoids the all-eggs-in-one-basket problem that necessarily afflicts approaches to substantive review premised upon a single doctrinal standard. The inadequacy of such an approach is evident from the fracturing of *Wednesbury* into the several variants mentioned above—which, among other things, acknowledged that standard *Wednesbury* was insufficiently attuned to the need for greater judicial oversight of decisions impacting upon particularly valuable norms.[99] The obverse problem is illustrated by the need, in systems that rely exclusively upon proportionality, to invest that test, in appropriate circumstances, with a more deferential character either through reliance upon adjudicative-deference techniques or by lightening the justificatory burden by transforming it into one that, in substance, requires little (if anything) more than bare rationality.[100] My intention here is not to reopen the reasonableness-*versus*-proportionality debate, but simply to point out that approaches based upon a single standard are insufficient on their own, precisely because they cannot (unless manipulated beyond recognition)[101] capture the full richness of the considerations that

[99] See generally Laws, '*Wednesbury*' (n 62).

[100] See, eg the cases cited in nn 72–74.

[101] Eg by turning proportionality into something that requires nothing other than bare rationality.

ought to inform the respective roles of judge and decision-maker. Nor, admittedly, are the notions of intrinsic and adjudicative deference that I have sketched in this chapter a panacea: but they do, I argue, provide a framework within which to engage more openly with the full range of relevant issues.

The complexity of those issues can be illustrated by two respects in which there is a degree of slippage between the two types of deference. First, although the extent and nature of the justificatory burden should be informed primarily by reference to the normative significance of the at-risk value, concerns pertaining to the judge–administrator relationship are nevertheless relevant to burden-setting too. The most obvious manifestation of this phenomenon is that, in relation to the substance of the decision, the administrator is never placed under a justificatory burden so heavy as to require it to demonstrate the *correctness* of the decision.[102] That is, the judicial analysis is never (or should never be) so crude as to reduce to asking whether the court *agrees* with the impugned decision (as distinct from asking whether it is reasonable, necessary, proportionate, and so on). It follows, then, that while institutional and constitutional considerations relating to the judge–administrator relationship find expression primarily through adjudicative deference when the burden-discharge analysis is undertaken, such considerations can—and should—also impact upon the earlier burden-setting task.

It follows that, even when more demanding tools such as proportionality are in play, substantive judicial review remains shot through with a residue of intrinsic deference that avoids setting the justificatory burden in a way that would (but for adjudicative deference) collapse the appeal–review distinction. Putting the matter another way, institutional and constitutional factors should operate to ensure that the burden-setting process only ever requires the reviewing court to perform a burden-discharge analysis that is *potentially* consistent with the proper judicial role (even if, in the particular circumstances of the case, the intrusiveness of the burden–discharge analysis needs to be reduced through reliance upon adjudicative deference). The fact that institutional and constitutional concerns have a degree of purchase in relation to intrinsic deference does not, however, wholly elide the two forms of deference. Normative considerations remain the focus of analysis at the burden-setting stage, and are the primary determinant of the degree of deference that should be exhibited so as to afford latitude to the

[102] This may be contrasted with judicial review of the decision-maker's interpretation of the law, as distinct from review of the decision itself. In the former context, the default position (at least in English law) is a correctness requirement. This reflects a generally-settled (albeit not uniformly held) view that institutional and constitutional considerations play out differently here, making the extension of latitude to the decision-maker, via intrinsic deference, inappropriate (or at least less appropriate).

decision-maker. In contrast, institutional and constitutional considerations going to the judge-administrator relationship serve a residual, backstop function during the burden-setting process, whilst assuming centre stage, through the doctrine of adjudicative deference, once the burden-discharge analysis gets underway.

Slippage between intrinsic and adjudicative deference arises in a second respect, too, demonstrating that the relationship between the concepts—or, more precisely, between the concerns that underpin them—is a two-way one. Just as the concerns that animate adjudicative deference may serve a residual, backstop function at the burden-setting stage, thereby informing the level of intrinsic deference, so may the reverse phenomenon occur. That is, considerations relevant principally to intrinsic deference may also exert a degree of influence in relation to adjudicative deference, in that constitutional or institutional arguments in favour of such deference may, to some extent at least, be undercut by the fundamentality of the at-risk norm. Indeed, the very fact that normative considerations can, and do, operate so as to influence the extent of the justificatory burden suggests that the institutional and constitutional concerns that may invite adjudicative deference are acknowledged to have a variable degree of purchase. Placing the decision-maker under a relatively heavy justificatory burden creates at least the potential for a more searching form of scrutiny. And whilst concerns about the appropriateness of such scrutiny are not wholly eclipsed by the fundamentality of the at-risk norm, they nevertheless fall to be evaluated in the light of the importance attached to judicial protection of particularly valuable norms. The imposition of a heavier justificatory burden thus raises the *possibility* of a more searching form of review, the extent to which that possibility becomes a reality turning upon the force—viewed *in context*—of the concerns that animate adjudicative deference. In this way, the capacity of such concerns to moderate the sharpness of review may itself be reduced by the fundamentality of the norms at stake.

This phenomenon is most obviously apparent when that norm takes the form of an absolute right: in that context there is not, in the usual way, any scope for adjudicative deference, the fundamentality of the norm—as reflected in the unqualified character of the right—foreclosing upon the possibility of such deference. Properly understood, however, a binary distinction does not fall to be drawn between situations (involving absolute rights) in which the concerns that animate adjudicative deference have no purchase, and all other situations, in which they do. Rather, the *extent* of their purchase is a function of the fundamentality of the at-risk value. Acknowledging the existence of such a relationship is crucial if we are properly to account for the absence of a 'feedback loop' between the two forms of deference, whereby any increase in the justificatory burden risks being offset by a commensurate ratcheting up of adjudicative deference. The result would be an unwavering approach to substantive review, the two forms of deference taking the form of participants in a zero-sum game. Recognising that the purchase of adjudicative-deference concerns falls to be evaluated in the light of—and that they may therefore be curtailed by—the sort of normative considerations that, in the first place, invite the allocation of a heavy justificatory burden helps to avoid this difficulty.

This analytical framework does not pretend, or aim, to offer easy answers. Determining what substantive review should look like in any given set of circumstances is a complicated business, but it can be made more consistent and transparent if the nature of its complexity is acknowledged, and tools to facilitate principled engagement with that task articulated. Like the task for which they are designed, the relationship between intrinsic and adjudicative deference is not a simple one: and the position is certainly not that they exist wholly in isolation from one another. It would be surprising if it were. The two forms of deference are united in a single endeavour: namely, delivering a level and type of judicial scrutiny that is appropriate in the circumstances of the case. Viewed thus, the two types of deference exist not as entirely separate concepts, but as distinct-yet-related aspects of a single concept. The distinctions between their respective roles, and between the concerns that animate them, are sufficient to tell against their wholesale elision. Yet to present them as entirely separate would be to risk oversimplifying the complexity of the issues that are at stake here. The better view, then, is to consider intrinsic and adjudicative deference as different but overlapping lenses through which to understand and determine the role that the court should play in any particular circumstance in which it is called upon to engage in substantive review.

VIII. SOME CONCLUSIONS ON THE TOPOGRAPHY OF SUBSTANTIVE REVIEW

It is not the purpose of this chapter to tackle directly the question whether proportionality should eclipse *Wednesbury* by becoming the sole doctrinal vehicle for undertaking substantive judicial review. That I consider the answer to that question to be 'no' will be clear from what I have already said, but I reach that conclusion not by means of a side-by-side comparison of the two tests or a reckoning of their relative strengths and weaknesses. Instead, that conclusion is informed by my argument that the forms which front-line administrative-law doctrine should take ought to be determined by thoroughgoing engagement with underlying normative, institutional and constitutional considerations. My argument is not that front-line doctrinal tools such as reasonableness, necessity, fair balance and proportionality should be eschewed, but that their role should be properly understood. They represent different, but related, ways of testing whether a decision is adequately justified. Deciding which tools to take out of the substantive-review toolbox, and deciding precisely how they should be deployed, are decisions that represent conclusions drawn from an evaluation of the context, including the importance of the norm that is at stake and the appropriateness of judicial review bearing in mind the institutional and constitutional constraints to which the court is subject. Engaging with such issues will—and should—produce doctrinal conclusions: that, for example, a decision-maker should be placed under a heavy justificatory burden (by being called upon to demonstrate the *proportionality* of the measure), but that, at the *fair-balance* stage of the proportionality analysis, *adjudicative deference* is warranted because the nature of the issue engages the democratic accountability of the executive body.

I am not, therefore, calling for an adoctrinal approach, far less for the replacement of doctrine with the superficially attractive but intellectually empty notion that '[i]n law context is everything'.[103] Nor am I endorsing the 'simplicity' school of thought associated with prominent New Zealand judges, including, most notably, Sir Robin Cooke[104] and, more recently, Dame Sian Elias.[105] More recently still, Lord Carnwath appeared to express sympathy with this sort of approach when he endorsed the view that, in substantive-review cases, courts should simply ask themselves 'whether something had gone wrong of a nature and degree which required the intervention of the court and, if so, what form that intervention should take'.[106] Unlike adherents of the simplicity school, I do not advocate the excision of doctrinal nicety on the ground that it sits in tension with the contextualist impulse. Doctrine remains a valuable, indeed essential, part of administrative law, preventing its collapse into a quagmire of well-intentioned judicial discretion.[107]

I recognise that the difference between my position and that of the proponents of simplicity may seem slight, but I consider it to be important. On my analysis, the tension between contextualism and doctrine is one that need not arise provided that the latter is understood as something that

[103] *Daly* (n 40) [28] (Lord Steyn).

[104] R Cooke, 'The Struggle for Simplicity in Administrative Law' in M Taggart (ed), *Judicial Review of Administrative Action in the 1980s: Problems and Prospects* (Oxford, Oxford University Press, 1986); R Cooke, 'The Discretionary Heart of Administrative Law' in C Forsyth and I Hare (eds), *The Golden Metwand and the Crooked Cord: Essays on Public Law in Honour of Sir William Wade* (Oxford, Clarendon Press, 1998).

[105] S Elias, 'Administrative Law for "Living People"' (2009) 68 *Cambridge Law Journal* 1. See also Elias CJ's contributions to an exchange with counsel in *Ye v Minister for Immigration* [2009] NZSCC 76, as set out in Knight (n 61) 400–401.

[106] R Carnwath, 'From judicial outrage to sliding scales—where next for *Wednesbury*?' (Annual Lecture, Constitutional and Administrative Bar Association, November 2013). Carnwath was citing with approval from the judgment of Lord Donaldson MR in *R v Take-over Panel, ex p Guinness plc* [1990] 1 QB 146, 160.

[107] See further C Forsyth, 'Showing the Fly the Way out of the Flybottle: The Value of Formalism and Conceptual Reasoning in Administrative Law' (2007) 66 *Cambridge Law Journal* 325.

grows out of the former. Doctrine, in other words, can be the servant of a context-sensitive approach which recognises that the core task of the courts is to determine whether the impugned decision is justified, but which also acknowledges that what justification boils down to is a question that can be answered only within the particular circumstances of the individual case.

The notions of intrinsic and adjudicative deference—which are themselves doctrinal constructs—are, I have argued, tools that can enable courts to engage with questions of justification in a way that is context-sensitive but which does not sacrifice the structural rigour that doctrine is capable of injecting into the judicial process. Viewed thus, deference—rather than being something to be applied if not as an afterthought, then at least as a consideration that is secondary to the choice of doctrine—occupies the centre stage, as a tool that helps to give concrete meaning to the core concept of justification, and doctrinal shape to the performance of a necessarily contextual judicial task. I have no doubt that this approach leads to a 'rainbow of review', as Michael Taggart put it.[108] But it is a rainbow that is calibrated in a finer-grained way than the notion of bifurcation permits, and one in which doctrine fulfils a function that is subsidiary to, and reflective of, the deeper considerations—normative, institutional and constitutional—that are necessarily in play when courts engage in substantive review.

[108] Taggart (n 1).

5

Against Unification

JASON NE VARUHAS*

I. INTRODUCTION: BIFURCATION OR UNIFICATION?

In 2003 Taggart observed:[1]

> There is an important debate, yet to occur in the United Kingdom, about whether or not British public law will bifurcate into human rights law and general administrative law (ie, the area left when you subtract rights-centred litigation). Some will argue that the unreformed or classic model of administrative law should survive in the latter area. I can see no advantage in maintaining an administrative law rump, cut off from developments in human rights law. But that is a matter for another day.

When that day came, Taggart had changed his mind: 'I come down on the side of bifurcation'.[2] In particular he opposed a proposition he had earlier defended: that the proportionality method, derived from human rights law, ought to be mainstreamed across the common law of judicial review (CLR), not only to become the standard of substantive review, but to become, along with the idea of 'fundamental values', the central concern of a reinvented, 'constitutionalised' and 'unified' public law.[3] In turn, others, most

* Senior Lecturer, Faculty of Law, University of New South Wales and Fellow of Christ's College, University of Cambridge. My thanks to Mark Aronson, Paul Daly, Mark Elliott, David Feldman, Cora Hoexter, Peter Turner, Nicola Varuhas and Greg Weeks for helpful discussions and/or comments. A draft was presented at a UNSW Faculty of Law Staff Seminar and I am grateful to participants for a stimulating discussion. It is fitting that this chapter addresses proportionality, among other things, as the first contact I had with Mike Taggart was in an email exchange concerning a paper on proportionality that I had written as a student in my final year of Law School in Wellington. It is indicative of his support of students and young scholars that despite never having met me, Mike replied promptly to an email asking if he would look at the paper, saying he would gladly read it, and generous, thought-provoking comments followed. Views and errors are my own.

[1] M Taggart, 'Reinventing Administrative Law' in N Bamforth and P Leyland (eds), *Public Law in a Multi-Layered Constitution* (Oxford, Hart Publishing, 2003) 311, 334 fn 144.

[2] M Taggart, 'Proportionality, Deference, *Wednesbury*' [2008] *New Zealand Law Review* 423, 478.

[3] D Dyzenhaus, M Hunt and M Taggart, 'The Principle of Legality in Administrative Law: Internationalisation as Constitutionalisation' (2001) 1 *Oxford University Commonwealth Law Journal* 5; M Taggart, 'The Tub of Public Law' in D Dyzenhaus (ed), *The Unity of Public Law* (Oxford, Hart Publishing, 2004).

prominently Hunt, have argued that Taggart was wrong to shift position: 'the bifurcation of public law into rights and non-rights cases ... would be a seriously retrograde step'.[4]

This chapter argues that the position Taggart ultimately reached was correct.

Let us first clarify the terms of the debate. First, despite participants making claims about the bifurcation of *public law*, the debate does not concern all fields of doctrine that could potentially be said to comprise public law. For example, review on EU grounds, the law of Parliament, public sector equality duties, the law of inquiries and the ombudsman, or actions in tort against officials do not form part of the debate. When one considers the substance of what is being debated, the debate concerns two sub-fields of public law only: the law under the Human Rights Act 1998 (HRA) (or, in other jurisdictions, analogous rights-instruments), and CLR.

Second, the crux of the debate is whether these two fields are being and/or ought to be integrated so that they are functionally aligned and characterised by common or interrelated 'norms, concepts, and doctrines',[5] and in particular and most importantly for opponents of bifurcation, whether proportionality ought to be mainstreamed across CLR. In short, those who oppose bifurcation—such as Dyzenhaus, Hunt and Taggart in his earlier writings—favour unification of the CLR around a set of 'rights' and other 'fundamental values' and organised around the 'central concepts' of 'justification' and 'due deference', with proportionality the principal, possibly only tool for testing the justifiability of administrative action within this unified field.[6] Some judges too have speculated that 'in time' some sort of 'synthesis may emerge' between human rights law and the CLR, and consonant with this view, have observed that elements of proportionality may have a role outside of HRA and EU contexts.[7]

Third, those who oppose 'bifurcation' make two types of claim: a descriptive claim that the law under the HRA and the CLR *are* being integrated into a unified whole,[8] and a normative claim that they *ought* to unify.[9] As is so often the case in public law scholarship, participants in the debate seldom delineate the two types of claim. Further, the descriptive claim is intimately tied to the normative claim: if one demonstrates that the law is

[4] M Hunt, 'Against Bifurcation' in D Dyzenhaus, M Hunt and G Huscroft (eds), *A Simple Common Lawyer: Essays in Honour of Michael Taggart* (Oxford, Hart Publishing, 2009) 120.

[5] Ibid, 103.

[6] Dyzenhaus, Hunt and Taggart (n 3); Hunt (n 4).

[7] *Kennedy v The Charity Commission* [2014] UKSC 20, [46], [54].

[8] Eg Taggart, 'Tub' (n 3); Dyzenhaus, Hunt and Taggart (n 3) (describing a series of developments which the authors consider evince constitutionalisation and unification of public law); Hunt (n 4) 100–03, 121. See also Taggart 'Reinventing' (n 1); T Poole, 'The Reformation of English Administrative Law' (2009) 68 *Cambridge Law Journal* 142 (both claiming administrative law is being reorganised around the idea of 'rights').

[9] Dyzenhaus, Hunt and Taggart (n 3) particularly 23ff; Hunt (n 4) 105ff.

already moving in a particular direction the normative claim that it ought to move in that direction appears less radical, and is more likely to hold sway.

This chapter challenges both claims.

First, the chapter demonstrates that the law under the HRA and CLR are distinct fields, each performing a radically different set of functions. This is important as it offers a corrective to the inaccurate narrative of unification; these two fields are far from being aligned. Further, this analysis demonstrates that it makes no sense to argue that the law ought not to bifurcate. The law *is* bifurcated. The normative debate is therefore more accurately one over *unification*. This exercise, of demonstrating how very different the concerns of each field are, is also of great importance when it comes to considering how the law ought to develop (or not). One cannot sensibly make claims about whether and how the law should change without a sound understanding of what the law is.

Second, the chapter argues that it is difficult to make sense of normative claims for unification, given the two fields are fundamentally distinct. Claims for unification are akin to claiming that the law of torts and equity should be unified; the proposition is perplexing. The chapter rejects arguments against the status quo. A general weakness of these arguments is that they fail to grasp the distinctive nature of human rights law and of the CLR. The chapter then considers two models of unification: constitutionalisation and privatisation. The fundamental problem with the first is that it seeks to transmute CLR into a new body of constitutional law. Apart from creating the equivalent of a legal constitution by stealth, as the UK would gain a new body of constitutional law it would lose its body of administrative law, which performs distinct and valuable functions. Further, these theorists fail to offer a convincing normative argument for shifting the general focus of public power away from the public interests which Parliament intended that the power should be used to secure, to judicially created values. The privatisation model would turn CLR into an outpost of private law. Again, no convincing normative justification is offered for altering the focus of public power *in general* away from pursuit of the public good to the protection of special interests of individuals. The concerns underpinning the constitutionalists' claims would be better met by their arguing for recognition of a novel body of constitutional law rather than arguing that the CLR ought to be 'constitutionalised'. The concerns of protagonists of privatisation would be better met by their mounting serious normative arguments for recognition of new private law actions to protect those interests they consider most valuable.

The bifurcation debate is of significance for the more general *Wednesbury*/proportionality debate.[10] In particular, it brings into focus an issue of considerable significance which has largely been ignored in that debate.

[10] There are too many sources to cite here.

That is, doctrinal categorisation and the normative significance of doctrinal categories. Ironically those who support unification bring this into focus by downplaying the existence or normative significance of any meaningful boundary between CLR and human rights law. Within the *Wednesbury*/ proportionality debate insufficient attention (often none) has been paid to doctrinal context in explaining why particular substantive standards prevail in certain fields, and in debating what substantive standards ought to prevail in particular fields. This debate has too often focused on 'formal' concerns such as the transparency or structure of particular methods, which are neither here nor there, and distract from deeper concerns.[11] Different bodies of public law perform radically different functions. Recognising this enables us to rationalise the very different substantive norms applied within the two fields. Indeed, close attention to the distinctive nature of each field reveals that within human rights law proportionality is not a ground of review at all, but a defence to a claim of breach of a personal right. Thus, there is not even conceptual or functional unity as between the two phenomena being compared.

Part II contrasts the CLR and the law under the HRA, demonstrating the fundamental functional divide between the fields, as well as examining examples of legal development which purportedly suggest a move towards unity. Part III considers and rejects claims that the two fields ought to merge.

II. THE COMMON LAW OF REVIEW AND THE LAW UNDER THE HRA

Those with a normative preference for unification claim that human rights law and CLR *are* moving towards unity. They make such claims expressly, and they are implied in their arguing 'against bifurcation'[12] and their framing the debate as one 'about whether or not British public law *will* bifurcate into human rights law and general administrative law';[13] both statements suggest that the two fields are *not currently* meaningfully distinct. This part offers a corrective to such flawed accounts.

Consideration of significant features of CLR and human rights law indicate that they are distinct bodies of doctrine which perform radically different functions. While each performs a range of functions the primary function of human rights law is, like certain actions in tort, to afford strong

[11] This is also what I take to be Mark Elliott's taking-off point in 'From Bifurcation to Calibration: Twin-Track Deference and the Culture of Justification' (ch 4 in this volume)—ie the debate needs to move beyond 'side-by-side comparison of the two tests [ie proportionality and *Wednesbury*] or a reckoning of their relative strengths and weaknesses' to 'underlying concerns that ought to be in the driving seat'.

[12] Hunt (n 4).

[13] Taggart, 'Reinventing' (n 1) 334 fn 144 (emphasis added).

protection to and vindicate fundamental *individual, personal interests*, whereas the primary function of CLR is to ensure that public power is exercised properly and in the *public interest*. In turn, this functional divide serves to explain why each field is characterised by different norms, concepts and methodologies. The part goes on to consider developments which unification theorists claim are indicative of a move to unity. They indicate no such thing.

A. The Law of the HRA

The primary function of human rights law, and the law's individualistic rights-based nature, are evident in its significant features, only a sketch of which is possible here. These features are similar to those of actions in private law, such as torts actionable per se, which have long afforded strong protection to basic interests.[14] In the following discussion I draw some parallels with tort, where relevant, in order to illustrate how starkly human rights law contrasts with CLR.

a. Standing and Assignment

In general only the individual rights-holder may bring a claim under the HRA,[15] and their claim may not be assigned.[16] That standing rules are limited to 'victims', that is, those directly affected by the impugned administrative action, suggests that the norms protected by human rights law are personal and specific to individuals, and that the law's focus is the protection of personal interests. In turn, this narrow approach to standing supports the individualist view of rights as the property of their holders.[17] Reinforcing this conclusion is that standing in fields such as tort and contract, which are typically conceptualised as based in individual rights, is similarly narrow,[18] while it is similarly the case in tort that actions

[14] On these torts see generally, JNE Varuhas, 'The Concept of "Vindication" in the Law of Torts' (2014) 34 *Oxford Journal of Legal Studies* 253.

[15] Human Rights Act 1998 (UK) (HRA 1998), s 7. There are exceptions, which are explicable by reference to the law's vindicatory, protective function: *Rabone v Pennine Care NHS Trust* [2012] 2 AC 72; JNE Varuhas, 'Liability under the Human Rights Act 1998: The Duty to Protect Life, Indirect Victims and Damages' [2012] *Cambridge Law Journal* 263.

[16] *Nassau Verzekering Maatschappij NV v Netherlands* App no 57602/09 (ECtHR, 4 October 2011).

[17] J Miles, 'Standing in a Multi-Layered Constitution' in N Bamforth and P Leyland (eds), *Public Law in a Multi-Layered Constitution* (Oxford, Hart Publishing, 2003) 404. I elaborate on this claim, and the sense in which Convention rights entail genuine individual claim-rights, in JNE Varuhas, 'The Reformation of English Administrative Law? "Rights", Rhetoric and Reality' (2013) 72 *Cambridge Law Journal* 369, especially 396ff.

[18] *Morris v Beardmore* [1981] AC 446, 454E; *R v Inland Revenue Commissioners, ex p National Federation of Self-Employed and Small Businesses Ltd* [1982] AC 617 (*IRC*), 639.

considered 'essentially personal', such as defamation or false imprisonment, are not assignable.[19] Reinforcing that rights are personal to individuals, as opposed to say, free-standing standards of legality, are consistent judicial statements to the effect that rights belong to and are specific to the claimant.[20] Further, the Supreme Court has said that 'decisions founded on human rights are essentially individual'; a determination of breach is a determination only in respect of the specific claimant's rights.[21]

b. Actionable per se

In common with torts actionable per se, a claimant in human rights law need not demonstrate that the rights-violation has left them materially worse off in order to bring a claim.[22] All that a claimant must show, in general, is that their protected interests have been infringed. An interference may well leave a victim materially better off, but it remains the case that their basic interests ought not, given their fundamental importance, to have been interfered with. They ought to be inviolate.

c. Strict Liability

Liability is generally strict rather than fault-based. All a claimant needs to show in order to establish a prima facie case of liability is that he has suffered interference with his interests, while a defendant authority may be held liable for interference even if they acted reasonably, with meticulous care or with benevolent intentions.[23] This reflects the prime importance the law places on fundamental interests and their protection against outside interference.

d. Defences

For some rights such as that against torture there is no defence other than express authorisation in statute.[24] For other rights there may be a general

[19] *Glegg v Bromley* [1912] 3 KB 474, 488; *24 Seven Utility Services Ltd v Rosekey Ltd* [2003] EWHC 3415, [25].

[20] These rights do not exist in the air but are 'the rights of the applicants', 'the Convention rights of these particular young people', 'his' or 'her' rights etc: *R (Quila) v Secretary of State for the Home Department* [2012] 1 AC 621, [44], [61]; *Belfast City Council v Miss Behavin' Ltd* [2007] 1 WLR 1420, [12]–[13], [15]–[16], [20], [90]; *R (Begum) v Governors of Denbigh High School* [2007] 1 AC 100, [48], [59]; *Rabone* (n 15) [107]; *Tweed v Parades Commission for Northern Ireland* [2007] 1 AC 650, [5]; *R (Wilkinson) v Broadmoor Special Hospital Authority* [2002] 1 WLR 419, [61]–[62]; *Bank Mellat v Her Majesty's Treasury (No 2)* [2013] 3 WLR 179, [21] (substantive appeal).

[21] *Quila* (n 20) [59], [80].

[22] *Cullen v Chief Constable of Royal Ulster Constabulary* [2003] 1 WLR 1763, [81].

[23] Eg *MS v UK* (2012) 55 EHRR 23; *ZH v Commissioner of Police of the Metropolis* [2013] 1 WLR 3021; *P v Cheshire West and Chester Council* [2014] UKSC 19.

[24] *Gäfgen v Germany* (2011) 52 EHRR 1, [101]–[108]; HRA 1998, s 6(2).

defence of proportionality,[25] while for others more specific grounds of justification are enumerated.[26] But all such defences are confined to protecting the most important of countervailing interests, such as national security or public order.[27] Further the criteria for justification are in general strict, defences are construed narrowly, the onus of justification rests with the defendant, and the courts may probe the factual foundations of asserted justifications.[28] These features again reflect the importance placed by the law on the claimant's interests, and also the strong legal protection afforded to those interests.

e. Remedies

Remedies are discretionary in human rights law.[29] But the discretion to refuse relief altogether is very narrow given the demands of Article 13 of the Convention (the right to an effective remedy), which the remedial provisions of the HRA were intended to implement[30] and which requires provision of effective redress for rights-violations, and admits very few exceptions. Importantly damages are an available remedy under the HRA.[31] This is significant because provision for monetary redress affords a further layer of protection to the underlying interests, but also because this remedy again suggests an individualist focus. Damages claims are 'paradigms of personal claims',[32] as the remedy redresses losses personal to specific individuals.

f. Procedure

Human rights claims may be brought via ordinary procedure, alongside other claims based in individual rights such as those in tort, and courts have gone so far as to indicate that certain types of human rights claim *ought* to be brought via ordinary procedure.[33] Where such claims are made via review procedure, the usual restrictions, for example on discovery and

[25] Eg European Convention on Human Rights (ECHR), art 8(2).

[26] Eg ECHR, arts 2(2), 5(1)(a)–(f).

[27] Eg see those countervailing interests in ECHR, art 8(2).

[28] Eg *Marcic v Thames Water Utilities Ltd* [2004] 2 AC 42, [37]; *Quila* (n 20) [44]; *Kallis and Androulla Panayi v Turkey* App no 45388/99, (ECtHR, 27 October 2009) [52]; *Smith and Grady v UK* (2000) 29 EHRR 493, [94], [99]–[100]; *R (Daly) v Secretary of State for the Home Department* [2001] 2 AC 532, [27]; *Bank Mellat* (n 20) [20].

[29] HRA 1998, s 8(1).

[30] *Re S (Minors)* [2002] 2 AC 291, [61]; HL Deb 19 January 1998, vol 584, col 1266 Lord Irvine of Lairg; HL Deb 29 January 1998, vol 585, col 385 Lord Irvine of Lairg; HC Deb 20 May 1998, vol 312, col 979 Mr Jack Straw.

[31] HRA 1998, s 8(2)–(5); *R (Faulkner) v Secretary of State for Justice* [2013] 2 AC 254.

[32] J Beatson, '"Public" and "Private" in English Administrative Law' (1987) 103 *Law Quarterly Review* 34, 45.

[33] *Ruddy v Chief Constable of Strathclyde* [2012] UKSC 57; *Wilkinson* (n 20) [61]; *ID v Home Office* [2006] 1 WLR 1003, [105].

cross-examination, have been loosened so that, in significant respects, the procedure comes to resemble ordinary procedure.[34] In loosening these restrictions courts have drawn direct analogies with claims in tort, while courts have extended the limitation period for human rights claims to match those for torts, so that human rights claimants are not disadvantaged.[35] All of this is of a piece with the long-standing judicial view that claims of individual right ought not to be subject to those restrictions on access to court imposed by review procedure.[36]

g. Substantive Questions for the Judiciary

In human rights claims the judiciary exercises final, determinative authority over substantive questions that arise in the context of the claim. This is because human rights claims are claims of individual right. Within the separation of powers, claims of individual right are for courts to determine; resolution of claims of right is the quintessential judicial function, the 'benchmark' of judicial power.[37] Thus questions over the scope of the right or breach are for the court. For example, in a claim that a public authority has failed to fulfil its positive operational duty under Article 2 to protect the claimant from threats to his life, the court applies the relevant legal tests in the same manner as it would apply elements of a tort to facts in determining liability. It is for the court to determine whether a risk was 'real and immediate', whether the authority knew or ought to have known of the risk, and if so whether the public authority took all reasonable steps required to prevent that risk from materialising; these questions are 'objectively considered' and determined by the court.[38] It is not surprising that Lady Hale has observed of such cases: 'A claim such as this ... is more in the nature of a claim in tort than for judicial review.'[39]

Just as in tort, it is for the court to determine whether a defence of justification, such as proportionality, has been established. Thus, for example, in respect of proportionality, the courts have held that they must 'make a value judgment, an evaluation' for themselves:[40] 'Proportionality must be judged objectively, by the court'.[41] Lord Hoffmann, contrasting the approach in

[34] *Tweed* (n 20); *Wilkinson* (n 20) [25]–[26].

[35] *Wilkinson* (n 20) [24], [56]–[59], [62]; *Dobson v Thames Valley Utilities Ltd* [2011] EWHC 3253, [1072]–[1074].

[36] *Roy v Kensington and Chelsea and Westminster Family Practitioner Committee* [1992] 1 AC 624, 654.

[37] *Kable v Director of Public Prosecutions (NSW)* (1996) 189 CLR 51, 123.

[38] *Rabone* (n 15) [43]; *Van Colle v UK* (2013) 56 EHRR 23, [95]; *Re Officer L* [2007] 1 WLR 2135, [20]–[21].

[39] *Rabone* (n 15) [108].

[40] *Denbigh* (n 20) [30].

[41] Ibid; *Tweed* (n 20) [55]; *R (Williamson) v Secretary of State for Education and Employment* [2005] 2 AC 246, [51].

human rights claims with the approach to protection of human rights at common law (see further below), in *Miss Behavin'*, said 'the question is ... whether there has actually been a violation of the applicant's Convention rights and not whether the decision-maker properly considered the question of whether his rights would be violated or not'.[42] Similarly, Lord Carnwath has said that in HRA cases '[t]he court's function ... is to decide for itself whether the decision was in accordance with Convention rights; it is not a purely reviewing function'; 'Under the HRA ... the claimant would have a right to full merits review by the court, again on fact and law'.[43] Of course a court, in adjudicating the defence, may give 'weight' to a balance struck by an official, just as courts ordinarily give weight to relevant considerations and the judgement of persons with particular expertise.[44] But the crucial point is that it is nonetheless the court's determination of proportionality that is determinative.[45]

Given these core features of proportionality and human rights adjudication more generally it is curious that prominent commentators frequently describe proportionality as a ground of review,[46] some going so far as to describe it as a 'free-standing principle'.[47] Proportionality is not a ground of review calling for exercise of the court's supervisory jurisdiction. Rather it is a defence in a claim of right, and the courts' role is not to exercise a reviewing function, but to exercise determinative judgement over whether the defence is proven. It is therefore a fundamental error to include proportionality under the HRA on a scale or rainbow of general standards of substantive review;[48] it is a functionally and conceptually distinct phenomenon from review standards. Including proportionality on such a spectrum is as misplaced as including the test of 'reasonable standard of care'—the criterion for breach of duty in negligence applied against public authorities—or 'reasonableness' *simpliciter*—the obligation imposed by the Article 2 positive operational duty—on the spectrum. This is also why it is a false move

[42] *Miss Behavin'* (n 20) [12]–[15], [31], [44] (Lady Hale made exactly the same point); *Denbigh* (n 20) [29]–[31]; *Huang v Secretary of State for the Home Department* [2007] 2 AC 167; *Quila* (n 20) [46], [61], [91]; *E v Chief Constable of the Royal Ulster Constabulary* [2009] 1 AC 536, [13], [52] onwards.

[43] *Kennedy* (n 7) [244].

[44] *Huang* (n 42) [16]; *Bank Mellat* (n 20) [129].

[45] *Miss Behavin'* (n 20) [31], [37].

[46] Eg P Craig, 'The Courts, the Human Rights Act and Judicial Review' (2001) 117 *Law Quarterly Review* 589, 594–96; P Craig, *Administrative Law*, 7th edn (London, Sweet & Maxwell, 2012) [20-033]–[20-034]; P Craig, 'Proportionality, Rationality and Review' [2010] *New Zealand Law Review* 265, 293.

[47] T Poole, 'Between the Devil and the Deep Blue Sea: Administrative Law in an Age of Rights' in L Pearson, C Harlow and M Taggart (eds), *Administrative Law in a Changing State: Essays in Honour of Mark Aronson* (Oxford, Hart Publishing, 2008) 34.

[48] Eg Taggart, 'Proportionality' (n 2) 451ff; H Woolf and others, *De Smith's Judicial Review*, 7th edn (London, Sweet & Maxwell, 2013) 635.

to argue that proportionality should be read across from human rights law as a possible *substitute* for *Wednesbury*.

Proportionality is not a free-standing review ground. It depends, for its applicability and application, on the claimant first demonstrating that their right has been infringed. Where this is demonstrated, in respect of some but not all rights, the defendant may raise proportionality as a defence. The onus is on the defendant to make this out on the balance of probabilities because it is for defendants to prove defences. Further, proportionality is only one type of defence to a rights-claim. It is therefore odd and striking that it is so often wrongly presented not only as a free-standing head of review, but as *the* head of review under the HRA.[49] For example, in claims concerning Articles 2–7 and 12–13, competing interests may be weighed, but the structured proportionality method associated with Articles 8–11 is not applied. The method is not relevant to the majority of Convention rights, excluding Protocols.

Thus, the courts' role in human rights actions derives from their being engaged in adjudication of claims of individual right, which courts have ultimate power and responsibility to determine.[50] In contrast, as we shall see, at common law the court performs a very different function, exercising a secondary, supervisory jurisdiction.

h. Miscellaneous

A miscellany of other features is indicative of human rights law's primary function of affording strong protection to fundamental interests. There is a strong interpretive obligation on courts to construe legislation compatibly with human rights. Courts may examine primary legislation for compatibility with human rights; these rights are so fundamental that even statute ought to be examined for consistency with them. Convention rights have been interpreted as casting not only negative duties of non-interference, but also positive duties, including duties on authorities to prevent third parties from interfering with individuals' interests, adding a further layer of protection to those interests and vindicating the value which the law places upon them.

[49] See the references in n 46; Poole (n 47) 41; Poole (n 8) 146.

[50] In this respect there is an important difference between the approach of UK courts to rights adjudication, and the approach of courts in some other common-law jurisdictions, where such adjudication has, in certain respects, been subordinated to pre-existing CLR principles: see *Doré v Barreau du Québec* [2012] 1 SCR 395, Geiringer's and Walters' contributions to this collection (chs 13 and 15), and H Wilberg, 'The Bill of Rights in Administrative Law Cases: Taking Stock and Suggesting Some Reassessment' (2013) 25 *New Zealand Universities Law Review* 866.

Thus, the primary function of human rights law, manifest in its fundamental features, is protection and vindication of individuals' basic rights and interests. The law's function is analogous to bodies of private law, such as torts actionable per se, which have long afforded strong protection to similarly basic interests in liberty, physical integrity and property, through positive, individual legal rights. These strong links between tort and human rights law can be obscured, and unfortunately often are obscured by fuzzy thinking in terms of a grand division between public and private law.

B. Common Law of Review

Fundamental features of CLR indicate that its focus is the near-complete inverse of that of human rights law. In human rights law the focus is upon ensuring strong protection and vindication of personal, individual interests, whereas the primary function of CLR is to ensure public powers are exercised properly—that is, in accordance with axiomatic ideas of good administration—and in the public interest; another way of putting this is that the primary role of CLR is to ensure public power is not misused or abused. While human rights law focuses on the interests of private individuals and their protection in the face of administrative action motivated by a concern for the public interest (individual-regarding), the common law's focus is squarely on public officials and regulation of the exercise of public power *itself*, ensuring it is exercised as it ought to be in the public interest (public-regarding). That the law's focus is on the common good is not to say the law evinces no concern for individuals. It does, as discussed below. But the concern is subsidiary, and the manner in which the law approaches this concern is moulded by its primary functions.

a. Standing

In stark contrast to the narrow, rights-based standing rules under the HRA, standing rules at common law are exceptionally liberal. The courts have recognised that exercise of the court's supervisory jurisdiction necessarily requires a different approach to standing from the rights-based approach in other fields.[51] In order to be granted standing applicants need not demonstrate that they have been personally or directly affected by the challenged administrative action, so that public-spirited individuals and pressure groups are routinely granted standing where they can demonstrate

[51] *AXA General Insurance Ltd v HM Advocate* [2012] 1 AC 868, [169]–[170]; *Walton v Scottish Ministers* [2012] UKSC 44, [90]–[94]; *O'Reilly v Mackman* [1983] 2 AC 237, 275; *IRC* (n 18) (Lords Diplock and Scarman).

an arguable case that administrative action is unlawful.[52] The reason for these wide rules is that CLR protects something we all have a legitimate interest in: the proper exercise of public power in the public interest. It is true that individual detriment is a factor that goes to standing. But it is in the nature of an indicator of the genuineness of the applicant's claim. That is, it tells against the application being 'prompted by an ill-motive' or the applicant being 'a mere busybody or a trouble-maker', such that standing should be denied for abuse of process.[53] Questions over assignment do not arise because claims are not the 'property' of any one individual or entity.

b. Remedies

The law's basic concerns are evident in the range of available remedies. Remedies are limited to specific-type relief, such as quashing and prohibiting orders, or injunctions, and declaratory relief. These remedies are geared towards regulating and guiding public power so that it is exercised as it ought to be.[54] Damages are not available,[55] and would be out of place, given they are concerned to remedy setbacks *personal* to specific individuals pursuant to breach of individual rights. In turn, the absence of a damages remedy reflects that the basic norms within CLR are not individual rights, given the nexus in English law between individual rights and the damages remedy.[56]

The courts exercise an ultimate discretion over whether to grant relief and what relief to grant. This allows the courts maximal flexibility to tailor, on a case-by-case basis, their interventions according to the demands of the public interest and administrative process. The court has[57]

> an ultimate discretion whether to set [decisions] aside and may refuse to do so in the public interest ... such decisions affect a very wide public which will not be parties to the dispute and ... their interests have to be taken into account as much as those of the immediate disputants.

For example, it is not uncommon for courts to declare administrative action unlawful but leave it intact, so as not to undermine public interests in

[52] *IRC* (n 18); *Gillick v West Norfolk and Wisbech Area Health Authority* [1986] AC 112, 191–93; *R v Secretary of State for Foreign and Commonwealth Affairs, ex p World Development Movement Ltd* [1995] 1 WLR 386 (*WDM*); *Walton* (n 51) [94]; *R v Somerset County Council, ex p Dixon* [1998] Env LR 111, 121.

[53] *R (Feakins) v Secretary of State for the Environment, Food and Rural Affairs* [2004] 1 WLR 1761, [23]; *Walton* (n 51) [92], [94], [153].

[54] *Gillick* (n 52) 192.

[55] Eg *X (Minors) v Bedfordshire County Council* [1995] 2 AC 633, 730–31; *Mohammed v Home Office* [2011] 1 WLR 2862; *Watkins v Secretary of State for the Home Department* [2006] 2 AC 395, [26].

[56] *Bourgoin SA v Ministry of Agriculture, Fisheries and Food* [1986] QB 716, 761, 767.

[57] *R v Panel on Take-overs and Mergers, ex p Datafin plc* [1987] 1 QB 815, 840–41.

administrative certainty and finality.[58] Relief may be denied altogether on the basis of public interest concerns.[59] The legitimate interests of the applicant may be relevant but if they are at odds with the demands of the administrative process they are likely to be trumped.[60] More recent dicta suggest a narrowing of the remedial discretion to refuse relief altogether.[61] However, such dicta are in general premised on the idea that public life ought to be conducted lawfully, rather than in a concern for, say, ensuring strong protection of individual rights and interests.[62] It is also not uncommon to find the narrowness of the discretion being emphasised in cases where relief is in fact denied.[63] In human rights law there is far less scope for denial of relief given the requirement of a right to an effective remedy and the underlying policy of strong protection and vindication of basic interests.

c. Presumption of Validity and Onus

In contrast to human rights law, where burdens of justification lie with the defendant, at common law administrative action is presumed valid and the burden lies on the applicant to demonstrate unlawfulness.[64] This reflects the public interest focus of the law. The presumption serves to protect public interests in administrative certainty and citizen compliance with administrative decisions. Further, it allows the administration to pursue public goals secure in the knowledge that the court's 'default setting' is non-intervention.

d. Procedure

The procedure by which review applications are streamed provides for many safeguards—severe restrictions on disclosure and oral evidence, a

[58] Ibid, 842.

[59] Eg *R v Monopolies and Mergers Commission, ex p Argyll* [1986] 1 WLR 763; *Walton* (n 51) [103], [131], [155]–[156]; *R (Edwards) v Environment Agency* [2009] 1 All ER 57, [65]; *R (Hurley) v Secretary of State for Business Innovation and Skills* [2012] HRLR 13, [99].

[60] *Argyll* (n 59) 774–75.

[61] Eg *Berkeley v Secretary of State for the Environment, Transport and the Regions (No 1)* [2001] 2 AC 603, 608, 616; *R (C (A Minor)) v Secretary of State for Justice* [2009] QB 657; *R (Corbett) v Restormel Borough Council* [2001] EWCA Civ 330, [17], [32], [34].

[62] Eg *C (A Minor)* (n 61) [41], [49], [54]–[55]; *R v Lincolnshire County Council, ex p Atkinson* (1996) 8 Admin LR 529, 550; *Corbett* (n 61) [32]; T Bingham, 'Should Public Law Remedies Be Discretionary?' [1991] *Public Law* 64.

[63] *Edwards* (n 59) [63]–[65]; Hurley (n 59) [99]; *R (Child Poverty Action Group) v Secretary of State for Work and Pensions* [2012] EWHC (Admin) 2579, [64]–[77]; *R (English Speaking Board Ltd) v Secretary of State for the Home Department* [2011] EWHC (Admin) 1788, [62]–[63]; *Atkinson* (n 62) 550.

[64] *F Hoffmann-la Roche & Co v Secretary of State for Trade and Industry Respondent* [1975] AC 295, 366ff; *R v Boundary Commission for England, ex p Foot* [1983] QB 600, 634, 637; *R v Lancashire County Council, ex p Huddleston* [1986] 2 All ER 941, 945. It may be that in some cases the onus does not make a great practical difference. However, allocation of onus, as a structural feature of the law, is an important signal of the law's concerns.

requirement at the outset for full, candid affidavits verifying the facts relied on by the applicant, a very short limitation period, and a permission stage—which serve to protect authorities from tardy and unmeritorious claims which could cause them delay, uncertainty and disruption in their pursuit of the common good.[65] These features, and their discretionary control by the courts, also operate to preserve public resources, of the authority and the court. The courts may also, more generally, take it upon themselves to cut down access to the courts if public interests in rationing of scarce resources so demand.[66] Whereas such restrictions would constitute undue impediments on individual access to court for protection of one's human rights and impede robust determination of HRA claims, which often raise complex factual questions, such restrictions are at one with the CLR's basic concerns.

e. Supervisory Jurisdiction

Judicial review is a secondary, supervisory, 'long stop'[67] jurisdiction, and a measure of last resort.[68] The principal reasons for this are grounded in the functions of the law. First, it is first and foremost for the official who has been bestowed with the relevant power by Parliament to determine what lies in the interests of the public. Second, administrators know a great deal more about good administration than judges. Third, if judges intervene too readily in administrative decisions, they may end up undermining pursuit of the public interest and administrative effectiveness. In this way pursuit of good administration and regulation of public power in the public interest forms the rationale for review, *and also* the rationale for restraint in its exercise.

f. Grounds

The grounds on which courts may find administrative action unlawful also reflect the underlying functions of the law.

Judges consistently emphasise that public power is only to be used for the public good. Of course, it is not for the judges to determine what lies in the public interest: whereas judges 'are equipped to find legal rights and administer, on well-known principles, discretionary remedies', 'decisions to be made as to the public interest are not such as courts are fitted

[65] CLR is not characterised by such stringent safeguards in all common-law jurisdictions, albeit as judicial review grows we may witness moves towards the English model elsewhere. See, eg Courts Reform (Scotland) Bill 2013, s 85.

[66] *R (Cart) v The Upper Tribunal* [2012] 1 AC 663.

[67] *R v Panel on Take-overs and Mergers, ex p Guinness plc* [1990] 1 QB 146, 177; *R v Secretary of State for the Home Department , ex p Brind* [1991] 1 AC 696, 765.

[68] *R v Chief Constable of Merseyside, ex p Calveley* [1986] QB 424.

or equipped to make'.[69] Rather, the judicial role on review is to keep administrators broadly 'on track', ensuring public power has genuinely been exercised according to the concern for the common good underlying its grant by Parliament. It has consistently been maintained by courts that public power is conferred 'for the public good',[70] 'for the public benefit',[71] 'for public purposes',[72] for the 'protection of the public',[73] or to be carried out 'in the public interest',[74] 'in the interests of the public generally'[75] rather than for the interests of any one individual.[76] It has been made clear at the highest level that 'in a legal system based on the rule of law executive or administrative power "may be exercised only for the public good" and not for ulterior and improper purposes', and that public officers 'must always act for the public good'.[77] This follows from the premise, recognised at Supreme Court level, that '[e]very public body exists for the service of the public'.[78] From this premise one can readily rationalise axiomatic grounds. Acting for improper purpose, taking into account extraneous concerns, or acting with bias are all clear ways in which administrators may deviate from the reasons why they have been bestowed with public power by Parliament; the common-law grounds exist to keep them 'on track'. When the court intervenes, it does so 'on behalf of the public'[79] or, put another way, 'in defence of the citizenry'.[80]

Similarly, where an administrator acts perversely, this is indicative of a decision-maker going 'off-course' and deviating from their task of genuine pursuit of the common good. In such cases the courts may intervene on the *Wednesbury* ground. Below that threshold courts will be reluctant to intervene given there is—as emphasised in the jurisprudence—scope for reasonable disagreement as to what lies in the common good, such that even strong disagreement with the decision-maker's reasoning or an outcome is not sufficient basis for holding the decision unlawful, even where basic interests are at stake.[81] In this way the 'emphatic language' of the

[69] *Gouriet v Union of Post Office Workers* [1978] AC 435, 482.

[70] *Stovin v Wise* [1996] AC 923, 935D, 951H.

[71] *Cutler v Wandsworth Stadium Ld* [1949] AC 398, 408.

[72] *X v Bedfordshire* (n 55) 737; *Swain v Law Society* [1983] 1 AC 598, 618.

[73] *Swain* (n 72) 607.

[74] *R (Niazi) v Secretary of State for the Home Department* [2008] EWCA Civ 755, [41].

[75] *Financial Services Authority v Sinaloa Gold plc* [2013] 2 AC 28, [31], [33].

[76] See, generally, H Woolf, 'Public Law–Private Law: Why the Divide? A Personal View' [1986] *Public Law* 220.

[77] *Three Rivers District Council v Governor and Company of the Bank of England (No 3)* [2003] 2 AC 1, 190, 196.

[78] *Kennedy* (n 7) [107].

[79] *Guinness* (n 67) 193G.

[80] *Datafin* (n 57) 839.

[81] *Kruse v Johnson* [1898] 2 QB 91, 100; *Foot* (n 64) 626; *R (McDonald) v Kensington and Chelsea Royal London Borough Council* [2011] 4 All ER 881, [31]; *Brind* (n 67) 765–66.

Wednesbury standard stands as a totem of non-intervention; it is designed 'to drive home the message' that it is for the decision-maker to determine what lies in the interests of the public.[82] In this respect it is worth recording that those who focus on and criticise variations in the formulation of the test put too much weight on often semantic linguistic variations, at the expense of trying to understand what the law is seeking to do. All formulations have one thing in common—they stand as a 'symbol', a marker of non-intervention.[83]

Another reason for the high threshold is the existence of the more specific or targeted grounds. If the applicant fails to make out such a ground, of which there are now a large number and which have been broadened over time,[84] it makes sense that a very cautious approach would be taken to intervention on a *general* inquiry into quality. And indeed, it has very often been the case that where judges do conclude that a decision is unreasonable, this is 'a way of saying that the decision is tainted by various specific breaches of administrative law principles'.[85] The availably of the specific grounds is also the reason why it is wrong to criticise *Wednesbury* on the basis that it is difficult for the applicant to get 'beyond the court door', given the high threshold.[86] An applicant is expected to get in the court door on the basis of specific grounds, with *Wednesbury* serving as a safety net, only to be resorted to if specific grounds fail. *Wednesbury is* and *is meant to be* a marginal ground.

A central concern of CLR is to ensure public power is exercised according to basic expectations of good administration. Thus it has been said that courts and administration form a 'partnership' 'in the public interest', 'based on a common aim, namely the maintenance of the highest standards of public administration'.[87] Bias, decision-making based in irrelevant

[82] *Brind* (n 67).

[83] Taggart, 'Proportionality' (n 2) 425, 436, 471. There are examples of courts applying a much lower threshold of intervention. These ought to be met with robust criticism: eg *R (Bradley) v Secretary of State for Work and Pensions* [2009] QB 114 (see JNE Varuhas, 'Governmental Rejections of Ombudsman Findings: What Role for the Courts?' (2009) 72 *Modern Law Review* 102); *R (Litvinenko) v Secretary of State for the Home Department* [2014] EWHC 194 (see JNE Varuhas, 'Ministerial Refusals to Initiate Public Inquiries: Review or Appeal?' [2014] *Cambridge Law Journal* 238).

[84] At times unification theorists seem to suggest that bifurcation would leave non-rights cases to be governed by the 'classic', 'unreformed' model of administrative law, and subject to 'narrowly conceived grounds' (Hunt (n 4) 102–104). Such claims are liable to mislead, if interpreted as suggesting that the 'classic model' accurately captures contemporary CLR. The 'classic model', a narrow, 'private law' model of review, was, between the 1950s and 1980s, gradually recalibrated as a 'public interest' model, with consequent significant expansion and development of the grounds: C Harlow, 'A Special Relationship? American Influences on Judicial Review in England' in I Loveland (ed), *A Special Relationship? American Influences on Public Law in the UK* (Oxford, Oxford University Press, 1995).

[85] Taggart, 'Proportionality' (n 2) 471, 479.

[86] Eg Craig, 'Proportionality' (n 46) 294, 299.

[87] *Datafin* (n 57) 842; *Huddleston* (n 64) 945, 947; see also *Cart* (n 66) [89].

concerns and acting for an improper purpose are all at variance with how one would expect public power to be exercised. Using a power bestowed for purpose X for purpose Y or acting according to one's prejudices cannot be considered permissible exercises of public power. In addition, making decisions based on material factual errors or without regard to material information, acting contrary to clear representations made to a person or group or suddenly deviating from entrenched practice with no good reason, or making decisions in respect of individuals without affording them notice, consulting them or affording them an opportunity to be heard is not in accord with basic expectations of good administrative practice. It will, in turn, lead to unreliable decision-making, which is not in the public interest or, in truth, anyone's interest.[88]

Strict ultra vires has not so far been mentioned. Given the public interest ethos of CLR, one might explain this ground on the basis that it is in the public interest that the administration obey the law.[89] One might also contend that where administrators abide the express terms of the empowering statute they are acting consistently with the demands of the public interest, as determined by Parliament which has ultimate authority to determine what lies in the interests of the polity and the purposes for which public power may be used. But one probably does not require such explanations. The ultra vires ground simply follows from a society being governed through law; addressees of those laws are under a duty to abide by them. This is true of citizen and official actor alike. However, it is worth observing that maintenance of the public interest in lawful decision-making may be dependent on other public interest concerns, such as those in final and effective administrative decision-making. This is clearest at the remedies stage, where either the demands of good administration or public interest may counsel against nullification of an unlawful decision,[90] and at the leave stage where public interests such as those in administrative certainty

[88] Eg *E v Secretary of State for the Home Department* [2004] QB 1044, [64], [66]; *Bank Mellat* (n 20) [32]. Some features of the natural justice 'core' of procedural fairness could suggest a principal focus upon the interests of the individual subject to the procedure. For example, it has been held that the individual can consent to waiver of natural justice requirements (*R (Hill) v Institute of Chartered Accountants in England and Wales* [2014] 1 WLR 86). The fact that the obligation can be waived simply because the individual consents might be taken to suggest that there is no wider public interest at stake (although it may be that such public interest concerns simply did not arise in *Hill*). In addition, courts have at times, but not consistently, placed emphasis on the impact unfair procedures may have on individuals: *R (Osborn) v Parole Board* [2013] 3 WLR 1020. However, these features are not determinative. Further, the individualist conception cannot explain, for example, wide standing, why procedural fairness is an aspect of a supervisory jurisdiction, or why damages may be recovered for breach of procedural individual rights under the HRA, but not of natural justice requirements.

[89] Eg *R (CJ) v Cardiff City Council* [2011] EWCA Civ 1590, [21]; *AXA* (n 51) [169] (Lord Reed describing review proceedings which serve to preserve the rule of law as implicating the 'public interest').

[90] Text to nn 54–63 above.

and speedy administrative decision-making may tell against grant of leave to a delayed application which entails arguable claims of unlawfulness.[91] This is reflective of the overarching concern of review with protection of the public good.

Overall, the principal function of the CLR is to ensure public power is exercised properly and in the public interest. Individual rights and interests may, and often will, be protected by the operation of the CLR, individuals may bring applications motivated by a desire to protect their interests, and the law may, as we shall see, require that individual interests be given consideration in certain contexts. But protection of the individual is not the law's principal concern. The law's concern is not with individual wrongs, but public wrongs. That is, breaches of duties owed to the public as a whole or to sections of the public, for the benefit of the public: 'Public law is not at base about rights, even though abuses of power may and often do invade private rights; it is about wrongs—that is to say misuses of public power'.[92] This is why, for example, unaffected members of the community are entitled to initiate proceedings, and why damages for personal loss are not available and would be out of place.

Some may criticise CLR as 'ruthless' or 'heartless' for its lack of concern for the individual, but this is akin to criticising the law of construction contracts on the basis that it does not evince a primary concern for human rights; it is simply not the focus of that field. And it does not follow that individual rights and interests are vulnerable in the face of executive power. Other bodies of law exist specifically to afford strong protection to the most important of individual interests, such as human rights law and tort.

C. Unification?

CLR and human rights law perform fundamentally different functions, and this difference is reflected in significant structural differences between the fields. It thus seems difficult to imagine how the two fields could be moving to unity. In making such claims unification theorists focus on a small selection of common-law developments, which typically entail adoption of something akin to proportionality. The 'usual suspects' include the test for reasonableness review where 'human rights' are at stake, the principle of legality and the reason-giving duty. On closer analysis these developments do not support the grand claims made.

[91] Senior Courts Act 1981, s 31(6).

[92] *Dixon* (n 52) 121. See also *IRC* (n 18) 648, 651–53; *Bourgoin* (n 56) 761; Varuhas (n 17) 408–11; Woolf (n 76); Lady Hale, 'Who Guards the Guardians?' (Speech to the Public Law Project Conference, 14 October 2013) 2 (available at: http://supremecourt.uk/docs/speech-131014.pdf).

First, it is important to record that basic doctrines of review which form the bread and butter of the Administrative Court's work are never or seldom mentioned by unification theorists. These include ultra vires, relevant considerations, improper purpose, unlawful delegation, unlawful fettering, and aspects of procedural fairness, such as requirements for hearings and notice and so on. While these doctrines continue to evolve, they have not undergone any radical recalibration based in rights or proportionality. Further, emergent fields such as review for factual error[93] or consultation[94] are at one with traditional concerns. They are not explicable by reference to a 'culture of justification', given that consultation and factual premises are inputs into the decision-process rather than justifications for outcomes. Further, these developments are justified expressly by reference to orthodox concerns: good administration and fair process.[95] Thus, *if* there is evidence of radical recalibration, it is confined to a few pockets of review. In turn, that the evidence is so confined suggests it is not symptomatic of a wider trend.

Let us turn to *Wednesbury*. Anxious scrutiny is and remains the general test of substantive review at common law where 'human rights' are at stake. It is important to pause here to explain the nature of this test, as it is often invoked as emblematic of a move towards the 'righting' of administrative law, and/or the emergence of a culture of justification, and it is sometimes argued that the anxious scrutiny test is equivalent to the structured proportionality test in human rights law.[96] It is none of these things. Rather, the anxious scrutiny test is illustrative of CLR's two traditional concerns: regulation of public power in the public interest, and in accordance with principles of good administration.

In the late 1980s it was established that where an individual's 'right to life', the 'most fundamental of all human rights', is at stake, the 'basis of the decision must surely call for the most anxious scrutiny'.[97] However, what this effectively amounted to was a requirement that the decision-maker take into account the impact of his decision on the applicant's rights, and ask himself whether that impact is justifiable: 'If the Secretary of State has asked himself that question and answered it ... in the light of all relevant evidence, the court cannot interfere'.[98] In a later decision, *Brind*, the House

[93] Eg *E* (n 88); *IA v Secretary of State for the Home Department* [2014] 1 WLR 384, [54] onwards.

[94] Eg *R v Brent London Borough Council, ex p Gunning* (1986) 84 LGR 168; *R (Niazi) v Secretary of State for the Home Department* [2008] EWCA Civ 755; *Draper v Lincolnshire County Council* [2014] EWHC 2388 (Admin).

[95] Factual error: *E* (n 88) [64], [66]: the Court explaining that the basis for recognition of the doctrine is ensuring correct results, which is in the interest of all. Consultation: *Niazi* (n 93) [30], [50].

[96] Taggart, 'Proportionality' (n 2) 448–49; Dyzenhaus, Hunt and Taggart (n 3) 18–20.

[97] *R v Secretary of State for the Home Department, ex p Bugdaycay* [1987] 1 AC 514, 531.

[98] Ibid, 532.

of Lords held that a court could intervene even where the right question had been asked but only if the balance struck by the decision-maker was *Wednesbury* unreasonable; the courts approaching such cases 'on a conventional *Wednesbury* basis adapted to a human rights context', rather than on the basis they are directly enforcing rights.[99] Thus, in *Brind* Lord Bridge said:[100]

> The primary judgment as to whether the particular competing public interest justified the particular restriction imposed falls to the Secretary of State to whom Parliament has entrusted the discretion. But we are entitled to exercise a secondary judgment by asking whether a reasonable Secretary of State, on the material before him, could reasonably make that primary judgment.

The court's role thus remains supervisory and secondary, such that considerable scope is maintained for reasonable disagreement. Courts emphasise that even though they could well see criticisms of particular administrative decisions they could only intervene if the balance struck was perverse.[101] Whereas under the HRA it is for the court to determine objectively, for itself, whether a rights-interference is justifiable, because the courts are adjudicating claims of right, courts do not have such role under *Wednesbury*, where they are exercising a supervisory jurisdiction. The extra burden imposed by anxious scrutiny is merely that where a decision-maker makes a decision which could affect a basic right, he or she has an obligation to take that into account as a concern relevant to the exercise of his or her public power, and to consider whether prejudice to that right is warranted in the public good. But if this is done, the balance struck by the decision-maker is unlikely to be disturbed.

This approach is reflective of the primary functions of CLR. While the law evinces some concern for individual interests, protection of individual interests is not its principal function. The principal concern underlying anxious scrutiny is the traditional concern of facilitating *good administrative practice*: to ensure that the decision-maker turns his mind to and considers all relevant considerations, one of which is prejudice to basic interests. As Lord Carnwath said recently, even in anxious scrutiny cases, 'the role of the courts is often more about process than merits'.[102] In another recent case, giving the judgment of the Supreme Court, he said that the concern underpinning anxious scrutiny is 'the need for decisions to show by their reasoning that every factor which might tell in favour of an applicant has been properly taken into account'.[103] The focus is on the *manner* of the exercise

[99] *Brind* (n 67); *R v Ministry of Defence, ex p Smith* [1996] QB 517, 540, 554.
[100] *Brind* (n 67) 748–49.
[101] Ibid, 749; *Smith* (n 99) 566.
[102] *Kennedy* (n 7) [245].
[103] *Secretary of State for the Home Department v MN and KY* [2014] UKSC 30, [31].

of power itself, rather than securing actual protection or enforcement of the 'right': '*Good public administration requires* a proper consideration of the legitimate interests of individual citizens ... But in judging the relevance of an interest, however legitimate, regard has to be had to the purpose of the administrative process concerned.'[104]

Therefore, the manner in which human rights are taken into account is moulded by the goals of the law. Human rights call for a modified approach because an element of good administration is that administrators should at least turn their minds to legitimate interests that may be affected by their action, and this is especially so where basic interests may be prejudiced. But only if there is something clearly wrong with the way in which this is done will the court intervene. This approach stands in stark contrast to the courts' role in human rights law, and this in turn is illustrative of the different principal functions of each field.

On top of claims that anxious scrutiny is itself illustrative of a move to unity, some go even further and claim or imply that proportionality under the HRA has replaced *Wednesbury* where human rights are at stake.[105] This is plainly wrong. The HRA created a new cause of action that subsists *in parallel* to CLR. The HRA does not alter CLR. It is further claimed that structured proportionality is now a test of substantive review *at common law*, where constitutional or human rights are at stake.[106] This is highly questionable. Such claims are often not supported by serious doctrinal exegesis or authority.[107] Where authority is cited it turns out that either, as already discussed, anxious scrutiny is wrongly being conflated with proportionality[108] or, as in *De Smith's Judicial Review*,[109] the cases cited do not concern the common-law test for substantive review at all, but the principle of legality.[110] The principle of legality is a principle of statutory interpretation. Where proportionality has been applied, it has been as an aspect of an interpretive enterprise rather than as a free-standing review standard.

[104] *Argyll* (n 59) 774 (emphasis added).

[105] Taggart, 'Proportionality' (n 2) 470; Poole (n 8) 146–47 (saying there has been 'a move from *Wednesbury* to proportionality').

[106] Eg *De Smith* (n 48) 599, 613–14, 632–35.

[107] Eg Taggart, 'Proportionality' (n 2) 448–49.

[108] Ibid.

[109] *De Smith* (n 48) 613–14, 633 cites *R v Secretary of State for the Home Department, ex p Leech (No 2)* [1994] QB 198 and Lord Bingham's speech in *Daly* (n 28). But *Leech* expressly concerned vires: 'The principal question arising on this appeal is whether rule 33(3) is ultra vires section 47(1) of the Act of 1952' (202E, 208B, 216–17, 218C). Lord Bingham's speech in *Daly* may be the most misinterpreted in English public law. His Lordship framed the issue in near-identical terms to *Leech*: 'Section 47(1) of the 1952 Act does not authorise such excessive intrusion, and the Home Secretary accordingly had no power to lay down or implement the policy in its present form' ([21], and see [31]; *Huang* (n 42) [13]). *R v Lord Chancellor, ex p Witham* [1998] QB 575 is also cited. Again, this is a *legality* case.

[110] Such error is regrettable, not least because the higher judiciary have relied uncritically upon the relevant passages of *De Smith*: eg *Kennedy* (n 7) [55].

Anxious scrutiny remains the test for substantive review where human rights are at stake, as it was in the pre-HRA era; no authority holds otherwise. Indeed, there has been so little development in this field over the last decade that Dyson LJ's dicta in *ABCIFER*[111] and Lord Cooke's dicta in *Daly*,[112] in the early 2000s and predicting *Wednesbury*'s demise and potential replacement with proportionality, have taken on the quality of one's recollection of attending a Def Leppard concert in the early '80s: a distant memory from a heady bygone era. However, such heady memories can be hard to shake and Lord Mance's judgment in the recent Supreme Court decision in *Kennedy* contains a jolting 'blast from the past'. Lord Mance opined that on the facts he would 'find it difficult to think' that there would be any 'significant difference in the nature or outcome of a court's scrutiny' of the administrative decision whether the challenge was brought at common law or for breach of Article 10.[113] He also suggested that facets of the proportionality test such as suitability, necessity and balance may be relevant even outside HRA or EU challenges.[114] But, as in *ABCIFER* and in *Daly*, this was all obiter. It is not clear whether Lord Mance envisioned that his dicta foreshadowed radical change, given most of his analysis was supported by reference to anxious scrutiny cases and cases emphasising the context-sensitive nature of review—which has long been accepted—while he did not expressly question *Wednesbury*'s continued role.[115] Further, other majority judges, such as Lord Toulson, said that '[t]he normal standard applied by a court reviewing a decision of a statutory body is whether it was unreasonable in the *Wednesbury* sense (ie beyond rational justification)', indicating that *Wednesbury* remains alive and well.[116] Since *Kennedy*, the Supreme Court, in a unanimous decision, proceeded on the basis that classic anxious scrutiny is the relevant standard at common law in human rights cases.[117] And most importantly of all, for those interested in what the law *is*, the Supreme Court's consistent recent practice has been to apply *Wednesbury* as the standard of substantive review at common law, including in a series of cases where basic interests were at stake, *without question*.[118]

In this light Lord Carnwath's observations in *Kennedy* come closest to capturing the prevailing legal position: 'it is *at best* uncertain to what extent

111 *R (Association of British Civilian Internees: Far East Region) v Secretary of State for Defence* [2003] QB 1397 (*ABCIFER*), [32]–[37].

112 *Daly* (n 28) [32].

113 *Kennedy* (n 7) [51], [56].

114 Ibid, [54].

115 Ibid, [51]–[55].

116 Ibid, [132].

117 *MN* (n 103) [31].

118 Eg *McDonald* (n 81) (*Wednesbury* pleaded concurrently with Article 8 claim); *R (Lumba) v Secretary of State for the Home Department* [2012] 1 AC 245, [30] (*Wednesbury* applied in the form of the *Hardial Singh* principles, where liberty at stake); *R (KM) v Cambridgeshire County Council* [2012] UKSC 23 (provision of welfare services to disabled person).

the proportionality test' has a role at common law.[119] For over a decade many commentators have subscribed to the view that '*Wednesbury* unreasonableness lingers on with the Sword of Damocles hanging over it'.[120] Tellingly, that sword never fell. For all the dicta, debate and speculation, *Wednesbury* endures.

There is no doubt that proportionality has been applied as an aspect of the principle of legality.[121] But just as one swallow does not make a summer, so too does one development not render human rights law and the CLR functionally unified, nor is it indicative of a macro-trend towards unification. Furthermore, context is crucial in understanding both anxious scrutiny and the proportionality element of the legality principle. Both have their origins in pre-HRA jurisprudence, at a time when English courts were under pressure to ensure compliance with ECHR requirements, in the absence of any domestic human rights instrument. That courts were fully aware of the importance of UK compliance with supranational obligations is evinced by the fact that major anxious scrutiny and legality cases, such as *Brind*, *Smith*, *Leech*, and *Simms*, all refer to the UK's supranational obligations.

However, as observed above, it is striking that *Wednesbury* has not developed since the passing of the HRA. Courts continue to make use of the principle of legality. But significantly, since the advent of the HRA, one is hard pressed to find *proportionality* deployed in a legality analysis in the manner in which it was in pre-HRA decisions such as *Leech* and *Simms*.[122] Without proportionality the principle loses its justificatory dimension, and is simply an extension of the old maxim that common law rights may only be frustrated by express words.[123] The explanation for this back-tracking on and stymieing of rights-based and justificatory developments is clear.[124] As Lord Rodger observed so candidly in *Watkins*, referring to the courts' increased recourse to the language of 'rights' in some review contexts:[125]

> In using the language of 'constitutional rights', the judges were, more or less explicitly, looking for a means of incorporation [of the ECHR] avant la lettre, of having the common law supply the benefits of incorporation without incorporation. Now the [HRA] is in place, such heroic efforts are unnecessary.

[119] *Kennedy* (n 7) [246] (emphasis added).

[120] Taggart, 'Proportionality' (n 2) 470–71.

[121] Varuhas (n 17) 387–88.

[122] Eg *R (Morgan Grenfell & Co Ltd) v Special Commissioner of Income Tax* [2003] 1 AC 563; *Ahmed v HM Treasury* [2010] 2 AC 534; *Al-Rawi v Security Service* [2012] 1 AC 531; *Assange v Sweden* [2012] 2 AC 471; *Bank Mellat* (n 20) (jurisdiction issue).

[123] Eg *Ledwith v Roberts* [1937] 1 KB 232, 255; *Morris* (n 18) 455, 461–62, 463–65.

[124] Similar stymieing effects are observable elsewhere, eg in tort: *Watkins* (n 55) [26], [64], [73]; *Van Colle v Chief Constable of Hertfordshire* [2009] 1 AC 225, [136]; *Wainwright v Home Office* [2004] 2 AC 406; cf *Campbell v MGN Ltd* [2004] 2 AC 457.

[125] *Watkins* (n 55) [64].

The HRA has introduced a body of law dedicated to affording direct protection of basic interests. There is now no need to stretch the functional and conceptual coherence of CLR to ensure compliance with supranational commitments, or adequate protection of basic interests. Against this background, some may view it as more than mere coincidence that Lord Mance's observations in *Kennedy*, which could be interpreted as gesturing towards alignment of CLR with the law under the HRA, came at a time when senior Ministers were mooting repeal of the HRA. Where courts alter doctrine according to such extrinsic concerns, the result is nearly always to introduce confusion and incoherence into the law.

Reason-giving may be dealt with briefly. It is correct that the 'trend of the law has been towards an increased recognition of the duty upon decision-makers of many kinds to give reasons'.[126] However, the duty has not been 'reinvented' as a generalised obligation as champions of unification wished.[127] In England this seems unlikely to change, at least in the short run, in light of recent authority.[128] Further, if this obligation were generalised such development would not necessarily be premised on the idea that all administrative decisions ought to be capable of some sort of objective justification. Such development could be rationalised according to orthodox concerns. For example, it is in the public's interest to know why decisions have been made, and reason-giving may promote good administrative practice by requiring decision-makers to think through their decisions methodically.

More generally, extravagant claims have been made, that 'administrative law' or 'public law' has undergone a rights-based 'reformation', being 'reinvented' as a rights-based order.[129] I have examined these highly ambiguous claims elsewhere.[130] They are misplaced. The HRA introduced a new, genuinely rights-based order into public law. But this did not entail across-the-board change; it only entailed the *addition* of a rights-based order, which exists in parallel to established public law fields, which have not been reinvented.

Lastly, it is inevitable that there will be 'spill-overs' or interactions between human rights law and CLR. Indeed, there have been a range of different types of interaction.[131] However, some interaction between fields, such as the odd instance of an idea from one field informing development of a particular doctrine in the other, far from indicates a trend to unity.

[126] *Stefan v GMC* [1999] 1 WLR 1293, 1300.

[127] Dyzenhaus, Hunt and Taggart (n 3) 23; Taggart, 'Reinventing' (n 1) 333.

[128] *R (Hasan) v Secretary of State for Trade and Industry* [2008] EWCA Civ 1312, [8]; *Gupta v GMC* [2002] 1 WLR 1691.

[129] Poole (n 8); Taggart, 'Reinventing' (n 1).

[130] Varuhas (n 17).

[131] ibid, 391–92.

It is unsafe to extrapolate from a few particular instances to a general descriptive claim of radical change.

III. OUGHT THE LAW TO UNIFY?

The CLR and human rights law have radically different structures, are characterised by very different norms, concepts and methods, and perform fundamentally distinct functions. In this light it is difficult to make sense of normative claims for 'unification': how could one sensibly unify a field concerned with preservation of the public interest and a field concerned with preservation of individual interests? It is also difficult to see why unification is desirable. Each field performs distinctly valuable functions. The CLR seeks primarily to ensure public power is exercised according to basic precepts of good administration and in the public interest. The focus is on exercise of power itself, and guarding against misuse or abuse of that power. Human rights law, on the other hand, ensures fundamental human interests are afforded strong protection against interference. In combination the fields ensure public power is exercised properly and in the public interest, and that fundamental individual interests are afforded strong protection in the face of power properly exercised for the common good. This all strikes me as perfectly sensible.

A. Arguments Against a Bifurcated Public Law

Let us consider the unification theorists' apparently 'powerful arguments'[132] against the status quo, and then move to consider, in the next part, their 'vision' of a unified order. I concentrate on those arguments against the status quo made by Hunt in his essay entitled 'Against Bifurcation', while also discussing common arguments made in the *Wednesbury*/proportionality debate, which bear on matters at hand.

Hunt argues that public law cannot easily be divided into a 'rights' side and a 'public wrongs' side, thereby undermining the argument that proportionality should only apply in the rights-sphere. The basis for this claim appears to be that:[133]

> While the ground for complaint in administrative law cases [read: CLR] may often appear to be one of maladministration or public wrong, rather than breach of a human right, what brings the applicant in a judicial review case to the point of litigating is often that the decision has had an adverse impact on an underlying right or interest of fundamental importance to the affected person, and that

[132] Hunt (n 4) 105.
[133] Ibid, 106.

underlying right or interest is often within the scope of what is recognised to be a fundamental right.

This is a strange argument that confuses a litigant's subjective motivation for bringing an application with the nature of the wrong in respect of which the application is made as a matter of law. I may bring a claim in battery against someone who punches me because it would allow me to test some claims I once made in an article about damages. That this is my motivation does not alter the normative basis of the claim: breach of a personal right not to be beaten up. Similarly, if I bring an application on the ground of improper purpose, motivated by a concern to protect certain of my basic interests, my subjective motivation does not alter the normative basis of the claim—a claim of public wrong. Thus, delineating rights-based claims and claims of public wrong is only difficult if one confuses subjective motivation for bringing a claim with the nature of the wrong. Otherwise delineating different types of wrong is very easy: HRA claims are claims of personal wrong, common-law claims are claims of public wrong.[134]

A further source of unease for unification theorists is that it is inconsistent that where administrative action touches on human rights, challenges will be approached one way under the HRA—for example proportionality will be applied—and another way at common law.[135] But such difference is explicable by reference to doctrinal context. A human rights claim is a claim of right within a body of law specifically constituted to protect fundamental interests. A CLR claim is a claim that a court should exercise a secondary jurisdiction to ensure public power is used as it ought to be. Given these differences it makes perfect sense that different approaches are taken. Further, with the existence of the HRA, there is no further need to distort the coherence of CLR to afford protection to individual interests. Some may respond that certain rights are not included in the HRA but should be afforded strong protection. If one feels this way one should argue for amendment of the HRA or development of a new field to protect other classes of rights, rather than make arguments the logical consequence of which would be distortion of the common law's coherence.

Dyzenhaus, Hunt and Taggart pegged their argument for unification partly on their view that 'the traditional role of the common law' is 'as

[134] Note that there is some confusion as to the nature of a public wrong. For example, Craig says of *Wednesbury* that, '[w]e should not live in a world in which "public wrongs" are subject to no meaningful judicial scrutiny' (Craig, 'Proportionality' (n 46) 279). This is confused: it is the establishment of a ground of review that denotes a public wrong. Therefore, wherever a public wrong is found, the judiciary would have meaningfully scrutinised the challenged decision.

[135] In 2001 Taggart wrote, with Hunt and Dyzenhaus, that the idea of a 'bifurcated public law' was 'unappealing'; it was not desirable for 'certain issues involving selected rights [to be] determined one way, and other interests outside the charmed constitutional circle [to be] determined another [way]' (Dyzenhaus, Hunt and Taggart (n 3) 31).

the repository of all the values considered to be fundamental in contemporary society'.[136] First, this is a grand claim that is unsubstantiated. Has freedom of speech not long been cherished in Britain? Yet it was not until recently afforded positive legal protection. An Englishman's home may be his castle, but the common law traditionally afforded no direct protection to privacy. Second, the common law, in actions and applications for prerogative writs/orders alike, has not traditionally fastened on values, but rather remedies.[137] Third, whether or not the common law is or ought to be a repository of all fundamental values, it is not clear why one sliver of the common law, CLR, should be burdened with the task of recognising everything that is good in society.

There is also a concern that whereas interests protected by the HRA are afforded strong protection, other interests which are not 'fundamental', but are still important, are afforded far less protection by *Wednesbury*.[138] The problem is again that this assumes that proportionality and *Wednesbury* are different points on the same spectrum of review, such that it is incongruous that there is a big jump in the intensity of scrutiny from human rights cases to cases concerning important-but-not-quite-fundamental interests. There is in fact no incongruity, given proportionality is a defence to a claim of individual right, whereas *Wednesbury* is a general ground of review applied in exercise of a supervisory jurisdiction; the two are incomparable. If it is felt that there are private interests that are not fundamental but warrant protection and are not already protected adequately, then one ought to argue for their direct protection within a dedicated body of law, just as human rights are protected via the HRA and equality is protected by dedicated legislation.

Various other arguments are made. Some argue that the CLR increasingly recognises 'substantive principles', and '[i]t is not clear why these substantive principles are not just as capable of anchoring the proportionality methodology'.[139] What is missing is a positive argument. X may logically ground the proportionality method, but why should it? Other formalistic arguments, which focus on adjectival features of the law, and pass over deeper normative questions of ultimate importance, are also made. Some are clear non-starters, such as the claim that it would make the law 'simpler' if proportionality applied across the board.[140] The law would be simpler still if the only basis upon which a court could impugn administrative action was where an express statutory term was breached. It is commonly claimed that proportionality is more transparent and structured than

[136] Ibid, 32.
[137] *Davy v Spelthorne Borough Council* [1984] AC 262, 276.
[138] Craig, 'Proportionality' (n 46) 279, 294.
[139] Hunt (n 4) 106.
[140] Craig, 'Proportionality' (n 46) 273.

Wednesbury.[141] This may or may not be correct, and is likely to vary from one case to the next, and ultimately depend on each judge's commitment to transparency and structured reasoning rather than the exact test applied. To address the matter definitively would require serious research into multiple proportionality and rationality decisions. Even given such research it may be difficult to settle the debate given evaluative criteria, such as a metric of transparency, are likely to be difficult to formulate precisely and apply. In any case, transparency and structure are formal concerns. They will always be second-order concerns. The first-order concern is a convincing normative case for unification. As we shall see, that is lacking, rendering secondary concerns beside the point.

Lastly, it appears that there is an emergent concern among some judges that CLR is somehow being 'eclipsed' by the HRA and associated Strasbourg jurisprudence, and that the common law's 'priority' needs to be asserted.[142] Some, it seems, would meet this concern by developing CLR so that it mirrors aspects of human rights law.[143] The exact nature of the concern is not clear, and whether it is well founded and warrants legal change cannot be addressed fully here. However, I offer some observations.

First, if any strategy is virtually certain to render the common law otiose, and entail subordination of CLR to human rights norms, it is this strategy. CLR will become a colony of human rights law, add little to functions performed by the HRA, and lose its distinctiveness.

Second, if there are good arguments for developing CLR, it ought to be in line with the field's underlying concerns, so that the CLR continues to perform a *distinctively* valuable function, updated, if necessary, to meet contemporary conditions.

Third, recent developments in, for example, procedural legitimate expectations, consultation, adherence to published policy,[144] publication,[145] and factual error, suggest the CLR continues to develop vibrantly and

[141] The literature is replete with such claims and counter-claims. For serious analysis of *Wednesbury*'s structure see, P Daly, '*Wednesbury*'s Reason and Structure' [2011] *Public Law* 238. But note that many of the examples discussed are comparative, and concern legality review. Further, while the article is a fine contribution, one cannot help but feel that the structure identified by Daly is one constructed and imposed by him, rather than one manifest in the case law. Also, Daly claims that the structure he imputes evinces a 'culture of justification'. This is questionable for the same reasons that the claim that proportionality evinces such a culture is questionable: see text to n 155. Simply because a defendant must provide some justification to the court to escape liability does not in itself suggest that the law upon which the legal claim is based is founded in a theory of justification (or it means that most fields of law are, rendering it a weak explanatory idea); rather the practice of a defendant justifying their acts is a general feature of adversarial litigation in any field.

[142] *Osborn* (n 88) [54]–[63]; *Kennedy* (n 7) [46], [133].

[143] Eg *Kennedy* (n 7) [46]–[56]; and see text to nn 113–114 above.

[144] *Lumba* (n 118).

[145] *R (Reilly) v Secretary of State for Work and Pensions* [2014] AC 453.

flourish, while all of these developments carry forward the law's distinctive underlying functions, and thus suggest a promising path forward for the CLR. Further, one is hard pressed to identify cases in the Administrative Court which do not raise common-law grounds; applications based in these grounds are pervasive. Of course, reasonableness has not developed a great deal recently. But reasonableness is a safety-net. It is not at the centre of the review jurisdiction. Reasonableness took on greater prominence as it was stretched to ensure compliance with ECHR requirements. But there is no longer any need to distort the law's functional coherence.

Fourth, underlying the concern is an idea that CLR and the HRA are institutional competitors. They are not. They complement each other, one protecting the public, the other, individuals. Naturally, in cases concerning basic interests the HRA will take priority. But this is as it ought to be: the HRA was passed specifically to protect basic interests, while individual interests are not the CLR's primary concern.

B. Two Visions of a Unified Public Law: 'Constitutionalisation' and 'Privatisation'

Here I consider two prominent visions of a unified public law, which emerge from the literature. Neither is based in convincing normative arguments, and each is seriously under-theorised in significant respects.

i. Constitutionalisation

One set of unification theorists argue for the unification of public law through the 'constitutionalisation' of administrative law, that is, CLR. In many respects their vision is ambiguous. Much emphasis is placed on arguments against bifurcation, but when it comes to explaining the putative unified order we are told: 'It is far too early to say precisely how this new constitutionalism will look.'[146] It is hard to assess an argument when one is not clear what precisely is being argued for. However, at a high level of abstraction it seems that unification theorists see the theoretical foundation of this brave new order of public law as a particular conception of 'democratic legal culture', a 'culture of justification'; and see the function of public law in general as being to test reasons for decisions according to a set of 'fundamental values', allied with a proportionality method, that would be mainstreamed across this new order of public law. I am not sure, because the claims are ambiguous, whether the CLR as we know it is to be supplanted by this new order. But indications are that this is the normative

[146] Hunt (n 4) 121.

preference of unification theorists. To maintain the CLR as we know it would be to maintain a bifurcated public law: one field concerned with fundamental values and justification, and one that is not. Rather, their vision is for public law *as a whole*—an 'entirely reconceived public law'[147]—to be 'founded' on protection of 'fundamental values' (foremost among these values, 'fundamental human rights') and 'generalis[ation of] the methodology of constitutional balancing to the common law of judicial review'.[148] Put another way, this 'integrated' order will be 'rooted' in 'fundamental' 'values' and 'organised around' 'justification' (read: proportionality) and 'deference'.[149] Ideas that were central, such as jurisdiction, will become obsolete.[150] Axiomatic doctrines such as relevant considerations are dismissed as 'not go[ing] far enough'.[151] Wherever the abstract vision of the reformed order is set out, no mention is made of existing grounds.[152] In any case, even if these doctrines were permitted to survive, there is a risk that they would be rendered otiose, as applicants would not bother pleading them, instead jumping to a proportionality claim, given the strictures and all-encompassing nature of a general proportionality head. *Wednesbury* is a residual safety net; a generalised proportionality standard would be the 'go-to' ground.[153]

Two important points need to be made before going on to consider the substance of this vision of public law.

First, human rights law is not concerned with protecting fundamental values. It is concerned with personal, individual rights, which protect personal, individual interests. This is significant in that when unification theorists argue for protection of other phenomena in the same manner that some rights are protected under the HRA (for example, application of proportionality) they do so by equating those phenomena with human rights on the basis that both are instances of fundamental values.[154] But this analogy is false. For example, proportionality applies in the manner it does in human rights law—that is, a high burden of justification with the judiciary exercising determinative judgement over justification—because the question arises in *a claim of fundamental right* (as opposed to one of value, or interest), while the burden is placed on the defendant because proportionality is a *defence to a rights-breach*. Further, there is no acknowledgement in this analogical argument that proportionality only applies to some rights. Does the fact that different, often more specific and rule-based

[147] Ibid, 100, 103.
[148] Dyzenhaus, Hunt and Taggart (n 3), 6–7, 30–34.
[149] Hunt (n 4) 100, 103.
[150] Dyzenhaus, Hunt and Taggart (n 3) 31–32.
[151] Ibid, 31.
[152] Eg Hunt (n 4) 121.
[153] Taggart, 'Proportionality' (n 2) 438–39.
[154] Eg Dyzenhaus, Hunt and Taggart (n 3) 30–31; Hunt (n 4) 106.

tests of justification, apply to different rights under the HRA not in itself indicate that a one-size-fits-all approach is not appropriate, or at least that consideration should be given to approaches beyond means-ends analysis?

Human rights law is not 'organised around'[155] the concept of justification, nor is its goal to foster such culture, even if that may be the *effect* of the practical operation of certain doctrines, such as proportionality. Again, this is significant because unification theorists tend to present their argument for such a culture as an extension of what already exists in human rights law. The law's principal concern is affording strong protection to fundamental rights. A strict approach is taken to defences because of this. In turn a defendant may bear a heavy burden of justification if they are to prove a defence. But requiring government to account for itself is not why human rights law exists in the first place. Unification theorists get this wrong because of their preoccupation with proportionality. To draw out the point, if someone brings an arguable claim against me in tort, contract, restitution, equity and so on, and I wish to defend that claim, then I must go to court to try to justify my actions that are the subject of the claim; I may bear a heavy burden. It does not follow that the very function of these fields is to foster a culture of justification within civil society.

Second, and of utmost importance: why should introduction of a body of law concerned with fundamental values come *at the expense of* CLR, as we know it? Unification theorists consistently describe their argument as one for the 'constitutionalisation' of administrative law. This exactly captures what is being argued for: a phenomenon akin to a 'legal constitution',[156] that is a legal statement of and legal protection of values fundamental to British society. This description also makes clear that the vehicle for creation of this new order is gradual recalibration of administrative law, or what I have described as the CLR. Putting aside that these theorists face an uphill, likely Sisyphean task to mount a convincing argument that this change should be brought about by judges—especially when they envision that the relevant values may include 'economic, social and cultural rights'[157]—why choose CLR as the vehicle? Here we find a common play by those advocating a novel development. If one was to argue for recognition of a whole new field, especially one as controversial as a novel constitutional order, one may find it difficult to have one's argument taken seriously, even if it is thought-provoking. But if one uses an existing field as a vehicle, and shows that the law is apparently moving in the direction of the normatively desired change anyway, such that one's argument is presented as one concerning the natural end-point of observed developments, one stands a better chance that one's argument will be taken seriously. Further, to ground some novel

[155] Hunt (n 4) 100; Dyzenhaus, Hunt and Taggart (n 3) 30.
[156] Hunt (n 4) 108.
[157] Ibid, 106.

development in an existing, accepted field affords judges a cloak of legitimacy for bringing about what are in truth radical changes.

A central problem with unification theorists' normative vision is that as the UK gains a fully-fledged legal constitution by stealth, it would simultaneously lose its body of administrative law. This would be a most undesirable state of affairs, given that a significant body of law, which performs a crucial function, distinct from human rights law or the new constitutional order, would be lost. Unification theorists should argue for a new body of constitutional law, which would sit alongside CLR, just as the HRA does, instead of seeking to achieve their normative aims by distorting existing fields. Consider the state of affairs in countries such as Australia and the United States which have written constitutions. The adoption of a legal constitution is not at the expense of administrative law; rather, administrative law exists in tandem with constitutional law, performing distinctly valuable functions.

Now let us move on to the substance of this vision of a unified public law. At the core of the unification theorists' vision is the protection of fundamental values. But all of the values mentioned by these theorists are already afforded legal protection, which in turn begs the question: why is a radical recalibration of CLR required to afford these values protection? For example, the fundamental value consistently invoked by unification theorists is human rights, but these are protected by the HRA, as well as other fields, such as the torts actionable per se. 'Non-retrospectivity' is mentioned, but retrospectivity is guarded against by long-standing maxims of construction and human rights.[158] 'Access to court' is mentioned but this is protected by the principle of legality,[159] contempt of court,[160] and Article 6.[161] Property is mentioned.[162] This is astonishing given that proprietary interests are the most strongly protected interests of all in English law, *and* also protected by the HRA.[163] Consistency of treatment is mentioned,[164] but this is protected by various areas of law including procedural legitimate expectations, anti-discrimination legislation, and Article 14. Children's rights are thrown into the mix,[165] but the general human rights of children are protected by the HRA and special considerations may apply in that context where a child's interests are at stake,[166] while elaborate statutory schemes exist specifically

[158] ECHR, arts 6, 7; *R (Reilly) v Secretary of State for Work and Pensions* [2014] EWHC 2182 (Admin).

[159] Eg *Raymond v Honey* [1983] 1 AC 1.

[160] Ibid.

[161] Eg *Silver v UK* (1983) 5 EHRR 347.

[162] Eg Taggart, 'Proportionality' (n 2) 468–69; Hunt (n 4) 106.

[163] ECHR, Protocol 1, art 1. Indirect protection is afforded by other Articles, such as Article 8.

[164] Hunt (n 4) 106.

[165] Dyzenhaus, Hunt and Taggart (n 3).

[166] Eg in the privacy context: *Murray v Express Newspapers plc* [2009] Ch 481; *ZH (Tanzania) v Secretary of State for the Home Department* [2011] 2 AC 166.

to protect children.[167] A further concern is that so many values are invoked by unification theorists that one wonders whether there are any values that are not fundamental, and whether there could ever be an administrative decision that did not touch on a fundamental value.

Questions also arise over derivation of these values. What makes a value fundamental? Are all fundamental values equal? If not, should the same tests of justification apply to all of them? It is difficult to find concrete answers to these questions. We are told that the common law, as it evolves, comes to recognise new values, and that international treaties may give guidance.[168] This is all very well (if one does not care for problems of democratic deficit),[169] but it does not tell us why particular values should or should not be selected for protection. For example, there are many international treaties that provide for a range of things; how are we to know which encapsulate fundamental values, and which of those values should be protected by review and which should not? Unification theorists give some rough guidance, but it is rather vague, and very little justification is offered for the criteria propounded.[170]

If we do not have properly worked-out criteria, there is a risk that the enterprise simply depends on individual preference. But there are also difficulties in figuring out objective criteria, given what values we each consider fundamental is likely to depend on our background political and/or moral concerns. The values identified by unification theorists are, invariably, grounded in a particular view of what is important, which is inevitably political, yet that view is unarticulated. For example, why are legislative democratic authority, social solidarity or economic efficiency not among those values mentioned by such theorists? In turn one may query whether this is not an attempt to foist a legal constitution based in a particular political ideology on the polity—a political ideology the polity may very well reject if given the opportunity to vote on it. That reasonable people in a society disagree in good faith as to what is fundamental to that society, and that these values are ones that are to stand in the name of the polity, are just two of the reasons why constitutional statements of fundamental values are generally left to representative legislatures to decide through a public, inclusive process, or the polity to vote upon in a referendum, for example. If, despite these concerns, one were to nonetheless maintain one's commitment to this judicially enacted new public law, one might have thought that the first place one might look for an objective basis for distillation of values is the parent statute.[171]

[167] Eg Children Act 1989, particularly s 1 (making the welfare of the child the dominant concern in certain types of litigation). For a comparative example of child protection legislation which imposes duties on public entities see Vulnerable Children Act 2014 (NZ).

[168] Dyzenhaus, Hunt and Taggart (n 3) 32–33.

[169] These concerns are touched upon only lightly by unification theorists: eg ibid, 33.

[170] Ibid, 32–33.

[171] Eg *Kennedy* (n 7) [43]–[49], [51], [55]–[56].

We are told that the foundation for this brave new order would be 'a particular conception of democratic legal culture—the culture of justification—in which decision-makers are obliged to justify their decisions by showing either how the decisions conform to the fundamental values or that they are justifiable departures from the values'.[172] Put aside that this seems to be a description of the putative unified order rather than a normative justification for it, it is far from self-evident that we should accept this idea, even though it is often stated as though it were self-evident. This is one of many competing views in the interminable debate as to what the theoretical foundation of public law ought to be, assuming we ought to base the entirety of public law on a single theoretical foundation, which, again, is far from self-evident.

We are also told that a decision can only have authority if good reasons are given for it.[173] Now, good reasons are one source of authority, but are there not others such as authority based in democratic, technocratic or procedural legitimacy? As discussed below, justification is only one 'good', and giving full effect to it may have negative effects on other 'goods', which in turn could render justificatory practices 'simultaneously legitimating *and delegitimating*'.[174] Further, assume we accept that decisions should be backed by good reasons, what is a good reason and who should decide whether reasons are good enough? These are difficult questions, not least because we are likely to quite reasonably disagree as to what reasons count as good or not. It would be one thing to claim that decisions should be backed by reasons which, say, genuinely engage with the matter for decision and meet certain basic standards of defensibility, so we know that power has not, for example, been exercised arbitrarily or capriciously, and so that individuals affected by exercise of public power, and the public, understand the basis for the decision. That is, reasons that will lead us to accept a decision, even if we seriously disagree with it, 'as a plausible instance of rational collective action'.[175] This would meet the concern that citizens should not be treated as 'subjects': if individuals are afforded reasons which explain

[172] Dyzenhaus, Hunt and Taggart (n 3) 34.

[173] Hunt (n 4) 108–109 drawing on D Dyzenhaus and M Taggart, 'Reasoned Decisions and Legal Theory' in DE Edlin (ed), *Common Law Theory* (Cambridge, Cambridge University Press, 2007). The philosophical foundation for such arguments may be theories of public reason. But there are many variants of such theories, they are open to all sorts of objections (including some of the arguments made here), there are competitor theories, and acceptance of such theories does not necessarily commit one to the vision of public law supported by unification theorists. See, eg J Mashaw, 'Public Reason as Process and Substance' (Paper delivered at Public Law Conference: 'Process and Substance in Public Law', University of Cambridge, 15–17 September 2014; paper on file with the author); D Enoch, 'The Disorder of Public Reason' (2013) 124 *Ethics* 141; 'Against Public Reason' (available at http://law.huji.ac.il/upload/AgPubRea.pdf).

[174] Mashaw (n 173) 1 (emphasis added).

[175] Ibid, 10.

an administrative decision, which directly affects them, as a plausible one implementing the public goals embedded in the parent statute, they are treated as moral agents capable of responding to reasons, rather than subjects of a command. The unification theorists' claims go well beyond this. The general (largely proceduralist) idea that broadly defensible reasons should be given for the exercise of power needs to be decoupled from the unification theorists' more radical claims that power must be justified specifically in terms of judicially-created substantive values based in a particular political ideology, with the adequacy of justifications in terms of those substantive, value-laden criteria being determined finally and objectively by the judiciary in every case.

The core concern here is that it is difficult to locate any convincing justification for the radical shift in the focus of public power, away from the public interests for which the power was conferred by a democratically-elected legislature, to judge-made fundamental values over which the judges exercise determinative judgment. Whereas it was Parliament's determination, taken for the common good, that the decision-maker should use his or her powers to pursue public interest X, under the unified system of public law this public concern will be transmuted into a countervailing factor, only possibly being of relevance as part of an explanation for deviation from a judicially-recognised fundamental value. The principal, indeed sole concern on judicial review, will be whether the exercise of power conformed to values the judges consider fundamental, and if not, whether a judge thinks countervailing concerns can justify departure. In this way Parliament's intent is supplanted by judicial intent. The principal concern for the administration, determined by the judiciary, shall be that power is exercised according to the demands of judicially-articulated values. This is both radical and deeply troubling.

The idea of a culture of justification was a response to and is given as an alternative to a 'culture of authority'. Mureinik, the originator of the culture of justification, associated the culture of authority with apartheid South Africa, in which fear was used to force obedience.[176] Given that context, one can fully understand the motivations for wanting to locate strong 'counterweights' to governmental power outside the ruling 'social monolith'.[177] This background brings into focus the extent to which context bears on what approach to review is normatively desirable and justified.

There are features of Parliament, the administration, the legal system, and institutional and other mechanisms for checking and holding power to account in the contemporary UK (within and outside the UK legal system), that set each apart from their counterparts in apartheid South Africa, and

[176] E Mureinik, 'A Bridge to Where? Introducing the Interim Bill of Rights' (1994) 10 *South African Journal on Human Rights* 31, 32.

[177] Ibid.

which imbue legislative and administrative decisions with a far greater degree of legitimacy-based authority, than decisions of the equivalent institutions in apartheid South Africa. As a matter of institutional design one may be receptive to an argument for objective judicial scrutiny of administrative decisions by reference to judicially recognised fundamental values where decisions and empowering legislation emanate from wicked, utterly illegitimate institutions or where a jurisdiction is transitioning out of such regime (assuming judges do in fact sit outside the ruling social monolith). But such judicial approach may be quite inappropriate and unjustified where decisions and empowering legislation are made by institutions imbued with a high degree of legitimacy. In other words, whether one favours a culture of justification, as conceptualised by unification theorists (a culture of judicial authority?) or not, is very much dependant on context, and in particular the legitimacy of institutions which have the authority to decide.

Further, it is worth recording that Mureinik himself saw enactment of the Interim South African Constitution—a *written constitution* that was the product of a *political process*—as the potential 'bridge' from a culture of authority to a culture of justification. The Bill of Rights was to be the 'chief strut'.[178] In the UK we have such an instrument, and it is, as already discussed, therefore unclear why the common law must nonetheless develop to resemble an outpost of human rights law. It is further interesting to observe that Mureinik seemed to recognise, unlike contemporary protagonists of justification, a difference in focus as between human rights law and administrative law, even within an organising framework of a culture of justification. In *administrative law* a culture of justification goes to the 'soundness of the *process* of deciding', with a strong emphasis on reason-giving and on reasons being plausible, and other requirements that will facilitate a 'thorough and disciplined decisionmaking *process*'.[179] Such concern is very close in nature to traditional concerns of the common law, and is a long way from unification theorists' vision of administrative law, within which judges would routinely scrutinise the substance of decisions in terms of substantive values they have determined to be fundamental. Other orthodox concerns also find reflection in Mureinik's arguments: reason-giving obligations can be 'an instrument for improving governance' but should not 'frustrat[e] it' by over-burdening administrators: requirements that were too extensive, such as holding the decision to be based only on those reasons within a statement of reasons, 'might undermine government altogether'.[180] Such concern for governance and sensitivity to administrative practicalities stands in contrast to contemporary writing on the culture of justification.

[178] Ibid.
[179] Ibid, 41 (emphasis added).
[180] Ibid, 41–42.

ii. Privatisation

Others, such as Craig, do not explicitly frame their normative claims as claims for unification, but this is arguably their effect. This group of commentators do not argue that values ought to anchor proportionality, but envision that individual rights and interests, whether fundamental or not, should anchor a new proportionality method at common law. Although Craig does not go as far as protagonists of constitutionalisation in arguing that proportionality should sweep away existing review doctrines, the consequence of his arguments would be that a central focus in review of exercise of public power will be its impact on individual rights and interests—replicating the focus in human rights law, albeit extending it significantly beyond the most important rights. But Craig offers no serious normative argument to justify a radical shift of focus in CLR from a concern for the public interest to a concern for private interests. His normative argument rests on the importance of reasoned justification, structure in judicial analysis and simplicity.[181] For example, he asserts that the normative argument for proportionality 'rests ultimately on the belief that exercise of power requires reasoned justification of the kind provided for by the proportionality inquiry'.[182]

Putting aside the circularity of this argument, it does not address the fundamental shift that acceptance of it would entail: why should the focus of public power in general, and not only where basic interests are at stake, be upon special interests of individuals and legal entities, such as corporations, rather than what would best serve the community as a whole? As Brennan J observed in *Quin*, this could very well have the effect of skewing the exercise of public power to those willing to risk the costs of litigation, including 'the rich, the powerful, or the simply litigious'.[183] As he also said in the same case, if review were to provide 'remedies to protect interests, falling short of enforceable rights,[184] which are apt to be affected by the lawful exercise of executive or administrative power … the courts would be asserting a jurisdiction, in protection of individual interests, to override the law by which a power to affect those interests is conferred on the [decision-maker]'—power conferred 'to advance the interests of the public'.[185] As Lord Scarman observed in *IRC*, if interference with an individual right or interest is necessary for the court to intervene, review becomes 'no more than a remedy for a private wrong'.[186]

[181] Craig, 'Proportionality' (n 46) 271–73.

[182] Ibid, 271–72.

[183] *Attorney-General (NSW) v Quin* (1990) 170 CLR 1, 37.

[184] If rights are enforceable, as under the HRA 1998, then there is no need for review to protect them, given that one could bring a claim directly enforcing one's rights.

[185] *Quin* (n 183) 34–35.

[186] *IRC* (n 18) 653.

English law already recognises a field constituted to protect private interests: private law. In accordance with the principle of equality that body of law applies, in principle, to public officials. Why is further protection of individual interests required, especially given that, inter alia, the HRA, employment, competition, consumer and equality legislation have plugged the most significant gaps in protection? And if further protection is warranted, why should that be through CLR? Further, if CLR is to protect private interests, should it stretch to protection of any possible interest? Craig does not appear to lay down any limits or criteria in this respect: any decision which burdens an individual would in principle be open to a proportionality challenge. We would need a good argument as to why each possible individual interest potentially affected by administrative action warrants *legal* protection. Further, if good arguments were found, would it not be preferable that claims concerning low-level interests be left to informal, cost-effective mechanisms such as ombudsmen? Such possibilities are not considered by protagonists of the privatisation of public law.

More generally, what are the drawbacks of a system of public law in which all government decisions are potentially required to be justified to the satisfaction of courts on a proportionality basis and by reference to 'values' or private interests? One only need look to the concerns that justify the current supervisory approach. Public interests in administrative certainty, flexibility, efficiency, effectiveness and expeditiousness, in the performance of public functions which ultimately serve the interests of all, may be seriously compromised by enabling persons to challenge any administrative decision on the open-ended basis that an incursion upon any one of a number of amorphous values was not sufficiently justified.[187] There would also be knock-on effects elsewhere in the legal system which would affect important public interests and which have not been considered by any participant in these debates. For example, if administrative action is more easily and more frequently found unlawful, public officers will less often be able to rely on the defence of lawful excuse in tort claims, potentially exposing government to far greater liability in damages.

Craig acknowledges some of these concerns, but concludes, after brief analysis, that 'there is no reason to believe that [adoption of proportionality] will lead to increased litigation or legal uncertainty, thereby interfering with the public body's ability to carry out its mandate'.[188] It would be one thing to acknowledge that we cannot be certain what the effects of mainstreaming proportionality would be but to dismiss such concerns in absolute terms after limited consideration is simply not credible.

[187] J King, 'Proportionality: A Halfway House' [2010] *New Zealand Law Review* 327.
[188] Craig, 'Proportionality' (n 46) 283.

Further, there is good reason to consider that adoption of either vision of a unified public law will cause serious uncertainty, given the highly fact-specific nature of core aspects of this new field, such as deference and proportionality balancing. In the vast majority of cases, if not every case, there will be questions over which values or interests out of a non-exhaustive list are in issue, the contours of those values and interests, how deference should be calibrated on the particular facts of the case, identification of relevant competing concerns on the facts, and how the balance between concerns should be struck on the facts. It is difficult to know how a street-level official, working at Job Centre Plus or as a clinician in the NHS, should proceed in the face of such uncertainty. In terms of litigation, there may be some clear cases but in most cases one would not envy a lawyer trying to advise either party as to the likely outcome. In turn, formal rule-of-law values in certainty and consistency are likely to be seriously undermined, as they are wherever broad fact-dependant balancing tests are adopted.

Sure, the precise boundaries of *Wednesbury* can be uncertain. But this has to be viewed in the light of the various formulations of the test sharing in common that they stand as totems of non-intervention, with judicial intervention only warranted where something has gone seriously wrong. That intervention based on substantive reasoning or outcome will be rare offers a degree of certainty on the basis of which parties can organise their affairs. Of course, human rights litigation entails much of the uncertainty that would be associated with a unified public law. But the existence of such uncertainty is another reason for not adding even further uncertainty in the field of public law, while the adoption of either vision of a unified public law would introduce *widespread* uncertainty as proportionality would be relevant in most public law cases.

Do the drawbacks outweigh any benefits of a unified system or do the drawbacks require modification of the legal approach? Even if one accepts fostering a culture of justification as desirable, the unification theorists do not explain why this ought to be the exclusive or predominant concern of public law, at the potential expense of other important concerns.[189] Further, will the envisioned system of public law actually deliver such culture—it may produce a culture of tick-box compliance and distrust—and even if it did help to foster such culture, would it be relatively more effective than other possible techniques, such as implementation of organisational measures within authorities to encourage justification? Do such alternative techniques have fewer drawbacks? One cannot take unification theorists' claims seriously unless they engage seriously with these questions. In the

[189] Others, such as Craig, ibid, take a less extreme approach, maintaining the specific grounds should not be swept away by proportionality.

absence of justification for radical recalibration of the law unification theorists have failed to meet their own standards; the status quo should be retained. This was the logic of the position reached ultimately by Taggart after wrestling with these matters through his career.

IV. CONCLUSION

In Hunt's view a central issue for Taggart's generation of public lawyers is 'how to reconcile the apparently competing instincts of administrative lawyers on the one hand and human rights lawyers on the other about the appropriate role of the courts'.[190] The answer is that these competing instincts—if there are such general propensities—do not require reconciliation. More fundamentally, it is difficult to see how they could be reconciled sensibly, nor why we would want to reconcile them.

The courts' role is legitimately different in human rights claims compared to that in common-law claims, and derives from the functional distinction between the fields. CLR is concerned to ensure proper exercise of public power in the public interest, whereas human rights law is concerned to protect fundamental, individual rights. Within CLR the normative ground for intervention is a public wrong, whereas human rights law is based in individual, personal wrongs. There has not been a doctrinal move to unity. If one is of the view that there are fundamental values or rights or interests that warrant strong protection through law, which are not already afforded adequate protection, then one should make a fully-fledged, serious normative argument to justify why those phenomena in particular ought to be afforded direct protection. But this should not be through CLR, because such matters are not the concern of that field, while a valuable public law function—regulation of public power in the public interest—would be lost or compromised seriously if the CLR were transformed into the equivalent of a written constitution or an outpost of private law. More generally, convincing arguments would be required to justify judicial creation of the equivalent of a written constitution, and general refocusing of public power away from the interests of the public as determined by Parliament to judicially created values or specific interests of persons. Those arguments are yet to be located, and are likely to prove illusive.

While I cannot agree with Taggart's view that public law is moving towards unity, I agree firmly with his reservations over unification, based in

[190] Hunt (n 4) 100.

concerns over indeterminacy, judicial discretion and judicial supremacy.[191] The unification theorists, like those who make less grand—yet still radical—claims that proportionality ought to supplant *Wednesbury*, have not made their case. The position remains that stated by Taggart in 2008: there is yet to be identified 'a compelling normative justification for the significant shift in discretionary power away from the delegates of the statutory power to the judges'.[192] Normative claims for unification should be repudiated.

[191] Taggart, 'Proportionality' (n 2) 477ff.
[192] Ibid, 478–79.

6

Substantive (Procedural) Review in Australia

MATTHEW GROVES* AND GREG WEEKS**

I. INTRODUCTION

MIKE TAGGART PROBABLY knew that, no matter how widely his proposed alternative to the variable intensity review standard was embraced, it would always be unlikely to receive judicial approbation in Australia.[1] After all, he had noted a streak of 'exceptionalism' in Australia's approach to judicial review in an article[2] which, while open to reasoned criticism,[3] contains an undeniable kernel of truth.[4] Australia *does* stand apart from the rest of the common-law world in several vital respects. To take but two examples: the High Court of Australia adheres to the concept of jurisdictional error, although the distinction between jurisdictional and non-jurisdictional errors of law has long been abandoned elsewhere in the word;[5] and it applies a strict

* Professor of Law, Monash University

** Lecturer in Law, University of New South Wales. We thank Mark Aronson for comments in writing this chapter. Any errors are ours alone.

[1] M Taggart, 'Proportionality, Deference, *Wednesbury*' [2008] *New Zealand Law Review* 423.

[2] M Taggart, '"Australian Exceptionalism" in Judicial Review' (2008) 36 *Federal Law Review* 1. The title of Taggart's article alludes to the extensive literature discussing American exceptionalism on constitutional grounds.

[3] M Aronson, 'Process, Quality, and Variable Standards: Responding to an *Agent Provocateur*' in D Dyzenhaus, M Hunt and G Huscroft (eds), *A Simple Common Lawyer: Essays in Honour of Michael Taggart* (Oxford, Hart Publishing, 2009) 5.

[4] Justice Gageler does not agree, having recently commented that the Australian 'constitutional paradigm alone … does not warrant or sustain an approach to administrative law that so diverges from that which exists elsewhere as fairly to attract the label of "Australian exceptionalism"': S Gageler, 'The Constitutional Dimension' in M Groves (ed), *Modern Administrative Law in Australia: Concepts and Context* (Melbourne, Cambridge University Press, 2014) 165, 176.

[5] See, eg *R v Lord President of the Privy Council, ex p Page* [1993] AC 682. The distinction appears to have been 'interred, without tears' in jurisdictions outside Australia, as Kirby J hoped that it would be in Australia: *Re Minister for Immigration and Multicultural Affairs, ex p Miah* (2001) 206 CLR 57, 123 [212]. His Honour's view has not commanded majority support in the High Court.

form of the separation of judicial power. These principles support a relatively limited conception of judicial power which, in turn, is invoked to define and confine the limits of judicial review. The grounds of review are similarly limited, such as the strictly attenuated form of reasonableness review, which has traditionally been available in Australia only on the *Wednesbury* standard.[6] These positions are all traced directly either to the text or the design of the Australian *Constitution*.[7] There is a strong link between the constitutional 'exceptionalism' ascribed respectively to Australia and to the United States, both of which have a written constitution.[8]

The one thing that cannot be traced to the Australian *Constitution*—and the lack of which truly causes Australia to be an exception to the rest of the common-law world—is any kind of enumeration of the rights held by Australian residents or citizens.[9] Such rights as Australians have are creatures of the common law.[10] Intensification of qualitative review beyond the *Wednesbury* standard in other jurisdictions has gone hand in hand with statutory or constitutional rights protection.[11] No such rights protection currently exists at Commonwealth level in Australia and there is no likelihood that that circumstance will change in the foreseeable future. However, we decline to conclude that this necessarily means that Australian courts will not move to apply a variable intensity reasonableness standard. Indeed, the High Court's decision in *Minister for Immigration and Citizenship v Li*[12] indicated that it is already open to giving *Wednesbury* a broader application, although the reasons given by the Court did not make clear the basis on which this may occur.

[6] *Associated Provincial Picture Houses Ltd v Wednesbury Corporation* [1948] 1 KB 223. This used to apply only to exercises of discretion which could be characterised as 'lunatic', although the High Court has recently signalled it may move on this point: *Minister for Immigration and Citizenship v Li* (2013) 249 CLR 332. See part III below.

[7] The most influential view on these subjects is the judgment of Brennan J in *Attorney-General (NSW) v Quin* (1990) 170 CLR 1.

[8] See M Cohen-Eliya and I Porat, *Proportionality and Constitutional Culture* (Cambridge, Cambridge University Press, 2013) 1. It is perhaps unsurprising that both countries have found that the international influence of their constitutional jurisprudence is reducing.

[9] After his retirement, Sir Anthony Mason expressed broad agreement with Taggart's label of 'exceptionalism' as appended to Australian judicial review jurisprudence but commented that 'it seems to me that Mike does not appreciate how deep-seated are some of the considerations that led to the present state of Australian administrative law and that Australian exceptionalism can be explained partly, though not wholly, by Australia's non-adoption of a charter of rights and the attitudes that underlie that non-adoption': Sir Anthony Mason, 'Mike Taggart and Australian Exceptionalism' in Dyzenhaus, Hunt and Huscroft (eds), (n 3) 179, 179. Mason did not consider whether the absence of a bill or charter of rights at the federal level is as much a symptom as a cause of Australian principles.

[10] See, eg M Groves, 'The Insecurity of Fairness in Security Cases' (2013) 24 *Public Law Review* 155, 155.

[11] Mason, 'Mike Taggart and Australian Exceptionalism' (n 9) 183.

[12] *Minister for Immigration and Citizenship v Li* (n 6).

If Australian courts are open to some form of variable intensity review, the question will ultimately be onto what body of principle the courts will attach such a doctrine in the absence of statutory or constitutional rights protection. The existence of such an 'anchor point' is required on the normative basis that only a matter involving a 'fundamental value' will justify a more intrusive form of review, and on the methodological basis that a more onerous or heavily structured conception of the *Wednesbury* ground requires that the value (or values) at issue be clearly articulated so the court can properly assess whether its prima facie infringement can be justified.[13] Several possible 'anchor points' have been suggested, such as community values,[14] or the principle of legality.[15] We doubt that either of these will suffice to support such a fundamental change of direction by the Australian judiciary. We will instead explore the possibility that there is already a body of rights which has been judicially recognised and that these may ultimately allow the courts to give *Wednesbury*, at least, a less restrictive reading than has been the norm in Australia for many decades.[16]

II. CONSTITUTIONAL FRAMEWORK

One conclusion which appears to be open is that the Australian judiciary is an exception to the rest of the common-law world only as a result of the particular political settlement in Australia which has given the judiciary a limited field of operation and little or no scope for substantive (as opposed to 'formalist') reasoning. Put another way, each democracy decides for itself what courts can do and what is reserved for the politically accountable arms of government. Australia's judiciary, on this supposition, has simply been given less to do than, say, Canada's, which is required to decide matters subject to the *Charter of Rights and Freedoms 1982*.[17]

[13] See M Elliott, 'From Bifurcation to Calibration: Twin-Track Deference and the Culture of Justification' (ch 4 in this volume).

[14] The Chief Justice of Australia has suggested that the norms of fairness are 'important societal values' that extend 'well beyond the confines of the courtroom in judicial proceedings': Hon R French, 'Procedural Fairness—Indispensable to Justice?' (speech to the University of Melbourne Law Students' Society, 7 October 2010) 22 (available at: http://www.hcourt.gov.au/assets/publications/speeches/current-justices/frenchcj/frenchcj07oct10.pdf).

[15] Professor Aronson referred to the principle of legality as being 'currently fashionable', with the clear implication that it lacks the permanence of other legal concepts: M Aronson, 'Statutory Interpretation or Judicial Disobedience?' (3 June 2013) *UK Constitutional Law Group Blog*, available at: ukconstitutionallaw.org/2013/06/03/mark-aronson-statutory-interpretation-or-judicial-disobedience/. See also the cases referred to in D Meagher, 'The Common Law Principle of Legality in the Age of Rights' (2011) 35 *Melbourne University Law Review* 449, 451, fn 14.

[16] Even prior to *Wednesbury* (n 6), Australian courts tended to apply the equivalent principle in a fashion which allowed little scope for interference in the merits of a matter; see, eg *R v Connell, ex p Hetton Bellbird Collieries Ltd* (1944) 69 CLR 407, 432 (Latham CJ).

[17] Part I of the Constitution Act 1982 (Canada).

The role of constitutional structures is not a complete or convincing explanation for the relatively formalist approach of the High Court because Australia's constitutional arrangements do not deny courts and judges considerable latitude to determine much about the legal relationships between the different arms of government,[18] and therefore, of course, much about the proper constitutional role of the courts. Should Australia ever adopt a constitutional, or even statutory, rights-protecting document, the extent of the judiciary's role would almost certainly change.[19] For the moment, however, Australian judges conceive their position and function by reference to constitutional principles that both entrench and limit that role. Commentators regularly note that the Australian *Constitution* does not directly recognise or protect many rights,[20] though many of the principles devised as part of the Australian conception of the separation of powers operate to secure the role of the courts and their inherent ability to protect the rights and interests of individuals. These constitutional principles may largely avoid the open language of rights but they contain whispers of it.

The strict Australian version of the separation of powers has long served to distinguish and limit the constitutional role of courts and administrative tribunals and officials.[21] At its simplest, the doctrine precludes judicial bodies and their officers from exercising any substantial non-judicial functions and places similar restrictions on the exercise of judicial functions by non-judicial bodies such as tribunals or officials. These principles largely developed as restrictions on the powers of the Commonwealth parliament to enact legislation which contradicted the requirements of the separation

[18] A Stone, 'Judicial Review Without Rights' (2008) 28 *Oxford Journal of Legal Studies* 1, though see the reply made in J Goldsworthy, 'Structural Judicial Review and the Objection from Democracy' (2010) 60 *University of Toronto Law Journal* 137.

[19] Precisely how and how much it might change is another matter. English commentators have suggested that the commencement of the Human Rights Act 1998 (UK) caused a seismic shift in the relationship between the courts and the legislature by expanding both the range of decisions the courts are able to review and their institutional competence to do so. See, eg J Jowell, 'Parliamentary Sovereignty Under the New Constitutional Hypothesis' [2006] *Public Law* 562. Australian courts have long approached those issues robustly and have done so in reliance upon their constitutionally entrenched position which provides, among other things, a power to declare legislation invalid on constitutional grounds. Enactment of a rights protecting document might alter and broaden the scope of review by Australian courts by enabling them to undertake a more substantive form of human rights review than current constitutional principles allow in judicial review. The likelihood of such change would depend on both the precise terms of the document and whether it took the form of legislation or a constitutional amendment.

[20] Australia has no statutory bill or charter of rights at the federal level but there is statutory rights protection in one state and one territory: Human Rights Act 2004 (ACT); Charter of Human Rights and Responsibilities Act 2006 (Vic).

[21] Following the doctrine in *R v Kirby, ex p Boilermakers' Society of Australia* (1956) 94 CLR 254. The doctrine traced to that case is well embedded but has some prominent dissenters; see, eg Sir Anthony Mason, 'Judicial Review: A View from Constitutional and Other Perspectives' (2000) 28 *Federal Law Review* 331, 339.

of powers. These same principles underpinned the assignment of sharply different functions to courts and tribunals in the radical Australian reforms to administrative law in the 1970s. The main reform affecting the courts was the codification of judicial review.[22] The more radical reform was the creation of the Commonwealth Administrative Appeals Tribunal (AAT), which was granted *de novo* appellate jurisdiction over decisions made under a vast number of federal statutes. The AAT was empowered to remake administrative decisions, according to the merits of the material placed before it.[23]

Judicial and merits review in Australia cannot be understood in isolation. Each operates by reference to the other.[24] The key remedy that lies beyond the reach of judicial review and its grounds—a new decision reached after a qualitative assessment of the evidence—is the defining feature of merits review.[25] The availability of merits review makes the remedial limits of Australian judicial review and its grounds more understandable and arguably acceptable.[26] As with so much else about Australian judicial review, the influence of the AAT was one of pragmatism rather than principle.[27] That was changed by *Quin's* case,[28] where Brennan J signalled the true emergence of the Australian *Constitution* as the ultimate foundation of judicial review.[29] His Honour drew upon the doctrine established in *Marbury v Madison*,[30] which asserted judicial review of legislative action, to explain the purpose, nature and limits of judicial review of administrative action. Brennan J reasoned that the division and allocation of powers and functions in Australia's constitutional arrangements necessarily limited

22 Administrative Decisions (Judicial Review) Act 1977 (Cth) (ADJR Act 1977). This jurisdiction was invested in a new court to hear such claims: Federal Court of Australia Act 1976 (Cth). The wider package of reforms included the Administrative Appeals Tribunal Act 1975 (Cth) (AAT Act 1975), the Ombudsman Act 1976 (Cth) and the Freedom of Information Act 1982 (Cth).

23 AAT Act 1975 (Cth) s 43.

24 We therefore reject suggestions that merits review is a thinly disguised form of judicial review, made in P Cane, 'Merits Review and Judicial Review: The AAT as Trojan Horse' (2000) 28 *Federal Law Review* 213, 220–43.

25 The principles governing merits review have been fashioned by courts and tribunals rather than the legislature: R Creyke, 'Tribunals and Merits Review' in M Groves (ed), *Modern Administrative Law in Australia* (n 4).

26 cf P Cane, 'The Making of Australian Administrative Law' (2003) 24 *Australian Bar Review* 114.

27 See, eg *Australian Broadcasting Tribunal v Bond* (1990) 170 CLR 321, 341 where Mason CJ reasoned that the jurisdiction of the AAT was one reason courts should approach judicial review of findings of fact very cautiously.

28 *Quin* (n 7).

29 Prior to his appointment to the High Court, Stephen Gageler frankly conceded that High Court cases before *Quin* had 'proceeded without apparent need for reference to any overarching theory of judicial review': 'Impact of Migration Law on the Development of Australian Administrative Law' (2010) 17 *Australian Journal of Administrative Law* 92, 95.

30 *Marbury v Madison* 5 US 137 (1803).

the power and role of each arm of government by reference to that of the others. His Honour explained:[31]

> The duty and jurisdiction of the court to review administrative action do not go beyond the declaration and enforcing of the law which determines the limits and governs the exercise of the repository's power. If, in doing so, the court avoids administrative injustice or error, so be it; but the court has no jurisdiction to simply cure administrative injustice or error. The merits of administrative action, to the extent that they can be distinguished from legality, are for the repository of the relevant power and, subject to political control, for the repository alone.

The important step of this and other parts of Brennan J's reasoning was its assimilation of the conceptual justifications for constitutional and non-constitutional review, so that the two 'were henceforth manifestations of one and the same constitutional duty of a court to police (declare and enforce) the whole of the law (constitutional and legislative) that limits and conditions' the power of those who exercise statutory or public power.[32] Brennan J expounded constitutional principles in a broad sense.[33] Subsequent decisions quickly fastened onto the unique jurisdiction in section 75(v),[34] which entrenches the power of the High Court to issue the judicial review remedies of mandamus, prohibition and injunctions against federal officials.[35] When the High Court subsequently made a strident assertion of its constitutionally secured role in the face of a wide-ranging privative clause, it also made clear that section 75(v) secured 'an entrenched minimum provision of judicial review'.[36] But the constitutional settlement that secures judicial review also limits it from entering what Brennan J described in a paper as 'the lush field of policy'[37] or other aspects about the merits of decisions.

This constitutional settlement also leaves many issues unresolved because it is guided by principles that say little about the content of the law the High Court is mandated to declare and uphold.[38] The notion of jurisdictional

[31] *Quin* (n 7) 35–36.

[32] Gageler, 'The Constitutional Dimension' (n 4) 172.

[33] So broad, in fact, that the key pages of his reasoning contained no mention of the Australian *Constitution* or any of its provisions: M Groves, 'Federal Constitutional Influences on State Judicial Review' (2011) 39 *Federal Law Review* 399, 402.

[34] Mark Leeming has noted that s 75(v) 'is the *only* class of matter in ss 75 and 76 which lacks a close counterpart in the United States Constitution': M Leeming, *Authority to Decide: The Law of Jurisdiction in Australia* (Annandale, New South Wales, Federation Press, 2012), 246 (original emphasis).

[35] The reasoning of Brennan J attracted support from a majority of the High Court in *Re Refugee Review Tribunal* (2000) 204 CLR 82.

[36] *Plaintiff S157/2002 v Commonwealth* (2003) 211 CLR 476, 513 [103] (Gaudron, McHugh, Gummow, Kirby and Hayne JJ). This finding sounded the death knell for legislation purporting to exclude or limit that constitutionally-based jurisdiction. The same also proved true for legislation imposing significant procedural restrictions, such as inflexible time limits, on that jurisdiction: *Bodruddaza v Minister for Immigration and Multicultural Affairs* (2007) 228 CLR 651.

[37] Sir Gerard Brennan, 'Purpose and Scope of Judicial Review' (1986) 2 *Australian Bar Review* 93, 111.

[38] A lacuna acknowledged by S Gageler, 'The Constitutional Dimension' (n 4) 175–77.

error, for example, provides the touchstone for the High Court to assert its power to define and police the law but operates more as a label of conclusion than a useful analytic concept.[39] It is given meaning by the examples of its occurrence.[40] It is therefore no surprise that, while the Court remains wedded to a clear distinction between judicial and merits review for constitutional reasons, it has been unable to separate the two in any practical sense. That problem is acute at the boundaries of judicial review where some grounds may edge towards merits review. Gleeson CJ conceded that a robust use of the unreasonableness ground made many think that the merits/review divide 'is not always clear cut', but he maintained 'neither is the difference between night and day; and twilight does not invalidate the distinction between night and day'.[41] The leap of faith required is not clear. Must we accept that we cannot see the merits/review divide clearly, or that the judges cannot? We can at least see the uncertainty into which Taggart's variable intensity standard would step in Australia. We are unsure whether it would add to constitutional uncertainty or provide a 'wobbly stepping stone' between the protected terrain of the judicial and executive arms of Australian government.[42]

One consequence of the Australian focus on constitutional principles has been an increasing tendency of its courts to explain decisions by reference to concepts and processes that fit most comfortably within the well-settled constitutional realm of the courts. Few fit more comfortably within the judicial role than statutory interpretation. However, as Etienne Mureinik commented, 'the intention of the legislature is notoriously a vessel into which all manner of content can, in practice if not in propriety, be poured'.[43] That suggestion is well illustrated by the differing stringency with which the High Court has interpreted procedural requirements which provide it with both power and latitude over the conduct of the hearings of migration tribunals. In some cases, for example, the High Court has enforced statutory requirements for notice of hearings with such literalism that it has overturned decisions even though there was no doubt actual notice was provided to applicants.[44] Yet in other cases, the High Court has adopted a more purposive approach that has allowed decisions to stand

[39] A problem frankly conceded by the Full Federal Court in *SDAV v Minister for Immigration and Multicultural and Indigenous Affairs* (2003) 199 ALR 43, [27].

[40] M Aronson, 'Jurisdictional Error and Beyond' in M Groves (ed), *Modern Administrative Law in Australia* (n 4) 248, 260. Aronson stated that, while jurisdictional error is 'a conclusory label for all sorts of faults, its consequences are usually more straightforward', ibid, 253.

[41] M Gleeson, 'Judicial Legitimacy' (2000) 20 *Australian Bar Review* 4, 11.

[42] The quoted words come from M Taggart, 'Legitimate Expectation and Treaties in the High Court of Australia' (1996) 112 *Law Quarterly Review* 50, 54.

[43] E Mureinik, 'Administrative Law in South Africa' (1986) 103 *South African Law Journal* 615, 616.

[44] *SAAP v Minister for Immigration and Multicultural and Indigenous Affairs* (2005) 228 CLR 294, 322 (McHugh J), 345–46 (Kirby J), 354–55 (Hayne J).

because the tribunal has met the purpose but not the letter of notice provisions.[45] Such shifts may simply illustrate the balance that courts always strive to seek between the purpose of legislation and the rights affected by that legislation.[46] As with all things in Australian public law, the issue has a strong constitutional dimension. At the abstract constitutional level, the High Court remains well within its defined constitutional role—to declare and apply the law—in taking a purposive approach because it simply gives effect to the 'imperative duties or inviolable limitations or restraints' that legislative powers and procedures may constitute.[47] The indeterminate and shifting level of compliance with legislative procedures that the courts require from tribunals and other administrative officials does not simply highlight their constitutional supremacy. It arguably provides a form of substantive review that is masked with constitutional language.

III. THE MYSTERY OF *LI*

The capacity of Australian courts to provide substantive relief in judicial review matters was, until recently, exceptionally stable and appeared unlikely to change. In brief, it has been considered definitional to Commonwealth judicial review in Australia that courts can provide relief where a jurisdictional error has been made, but that relief was only ever of a procedural kind.[48] Australian courts would remit a matter to the original decision-maker to be re-made according to law but never enter into the merits of a matter. The merits/legality border was nervously observed from the judicial side. The very fact of the central place of administrative tribunals in the administrative law reforms of the 1970s is perhaps the most pertinent illustration of this but, as was explained above, it seems clear that the merits/legality divide in Australia was both a cause and an effect of the distinction those reforms drew between judicial and merits review. One ground of review came closer than any other to the 'porous'[49] boundary between the merits and legality and that was *Wednesbury*

[45] *Minister for Immigration and Citizenship v SZIZO* (2009) 238 CLR 627, 640 [35] (*per curiam*).

[46] TRS Allan, 'Democracy, Legality and Proportionality' in G Huscroft, B Miller and G Webber (eds), *Proportionality and the Rule of Law* (New York, Cambridge University Press, 2014) 205, 218–23.

[47] The quoted phrase of Dixon CJ in *R v Metal Trades Employers' Association, ex p Amalgamated Engineering Union, Australian Section* (1951) 82 CLR 208, 248 was endorsed by the plurality in *Plaintiff S157* (n 36) 489 [21].

[48] Though the elastic and expanding scope of jurisdictional error in Australia means that relief on this basis can be issued against a multitude of errors which increasingly resemble a list of all of the grounds of judicial review.

[49] J Spigelman, 'The Integrity Branch of Government' (2004) 78 *Australian Law Journal* 724, 732.

unreasonableness, which asks a court to look at the quality of a decision and is further removed from the procedural examination that is required by other grounds.[50] Even before the case which gave *Wednesbury* unreasonableness its name,[51] the High Court of Australia had indicated that it took a conservative view of the application of that ground.[52] Little changed for the best part of the next seven decades.

It is too early to say whether *Li*[53] is a revolutionary decision; doubt remains as to the full meaning and scope of the High Court's judgments, which both hinted at a significant change of direction[54] and did so without any ostensible recourse to values. What is clear, however, is that the Court not only upheld the decision of the Full Federal Court to grant relief,[55] but unanimously did so on the basis that the challenged decision was unreasonable. The court below had, by contrast, relied essentially on the Migration Review Tribunal's (MRT's) failure to adhere to statutory procedures, and thereby followed a venerable line of High Court decisions which had packaged all manner or procedural and substantive errors under the rubric of some sort of miscarriage of the statutory duties or procedures to which migration tribunals are subject.[56]

Furthermore, the judgments handed down by the High Court each reached their conclusions outside the specific principles of *Wednesbury* unreasonableness. On the facts, Ms Li's claim would not have met the previously established requirement that a decision be 'absurd' before it could be invalidated on the ground that it was unreasonable in the *Wednesbury* sense.[57] However, the plurality judgment abandoned this standard, holding that:

> The legal standard of unreasonableness should not be considered as limited to what is in effect an irrational, if not bizarre, decision—which is to say one that is so unreasonable that no reasonable person could have arrived at it—nor should Lord Greene MR be taken to have limited unreasonableness in this way in his judgment in Wednesbury.[58]

[50] G Weeks, 'The Expanding Role of Process in Judicial Review' (2008) 15 *Australian Journal of Administrative Law* 100.

[51] *Wednesbury* (n 6).

[52] *Hetton Bellbird Collieries* (n 16) 432 (Latham CJ).

[53] *Minister for Immigration and Citizenship v Li* (n 6).

[54] While the reasoning of French CJ and the plurality might cause one to sense 'a lowering of the barrier to judicial review of administrative decisions', the statements in question were merely dicta and it is therefore difficult to be sure about their long term import: see The Hon J Basten, 'Judicial Review of Executive Action: Tiers of Scrutiny or Tears of Frustration?' in N Williams (ed), *Key Issues in Judicial Review* (Annandale, New South Wales, Federation Press, 2014) 45.

[55] *Minister for Immigration and Citizenship v Li* (2012) 202 FCR 387.

[56] Though the High Court now appears more reluctant to find such errors arising from technical or trivial issues. See, eg *SZIZO* (n 45).

[57] As a senior Australian judge put it, 'this was not a promising case, on one view, for a restatement of fundamental principle': Basten, 'Judicial Review of Executive Action' (n 54) 42.

[58] *Minister for Immigration and Citizenship v Li* (n 6) 364 [68] (Hayne, Kiefel and Bell JJ); cf 377–78 [113] (Gageler J).

The hold that *Wednesbury* has exercised over the imaginations of Australian administrative lawyers has always been in inverse proportion to the regularity of its application.[59] From time to time, it has been re-evaluated,[60] but has for over two decades been applied in an extremely minimalist fashion.[61] The High Court's departure from the established approach may justify the conclusion that *Li* 'may mark the commencement of the next large step' in the development of Australian administrative law.[62]

Briefly, the facts of the case were that Ms Li had applied for a visa under the Migration Act 1958 (Cth) but had supplied false information about her employment history in support of her application, which caused the MRT to set aside her skills assessment. She sought a new skills assessment, which confirmed that her work experience met the required criterion but contained other errors. Through her migration agent, she informed the MRT of this problem and sought an adjournment. The MRT refused this application and stated that it was 'not prepared to delay any further', since Ms Li had had 'enough opportunities to present her case'.

The MRT's powers are specified in legislation, relevantly including:[63]

353 Tribunal's way of operating

(1) The Tribunal shall, in carrying out its functions under this Act, pursue the objective of providing a mechanism of review that is *fair, just, economical, informal and quick*.

(2) The Tribunal, in reviewing a decision:

(a) is not bound by technicalities, legal forms or rules of evidence; and

(b) shall act according to *substantial justice and the merits of the case*.

…

357A Exhaustive statement of natural justice hearing rule

(1) This Division is taken to be an exhaustive statement of the requirements of the natural justice hearing rule in relation to the matters it deals with.

…

(3) In applying this Division, the Tribunal *must act in a way that is fair and just*.

…

360 Tribunal must invite applicant to appear

(1) The Tribunal must invite the applicant to appear before the Tribunal to give evidence and present arguments relating to the issues arising in relation to the decision under review.

[59] See, eg *A v Pelekanakis* (1999) 91 FCR 70, 89 [89] (Weinberg J).

[60] For example, it was held to apply only to exercises of discretion and not to fact-finding following the High Court's decision in *Minister for Immigration & Multicultural Affairs, ex p Applicant S20/2002* (2003) 198 ALR 59.

[61] This approach can be traced, at least, to the decision of Brennan J in *Quin* (n 7) 36.

[62] Basten, 'Judicial Review of Executive Action' (n 54) 35.

[63] Migration Act 1958 (Cth) (emphasis added).

The Full Federal Court was divided on whether these provisions had been followed and also whether they imposed procedural duties upon the MRT, or perhaps even more substantive obligations. Collier J took a narrower view of section 360 and the other procedural provisions noted above than her judicial colleagues, holding that they were 'exhortative' and aspirational and did not create a procedural requirement to be followed by the MRT in addition to requirements imposed elsewhere in the Act.[64] Her Honour found that the MRT had not provided the opportunity required by section 360 because it had failed to consider the application for an adjournment properly.[65] According to this view, the obligation to provide a proper invitation to a hearing included a duty to properly consider an application for an adjournment.[66]

Greenwood and Logan JJ held that the MRT had committed a jurisdictional error by failing to act in a manner that was 'fair' for the purposes of sections 353(1) and 357A(3).[67] Their Honours made clear that the denial of the adjournment was no mere procedural breach or erroneous exercise of a discretion. The error went to the very heart of the Tribunal's functions because 'when a tribunal fails in this way to offer an opportunity to be heard, it fails to discharge its core *statutory function* of *reviewing* the decision of the Minister or his delegate'.[68] This error meant that the MRT had failed to grant Ms Li a 'meaningful' opportunity to appear as required by section 360.[69] That reasoning represents one side of a sharp division within the Federal Court about the precise requirements of s 360. Some cases have accepted that the statutory duty of the tribunal to invite an applicant to appear before it requires any invitation to be 'real and meaningful' rather than 'a hollow shell or an empty gesture'.[70] According to this view, invalidity occurs because the failure to provide a meaningful invitation to appear leads to a failure in the core statutory mission of the tribunal. The difficulty with this approach is that the 'core statutory function' of the tribunal, and usually also the conduct which is said to have led to a failure of that function, are not clearly stated or required by the statute. Consideration of that issue frequently leads courts to assess the quality of the invitation in light of the subsequent hearing that was conducted.[71] It is not hard to see why an interpretive gloss upon the invitation to appear and make arguments about issues has been used by courts as a vehicle for a qualitative assessment of the subsequent hearing of those issues. The statutory duty of invitation to

[64] *Minister for Immigration and Citizenship v Li* (FC) (n 55) [83].
[65] Ibid, [85].
[66] Ibid, [87], [102].
[67] Ibid, [28]–[30].
[68] Ibid, [27] (emphasis in original).
[69] The lingering disagreement within the Federal Court on this issue is explained in *Minister for Immigration and Citizenship v SZNVW* (2010) 183 FCR 575.
[70] *Mazhar v Minister for Immigration and Multicultural Affairs* (2000) 64 ALD 395, [31]. The notion of a 'real and meaningful' invitation can be traced to *Minister for Immigration and Multicultural and Indigenous Affairs v SCAR* (2003) 128 FCR 553.
[71] A point acknowledged by Perram J in *SZNVW* (n 69) [75].

attend and present evidence and arguments about the 'issues arising' seems apt to invite some assessment of what has arisen and how the relevant duty and consequent arguments were addressed, particularly when that duty exists in conjunction with one to act 'fairly and justly'.

In the High Court, French CJ held that section 353 was not 'expressed in terms or in a context which would support a claim of jurisdictional error based on ... non-observance',[72] but alone of the three judges expressed the view that the MRT had denied Ms Li procedural fairness by acting contrary to section 357A(3).[73] Gageler J agreed with Collier J that the two relevant statutory provisions 'are couched in language that is broad and that is best seen to be exhortatory or aspirational'.[74] The plurality judgment of Hayne, Kiefel and Bell JJ also held that section 353(1) was 'intended to be facultative, not restrictive'[75] but made no determination as to section 357A(3).[76] The net result of these differently reasoned judgments in the High Court is that there was no majority support for the position taken by Greenwood and Logan JJ, which made the statutory exhortations to 'fairness' substantively enforceable.

Consequently, the High Court dismissed the Minister's appeal on the basis that the MRT had behaved unreasonably in exercising its discretion to deny an adjournment. What is most intriguing about the three judgments is that they did not decide that the MRT had behaved unreasonably in the *Wednesbury* sense (at least as that test had previously been understood), nor did they define the MRT's unreasonableness in precisely the same way. The basis of the result in *Li* might therefore amount to a new approach to unreasonableness as a basis of jurisdictional error, though all members of the High Court affirmed the existence of some of the long-standing problems surrounding unreasonableness.

That is not to say that it represents a complete break from the High Court judges' previous approaches. This point is perhaps best illustrated by reference to the judgment of French CJ, who has long placed procedural fairness issues at the forefront of his judicial review analyses.[77] Here, his Honour found that the privative clause in section 357A(1) of the Migration Act did not apply because the relevant division of the Act[78]

> does not deal with the matter of an application by an applicant for an adjournment in order to provide additional material or, as in this case, the provision of a third party assessment the existence of which is a criterion for the grant of the

[72] *Minister for Immigration and Citizenship v Li* (n 6) 342–43 [12].

[73] Ibid, 347 [21]. We shall return to this point.

[74] Ibid, 372 [96].

[75] Ibid, 348–49 [52].

[76] Ibid, 362 [62].

[77] A notable exception was his Honour's dissenting opinion in *Minister for Immigration and Multicultural Affairs v SZFDE* (2006) 154 FCR 365, which was upheld by the High Court: *SZFDE v Minister for Immigration and Multicultural Affairs* (2007) 232 CLR 189.

[78] *Minister for Immigration and Citizenship v Li* (n 6) 346 [18].

> visa. The common law hearing rule of procedural fairness applies to the process for making a decision to grant or refuse an adjournment in such cases and informs its legal consequences where a person is said to have been deprived by a refusal of a reasonable opportunity for a hearing.

French CJ suggested that the Minister's submission that 'the present case was not really about procedural fairness at all' was 'antithetical to the legislative direction and facultative purpose of section 353 and indeed that of section 357A(3)'.[79] This statement is one of the few occasions on which the High Court referred to the values on which it relied in undertaking a significant change in direction on the subject of judicial review of poor quality decision-making. On the whole, however, the court's rationale remains unclear. Is *Li* another implied limitation on the exercise of statutory powers, like natural justice? Does it extend that limitation, now so recognised in natural justice, to unreasonableness? Is the High Court thinking about adopting a more substantive review approach while also drifting away from close reliance on the principles of statutory interpretation? It is not clear why so many potentially wide-ranging issues were approached with such an absence of context.

While concurring with the plurality judgment, French CJ entered into far less analysis of the MRT's alleged unreasonableness than the other members of the Court. It is significant that, when he did, his Honour cited the judgment of Dixon CJ in *Klein v Domus*.[80] Just above the passage cited by French CJ, Dixon CJ said[81]

> that wherever the legislature has given a discretion [without defining the grounds on which the discretion is to be exercised] you must look at the scope and purpose of the provision and at what is its real object. If it appears that the dominating, actuating reason for the decision is outside the scope of the purpose of the enactment, that vitiates the supposed exercise of the discretion.

Dixon J had earlier stated that if the holder of a discretion

> does not address himself to the question which the sub-section formulates, if his conclusion is affected by some mistake of law, if he takes some extraneous reason into consideration or excludes from consideration some factor which should affect his determination, on any of these grounds his conclusion is liable to review. *Moreover, the fact that he has not made known the reasons why he was not satisfied will not prevent the review of his decision.*[82]

[79] Ibid, 346–47 [19]–[20]; cf L Pearson, '"Fair is Foul and Foul is Fair": Migration Tribunals and a Fair Hearing' in M Groves (ed), *Modern Administrative Law in Australia* (n 4) 416, 437.

[80] *Klein v Domus Pty Ltd* (1963) 109 CLR 467, 473. See also *Minister for Immigration and Citizenship v Li* (n 6) 363–64 [67] (Hayne, Kiefel and Bell JJ); 376 [109] (Gageler J).

[81] *Klein v Domus* (n 80) 473.

[82] *Avon Downs Pty Ltd v Federal Commissioner of Taxation* (1949) 78 CLR 353, 360 (emphasis added). This reasoning draws implicitly on the earlier judgment of Latham CJ in *Hetton Bellbird Collieries* (n 16) 432.

In other words, if no good reason could be posited for a decision in respect of which the decision-maker had offered no reasons, a court may assume there is none. These dicta were really an extension of the reasoning of Dixon, Evatt and McTiernan JJ in *House v The King*, in which their Honours stated that an 'unreasonable or plainly unjust' result may point to the miscarriage of a judicial discretion, despite the fact that the 'nature of the error of law may not be discoverable'.[83] McHugh and Gummow JJ have noted elsewhere[84] that both this passage in *House v The King* and Lord Greene's speech in *Wednesbury* have in common a connection to the House of Lords' decision in *Sharp v Wakefield*,[85] which distinguished lawful exercises of discretion, done 'according to the rules of reason and justice, not according to private opinion', from 'arbitrary, vague, and fanciful' exercises of discretion. In Australia, this is taken to mean an exercise of discretion almost completely unsupported by reasons. Recent English authority has sought to extend this principle to reasoning for discretionary decisions deemed by the court to be deficient on the merits.[86] It is unthinkable that such authority could be applied in Australia.

The decisions in *Sharp v Wakefield* and *Klein v Domus* were cited by all three judgments in the High Court, in addition to which *House v The King* and *Avon Downs* were cited by two.[87] This points clearly to the basis on which the High Court found that the MRT had exercised its discretionary power unreasonably, which was that its refusal to adjourn because it 'consider[ed] that the applicant [had] been provided with enough opportunities to present her case and [was] not prepared to delay any further' looked arbitrary. Without the MRT having provided reasons with any real detail, it was open to the High Court to find that the MRT lacked a lawful reason for exercising its discretion as it did. In an age where reasoned decisions are the norm, it is somewhat unusual to see the line of cases cited

[83] *House v The King* (1936) 55 CLR 499. The interaction of these three judgments was noted by the plurality: *Minister for Immigration and Citizenship v Li* (n 6) 363–65 [67]–[69] (Hayne, Kiefel and Bell JJ).

[84] *Applicant S20* (n 60) 75.

[85] *Sharp v Wakefield* [1891] AC 173, 179–80 (Lord Halsbury LC). This decision was cited by all three High Court judgments in *Minister for Immigration and Citizenship v Li* (n 6) 349 [24] (French CJ); 363 [65] (Hayne, Kiefel and Bell JJ); 370–71 [90] (Gageler J).

[86] *R (Litvinenko) v Secretary of State for the Home Department* [2014] EWHC 194 (Admin).

[87] Another aspect of the reasoning which applied *House v The King* (n 83) stems from the fact that that case was about when it will be appropriate for a court to overturn the exercise of a discretion. In *Minister for Immigration and Citizenship v Li*, Gageler J considered that the MRT's exercise of its discretion to refuse an adjournment was entirely within the sort of matters in which judges are experts. Finding that the MRT exercised its discretion unreasonably no doubt stemmed from an innate understanding of how a similar discretion would properly be exercised in judicial proceedings: *Minister for Immigration and Citizenship v Li* (n 6) 377 [112]; cf Basten, 'Judicial Review of Executive Action' (n 54) 46.

by the High Court applied directly.[88] Perhaps this is the basis upon which Gageler J was able to make the (at first blush, breathtaking) statement that *Li* was a 'rare case' which will do nothing to affect the stringency of the test in *Wednesbury*.[89]

We take the contrary view that, if *Li* was not in fact a very ordinary case, it might well have been so but for the manner with which the MRT dealt with it. By definition, cases in which *Wednesbury* is relied upon are those in which an administrative discretion is under challenge. There is nothing so unusual about the facts of *Li* in this regard. How, then, did it come to such an unusual conclusion in the High Court? We take the view that all three judgments can be traced back to the fact that the MRT gave inadequate reasons for its decision to refuse a further adjournment.[90] The references to the cases referred to above seems to support this view, since they are generally taken to stand for the proposition that, where no good reason has been given by a decision-maker, a judicial review court may conclude that one did not exist. This was standard reasoning at a time when few non-judicial decisions were supported by reasons but has been more frequently referred to than applied over the last 40 years.

Since then, the High Court declined in *Osmond's* case[91] to find that there is a common-law right to reasons for non-judicial decisions, holding that any such right should be conferred by legislation.[92] It may be, however, that

[88] The exception to this proposition is *House v The King* (n 83), which is usually cited for an associated but different point relating to the exercise of appellate jurisdiction.

[89] *Minister for Immigration and Citizenship v Li* (n 6) 377–78 [113].

[90] In a subsequent case regarding a refusal by the MRT to adjourn proceedings, a particularly strong Full Federal Court (Allsop CJ, Robertson and Mortimer JJ) applied *Li*, but on the basis that a failure to *consider* the adjournment request actively, 'on its merits and in context at the time it was made', was not 'a legally reasonable exercise of power': *Minister for Immigration and Border Protection v Singh* [2014] FCAFC 1, [66]. This seems to suggest that *Li* might extend beyond insufficiently reasoned exercises of discretion. Prior to *Li* such a problem would most likely have been held a constructive failure to exercise jurisdiction. See, eg *Minister* for *Immigration and Multicultural Affairs v SZIAI* (2009) 83 ALJR 1123, 1125 [25] (possible error by tribunal for failure to exercise power to inquire in a cases where inquiry might clearly be called for).

[91] *Public Service Board of New South Wales v Osmond* (1986) 159 CLR 656. Mike Taggart was critical of the High Court's failure to bridge the gap between acknowledging that it is desirable for administrative decision-makers to provide reasons for their decisions: M Taggart, '*Osmond* in the High Court of Australia: Missed Opportunity' in M Taggart (ed), *Judicial Review of Administrative Action in the 1980s* (Auckland, Oxford University Press, 1986) 53. He was keeping good company. Michael Kirby deplored the High Court's decision in *Osmond*, which unanimously overturned Kirby's own decision in the NSW Court of Appeal just after Kirby had delivered a paper on the common law right to reasons at an administrative law conference organised by Mike Taggart: The Hon M Kirby, 'Accountability and the Right to Reasons' in M Taggart (ed), *Judicial Review of Administrative Action in the 1980s* (Auckland, Oxford University Press, 1986) 36. See the account in AJ Brown, *Michael Kirby: Paradoxes and Principles* (Annandale, NSW, Federation Press, 2011), 197–98. We do not share the criticisms of *Osmond* advanced by Taggart and Kirby. See the analysis in M Groves, 'Reviewing Reasons for Administrative Decisions' (2013) 35 *Sydney Law Review* 627.

[92] The High Court referred specifically to the ADJR Act 1977 (Cth) s 13. A number of other legislative provisions which confer a limited right to reasons have been based on this section.

there has now been a change in tone, if not in substance, from the High Court. The application of *Wednesbury* in *Li* may indicate that the High Court sanctions a wider application of that ground in order to ensure that a greater number of non-judicial decisions are supported by reasons. While this may not amount to a back-door way around *Osmond*, it may nonetheless reduce the circumstances in which administrative decision-makers can safely exercise discretion without supporting their decision by an extensive statement of reasons. On the other hand, the High Court may have done no more than to reassert the accepted principle that the duty to provide reasoned decisions is variable and is more demanding as the decision-maker in question comes closer to performing a judicial function.[93] If, as McHugh JA thought in *Soulemezis*,[94] this duty 'rests on ... the principle that justice must not only be done but it must be seen to be done', then it is readily understandable that the High Court might seek to apply it to tribunals such as the MRT, notwithstanding that it is not an adversarial body in the sense that courts are.[95]

It follows from this that the High Court is unlikely to have intervened at all if the MRT had provided a fuller statement of reasons for its refusal to grant an adjournment[96] and those reasons did not disclose a jurisdictional error. What is interesting about that conclusion is simply that, while the MRT erred in saying little more than that Ms Li had 'been provided with enough opportunities to present her case' and concluding that it was 'not prepared to delay any further',[97] it did not necessarily err in refusing to grant the adjournment sought. If the tribunal had provided a fully reasoned justification, the High Court would not have been able to infer that the MRT had acted unreasonably in the sense amounting to jurisdictional error even if its reasons were illogical or contained errors of fact.[98]

[93] The High Court has made clear that the judicial duty to give reasons for decisions is not absolute. See, eg *Wainohu v New South Wales* (2011) 243 CLR 181, 215 [56] where French CJ and Kiefel J explained that the constitutional duty of judges to provide reasons 'does not apply to every interlocutory decision, however minor' and that the detail required in reasons must 'vary according to the nature of the jurisdiction which the court is exercising and the particular matter the subject of the decision'.

[94] *Soulemezis v Dudley (Holdings) Pty Ltd* (1987) 10 NSWLR 247, 278.

[95] For example, the Secretary of the Department of Immigration is not represented in hearings before the MRT, but may provide 'written argument relating to the issues arising in relation to the decision under review': Migration Act 1958 (Cth) s 358(2). The High Court has made clear that this and other legislative adjustments to the traditional adversarial practice of the courts does not make the MRT an inquisitorial body in a full or pure sense: *SZIAI* (n 90) [18] (French, Gummow, Hayne, Crennan, Kiefel and Bell JJ); *SZBEL v Minister for Immigration and Multicultural and Indigenous Affairs* (2006) 228 CLR 152, 164 [40] (Gleeson CJ, Kirby, Hayne, Callinan and Heydon JJ).

[96] The MRT is obliged by legislation to provide reasons: Migration Act 1958 (Cth) s 368(1)(b).

[97] *Minister for Immigration and Citizenship v Li* (n 6) 338–39 [3]. This is all the more so because the Minister had conceded that the grounds upon which the adjournment had been requested were 'coherent': Pearson, 'Fair is Foul and Foul is Fair' (n 79) 437.

[98] *L&B Linings Pty Ltd v WorkCover Authority of New South Wales* [2012] NSWCA 15 [57] (Basten JA).

Subject to legislation, the MRT is allowed to govern its own process. Given that it is able to 'adjourn the review from time to time'[99] and is required in any case to pursue the objective of providing review that is economical and quick,[100] it must be open to such a busy tribunal, operating under considerable pressure of time and resources, to decide that a given applicant has had sufficient opportunity to make his or her case. Gageler J articulated the view that the MRT would not fall into jurisdictional error as a result of the 'mere erroneous application' of these compulsory considerations, but only by their 'neglect'.[101] On this interpretation, *Li* stands for the proposition that a tribunal wishing to refuse an adjournment must make its statement of reasons utterly clear in order to avoid a finding of unreasonableness.

Ultimately, we do not share the confidence expressed by Gageler J that the judgments in *Li* will not 'be taken as encouragement to greater frequency' in applying *Wednesbury* or in finding unreasonableness, if that is now a different thing.[102] Our doubts stem from the fact that there has been a subtle but clear change in the way that the evidentiary burden in relation to the unreasonableness ground is to be handled. Previously, all that a government party needed to do to avoid a finding of *Wednesbury* unreasonableness was to posit some possible, even if improbable, valid reason for the exercise of power under question. This was not a task which tested any competent government counsel. Now, however, the judgments of the plurality and Gageler J have set a much lower bar for applicants.

IV. VALUES

Why might the High Court have taken the unexpected steps that it did in *Li*? The answer surely lies in the wider context of *Li* and the torrent of migration decisions that continue to flow into the High Court. The answer is context, though one that is never mentioned openly by the courts. Lord Steyn made his often quoted point that '[i]n law context is everything'[103] when explaining the different considerations that might arise in judicial and human rights review in light of the Human Rights Act 1998 (UK). There may be disagreement in England about the merit of the doctrinal changes which that statute has triggered in English public law but most would agree that the enactment of human rights and consequential responsibilities for

[99] Migration Act 1958 (Cth) s 363(1)(b).

[100] As well as fair, just and informal: Migration Act 1958 (Cth) s 353(1).

[101] *Minister for Immigration and Citizenship v Li* (n 6) 372–73 [97]. See Pearson, 'Fair is Foul and Foul is Fair' (n 79) 425–27.

[102] *Minister for Immigration and Citizenship v Li* (n 6) 377–78 [113].

[103] *R (Daly) v Secretary of State for the Home Department* [2001] 2 AC 532, 548 [28].

public authorities has served a crucial role.[104] Context in the sense of an explanation for ebbs and flows in legal doctrine is surely not limited to positive action by the legislature. It can also take the form of inaction. In the dying years of the apartheid regime in South Africa, Mureinik suggested that:[105]

> The body of opinion that favours a Bill of Rights enforced by judicial review is no longer marginal, and it enjoys weighty judicial support. Until it prevails, we shall no doubt observe the judges resorting, in order to promote the values which ought to be protected by such an instrument, to ever bolder conceptions of what is permissible in the name of interpretation.

The relevance of such reasoning to Australia is obvious but so also is Mureinik's added caution from South Africa that:[106]

> [T]he moral authority of the judiciary is expanding into the space vacated by the contraction of the moral authority of the executive and the legislature. Like equity, morality abhors a vacuum. And as the moral authority of the judicial system is expanding, so is what is conceived to be its core; so, that is to say, is its moral heart.

The moral gap in Australian law in the last 20 years or so has arguably arisen through the enactment of what must be some of the most complex and draconian migration legislation in the developed world. That legislation is matched by political rhetoric so harsh it would astonish outside observers.[107] The decisions of the High Court regularly feature heavily in this debate, though the Court mentions the wider political and media obsession in Australia about migration rarely and with a delicacy beyond the reach of most politicians.[108] The absence of a Bill or Charter of Rights at Commonwealth level and the gaping unfairness of much about Australian migration law might each provide strong reasons for strident assertions by Australian courts of their entrenched and protected jurisdiction. Perhaps it can also explain how courts conceive their role in that structure in terms of a 'duty' to declare and apply the law. A key aspect of that judicial role in recent times has been to keep draconian migration legislation (or, perhaps

[104] We take no stand on this issue except to acknowledge the force of the differing views in T Poole, 'The Reformation of English Administrative Law' (2009) 68 *Cambridge Law Journal* 142 and J Varuhas, 'The Reformation of English Administrative Law? "Rights", Rhetoric and Reality' (2013) 72 *Cambridge Law Journal* 369.

[105] Mureinik, 'Administrative Law in South Africa' (n 43) 616.

[106] Ibid.

[107] A vivid illustration is provided by an account of events in a notorious migration incident which occurred prior to the federal election in 2001 in D Marr and M Wilkinson, *Dark Victory* (Crows Nest New South Wales, Allen & Unwin, 2003).

[108] See, eg *M70/2011 v Commonwealth* (2011) 244, CLR 144, 157–58 [1]–[2] (the *Malaysian Declaration* case) where French CJ acknowledged that the case arose in a 'strongly contested area of public policy' but then added that the role of the High Court in this wider debate was simply to decide the matter according to law.

most likely, its creators in the executive government) at bay. But an identification of that function does not explain precisely what is sought to be protected and why. Gageler J was mindful of that problem in a recent paper which commented that the constitutional demarcation which guides the High Court merely 'allows identification of the relevant questions'.[109] His Honour thought the key questions were not the grounds a court might apply to limit the power of administrative officials but the source and substantive content of the law they might invoke to do so. We suggest the even more pressing question is what exactly the courts seek to protect and why. What values lie behind the protective doctrines of the courts? The answer must surely lie in the basic or fundamental values that courts and their judges believe are worth protecting.

Reference to certain fundamental, shared values is also one of very few ways that courts might look to make substantive review 'grip' on existing law. This option becomes problematic, not to say controversial, where reference to the fundamental nature of rights or values tends to beg the question of not only what values are fundamental but why they are so.[110] Values are often referred to, albeit more frequently in compendium form than individually: it is easier to assert that people in Australia share 'values' than it is to nominate the individual values that are shared.[111] Any attempt to justify judicial intervention based on the infringement of values therefore suffers from two essential flaws. First, it is inevitably an ex post facto exercise in generalising what judges think that Australian values might be, which is necessarily conducted on shifting sands. The second problem with values is that their use rests on the unlikely assumption that there are core values which are both widely shared and also understood in the same way by those who share them.[112] Such difficulties point to more fundamental questions about supposedly fundamental values. How are values, even those to which the adjective 'fundamental' is appended, able to be identified, and subsequently applied, in the event that they are contested?

[109] Gageler, 'The Constitutional Dimension' (n 4) 172.

[110] A similar problem exists in attempts to determine whether interests are rights that warrant protection by proportionality based rights review: K Möller, 'Proportionality and Rights Inflation' in G Huscroft, B Miller and G Webber (eds), *Proportionality and the Rule of Law* (New York, Cambridge University Press, 2014). The line dividing rights from mere interests is one that must be drawn if Taggart's bifurcation concept (Taggart (n 1)) is to be made to work.

[111] For example, the celebrated Australian belief in a 'fair go' depends in fact upon to whom the 'fair go' is being offered, a proposition that can be proved by listening to talkback radio or reading the comments section below online news reports. French CJ placed great weight on the notion of a 'fair go': French, 'Procedural Fairness—Indispensable to Justice?' (n 14).

[112] Loughlin saw that problem early in the debate about fairness, when he cautioned that acceptance of the concept might be based on 'an imaginary consensus' about its content: M Loughlin, 'Procedural Fairness: A Study of the Crisis in Administrative Law Theory' (1978) 28 *University of Toronto Law Journal* 215, 238.

The 'principle of legality' is sometimes considered to be a relatively modern phenomenon but it is a much older concept.[113] In Australia, the principle is usually associated with the oft-quoted and frequently endorsed words of O'Connor J in *Potter v Minahan*:[114]

> There are certain objects which the legislature is presumed not to intend; and a construction which would lead to any of them is therefore to be avoided.... One of these presumptions is that the legislature does not intend to make any alteration in the law beyond what it explicitly declares ... either in express terms or by implication; or, in other words, beyond the immediate scope and object of the Statute. In all general matters beyond, the law remains undisturbed. *It is in the last degree improbable that the legislature would overthrow fundamental principles, infringe rights, or depart from the general system of law, without expressing its intention with irresistible clearness*; and to give any such effect to general words, simply because they have that meaning in their widest, or usual, or natural sense, would be to give them a meaning in which they were not really used.

If the principle of legality can be traced back for over a century, it is nonetheless true that it has more recently enjoyed an image relaunch,[115] under which it has a sharper, rights-based focus. This is to some extent a matter of emphasis rather than substance, though in Australia the two have long blurred. In *R v Snow*, the High Court held by a majority that nothing in section 73 of the *Constitution* set aside the common-law presumption that no appeal lay from a verdict of 'not guilty'.[116] This reasoning can be viewed as including some rights analysis,[117] given that the defendant had been

[113] Lord Hoffmann's speech in *R v Secretary of State for the Home Department, ex p Simms* [2000] 2 AC 115 is usually considered the source of the modern UK enunciation of the principle. Lord Steyn had earlier noted that the 'idea [behind the principle of legality] is even older' than Benson's *On the Interpretation of Statutes*, which was cited in the earliest Australian case: *R v Secretary of State for the Home Department, ex p Pierson* [1998] AC 539, 587. His Lordship traced the concept back to a speech of Sir John Romilly MR in *Minet v Leman* (1855) 20 Beav 269, 278. Others trace the essential principle back as far as Lord Mansfield's speech in *Somerset v Stewart* (1772) Lofft 1, 98 ER 499. See Meagher, 'The Common Law Principle of Legality in the Age of Rights' (n 15) 452–53.

[114] *Potter v Minahan* (1908) 7 CLR 277, 304 (emphasis added). His Honour was citing Sir Peter Benson Maxwell, *On the Interpretation of Statutes* 4th edn (London, Sweet & Maxwell, (1905) 121–22.

[115] Taggart noted that the long-standing presumption that general statutory words cannot override fundamental rights was 'powerfully rebranded' as the principle of legality in connection with the increased status of human rights in judicial interpretation in both New Zealand and the UK: Taggart (n 1) 431.

[116] See *The King v Snow* (1915) 20 CLR 315, 322 (Griffith CJ). Isaacs and Higgins JJ dissented. Isaacs J contended that the principle relied upon by the majority did not exist (351–53). Higgins J argued that the presumption was not confined to acquittals (353–54). See DC Pearce and RS Geddes, *Statutory Interpretation in Australia*, 8th edn (Chatswood, New South Wales, LexisNexis, Butterworths, 2014) 242.

[117] Pearce and Geddes make the point that there are separate presumptions against the alteration of common law doctrines and the invasion of common law rights but that most cases do not distinguish between the two: Pearce and Geddes (n 116) 243. It is, however, a feature often associated with 'rights cases' that the court is called upon to consider procedural (and not

charged during wartime with an offence under the Trading with the Enemy Act 1914 (Cth), described by Isaacs J as 'one of unparalleled gravity'.[118] The analysis of the majority has been upheld into this century, meaning that a specific statutory power is required before the Crown can appeal against an acquittal or a sentence imposed following conviction.[119]

Application of the principle of legality has more recently been typified by cases like *Coco v R*,[120] in which the High Court held as a matter of statutory interpretation that the legislature would not intend to authorise trespass without making such intention pellucidly clear. The true purpose, of course, was to make the legislative branch politically accountable for any retraction of fundamental rights or freedoms, with the judicial branch purporting not to know what the legislature intended unless its intentions were politically visible. An insistence on clear legislative language before finding an intention for fundamental norms to be infringed upon seems now to be the standard judicial response, which seems to reduce the principle of legality to a judicial requirement of unambiguous statutory drafting.[121] Linking this process to democratic principles, or (if it is different) to political accountability, has been described as a 'relatively novel component' in the modern principle of legality.[122]

This has more or less been the accepted approach to the principle of legality for over a century. So what does it mean when we (and others) contend that it is a more 'modern' phenomenon, or has at least changed in some way since *Potter v Minahan*?[123] When the Australian High Court now invokes the principle, it does not necessarily rely only on the principles articulated by O'Connor J. Rather, it seems to apply the implicit interpretive presumptions of the principle of legality with such force that they move the principle towards encapsulating some form of right. The basis of this

only substantive) rights; see, eg *Evans v New South Wales* (2008) 168 FCR 576 ('*The World Youth Day Case*') (French, Branson and Stone JJ); *Coco v R* (1994) 179 CLR 427; *Pierson* (n 113) 589 (Lord Steyn).

[118] *R v Snow* (n 116) 330 (Isaacs J). The language employed by Isaacs J in this and following passages was, to say the least, passionate.

[119] Pearce and Geddes (n 116) 242–43.

[120] *Coco* (n 117). Meagher noted that the Australian 'judicial reassertion of the principle of legality' was underway some years before the equivalent process in the UK: Meagher, 'Principle of Legality in the Age of Rights' (n 15) 454.

[121] M Aronson and M Groves, *Judicial Review of Administrative Action*, 5th edn (Pyrmont, NSW, Thomson Reuters, 2013) 177.

[122] Ibid. Some judges and commentators have, however, indicated a preference for elevating such norms to a constitutional status, thereby protecting them 'against legislative reversal'; see the authorities cited at Aronson and Groves, *Judicial Review of Administrative Action* (n 121) 176, fn 443.

[123] McHugh J warned that the presumption against the legislative incursion of common law rights was 'admittedly weak these days': *Gifford v Strang Patrick Stevedoring Pty Ltd* (2003) 214 CLR 269, 284 [36]. One of the cases cited by his Honour was *Potter v Minahan* (n 114), which is typically invoked by Australian judges to make precisely the opposite point.

substantive (rather than merely procedural) rights protection by the principle of legality in modern Australian law can be traced back to both *Coco* and the speech of Lord Steyn in *Pierson*, which was approved by Gleeson CJ in *Electrolux* in the following terms:[124]

> Lord Steyn described the presumption [against modification or abrogation of fundamental rights] as an aspect of the principle of legality which governs the relations between Parliament, the executive and the courts. The presumption is not merely a common sense guide to what a Parliament in a liberal democracy is likely to have intended; it is a working hypothesis, the existence of which is known both to Parliament and the courts, upon which statutory language will be interpreted. The hypothesis is an aspect of the rule of law.

Meagher has described the passage from Gleeson CJ's judgment in *Electrolux* as emphasising the 'constitutional significance' of the principle of legality.[125] That appeared more so when the passage was approved by a majority of the High Court in *Saeed*.[126]

Ultimately, the (small-c) constitutional significance of the principle of legality is found in the scrutiny applied by courts before allowing rights to be removed by legislation, rather than in any substantive protective mechanism. Once this is accepted, the question becomes what principles or values are sufficiently 'fundamental' to attract the interpretive protection of the principle of legality? Australian cases which have held various rights to be fundamental have done little to explain how or why those rights are so designated.[127] The High Court illustrated this problem in *Saeed* when it declared natural justice to be a fundamental principle but shed no new light on natural justice, or on why earlier cases which had stressed the difficulty of any legislative exclusion of the doctrine had not explained it as a fundamental principle or right.[128] Gageler J recently offered a more extended explanation when he stated that:[129]

> Application of the principle of construction is not confined to the protection of rights, freedoms or immunities that are hard-edged, of long standing or recognised and enforceable or otherwise protected at common law. The principle extends

[124] *Electrolux Home Products Pty Ltd v The Australian Workers' Union* (2004) 221 CLR 309, 329 [21].

[125] Meagher, 'Principle of Legality in the Age of Rights' (n 15) 455. That phrase should not be understood as protecting rights from statutory reversal in the manner of a 'constitutionally entrenched' right, such as to judicial review before the High Court in its original jurisdiction: *Plaintiff S157* (n 36).

[126] *Saeed v Minister for Immigration and Citizenship* (2010) 241 CLR 252, 259 [15] (French CJ, Gummow, Hayne, Crennan and Kiefel JJ).

[127] Meagher has compiled a list of rights that have been held to be fundamental, although we would warn that some, like the rights of access to courts and freedom of expression, are conditional only: Meagher, 'Principle of Legality in the Age of Rights' (n 15) 456–57.

[128] *Saeed* (n 126) 259 [15] (French CJ, Gummow, Hayne, Crennan and Kiefel JJ).

[129] *Lee v Crime Commission (NSW)* (2013) 87 ALJR 1082, 1152 [313].

> to the protection of fundamental principles and systemic values. The principle ought not, however, to be extended beyond its rationale: it exists to protect from inadvertent and collateral alteration rights, freedoms, immunities, principles and values that are important within our system of representative and responsible government under the rule of law; it does not exist to shield those rights, freedoms, immunities, principles and values from being specifically affected in the pursuit of clearly identified legislative objects by means within the constitutional competence of the enacting legislature.

This account of the principle of legality may be lucid but it offers little help in understanding which values and principles will be shielded. It is almost implicit in the nature of judicial protection of values that only the judiciary can say when a fundamental value has been encroached upon, if it does not fall within the established categories of protected values.[130] This is, in a sense, an obvious point of difference between a common-law system of rights protection and one which relies upon the protection of enumerated rights (although history has shown that the latter system is by no means a guarantor of certainty).[131] The absence of an agreed list of fundamental values has been seen as a 'major objection to the argument that the courts provide all the protection of rights which is necessary'.[132] This criticism seems to amount to an argument that any failure to codify rights (in the manner of a Bill of Rights) means that the common-law approach is inadequate. Without more, we cannot accept that proposition. The common law has always operated based on precedent. If the learned authors of *Statutory Interpretation in Australia* have been able to identify the relevant precedents, it should not be impossible for trained lawyers to continue to follow their example. Furthermore, it is not unduly cynical to say that an approach that leaves courts with greater flexibility makes it more certain that they will interpret statutory provisions in such a way that confers the utmost protection to the values they hold to be fundamental. This cynical conclusion points to a position not unlike that reached by Australian courts in the flexible approach of the *Project Blue Sky* case[133] in the interpretation of statutory procedural requirements. One could simply substitute

[130] There does not seem to be an accepted list of recognised principles except at Pearce and Geddes (n 116) 255–59.

[131] Professor Pearce has also suggested that the common law principles which are protected by the principle of legality are broader than the 'types of rights that might be the subject of a Bill of Rights': D Pearce AO, 'Principle of Legality and Human Rights' (Paper presented at the Public Law Weekend 2013, 15 November 2013).

[132] Ibid.

[133] *Project Blue Sky Inc v Australian Broadcasting Authority* (1998) 194 CLR 355. This case replaced the old mandatory/directory distinction as a guide to determine whether statutory procedural requirements should be followed with an approach that requires an interpretive assessment of whether the legislature is presumed to have intended a decision made without compliance of a procedure to be valid or invalid. The new approach is a vague, impressionistic one.

'legislative intention' for 'fundamental rights/values' to fashion a very similar judicial discretion.

The point remains that legislation drafted with the necessary clarity can validly override common-law principles, whether or not they are characterised as 'fundamental'. McHugh J explained the problem as follows in a speech:[134]

> Australia is a multi-cultural society, which is constantly undergoing rapid social and economic change. It is extremely difficult for present-day judges to know what are the permanent or enduring values in contemporary Australian society. Bedrock values of the nation have been overturned in recent years.

Only two years later in *Malika Holdings*, his Honour strongly doubted whether norms could be protected from legislative infringement simply because they were described as 'fundamental'. The problem, his Honour explained, simply opened new questions about when and why principles became fundamental because:[135]

> What is fundamental in one age or place may not be regarded as fundamental in another age or place. When community values are undergoing radical change and few principles or rights are immune from legislative amendment or abolition, as is the case in Australia today, few principles or rights can claim to be so fundamental that it is unlikely that the legislature would want to change them. No doubt there are fundamental legal principles ... But care needs to be taken in declaring a principle to be fundamental.

McHugh J thus recognised that even 'fundamental' norms and values are vulnerable to legislative change in a legal system where almost none are constitutionally protected.[136] This is where the principle of legality, as it is applied in Australia, differs from the modern application of a principle under the same name in the UK. The 'contemporary renaissance' of the principle of legality in the UK is firmly connected to the dominant presence of human rights in the law of that country.[137] A principle of legality in these circumstances does not, of course, have to do the same amount of work as

[134] Justice M McHugh, 'The Judicial Method' (1999) 73 *Australian Law Journal* 37, 46. His Honour drew upon the earlier comment of Kirby J that 'Australia is a multi-cultural society where the "permanent values" of the people are often hard to find': Justice M Kirby, 'Judicial Activism' (1997) 16 *Australian Bar Review* 11, 14.

[135] *Malika Holdings Pty Ltd v Streeton* (2001) 204 CLR 290, 298–99 [28]–[29]. This passage was cited with approval in *The World Youth Day Case* (n 117) 593 [69].

[136] The few exceptions include freedom of religion (s 116) and jury trial for indictable offences under Commonwealth laws (s 80). There are also certain implied rights, relating to freedom of political communication (see *Lange v Australian Broadcasting Corporation* (1997) 189 CLR 520) and the right to freedom from lawful detention in the form of a requirement that detention be clearly justified by law (see *Chu Kheng Lim v Minister for Immigration Local Government and Ethnic Affairs* (1992) 176 CLR 1).

[137] Meagher, 'Principle of Legality in the Age of Rights' (n 15) 453. However, we see much force in the sceptical assessment given in Varuhas, 'The Reformation of English Administrative Law' (n 104).

the principle of legality discussed by McHugh J. Nor is it as vulnerable, to the extent that there is an external source of protection available for enumerated rights.[138]

The principle of legality provides a more fragile protection of rights in Australia than they are provided in countries which have statutory or constitutional protection of enumerated rights.[139] Paradoxically, given that context, the principle of legality's operation has been employed as a central argument by those opposed to Australia adopting a bill of rights.[140] It is trite to observe that the status of individual 'fundamental' rights in Australia is most uncertain, but what of the rights which have already been accepted by the courts? Gleeson CJ listed certain 'established principles' in his judgment in *S157*, all of which 'are relevant to the resolution of the question of statutory construction'.[141] These included favouring a construction which accords with Australia's international obligations in cases of ambiguity, requiring 'unmistakable and unambiguous language' before imputing to the legislature 'an intention to abrogate or curtail fundamental rights or freedoms', applying the rule of law in the sense of preventing executive action 'from exceeding the powers and functions assigned to the executive by law and [protecting] the interests of the individual … accordingly',[142] construing privative clauses 'by reference to a presumption that the legislature does not intend to deprive the citizen of access to the courts, other than to the extent expressly stated or necessarily to be implied',[143] and construing privative clauses by 'a consideration of the whole Act' and attempting to reconcile it to the rest of the legislation.[144]

French CJ has extra-curially suggested a similar list, requiring that public statutory power be exercised lawfully, in good faith, rationally and fairly.[145] While stating that these are 'common law principles', French CJ (like Gleeson CJ in *S157*) attached a constitutional significance to them, saying that the principles are required by the 'framework of constitutional and administrative law'. Elsewhere, his Honour has explained that the

[138] In the UK, Parliament could repeal the non-constitutional Human Rights Act 1998 (UK). It could also withdraw from the European Convention on Human Rights, and indeed the Conservative party has said that it would already have done so if it were not part of a coalition government.

[139] In jurisdictions with statutory bills of rights, the rights interpretation provisions are applied only after common law interpretive provisions like the principle of legality: see Meagher, 'Principle of Legality in the Age of Rights' (n 15) 455–56.

[140] Pearce, 'Principle of Legality and Human Rights' (n 131).

[141] *Plaintiff S157* (n 36) 492 [28].

[142] *Church of Scientology Inc v Woodward* (1982) 154 CLR 25, 70 (Brennan J).

[143] *Public Service Association (SA) v Federated Clerks' Union* (1991) 173 CLR 132, 160 (Dawson and Gaudron JJ).

[144] *Plaintiff S157* (n 36) 492–93.

[145] Chief Justice R French, 'Public Law—An Australian Perspective' at the Scottish Public Law Group (Edinburgh, 6 July 2012) [16].

protection of non-constitutional rights can still incorporate a constitutional dimension because:[146]

> Although Commonwealth statutes in Australia are made under a written constitution, the Constitution does not in terms guarantee common law rights and freedoms against legislative incursion. Nevertheless, the interpretive rule [in *Potter v Minahan*] can be regarded as 'constitutional' in character even if the rights and freedoms which it protects are not.

It is the very fact that the principle of legality has developed through the common law that means it can claim to 'reflect fundamental assumptions' and may therefore be seen as having a 'quasi-constitutional' basis.[147]

What comes of the fact that the interpretive presumptions noted by Gleeson and French CJJ provide a constitutionally-mandated protection of rights which are not otherwise protected, when all that is required to infringe upon those 'rights' is pellucid clarity in legislation? McHugh J has described the existing protection as weak. This view has featured strongly in the arguments of those who would prefer Australia to adopt a statutory or constitutional system of protecting certain enumerated rights, but others have noted that some rights-protecting instruments operate in a similar way and with similar judicial results to the principle of legality.[148]

French CJ approached the issue from a different direction in a speech when he explained one of the few principles that gained general acceptance within the High Court when it considered the interpretive power of the Victorian statutory charter of rights in *Momcilovic v R*.[149] Section 32(1) of the Victorian Charter[150] requires courts to interpret 'all statutory provisions … in a way that is compatible with human rights' so far as this is consistent with their purpose. French CJ thought that neither that provision nor any common-law principle allowed a court to rewrite or distort the meaning of a statute. He subsequently explained that the interpretive provision of the Victorian Charter[151]

> resembles the common law principle of legality which is an important rule for the interpretation of statutes. That rule takes the form of a strong presumption that if on one interpretation a statute would infringe common law rights and freedoms

[146] Chief Justice R French, 'Litigating in a Statutory Universe' at the Victorian Bar Association 2nd Annual CPD Conference—the New Litigation Landscape: Challenges and Opportunities (Melbourne, 18 February 2012) 19.

[147] D Meagher, 'The Principle of Legality and the Judicial Protection of Rights—*Evans v New South Wales*' (2009) 37 *Federal Law Review* 293, 310. Meagher was quoting James Spigelman, *Statutory Interpretation and Human Rights* (St Lucia, Queensland, University of Queensland Press, 2008) 56.

[148] Meagher, 'The Principle of Legality and the Judicial Protection of Rights—*Evans v New South Wales*' (n 147) 306–309.

[149] *Momcilovic v R* (2011) 245 CLR 1.

[150] Charter of Human Rights and Responsibilities Act 2006 (Vic).

[151] Hon RS French, 'Unelected Judges in a Representative Democracy' (speech to the St Thomas More Society, Sydney, 22 June 2012) 13.

> and on another interpretation it would not the latter interpretation is to be preferred. It is important to observe that the interpretation which is chosen under this rule must be one that is open on the language of the statute and not the result of simply rewriting it. In that constraint the rule preserves the proper constitutional relationship between the courts and the Parliaments.

The weaknesses which have been noted in the principle of legality, particularly the fact that it amounts to nothing more than a principle of statutory construction, should not be overstated. The principle has been applied on many occasions in Australian courts.[152] Furthermore, the fact that a law properly made by Parliament in unambiguously clear terms might infringe on a 'fundamental' right might conceivably be a cause for concern. However, given that the Parliament will have been obliged to 'accept the political cost' of its legislation and can expect to be held accountable in the usual democratic fashion,[153] one might query whether such concern would be on a rule of law basis. Meagher has commented that the judiciary is not faced with the same criticism where it employs the principle of legality to oblige Parliament to consider rights at the time of passing legislation as it would be if it were empowered to criticise or invalidate legislation on rights grounds.[154]

One approach is typified by the concurring judgment of Stewart J in *Jacobellis v Ohio*,[155] a case in which the United States Supreme Court was asked to determine whether exhibition of a certain film failed to be protected under the First Amendment on the basis that the film was 'hard-core pornography'. Rather than 'trying to define what may be indefinable', as his Honour argued the Court had done unsuccessfully in relation to similar issues in previous cases, Stewart J said simply:[156]

> I shall not today attempt further to define the kinds of material I understand to be embraced within [the] shorthand description [of hard-core pornography], and perhaps I could never succeed in intelligibly doing so. But *I know it when I see it*, and the motion picture involved in this case is not that.

The key phrase of Stewart J's brief judgment achieved significant fame.[157] It is frequently cited in US judgments[158] and has been praised for 'candidly' acknowledging that traditional modes of judicial reasoning are limited.[159]

[152] Pearce and Geddes (n 116) 255–59.

[153] Meagher, 'The Principle of Legality and the Judicial Protection of Rights—*Evans v New South Wales*' (n 15) 309.

[154] Ibid, 310.

[155] *Jacobellis v Ohio* (1964) 378 US 184.

[156] Ibid, 197 (emphasis added).

[157] Indeed, a level of fame which the judge himself came to regret: P Gewirtz, 'On "I Know It When I See It"' (1996) 105 *Yale Law Journal* 1023, 1025, *Quin* (n 7).

[158] Variants have been noted in other jurisdictions, such as the 'well known elephant test' cited by Stuart-Smith LJ in *Cadogan Estates Ltd v Morris* [1998] EWCA Civ 1671 [17].

[159] RA Posner, *Law and Literature: A Misunderstood Relation* (Cambridge, Mass, Harvard University Press, 1988) 308.

It has inspired at least one lengthy analysis and defence.[160] It is not our purpose to determine whether Stewart J was a model for a more sensitive kind of judicial method, which goes beyond the merely rational to take account of the emotional realm.[161] Our comment is simply that Stewart J determined an issue about contested values through the application of an inherently subjective standard: *he* would know hard-core pornography when *he* saw it.[162] Such a standard is by definition impossible to replicate and lacks even the doubtful justification of being sourced to 'community values'.[163]

This is not to deny that some judicial decisions should be made intuitively, rather than as a result of extensive consideration of evidence.[164] Standards, such as the *Wednesbury* ground of judicial review, which have been applied in Australia qualitatively to exclude only the most extreme cases,[165] can be properly applied with alacrity. If it is not clear upon the first examination whether the ground has been made out, the situation is unlikely to become clearer following extensive consideration because what is being looked for is a flagrant breach of the norm. The difference between such an application of a qualitative ground of review and a decision based upon values-laden findings is that, as much as it has been suspected or even feared for straying too close to the merits,[166] *Wednesbury* has had a relatively stable and well-understood content. This is certainly the case in Australia, where for many years it was given almost the minimum possible scope, but is also true of other countries, such as Canada and the UK. Any decision based upon a determination of values is more likely to draw extensively from the judge's subjective views.[167]

This problem is clearly not limited to unreasonableness, whether in the form of *Wednesbury* or something else. It is a mistake to think that judges can apply a strictly mechanical, value-free method which, in judicial review matters, determines nothing more than the limits of jurisdiction.[168] Stephen Gageler has noted that patrolling the express statutory limits of authority

[160] Gewirtz, 'On "I Know It When I See It"' (n 157).

[161] Ibid, 1028–38.

[162] Professor Gewirtz conceded this point, although he evidently did not see it as a problem: ibid 1037–38.

[163] Basten JA acknowledged the difficulty of such a standard in an extra-curial address: The Hon Justice Basten, 'Judging Community Standards and Mores' (Roseville Rotary Club, 17 April 2013).

[164] See G Weeks, 'Litigating Questions of Quality' (2007) 14 *Australian Journal of Administrative Law* 76, 81–83.

[165] This interpretation is now subject to the High Court's decision in *Minister for Immigration and Citizenship v Li* (n 6).

[166] *Quin* (n 7) 36–37 (Brennan J).

[167] Judges, like anyone else, have varying degrees of familiarity with concepts that are considered to be well-understood in the wider populace: see F Dominello, 'Popular Culture' in AR Blackshield, M Coper and G Williams (eds), *The Oxford Companion to the High Court of Australia* (South Melbourne, Vic, Oxford University Press, 2001).

[168] See *SDAV* (n 39) 49–50 [27] (Hill, Branson and Stone JJ).

is rather less difficult than keeping administrative decision-makers within the limits of terms merely implied by statute, but that function invites more questions than it usually answers. He asked:[169]

> What are the limits to be implied? By what standards are implications to be drawn? Is truly value-free implication possible? Is it even desirable? Can the result in *Plaintiff S157/2002*[170] itself be adequately explained except by reference to values? Under the rubric of jurisdictional error, we have perhaps already reached the point where some limitations on power will be implied by way of presumption in the absence of a tolerably clear manifestation of legislative intention to the contrary. If so, what is it precisely that gives rise to the relevant presumption?

Jurisdictional error describes when courts have the capacity to grant remedies in judicial review proceedings but it tells us nothing about what values apply in determining its ambit. Nonetheless, it is clear that the High Court, of which Gageler J is now a member, must be driven by such values. What are they, and how do we find out? The answer might lie in the possibility that the values in question are not to be inferred from the character of the nation as a whole, but are instead a set of objectively observable values which attach not to the people but to the *law*. The existence of 'administrative law values' has been assumed by several leading authors,[171] albeit with the caveat that such a list cannot be finite.[172] Precisely where the interpretive approach of Australian courts, or the novel one taken in *Li* specifically, fit within a list of values is unclear, though we suggest that later cases exploring the boundaries and requirements of *Li* may also shed some light on just what the High Court was mindful to protect.

V. CONCLUSION

The rebirth of judicial review in the 1960s is a common article of faith.[173] So is the idea that the subsequent developments in judicial review were for the good of most.[174] The reality, as always, is more complicated than such a brief account can reflect but, with that reservation, such a version

[169] Gageler, 'Impact of Migration Law on the Development of Australian Administrative Law' (n 29) 104–105.

[170] *Plaintiff S157* (n 36).

[171] See, eg M Taggart, 'Reinvented Government, Traffic Lights and the Convergence of Public and Private Law' [1999] *Public Law* 124, 127–28; Aronson and Groves, *Judicial Review of Administrative Action* (n 121) 1 (values as 'ideals of good government according to law').

[172] C Harlow and R Rawlings, *Law and Administration*, 3rd edn (Cambridge, Cambridge University Press, 2009) 48.

[173] Credit for this is frequently given to the judges who decided a trinity of cases, being *Padfield v Minister of Agriculture, Fisheries and Food* [1968] AC 997; *Anisminic Ltd v Foreign Compensation Commission* [1969] 2 AC 147; *Ridge v Baldwin* [1964] AC 40.

[174] Taggart, 'Proportionality, Deference, *Wednesbury*' (n 1) 429.

of history is generally true.[175] Australia was again the exception to many of the most 'aggressively' developed grounds of review—as Mike Taggart put it, Australia was 'once again ... out of step' with the common-law world.[176] Although we concede that Australia is something of an easy mark for those who would either point out the comparative joylessness of its judicial review tradition or—as Taggart deftly did—express concern that 'Australian exceptionalism [might become] isolationism',[177] we contend that Australia is isolated from the more free-wheeling developments of judicial review in the common-law world only so far as Australian courts have imposed constitutional constraints upon themselves. Those constraints appear to weigh against a variable intensity standard, along with many other novel principles of judicial review, so far as it is expressed as a danger to the merits/review divide.

Whether that wider position is one of isolation is another matter. More difficult still is the question whether isolation is an entirely bad thing, since it largely reflects Australia's adherence to a mode of governance which suits it well, even if one accepts that the borders upon which power is divided and allocated are less than clear. Some consider Australia fortunate that its judicial branch is not given the multitude of tasks and the expectation of 'righting every wrong' which appears to have become the lot of the English judiciary. The controversy generated by that task has become a political football in England.[178] Australia has at least not experienced the adoption of a Bill or Charter of Rights only then to experience the same problem, but it has experienced a political and constitutional battle about migration law on a scale like no other nation. The strong constitutional principles devised by Australian courts have allowed them to cast a veil of constitutional legitimacy over much of their decision-making, so that they may regularly stymie important government policies or legislation but in the guise of courts and judges simply performing their constitutional duty. *Li* marks a curious step beyond that hitherto protected position because it seems almost destined to draw courts more closely into the heart of decision-making. Where that first step may lead remains to be seen.

[175] For example, *Anisminic* (n 173) is often cited as the modern origin of the decline of jurisdictional error in English law, without recognition that the doctrine was central to the reasoning in that case.

[176] Taggart, 'Proportionality, Deference, *Wednesbury*' (n 1) 429, fn 29.

[177] Taggart, 'Australian Exceptionalism' (n 2) 30.

[178] The senior party in the UK's ruling coalition may seek a referendum to withdraw from the ECHR (www.letbritaindecide.com). The plans of the Conservative Party seem elusive. A senior Minister of the coalition government has continually criticised 'Labour's Human Rights Act' and has suggested repeal of that statute followed by the enactment of one that supposedly ensures the primacy of British, rather than European, courts and legal principles. See: www.conservativehome.com/platform/2014/10/chris-grayling-mp-our-plan-to-protect-human-rights-while-making-the-european-court-advisory-only.html.

7

A Rainbow of One Colour? Judicial Review on Substantive Grounds in South African Law

CORA HOEXTER*

I. INTRODUCTION

AFTER CENTURIES OF white minority rule and more than 40 years of institutionalised racial oppression, constitutional democracy was introduced into South Africa two decades ago. A justiciable Bill of Rights appeared in the interim Constitution of 1993[1] and is also a feature of the 'final' Constitution of 1996;[2] and the many rights listed there are protected by the principle of constitutional supremacy[3] and an express limitation clause.[4]

Rights to just administrative action were a dramatic innovation in section 24 of the interim Constitution and subsequently in section 33 of the 1996 Constitution. By virtue of section 33, everyone acquired an unqualified right to administrative action that is lawful, reasonable and procedurally fair, as well as a more qualified right to written reasons for administrative action.[5]

* Professor of Law, University of the Witwatersrand, Johannesburg.

[1] Constitution of the Republic of South Africa, Act 200 of 1993, which entered into force on 27 April 1994.

[2] Constitution of the Republic of South Africa, 1996 (hereafter simply 'the Constitution' except where the context calls for qualification). Most provisions came into force on 4 February 1997.

[3] Section 2 states: 'This Constitution is the supreme law of the Republic; law or conduct inconsistent with it is invalid, and the obligations imposed by it must be fulfilled.' Supremacy of the Constitution is also a founding value in terms of s 1*(c)* of the Constitution.

[4] In terms of s 36, a limitation of rights may be justified if it is shown to be 'reasonable and justifiable in an open and democratic society based on human dignity, equality and freedom'. In order to qualify, however, any such limitation must be authorised by 'a law of general application'.

[5] Section 33, headed 'Just administrative action', reads as follows:

(1) Everyone has the right to administrative action that is lawful, reasonable and procedurally fair.

These new rights changed the orientation of South African administrative law ineluctably. Previously judicial review had always had a common-law basis; now it was constitutionalised and indeed 'righted'. Rights-based review became the norm in respect of exercises of public power, and common-law review became the exception:[6] a pathway to review reserved for exercises of *private* power that had traditionally been reviewable, such as the disciplinary decisions of churches and clubs. Importantly, too, judicial review no longer existed at the mercy of parliamentary sovereignty, but was now guaranteed by the supremacy of the Constitution.[7]

Given the sweeping nature of section 33, there was an understandable fear of what the effects might be of unleashing this right on an unprepared public administration. Section 33(3) of the Constitution thus mandated national legislation to 'give effect to' the rights in section 33(1) and (2) by a certain date, failing which the section 33 rights would apply directly. The legislation would provide detail and also limit the scope of the rights to some extent, it was understood—and this impression was reinforced by the constitutional mandate to 'promote an efficient administration'.[8] Draft legislation was produced by the South African Law Reform Commission in August 1999[9] and, after rather heavy amendment by Parliament, was enacted in the form of the Promotion of Administrative Justice Act 3 of 2000 (PAJA). The statute entered into force at the end of that same year and thus became the primary or default pathway to judicial review in administrative law.

(2) Everyone whose rights have been adversely affected by administrative action has the right to be given written reasons.
(3) National legislation must be enacted to give effect to these rights, and must–
  (a) provide for the review of administrative action by a court or, where appropriate, an independent and impartial tribunal;
  (b) impose a duty on the state to give effect to the rights in subsections (1) and (2); and
  (c) promote an efficient administration.

[6] The position is thus quite different from jurisdictions where common-law review is still regarded as the standard or dominant type and human rights review as somewhat atypical. As to the bifurcation between the two in the UK, see, further, J Varuhas, 'Against Unification' (ch 5 in this volume); and for a survey of several jurisdictions in relation to proportionality review, see C Geiringer, 'Process and Outcome in Judicial Review of Public Authority Compatibility with Human Rights: A Comparative Perspective' (ch 13 in this volume).

[7] See, further, C Hoexter, 'The Constitutionalization and Codification of Judicial Review in South Africa' in C Forsyth and others (eds), *Effective Judicial Review: A Cornerstone of Good Governance* (Oxford, Oxford University Press, 2010) 43, 46.

[8] See s 33(3)*(c)*, and see, further, C Hoexter, *Administrative Law in South Africa*, 2nd edn (Cape Town, Juta & Co Ltd, 2012) 245–47.

[9] The Law Commission's project committee (of which I was a member) began work in January 1999 and managed to issue its *Report on Administrative Justice* with draft legislation in August of that year. A few weeks earlier, in July, it had benefited tremendously from a workshop of experts convened by Professor Jeffrey Jowell QC at Leeds Castle in Kent. Participants in this star-studded event included Professors Michael Asimow, Paul Craig, David Mullan, Jost Pietzcker, Cheryl Saunders and Michael Taggart.

The PAJA is considerably more hedged about than the constitutional rights, and some of the grounds of review listed in section 6 of the statute are more conservative than those proposed by the Law Commission. In spite of this, substantive grounds of review have burgeoned since its enactment. As I shall explain in part II of this essay, the PAJA's *Wednesbury*-like ground of unreasonableness has been interpreted liberally by the Constitutional Court, and a new substantive ground has been created by the Supreme Court of Appeal[10] to allow for review of non-jurisdictional mistakes of fact.

Another and even more remarkable development dealt with in part III of this essay is the virtual collapse of a scheme of twin-track review that developed early in the democratic era. This scheme initially allowed for more intense scrutiny of 'administrative action' in terms of section 33 and the PAJA and considerably less intense scrutiny of non-administrative action under a residual principle of legality, seeming to evoke Taggart's preference for bifurcation between cases implicating rights and those involving mere 'public wrongs'.[11] But the content of principle of legality has developed so rapidly that it has begun to resemble review under the PAJA itself. In particular, the differences between 'minimum' rationality and rationality under the PAJA have become blurred, and the requirement of rationality has itself spawned further duties in the form of procedural fairness and the giving of reasons. The result is that there is little or no advantage today in bringing a review challenge under the PAJA rather than under the principle of legality. Indeed, with bland disregard for the principle of subsidiarity, the courts have increasingly allowed the legality track to be used even in respect of decisions that may amount to 'administrative action', and have not actually been shown not to qualify as such.

In short, the substantive grounds of review both in and outside the PAJA have expanded to meet what seems to be an insatiable demand and, as Taggart might have described it, any remaining 'accountability vacuum'[12] is capable of being filled—but perhaps at the expense of nuance. Ironically, this burgeoning of substantive review has occurred in the context of the

[10] This court came into being when the Union of South Africa was created in 1910. It was the apex court under its original name, the Appellate Division of the Supreme Court of South Africa. Under the 1996 Constitution it was renamed the Supreme Court of Appeal and, in a system of two highest courts, was the highest court of appeal in all but constitutional matters. By virtue of Constitution Seventeenth Amendment Act of 2012, which came into force on 23 August 2013, the Constitutional Court has now become the apex court in *all* matters, and (notwithstanding its name) the Supreme Court of Appeal has become an intermediate court of appeal between the High Court and the Constitutional Court.

[11] M Taggart, 'Proportionality, Deference, *Wednesbury*' [2008] *New Zealand Law Review* 423, 465ff. In South Africa, review under the principle of legality is akin to 'regular' review in common-law jurisdictions in that it is not centred on rights. But the comparison cannot be pushed too far—for unlike the common law of review, the principle of legality has a constitutional basis.

[12] M Taggart, 'The Province of Administrative Law Determined?' in M Taggart (ed), *The Province of Administrative Law* (Oxford, Hart Publishing, 1997) 1, 3.

courts' increasing acknowledgment of the need for a doctrine of deference or respect in South African administrative law.

In part IV of the essay I offer some reasons that may help to explain these interesting developments.

II. THE COURTS' INTERPRETATION OF SECTION 6 OF THE PAJA

As indicated above, the courts have been bold in their interpretation of the grounds of review in the PAJA. In this part I outline the expansion of the *Wednesbury*-like ground of unreasonableness in section 6(2)*(h)* of the PAJA and the recognition of 'material mistake of fact' as an extension of the existing statutory grounds.

A. Rationality and Unreasonableness

Apart from codifying a number of familiar common-law grounds, such as ulterior purpose and irrelevant considerations, the PAJA contains an explicit ground of 'rational connection' in section 6(2)*(f)*(ii). This provision allows for review of administrative action that is not rationally connected to:

(aa) the purpose for which it was taken;
(bb) the purpose of the empowering provision;
(cc) the information before the administrator; or
(dd) the reasons given for it by the administrator.

This formulation must count as a fairly searching ground of rationality review. On the other hand, it does not seem to add much more than fresh terminology to what would have been implied by the old and well-established common-law grounds of abuse of discretion, such as arbitrariness and 'failure to apply the mind'. As our courts have often said, a rationality test is not the same thing as a test for correctness, and it certainly does not entitle the court to impose its own preferences on the administrator. One High Court judge has expressed this by describing the PAJA ground as 'relatively deferential'.[13] At any rate, the ground evidently did not frighten the legislature. The formulation quoted above was proposed in precisely these terms by the Law Commission, accepted without any amendment by the Parliamentary Portfolio Committee on Justice, and was duly enacted.

In what proved to be a more controversial proposal, the Law Commission put forward a combined ground of review of unreasonableness-plus-

[13] Davis J in *Nieuwoudt v Chairman, Amnesty Subcommittee, Truth and Reconciliation Commission* 2002 (3) SA 143 (C), 155G–H.

disproportionality. The proposed ground was clause 7(1)*(g)* of the Law Commission's Bill, and it allowed for judicial review where

> the effect of the action is unreasonable, including any:–
>
> (i) disproportionality between the adverse and beneficial consequences of the action; and
> (ii) less restrictive means to achieve the purpose for which the action was taken.

This proposal was partly a reaction against the tight constraints of the pre-democratic era, when the courts relied heavily and rather mechanically on the classification of functions to govern and restrict the application of certain grounds of review. Probably the most notorious feature of South Africa's common law was its test of 'symptomatic unreasonableness', for the courts were very reluctant to acknowledge a ground of unreasonableness as such. While the rule in *Kruse v Johnson*[14] offered an exception for decisions that could be labelled 'legislative', and while another exception was eventually created for decisions of a 'purely judicial' nature,[15] it was not possible to review mere 'administrative' decisions whose results were unreasonable. However, the courts were prepared to treat a result of sufficiently *gross* unreasonableness as a symptom of some sort of illegality or irregularity—typically one of the established and safe-sounding grounds of abuse of discretion: mala fides, ulterior 'motive' (which really meant 'purpose') and failure to apply the mind.[16]

This test of 'symptomatic' unreasonableness became even more deferential as time went on, and in a judgment from the 1970s the Appellate Division indicated that only gross unreasonableness of a really 'striking degree' would warrant the inference of abuse of discretion.[17] Interestingly, a similarly restrained formula was proposed by the African National Congress (ANC) during the constitutional negotiations. The ANC, then a liberation movement, evidently foresaw its future as the majority party in government when it proposed a highly deferential test of 'such gross unreasonableness ... as to amount to manifest injustice'.[18]

As to the proportionality-driven nature of the proposed PAJA ground, in the Law Commission's deliberations there was strong support for having proportionality as well as rationality and reasonableness as general grounds in the PAJA. This accorded with the understanding that 'reasonableness'

[14] *Kruse v Johnson* 1898 (2) QB 91.

[15] *Theron v Ring van Wellington van die NG Sendingkerk in Suid-Afrika* 1976 (2) SA 1 (A) established a 'no reasonable evidence' review ground for decisions dubbed 'purely judicial' because they were characterised by the application of rules rather than policy.

[16] *Union Government (Minister of Mines and Industries) v Union Steel Corporation (South Africa) Ltd* 1928 AD 220, 237.

[17] *National Transport Commission v Chetty's Motor Transport (Pty) Ltd* 1972 (3) SA 726 (A), 735G–H.

[18] See the ANC's proposed Bill of Rights in (1991) 7 *South African Journal on Human Rights* 110.

encompassed more than just 'rationality',[19] and that the ingredient of proportionality was what distinguished the two concepts.[20] A few traces of the proportionality doctrine were already to be found in the South African common law: for instance, in a celebrated case involving emergency detention during the 1980s, the Court of first instance had laid emphasis on the element of necessity.[21] There was also academic support for proportionality.[22] It would perhaps be going too far to say that the Law Commission hoped proportionality would introduce 'discipline and restraint', potential benefits that Mullan has identified in the Canadian context.[23] However, it certainly saw proportionality as a way of adding structure, meaning and transparency to the otherwise rather blank concept of unreasonableness.[24]

Most significantly, South Africans had recently discovered the attractions of proportionality as a feature of the limitation clause in the interim Constitution. That provision permitted limitations that were 'necessary' as well as reasonable and justifiable 'in an open and democratic society based on freedom and equality'. Its successor, section 36 of the 1996 Constitution, was a source of even more direct inspiration. This provision includes a list of factors to be taken into account in assessing the justifiability of a limitation, and the last of these (and the most important in practice) is the existence of 'less restrictive means to achieve the purpose' of the limitation. Those words were imported directly into the Law Commission's proposed ground of review for unreasonableness.

As things turned out, however, the wording of the proposed ground did not find favour with the legislature's Portfolio Committee on Justice. It was ultimately omitted from the PAJA, and replaced with a *Wednesbury*-type ground of unreasonableness. Its replacement, section 6(2)*(h)* of the PAJA, enables a court to review administrative action where

> the exercise of the power or the performance of the function authorised by the empowering provision, in pursuance of which the administrative action was purportedly taken, is so unreasonable that no reasonable person could have so exercised the power or performed the function.

[19] A view confirmed by the Constitutional Court in cases such as *Bel Porto School Governing Body v Premier, Western Cape* [2002] ZACC 2; 2002 (3) SA 265 (CC), [46] and *Khosa v Minister of Social Development* [2004] ZACC 11; 2004 (6) SA 505 (CC), [67].

[20] For judicial support, see, eg *Roman v Williams NO* 1998 (1) SA 270 (C), 282C and 284I; *Eastern Metropolitan Substructure v Peter Klein Investments (Pty) Ltd* 2001 (4) SA 661 (W), [36]; the minority judgment of Mokgoro and Sachs JJ in *Bel Porto SGB* (n 19) [166]; and that of Sachs J in *Minister of Health v New Clicks South Africa (Pty) Ltd* [2005] ZACC 14; 2006 (2) SA 311 (CC), [637].

[21] *Dempsey v Minister of Law and Order* 1986 (4) SA 530 (C), overturned on appeal in *Minister of Law and Order v Dempsey* 1988 (3) SA 19 (A).

[22] See, eg JR de Ville, 'Proportionality as a Requirement of Legality in Administrative Law in Terms of the New Constitution' (1994) 9 *SA Public Law* 360.

[23] D Mullan, 'Proportionality—A Proportionate Response to an Emerging Crisis in Canadian Judicial Review Law?' [2010] *New Zealand Law Review* 233, 264.

[24] See, further, in this regard P Craig, 'Proportionality, Rationality and Review' [2010] *New Zealand Law Review* 265.

Like the definition of a 'decision' in section 1 of the PAJA, which was taken almost verbatim from Australia's Administrative Decisions (Judicial Review) Act 1977 (Cth), this ground seems to have been inspired by the Australian legislation.[25]

Whatever its provenance, the section 6(2)*(h)* ground dismayed many South African administrative lawyers. Not only did it omit any reference to proportionality, but its cautious and circular formulation seemed to resonate with our conservative pre-1994 common law and to be quite out of step with the new and progressive Constitution. In truth, the wording of section 6(2)*(h)* was less extreme than any of the pre-democratic formulations outlined above. Nevertheless, it was a highly unpopular choice with the academy—a group consisting mostly of white liberals who were steeped in scholarly criticism of *Wednesbury* and determined not to perpetuate the exaggerated deference associated with the pre-1994 era.

We need not have worried. Within three years of the coming into force of the PAJA the Constitutional Court had an opportunity to pronounce on the meaning and scope of section 6(2)*(h)* in *Bato Star Fishing (Pty) Ltd v Minister of Environmental Affairs*.[26] There the Court interpreted section 6(2)(*h*) as simply a test of unreasonableness rather than gross unreasonableness. This was partly on the basis of section 33(1) of the Constitution, for the Court found that the provision had to be interpreted in conformity with the constitutional right and its standard of unqualified reasonableness.

Referring to the approach of Lord Cooke in *International Trader's Ferry*,[27] O'Regan J held that a decision will be reviewable if it is one that a reasonable decision-maker could not reach.[28] This would always depend on the circumstances of the case, and the Court laid down various factors for deciding what is reasonable in a particular case. Notably, some of these factors seem to invite a proportionality inquiry. Apart from the nature of the decision, the identity of the decision-maker and the reasons given for the decision, O'Regan J mentioned 'the range of factors relevant to the decision', 'the nature of the competing interests involved' and the impact of the decision 'on the lives and well-being of those affected'.[29] So proportionality, rejected by Parliament, seemed to be brought in by the back door.

Proportionality in the sense of balance is given further expression in the concept of 'reasonable equilibrium' that was popularised by *Bato Star*. The challenge in this instance was brought by an aggrieved applicant who had been awarded a smaller deep-sea fishing quota for hake than it had applied for under the Marine Living Resources Act 18 of 1998. Such allocations

[25] Sections 5(2)*(g)* and 6(2)*(g)* of the Australian Act both refer to 'an exercise of a power that is so unreasonable that no reasonable person could have so exercised the power'.

[26] *Bato Star Fishing (Pty) Ltd v Minister of Environmental Affairs* 2004 ZACC 15; 2004 (4) SA 490 (CC).

[27] *R v Chief Constable of Sussex, ex p International Trader's Ferry Ltd* [1999] 2 AC 418.

[28] *Bato Star Fishing* (n 26) [44].

[29] Ibid, [45].

are a nice illustration of complex decision-making, as they involve large numbers of applicants and widely ranging criteria, some of which are in tension with each other. In *Bato Star* the administrator had to take account of the need to admit new entrants from previously disadvantaged communities while not losing sight of the importance of experience, past performance and past investment in the fishing industry. The Court judged the decision in this instance to be reasonable, since a reasonable equilibrium had been struck between the various competing considerations.[30] Since then the idea of reasonable equilibrium has been used in a number of cases. In a challenge to the appointment of a school principal, for instance, the Supreme Court of Appeal ruled that the administrator had failed to reach a reasonable equilibrium between the various interests that had to be taken into account: it had given too much weight to equity considerations and had disregarded other factors such as the interests of the governing body and of the school itself.[31]

Notably, *Bato Star* was also the Constitutional Court's first explicit attempt to enunciate a doctrine of deference or respect in South African administrative law. The need for such a doctrine, and some tentative suggestions of my own in this regard, had been acknowledged by Cameron JA for the Supreme Court of Appeal in *Logbro Properties CC v Bedderson NO*[32] a year or two before, and had been taken further by the same Court in the *Bato Star* matter itself.[33] There Schutz JA had recognised that:[34]

> Judicial deference is particularly appropriate where the subject-matter of an administrative action is very technical or of a kind in which a Court has no particular proficiency. We cannot even pretend to have the skills and access to knowledge that is available to the Chief Director. It is not our task to better his allocations, unless we should conclude that his decision cannot be sustained on rational grounds. That I cannot say. Accordingly I am of the view that the attack based on capriciousness must also fail.

On further appeal to the Constitutional Court, O'Regan J conceived of deference or 'respect' (her preferred term)[35] as flowing from the separation of powers. It was constitutionally appropriate, she held, for a court to show respect to a decision 'that requires an equilibrium to be struck between a

[30] Ibid, [49]–[54].

[31] *Head, Western Cape Education Department v Governing Body, Point High School* [2008] ZASCA 48; 2008 (5) SA 18 (SCA), [16].

[32] *Logbro Properties CC v Bedderson NO* [2002] ZASCA 135; 2003 (2) SA 460 (SCA), [20]–[22], referring to C Hoexter, 'The Future of Judicial Review in South African Administrative Law' (2000) 117 *South African Law Journal* 484, 501–502.

[33] *Minister of Environmental Affairs and Tourism v Phambili Fisheries (Pty) Ltd; Minister of Environmental Affairs and Tourism v Bato Star Fishing (Pty) Ltd* 2003 ZASCA 46; 2003 (6) SA 407 (SCA).

[34] Ibid, [53].

[35] *Bato Star Fishing* (n 26) [46]–[47]. As she explained there, 'respect' was preferable because it lacked the 'overtones of servility' mentioned by Lord Hoffmann in *R (on the application of Prolife Alliance) v British Broadcasting Corporation* [2003] UKHL 23; [2004] 1 AC 185, [75]–[76].

range of competing interests or considerations and which is to be taken by a person or institution with specific expertise in that area'.[36]

This conception of deference has since served in a few cases to explain the courts' reluctance to interfere with a complex decision taken by an administrator with some expertise in the matter.[37] But the doctrine has not developed beyond this, a point I shall return to in the last part of this essay.

B. Non-Jurisdictional Mistake of Fact

The Constitutional Court's expansive interpretation of section 6(2)*(h)* of the PAJA in *Bato Star* is more than matched by the creation of a new ground of review by the Supreme Court of Appeal. In 2003 this court boldly set about establishing the ground of 'material mistake of fact' and reading it into an existing ground of review in the PAJA. Material mistake of fact has since become a prominent ground of review that is typically relied on where a decision has been made on the basis of inaccurate information placed before an administrator.

Again, the historical background is illuminating. The South African common law had always followed the English tradition of distinguishing between jurisdictional and non-jurisdictional errors. The former were reviewable, the latter not. As regards errors of law, the dichotomy lost much of its force after the important case of *Hira v Booysen* in 1992,[38] where the Appellate Division found a new basis on which to identify reviewable errors of law. This was linked to the intention of the legislature, and depended on whether the power in question was highly discretionary or required more objective ('judicial') judgement. But the law remained unchanged in relation to non-jurisdictional errors of fact, the last bastion of the distinction between appeal and review. As a High Court explained it in 1997,[39]

> it is not open to this Court to set aside a discretionary decision by a functionary, acting within his powers, merely because he made a mistake of fact … Where the

[36] *Bato Star Fishing* (n 26) [48].

[37] Examples include *Associated Institutions Pension Fund v Van Zyl* [2004] ZASCA 78; 2005 (2) SA 302 (SCA), [39] (a case involving actuarial calculations); *Joubert v National Commissioner for the South African Police Service* [2005] ZAGPHC 238 (decision of medical board); *Lazarides v Chairman of the Firearms Appeal Board* [2005] ZAGPHC 221 (decision of firearm appeal board); *Foodcorp (Pty) Ltd v Deputy Director-General, Department of Environmental Affairs and Tourism: Branch Marine and Coastal Management* [2005] ZAWCHC 59; 2006 (2) SA 199 (C), 211G–H (allocation of fishing quotas); *Laingville Fisheries (Pty) Ltd v Minister of Environmental Affairs and Tourism* [2008] ZAECHC 28 (allocation of fishing quotas); *Corrans v MEC for the Department of Sport, Recreation, Arts and Culture* [2009] ZAECGHC 17; 2009 (5) SA 512 (ECG), [21]–[23] (decision of heritage authority); *Legal Aid Board v The State* [2010] ZASCA 112, [45]–[49] (decision of Legal Aid Board).

[38] *Hira v Booysen* [1992] ZASCA 112; 1992 (4) SA 69 (A).

[39] *De Freitas v Somerset West Municipality* 1997 (3) SA 1080 (C), 1084E–H.

> functionary had the power to decide and applied his mind, the decision can as a general rule not be set aside, even if on the merits it is 'wrong' and in making it the functionary made an error of fact. To hold otherwise would be to turn basic principles of administrative law relating to discretionary decisions on their heads.

Non-jurisdictional mistakes of fact could, in theory at least, be challenged on the traditional grounds of abuse of discretion. One could, for instance, claim failure to apply the mind or, to use the more modern terminology, irrationality. But these grounds were practically useless in most instances, and inevitably so where incorrect facts had been placed before the decision-maker by another official. The decision would be bad, but not as a result of irrationality or a lack of good faith.

When the PAJA was enacted, it generously acknowledged the position after *Hira v Booysen* by allowing for review where administrative action 'was materially influenced by an error of law' (section 6(2)*(d)*). It also acknowledged the reviewability of jurisdictional mistakes of fact by allowing for review where 'a mandatory and material procedure or condition prescribed by an empowering provision was not complied with'. Unsurprisingly, no mention was made of non-jurisdictional mistakes of fact. But this did not deter the Supreme Court of Appeal when, in *Pepcor Retirement Fund v Financial Services Board*,[40] it created 'material mistake of fact' as a new ground of review. The Court did not actually rely on the PAJA at all, as the dispute had arisen before the statute came into force. Instead the Court relied mainly on the constitutional principle of legality, a topic discussed in more detail below.[41] It took inspiration also from dicta in English law. It referred in particular to the judgment of Scarman LJ in the *Tameside* case,[42] and to Lord Slynn's acknowledgment of the need for such a ground of review in the case of *R v Criminal Injuries Compensation Board, ex p A*.[43]

The problem in *Pepcor* was that a decision had been made by the Registrar of Pension Funds on the basis of what proved to be incorrect actuarial information provided to him. The financial consequences were considerable, and the Registrar went to court seeking to have his own decision set aside. Cloete JA held for the Supreme Court of Appeal:[44]

> In my view, a material mistake of fact should be a basis on which a Court can review an administrative action. If legislation has empowered a functionary to make a decision, in the public interest, the decision should be made on the

[40] *Pepcor Retirement Fund v Financial Services Board* [2003] ZASCA 56; 2003 (6) SA 38 (SCA).

[41] Part III.

[42] *Secretary of State for Education and Science v Tameside Metropolitan Borough Council* [1977] AC 1014.

[43] *R v Criminal Injuries Compensation Board, ex p A* [1999] 2 AC 330, 344G–345C.

[44] *Pepcor Retirement Fund v FSB* (n 40) [47].

> material facts which should have been available for the decision properly to have been made. And if a decision has been made in ignorance of facts material to the decision and which therefore should have been before the functionary, the decision should … be reviewable … The doctrine of legality … requires that the power conferred on a functionary to make decisions in the public interest, should be exercised properly, ie on the basis of true facts; it should not be confined to cases where the common law would categorise the decision as *ultra vires*.

The ground would not apply in an absolute fashion, the Court explained, for factors such as the public interest and any prejudice to one or other of the parties would be relevant to the reviewability of mistake of fact in a particular case.[45] In this instance, however, there were no factors militating against reviewability. On the contrary, there was a strong public interest in the proper regulation of pension funds and no question of prejudice to either of the parties.[46]

In *Pepcor* the Court suggested that for purposes of the PAJA, the new ground of material mistake of fact could be encompassed by or be regarded as an extension of the existing ground of section 6(2)*(e)*(iii): taking into account irrelevant considerations or failing to take into account relevant ones. This suggestion was taken up by the Supreme Court of Appeal in *Chairpersons' Association v Minister of Arts and Culture*,[47] which concerned a decision to change the name of a town. Here the Minister had approved the name change on the basis of a memorandum from his Director-General. The memorandum gave the impression that the community had been properly consulted about the proposed change, which turned out not to be so, and the Court set aside the approval on the basis of section 6(2)*(e)*(iii) of the PAJA.[48]

As to the limits of the ground of review, the Supreme Court of Appeal stressed in *Pepcor* and has reiterated since that the ground should not be employed 'so as to blur, far less eliminate' the fundamental distinction between review and appeal.[49] By way of an example, it suggested that a court would not be able to interfere on this ground where a functionary has been entrusted with 'both the power to determine what facts are relevant to the making of a decision, and the power to determine whether or not they exist'.[50] But this example was not a particularly helpful one, for in such

[45] Ibid, [49].

[46] Ibid, [48].

[47] *Chairpersons' Association v Minister of Arts and Culture* [2007] ZASCA 44; 2007 (5) SA 236 (SCA).

[48] In a subsequent case, *Chairman, State Tender Board v Digital Voice Processing (Pty) Ltd* [2011] ZASCA 202; 2012 (2) SA 16 (SCA), [34], Plasket AJA pointed out that the ground could just as easily be accommodated under s 6(2)(i) of the PAJA, the catch-all ground of 'otherwise unconstitutional or unlawful'.

[49] *Pepcor Retirement Fund v FSB* (n 40) [48], and see also, eg *Government Employees Pension Fund v Buitendag* [2006] ZASCA 166; 2007 (4) SA 2 (SCA), [12].

[50] *Pepcor Retirement Fund v FSB* (n 40) [48].

a situation an error would surely be reviewable in any event as a matter of *jurisdictional* fact. Clearer limits have been set in the most recent case, *Dumani v Nair*,[51] where Cloete JA wrote a separate judgment outlining the development of material mistake of fact so far. The ground should not be confused with an appeal, he said, particularly because it does not entitle the decision-maker to consider the matter afresh and also because it is confined to facts that are established in the sense of being 'uncontentious and objectively verifiable'.[52] This qualification was again inspired by dicta in English law,[53] and its purpose is to mark off an area of judgment that is the administrator's preserve.[54] In *Dumani's* case it meant that a presiding officer's assessment of evidence in a disciplinary matter was not reviewable on the ground of material mistake of fact.

Material mistake of non-jurisdictional fact is now well-established as a ground of review in South African law. Meanwhile, there has also been significant development in the area of jurisdictional facts. Until 2008 South African law observed the distinction, made famous by *Liversidge v Anderson*,[55] between jurisdictional facts that are required to exist in an objective sense and those that need merely exist in the subjective judgement of the administrator—signalled by subjective language such as 'if in his opinion' or 'is satisfied'. In *Walele v City of Cape Town*, however, where an 'is satisfied' clause was in issue, the Constitutional Court held as follows:[56]

> In the past, when unreasonableness was not taken as a self-standing ground for review, the [decision-maker's] *ipse dixit* could have been adequate. But that is no longer the position in our law. More is now required if the decision-maker's opinion is challenged on the basis that the subjective precondition did not exist. The decision-maker must now show that the subjective opinion was based on reasonable grounds.

The result is that in South African law all jurisdictional facts are objectively justiciable today, quite irrespective of their wording.[57]

[51] *Dumani v Nair* [2012] ZASCA 196; 2013 (2) SA 274 (SCA).

[52] Ibid, [32].

[53] Cloete JA referred to *E v Secretary of State for the Home Department* [2004] EWCA Civ 49, [2004] QB 1044, [66] (Carnwath LJ). See, further, Forsyth and Dring, 'The Final Frontier' (n 7) 245, 250ff.

[54] See Forsyth and Dring (n 53) 258.

[55] *Liversidge v Anderson* [1942] AC 206.

[56] Jafta AJ in *Walele v City of Cape Town* [2008] ZACC 11; 2008 (6) SA 129 (CC), [60] (footnotes omitted), confirming an approach presaged in High Court judgments such as *Camps Bay Ratepayers and Residents' Association v Minister of Planning, Culture and Administration, Western Cape* 2001 (4) SA 294 (C), 321B–C.

[57] See, further, C Plasket, 'Playing Catch-Up: The South African Constitution, Administrative Law and Jurisdictional Facts' in M Carnelley and S Hoctor (eds), *Law, Order and Liberty: Essays in Honour of Tony Mathews* (Scottsville, University of KwaZulu-Natal Press, 2011) 75.

III. TWIN-TRACK REVIEW AND ITS COLLAPSE

The second main phenomenon I want to highlight in this essay is a scheme of twin-track review that was developed by the Constitutional Court—and its virtual collapse in recent years. This scheme initially allowed for more intense scrutiny of 'administrative action' in terms of section 33 and the PAJA and considerably less intense scrutiny of non-administrative action under the principle of legality. This bifurcation can be compared to Taggart's preference for higher-intensity review in cases implicating rights and lower-intensity review in other cases.[58] However, there are important differences between it and the bifurcation that has been identified in jurisdictions such as the UK, where common-law review remains the standard or dominant type.[59] In the South African bifurcation both of the tracks are *constitutional* ones: rights-based review is supposed to be the standard type and principle-of-legality review the backstop. Common-law review has no place in this bifurcation and indeed it has very limited relevance nowadays, for its use is confined to exercises of private power that attract the general principles of administrative law. Furthermore, review of administrative action is 'rights-based' in the specific sense that the section 33 rights are implicated. (That said, it is quite usual for other constitutional rights, particularly socio-economic rights, to be implicated as well. Indeed, the array of constitutional rights is so wide that it is difficult to think of administrative action that does not touch one or another of them.)

The principle of legality was evidently envisaged as a residual pathway to review, a track for the review of exercises of public power not amounting to administrative action, and it was held to demand merely lawful authority, good faith and a minimum requirement of rationality. It was to act as a mere backstop or safety net.[60] However, this scheme proved to be of very short duration, for as I explain in this part, the principle of legality has acquired a vibrant life of its own. Evidence of this is that the ground of material mistake of fact was created with reference to it.[61] Recently the supposedly low-intensity rationality test associated with the principle of legality has become far more rigorous in practice, to the extent that it now mimics the harder-look rationality ground listed in the PAJA. And most dramatically, the element of rationality has spawned further requirements of good administration. In recent cases it has been held respectively to demand procedural fairness and the giving of reasons—a feat achieved quite simply by characterising procedural fairness as an obvious aid to rationality, and reason-giving as essential evidence of rationality. So in

[58] Taggart, 'Proportionality, Deference, *Wednesbury*' (n 11).
[59] See, further, Varuhas (n 6) and Geiringer (n 6).
[60] See *Minister of Health v New Clicks South Africa* (n 20) [97].
[61] See part II.

a very short time the principle of legality has expanded into something resembling the PAJA itself.

A. The Early Development of the Principle of Legality

In the pre-1994 era virtually any official conduct was reviewable in administrative law. Thus all official conduct had to comply with the basic requirements of legality, such as the need for lawful authority and jurisdiction. However, not all of it could be reviewed on the far more burdensome grounds of unreasonableness and procedural fairness for, as already indicated in relation to the former, the 'classification of functions' was used as a device to restrict the application of such grounds of review.[62] This position was almost reversed under the 1996 Constitution, since under section 33(1) everyone acquired unqualified rights to be treated lawfully, reasonably and fairly by officialdom. Under section 33(1), then, all the grounds of review evidently applied in all cases—but only if the action in question qualified as 'administrative action'. Other action was apparently immune from challenge.

The new demarcation was wholly unfamiliar to South Africans, and the Constitution offered no definition of it. It thus fell to the courts to work out the meaning of 'administrative action', and the Constitutional Court, in particular, was soon given several opportunities to distinguish such action from decisions having a legislative or executive character, say (for as in most jurisdictions today, it is not the functionary but the nature of the function that counts). As it elaborated on the meaning of the term, it was apparent to the Court that a safety net of some sort would have to be developed to deal with exercises of public power that were not administrative but that nevertheless required some degree of public-law control. So it began the process of replicating some of the ordinary requirements of administrative law and making them applicable to *all* exercises of public power.

The Court first identified the principle of legality in 1998 in the *Fedsure* case,[63] at a time when the interim Constitution still applied. The question in *Fedsure* was the nature of resolutions made by a city council relating to its budget. The Court held that the resolutions clearly did not amount to administrative action under the interim Constitution because in making

[62] Classification of this kind and for this purpose eventually fell out of favour in the late 1980s, and its complete abandonment in the context of procedural fairness was noted by the Appellate Division in *South African Roads Board v Johannesburg City Council* 1991 (4) SA 1 (A), 10J.

[63] *Fedsure v Greater Johannesburg Metropolitan Council* [1998] ZACC 17; 1999 (1) SA 374 (CC).

them, the council had acted as a deliberative legislative body and had exercised original law-making power.[64] But the Court went on to say that, in accordance with the rule of law, local government still had to act within the powers conferred on it.[65] This, it said, was by virtue of the principle of legality, an aspect of the rule of law. The rule of law doctrine itself was not specifically mentioned in the interim Constitution but, the Court held, was nevertheless immanent in it. In a dictum that has been repeated hundreds of times since then, the Court said:[66]

> It seems central to the conception of our constitutional order that the legislature and executive in every sphere are constrained by the principle that they may exercise no power and perform no function beyond that conferred upon them by law.

Significantly, the Court also seemed to see the principle of legality as the more general constitutional counterpart of the right to lawful administrative action.[67]

The Court soon had an opportunity to apply the principle of legality again. The President had appointed a commission of inquiry into the state of rugby in South Africa, and his power to do so was challenged in 1999 in the *SARFU* case.[68] Again, the appointment of such a commission was found not to be administrative action. But, the court emphasised, there were other constraints on the exercise of the President's power, and these included the principle of legality. It added two new ingredients to the principle, requiring the President to act in good faith and not to misconstrue his powers.[69]

A few months after this, the Constitutional Court developed the principle of legality again in a case involving the *Pharmaceutical Manufacturers Association*.[70] This case concerned the Medicines Act,[71] a statute regulating the sale and possession of medicinal drugs, which the President had proclaimed into force on the understanding that various schedules and regulations essential to its enforcement had already been produced. It turned out that they had not been, and their absence made the statute completely unworkable. This situation prompted a challenge to the legality of the proclamation. The Court held that the President's decision to bring a statute into operation lay closer to the legislative than to the administrative process, and did not constitute administrative action. Nevertheless, it was

[64] Ibid, [41], [45].

[65] Ibid, [56].

[66] Ibid, [58].

[67] Ibid, [59].

[68] *President of the Republic of South Africa v South African Rugby Football Union* [1999] ZACC 11; 2000 (1) SA 1 (CC).

[69] Ibid, [148].

[70] *Pharmaceutical Manufacturers Association of SA: Re ex p President of the Republic of South Africa* [2000] ZACC 11; 2000 (2) SA 674 (CC).

[71] South African Medicines and Medical Devices Regulatory Authority Act 132 of 1998.

a requirement of the rule of law that the exercise of public power not be arbitrary. Decisions must be 'rationally related to the purpose for which the power was given, otherwise they are in effect arbitrary', said the Court.[72] And it held that while he had clearly acted in good faith, the President's premature or badly timed exercise of his power was 'objectively irrational' and had to be set aside on that basis.[73] So it was that in this case the crucial requirement of rationality was established as a minimum threshold requirement applicable to the exercise of all public power by members of the executive and other functionaries.[74]

B. The Meaning and Content of Rationality

As conceived and described by the Constitutional Court in *Pharmaceutical Manufacturers Association*, the minimum threshold test of rationality is clearly distinguishable from the more rigorous and searching ground of rationality laid down in section 6(2)*(f)*(ii) of the PAJA (quoted above).[75] The role envisaged for it was evidently that of a safety net for cases of non-administrative action, and indeed the Constitutional Court predicted that findings of 'objective irrationality' would be rare.[76] One example is *Kruger v President of the Republic of South Africa*,[77] where an arbitrary selection of legislative provisions had been proclaimed into force by the President. As in *Pharmaceutical Manufacturers Association*, the proclamation did not count as administrative action; and, as in the earlier case, the Constitutional Court set aside the proclamation as 'objectively irrational'.[78]

More recently, however, the minimum rationality test seems to have become blurred with the PAJA test so that it is becoming more difficult to discern the differences between the two. A notable case in this regard is *SA Predator Breeders' Association*,[79] which concerned a challenge to regulations governing the 'canned hunting' of lions. At the time there was no certainty as to whether regulations qualify as administrative action,[80] so

[72] *Pharmaceutical Manufacturers Association* (n 70) [85].
[73] Ibid, [89] and [90].
[74] Ibid, [90].
[75] Part II A.
[76] *Pharmaceutical Manufacturers Association* (n 70) [90].
[77] *Kruger v President of the Republic of South Africa* [2008] ZACC 17; 2009 (1) SA 417 (CC).
[78] Ibid, [52].
[79] *SA Predator Breeders' Association v Minister of Environmental Affairs and Tourism* [2010] ZASCA 151; [2011] 2 All SA 529 (SCA).
[80] In *Minister of Health v New Clicks* (n 20) the Constitutional Court had been unable to agree on this issue. However, in a case decided before *Predator Breeders' Association*, the Supreme Court of Appeal seems to have assumed that *New Clicks* did decide the question and that regulations are indeed administrative action: *City of Tshwane Metropolitan Municipality v Cable City (Pty) Ltd* [2009] ZASCA 87; 2010 (3) SA 589 (SCA), [10]. Since then, other courts have made the same assumption.

the challenge was brought under the principle of legality and the Court purported to apply the principle in *Pharmaceutical Manufacturers Association*. However, the rationality test actually applied by it resembled that in section 6 of the PAJA. The Court referred not only to the purpose for which the power was given, but also to the need for a rational link between the decision and the facts and information before the decision-maker, and rather tellingly, the Court referred to case law decided under the PAJA ground.[81]

Another case that blurs the distinction is *Democratic Alliance v President of the Republic of South Africa*,[82] a *cause célèbre* concerning the President's decision to appoint a new National Director of Public Prosecutions. There was serious doubt about whether the President's choice, Mr Menzi Simelane, was a 'fit and proper' person of integrity and experience, as required by the Constitution and the relevant legislation. Indeed, the appointment struck many people as perverse: Simelane had been a Director-General of the Department of Justice, and the President was aware that in that capacity his integrity had been impugned by a commission of inquiry and that the Public Service Commission had recommended disciplinary action against him. In the result the legality and rationality of the decision were successfully challenged by a political party, the Democratic Alliance, and the appointment was set aside by the Constitutional Court.

In this case it was common cause that the decision was executive in nature, and the Democratic Alliance did not push for a diagnosis of administrative action. Thus the Court again purported to apply the basic rationality test laid down in *Pharmaceutical Manufacturers Association*. It described this test as the 'lowest possible threshold' and explained that the point of this restrained inquiry was to give the legislature and executive the widest possible latitude within the limits of the Constitution.[83] But in the next breath the Court indicated that there is no difference between the meaning and content of rationality in the two contexts of executive and administrative decision-making. It would be wrong, the Court said, to suppose that 'whether the means are rationally related to the ends in executive decision-making somehow involves a lower threshold' than in the case of administrative action, for:[84]

> Rationality does not conceive of differing thresholds. It cannot be suggested that a decision that would be irrational in an administrative law setting might mutate into a rational decision if the decision being evaluated was an executive one. ... Either the decision is rational or it is not.

[81] *Predator Breeders' Association* (n 79) [28].

[82] *Democratic Alliance v President of the Republic of South Africa* [2012] ZACC 24; 2013 (1) SA 248 (CC). See, further, L Kohn, 'The Burgeoning Constitutional Requirement of Rationality and the Separation of Powers: Has Rationality Review Gone Too Far?' (2013) 130 *South African Law Journal* 810, 833–35.

[83] Ibid, [42], with reference to the Constitutional Court's judgment in *Affordable Medicines Trust v Minister of Health* [2005] ZACC 3; 2006 (3) SA 247 (CC), [83] and [86].

[84] *Democratic Alliance v President* (n 82) [44].

The Court had already indicated that 'both the process by which the decision is made and the decision itself must be rational'.[85] In this regard, 'everything done in the process of taking th[e] decision constitutes means towards the attainment of the purpose for which the power was conferred', including a failure to take into account relevant considerations[86] (in this instance, the doubt cast on Simelane's integrity).

In view of these developments, it is fair to say that the 'lowest possible threshold' bears an increasing resemblance to the more rigorous rationality that is demanded by the PAJA.

C. The Extension of Rationality to Other Principles of Good Administration

In 2009 came the first attempt to make the principle of legality cover procedural fairness as well as legality and rationality. This was in the *Masetlha* case,[87] where the President had dismissed the head of South Africa's National Intelligence Agency, Mr Billy Masetlha, and the question arose whether the President ought to have given him a hearing before firing him. The Court held that this was a special executive type of dismissal that did not attract labour rights or the rights to just administrative action. It was indeed governed by the principle of legality and the rule of law, a doctrine that did not extend as far as procedural fairness.[88] But one member of the court, Ngcobo J, held that the existing requirement of *rationality* demanded procedural fairness. In a dissenting opinion he reasoned that because hearing both sides tends to minimise arbitrariness, it was irrational for the President not to give Masetlha a hearing before firing him.[89]

A year later came the *Albutt* case,[90] which concerned the President's power to pardon offenders in terms of section 84(2)*(j)* of the Constitution. South Africa had established a truth and reconciliation process in the early years of democracy, but not everyone had participated in it. As a sort of mopping-up process, the President announced a special new regime for pardoning offenders who had committed politically motivated offences and who had, for whatever reason, not been part of the earlier process. The aims of the dispensation were to promote reconciliation and nation-building. However, the President decided that victims of such offences or

[85] Ibid, [34].

[86] Ibid, [36], [39] and [40].

[87] *Masetlha v President of the Republic of South Africa* [2007] ZACC 20; 2008 (1) SA 566 (CC).

[88] Ibid, [77]–[78].

[89] Ibid, [184]–[186].

[90] *Albutt v Centre for the Study of Violence and Reconciliation* [2010] ZACC 4; 2010 (3) SA 293 (CC).

their families would not be heard in the pardoning process. This decision was challenged and eventually came before the Constitutional Court under a new Chief Justice, Sandile Ngcobo.

In the Court below[91] it was argued for the President that a pardon involved the use of executive rather than administrative action. But the government lost that round: it was held that the decision was in fact administrative action; that the procedural fairness provisions of the PAJA were applicable; and therefore that victims of an offence would be entitled to a hearing before a presidential pardon could be granted.

On appeal the Constitutional Court agreed that victims had to be heard, but on a different basis. Even though the administrative action question was fully argued before it, the Court was unwilling to confront this issue. The inquiry, it said, would raise all sorts of difficult questions, such as whether this was really action of an executive kind and if so, whether it was permissible for the PAJA to 'reclassify' executive action as administrative action.[92] Instead the court preferred to rely on the principle of legality. Using the existing requirement of rationality as he had done in the *Masetlha* case, Ngcobo CJ reasoned that it would be irrational for the President to pardon offenders without hearing from their victims. The participation of victims was crucial to the achievement of the particular objectives of nation-building and national reconciliation, and the President would not be in a position to establish an offender's motive without hearing both perpetrator and victim.[93]

So the Court did not identify procedural fairness as a separate or independent requirement dictated by the principle of legality, but chose to reason more cautiously. The Chief Justice was also careful to stress that his reasoning did not necessarily apply to all pardons but only to this particular dispensation with its particular objectives, and he criticised the High Court for reasoning in relation to pardons in general[94]—thus leaving plenty of room for future courts to find that rationality demands procedural fairness in some but not necessarily in all cases. But it is difficult to think of a decision whose rationality would not be enhanced by hearing both sides impartially, so there seems plenty of scope for the further development of procedural fairness as a requirement of the rule of law. This tends to be confirmed by the case of *Minister of Home Affairs v Scalabrini Centre*,[95] which concerned a challenge to a decision to close the Cape Town Refugee Reception Office: a piece of non-administrative action, according to the

[91] *Centre for the Study of Violence and Reconciliation v President of the Republic of South Africa* [2009] ZAGPPHC 35.

[92] *Albutt* (n 90) [80].

[93] Ibid, [68] and [70]–[72].

[94] Ibid, [75]–[76].

[95] *Minister of Home Affairs v Scalabrini Centre* [2013] ZASCA 134; 2013 (6) SA 421 (SCA).

Supreme Court of Appeal. Here, too, the Court ruled that that the failure to consult with interested parties before making the decision rendered it irrational—more particularly because the authorities had undertaken to consult with organisations including the respondent on any proposal to close the Cape Town office.[96]

In the *ARMSA* case[97] the Constitutional Court seemed to regret its creativity in *Albutt*. The *ARMSA* matter concerned the President's determination of a salary increase for magistrates, which the Court held was executive rather than administrative action. Responding to an argument that the President ought to have consulted the Association of Regional Magistrates or its members, the Court ignored its previous approach in *Albutt* and simply reasserted the *Masetlha* proposition that unless a hearing is specifically called for by the enabling legislation, procedural fairness is not a requirement for the exercise of executive powers.[98] It went so far as to state that 'a procedural fairness challenge *is not competent* because the decision ... did not amount to administrative action'.[99] This assertion had a somewhat disingenuous air, for no mention was made of the possibility of bringing in procedural fairness via rationality, or that this was actually done in *Albutt*. More recently, however, in *Motau*, the Court was willing to admit that 'procedural fairness obligations may attach independently of a statutory obligation', either as a requirement of rationality or as a stand-alone requirement of the principle of legality, or possibly 'some other principle'.[100]

Meanwhile, it has been established by the Supreme Court of Appeal that the principle of legality may require reasons to be given for non-administrative action. *Judicial Service Commission v Cape Bar Council*[101] concerned a selection decision of the Judicial Service Commission (JSC)—a type of decision that is specifically excluded from the definition of administrative action in the PAJA. The JSC had decided not to recommend certain well-qualified candidates for judicial office, preferring to leave the vacancies open, and it declined to give reasons for its decision. However, the Court

[96] Ibid, [70]–[72].

[97] *Association of Regional Magistrates of Southern Africa v President of the Republic of South Africa* [2013] ZACC 13; 2013 (7) BCLR 762 (CC).

[98] Ibid, [59].

[99] Ibid, (my emphasis).

[100] *Minister of Defence and Military Veterans v Motau* [2014] ZACC 18, [81]–[83], again in the context of executive action. By contrast, the Court has stated that 'fairness is not a requirement in the rationality enquiry' that is applied to original legislation: *Law Society of South Africa v Minister of Transport* [2010] ZACC 25; 2011 (1) SA 400 (CC), [39].

[101] *Judicial Service Commission v Cape Bar Council* [2012] ZASCA 115; 2013 (1) SA 170 (SCA). It had previously been confirmed in *Mphahlele v First National Bank of SA Ltd* [1999] ZACC 1; 1999 (2) SA 667 (CC), [12] that the rule of law requires *judges* to give reasons for their decisions, and in *Wessels v Minister for Justice and Constitutional Development* [2009] ZAGPPHC 81; 2010 (1) SA 128 (GNP) a High Court expressed support, obiter, for the same principle in relation to administrative officials.

reasoned that like all other exercises of public power, the selection of judges has to be performed rationally, in accordance with the principle of legality.[102] It went on to hold that if properly called upon to do so, the JSC had to *demonstrate* that rationality by giving reasons for its decisions—for if this were not so, the JSC would effectively be immune from a challenge based on rationality.[103]

D. The Future of Legality

In constitutional litigation the normal order of things is to rely on a more specific or lower-level norm in preference to a more general or higher-level one. The Constitutional Court has been strict about this principle of subsidiarity in relation to applications for review based on section 33 of the Constitution: it has not allowed litigants to 'go behind' the PAJA by resorting directly to the constitutional rights.[104] One would expect a similar attitude to prevail in relation to the principle of legality. Indeed, it is arguably a norm at an even higher level than section 33, for it has been characterised as the more general constitutional counterpart of the right to lawful administrative action.[105] However, the Court has been strangely tolerant of applications based on the principle of legality instead of the PAJA, and has quite often permitted them even when it has not yet been established that the PAJA is inapplicable because the action is not administrative.[106] And in the *Albutt* case (discussed in section C above) the Constitutional Court actually reversed the normal order of things by holding that since the case could be resolved by the principle of legality, there was no need to ask whether the PAJA was applicable. This was an 'ancillary' question that should not be reached, and indeed it would be contrary to sound judicial policy to do so.[107]

This approach was adopted by a High Court a few months later[108] but has not featured in the more recent case law, and was quietly repudiated by the Constitutional Court in *Motau*.[109] That is just as well, for if it were to

[102] *JSC v Cape Bar Council* (n 101) [21]–[22] and [43].

[103] Ibid, [44]–[45].

[104] See, especially, *Minister of Health v New Clicks* (n 20) [96]; *Mazibuko v City of Johannesburg* [2009] ZACC 28; 2010 (4) SA 1 (CC), [73].

[105] See the text to n 67 above.

[106] See, further, Hoexter, *Administrative Law in South Africa* (n 8) 134–35.

[107] *Albutt* (n 90) [82].

[108] *Southern African Litigation Centre v National Director of Public Prosecutions* [2012] ZAGPPHC 61; 2012 (10) BCLR 1089 (GNP), [18]. The judgment was largely upheld on appeal, but the Supreme Court of Appeal made no reference to this approach of avoiding the PAJA: *National Commissioner of the South African Police Service v Southern African Human Rights Litigation Centre* [2013] ZASCA 168; 2014 (2) SA 42 (SCA).

[109] *Minister of Defence v Motau* (n 100) [27], where Khampepe J observed in a footnote: 'The correct order of enquiry is to consider, first, whether PAJA applies, and only if it does not, what is demanded by general constitutional principles such as the rule of law.'

be followed generally it would destroy the status of the PAJA as the primary or default pathway to judicial review in administrative law. It is difficult for the PAJA to compete with the principle of legality because the latter is so very attractive: it is simple, general and flexible and can evidently be made to mean whatever the court wants it to mean. The PAJA is far more detailed and less user-friendly. Its definition of administrative action is overly complicated and tries to exclude too much;[110] and section 7 of the PAJA contains procedural obstacles in the form of a strict six-month time limit for applications for review and a rather onerous duty to exhaust internal remedies. By contrast, the principle of legality attracts the more flexible and less irksome common-law versions of these requirements.[111]

So a parallel universe of administrative law is being created by the courts; a new common law for the constitutional era, as it were. As shown by the discussion above, the content of the principle of legality has grown very rapidly and there seems no reason why it should not, in time, replicate every one of the grounds of review in the PAJA. The principle seems infinitely manipulable. So far, however, the courts have not applied procedural fairness or reason-giving as independent requirements, and they have stopped short of making the principle cover unreasonableness in the sense of disproportionality;[112] so to that extent, a system of bifurcation still reigns in South African public law.

IV. RIGHTERS OF EVERY WRONG

As shown in this essay, substantive grounds of review have burgeoned in a remarkable fashion over the last decade. In the process, some of the nuances introduced by the legislature or originally envisaged by the courts have been diminished. The legislature's deliberate choice of *Wednesbury*-type review has been expanded and interpreted to include proportionality; material mistake of fact has become a ground of review; the careful distinction between 'minimum' rationality and PAJA rationality is increasingly difficult to discern; and minimum rationality itself has been held to imply further principles of good administration in the form of procedural fairness and reason-giving. All of this has been achieved by the courts and in a remarkably short time. But what explains these developments?

[110] See, further, Hoexter, 'Constitutionalization and Codification' (n 7) [53]–[55].

[111] In the UK, common-law review entails *greater* procedural restrictions than human-rights review: see Varuhas (n 6). But these different positions are not particularly surprising when one considers that common-law review remains the standard or dominant type in the UK, and that review under the PAJA is intended to be the standard or dominant type in South Africa.

[112] In his minority judgment in *Minister of Health v New Clicks* (n 20), Sachs J indicated his willingness to extend the principle to encompass proportionality when judging the lawfulness of subordinate legislation.

Psychology has almost certainly played a role, particularly in relation to the expansion of section 6(2)*(h)* of the PAJA. The sins of the past still exercise a strong influence on South African lawyers and judges—perhaps especially in administrative law, for between 1948 and 1994 this branch of the law was an essential adjunct to the enforcement of the apartheid system.[113] As I indicate below, in the hands of the courts it was sometimes also able to serve as an instrument for protecting rights; but even so, I think the essential problem is that in the context of administrative law, deferential tests evoking 'symptomatic' and gross unreasonableness are ineluctably associated with the apartheid era. There is certainly an argument that South Africa did not really need a general ground of unreasonableness after 1994, and indeed I have always believed that in their fully developed form, the grounds of abuse of discretion are capable of doing much the same work. But reasonableness review was and remains laden with political and emotional significance for South African lawyers,[114] and it may be that the *Wednesbury*-like ground in section 6(2)*(h)* of the PAJA was simply too redolent of the past to be acceptable.

More generally, however, I suggest that the developments outlined in this essay are part and parcel of the extraordinarily prominent role played by the courts in South African public law, not only today but also in the past. A feature of the South African system is the widespread perception of the courts as 'unproblematic righters of every wrong'.[115] As I explain in this part, there is and always has been a great deal of work for the courts to do in administrative law, and an unusually large accountability vacuum for them to fill. These realities help to explain why South Africans are so inclined to turn to the courts in public-law matters, and why the courts are so inclined to respond favourably.

A. The Traditional Prominence of Judicial Review

A readiness to turn to the courts is part of our inheritance from the apartheid era. Though it seems (and is) paradoxical in the light of the courts' often submissive response to legislative and executive excesses during that era, the courts also played a not insignificant role in protecting individual rights. Parliament was sovereign and could, and did, authorise all sorts of invasive action on the part of the executive, but the courts were sometimes both

[113] See, eg J Dugard, *Human Rights and the South African Legal Order* (Princeton, Princeton University Press, 1978); I Evans, *Bureaucracy and Race* (Berkeley and Los Angeles, University of California Press, 1997).

[114] C Hoexter, 'Standards of Review of Administrative Action—Review for Unreasonableness' in J Klaaren (ed), *A Delicate Balance: The Place of the Judiciary in a Constitutional Democracy* (Claremont, Siber Ink, 2006) 61, 61.

[115] Taggart, 'Proportionality, Deference, *Wednesbury*' (n 11) 453.

able and willing to soften its impact. They did this by applying principles of administrative law.

A good illustration is the courts' treatment of ouster or privative clauses, which were routinely overridden by them even during periods of extreme judicial restraint. For instance, the Appellate Division famously held an ouster clause to be ineffective in *Minister of Law and Order v Hurley*,[116] a case relating to arrest and detention during a state of emergency (though the arrest and detention were effected under ordinary legislation rather than emergency regulations). The clause excluded review of action taken 'in terms of' a legislative provision, and the Court reasoned that an unlawful arrest and detention could not qualify as such action. And that is only one example. Budlender remarked in 1993 that almost all of the major human-rights advances of the previous two decades had been achieved by means of the courts' use of administrative-law principles: they had used these principles to promote freedom of movement and access to public amenities, and to impose limits on emergency powers.[117] Albeit not in a consistent manner, administrative-law review was quite often made to operate as a rudimentary charter of rights.

This is not so surprising when one considers that judicial review was really the only reliable safeguard in existence before 1994.[118] Remarkably, there were no other constraints worth mentioning on exercises of public power. There was no right of access to information, no public participation to speak of, and no ombudsman of any kind until 1979—and then a rather feeble one.[119] Administrative appeals were largely under the control of the executive and were not known for their impartiality or reliability. As a result, the courts represented the only realistic chance of having one's rights protected. This position was reflected in the legal education of the time, which generally assumed that there was nothing more to administrative law than judicial review, and which paid little or no attention to non-curial processes and safeguards.[120] And it was typified by a Law Commission report which admitted the lack of a coherent system of administrative appeals and saw the solution to this problem in the extension of the existing grounds of review.[121]

[116] *Minister of Law and Order v Hurley* 1986 (3) SA 568 (A).

[117] G Budlender, 'The Accessibility of Administrative Justice' [1993] *Acta Juridica* 128, 128.

[118] See, further, Hoexter, 'Future of Judicial Review' (n 32).

[119] The jurisdiction of the Advocate-General (introduced by the Advocate-General Act 118 of 1979) was essentially limited to the misuse of public money, and the office was not easily accessible to ordinary South Africans.

[120] Baxter saw this phenomenon as part of the lawyer's traditional aversion to policy: LG Baxter, 'Legal Education and Public Policy', his inaugural lecture delivered at the University of Natal, Pietermaritzburg (1984).

[121] South African Law Commission, *Report* (Project 24) (1992) 50.

A related point is that most people trusted the judiciary more than they trusted the legislature and executive; or more accurately, they mistrusted it less. Judges evidently maintained their aura of detachment and dignity even while enforcing the laws of apartheid;[122] and while many apartheid-era judges suffered from executive-mindedness, they retained at least their formal independence. As Forsyth puts it, '[t]he judges were never corrupt and did not take orders from politicians'.[123] Cameron, writing towards the end of the apartheid era, suggested that the judiciary could still claim a degree of 'professionalism and relative autonomy that few would seek to pass off as discreditable'.[124]

All this fostered a distinctly 'pro-review' attitude. As I have explained in more detail elsewhere,[125] the energies of anti-apartheid lawyers were always directed towards the *expansion* of the grounds of review. It was starkly simple in those days: the more judges interfered with governmental decision-making, the better things would be. And that general attitude did not necessarily go into reverse when the new democratic regime was introduced together with constitutional supremacy and a justiciable Bill of Rights.

B. The Continuing Prominence of Judicial Review

The judiciary has a hugely enhanced role in South Africa's constitutional democracy. From the remedial point of view, the courts no longer need to 'claim space and push boundaries to find means of controlling public power'.[126] For one thing, they have been made more accessible by means of extremely generous provisions as to standing. Section 38 of the Constitution, which relates to infringements of the Bill of Rights, is radically different from the more parsimonious common law in this regard. It expressly invites litigants to act on behalf of others, to represent a class and to vindicate the public interest, and for good measure it permits an association to act in the interest of its members. The courts also enjoy very wide remedial powers by virtue of sections 38[127] and 172[128] of the Constitution,

[122] See, generally, R Suttner, 'The Ideological Role of the Judiciary' (1984) 13 *Philosophical Papers* 28.

[123] C Forsyth, 'The Judiciary under Apartheid' in C Hoexter and M Olivier (contributing eds), *The Judiciary in South Africa* (Cape Town, Juta & Co Ltd, 2014) 26, 66.

[124] E Cameron, now a judge of the Constitutional Court, in 'Nude Monarchy: The Case of South Africa's Judges' (1987) 3 *South African Journal on Human Rights* 338, 339.

[125] See, further, Hoexter, 'Future of Judicial Review' (n 32).

[126] Chaskalson P in *Pharmaceutical Manufacturers Association* (n 70) [45].

[127] Section 38 permits a court to grant 'appropriate relief, including a declaration of rights'.

[128] In terms of s 172(1)*(b)*, a court 'may make any order that is just and equitable'.

and in terms of section 172(1)*(a)* they are obliged to strike down any law or conduct found to be inconsistent with any part of the Constitution.

Then, too, the substance of the transformative democratic Constitution exerts its own pressures and constantly challenges the courts to push the boundaries. The Constitution includes rights of an ambitious and inspiring nature, including justiciable socio-economic rights.[129] It contains explicit duties on the state, including the general duty in section 7(2) to 'respect, protect, promote and fulfil' all rights. It is also replete with values, including but not limited to the founding values in section 1.[130] These and other provisions suggest that the Constitution envisages nothing less than 'transformative adjudication', one aim of which is the achievement of a culture of justification in all public-law interactions.[131] In the circumstances, the courts are under unusual pressure to 'perform'.

They also have many opportunities to do so. One of the features of our adolescent democracy is that the authority of the Constitution and the rule of law are constantly being tested by wayward executive and administrative action. South Africa's political leaders are relatively inexperienced—most were completely new to governance in 1994—and the quality of public administration remains very uneven.[132] As the law reports reveal, administrative skill, expertise and experience undoubtedly do exist, but in patches. One cannot count on the presence of these attributes in all or even most areas of the public administration. Only a decade ago appalling anecdotes were related of officials who had never actually laid eyes on the enabling legislation in terms of which they were required to act.[133] The sad truth is that little has changed in some departments, where decisions continue to be taken by untrained or barely trained administrators. In others, the courts have diagnosed problems including 'lack of capacity, incompetence, inefficiency, fraud and corruption'.[134]

[129] See s 26 (the right to housing), s 27 (rights to health care, food, water and social security), s 28 (children's rights), and s 29 (rights to education). Some of these are conferred in unqualified terms, such as the children's rights and the right to a basic education.

[130] Another important source of values is s 195, which records the basic values and principles governing the public administration.

[131] See especially D Moseneke, 'The Fourth Bram Fischer Memorial Lecture: Transformative Adjudication' (2002) 18 *South African Journal on Human Rights* 309; C Hoexter, 'Judicial Policy Revisited: Transformative Adjudication in Public Law' (2008) 24 *South African Journal on Human Rights* 281, 286–87.

[132] See, eg R de Kadt and J Hudson, 'South Africa's Democracy in 2014: Fragile or Robust? (2014) 72 *Focus* 4, 10, who give the Treasury and the South African Revenue Service as examples of efficient departments. Many are inefficient, however, and some grossly so.

[133] See, eg JH Wessels, 'Training on the Promotion of Administrative Justice Act 3 of 2000' in H Corder and L van der Vijver (eds), *Realising Administrative Justice* (Claremont, Siber Ink, 2002) 118, 119.

[134] Wallis J in *Thusi v Minister of Home Affairs* [2010] ZAKZPHC 87; 2011 (2) SA 561 (KZP), [1].

Corruption is a problem often experienced by societies in transition. It is one of the most painful of current South African realities, and undoubtedly exacerbates the accountability vacuum. It has become endemic in the public administration and has been described by the Constitutional Court as a 'pernicious threat to our collective enterprise to entrench a just and democratic society'.[135] In 2013 the Corruption Perceptions Index of Transparency International, which measures perceived levels of public corruption, ranked South Africa seventy-second out of 177 countries with a score of 42, just below the average of 43.[136] That may not seem too bad, but it is depressingly far below the score of 91 achieved by the least corrupt countries in the world (Denmark and New Zealand). In a local survey by Corruption Watch, a non-governmental organisation, one in four South Africans admitted to paying a bribe when interacting with public institutions or services in the course of 2013.[137] The one glimmer of good news is that apparently South Africans are becoming less tolerant of public corruption.[138]

It is, of course, true that judicial review is no longer the only safeguard against the abuse of public power, for the range of other methods of control has increased greatly since the pre-democratic era. In particular, Chapter 9 of the 1996 Constitution creates a number of institutions to support constitutional democracy, including the Human Rights Commission, the Auditor-General and the Public Protector, an ombudsman of general jurisdiction that reports to Parliament. The Chapter 9 institutions form the core of a growing integrity system. In fact, while the concept of an integrity 'branch' of government[139] is novel to South Africans, these bodies would certainly qualify on the definition of such a branch proposed by Brown: '[A] small number of permanent institutions, whose function is solely or primarily to ensure that other governmental institutions and officials exercise the powers conferred on them for the purposes for which they were conferred.'[140] Today South Africans enjoy various other public-law safeguards, too, such as opportunities for public participation in legislative processes[141] and a

[135] *Glenister v President of the Republic of South Africa* [2011] ZACC 6; 2011 (3) SA 347 (CC), [172].

[136] Transparency International, *Corruption Perceptions Index 2013*, available at: cpi.transparency.org.

[137] See *Legalbrief* 4 April 2014, available at: www.legalbrief.co.za.

[138] South African Press Association, 'Corruption Remains High in SA—Index' *news24* 3 December 2013, available at: www.news24.co.za.

[139] As originally described by the Hon JJ Spigelman AC in 'The Integrity Branch of Government' (2004) 78 *Australian Law Journal* 724.

[140] AJ Brown, 'The Integrity Branch: A "System", an "Industry", or a Sensible Emerging Fourth Arm of Government?' in M Groves (ed), *Modern Administrative Law in Australia* (Cambridge, Cambridge University Press, 2014) 301, 313.

[141] Duties are placed on the two houses of Parliament, the National Assembly and the National Council of Provinces to facilitate public involvement in their legislative and other processes, by ss 59 and 72 of the Constitution, and similar duties are placed on provincial legislatures by s 118.

right of access to information contained in section 24 of the Constitution and given effect to in an Act of Parliament.

The sad reality, however, is that over the last two decades the integrity system has not proved nearly as effective as it may appear on paper, and not nearly effective enough to discourage resort to judicial review by public-interest organisations, opposition parties and the media. In practice, litigation is often needed to reinforce the integrity system. In relation to access to information, for instance, it was estimated in 2012 that fewer than half of the country's government departments were actually complying with the provisions of the Promotion of Access to Information Act 2 of 2000, and it was apparent that far too many departments simply ignore or 'mutely refuse' requests for access.[142] The result is that compliance often has to be enforced by the courts.

Another example of this is the office of Public Protector, which was for many years dubbed the 'ANC Protector' as a result of the incumbent's apparent reluctance to investigate or criticise members of the governing party, the African National Congress. This reluctance reached its apogee a few years ago in the Public Protector's investigation into the 'Oilgate' scandal, in which the ANC was alleged to have received large sums of public money illicitly. The bland and superficial report[143] which followed the investigation was challenged on review, and the Supreme Court of Appeal ultimately found that there had been no real investigation at all, and no serious attempt made to uncover the truth.[144]

Unlike some of her predecessors the courageous current incumbent, Thuli Madonsela, has not hesitated to expose malfeasance wherever she has found it, but unfortunately that is no guarantee that consequences will follow or that action will be taken against wrongdoers. An illustration is the Public Protector's recent report on security upgrades effected at vast public expense on the President's private homestead at Nkandla.[145] The report found that some of the upgrades had had nothing to do with security, that they represented opulence on a grand scale and that the President had benefited unduly from such expenditure; and it called upon him to repay a reasonable percentage of those costs.[146] However, nothing short of a court order is likely to make the President comply. Indeed, at the time of writing he had already missed his own deadline for responding to the report.[147]

142 Anonymous, 'Government Fails to Inform the People', *Business Day* 6 August 2012, available at: www.bdlive.co.za.

143 Public Protector, *Report on an Investigation into an Allegation of Misappropriation of Public Funds by the Petroleum Oil and Gas Corporation of South Africa, Trading as PetroSA, and Matters Allegedly Related Thereto* (2005).

144 *Public Protector v Mail & Guardian Ltd* [2011] ZASCA 108; 2011 (4) SA 420 (SCA).

145 Public Protector, *Secure in Comfort*, Report 25 of 2013/14 (March 2014).

146 Ibid, see the Executive Summary especially at 68.

147 See, eg C Kgosana, 'Jacob Zuma Misses Own Nkandla Deadline' *City Press* 17 July 2014, available at: www.citypress.co.za.

C. Judicial Review of Political Disputes

For all the reasons given above, judicial review remains a tremendously significant and popular method of holding the government to account—even in highly discretionary or political matters. Overseas observers often remark on this, pointing out that disputes that would be resolved by political means at home are routinely subjected to judicial review in South Africa. This phenomenon is well illustrated by some of the cases already mentioned in this essay. Three of these concerned powers of the President having a distinctively political flavour: his power to grant pardons,[148] his dismissal of the head of the National Intelligence Agency[149] and his appointment of a controversial Director of Public Prosecutions.[150] Two other cases referred to in this essay concerned the conduct of supposedly independent bodies created by the Constitution and necessarily enjoying considerable discretion in the performance of their functions: a decision of the Judicial Service Commission not to recommend certain candidates for judicial office[151] and the Public Protector's report on the 'Oilgate' affair.[152] More recently, a public-interest organisation took on review the decision of another such body, the National Prosecuting Authority, to withdraw an array of criminal charges against the Head of Crime Intelligence, as well as the decision of the Commissioner of Police to withdraw disciplinary charges against him and to reinstate him in his post.[153] It is interesting to note, too, that only one of these challenges (*Masetlha*)[154] was unsuccessful.

Cases such as these might count as exceptional in some jurisdictions, but here they are nothing unusual. Every exercise of public power is justiciable to some extent at least—the Constitutional Court confirmed that proposition a decade ago[155]—and it seems that no exercise of public power is too political to be taken on review. However, the courts are increasingly expressing their discomfort with this state of affairs. In *Mazibuko NO v Sisulu NO*,[156] in which the leader of the opposition sought to direct the

[148] *Albutt v Centre for the Study of Violence and Reconciliation* (n 90).

[149] *Masetlha v President* (n 87).

[150] *Democratic Alliance v President* (n 82).

[151] *Judicial Service Commission v Cape Bar Council* (n 101).

[152] *Public Protector v Mail & Guardian Ltd* (n 144).

[153] *Freedom Under Law v National Director of Public Prosecutions* [2013] ZAGPPHC 271; 2014 (1) SA 254 (GNP). The judgment of the High Court was taken on appeal and was recently upheld in part by the Supreme Court of Appeal in *National Director of Public Prosecutions v Freedom Under Law* [2014] ZASCA 58.

[154] *Masetlha* (n 87).

[155] *Kaunda v President of the Republic of South Africa* [2005] ZACC 5; 2005 (4) SA 235 (CC), [78] (a case concerning a request for diplomatic protection).

[156] *Mazibuko NO v Sisulu NO* [2012] ZAWCHC 189; 2013 (4) SA 243 (WCC).

Speaker of the National Assembly to schedule a motion of no confidence in the President, Davis J was driven to observe:[157]

> Courts do not run the country, nor were they intended to govern the country. There is a danger in South Africa ... of the politicisation of the judiciary, drawing the judiciary into every political dispute as if there is no other forum to deal with a political impasse relating to policy or disputes which clearly carry polycentric consequences beyond the scope of adjudication.

He also remarked that '[a]n overreach of the powers of judges' would place our constitutional democracy in jeopardy.[158]

Another recent example is *National Treasury v Opposition to Urban Tolling Alliance*,[159] a case concerning the highly unpopular decision to introduce e-tolling on highways in the province of Gauteng. The High Court had granted an interim interdict restraining the implementation of the e-tolling regime. On appeal, having noted that the ordering of public resources inevitably entails 'policy-laden and polycentric decision-making', the Constitutional Court went on to deplore the High Court's 'deafening silence' on the separation of powers and its relevance to the granting of such a remedy.[160] In a separate opinion in the same case, Froneman J remarked that: 'The playing field for the contestation of executive-government policy is the political process, not the judicial one.'[161] One can perhaps discern the beginnings of an explicit 'political question' doctrine in dicta such as these.[162]

As noted earlier in this essay, South Africa already has a nascent doctrine of deference. The courts are generally aware of the limits of their constitutional and institutional competence, particularly in the area of socio-economic rights,[163] and it is more than a decade since the highest courts began to elucidate an explicit theory of deference or respect in the context of administrative law. Since then, the doctrine has served in a few cases to explain the courts' reluctance to interfere with a complex decision taken by an administrator with some expertise in the matter.[164] However, the doctrine has not been taken further than this, and it certainly has not acted as any sort of brake on the development, extension or application of substantive review grounds. Yet the relationship between deference and

[157] Ibid, 256E–G.

[158] Ibid, 256H–I.

[159] *National Treasury v Opposition to Urban Tolling Alliance* [2012] ZACC 18; 2012 (6) SA 223 (CC).

[160] Ibid, [68] and [72] in the judgment of Moseneke DCJ.

[161] Ibid, [93].

[162] On the need for such a doctrine, see, eg M Mhango, 'Separation of Powers and the Resolution of Political Questions in South Africa: A Comparative Analysis of Lessons from the United States and Ghana' (2014) 7 *African Journal of Legal Studies* (forthcoming).

[163] For an overview, see the judgment of O'Regan J in *Mazibuko v City of Johannesburg* (n 104) [46]–[68].

[164] See the cases listed in n 37.

such grounds surely deserves to be explored. In my view there is a definite need for further articulation of the principles that govern, or that ought to govern, judicial intervention and non-intervention in administrative law.[165]

V. CONCLUSION

Notwithstanding the emergence of an integrity system that includes a number of non-curial safeguards, South Africans seem to rely just as heavily on judicial review today as they did in the pre-democratic era—a time when administrative-law review was the citizen's only hope against executive excesses. As shown in this essay, the courts' scrutiny of public decision-making has become more and more intense over the past decade, both under the PAJA and in terms of the residual principle of legality, and the possibilities of substantive review seem simply to have expanded to meet a growing demand. As a result, the courts of the Rainbow Nation have increasingly contemplated a rainbow of review[166] in which all the colours are strangely alike.

I have suggested that this phenomenon is attributable to several factors, including the perception of the courts as the righters of every conceivable wrong, the possibilities and pressures of a transformative Constitution, the existence of a definite accountability vacuum and the absence of a fully developed doctrine of deference.

[165] Davis, for instance, has expressed the hope that the debate would move beyond expertise and the separation of powers towards a fuller consideration of the role of the courts in a constitutional democracy, particularly in a 'rights culture': D Davis, 'To Defer and When? Administrative Law and Constitutional Democracy' [2006] *Acta Juridica* 23, 34.

[166] Taggart, 'Proportionality, Deference, *Wednesbury*' (n 11) 451ff.

Part B

Deference on Questions of Law?

8

Deference on Questions of Law: A Survey of Taggart's Contribution and Themes in the Wider Literature

HANNA WILBERG AND MARK ELLIOTT

I. THE NATURE AND PURPOSE OF THIS SURVEY

AS EXPLAINED IN the introduction to chapter two, this collection of essays engaging with Professor Michael Taggart's work on substantive review, and building on that work, seems a good opportunity to attempt an overview of Taggart's work in this area and of the existing state of the debate—an overview which explores that work and sets out our personal best understanding of it, without seeking to evaluate or endorse it. Chapter two does this in relation to the first of the two themes pursued in this book, the debate about modern extensions of substantive review in the sense of review engaging the merits. In the present chapter, we attempt the same kind of overview in relation to the second theme, the debate about deference on questions of law.

II. EXPLORING TAGGART'S CONTRIBUTION

On the question of deference on questions of law, Taggart's main contribution addressed to audiences outside Canada dates back to 1997 and is entitled 'The Contribution of Lord Cooke to Scope of Review Doctrine in Administrative Law: A Comparative Perspective'.[1] In this part of our

[1] M Taggart, 'The Contribution of Lord Cooke to Scope of Review Doctrine in Administrative Law: A Comparative Common Law Perspective' in Paul Rishworth (ed), *The Struggle for Simplicity in the Law: Essays in Honour of Lord Cooke of Thorndon* (Wellington, Butterworths, 1997) 189 ('Scope of Review').

survey, we present a brief summary of the arguments in that essay, followed by an exploration of three questions. First, it seems helpful to shed some light on the Canadian arguments that are relied on but not spelt out in any detail in this essay. The second and third questions arise from reading Taggart's essay in the context of some of his other work on substantive review.

A. The 'Scope of Review' Essay

In his 'Scope of Review' essay, Taggart advocates 'recognition and refinement of a doctrine or theory of deference' in relation to questions of law and statutory interpretation. He considers possible reasons for the divergence between New Zealand and the North American jurisdictions on this point,[2] pointing out that the divergence with Canada is particularly puzzling in light of New Zealand's close attention to other aspects of Canadian public law, especially its Charter jurisprudence.[3]

The focus in the essay is on New Zealand's landmark *Bulk Gas* decision.[4] *Bulk Gas* established a strong, virtually irrebuttable presumption that Parliament does not intend to empower administrative decision-makers to determine questions of law conclusively.[5] In doing so, it followed dicta of Lord Diplock in *Racal*[6] and *O'Reilly*[7] that further developed the House of Lords' landmark decision in *Anisminic*.[8] It anticipated *Page*, where the House of Lords confirmed the same position.[9] The rationale was that 'it is the constitutional role of the superior Courts to interpret the laws enacted by Parliament'.[10] Courts therefore 'have the function of interpreting Acts of Parliament and the duty to correct any errors of law made'.[11]

Taggart's central critique of the *Bulk Gas* and *Page* approach is that it is founded on a series of 'controversial' and questionable assumptions:[12]

(1) That there is a right answer to questions of statutory interpretation.
(2) That, as experienced and talented lawyers, the judiciary are the best placed persons to provide that answer.
(3) That questions of 'law' are separate and distinguishable from policy, discretion and fact-finding.

[2] Ibid, 216–19.
[3] Ibid, 215.
[4] *Bulk Gas Users Group v Attorney-General* [1983] NZLR 129 (CA). The Court of Appeal was then still the highest local court, subject to appeals only to the Privy Council.
[5] *Bulk Gas* (n 4) 133, 136; Taggart, 'Scope of Review' (n 1) 195.
[6] *Re Racal Communications Ltd* [1981] AC 374 (HL).
[7] *O'Reilly v Mackman* [1983] 2 AC 237 (HL).
[8] *Anisminic Ltd v Foreign Compensation Commission* [1969] 2 AC 147 (HL).
[9] *R v Hull University Visitor, ex p Page* [1993] AC 682 (HL).
[10] Taggart, 'Scope of Review' (n 1) 192.
[11] Ibid, 195, referring to *Bulk Gas* (n 4) 133 and Lord Diplock in *Re Racal* (n 6) 382–83.
[12] Taggart, 'Scope of Review' (n 1) 203–204.

This set of assumptions is said to represent legal 'centralism'—an understanding of the law as one integrated, unified structure administered by the ordinary courts, which formed part of the basis for Dicey's version of the rule of law.[13] But Taggart points out that even though there is a long and strong centralist tradition in English public law, the *Bulk Gas/Anisminic* approach represents a recent move to an unprecedented extreme version of centralism. Historically and up until *Anisminic*, there was an element of legal pluralism, in that 'the Courts never claimed to determine conclusively the meaning of all "law"': the old jurisdictional doctrine limited the courts' role, and allowed them to leave some questions to the administrators. Errors of law within jurisdiction were open to review only if they appeared on the face of the record, and then only if there was no ouster clause.[14] Taggart agrees that this doctrine 'was too blunt an instrument' for the task, since there was no satisfactory basis for drawing the line between jurisdictional errors and those within jurisdiction. But he argues that 'the baby of pluralism should not be thrown out with the bath water of jurisdiction'; quoting Paul Craig, he points out that the 'central issue' remains 'the proper balance of power between Court and agency'.[15]

Taggart thus advocates 'consciously thinking of scope of review in terms of the appropriate allocation of interpretive authority between agencies and Courts', as the North Americans do to their advantage.[16] He touches on three more particular points, drawn from the Canadian (and US) jurisprudence. First, he considers that the decision-maker's expertise is the relevant criterion in determining who is best suited to make conclusive determinations of the law.[17] Secondly and relatedly, he criticises courts' implicit assumption that questions of statutory interpretation 'can be separated clearly from the economic, commercial or other contexts in which they arise. I do not believe that "law" and "policy" can be so neatly cleaved.'[18]

Thirdly, he criticises the 'short shrift' given to privative clauses in *Bulk Gas* and its progeny, noting that this is inconsistent with the courts' claim to be determining the allocation of interpretive authority by means of statutory interpretation.[19]

Taggart draws attention to some existing limits to the strong presumption that questions of law are for the courts.[20] First, *Bulk Gas* allows

[13] Ibid, 212. See further below, part II B i.

[14] Taggart, 'Scope of Review' (n 1) 212.

[15] Ibid, 213.

[16] Ibid, 211. Indeed, he regrets that the Canadian Supreme Court does not focus more directly and exclusively on that enquiry: he considers the retention of the concept of jurisdiction in this context 'a major mistake': ibid, 206.

[17] Ibid, 198.

[18] Ibid. For criticism of cleaving law from politics, see also ibid, 203–204, and the comment ibid, 218 doubting whether Lord Cooke's commitment to purposive interpretation fits with his Diceyan stance on error of law.

[19] Ibid, 199.

[20] Ibid, 196.

that where, having determined the meaning of the statutory test, 'there remains legitimate room for judgment in applying the test', the decision-maker's application of the test will be reviewed only on grounds of unreasonableness.[21] This is a particular instance of the perennially difficult law/fact divide: questions of fact, unlike questions of law, are for the decision-maker, subject only to unreasonableness review. The *Bulk Gas* dictum effectively extends the category of questions of fact to questions as to the application of broad or vague terms. Though Taggart does not refer to it, this is much like the House of Lords' decision in *South Yorkshire Transport*.[22] Secondly, *Bulk Gas* confines the judicial duty to correct errors to situations where the statute sets out a 'definite'[23] or 'ascertainable' test.[24] By implication, it would seem that in the absence of such a test the 'correctness' test must again be replaced by reasonableness review.[25] A third limit suggested in *Bulk Gas* is that the presumption in favour of judicial determination of questions of law may not apply where the primary decision-maker is an inferior court.[26] Taggart doubts this distinction.[27]

He also notes some isolated deviations from the *Bulk Gas/Anisminic* orthodoxy in the New Zealand and British case law. In a case called *Hawkins*,[28] Cooke P was apparently alone in reiterating the presumption against a decision-maker having power to determine questions of law conclusively.[29] A similar divergence from the orthodox approach is also identified in 'a neglected passage' in Lord Wilberforce's speech in *Anisminic* itself.[30] His Lordship there acknowledges that Parliament may sometimes 'concede a wide area to the authority', particularly where 'a degree of policy-making rather than fact-finding is involved'.[31] Crucially, Lord Wilberforce then concludes by rejecting any presumption in favour of courts having the final word on questions of statutory interpretation.[32]

Yet by and large the case law in New Zealand and the UK has adhered to the *Bulk Gas/Anisminic* majority approach without much deviation. While there are examples of ad hoc deference to particular decision-makers, such as welfare tribunals, for pragmatic reasons, and while 'notions of deference

[21] *Bulk Gas* (n 4) 136.

[22] *R v Monopolies and Mergers Commission, ex p South Yorkshire Transport Ltd* [1993] 1 WLR 23 (HL). For discussion, see M Elliott, *Beatson, Matthews and Elliott's Administrative Law: Text and Materials*, 4th edn (Oxford, Oxford University Press, 2011) 61, 66–68; P Craig, *Administrative Law*, 7th edn (London, Sweet & Maxwell, 2012) [16-026], [16-028].

[23] *Bulk Gas* (n 4) 135.

[24] Ibid, 136.

[25] Taggart, 'Scope of Review' (n 1) 196.

[26] *Bulk Gas* (n 4) 136; see also *Re Racal* (n 6) and *Page* (n 9).

[27] Taggart 'Scope of Review' (n 1) 197, and see, generally, 196–99.

[28] *Hawkins v Minister of Justice* [1991] 2 NZLR 530 (CA).

[29] Taggart, 'Scope of Review' (n 1) 200–201.

[30] Ibid, 216.

[31] *Anisminic* (n 8) 209.

[32] Ibid.

play a part in classifying issues or questions as ones of fact, mixed fact and law, and law',[33] Taggart considers such ad hoc or tacit treatment of deference unsatisfactory (which is where Mark Aronson's contribution to this volume disagrees[34]): 'the public are entitled to expect open and honest explanation by the Judges of what they are doing and why'.[35]

B. Some Questions and Puzzles

In light of this brief outline of Taggart's arguments, we now turn briefly to explore the meaning of the argument against Diceyan centralism, and to grapple with two puzzles about how these arguments fit within Taggart's wider work on substantive review.

i. Spelling Out the Argument Against Diceyan Centralism

In Canada, arguments for deference on questions of law draw on a broader dissenting tradition of court-scepticism. As we saw, Taggart's essay invokes these arguments in questioning the Diceyan 'centralist' assumptions underlying the correctness standard, but he does not give much detail. Mainstream readers in the UK and New Zealand may not be closely familiar with these arguments. More detail is to be found in a later article entitled 'Prolegomenon to an Intellectual History of Administrative law in the Twentieth Century: The Case of John Willis and Canadian Administrative Law', which outlines the work of scholars at Osgoode Hall and the London School of Economics promoting 'court-scepticism ... and deference' in administrative law.[36] But for a full discussion, readers need to turn to the Canadian sources[37]—including the contributions to this volume by Paul Daly and Mark Walters.[38] A short summary and some references may be helpful.

[33] Taggart, 'Scope of Review' (n 1) 202–203.

[34] M Aronson 'Should We Have a Variable Error of Law Standard?' (ch 10 in this volume). See also P Cane, 'Judicial Control of Administrative Interpretation in Australia and the United States' (ch 9 in this volume) for a defence of Australia's different solution.

[35] Taggart, 'Scope of Review' (n 1) 202.

[36] M Taggart, 'Prolegomenon to an Intellectual History of Administrative Law in the Twentieth Century: The Case of John Willis and Canadian Administrative Law' (2005) 43 *Osgoode Hall Law Journal* 223, 257–67. See also M Taggart, 'Reinvented Government, Traffic Lights, and the Convergence Between Public and Private Law' [1999] *Public Law* 124; M Taggart, 'Outside Canadian Administrative Law' (1996) 46 *University of Toronto Law Journal* 649, 655–56.

[37] See, eg H Arthurs, 'Rethinking Administrative Law: A Slightly Dicey Business' (1979) 17 *Osgoode Hall Law Journal* 1; J Evans, H Janisch and DJ Mullan, *Administrative Law: Cases, Text and Materials*, 4th edn (Toronto, Edmond Montgomery Publications, 1995) 28–31 and 820.

[38] P Daly, 'The Struggle for Deference in Canada' (ch 12 in this volume); M Walters, 'Respecting Deference as Respect: Rights, Reasonableness and Proportionality in Canadian Administrative Law' (ch 15 in this volume), text accompanying nn 38, 42–49.

The 'centralism' that is criticised by Taggart and the Canadian sources involves an insistence on conclusive judicial interpretation of all law, and on judicial avenues (judicial review and causes of action in tort) for redressing grievances against the state. That is the effect of Dicey's version of the rule of law, according to which government must be subject to the ordinary law, administered by the ordinary courts, and specialist tribunals are to be distrusted.[39] This also involves a positivist division between law and policy and a consequent rejection of contextualist interpretation—both associated in the Canadian literature with Dicey's doctrine of Parliamentary sovereignty as well as his version of the rule of law.[40]

Pluralism, in contrast, means acceptance and promotion of a broader range of avenues of redress; of a sharing of interpretive authority; and of a diversity of interpretation depending on context. Pluralism thus describes an aspect of those approaches to administrative law that have been labelled functionalist or 'green light', in contradistinction to the mainstream normative or 'red light' approach that is characterised, among other things, by a focus on judicial authority and control.[41] In such pluralist, functionalist or green light approaches, the advantages and disadvantages of the general courts and specialist alternative avenues are weighed up in deciding on the allocation of powers between them.

For the proponents of pluralism or functionalism, one of the chief disadvantages of courts and the general or 'ordinary' law is the individualist and conservative bias associated with them. Taggart points out that pluralism in practice first developed in Canada in an area in which the courts' politics had come under sustained fire—namely labour relations law.[42] More generally, scholars of this bent were 'deeply resentful of ... conservative judges twisting the pliable rules of statutory interpretation to favour the existing order, privileging the rich and powerful, and defeating the purposes of statutes intended to further the interests of the workers, the homeless, and the least well-off in society'.[43] To commentators who are politically inclined to

[39] Taggart, 'Scope of Review' (n 1) 218, quoting from D Mullan, 'Substantive Fairness Review: Heed the Amber Light!' (1988) 18 *Victoria University of Wellington Law Review* 293, 305; also Taggart, ibid, 190, 206, 211, and 212. For further Canadian sources, see, eg *National Corn Growers Association v Canada (Import Tribunal)* [1990] 2 SCR 1324, 1332–35; CM Flood and L Sossin (eds), *Administrative Law in Context*, 2nd edn (Toronto, Emond Montgomery Publications, 2013) chs 2, 10 and 11. See also, similarly, P Craig, 'Dicey: Unitary, Self-Correcting Democracy and Public Law' (1990) 106 *Law Quarterly Review* 105.

[40] Evans, Janish and Mullan (n 37) 29 and 30–31; Arthurs (n 37).

[41] See, eg Arthurs (n 37); Evans, Janisch and Mullan (n 37) 29–31. While the idea of deference on questions of law has attracted only limited attention in Britain, Australia or New Zealand, these jurisdictions do have their own proponents of functionalist or 'green light' approaches: see, especially, C Harlow and R Rawlings, *Law and Administration*, 3rd edn (Cambridge, Cambridge University Press, 2009); M Loughlin *Public Law and Political Theory* (Oxford, Clarendon Press, 1992).

[42] See Taggart, 'Scope of Review' (n 1) 205 and 217; Taggart, 'Prolegomenon' (n 36) 260.

[43] Taggart, 'Prolegomenon' (n 36) 257. For a nuanced account, see also J McLean, *Searching for the State in British Legal Thought* (Cambridge, Cambridge University Press, 2012) ch 6.

see the state as a force for good, and to look to Parliament for beneficial change, the role of administrative law should be to facilitate the effective implementation of regulatory schemes, rather than obstructing those schemes by a focus on protection of individual interests affected by them.[44]

Pluralist or functionalist approaches moreover stress the importance of contextual interpretation: if regulatory schemes are to be effectively implemented and delivered, they must be interpreted in light of the policy they are designed to serve, and in light of the practicalities of the particular scheme.[45] If that is the objective, then the agency charged with administering the scheme may well be better qualified to determine the best interpretation than a generalist court: specialist expertise and experience are relevant factors in allocating interpretive authority.[46]

ii. An Instance of Breaking Down the Law/Discretion Divide?

This rejection of a clear line between questions of law on the one hand and questions of policy, discretion and fact-finding could be described as breaking down the law/discretion divide. That is a phrase used by Taggart and others in a different context, but it seems similarly apposite here. The question that occurs to us is whether there is indeed a link between the two areas and arguments, and if so, how they relate. Taggart's writings address this question only obliquely.

In the different context of arguing that rights should be given greater protection by using interpretive presumptions to read down broad discretionary statutory powers, Taggart and his co-authors reject two traditional limits. First, they consider the traditional administrative law preoccupation with the reasoning process to be insufficient—rights must operate as substantive limits.[47] Secondly, they reject the *Brind* objection that interpretive presumptions are triggered only by statutory ambiguity, and that broad discretionary powers contain no such ambiguity.[48] They point out that determining the scope of a broad discretionary power is surely a matter of statutory interpretation,[49] and draw attention to the so-called 'principle of legality' which does involve reading down broad discretionary powers by reference to an interpretive presumption.[50] More broadly, Canadian

[44] Evans, Janish and Mullan (n 37) 30–31.

[45] Arthurs (n 37).

[46] Taggart, 'Scope of Review' (n 1) 198, 218; for a summary of competing positions on this, see also Taggart, 'Reinvented Government' (n 36) 135–36.

[47] J McLean, P Rishworth and M Taggart, 'The Impact of the New Zealand Bill of Rights on Administrative Law' in *The New Zealand Bill of Rights Act 1990* (Auckland, Legal Research Foundation, 1992) 62.

[48] *R v Secretary of State for the Home Department, ex p Brind* [1991] 1 AC 696 (HL).

[49] Citing *Padfield v Minister of Agriculture, Fisheries and Food* [1968] AC 997 (HL).

[50] D Dyzenhaus, M Hunt and M Taggart, 'The Principle of Legality in Administrative Law: Internationalisation as Constitutionalisation' (2001) 1 *Oxford University Common Law Journal* 5.

commentators reject what they present as the Diceyan compromise, where judges assert absolute control over questions of law but discretion is a lawless void.[51] In the context of rights and interpretive presumptions, breaking down the divide leads to an expansion of review or to more intensive review: an exercise of discretion may be unlawful not only if there was a flaw in the reasoning process or if it is *Wednesbury* unreasonable, but also if an interpretive presumption takes it outside the scope of the discretion.[52]

In the context of arguing for deference on questions of law, the divide between questions of law on the one hand and matters of discretion and policy on the other has also been questioned by Taggart and others,[53] as already mentioned. The point in this context is that the line is not as clear-cut as the Diceyan orthodoxy would have us believe—law and policy or discretion are really two ends of one spectrum rather than binary opposites. The distinction should therefore not be relied on as the sole basis for determining standards of review. Other factors are relevant, and may call for a deferential standard even on questions that fall closer to the legal end of the spectrum. In this context, then, breaking down the divide leads the courts to pull back and engage in less intensive review on some questions of law.

There does, then, appear to be a link between the two arguments. If the two are put together, the challenge to the law/discretion divide can be seen to cut both ways: it can lead both to expanded or intensified review of matters that would otherwise fall on the discretion side of the line, and to deferential review on matters that would otherwise fall on the law side of the line.

Whether Taggart and other commentators see these two arguments as linked in this way is not always immediately obvious, but there are at least some indications in favour of such a reading. A notable instance is the Canadian *Baker* case[54] and Taggart's discussion of this case. In *Baker*, the Canadian Supreme Court abandoned the distinction between law and discretion that had until then served to confine the Canadian contextual standards of review approach to questions of law.[55] The most obvious effect was the potential for more intensive review on questions that would

[51] D Dyzenhaus and E Fox-Decent, 'Re-thinking the Process/Substance Distinction: Baker v Canada' (2001) 51 *University of Toronto Law Journal* 193. On all of these points, see also M Taggart, 'Proportionality, Deference, *Wednesbury*' [2008] *New Zealand Law Review*' 423.

[52] For an argument cautioning against correctness review in this area, see H Wilberg, 'The Bill of Rights in Administrative Law Cases: Taking Stock and Suggesting Some Reassessment' (2013) 25 *New Zealand Universities Law Review* 866, 893–95.

[53] Taggart, 'Scope of Review' (n 1) 198, 203–204, 205, fn 69; P Daly, *A Theory of Deference in Administrative Law* (Cambridge, Cambridge University Press, 2012) 255–57; P Hogg, 'Judicial Review: How Much Do We Need?' (1974) 20 *McGill Law Journal* 157, 161–62; P Hogg, 'The Supreme Court of Canada and Administrative Law, 1949–1971' (1973) 11 *Osgoode Hall Law Journal* 187, 188–89.

[54] *Baker v Canada* (1999) 174 DLR (4th) 193 (SCC).

[55] Ibid, [53]–[55].

previously have been understood as falling on the discretion side, as clearly noted by Taggart[56] amongst other commentators.[57] However, both the Court and Taggart also note the potential for the breakdown to have the opposite effect: questions that would previously have attracted a correctness standard should now be subject to a variable standard of review, and hence potentially attract deference.[58]

iii. An Entirely Illusory Divide?

Some commentators and Canadian judges appear to subscribe to a view that takes the rejection of the law/discretion divide to its extreme. In that view, not only should this divide not result in radically different approaches on the two sides of the divide, and not only should it not be alone determinative; rather, the divide is entirely illusory and irrelevant for the standard of review. It is difficult to be certain which judges and commentators take this extreme stance. There is, however, one otherwise puzzling passage in Taggart's work that suggests he may have subscribed to this view.

In his late 'Proportionality' article, Taggart appears to imply that courts in the UK and New Zealand have come to accept that deference may be appropriate on questions of law: 'The courts *used to* apply a Diceyan-inspired correctness standard of review to the interpretation of statutory texts';[59] now, however, 'the word "deference" is very much in the air in the United Kingdom and New Zealand'.[60] While the focus in the 'Proportionality' article is on review of the substantive merits, these statements appear to concern questions of law as well, and to claim that deference has become established in that context. It is difficult to accept that as an accurate account of what courts in these jurisdictions say they do. It is true, at least if we look at commentators, that there is now much discussion of deference. But that is primarily in relation to the proportionality analysis in rights cases, and more generally in relation to substantive grounds of review such as *Wednesbury* unreasonableness and proportionality. It is also arguably true that there is much covert deference on questions of law in the case law. But with the exception of a few commentators seeking to challenge the orthodox approach (to be discussed below), deference is never explicitly discussed in relation to statutory interpretation in these jurisdictions.

[56] M Taggart, 'The Impact of Apartheid on Commonwealth Administrative Law' [2006] *Acta Juridica* 158, 203.

[57] See also D Mullan, 'Deference from *Baker* to *Suresh* and Beyond—Interpreting Conflicting Signals' in D Dyzenhaus (ed), *The Unity of Public Law* (Oxford, Hart Publishing, 2004) 21.

[58] *Baker* (n 54) [56]; Taggart, 'Impact of Apartheid', 204; also M Taggart, 'The Tub of Public Law' in D Dyzenhaus (ed), *The Unity of Public Law* (Oxford, Hart Publishing, 2004) 455, 469–70.

[59] Taggart, 'Proportionality' (n 51) 430 (emphasis added).

[60] Ibid, 424, also 454.

The solution to this puzzle may well be that Taggart was among those who entirely reject the distinction between review of the substantive merits and questions of law. If that was the view he took, the current widespread talk of deference on one side of the illusory law/discretion divide would for him have necessarily implied contemplation of deference on the other side as well. One of us presents an argument against such a complete rejection of the divide in this volume.[61]

III. THE WIDER DEBATE[62]

The wider literature on deference in relation to judicial review of questions of statutory interpretation discloses—perhaps unsurprisingly—a broad range of views. No attempt will be made to summarise the existing body of literature in this area; instead, three broad strands within it will be highlighted. Although they exhibit internal variety, those three strands within the debate can (loosely) be thought of in terms of defences of the expansive approach, arguments in favour of some degree of deference on questions of law, and questions concerning the viability and implications of the distinction between questions of fact and law.

A. Defences of the Expansive Approach

In jurisdictions, such as the UK and New Zealand, that embrace the expansive approach to error of law review, a certain paradox arises. Even though the expansive approach is relatively novel—it can be traced in the UK to *Anisminic*,[63] but was only firmly adopted in *Page*[64]—it is widely taken to represent orthodoxy. Yet it is, in one sense, in *tension* with administrative law orthodoxy. As Ivan Hare points out, central to that broader orthodoxy is the distinction between appeal and review: a distinction that could meaningfully be said to exist in this sphere only for 'as long as there were some questions of law which the inferior body could get wrong (in the eyes of the reviewing court) and yet not sacrifice its ultimate say'.[65] The expansive

[61] H Wilberg, 'Deference on Relevance and Purpose? Wrestling with the Law/Discretion Divide' (ch 11 in this volume).

[62] It seems to us that the argument against Diceyan centralism is the main line of argument for deference in Canada. That point has already been considered above in section II B i. The discussion in this section focuses on other aspects of the debate that are encountered principally in other jurisdictions.

[63] *Anisminic* (n 8).

[64] *Page* (n 9).

[65] I Hare, 'The Separation of Powers and Judicial Review for Error of Law' in I Hare and C Forsyth (eds), *The Golden Metwand and the Crooked Cord: Essays in Honour of Sir William Wade* (Oxford, Clarendon Press, 1988) 124.

approach, however, empties the distinction of content in the field of error of law.[66]

Hare argues that the elision of appeal and review in this field is so antithetical to conventional administrative law theory that the expansive approach to error of law 'cannot be accommodated within the traditional justification for judicial review', such that 'an alternative constitutional basis must be located'.[67] Hare is influenced in this conclusion not only by the implications of the expansive approach for the appeal/review distinction, but also by the way in which it can be—and has been[68]—used to facilitate judicial review in the face of a privative clause. As a result, argues Hare, the expansive approach may not be—and sometimes is not—consistent with a justification for judicial review grounded in the effectuation of legislative intention.[69] On this view, the machinery of ultra vires cannot readily be invoked in service of the expansive model of error of law review.

It might well be thought that Hare's conclusions as to the incompatibility between that approach and conventional administrative law theory points towards difficulties with the expansive approach itself.[70] Hare, however, argues that the incompatibility between that approach and conventional justifications for review demonstrates not the wrongness of that approach, but merely the insufficiency of those justifications. Some other justification is therefore required—which, says Hare, can be found in the form of the separation of powers doctrine. Courts, the argument runs, should determine the meaning of legislation—including by denying to administrative agencies the final say about the meaning of provisions that fall to be applied by such agencies—because it is courts that are best placed to decide what meaning legislation should bear.

For others, the justification might be found in the rule of law. And in systems, like those in the UK and New Zealand, that embrace both the expansive approach and parliamentary sovereignty, constitutional axioms such as the separation of powers and the rule of law are typically pressed into service in an attempt to reconcile *judicial* supremacy in matters of *interpretation* with *parliamentary* supremacy in matters of *legislation*. Such arguments are most obviously germane when a reviewing court is presented with (what appears to be) a preclusive provision. Classically, courts in the UK and New Zealand—in cases such as *Anisminic*[71] and *Bulk Gas*[72]—have taken the view that the judicial role is to interpret statutes and that it

[66] Ibid, 124.
[67] Ibid, 127.
[68] As in *Anisminic* (n 8).
[69] Hare (n 65) 125–27.
[70] P Daly, 'Deference on Questions of Law' (2011) 74 *Modern Law Review* 694, 699–706. See also Daly, *A Theory of Deference* (n 53) ch 6.
[71] *Anisminic* (n 8).
[72] *Bulk Gas* (n 4).

would be nonsensical for the legislature to circumscribe the authority of a decision-maker whilst denying courts the authority to determine what those limits actually are. In this way, very strong interpretative presumptions are brought to bear upon provisions that might otherwise be taken to oust the courts' interpretative function.

Others go further still. In *R (Cart) v Upper Tribunal*, Laws LJ,[73] resisting the suggestion that there had been an effective exclusion of the courts' judicial review jurisdiction, contends that the interpretation of legislative texts cannot legitimately be performed by the legislature or the executive, since that would make them 'judge in their own cause, with the ills of arbitrary government which that would entail'.[74] Nor could the interpretive function be performed 'by the public body which has to administer the relevant law: for in that case the decision-makers would write their own laws'.[75] Rather, the interpreter must be 'impartial, independent both of the legislature and of the persons affected by the texts' application, and authoritative', such that statutory interpretation is a role that '[o]nly a court can fulfil'.[76]

Laws LJ uses this conclusion to argue that courts can legitimately resist privative clauses even in legal systems—such as those of the UK and New Zealand—that incorporate legislative supremacy. Such resistance would 'not [be] a denial of legislative sovereignty, but an affirmation of it': the legislature's authority to make *law* would be undermined if the status of its enactments were degraded by virtue of being immune from interpretation by independent courts.[77]

Whether or not accepted at face value, Laws LJ's argument is genuinely one founded upon the separation of powers. In contrast, Hare's analysis—as Paul Daly points out[78]—is arguably not, since Hare's focus is not so much upon separation of powers as upon the courts' putative interpretive expertise.[79] This argument is quite different in nature from the one advanced by Laws LJ (albeit that both sail, whether or not appropriately, under the colours of the separation of powers). Laws LJ's argument is normative–constitutional in nature, in that it rests upon a vision of how authority is (or should be) divided. Hare's approach, in contrast, is of a more pragmatic kind: the courts' claim to interpretive monopoly is founded, on this view, not upon their special constitutional status, but, more mundanely, upon their technical interpretive prowess. In this regard, then, Hare's approach joins issue with the argument—advanced by many—against the expansive approach, on the ground that courts' superior expertise cannot and should not be taken for granted.[80]

[73] *R (Cart) v Upper Tribunal* [2009] EWHC 3052 (Admin), [2010] PTSR 824.
[74] Ibid, [37].
[75] Ibid, [37].
[76] Ibid, [37].
[77] Ibid, [38].
[78] Daly, 'Deference on Questions of Law' (n 70) 706.
[79] Hare (n 65) 130–36.
[80] See parts II A and II B i above; and the text below at n 87.

B. Arguments for Deference

A number of commentators, writing from the perspective of jurisdictions in which the expansive approach has become the orthodoxy, challenge that approach and argue instead in favour of some measure of deference.[81] As contributions to this aspect of the debate show, there are many different ways in which deference—or, to use a more neutral term, a less demanding standard of review—may be secured.

For some commentators, such as Rebecca Williams, old distinctions (between jurisdictional and non-jurisdictional matters, and between law and fact) should be eschewed in favour of a new distinction between questions whose unambiguous objectivity dictates that there can be only 'one correct answer' to them, and those questions that call for the exercise of some degree of 'discretion', the two categories respectively attracting correctness and reasonableness review.[82] For others, such as Trevor Allan, any attempt to lay down a bright-line distinction between circumstances attracting different standards of review is doomed to failure on account of insufficient nuance. Instead, Allan calls for a wholly contextual determination of what constitutes a 'rational division of responsibility, *in the particular case*, between court and agency'.[83] He thus emphatically rejects any doctrine of deference.

Paul Daly makes a particularly strong challenge to the expansive approach. He draws upon the approach now adopted in Canada and upon earlier Canadian literature advocating that approach,[84] but addresses his argument as much to the jurisdictions outside North America that continue to embrace the expansive approach. He argues that 'where legislative intent and practical considerations so suggest ... courts should defer to administrative interpretations of law by applying a less exacting standard of review'.[85] Daly's argument is built upon normative and pragmatic foundations that challenge the premises, described above, that Hare and Laws LJ adopt. On a normative level, Daly does not share Laws LJ's conviction that judicial bodies must, *because* they are judicial bodies, necessarily enjoy interpretive supremacy—not least because, within Daly's framework, legislative intention is accorded greater prominence, and so greater capacity to influence the allocation of interpretive competence as between judicial and administrative institutions.[86] Meanwhile, in pragmatic terms, Daly

[81] See, eg our discussion in part II above of the positions taken by Taggart and Craig.

[82] R Williams, 'When is an error not an error? Reform of jurisdictional review of error of law and fact' [2007] *Public Law* 793.

[83] TRS Allan, 'Doctrine and theory in administrative law: an elusive quest for the limits of jurisdiction' [2003] *Public Law* 429, 442.

[84] On which see Daly (n 38). The earlier Canadian literature is discussed in section II B i above.

[85] Daly, 'Deference on Questions of Law' (n 70) 696–97.

[86] Ibid, 699–706.

challenges the view that courts necessarily enjoy superior institutional competence in relation to interpretive matters, arguing that: 'The best answer to a question of law might come from a delegated decision-maker more familiar than a court with the particular area of law.'[87]

Significantly, the position Daly adopts in relation to judicial review of questions of law is not an isolated one, but one which forms part of a broader argument about the place of deference in administrative law—and hence about the relationship between judicial and administrative authority.[88] On this view, the debate about error of law review is a facet of a much broader debate that has deep constitutional roots concerning the extent (if any) of the legislature's capacity to allocate a share of interpretive authority to a non-judicial institution. To the extent that that question remains unanswered by definitive provision in a constitutional text—either because, as in the UK and New Zealand, no such text exists, or because whatever text does exist fails to answer the question—the question segues into a normative one about whether the legislature *ought* to be able to invest non-judicial bodies with a share of interpretive authority. And, to the extent that such capacity is ascribed to the legislature, further questions then arise about whether, in any particular situation, the legislature should actually be taken to have exercised that capacity by giving a share of interpretive authority to a non-judicial body. On this view, it is at this stage that second-order questions concerning relative institutional competence are most likely to arise, in that they go to the *wisdom*—as distinct from the *constitutional possibility*—of permitting institutions other than courts to determine what the law means; as such, they enjoy purchase in relation to the question whether the legislature has chosen to (as opposed to could) locate a share of interpretive authority outwith the judicial branch. It follows that questions about the appropriate standard of review in relation to error of law cannot be considered in isolation from underlying considerations pertaining to institutional and constitutional context.[89]

A different dimension of the debate about interpretive deference is brought out by Paul Craig. He expresses a degree of support for the rejection in the US and Canada of the expansive approach in favour of a greater degree of deference.[90] And although—as the voluminous jurisprudence and literature surrounding the US *Chevron* test[91] amply demonstrates—deviation from

[87] Ibid, 707.

[88] See, generally, Daly, *A Theory of Deference* (n 53).

[89] This is the line of thought pursued in P Cane, 'Judicial Control of Administrative Interpretation in Australia and the United States' (ch 9 in this volume).

[90] Craig, *Administrative Law* (n 22) 502–507. See also P Craig, 'Jurisdiction, Judicial Control, and Agency Autonomy' in I Loveland (ed), *A Special Relationship? American Influences on Public Law in the UK* (Oxford, Oxford University Press, 1995) 173.

[91] *Chevron USA Inc v NRDC* (1984) 467 US 837.

the expansive approach may produce complexity and uncertainty, Craig argues that such difficulties do not 'undermine the soundness of the premise' that there must be circumstances in which agencies retain some interpretive autonomy, subject to rationality review.[92] (It might be added that approaches such as those found in the US and Canada merely serve to make explicit difficulties that, under the expansive approach, exist in more clandestine form—a point we develop below in relation to the malleability of the law/fact distinction.)

Craig also acknowledges that any attempt to carve out distinct categories in this area—whether by reference to 'true' jurisdictional issues attracting (on the most recent Canadian approach) a correctness standard, or to the specificity of legislative intention (which, under the US approach, determines the applicable standard of review)—creates significant risks of judicial instrumentalism. Craig is thus alive to the possibility that—like the distinction between 'jurisdictional' and 'non-jurisdictional' questions—other devices that might be invoked in order to determine the applicable standard of review might be manipulated by courts. Ultimately, says Craig, it might be argued (albeit 'in cynical vein') that: 'The label rational basis would simply be reflective of a conclusion already reached that the court did not wish to intervene', while a 'test of rightness would indicate the opposite conclusion.'[93] However, Craig does not accept that this risk should necessarily stand in the way of an approach that explicitly countenances distinct standards of review: the challenge, he argues, is to fashion an approach that engages directly with questions about the 'desirability of judicial intervention'.[94] This comment perhaps underlines concerns about the recent Canadian move away from an approach that relied on a set of 'pragmatic and functional' factors which were designed to engage with precisely those questions.[95]

C. The Fact/Law Distinction

Even if it is accepted that questions of law are always questions for the court, this still leaves the difficulty of defining questions of law. The difficulty concerns in particular how questions of law are to be distinguished from questions of fact. In our view, this is simply a manifestation of the

[92] P Craig, 'Judicial Review and Questions of Law: A Comparative Perspective' in S Rose-Ackerman and P Lindseth (eds), *Comparative Administrative Law* (Cheltenham, Edward Elgar, 2010) 463.

[93] Craig, *Administrative Law* (n 22) 506.

[94] Ibid, 505.

[95] P Daly, 'The Unfortunate Triumph of Form over Substance in Canadian Administrative Law' (2012) 50 *Osgoode Hall Law Journal* 317. The point is also touched on in this volume: Daly (n 38).

same difficulty that has beset this aspect of administrative law for centuries: as Craig puts it, there is always a question as to 'when courts should substitute judgment and when some interpretative autonomy, subject to rationality review, should be accorded to the initial decision-maker'.[96] Traditionally, this has found expression in the distinction between 'jurisdictional' and 'non-jurisdictional' questions of law. Yet although the highly unsatisfactory nature of that distinction has led to its abandonment in some common-law systems, this has—unsurprisingly—not proven to be a magic bullet. Instead, the result has been the replacement of one problematic distinction with another: namely, the distinction between fact and law. For while defenders of the expansive approach insist that law (and hence statutory interpretation) must be for the courts, there are very few (if any) who think that all factual determinations are equally a matter for the courts (since, if they were, the distinction between appeal and review really would collapse).[97] It follows that the true import of the expansive approach to questions of law can only be appreciated by reference to how the fact/law distinction—and so the province of expansive review of questions lying on the 'law' side of the line—is understood. Furthermore, to the extent that the distinction is unstable and open to manipulation, that presents the risk that the distinction between appeal and review may collapse.

Before the expansive approach was cemented in England by the House of Lords' decision in *Page*[98]—but at a time when the direction of travel was already tolerably clear—Jack Beatson presciently wrote about the difficulties likely to attend its adoption. In particular, he observed that the rejection of any category of non-jurisdictional questions of law coupled with an 'analytic' approach to the characterisation of legal issues—that is, one that treats as a question of law every question involving the interpretation or application of a statutory text—would result in a '"total" reviewing power'[99] that would 'deprive administrative bodies of all their autonomy'.[100]

An obvious reaction to this conclusion (if accepted) is that unless the expansive approach is to be rejected, a more pragmatic approach to characterisation must be adopted in order to strike an acceptable balance between judicial control and agency autonomy. Thus the fact/law distinction would become the site of precisely the type of judicial manipulation that in the

[96] Craig (n 92) 463.

[97] For an instance of the most expansive view of review for error of fact, see C Forsyth and E Dring, 'The Final Frontier: The Emergence of Material Error of Fact as a Ground for Judicial Review' in C Forsyth and others (eds), *Effective Judicial Review: A Cornerstone of Good Governance* (Oxford, Oxford University Press, 2010) 245.

[98] *Page* (n 9).

[99] J Beatson, 'The Scope of Judicial Review for Error of Law' (1984) 4 *Oxford Journal of Legal Studies* 22, 41.

[100] Ibid, 42.

past occurred by reference to the distinction between jurisdictional and non-jurisdictional question of law. The scope for such manipulation is particularly obvious in relation to matters that involve the application of the law to the facts.

Some have argued that such 'mixed questions of fact and law' can be classified as different from pure questions of law, and can thus serve as a vehicle for less intensive review whilst leaving the correctness approach to 'purely' legal questions untouched. As Timothy Endicott notes, treating *all* application questions as questions of law would—if all questions of law are subject to correctness review—be 'intolerable': this really would result in the sort of 'total' reviewing power warned against by Beatson.[101] But Endicott argues that application questions need not and are not invariably treated as questions of law—and although the characterisation of application questions is perhaps especially susceptible to a pragmatic approach, Endicott argues that an analytical approach can in fact be brought to bear in this context.[102]

However, Endicott's approach still presupposes that pure questions of law are determinable by courts applying a correctness standard—the possibility of characterising application questions as questions of *fact* being a means of escape from the strictures of correctness review that would otherwise apply. The difficulty, as Beatson observes, is that error of law is, at best, an inadequate organising concept, because it 'avoids grappling with necessary questions of policy concerning the amount of autonomy that administrative [bodies] should be given' in relation to matters of law.[103] It follows that—unless it is felt that the answer to that question is, in all circumstances, 'none whatever'—some *other* way must be found of engaging with such policy concerns. Courts reluctant to engage in correctness review on questions of law might, for instance, interpret statutory purposes broadly and generously,[104] declare decisions or particular issues to be non-justiciable,[105] or exercise their discretion against awarding a remedy.[106]

[101] T Endicott, 'Questions of Law' (1998) 114 *Law Quarterly Review* 292, 307.

[102] On Endicott's preferred approach (ibid, 318), an application question should be treated as a question of law (and subject to correctness review) if 'the law requires one answer to the question'. The law will require one answer 'in a *clear* case of the application of the statutory language' and 'when the court exercises its legal power to elaborate the law so as to require (*or* interprets the statutory standard to require) one answer'. Endicott concedes that these amount to pragmatic considerations, but argues that the approach remains an analytical one because pragmatic considerations are, on this approach, relevant only to the *general* characterisation of the application question as opposed to its characterisation for the specific purpose of the particular situation.

[103] Beatson (n 99) 31.

[104] Ibid, 417; Wilberg (n 61).

[105] DR Knight, 'Mapping the Rainbow of Review: Recognising Variable Intensity' [2010] *New Zealand Law Review* 393, 424–26.

[106] Aronson (n 34).

Another possibility, of course, is that the law/fact distinction itself might be manipulated, as Beatson,[107] Taggart,[108] Dean Knight[109] and, in his contribution to this volume, Mark Aronson, have noted. Such manipulation might offer a way of carving out a degree of interpretive autonomy for decision-makers by means of characterising some questions of statutory interpretation as questions of law.

However, this cuts both ways: the malleability of the fact/law distinction might serve to *expand* the availability of correctness review by resulting in a broader range of matters being characterised as questions of law. This possibility was raised by Lord Carnwath in *Jones v First-tier Tribunal*, where he suggested that an expert tribunal with jurisdiction to deal with appeals on points of law might be justified in adopting a broad view of what constitutes a question of law so as to enable it to deploy its expertise to best effect.[110]

In surveying the wider debate, it is hard to resist the conclusion that it operates on two quite different levels—but that the distinction between those levels is ultimately an illusory one, as suggested in Aronson's contribution. In the first place, there is the question whether questions of law should always attract correctness review, or whether a more deferential standard should (sometimes) apply. Legal systems that opt for the former model—by embracing the expansive conception of error of law—appear to prefer a simple, uncompromising approach that prizes legality and certainty over other values such as administrative autonomy and acknowledgment of relative expertise. In doing so, they appear to turn their faces away from the second aspect of the debate that occurs in systems that acknowledge a role for deference: namely, the debate about *when* deference is warranted. Yet it is clear that precisely such a debate is engaged in, either overtly or covertly, whether a system opts for the expansive or for a more deferential approach. To put the matter another way, none of the major common-law systems actually treats every question of statutory interpretation as a matter that must inevitably attract correctness review. It follows that the real fault-line in the debate relates not to the question *whether* deference is ever appropriate. Rather, the principal site of disagreement is found in relation to questions pertaining to the *circumstances* in which deference is appropriate and the *means* by which deference, when it is appropriate, should be delivered.

[107] Beatson (n 99).
[108] See above, text accompanying n 33.
[109] Knight (n 105) 415–17.
[110] *Jones v First-tier Tribunal* [2013] UKSC 19, [2013] 2 AC 48, [46].

9

Judicial Control of Administrative Interpretation in Australia and the United States

PETER CANE*

I. INTRODUCTION

CANONICAL LEGAL TEXTS are texts the precise words, grammar, punctuation and other linguistic features of which are authoritative. Constitutions and legislation, whether primary or secondary, are the prime examples of canonical legal texts. Interpretation of canonical legal texts is the activity of determining what they mean. Every time a canonical legal text is applied, it is interpreted. This is true even where it is universally agreed that the relevant words of the text can reasonably bear only one meaning. Because application of canonical legal texts is a ubiquitous 'law job',[1] interpretation is, too.

In English law, the idea that certain legal texts are canonical developed gradually and matured probably in the nineteenth century. By that time, the clear modern distinction between law made by Parliament (legislation) and law made by courts (common law)—the former embodied in canonical texts but the latter not—had emerged on the back of the doctrine of parliamentary supremacy, which was formally established as the foundation of the English legal system at the end of the seventeenth century. In the medieval way of thinking, by contrast, all lawmaking, whether by Parliament or courts, was a process of giving expression to pre-existing principles.[2] It followed that interpretation of legislation would not begin (and should

* Distinguished Professor of Law, Australian National University. I am very grateful to Mark Aronson, Tony Connolly, Paul Daly, James Stellios and Hanna Wilberg for perceptive and helpful comments and to Zsofia Korosy for excellent research assistance. The research for this paper was partly funded by an Australian Research Council Discovery Project grant.

[1] To borrow Karl Llewellyn's famous term: W Twining, *Karl Llewellyn and the Realist Movement* (with Postscript) (London, Weidenfeld & Nicolson, 1985) 175–84.

[2] There were various views and theories about the source and content of such principles.

certainly not end) with the precise words, syntax and other linguistic features of the text, but with the pre-existing principles of which the text was an embodiment and expression.

Applying—and, therefore, interpreting—canonical legal texts is a characteristic activity of the executive branch of government,[3] understood broadly to include all those individuals and organisations that perform public functions and that are not identified as belonging either to the legislature or the judiciary. For convenience, I shall refer to them as 'administrators'. Of course, administrators not only interpret and apply the law: they also make law and adjudicate legal disputes. However, relative to lawmaking and adjudication, interpretation and application of the law dominate public administration. Conversely, although the legislature and courts interpret and apply canonical legal texts, the former does so only relatively rarely when testing the limits of its constitutional powers and in the administration of its own affairs, while the latter do so only when asked by the right person, at the right time and in the right way. For every instance of legislative or judicial interpretation and application of canonical law, there are countless instances of administrative interpretation and application. The metaphor of the tip of the iceberg gets nowhere near capturing the ratio of judicial (and legislative) to administrative interpretation and application of canonical law.

In practice, canonical law normally means what administrators—those most engaged in its application—say it means. This is as true of constitutional documents as it is of primary and secondary legislation ('statutes' and 'regulations' as I shall respectively name the latter two). For that reason, it is very important to understand how administrators go about interpreting canonical texts. However, I say nothing about that in this paper.[4] My topic here is theory, not practice. There are three relevant and related theoretical questions. First, who has the last word on what a canonical text means? Put differently, who is the supreme interpreter? Secondly, what account, if any, should judges take of administrators' interpretations in determining what a canonical text means? Thirdly, how should administrators go about interpreting canonical texts?

As we will see, in relation to statutes and regulations (at least) Australian and US law answer the second question differently.[5] Crudely and briefly, under Australian law (as under English law), there is only one correct answer to what any particular provision of a statute or regulation means,

[3] Eg *Bowsher v Synar* (1986) 478 US 714, 733 ('Interpreting a law enacted by Congress to implement the legislative mandate is the very essence of "execution" of the law.')

[4] My colleague and Australia's pre-eminent expert on statutory interpretation, Dennis Pearce, once said to me (with tongue not very far into cheek) that in deciding what the text of a statute means, administrators may not only start elsewhere but may never look at the text.

[5] The main focus in this paper in relation to both Australia and the US is federal law and the federal legal system.

and that is the answer given by the ultimate court in the system (the High Court, in the Australian case).[6] In this sense, only the High Court has power to interpret 'conclusively' or 'finally'. Under US law, by contrast, whether any particular provision of a statute or regulation has only one reasonably possible meaning, or more than one, is itself a question of interpretation. If, properly interpreted,[7] such a provision has more than one reasonably possible meaning, in certain circumstances a court should 'defer' to—in other words, adopt as the meaning of the provision—the alternative chosen by the administrator, even if the court itself would have chosen a different meaning. As I will suggest, the answer to this second question has implications for the answers to the first and third questions.

This contrast between (Anglo-)Australian law and US law has been frequently noted. In the literature, the rules about judicial control of administrative interpretation are often compared with those concerning judicial control of administrative fact-finding and policy-making. Under Australian law, when reviewing administrative fact-finding and policy-making, courts must defer to a greater or lesser extent. By contrast, under orthodox accounts of US law, courts are required to defer significantly less to administrative fact-finding and policy-making than to administrative interpretation.[8] As a normative matter, some writers consider the US position to be 'anomalous' and the Australian position to be more consistent with constitutional principles concerning the role of courts and the proper relationship between courts and administrators.[9] Conversely, some have argued that Australian (and English) law should accord some deference to administrative interpretations. However, as far as I can see, the existing literature does not offer a plausible (or, indeed, any) explanation of why Australian (or English) law is different from US law in this regard.

Suggesting such an explanation is the purpose of this paper. My aim is not to contribute to normative arguments about what the law should be, but rather to offer an explanation of why it is as it is. The normative and the explanatory are not unrelated: what *is* may affect what is *desirable*; but my views about what is desirable deserve no particular attention, and explanation is enough to be getting on with. The focus will be on the law relating to judicial control of administrative interpretation rather than administrative fact-finding or policy-making, and on interpretation of statutes and regulations. My basic argument will be that the difference between Australian and

[6] The same approach is applied to issues of procedural fairness both in Australia (P Cane and L McDonald, *Principles of Administrative Law: Legal Regulation of Governance*, 2nd edn (Melbourne, Oxford University Press, 2012) 125–26) and England (*Osborn v Parole Board* [2013] UKSC 61, [2013] 3 WLR 1020, [65]).

[7] Of course, this proviso itself raises a host of issues.

[8] Assume, for the moment, that there are reasonably clear, objective criteria for distinguishing between law, fact and policy.

[9] Eg S Breyer, 'Judicial Review of Questions of Law and Policy' (1986) 38 *Administrative Law Review* 363.

US law is explicable, at least partly, by reference to two models of the judicial function and the nature of judicial power. This explanation (unlike many theoretical accounts of administrative law)[10] depends on understanding not only the relationship between courts and administrators but, more generally, the relationships between the various major institutions of government.

II. THE LAW

A. US Law

First, it is necessary to give a somewhat more detailed account of the relevant law. In US law, there are three main varieties of judicial deference to administrative interpretation.[11] These are generally referred to as '*Skidmore* deference', '*Chevron* deference' and '*Seminole Rock* (or '*Auer*') deference' after their eponymous cases.[12] *Chevron* stands for the basic proposition that the court should accept the administrator's interpretation of a statutory provision that is reasonably open to more than one interpretation, even if the court itself would have preferred a different interpretation. This rule does not apply to statutes generally but only to the constitutive statute of the agency in question and other statutes that the agency is responsible for administering. However, it applies as much to provisions that determine the scope of the agency's authority (its 'jurisdiction') as to other provisions.[13] On the other hand, it does not apply to interpretations generally but only to those that have 'the force of law' or, for some other reason, deserve deference.[14] Interpretations that have the force of law are, effectively, those

[10] Eg P Daly, 'Deference on Questions of Law' (2011) 74 *Modern Law Review* 694.

[11] The discussion that follows is concerned primarily with departments and agencies rather than the President. An increasingly important vehicle for Presidential interpretation of statutes is the 'signing statement'. See, eg CA Bradley and AE Posner, 'Presidential Signing Statements and Executive Power (2006) 23 *Constitutional Commentary* 307, especially 344–56; Note, 'Context-Sensitive Deference to Presidential Signing Statements' (2006) 120 *Harvard Law Review* 597. Signing statements are sometimes considered part of the legislative history of a statute but at other times as administrative interpretations: DC Jenson, 'From Deference to Restraint: Using the *Chevron* Framework to Evaluate Presidential Signing Statements' (2007) 91 *Minnesota Law Review* 1908. Treating them as administrative interpretations raises two questions: (1) does the signing statement itself attract deference? and (2) does an interpretation by a department or agency based on a signing statement attract deference? Concerning the latter question, see NJ Leddy, 'Determining Deference: Examining When Courts Should Defer to Agency Use of Presidential Signing Statements' (2007) 59 *Administrative Law Review* 869. On deference to Presidential interpretations more generally, see CR Sunstein, 'Beyond *Marbury*: The Executive's Power to Say What the Law Is' (2006) 115 *Yale Law Journal* 2580, 2603–604.

[12] *Skidmore v Swift & Co* (1944) 323 US 134; *Chevron USA Inc v Natural Resources Defense Council* (1984) 467 US 837; *Bowles, Price Administrator v Seminole Rock and Sand Co* (1945) 325 US 410; *Auer v Robbins* (1997) 519 US 452.

[13] *City of Arlington, Texas v Federal Communications Commission* (2013) 133 S Ct 1863.

[14] *United States v Mead Corp* (2001) 533 US 218 as interpreted in *Barnhart, Commissioner of Social Security v Walton* (2002) 535 US 212.

embodied in regulations made by the agency or in agency common law (that is, law made in the process of adjudication by the agency), but not those embodied in 'soft law' or that support non-adjudicatory decisions (such as initial decisions about entitlement to social security benefits).[15]

Interpretations of statutory provisions that do not attract *Chevron* deference may nevertheless be accorded *Skidmore* deference. Under the latter, unlike the former, in cases where a provision is reasonably open to more than one interpretation, the court decides which interpretation is preferable. However, in doing so it takes account of the *agency's preferred* interpretation and asks whether that interpretation is the *preferable* interpretation.[16]

> We consider that the ... interpretations ... of the Administrator under this Act ... constitute a body of experience and informed judgment to which ... courts may properly resort for guidance. The weight of such a judgment in a particular case will depend upon the thoroughness evident in its consideration, the validity of its reasoning, its consistency with earlier and later pronouncements, and all those factors which give it power to persuade.

Whereas *Skidmore* and *Chevron* deference relate to interpretation of statutory provisions, *Seminole Rock* deference relates to interpretation by an agency of provisions in regulations that the agency itself has made. The basic rule is that the agency's interpretation of its own regulations is 'controlling unless "plainly erroneous or inconsistent with the regulation"'.[17] Put differently, whereas under *Chevron* an agency's interpretation of a statute will be 'controlling' only if the court considers it reasonable, under *Seminole Rock* an agency's interpretation of a regulation will be controlling unless the court considers it (in Anglo-Australian terminology) *Wednesbury*-unreasonable.

It is commonly argued that these various formulae are explanatory rather than dispositive, and that courts can and do deploy them strategically to achieve the results that they favour on grounds that may or may

[15] Note, however, that in US legal terminology such initial decisions would be called instances of '(informal) adjudication'. This is because the Administrative Procedure Act 1946 defines 'adjudication' effectively to mean any activity other than rule-making. In Anglo-Australian terminology, by contrast, 'adjudication' refers to a three-party mode of resolving disputes. The US distinction between 'formal' and 'informal' adjudication refers to differences in adjudicatory procedure.

[16] *Skidmore* (1944) 323 US 134, 140. At the time of this decision there was a strand of authority in favour of no deference to administrative decisions on 'pure questions of law'. Concerning more recent statements to this effect see CR Sunstein, '*Chevron* Step Zero' (2006) 92 *Virginia Law Review* 187, 190.

[17] *Auer* (1997) 519 US 452, 461. An interpretation embodied in a regulation will not attract *Seminole Rock* deference if it merely reproduces the terms of a statute: *Gonzales v Oregon* (2006) 546 US 243. Concerning judicial interpretation of regulations (which is logically prior to applying the *Seminole Rock* test) see KM Stack, 'Interpreting Regulations' (2012) 111 *Michigan Law Review* 355.

not be expressed.[18] For our purposes, however, this is as unimportant as the finer points of the various formulae themselves.[19] The significant thing is that US law[20] starts from the position that the power of interpretation is shared between courts and administrators.[21] Because courts sit at the end of the interpretive chain (as it were) they decide the nature and scope of the administrative power of interpretation, and the boundary of that power marks the limit of judicial deference. This is not considered inconsistent with the famous dictum of Marshall CJ in *Marbury v Madison* that 'it is emphatically the duty of the judicial department to say what the law is'.[22] *Marbury* established the power of the courts to determine not only the constitutionality of Congressional legislation but also the legality of executive action. However, it does not follow from either holding that the law allocates exclusive power of conclusive interpretation to the courts. Under US law (as made by the Supreme Court), power to interpret statutes and regulations conclusively is shared between the judiciary and the executive.

There are three strands of reasoning supporting more or less deference by courts to administrative interpretations, one formal and the other two substantive. The formal reason refers to the power of Congress to confer interpretive power on the executive: the Constitution does not expressly allocate interpretive power and does not prevent Congress from allocating a share of that power to the executive.[23] The second, substantive reason points to the expertise of administrative agencies in the policy areas for which they are responsible. An interpreter with expert knowledge and experience of the subject matter of legislation and regulations may be better equipped than a generalist court to interpret relevant provisions in a way that will best promote the purposes of the law being interpreted. Thirdly,

[18] Eg TJ Miles and CR Sunstein, 'Do Judges Make Regulatory Policy? An Empirical Investigation of *Chevron* (2006) 73 *University of Chicago Law Review* 823. But see MJ Richards, JL Smith and HM Kritzer, 'Does *Chevron* Matter?' (2006) 28 *Law and Policy* 444; CN Raso and WN Eskridge Jr, '*Chevron* as a Canon, not a Precedent: An Empirical Study of What Motivates Justices in Agency Deference Cases' (2010) 110 *Columbia Law Review* 1727.

[19] For detailed analysis see WN Eskridge and LE Baer, 'The Continuum of Deference: Supreme Court Treatment of Statutory Interpretations from *Chevron* to *Hamdan*' (2008) 96 *Georgetown Law Journal* 1083.

[20] Judge-made law, anyway. However, this position is arguably inconsistent with the Administrative Procedure Act 1946, which provides that 'the reviewing court shall decide all questions of law'.

[21] Even commentators who favour the overruling of *Chevron* do not propose replacing it with a rule of no deference: eg JM Beermann, 'End the Failed *Chevron* Experiment Now: How *Chevron* Has Failed and Why It Can and Should Be Overruled' (2010) 42 *Connecticut Law Review* 779. Concerning the role of the legislature in interpretation see nn 24 and 70 below.

[22] *Marbury v Madison* (1803) 5 US (1 Cranch) 137, 167. See, generally, HP Monaghan, '*Marbury* and the Administrative State' (1983) 83 *Columbia Law Review* 1.

[23] *United States v Mead Corp* (2001) 533 US 218. An alternative view is that there is a 'constitutionally inspired' default rule, subject to Congressional displacement, that resolving statutory ambiguity is an executive function: J Goldsmith and JF Manning, 'The President's Completion Power' (2006) 115 *Yale Law Journal* 2280.

it is said, courts should defer to administrators because, by virtue of being subject to Presidential oversight, administrators enjoy a degree of political legitimacy that courts lack.[24]

This last argument alerts us to an important underlying issue about the concept of 'interpretation'. A possible—and perhaps now the standard—reading of the *Chevron* decision is that the first step of deciding whether a provision is reasonably open to more than one meaning involves interpretation, while the second step of choosing between reasonable meanings involves policy-making.[25] Put in terms more familiar to Australian ears, the first step involves answering a question of law whereas the second step involves exercising discretion. As we have noted, under both US law and Australian law, the criterion for judicial review of administrators' answers to questions of law is different from the criteria for review of administrative fact-finding and policy-making respectively. However, choosing between reasonable interpretations of a provision on the one hand, and exercising discretion conferred by that provision on the other, cannot be distinguished from one another in a purely analytical way. Nor, indeed, is there any mechanical formula for deciding whether a provision is reasonably open to more than one interpretation. Fortunately, for present purposes we can ignore these complications. The concern here is not with how the various concepts (law, fact and policy) and the various criteria of review—no deference (otherwise known as '*de novo* review'),[26] *Skidmore* deference, *Chevron* deference, *Seminole Rock/Auer* deference, and those applicable to exercises of discretion—apply in particular cases, but only with their abstract significance and inter-relationship.

B. Australian Law

The leading Australian case on the topic is *Corporation of the City of Enfield v Development Assessment Commission*.[27] In their joint judgment, the plurality conceptualised the case as being about the standard of review

[24] *Chevron* (1984) 467 US 837, 864-66. Administrators are also subject to Congressional oversight, but this fact is not part of the argument for deference. See further n 70 below.

[25] ED Elliott, '*Chevron* Matters: How the *Chevron* Doctrine Redefined the Roles of Congress, Courts and Agencies in Environmental Law' (2005) 16 *Villanova Environmental Law Journal* 1; EV Foote, 'Statutory Interpretation or Public Administration: How *Chevron* Misconceives the Functions of Agencies and Why it Matters' (2007) 59 *Administrative Law Review* 673; RJ Pierce Jr, '*Chevron* and its Aftermath: Judicial Review of Agency Interpretations of Statutory Provisions' (1988) 41 *Vanderbilt Law Review* 301; Sunstein (n 11).

[26] Administrative interpretations of the Constitution and of statutes of general application, such as the Administrative Procedure Act, attract no deference.

[27] *Corporation of the City of Enfield v Development Assessment Commission* (1999) 199 CLR 135.

of administrative fact-finding, not administrative statutory interpretation—in other words, not as an issue of law but as issue of the application of law to facts. They distinguished between jurisdictional and non-jurisdictional facts. In relation to non-jurisdictional facts, the plurality said that:[28]

> The weight to be given to the opinion of the tribunal in a particular case will depend on the circumstances. These will include such matters as the field in which the tribunal operates, the criteria for appointment of its members, the materials upon which it acts in exercising its functions and the extent to which its decisions are supported by disclosed processes of reasoning.

In relation to jurisdictional fact-finding the plurality said that if (1) in all significant respects the evidence before the court is substantially the same as had been before the administrator; (2) the administrator's decision was confirmed at appellate level; and (3) by virtue of relevant expertise the administrator was specially equipped to decide the issue of fact, 'greater weight will be accorded than in cases in which one or more of these facts is absent'.[29]

Several points deserve to be made about these two holdings. First, both authorise courts to give what, in US law, is called 'deference' to administrative decisions. The approach in both instances bears significant similarities to *Skidmore* deference, not only in the reference to various factors but also in 'permitting rather than requiring recourse to the administrative decision'.[30] Secondly, one of the factors to be taken into account in relation to jurisdictional fact-finding is the expertise of the decision-maker. Like US courts, the High Court understands the relationship between the judiciary and the executive partly in terms of 'comparative institutional competence'. However, this concept has a different resonance in the US than in Australia. In the US, one of the main aims of reform of the civil service in the late nineteenth century, by the introduction of merit-based recruitment in place of the so-called 'spoils system', was to reduce the role of politics and increase that of expertise and 'science' in public administration.[31] By contrast, the prime justificatory characteristic of the public service in Australia (and England) is political neutrality (or, perhaps more accurately, serial bipartisanship), not expertise. In the Australian context, expertise is a special characteristic of some administrative decision-makers rather than an assumed characteristic of public administration generally. Indeed, traditionally the upper echelons of the public service have been predominantly populated by 'generalists'.

[28] Ibid, 154–55.
[29] Ibid, 155.
[30] Ibid, 155.
[31] See, eg DH Rosenbloom, R O'Leary and J Chanin, *Public Administration and Law*, 3rd edn (Boca Raton, CRC Press, 2010) 5–8.

Thirdly, in its general discussion of standards of review, the plurality approves a statement of Brennan J to the effect that courts should not concern themselves with the 'merits' (as opposed to the 'legality') of administrative decisions because these are properly subject to 'political' control.[32] For the High Court, as for US courts, the fact of political control is relevant to judicial control of administrative decision-making. However, whereas for US courts, political control provides a reason to give weight to certain administrative decisions, for the High Court it is a reason not to review certain decisions or, at least, not to review decisions on certain grounds. It is noteworthy that the possibility of political control does not figure in either of the sets of criteria relevant to review of administrative fact-finding. This is probably because these tests relate to fact-finding or to the application of law to facts. In the Australian way of thinking, politics are relevant to policy, but not to fact or law.

Concerning review of administrative statutory interpretation, the plurality speculates that the *Chevron* rule might encourage administrators to adopt 'one of several competing reasonable interpretations ... so as to fit the facts to the desired result' thus 'delegalising' the administrative process.[33] 'The fundamental consideration in this field of discourse', the plurality continues, referring to *Marbury v Madison*, is 'that an essential characteristic of the judicature is that it declares and enforces the law which determines the limits of the power conferred by statute on administrative decision-makers'.[34] We saw earlier that US courts do not consider the judiciary's power and obligation to enforce the law as inconsistent with deference to administrative interpretations. These dicta in *Enfield* suggest that the High Court does. Moreover, the plurality goes on to observe that Australian law draws a sharp distinction between the legality and the merits of administrative decisions, suggesting that for them (unlike US courts) declaring and enforcing the legal limits of public power is not only the judiciary's 'essential characteristic' but also its only proper task in reviewing administrative decision-making.[35] Conversely, for the plurality, conclusively declaring and enforcing the law is no part of the role of the

[32] *Corporation of the City of Enfield v Development Assessment Commission*, (n 27) 153.

[33] Ibid, 152.

[34] Ibid, 153. As has been noted, under US law *Chevron* applies to interpretation of provisions that establish the limits of power (jurisdiction) as much as to provisions that do not. In England, for all practical purposes, the distinction between jurisdictional and non-jurisdictional issues of law has been abolished, making all administrative decisions on issues of law reviewable. The position in Australia is complex. The distinction survives in some contexts (eg *Wingfoot Australia Partners Pty Ltd v Kocak* [2013] HCA 43), and remedies may be available for non-jurisdictional error of law, although not (perhaps) the full suite of judicial review remedies. It seems that the non-deferential approach applies to decisions on non-jurisdictional issues of law as much as to decisions on jurisdictional issues.

[35] KM Hayne, 'Deference—an Australian Perspective' [2011] *Public Law* 75, 76–77. Marshall CJ stated the latter proposition in *Marbury v Madison* (1803) 5 US 137, 170 but it has not had the effect in the US that it has had in Australia.

executive—it is an exclusively judicial power and responsibility. This may explain why the plurality eschews the language of 'deference': that term perhaps implies that the court is free to allocate the power of interpretation as between itself and the executive for 'prudential' reasons. The plurality in *Enfield*, by contrast, views the allocation of that power as pre-ordained by the Constitution: the court must not defer to administrative interpretations because the Constitution forbids it. On the other hand, the starting point of US law seems to be that the Constitution does not allocate the power of interpretation.

To summarise so far: under US judge-made, common law the power of interpreting statutes and regulations is shared between the judiciary and the executive. Under Australian law, by contrast, the interpretation of statutes (at least) is an exclusively judicial function allocated to federal courts (and State courts exercising federal jurisdiction) by the Constitution.

III. AN EXPLANATION

This brings us to the central question addressed in this paper: given that both the US Constitution and the Australian Constitution embody formal separation of executive and judicial power, how might we explain this fundamental difference in the law governing judicial control of administrative statutory interpretation? The explanation I will offer is based on a distinction between two different conceptions of the role of courts in the system of government, which I will call the 'subordinate judiciary' model and the 'coordinate judiciary' model respectively.

To understand this distinction some history is needed. First, the Anglo-Australian story. The English central courts (including and especially the common-law courts: King's/Queen's Bench and Common Pleas), like the English Parliament, grew out of the *Curia Regis* ('royal court'), the remote ancestor of today's Privy Council. In the medieval period neither institutional nor functional separation amongst organs of government was as strong as it was later to become. The judges not only adjudicated but also advised the monarch[36] and were actively involved in Parliament. They held office at the monarch's pleasure. Despite the emergence of courts as separate entities, the monarch and the Council (the membership of which, like that of today's Privy Council, included but was not limited to the senior government officials) continued to exercise considerable judicial power—for instance through the Court of Star Chamber. The distinctions we now draw between adjudication on the one hand, and administration

[36] Indeed, the Court of Chancery was presided over solely by the Lord Chancellor, a senior royal official, until the nineteenth century. To this day, the Privy Council in its judicial capacity advises the monarch.

and legislation on the other, were not nearly so clear. Adjudication was a tool of administration; and much legislation addressed petitions for relief made to the monarch by individuals, groups, communities and Parliament itself. Nor was the distinction between legislation and common law as sharp as it became later. In a meaningful sense, the role of the judges, like that of Parliament, was to support and assist the monarch to govern and administer the realm.

In the course of the seventeenth century, relationships between the various organs of central government were transformed. The domestic jurisdiction of the monarch-in-council was removed by Parliament in 1641. In 1701, the power to dismiss judges was transferred from the monarch to Parliament. The Bill of Rights 1689 marked the shift of 'sovereignty' from the monarch to (the monarch-in-) Parliament, which became the supreme legislator and monarch-maker. As a result of these changes, the common-law judges ceased to be an integral component of the machinery of government and agents of the monarch. Instead they became agents of Parliament and, in that capacity, interpreters and appliers of Parliament's sovereign will expressed in legislation. In *The Spirit of the Laws*, Montesquieu famously captured the outcome of the revolution in the concept of separation of powers. Blackstone interpreted that concept for an English audience in terms of separation of judicial power and independence of the judiciary.[37] A century later, Dicey made these ideas the foundation of his understanding of the rule of law, according to which it is the role of the 'ordinary' courts to define and police limits on executive power.[38]

The changed relationship between Parliament and the courts triggered the development of a much sharper distinction between law-making and law-interpretation than had existed in the medieval period and, eventually, a shift in modes of interpretation from an emphasis on purpose to a focus on the text. This shift was also encouraged by the development, in the nineteenth century, of responsible government and strong political parties, as a result of which the government gained effective control of the legislature, its legislative agenda and the drafting of legislation, the last of which became highly professionalised.[39] At the same time, the courts retained their

[37] JWF Allison, *The English Historical Constitution: Continuity, Change and European Effects* (Cambridge, Cambridge University Press, 2007) 78–83.

[38] AV Dicey, *An Introduction to the Study of the Law of the Constitution*, 10th edn (London, Macmillan, 1959) [1885]. LL Jaffe and EG Henderson, 'Judicial Review and the Rule of Law: Historical Origins' (1956) 72 *Law Quarterly Review* 345 argue that the basic idea of judicial control of executive action in the name of the rule of law had been developed by 1700.

[39] PS Atiyah and RS Summers, *Form and Substance in Anglo-American Law: A Comparative Study of Legal Reasoning, Legal Theory, and Legal Institutions* (Oxford, Clarendon Press, 1987) 315–23. On the influence of utilitarianism see R Stevens, *The English Judges* (Oxford, Hart Publishing, 2002) 62–63, 79–80.

independent role as makers of common law.[40] However, by the nineteenth century, the relationship between statute law and common law had been reconceptualised. Instead of both being seen (as in the medieval period) as expressions of pre-existing principles, they were both now thought of simply as products of institutional activity. This change was reflected in the development of a strong doctrine of *stare decisis* and rules of binding precedent. Because Parliament was now the sovereign law-maker and the courts were subordinate to Parliament, common law was subordinated to statute, which would prevail in case of conflict.[41]

In the subordinate judiciary model of the judicial function, courts are marginal actors in the system of government and subordinate agents of the sovereign legislature, in relation to which their main function is to interpret and apply statute law. Common law is subordinate to statute. Because there is a sharp distinction between making and interpreting law, interpretation focuses on the text and only secondarily on policy and purpose.

The subordinate judiciary model of the judicial function was well established in the Australian colonial legal systems by the time of Federation. Federation and the Constitution on which it was built did not represent a clean break or a constitutional fresh start. The Australian Constitution is better understood as a gloss on a pre-existing constitutional tradition, much of which was imported into the new Australian federal legal system. The subordinate judiciary model was one element of that tradition. Sir Owen Dixon was the leading exponent of the idea that the Australian Constitution had a common-law foundation;[42] and his doctrine of 'strict legalism'[43] expressed the subordination of the courts to the Constitution's maker—the British Parliament. Under that doctrine, the source of the judiciary's authority is the law, and the supreme source of law is Parliament—the British Parliament in the case of the Constitution and the Australian Parliament in the case of statutes.

Of course, the traditional subordinate judiciary model never applied to the Australian legal system in precisely the way it operated in England. Most significantly for present purposes, the Australian Constitution separates

[40] Moreover, in common-law systems, judge-made law provides the background against which legislation operates because in such systems, the common law that must provide the answers to legal questions that have not been answered by legislation rather than vice versa. The power (and duty) to interpret and apply legislation carries with it an obligation to work it into a complete and reasonably coherent system. This system-building function, which is characteristically judicial, cannot simply be described either as deciding what the law is or as making law.

[41] In more general and structural terms, Parliament decides the province of the common law. Of course, the judges' exclusive power of conclusive statutory interpretation carries with it the power to decide whether a conflict exists between common law and statute; and the courts have developed various presumptions against implied displacement of the common law.

[42] O Dixon, 'The Common Law as an Ultimate Constitutional Foundation' in *Jesting Pilot And Other Papers and Addresses* (Melbourne, The Law Book Co, 1965).

[43] Ibid, 247.

judicial power from executive and legislative power more formally and strictly than does the English constitution, and empowers the courts to enforce the Constitution against the legislature as well as the executive. The burst of state-building in the nineteenth and early twentieth centuries, coupled with the development of responsible government, which concentrates executive and legislative power, and the strengthening of the executive consequent on the rise of political parties, made an independent judiciary and separation of judicial power even more important for the protection of the individual against the state. In Australia, federalism further increased the need for a federal judiciary independent of the federal executive-legislative conglomerate. Thus, s 75(iii) and (v) of the Constitution[44] came to be seen as vital safeguards for the rights of the States against the Commonwealth and the individual against the government. Enforcing the 'rule of law' came to be seen not only as the characteristic judicial function but also the judiciary's exclusive prerogative. Moreover, this role had to be protected from taint by a strong prohibition on the performance of any other role by the judiciary except to a purely 'incidental' extent.[45]

My argument, then, is that the Australian rule that statutory interpretation is an exclusively judicial function can be explained in terms of the importation into the Australian federal legal system of the English subordinate judiciary model of the judicial function, the development of responsible government, the rise of political parties, the architecture of the first three chapters of the Australian Constitution, and the federal nature of the Australian system of government. In this institutional environment, courts see their exclusive guardianship of the rule of law as both the source of their authority and an essential protection for the federal compact and the rights of the citizen.

Now let us turn to the US history. The American Revolution and the US Constitution were both meant and understood as clean breaks from the colonial English heritage and fresh starts for a new polity. Both were understood in republican terms as expressions of the sovereignty of the people. The main institutions of the new state—legislature, executive and judiciary—were to be delegates of the people and 'perfectly coordinate'[46] to each other. The foundational principle of constitutional design was that rights—of individuals and the States—are best protected by dividing and sharing power between institutions. Division of power protects rights by

[44] Section 75(iii) confers original jurisdiction on the High Court in cases in which 'the Commonwealth, or a person suing or being sued on behalf of the Commonwealth, is a party'. Section 75(v) confers original jurisdiction in cases in which 'a writ of Mandamus or prohibition or an injunction is sought against an officer of the Commonwealth'.

[45] J Stellios, *The Federal Judicature: Chapter III of the Constitution, Commentary and Cases* (Chatswood, New South Wales, LexisNexis Butterworths, 2010) 79–96.

[46] A Hamilton, J Madison and J Jay, *The Federalist Papers* (with an Introduction by L Goldman) (Oxford, Oxford University Press, 2008) 250 (*Federalist* 49, Madison).

enabling one institution to check another, while giving various institutions a share in the exercise of a power protects rights by forcing institutions to compromise and cooperate to achieve desired ends. Thus, the Constitution establishes three separate institutions each with a characteristic function. However, each institution shares its characteristic function with other institutions. In other words, a characteristic function does not belong exclusively to the institution of which it is characteristic. For instance, the President shares legislative power with Congress by virtue of the powers to veto legislation and make legislative proposals. Congress shares administrative power with the President by virtue of the Senate's role in the appointment of executive officials and Congress's power to create and oversee executive departments and agencies. The judiciary shares legislative power with Congress and the President by virtue of its power to make (common) law, interpret statutes, and review legislation for consistency with the Constitution; and it shares executive power with the President by virtue of its power to control the bureaucracy by reviewing executive action for consistency with the Constitution and statute.

In Richard Neustadt's famous phrase, the US Constitution establishes a system of 'separated institutions sharing power'.[47] In the US system, power is diffused on the basis that diffused power is safe power. Of course, the sharing of power must be limited because 'where the *whole* power of one department is exercised by the same hands which possess the *whole* power of another department, the fundamental principles of a free constitution are subverted'.[48] For instance, while the President can veto Congressional bills, the Supreme Court has held that Congress may not veto rules made by the executive on the ground that this would involve an improper exercise of executive power by the legislature.[49] Similarly, although it was held as early as 1856 that Congress may confer judicial power on the executive,[50] adjudication of certain types of disputes is reserved to the judiciary.[51] Conversely, in 1930 it was held that awarding a radio licence was an 'administrative function' that could not be conferred on a court.[52] Nevertheless, fundamental to US constitutional theory and design is the idea that power can be controlled by giving various institutions a share in its exercise, thus creating competition between them to secure its use consistently with their own policy objectives. By contrast, the basic technique for controlling power in the Australian system can be encapsulated in the concept of separated institutions exercising separate powers. In particular, under the Australian

[47] RE Neustadt, *Presidential Power and the Modern Presidents* (New York, The Free Press, 1980) 34.

[48] *Federalist Papers* (n 46) 240 (*Federalist* 47, Madison).

[49] *Immigration and Naturalization Service v Chadha* (1983) 462 US 919.

[50] *Murray's Lessee v Hoboken Land and Improvement Co* (1856) 18 How 272 (USSC).

[51] Eg *Northern Pipeline Construction Co v Marathon Pipeline Co* (1982) 485 US 50.

[52] *Federal Radio Commission v General Electric Co* (1930) 381 US 464.

version of the subordinate judiciary model, judicial independence from the other organs of government and the separation of judicial power from executive and legislative power are seen as fundamental to controlling the exercise of power by the legislative-executive conglomerate.

The US coordinate model of the judicial function is based on the ideas that sovereignty resides in the people, that each of the three branches of government is a delegate of the people with an independent source of authority, and that liberty is best protected by creating competitive relationships between the branches, forcing them to cooperate with one another. Within this framework, one of the main functions of courts is to maintain a balance of legal power between the various branches and institutions of government, including the courts themselves. They do this by interpreting and enforcing the Constitution. Their authority to do so derives from the people, not from the Constitution itself: in enforcing the Constitution they enforce the will of the sovereign people. However, because the other two branches also derive their authority not from the Constitution but from the people, there are ongoing debates in the US about whether the power to interpret the Constitution belongs exclusively to the courts—whether, in other words, the US Constitution establishes judicial supremacy.[53] Ironically, by contrast, the Australian system is much more clearly one of judicial supremacy in this sense.[54] As we have seen, the marginalisation of courts following the English Revolution was accompanied by allocation to them of exclusive power of conclusive statutory interpretation. The incorporation of the subordinate judicial model into the Australian legal system brought with it not only that exclusive power of conclusive statutory interpretation but also exclusive and conclusive power to interpret the Constitution.[55]

[53] Eg MS Paulsen, 'The Most Dangerous Branch: Executive Power to Say What the Law Is' (1994) 83 *Georgetown Law Journal* 217; CL Eisgruber, 'The Most Competent Branches: A Response to Professor Paulsen' (1994) 83 *Georgetown Law Journal* 347; L Alexander and F Schauer, 'On Extrajudicial Constitutional Interpretation' (1997) 110 *Harvard Law Review* 1359; DE Johnsen, 'Functional Departmentalism and Nonjudicial Interpretation: Who Determines Constitutional Meaning?' (2004) 67 *Law and Contemporary Problems* 105; DA Farber, 'Legislative Constitutionalism in a System of Judicial Supremacy' in RW Bauman and T Kahana (eds), *The Least Examined Branch: The Role of Legislatures in the Constitutional State* (Cambridge, Cambridge University Press, 2006).

[54] M Stubbs, 'A Brief History of the Judicial Review of Legislation under the *Australian Constitution*' (2012) 40 *Federal Law Review* 227; G Appleby and A Webster, 'Parliament's Role in Constitutional Interpretation' (2014) 37 *University of Melbourne Law Review* 255. Of course, judicial interpretations of the Constitution can be overturned by formal amendment. The question is whether, short of that, judicial interpretations can 'be evaluated according to the standards set forth in the Constitution?' (SM Griffin, 'The United States of America' in D Oliver and C Fusaro (eds), *How Constitutions Change: A Comparative Study* (Oxford, Hart Publishing, 2011) 362).

[55] For an argument, based on the dynamics of responsible government, in support of judicial deference to the legislature in interpreting the Constitution see S Gageler, 'Foundations of Australian Federalism and the Role of Judicial Review' (1987) 17 *Federal Law Review* 161; 'Beyond the Text: A Vision of the Structure and Function of the Constitution' (2009) 32 *Australian Bar Review* 138.

These basic principles of institutional design have had a profound effect on the construction of the US bureaucracy. Because the President (by virtue of the responsibility to 'take care that the laws be faithfully executed')[56] and Congress (by virtue of its power to create departments and agencies)[57] share and, therefore, compete more or less vigorously[58] for control over the bureaucracy, the bureaucracy effectively constitutes a fourth branch of government, quasi-autonomous from both President and Congress and able to play one master off against the other. The autonomy of the bureaucracy is increased by the ability of Congress to protect administrative agencies from Presidential control by placing limitations on the President's power to remove senior executive officials. As a result, administrative agencies are able to operate as quasi-autonomous policy-makers and to compete with Congress and the President to achieve their policy objectives within the various constraints imposed on them by statute, Presidential Executive Orders and the politics of Presidential and Congressional oversight.

US courts, too, are quasi-autonomous policy-makers pursuing, we might say, various agendas of their own.[59] This is reflected, for instance, in (1) the blurring of the distinction between law and policy;[60] (2) more purpose-based and less text-focused modes of interpretation;[61] (3) a relatively loose doctrine of *stare decisis*[62] and relatively non-prescriptive rules of precedent;[63] (4) the phenomenon of public law, structural-reform litigation;[64] and (5) a broad, creative approach to the development of the common law.[65] A pertinent example of several of these phenomena (especially (2)

[56] US Constitution, Art II, s 3.

[57] Under the 'necessary and proper' clause: US Constitution, Art I, s 8[18].

[58] The level and nature of this competition is affected by the operation of party politics. Competition is strongest when the President's party controls neither House of Congress and weakest when it controls both.

[59] '... courts and the litigation system ... [play] an active role ... as one of the independent centers of policy formation and execution': PM Bator, 'Legalistic Constitutionalism and Our Ineffective Government' in LG Crovitz and JA Rabkin (eds), *The Fettered Presidency: Legal Constraints on the Executive Branch* (Washington DC, American Enterprise Institute, 1989) 267. For a positive (although somewhat dated) assessment by a judge and former legislator see R Neely, *How Courts Govern America* (Hew Haven, Yale University Press, 1981). For a more recent and much more negative, academic approach, see R Kagan, *Adversarial Legalism: The American Way of Law* (Cambridge Mass., Harvard University Press, 2001). Courts are 'quasi-autonomous' in the sense that except in relation to the Constitution, the policy (law) they make is subject to legislative reversal.

[60] Atiyah and Summers, *Form and Substance in Anglo-American Law* (n 39) ch 3.

[61] Ibid, 100–12. The approach to statutory interpretation is also affected by the facts that control of the legislative agenda is much more diffused in the US than in Australia and legislative drafting is less centralised and professionalised: ibid, 306–23.

[62] Ibid, 115–27.

[63] Ibid, 289–97.

[64] Ibid, 150–56.

[65] Ibid, ch 10. In the US federal system, most common (ie judge-made) law is 'dependent' in the sense of being generated, in theory at least, by judicial interpretation and application/implementation of the Constitution and statutes: TW Merrill, 'The Common Law Powers of Federal Courts' (1985) 52 *University of Chicago Law Review* 1. As an independent source

and (5)) is the very large body of common law regulating judicial review of administrative action that has been built on—and, to some extent, in defiance of—the spare provisions of the Administrative Procedure Act 1946.[66] There are, no doubt, various possible, and probably inter-related, explanations for the importance and strength of US courts as policy- (and law-) makers. Particularly pertinent in the present context is the relative weakness of the legislature and the executive. Because the President and Congress share legislative and executive power, neither is as strong as its counterpart under a system of responsible government such as the Australian.

Two aspects of the relative weakness of the President and Congress deserve particular mention. First, whereas Congress and the President compete more or less vigorously for control of the bureaucracy, the Australian bureaucracy has only one master—the executive. Furthermore, because of its non-statutory powers, the executive can control the bureaucracy largely without the need for legislation. The relative weakness of both Congress and the President in controlling the bureaucracy gives the judiciary the opportunity and pretext for exercising control in its own name.[67] By contrast, because of the power of the Australian executive over the bureaucracy and the marginal position of courts in the system of government, the judiciary cannot easily exercise control over the bureaucracy on its own account but must do so in the name of 'the rule of law'.

Secondly, whereas Congress and the President compete more or less vigorously for control of the legislative agenda and legislative outputs, the

of law, common law is mostly state law. The relationships between statute and dependent common law on the one hand and statute and independent common law on the other are necessarily different, reflecting two different concepts of legislative supremacy. In relation to independent common law, legislative supremacy implies that in case of conflict between statute and common law, statute prevails. In relation to dependent common law, legislative supremacy implies a more rather than less textualist, literalist, non-purposive approach to statutory interpretation, and a sharp distinction between law-making and law-interpretation (see, eg WN Eskridge Jr, 'Spinning Legislative Supremacy' (1989) 78 *Georgetown Law Journal* 319). Under this approach, courts are (subordinate) agents of the legislature, charged with application and interpretation of the laws it makes. Under a different approach, courts are (coordinate) partners with the legislature in the law-making project. In this model, (1) the particular role of the legislature is to make general rules without reference to particular situations, while the role of courts is to fine-tune those rules in the context of resolving particular disputes; and (2) interpretation is a form of law-making.

[66] KM Stack, 'The Statutory Fiction of Judicial Review of Administrative Action' in C Forsyth and others (eds), *Effective Judicial Review: A Cornerstone of Good Governance* (Oxford, Oxford University Press, 2010); JM Beermann, 'Common Law and Statute Law in US Federal Administrative Law' in L Pearson, C Harlow and M Taggart (eds), *Administrative Law in a Changing State: Essays in Honour of Mark Aronson* (Oxford, Hart Publishing, 2008) 45–69; JF Duffy, 'Administrative Common Law in Judicial Review' (1998) 77 *Texas Law Review* 113.

[67] RS Melnick, 'The Courts, Jurisprudence, and the Executive Branch' in JD Aberbach and MA Peterson (eds), *The Executive Branch* (Oxford, Oxford University Press, 2005) 455 (referring to *Marbury v Madison*: 'With one stroke, Marshall in effect established the federal judiciary as the president's rival for control of the federal bureaucracy.')

Australian executive has much greater control over Parliament. As a result, the Australian Parliament is a more efficient legislature than the US Congress, which is weakened not only by external competition from the Presidency, but also by internal fragmentation of power amongst committees and individual members, and by the relative weakness of political parties in Congress. The relative inefficiency of Congress as a law-maker leaves more room for the courts to make law than their Australian counterparts enjoy. Australian courts are more likely than US courts to decline to develop the law in a particular way on the ground that the task is properly left to the legislature. Moreover, because Congress, as a result of its inefficiency, is probably less likely than Parliament to reverse by legislation a court decision it does not like,[68] US courts may exercise less caution than Australian courts in broadly and creatively interpreting statutes and developing the common law. As Richard Neely graphically puts it: 'When the man in the [US] street is asked why courts legislate, he answers that courts must do what the other branches seem incapable of doing.'[69]

Against this background of coordinate institutions and shared powers, it is not difficult to understand the development of rules of deference that share out the power of interpretation between the judiciary and the executive.[70] Because the Constitution does not expressly allocate interpretive power, judicial 'deference' to administrative interpretation can be understood as constitutional common law—a judicial gloss on the Constitution designed to give more specific content to the underlying scheme that it establishes for the allocation of public power. For this reason, the language

[68] I know of no comparative data on legislative reversal of judicial interpretations of statutes. For US data, see WN Eskridge Jr, 'Overriding Supreme Court Statutory Interpretation Decisions' (1991) 101 *Yale Law Journal* 331.

[69] Neely (n 59) xi.

[70] The question of whether or not Congress also shares the power of statutory interpretation (which is, perhaps, implicit in the issue of the proper role of Congressional materials in statutory interpretation) is more difficult to answer. On the one hand, there is an argument that separation of the power to make law from the power of interpretation is fundamental to the Constitutional scheme: JF Manning, 'Constitutional Structure and Judicial Deference to Agency Interpretations of Agency Rules' (1996) 96 *Columbia Law Review* 612; WN Eskridge Jr, 'The New Textualism' (1990) 37 *UCLA Law Review* 621, 647–48, 653–54, 673–74. On the other hand, if interpretation of ambiguous statutes is understood (as in *Chevron*) as a mode of policy-making, it may be arguable that Congress (or, perhaps more realistically, its committees and sub-committees: RS Melnick, 'Administrative Law and Bureaucratic Reality' (1992) 44 *Administrative Law Review* 245, 251–55) has a role to play in the performance that function. Recall that one of the arguments for judicial deference appeals to the political accountability of administrators. Administrators are politically accountable not only to the President but also to Congress. It might seem to follow that Congress as well as the President may legitimately contribute to the interpretation of statutes, resolution of statutory ambiguity and filling of statutory gaps (LS Bressman, 'Procedures as Politics in Administrative Law' (2007) 107 *Columbia Law Review* 1749, 1807). In Australia, the use of legislative history to clarify the meaning of a statute is generally frowned upon: DC Pearce and RS Geddes, *Statutory Interpretation in Australia*, 7th edn (Chatswood, New South Wales, LexisNexis Butterworths, 2011) 77–78, 90–92.

of 'deference' has a quite different resonance in US law than it would have in Australian law. To the Australian way of thinking, judicial deference to administrative statutory interpretations would be inconsistent with the constitutional allocation of power whereas in the US system it can be understood as a specific outworking of that allocation.

My suggestion, then, is that the difference between the US and Australian rules governing judicial review of administrative statutory interpretation can be explained in terms of differences between the institutional structure and constitutional foundations of the respective systems of government of which courts are part and, more specifically, in terms of the difference between the coordinate and subsidiary models of the judicial function.

IV. A FURTHER QUESTION

This explanation raises a further intriguing question about the possible future development of the Australian rule, prompted by the fact that the Australian system has a dual constitutional heritage—responsible government from England and separated institutions from the US. So far as the model of the judicial function is concerned, for the first eight decades of Australian federation, the subordinate judiciary model prevailed. However, it is arguable that the enactment of the Australia Acts in 1986 has provided the catalyst for reconsideration by the High Court of the constitutional role of courts in the Australian system. It is not implausible to think that just as the US Constitution represented a clean break from America's English colonial heritage and a fresh start for a new polity, so the Australia Acts represent a clean break and a fresh start of sorts, and the creation of a new, independent politico-legal order. It is true, of course, that the Australian Constitution is still, technically, an enactment of the UK Parliament. In that sense, the authority of the courts still derives, like that of English courts, from the legislature. However, the High Court appears to have developed a new theory about the source of its authority: not the UK legislature via the Constitution but the Constitution itself.[71] There was a period in the 1990s when it seemed that the Court might adopt the US theory that the people are sovereign.[72] However, such a radical departure from the

[71] WMC Gummow, 'The Constitution: Ultimate Foundation of Australian Law?' (2005) 79 *Australian Law Journal* 167, 170–72; JT Gleeson and RA Yezerski, 'The Separation of Powers and the Unity of the Common Law' in JT Gleeson, JA Watson and RCA Higgins (eds), *Historical Foundations of Australian Law, Volume I: Institutions, Concepts and Personalities* (Sydney, The Federation Press, 2013) 322. By contrast, '[i]t is perhaps the defining characteristic of the UK system of government that Parliament, not the constitution, is supreme': R Masterman, *The Separation of Powers in the Contemporary Constitution: Judicial Competence and Independence in the United Kingdom* (Cambridge, Cambridge University Press, 2011) 20.

[72] See, eg *Australian Capital Television Pty Ltd v Commonwealth of Australia* (1992) 177 CLR 106, 138 (Mason CJ); *Theophanous v Herald and Weekly Times* (1994) 182 CLR 104, 171 (Deane J).

ideology of the rule of law has not gained acceptance.[73] Instead, it is said that the Court's authority is based directly on the Constitution, thus confirming the Court as its exclusive and supreme interpreter and enforcer. In pursuit of this reorientation, the Court is gradually rewriting history by, for instance, renaming the prerogative writs as 'constitutional writs'[74] and grounding the contracting power of the executive in section 61 of the Constitution rather than in the prerogative,[75] thus distancing itself from the Dixonian theory that the Australian Constitution has its roots firmly in the common law. The Court has even suggested a structural understanding of rules of statutory interpretation as 'an expression of the constitutional relationship between the arms of government with respect to the making, interpretation and application of laws' rather than as criteria of the intention of Parliament.[76]

The cases in which the High Court held that certain rights are implicitly protected by the Constitution may be seen as an early application of this changed understanding of the Court's place in the Constitutional regime.[77] These cases are significant not only because they strengthen the Court vis-à-vis the other branches, but also because the rights they acknowledge are grounded in the structure of the governmental system the Constitution establishes rather than on the idea of individual autonomy. This approach harks back to the early position in the US. The first ten amendments to the US Constitution, ratified in 1791 and known collectively as the Bill of Rights, were concessions to the anti-federalists. They were conceived as limitations on (federal) government power rather than protections for individual citizens. Not until well into the twentieth century when the human rights movement gathered momentum after the Second World War, did rights come to be understood, in the US and around the world, as fundamental attributes of human beings. The High Court of Australia has resisted that shift. Recently it has effectively blocked the creation of a justiciable, constitutional, autonomy-based rights regime of the type that has been adopted in other systems of responsible government such as the UK.[78] A central feature of such regimes is that instead of power to invalidate statutes they confer on courts power merely to declare a statutory provision to be incompatible with a protected right. In *Momcilovic v R* the Court

[73] See, eg *Lange v Australian Broadcasting Corporation* (1997) 189 CLR 520, 566–67.

[74] *Re Refugee Tribunal; ex p Aala* (2000) 204 CLR 82, [21], [138–39].

[75] *Williams v Commonwealth of Australia* (2012) 288 ALR 410 (HCA).

[76] *Zheng v Cai* (2009) 239 CLR 446, [28]; *Plaintiff S10/2011 v Minister for Immigration and Citizenship* (2012) 290 ALR 616, [97] (HCA).

[77] L Zines, *The High Court and the Constitution*, 5th edn (Sydney, Federation Press, 2008) ch 15. Cases in which the Court has developed the idea that due process guarantees may be implicit in the concept of judicial power may also be seen in this way: ibid, 273–94. Like the *Kable* and *Kirk* cases discussed later, they show the Court asserting itself to promote a strict, subordinate judiciary model of judicial power.

[78] Under the Human Rights Act 1998, which domesticated the European Convention on Human Rights.

held that making such a declaration is an exercise of non-judicial power that cannot be invested in a federal court or a State court exercising federal jurisdiction.[79] Instead, Australia has a human-rights regime that depends on Parliament, in its capacity as scrutineer of the executive, to monitor and promote compliance by Parliament in its legislative capacity (the Queen-in-Parliament).

Another manifestation of the Court's self-reorientation is its insistence on and development of the concept of a national, Australian common law.[80] This is made possible by the fact that, unlike the US Supreme Court, the High Court is a general court of appeal from State courts exercising State jurisdiction as much as from federal courts and State courts exercising federal jurisdiction. The creation of a national common law, as opposed to a set of State-specific common-law regimes, was not inevitable. It is one instance of what has been called 'judicial federalism',[81] based on a centralising interpretation of section 73(ii) of the Constitution.[82]

An example of judicial federalism more significant for present purposes is found in the *Kable* line of cases[83] and in *Kirk v Industrial Court (NSW)*.[84] The decisions in these two cases are built on two features of Australian constitutional arrangements. One is that State constitutions do not formally allocate power in the way it is allocated by the first three Chapters of the Australian Constitution. In particular, they do not formally allocate judicial power to courts. The other feature is the so-called 'autochthonous expedient'—the power of the Australian Parliament to confer federal jurisdiction on State courts. The basic idea underlying *Kirk* and the *Kable* cases[85] is that in order to be suitable repositories of federal jurisdiction, State courts must be fashioned (to an incompletely specified extent) on federal courts. Just as the Australian Constitution imposes certain limits on the power of the Commonwealth Parliament to legislate in relation to federal courts and federal judicial power, it also imposes certain (although not identical) limits on State Parliaments because State courts are components not only of State systems of government but also of the federal system, and because the High

[79] *Momcilovic v R* (2011) 245 CLR 1. The question of whether such a power could be conferred by State legislation on a State court exercising State jurisdiction was left open.

[80] L Zines, 'The Common Law in Australia: Its Nature and Constitutional Significance' (2004) 32 *Federal Law Review* 337.

[81] G Griffith and G Kennett, 'Judicial Federalism' in B Opeskin and F Wheeler (eds), *The Australian Federal Judicial System* (Melbourne, Melbourne University Press, 2000).

[82] J Stellios, 'The Centralisation of Judicial Power Within the Australian Federal System' (2014) 42 *Federal Law Review* 357. Section 73(ii) confers jurisdiction on the High Court to hear appeals from (inter alia) 'the Supreme Court of any State'.

[83] *Kable v DPP* (1996) 189 CLR 51; *Fardon v A-G (Qld)* (2004) 223 CLR 575; *International Finance Trust Co Ltd v NSW Crime Commission* (2009) 240 CLR 319; *South Australia v Totani* (2010) 242 CLR 1; *Wainohu v NSW* (2011) 243 CLR 181.

[84] *Kirk v Industrial Court (NSW)* (2010) 239 CLR 531.

[85] As well as *Momcilovic* (2011) 245 CLR 1.

Court is a general court of appeal from State courts not only on issues of federal law but also on issues of State law.[86]

A possible way of understanding these developments in judicial federalism is in terms of a shift from a subordinate judiciary model to a coordinate judiciary model of the role of the High Court in the system of government. It is widely argued that the reasons given by the Court for these various decisions are more or less weak legally, historically, theoretically and empirically.[87] The Court, it may be argued, has abandoned Dixonian strict legalism, with its implication that the Constitution is to be interpreted in essentially the same way as a statute, in favour of a creative, policy-driven approach to the Constitution that allows the Court to design and implement a new federal settlement and effectively to amend the Constitution by means other than those prescribed by the Constitution itself. Put bluntly and provocatively, in these cases the Court has re-invented itself as a quasi-autonomous policy-maker. Instead of being the creature and servant of the Constitution, the Court has made itself the Constitution's architect and master.

Accepting this highly speculative analysis purely for the sake of argument, what might be its implications for judicial review of administrative interpretation? Might the idea that the Court is, in certain respects at least, a coordinate rather than subordinate constitutional actor lead it to modify or abandon other elements of the subordinary judiciary model, in particular the principle that conclusive statutory interpretation is an exclusively judicial function? This seems extremely unlikely for several reasons. First, the model of a court and the judicial function that the High Court is seeking to embed in the State constitutions is, essentially, the Australian version of the subordinate judiciary model in which the constitutional role of the judiciary is to enforce the law and only to enforce the law. Ironically, the High Court has adopted a highly creative approach to the Constitution in order to pursue a policy of imposing on State legislatures a strict subordinate model of the judicial function.

Secondly, and more fundamentally, allocation to the judiciary of the power of conclusive statutory interpretation is inextricably bound up with three other fundamental features of Australian constitutionalism—Parliament's role as the peak law-making institution, responsible government and strong political parties. As a result of these features, power is not divided and shared between the legislature and the executive as it is in the US system. Nor is the bureaucracy quasi-autonomous as it is in the US system. The Australian system is not one in which power is divided and shared between quasi-autonomous policy-makers in the legislature, executive and

[86] Limits on what the High Court can do in hearing an appeal on an issue of State law imply limits on what State courts can do at first instance.

[87] Eg J Goldsworthy, '*Kable, Kirk* and Judicial Statesmanship' (2014) 40 *Monash University Law Review* 75.

bureaucracy. On the contrary, it is a system in which legislative power, executive power and bureaucratic power are concentrated in the elected government. In such a system, the rights and interests of individuals and the States cannot effectively be protected against abuse of federal power by competition between quasi-autonomous policy-makers. Rather, they need for their protection a strong, independent, monastically-separated judiciary. The exclusive power of conclusive statutory interpretation is a source of strength for the judiciary, and a powerful tool for controlling the legislative-executive-bureaucratic conglomerate and providing protection against abuse of the enormous combined powers of making and enforcing law that Australian governments possess. The judicial power of conclusive statutory interpretation is here to stay because Australia has a system of responsible government run by relatively strong, cohesive and disciplined political parties.

V. CONCLUSION

Finally, let us return to the first and third of the questions posed at the beginning of this paper. The first question, it will be recalled, concerns the identity of the supreme interpreter. Under Australian law, the answer is clear: the High Court is the supreme interpreter of the Constitution, statutes and regulations. This is not because the High Court is sovereign amongst organs of government but, to the contrary and consistently with the subordinate judiciary model, because the Court is the servant and mouthpiece of the Constitution and the law. In the post-Australia-Acts mythology of Australian constitutionalism, sovereignty resides in the Constitution and in law consistent with it. Australia is, in a strong sense, a rule-of-law state. Coupled with the related doctrine that there is only one correct answer to any question of law, the Court's function as supreme interpreter explains why, under Australian law, courts must not defer to administrative statutory interpretations.[88]

Under US law the answer to this first question is more complex. The standard modern view is that the Supreme Court is the supreme interpreter of the Constitution—although this view has never been uncontested.[89] By contrast, it seems that there is no supreme interpreter of statutes and regulations. The power to interpret is shared, at least between the judiciary and the executive. This explains why US courts are required, in certain

[88] As for administrative interpretations of the Constitution, it seems that administrators are required to assume that statutes are constitutionally valid: *Re Adams and Tax Agents Board* (1976) 1 ALD 251 (AAT) (re the Administrative Appeals Tribunal); D Pearce, *Administrative Appeals Tribunal*, 3rd edn (Chatswood, New South Wales, LexisNexis Butterworths, 2013) 21–23. Concerning Constitutional interpretation by US administrators, see JD Urick, '*Chevron* and Constitutional Doubt' (2013) 99 *Virginia Law Review* 375.

[89] M Tushnet, *The Constitution of the United States of America: A Contextual Analysis* (Oxford, Hart Publishing, 2009) 136–40.

circumstances, to defer to administrative interpretations of statutes and regulations.

The third question, it will be recalled, asks how administrators should go about interpreting statutes and regulations. Under Australian law the answer, once again, seems straightforward: both normatively and strategically, administrators should approach interpretation in precisely the way a court would, applying the same rules, principles and modes of reasoning.[90] From the doctrine that every question of law has only one correct answer, namely the answer given by the supreme interpreter, it follows—as a matter of practical logic, at least—that subordinate interpreters should mimic the supreme interpreter. US law does not subscribe to this doctrine. Rather it accepts that a question of law may be answerable in more than one reasonable way and that the power to interpret statutes and regulations is shared by courts and administrators. Courts defer to administrative interpretations on the basis of the expertise and political accountability of administrators. It would seem arguable, then, not only that administrators need not approach interpretation in the same way as courts but that they should not. Rather, they should bring their expert knowledge and the legitimate demands of their political masters to bear on the interpretive task in a way that courts do not and should not. This conclusion helps to explain why there is a robust debate in the US about how administrators should approach statutory interpretation[91] and no equivalent debate in Australia.

The difference between US and Australian law concerning the allocation of the power of interpretation, and judicial review of administrative interpretations of statutes and regulations, is a reflection of deeper and broader constitutional and institutional differences between the two systems of government and, in particular, different understandings of the role of courts in the system. In a late, characteristically sparkling contribution to administrative law scholarship Mike Taggart described this feature of Australian law as an instance of 'Australian exceptionalism' and as one of

[90] Pearce and Geddes, *Statutory Interpretation in Australia* (n 70) 17. Nevertheless, it is unlikely and, perhaps, inappropriate that administrators approach statutory interpretation in the same way as judges because whereas the prime role of administrators is to implement general policy and rules in relation to classes and categories of citizens, the prime function of courts is to protect particular individuals who object to the way they have been treated by administrators. Bureaucrats have an obligation to promote government policy that courts do not. See, further, P Cane, *Administrative Tribunals and Adjudication* (Oxford, Hart Publishing, 2009) 12–13.

[91] JL Mashaw, 'Norms, Practices, and the Paradox of Deference: A Preliminary Inquiry into Agency Statutory Interpretation' (2005) 57 *Administrative Law Review* 501; JL Mashaw, 'Agency-Centered or Court-Centered Administrative Law? A Dialogue with Richard Pierce on Agency Statutory Interpretation' (2007) 59 *Administrative Law Review* 889; PL Strauss, 'When the Judge is not the Primary Official with Responsibility to Read: Agency Interpretation and the Problem of Legislative History' (1990) 66 *Chicago-Kent Law Review* 321; RJ Pierce Jr, 'How Agencies Should Give Meaning to the Statutes They Administer: A Response to Mashaw and Strauss (2007) 59 *Administrative Law Review* 197.

many instances where Australian administrative law is out of step with that of other major common-law jurisdictions such as the US and Canada (but, in this instance, not England and New Zealand).[92] As one would expect of such a fine scholar, Mike also acknowledged that judgements of exceptionality presuppose a benchmark of normality. My perspective is quite different from his.[93] I start with the assumption that every legal system is a product of its own history and conclude that so far as judicial control of administrative interpretation is concerned, neither US law nor Australian law is exceptional. On the contrary, closer analysis shows how the law of both jurisdictions can be understood as a product of a unique combination of constitutional and institutional structures and interactions, a set of normative assumptions and a dynamic process of historical development.

[92] M Taggart, '"Australian Exceptionalism" in Judicial Review' (2008) 36 *Federal Law Review* 1, 10–11.

[93] It is also different from that of Richard Lucy (*The Australian Form of Government* (Melbourne, Macmillan, 1985) who argues that the British and American elements of the Australian system of government are mutually 'incompatible' or 'irreconcilable'. My concern is to understand and explain rather than to evaluate the interaction between these two elements.

10

Should We Have a Variable Error of Law Standard?

MARK ARONSON*

I. INTRODUCTION

MY BRIEF IS to explore the possibility of turning 'error of law' into a 'variable standard of review'. The language comes in part from New Zealand where the big questions concern the 'variability' of the 'grounds' of review, and in particular, the shape and place of the proportionality ground and its relationship with the 'unreasonableness' ground. But the language also has a distinctly Canadian accent, because Canada now has only two 'standards' (as distinct from grounds), namely, correctness and reasonableness.[1]

Correctness review looks like an appeal that is limited to the issue, process, or outcome that the court says the primary decision-maker is not allowed to get wrong. These used to be called 'jurisdictional' issues, but that term now has a greatly reduced meaning in Canada; and sometimes they were called 'collateral' or 'preliminary' issues, but in Canada as elsewhere, that language has also gone.

Where error of law is the ground of challenge, correctness review allows the court to replace the primary decision on the meaning of the governing law with its own. Reasonableness review, on the other hand, allows some leeway to the primary decision-maker, and the real question there is the extent of that leeway. Canada's reasonableness standard is now 'a big tent that will have to accommodate a lot of variables that inform and limit a court's review of the outcome of administrative decision making'.[2]

* Emeritus Professor of Law, University of New South Wales. I am grateful to Janina Boughey, Peter Cane, Paul Daly, Matthew Groves, Carol Harlow, David Mullan, Jason Varuhas, Greg Weeks and Hanna Wilburg for their comments and corrections, and to the Law Department of the LSE for hosting me whilst I wrote the bulk of this contribution.

[1] *Dunsmuir v New Brunswick* [2008] 1 SCR 190, [2008] SCC 9.

[2] Ibid, [144] (Binnie J).

Canada's twin standards replaced three standards—correctness, unreasonableness *simpliciter*, and something extremely deferential that English law would have called *Wednesbury* unreasonableness, but Canada called 'patent unreasonableness'.[3] Whether '*Wednesbury*' or 'patent', this level of unreasonableness was almost equivalent to 'lunatic'. The process of selecting one or other of the three standards was said to be an issue of statutory interpretation, conducted according to a 'pragmatic and functional approach'.[4] The reduction from three to two standards was meant to make things easier,[5] and the choice between 'correctness' on the one hand, and the extremely broad spectrum that is 'reasonableness' on the other, is still conducted in a pragmatic and functional way, but the Supreme Court now regards that label as unnecessary: '[W]e prefer to refer simply to the "standard of review analysis" in the future.'[6]

Canada still retains its grounds of review: improper purpose, breach of natural justice, irrelevant considerations, error of law, and so forth. But the real heat in Canadian judicial review literature concerns the *intensity* with which those grounds are applied, an intensity which varies between contexts, and in accordance with a large smorgasbord of relevant factors but very few fixed points of reference. Indeed, there might come a point at which the grounds of review will cease to retain their individual identities, and the real issue will be more simply described as being the intensity with which the judicial review court disagrees with the primary decision. It is not the purpose of this chapter to explore the pros and cons of Canada's approach in general. My focus is on the idea that the intensity of curial scrutiny for error of law might be as variable as the intensity for other grounds of challenge, and for the same reasons.

The more one pursues this idea, the more one becomes aware that the apex courts of Canada, the United States, England, Australia and New Zealand are all moved by roughly similar concerns not to interfere too much with primary decision-makers, but that they give effect to those concerns in apparently quite dissimilar ways. I will start by sketching the doctrinal positions of the United States and Canada, each of which has overt 'deference' doctrines. My principal focus at this point, however, will be on Canada whose institutional and political arrangements have a good deal more in common with those of England, Australia and New Zealand, to whose doctrinal positions I will then turn. Although each of those countries appears radically different at the doctrinal level, I will argue that their courts have something important in common, namely, a concern not to be too interventionist in the workings of administrative decision-makers,

[3] *Baker v Canada (Minister of Citizenship and Immigration)* [1999] 2 SCR 817.
[4] *UES, Local 298 v Bibeault* [1988] 2 SCR 1048, 1088–90.
[5] *Dunsmuir* (n 1) [32–33] and [43].
[6] Ibid, [63] (Bastarache and LeBel JJ).

tribunals and inferior courts. The important differences between the countries are not so much in their doctrines (although they are indeed strikingly different), but in their justifications for judicial self-restraint.

I will conclude that on this topic, at least, beyond the intrinsic interest of a comparative survey, perhaps the single most important lesson to be drawn is that there is no single answer. No country has provided a theory of everything, even for their own purposes, let alone for transplantation, and the search for a single answer is bound to provide more in the way of ex post rationalisation than ex ante predictability.

II. UNITED STATES

Imagine two models of a Clean Air Act, each of them dealing with specifically identified areas of a country where ageing factories are clustered, emitting vast amounts of pollutants. It was economically and politically impossible for the legislature to close them all down overnight, and equally impossible to draw up a selective 'hit list' because all the factories were to blame. The legislature decided to grandfather the existing arrangements, allowing existing pollution 'sources' to continue on condition that they got no worse. Any new sources, however, had to conform to radically more stringent emission standards. The efficacy of this compromise was substantially dependent on whether the entire industrial complex at a company site was to count as a single source, or whether the site would have as many sources as it had chimneys. The first model Act attempted a definition of 'sources', but it was so prolix as to be quite ambiguous. The second model empowered the regulatory agency to set its own guidelines as to what, in the public interest, would be treated as a source.

The United States Supreme Court in *Chevron USA Inc v Natural Resources Defense Council Inc*[7] read an Act that conformed to the first model as if it had conformed to the second model. Each style of statute would have been valid, but in a constitutional environment such as America's, which separates the judicial power from the legislative and executive powers, one would have thought that however imperfect, a statutory definition of 'sources' was part of the 'law'—after all, it was in the Act. The court, however, read it not as law, but as a delegation to the executive branch to make and vary not law (because in high theory, Congress cannot validly delegate law-making power) but policy.[8] The result was that agency

[7] *Chevron USA Inc v Natural Resources Defense Council Inc* (1984) 467 US 837.

[8] The high theory is clearly defective. Its effect is to characterise Executive rules not as legislation, but as policy, *because* the Executive made the rules. See Stevens J's concurrence in *Whitman v American Trucking Associations, Inc* (2001) 531 US 457. See also K Watts, 'Rulemaking as Legislating' (2015) 103 *Georgetown Law Journal* (forthcoming).

vacillations over time as to how it regulated changes to existing factory sites (and there were vacillations aplenty) were reviewable only against the fairly undemanding prohibition of 'arbitrary and capricious' action. To be fair, the Act's drafting history showed very clearly that the legislative committees had simply fudged their definition, leaving the hard job for others. But if they had really meant to leave it not to the courts but to the regulatory agency, why did the drafting conform to the first model rather than the second? Had the Act's definition of 'sources' been 'law', its meaning would have been an issue of statutory interpretation, and the courts have had the last word on such issues.

Perhaps, however, the credibility of *Chevron*'s interpretation of statutory intent is more dubious for outsiders than Americans. Judicial 'deference' to agency interpretations of their home statutes was well established before *Chevron*,[9] even if the rationalisations and rebadging wrought by that case were relatively new. More importantly, America's separation of powers does not deny to the Executive branch the power to have the last word on some matters of law: 'Our legal system presumes there will be continuing dialogue among the three branches of Government on questions of statutory interpretation and application.'[10]

Chevron's trigger (statutory ambiguity) may once have been clear (although that is debateable), but it has become extraordinarily unclear: how ambiguous must a regulatory statute be for it to raise the 'presumption'[11] that *Chevron* deference applies? Also, and in a move that underlines *Chevron*'s political basis of preferring an agency's accountability to the political branch over its accountability to the judicial branch, either its strength or even its applicability now depends on a number of preliminary preconditions that mirror the notice and comment processes of rule-making.[12] If *Chevron* is indeed triggered, however, then the agency interpretation will prevail provided only that it is reasonably open.

Chevron continues to generate much debate, even at the doctrinal level. Some American academics suggest that the answers in any given case depend not on doctrine, but on the judge's political leanings for or

[9] A Scalia, 'Judicial Deference to Administrative Interpretations of Law' [1989] *Duke Law Journal* 511.

[10] *United States v Home Concrete & Supply LLC* (2012) 132 S Ct 1836 (Kennedy J in dissent, but not on this point).

[11] Ibid (Breyer J for the court).

[12] *United States v Mead Corporation* (2001) 533 US 218, trenchantly criticised by A Scalia, 'Is *Chevron* Out of Gas? The State of Judicial Review 25 Years After *Chevron USA, Inc v Natural Resources Defense Council*', Keynote Address to Washington College of Law at American University, 24 April 2009, podcast available at: www.wcl.american.edu/podcast/audio/20090424_WCL_Chevron-Scalia.mp3.

against the current administration.[13] Others have called for *Chevron* to be overruled,[14] but that hardly seems likely; it may well be 'the most-cited US Supreme Court case in history',[15] and the Supreme Court recently defended it against an attempt to create a carve-out for 'jurisdictional' questions.[16]

Chevron dominates America's federal judicial review literature. Australia, England, and Canada certainly know about it, but none of those is likely to adopt it. Each of those countries in fact forbears from correcting *every* error of law, and each gives different explanations for that forbearance. Only Canada uses the language of deference, but it is a very different deference to *Chevron*'s, and is done without rebadging 'law' into 'statutory delegations' of the power to make 'policy'.

III. CANADA

Canada's overt deference doctrine predates *Chevron* by five years.[17] The Supreme Court appears initially to have applied it only to adjudicative tribunals,[18] but more recent decisions have extended deference beyond that line.[19]

Like America's *Chevron* deference, Canada's standard of review doctrine continues to promote a sizeable body of case law and academic commentary. Any exposition on my part would have a short shelf-life even if accurate,

[13] PH Schuck and DE Elliott, 'To the *Chevron* Station: an Empirical Study of Federal Administrative Law' [1990] *Duke Law Journal* 984; TJ Miles and CR Sunstein, 'Do Judges Make Regulatory Policy? An Empirical Investigation of *Chevron*' (2006) 73 *University of Chicago Law Review* 823; CR Sunstein, 'Beyond *Marbury*: the Executive's Power to Say What the Law Is' (2006) 115 *Yale Law Journal* 2580, 2600–602.

[14] JM Beermann, 'End the Failed *Chevron* experiment Now: How *Chevron* has Failed and Why it Can and Should be Overruled' (2010) 42 *Connecticut Law Review* 779.

[15] AR Gluck, 'The Federal Common Law of Statutory Interpretation: *Erie* for an Age of Statutes' (2013) 54 *William and Mary Law Review* 753, 798. Judicial deference to agency interpretations that they themselves make is generally known as *Auer* deference after a case of the same name. The Supreme Court has flagged its willingness to reconsider *Auer* deference, which violates a separation of powers principle against a lawmaker being vested with an interpretive power, and which might encourage agencies to draft their regulations in deliberately vague terms so as to maximise their future flexibility: *Decker v Northwest Environmental Defense Center* (2013) 133 S Ct 1326.

[16] *City of Arlington, Texas v Federal Communications Commission* (2013) 133 S Ct 1863, noted by the Canadian Supreme Court in *McLean v British Columbia (Securities Commission)* [2013] 3 SCR 895.

[17] *Canadian Union of Public Employees Local 963 v New Brunswick Liquor Corporation* [1979] 2 SCR 227.

[18] JM Evans, 'Standards of Review in Administrative Law' (2012) 26 *Canadian Journal of Administrative Law and Practice* 67, 74–76.

[19] See *McLean v British Columbia (Securities Commission)* [2013] 3 SCR 895 and *Agraira v Canada (Public Safety and Emergency Preparedness)* [2013] 2 SCR 559.

and would likely have in addition the usual failings of an outsider's perspective. Furthermore, Canada's deference doctrine did not spring fully-formed from a single case—it has been and remains a long work in progress. However, it might be worthwhile to try to capture some of Canada's present *arguments* for and against deference in the specific context of challenges for error of law, without attempting a snapshot of their relative *weights* in any particular Canadian context.

All inquiries into the appropriate standard of review acknowledge two boundary lines. Naturally, no deference is accorded to constitutional transgressions. Nor is deference given to transgressions of legislative meaning, a position sometimes tricked out in the language of democratic principle,[20] which can be somewhat misleading. 'Legislative meaning' is what remains at the end of a process of statutory construction that glosses statutory texts, not just in ways readily recognisable in other common-law countries, but also by application of the 'standard of review analysis' itself.[21] Between the two bookends of the Constitution and 'legislative meaning' stand rule of law values, Charter values, and highly pragmatic factors bearing upon administrative authority, efficiency, and effectiveness. No single factor is determinative, although the courts identified four factors as being of principal concern. These are: the presence or absence of a privative clause; the expertise or otherwise of the primary decision-maker; the purpose of the Act as a whole; and whether the disputed issue is one of law, fact or discretion.[22] There is some doubt, however, whether these factors really count for much these days, or whether the Supreme Court is moving towards one single, big, and very strong presumption that deference is owed to interpretations by adjudicative tribunals (and some other administrative decision-makers) of the law of their home statutes.

Privative clauses used to pull away from correctness and it used to be that their absence usually pulled the other way, but their relevance has now diminished.[23] Similarly, statutory appeal rights used to count towards correctness review and their absence used to count the other way, but this factor is now undercut by the fact that the standard of review

[20] See *Dunsmuir* (n 1) [27] (Bastarache and LeBel JJ): 'Judicial review seeks to address an underlying tension between the rule of law and the foundational democratic principle, which finds expression in the initiatives of Parliament and legislatures to create various administrative bodies and endow them with broad powers.'

[21] See *Pezim v British Columbia (Superintendent of Brokers)* [1994] 2 SCR 557, 589–90 and *Smith v Alliance Pipeline Ltd* [2011] 1 SCR 160, [106] (Deschamps J in dissent on this point, but not in the result).

[22] *Pushpanathan v Canada (Minister of Citizenship and Immigration)* [1998] 1 SCR 982; *Dunsmuir* (n 1) [64].

[23] Starting with *Pezim* (n 21) to which Rothstein J (in dissent) took extended exception in *Canada (Citizenship and Immigration) v Khosa* [2009] 1 SCR 339.

analysis applies not just in judicial review contexts, but also in the context of statutory appeals.[24]

Tribunal adjudications on issues within the core functions of their 'home statutes' usually get deference. This used especially to be the case where their jobs could be specialised and complex, and where they either had or (rather intriguingly) *could be expected to develop* substantial expertise. There are signs of restiveness at this extension of the 'expertise' rationale, partly because expertise has become a question of imputation (or even a strong presumption) rather than evidence, and partly because the courts have at times imputed expertise simply from the specialist nature of the adjudicative function, rather than from statutory signals (the most obvious being a strong privative clause) that the legislature itself wants the primary decision-maker to be ceded space as an expert.[25] An adjudicative tribunal that shares its adjudicative domain with the courts is accorded no deference.[26]

Tribunal adjudications within a complex regulatory framework also get deference, not just because of the expertise involved, imputed, or presumed, but also in recognition of the ongoing responsibilities of regulators, responsibilities that extend far beyond the adjudication of individual disputes.[27] Indeed, one sometimes gets the sense of Canada's standard of review analysis morphing into a *Chevron*-like allowance for the tribunal or other decision-maker to develop policy (characterised as regulatory, rather than political) in the guise of interpretation:[28]

> A higher degree of judicial deference is also warranted with respect to a tribunal's interpretation of the law where it plays a role in policy development ... [even though] its policies are not to be treated as legal pronouncements absent statutory authority mandating such treatment.

Correctness is in order for interpretive issues that have large ramifications beyond the primary decision-maker's home statute or on which the decision-maker lacks specialist expertise.[29]

Canada's case law on 'standard of review' remains a work in progress, and the judges clearly differ as to how readily they will accord deference to a primary decision-maker's answer to the relevant question of law. However, there is one point on which they have all agreed for well over

[24] As in *Pezim* (n 21), where reasonableness review applied despite the presence of statutory appeal rights.

[25] See the dissents in *Council of Canadians with Disabilities v VIA Rail Canada Inc* [2007] 1 SCR 650 (Deschamps and Rothstein JJ); *Khosa* (n 23); *Alliance Pipeline* (n 21) [80] (Deschamps J).

[26] *Rogers Communications Inc v Society of Composers, Authors and Music Publishers of Canada* [2012] 2 SCR 283.

[27] *Pezim* (n 21) 589 (Iacobucci J): 'It is important to note from the outset that the Act is regulatory in nature.'

[28] Ibid, 561 (Iacobucci J).

[29] Ibid, 590.

30 years,[30] and that is that they should not necessarily have the last word on all legal questions. And when they do accord deference on legal issues, it is not because they think that there is an error of law that is too trivial or unimportant to warrant superior court correction. They never describe their position as leaving 'wrong' but 'reasonable' decisions uncorrected; identifying 'error' is simply not part of the exercise:[31]

> It is sometimes said by judges that an administrator acting within his or her discretion 'has the right to be wrong'. This reflects an unduly court-centred view of the universe. A disagreement between the court and an administrator does not necessarily mean that the administrator is wrong.

Taggart's advocacy of variable intensity was clearly influenced by some, at least, of these Canadian developments.[32] Other contributions to this collection deal with the argument that one might properly confine intensified scrutiny to instances of potential infractions of human rights or fundamental common-law values. Canada, however, provides what may be a salutary lesson to be careful what you wish for. Canadian courts have the last word, of course, on Charter challenges to laws,[33] but not on questions as to whether administrative adjudicators have acted proportionately in individual matters involving potential Charter infractions; on those questions, Canada applies its administrative law standard of 'reasonableness'.[34]

IV. 'DEFERENCE' AND 'JURISDICTIONAL ERROR'

Any account of the variability of judicial scrutiny beyond the United States and Canada must start with some semantics. 'Deference' to non-curial interpretations of statute is not a winning way to approach the matter in the judicial review courts of either England[35] or Australia.[36] So expressed, the

30 Since *CUPE Local 963* (n 17).

31 *Dunsmuir* (n 1) [125] (Binnie J).

32 See M Taggart, 'The Contribution of Lord Cooke to Scope of Review Doctrine in Administrative Law' in P Rishworth (ed), *The Struggle for Simplicity in the Law: Essays for Lord Cooke of Thorndon* (Wellington, Butterworths, 1997) 189.

33 *R v Oakes* [1986] 1 SCR 103.

34 *Doré v Barreau du Québec* [2012] 1 SCR 395. The English position is not so clear: *R (SB) v Governors of Denbigh High School* [2006] UKHL 15, [2007] 1 AC 100.

35 *R (ProLife Alliance) v British Broadcasting Corporation* [2003] UKHL 23, [2004] 1 AC 185, 240; and *A v Secretary of State for the Home Department* [2004] UKHL 56, [2005] 2 AC 68, 155. 'Deference' is frequently accorded to human rights assessments made by public authorities, but the courts said that it would be an unnecessary distraction to have a deference *doctrine*, because precise calibration of deference would be unattainable: *Denbigh* (n 34); *Huang v Secretary of State for the Home Department* [2007] UKHL 11, [2007] 2 AC 167; *Belfast City Council v Miss Behavin' Ltd* [2007] UKHL 19, [2007] 1 WLR 1420; *E v Chief Constable of the Royal Ulster Constabulary* [2008] UKHL 66, [2009] 1 AC 536; *R (Quila) v Secretary of State for the Home Department* [2011] UKSC 45, [2012] 1 AC 621; *AXA General Insurance Ltd v Lord Advocate (Scotland)* [2011] UKSC 46, [2012] 1 AC 868.

36 *Enfield City Corporation v Development Assessment Commission* (2000) 199 CLR 135, 152–53.

idea conveys for some a sense of cringing subservience, or an abdication of the judicial responsibility to declare the law. Other terms are needed. 'Non-jurisdictional error' used to be the principal vehicle for varying the intensity of judicial scrutiny, although English doctrine has now replaced that with an increasingly strong sense of judicial discretion.

There was a time when the concepts of 'jurisdiction', or 'preliminary' or 'collateral' issues figured prominently in the judicial review case law of Canada, England, Australia and New Zealand. Canada and Australia still talk of 'jurisdictional error', although it bears a very narrow meaning in Canada these days, and has become a conclusory term in Australia. England and New Zealand, on the other hand, no longer use 'jurisdictional error', although 'ultra vires' is still an organising (albeit contested) principle.

For its critics, 'jurisdictional error' had at least three major flaws. First, its theoretical purity as something determinable at the outset of an inquiry or process had never been wholly accurate in representing how the courts actually used the term. By the mid-twentieth century, the disconnect between theory and practice was so vast as to demand a better theory. Everyone everywhere has rejected the so-called pure theory of jurisdiction.[37] Secondly, 'jurisdictional error' focused on issues of process rather than substance, but substantive errors could be disguised as process mistakes (most obviously in the case of review for failing to take account of a mandatory consideration). In any event, substantive review at the margins was openly acknowledged in the case of decisions so absurd as to be *Wednesbury* unreasonable, with the result that administrators could have 'jurisdiction' right up to the end of the process, at which point they would 'lose' it. Thirdly, and partly as a consequence of the courts having to struggle with these difficulties, it became fashionable for cynics[38] and theoretical reductionists alike to see 'jurisdictional error' as the infinitely manipulable plaything of the judges, who could and did use it to achieve their desired outcomes in any particular case without any genuine regard either to statutory interpretation or administrative practicalities.

My concern here is not with the wider debates about 'jurisdictional error', but with their impact upon the case for a variable standard of review for error of law. Non-jurisdictional error was the flip-side of jurisdictional error, even where the error was one of law. Without descending into the detail, one can say of the common law that in the run-up to *Anisminic Ltd v Foreign Compensation Commission*,[39] most jurisdictional errors were of

[37] *Anisminic Ltd v Foreign Compensation Commission* [1969] 2 AC 147; *Kirk v Industrial Court (NSW)* (2010) 239 CLR 531, 569–71. The pure theory still applies to US courts, but not to administrative agencies: *Arlington v Federal Communications Commission* (2013) 133 S Ct 1863. *CUPE Local 963* (n 17) 233 rejected the language of 'preliminary' or 'collateral' issues, preferring instead to see 'jurisdiction' as being 'typically' determinable at the outset. For criticism of the distinction, see Evans (n 18) 71–73.

[38] The most obvious example being Lord Denning MR in *Pearlman v Harrow School* [1979] QB 56, 69–70.

[39] *Anisminic* (n 37).

law rather than fact;[40] errors of law were increasingly likely to be categorised as jurisdictional; and certiorari could reach non-jurisdictional errors of law provided that they were apparent on the face of the decision-maker's record.[41] The Tribunals and Inquiries Act 1958 (UK) provided a further boost to certiorari's reach by requiring tribunals to give reasons for their decisions, and quite apart from the common-law's judicial review remedies, the same Act also provided direct appellate access to the High Court from an increasing number of tribunals on all questions of law. In other words, redress for error of law was *already* subject to variable standards, according to whether the error was jurisdictional, non-jurisdictional but ex facie, or appellable without regard to those common-law distinctions.

V. ENGLAND

Anisminic may well have constituted a clear example of the manipulability of the distinction between jurisdictional and non-jurisdictional legal errors, but its doctrinal statements were equally clear in the importance of maintaining that distinction—it was deployed to get around a privative clause. Lord Wilberforce even disowned any bias for or against categorising questions of statutory interpretation as either jurisdictional or non-jurisdictional.[42] *Anisminic*'s English successors, however, treat that case as having been considerably more radical.[43] After an initial dalliance with an interpretive presumption that all legal errors are jurisdictional except those committed by inferior courts,[44] the House of Lords opted for treating them all as reviewable no matter who their author,[45] and dropped the language of 'jurisdictional error'.

Shortly after *Anisminic*, and going against the prevailing fashion,[46] Jack Beatson had issued an early warning of the dangers inherent in judicial review's extension to all legal errors.[47] He made two predictions, each of which has come to pass. First, the extension turned on a distinction between errors of fact and law that was in danger of becoming no less

[40] 'Jurisdictional' or 'precedent' fact was the exception.

[41] Certiorari's reach beyond jurisdictional error was 'rediscovered' as late as 1952: *R v Northumberland Compensation Appeal Tribunal, ex p Shaw* [1952] 1 KB 338.

[42] *Anisminic* (n 37) 209.

[43] *Boddington v British Transport Police* [1999] 2 AC 143, 154; *R (Cart) v Upper Tribunal* [2011] UKSC 28, [2012] 1 AC 663, 676, 683 and 702; *Eba v Advocate General for Scotland* [2011] UKSC 29, [2012] 1 AC 710, 718–19.

[44] See *Pearlman* (n 38); *South East Asia Fire Bricks Sdn Bhd v Non-Metallic Products Manufacturing Employees Union* [1981] AC 363; *Re Racal Communications Ltd* [1981] AC 374.

[45] *R v Hull University Visitor, ex p Page* [1993] AC 682.

[46] Commencing with B Gould, 'Anisminic and Judicial Review' [1970] *Public Law* 358.

[47] J Beatson, 'The Scope of Judicial Review for Error of Law' (1984) 4 *Oxford Journal of Legal Studies* 22.

manipulable than that between jurisdictional and non-jurisdictional legal error.[48] Secondly, and even without result-oriented manipulation, 'error of law' was so broad a category error as to be in serious need of a counterbalance, which would most likely take the form of an enhanced judicial discretion to decline relief.

The Supreme Court said in *R (Cart) v Upper Tribunal*[49] that it was now too late to resurrect the terminology of 'jurisdictional error', and that its distinctions were immaterial from the complainant's perspective, and unprincipled from a rule of law perspective. Non-jurisdictional errors on a point of law of general public importance could be 'egregious and obvious', 'whereas a one-off jurisdictional error of no general significance' would be reviewable.[50] Better, according to the Supreme Court, to maintain the doctrinal position reached after *Anisminic* that all legal errors are reviewable, and counterbalance that with a judicial discretion to decline relief, a discretion now to be informed by both functional and rule of law considerations. *Cart*'s context was the relationship between the 'regular' courts and the recently rationalised tribunal system, which had replaced a plethora of separate tribunals with a First-tier Tribunal and an Upper Tribunal. The Upper Tribunal supervises the First-tier, is headed by judges, and has its own judicial review powers if a judge is sitting.

Cart noted that the judicial discretion to decline relief had long been a feature of judicial review, exercised according to a number of well-established principles, including that judicial review was a remedy of last resort, generally to be used after exhaustion of alternative appellate redress. But *Cart* took that a step further. Applicants dissatisfied with a First-tier decision can seek an internal review (which is usually conducted on the papers), or seek leave to appeal to the Upper Tribunal (once again, usually decided on the papers), but in either case, a full 'second look' at the legal question is usually limited to cases raising issues of general public importance. *Cart* said that permission to seek judicial review of the Upper Tribunal would be filtered by the same criteria, because anything more would be a waste of scarce judicial resources in the pursuit of an improbable error of law: 'The rule of law is weakened, not strengthened, if a disproportionate part of the court's resources is devoted to finding a very occasional grain of wheat on a threshing floor full of chaff.'[51]

It is true that *Cart* had involved special questions as to the availability and intensity of judicial review of the unique and very court-like Upper Tribunal, but *Cart*'s reasoning had explicitly attempted a reconciliation

48 *E v Secretary of State for the Home Department* [2004] EWCA Civ 49, [2004] QB 1044 said that an acknowledged error of a material fact was an error of law.

49 *Cart* (n 43).

50 Ibid, 702 (Lord Dyson).

51 Ibid, 700 (Lord Brown).

of inconsistent streams of judicial authority as to the intensity of judicial scrutiny of the decisions of expert tribunals.[52] At one extreme were cases involving asylum and immigration decisions, which the courts tended to review with 'anxious scrutiny', an approach paradoxically, that had led to a legislative backlash against judicial review.[53] At the other extreme were matters involving social security decisions, where the courts had long propounded a 'hands off' policy on the proviso that applicants have ample access to legally well-qualified tribunals who would be[54]

> sufficiently expert to be able to take an independent and robust view, particularly in cases where the government agency has gone wrong. It must be in a position to see through what the relevant sponsoring department is saying when it is arguing the case.

Two years after *Cart*, although curiously without any reference to it, the Supreme Court vindicated both of Beatson's predictions in *Jones v First-tier Tribunal*.[55] Distinguishing between errors of fact and law has always been fraught, and always sensitive to context, but one proposition used to be virtually axiomatic. Where decision-makers had committed no legal error in the process of finding the relevant facts, and where they had articulated and understood the correct legal test, then their application of that test to those facts was classically characterised as an issue of fact.[56] Exceptions started to appear where the court thought that the primary decision-maker's application of the law to the facts was perverse, or beyond any permissible 'either way' margin,[57] but these were sometimes rationalised on the basis that the law must somehow have been misunderstood. *Jones* has shifted the goal posts even further, at least in relation both to the Upper Tribunal's supervision of the First-tier Tribunal, and to the Court of Appeal's supervision of the Upper Tribunal.

Jones dealt with the availability of criminal injuries compensation for third party injuries suffered as a result of suicides on the road or rail systems. The rules dictated that there had to be a crime of violence, which meant that persons committing suicide (which is no crime) had either to have intended harm (which would be highly improbable) or at the very least, they must have actually foreseen some harm to others. If one or other of those mental

[52] See especially ibid, 686–87. See also *Daejan Investments Ltd v Benson* [2013] UKSC 14, [2013] 1 WLR 854, [89] (Lord Hope, dissenting, but not relevantly to this point).

[53] *Cart* (n 43) [50] (Lady Hale): 'Had [the courts] adopted the same restraint in asylum as in social security cases, it might not have been thought necessary to introduce statutory review procedures. Ironically, therefore, the more troubling the context, the more necessary it has seemed to limit the availability of judicial review.'

[54] *Cooke v Secretary of State for Social Security* [2001] EWCA Civ 734, [2002] 3 All ER 279, [15] (Lady Hale).

[55] *Jones v First-tier Tribunal* [2013] UKSC 19, [2013] 2 AC 48.

[56] See M Aronson and M Groves, *Judicial Review of Administrative Action*, 5th edn (Pyrmont, Thomson Reuters, 2013) [4.240]–[4.260].

[57] T Endicott, 'Questions of Law' (1998) 114 *Law Quarterly Review* 292, 302–303.

elements were satisfied, the Supreme Court said that the offence was necessarily a 'crime of violence'. The antecedent problem, however, was that primary decision-makers had been coming to different conclusions about the deceased's mental states, given that there was usually no hard evidence either way. Appeals and judicial review were limited to errors of law.

The Supreme Court acknowledged that whilst a finding on the deceased person's state of mind (knowledge or deliberate recklessness) might not fit the traditional definition of a decision on a point of law, the Upper Tribunal could treat it as a legal issue in order to impose consistency. The courts on appeal or judicial review could also treat the matter as a question of law, but should exercise self-restraint in the interests of expediency, giving room for the Upper Tribunal to impose its authority and expertise on the First-tier Tribunal:[58]

> [T]he division between law and fact in such classification cases is not purely objective, but must take account of factors of 'expediency' or 'policy'. Those factors include the utility of an appeal, having regard to the development of the law in the particular field, and the relative competencies in that field of the tribunal of fact on the one hand, and the appellate court on the other. Secondly, even if such a question is classed as one of law, the view of the tribunal of fact must be given weight.
>
> [E]xpediency requires that, where Parliament has established such a specialist appellate tribunal in a particular field, its expertise should be used to best effect, to shape and direct the development of law and practice in that field.

The court's references to the relative expertise of the First-tier Tribunal and the Upper Tribunal are, frankly, entirely unconvincing. Judicial self-restraint on the basis of expertise is sometimes a convincing rationale, but not in this context. After all, the regular courts have long tried the more serious criminal cases, which have all required detailed inquiry into the state of mind of the accused person. There is no reason to suppose that the regular courts are less capable than the tribunals beneath them on the issue of a deceased's mental state. A more likely explanation of *Cart* and *Jones* is that the courts are in the process of developing a highly pragmatic and flexible approach to the appropriate level of scrutiny, not just by themselves, but also within the tribunal hierarchy. *Cart* said repeatedly that it was setting the appropriate level of scrutiny by reference to the judges' view of the demands of the rule of law; it even used the word 'proportionate' for that purpose:[59]

> [T]he scope of judicial review is an artefact of the common law whose object is to maintain the rule of law—that is, to ensure that, within the bounds of practical possibility, decisions are taken in accordance with the law, and in particular the law which Parliament has enacted, and not otherwise. Both tribunals and the

[58] *Jones* (n 55) [46] (Lord Carnwath, quoting himself in 'Tribunal Justice, a New start' [2009] *Public Law* 48, 63–64).

[59] *Cart* (n 43) [37] (Lady Hale).

> courts are there to do Parliament's bidding. But we all make mistakes. No-one is infallible. The question is, what machinery is necessary and proportionate to keep such mistakes to a minimum?

Jones went further, because it sanctioned not just judicial self-restraint, but also an interventionist posture on the part of the Upper Tribunal in order to produce consistency in what on any view was really an issue of fact.

In effect, *Cart* and *Jones* saw the Supreme Court playing a role in devising a system of accountability both to the tribunals *and* (but only as a long-stop) the courts. The criteria will be flexible—the relative expertise of the primary decision-makers and of the tribunals and courts, whether the decisions beneath the court level are basically consistent on issues both of law and fact, the complexity of the issues, whether the non-government parties have access to truly independent scrutiny, and whether that access is sufficient having regard to a number of factors including the amount at stake and the need for administrative effectiveness and efficiency. This is judicial self-restraint, although it is a far cry from North America's 'deference' cousins, which have long struggled to formulate generalist criteria operating across the whole spectrum of administrative decision-making.

VI. AUSTRALIA

England's common-law review for error of law aligned itself with its more liberal statutory developments, but Australian common law did not follow suit. Nor have the Australian statute books followed the English model in all respects. Australian common law retains the language of jurisdictional error, and with it, the concept of a non-jurisdictional error of law.[60] Moreover, it is an important concept in light of the starkly different stances taken by the legislatures towards judicial review and appeals in different substantive contexts.

On the one hand, and to some extent influenced by the English model, statutes have boosted access to judicial review and appeals for all or most errors of law in a wide range of circumstances. They have done this in three principal ways. First, statutory schemes for judicial review typically declare 'error of law' *simpliciter* to be a review ground.[61] Secondly, and as a more limited alternative, they have added further emphasis to the pervasive statutory duties to give reasons, by deeming that reasons form part of the decision-maker's record; the result is to extend access to certiorari

[60] *Craig v South Australia* (1995) 184 CLR 163.

[61] Eg s 5(1)(f) of the Administrative Decisions (Judicial Review) Act 1977 (Cth) allows review of a huge range of Commonwealth administrative decisions if they involve an error of law, 'whether or not the error appears on the record of the decision'.

for non-jurisdictional error of law apparent upon the face of the record.[62] Thirdly, appeals for error of law or on questions of law are widely available from most tribunals[63] and many administrative or regulatory decisions.

On the other hand, Australia has a long history of fierce-looking privative clauses, restricting access to both appeals and judicial review. For example, a full *de novo* appeal on the merits is available in respect of most adverse immigration decisions, but that is to a tribunal, not the courts. Parliament has gone almost as far as it can to restrict access to judicial review in immigration law, deploying a privative clause that attempts to shield from judicial scrutiny not just 'decisions' (which is easily avoided by being restricted to valid decisions),[64] but also *purported* decisions. However, because all Australian parliaments (State,[65] Commonwealth,[66] and Territorial[67]) are constitutionally incapable of abolishing judicial review, seemingly judge-proof privative clauses have either to be dismissed as invalid, or acknowledged as perhaps providing an interpretive indicator of the breadth of the decision-maker's power,[68] although that latter option has to date remained entirely theoretical.[69] It will be recalled that Canada, by contrast, treats the existence of a privative clause as one of its pro-deference factors.

The net result is that judicial review on common-law principles remains available for jurisdictional errors of all kinds, leaving the legislatures free to extend the reach of review or appeal, but equally free to abolish judicial review for non-jurisdictional errors of law. The High Court said that the distinction between jurisdictional and non-jurisdictional errors is 'useful',[70] by which it probably meant that the distinction permits the drawing of sensible compromises between enforcing compliance with a proper interpretation of the law, and the administrative necessity for finality in administrative decision-making.

It follows that, as with the other countries in this survey, Australia already has a variable standard for redressing error of law, a standard that turns for the most part upon the distinction between jurisdictional and non-jurisdictional legal errors. The High Court recognises that there is no magic bullet for predicting how this critical distinction will play out in different contexts, because different contexts will inevitably produce different

[62] See, eg Supreme Court Act 1970 (NSW), s 69; Administrative Law Act 1978 (Vic), s 10.
[63] Eg Administrative Appeals Tribunal Act 1975 (Cth), s 44.
[64] *Minister for Immigration and Multicultural Affairs v Bhardwaj* (2002) 209 CLR 597, 614–15; *Plaintiff S157/2002 v Commonwealth* (2003) 211 CLR 476, 506.
[65] *Kirk v Industrial Court (NSW)* (2010) 239 CLR 531.
[66] Constitution, s 75 (v); *Plaintiff S157/2002* (n 64).
[67] *DPP v Martin* (2014) 286 FLR 120, [104].
[68] *Plaintiff S157/2002* (n 64); *Kirk* (n 65) [93].
[69] Aronson and Groves (n 56) [17.170].
[70] *Kirk* (n 65) 576, 581.

compromises between the need for administrative finality and the rule of law demand for compliance with the law.[71]

'Jurisdictional error' has in Australia become a term of conclusion, representing all of the grounds for alleging that decision-makers lacked legal authority to decide as they have done. The dividing line between errors that are jurisdictional and those that are not has so far been drawn by reference to the usual principles of statutory interpretation, principles that are informed as much by legal values and judicial culture as by a curial sense of the functionality demands of the particular statutory context. Quoting Louis Jaffe,[72] the High Court said that whether a question is to be categorised as 'jurisdictional'[73]

> is almost entirely functional: it is used to validate review when review is felt to be necessary ... If it is understood that the word 'jurisdiction' is not a metaphysical absolute but simply expresses the gravity of the error, it would seem that this is a concept for which we must have a word and for which the hallowed word ['jurisdictional'] is justified.

Having said that, however, there is a reasonably clear rule of thumb which may even be an interpretive presumption. The 'jurisdiction' of inferior and superior courts includes the power to have the last word (subject to statutory appeal rights, if any) on most questions of law that may be expected to arise as part of the core work of the relevant court.[74] There is some debate as to whether the same or a similar rule of thumb applies to court-like tribunals whose members are legally qualified.[75]

The big issue which is yet to be resolved is whether there are any constitutional limits upon the legislative ability to grant powers of such broad scope (so-called 'plenary provisions') that, in practice, there never could be a 'jurisdictional error'.[76]

A cynic might say that this is all a smokescreen for judicial discretion, and that it would be preferable to take the Canadian lead which, for all its indeterminacy, at least has the virtue of intellectual honesty. That was Mike Taggart's view,[77] although he was no cynic, but it is a view that pays too little credence to the Australian courts' determination to approach the

[71] Ibid, 573–74.

[72] L Jaffe, 'Judicial Review: Constitutional and Jurisdictional Fact' (1957) 70 *Harvard Law Review* 953, 963 (footnote omitted).

[73] *Kirk* (n 65) 570–71.

[74] *Craig* (n 60).

[75] Aronson and Groves (n 56) [4.360].

[76] W Bateman, 'The *Constitution* and the Substantive Principles of Judicial Review: The Full Scope of the Entrenched Minimum Provision of Judicial Review' (2011) 39 *Federal Law Review* 463; Aronson and Groves (n 56) [17.290].

[77] See Taggart (n 32); M Taggart, '"Australian Exceptionalism" in Judicial Review' (2008) 36 *Federal Law Review* 1, 8–10.

matter from the perspective of rules rather than discretion. It would be unfair to respond that the Australian judges are fooling themselves.

A reductionist elision of rule-based and discretion-based judging is neither useful nor accurate in this context. All countries in this survey acknowledge in one way or another the utility of being able to vary the intensity of scrutiny for error of law according to statutory and administrative context. The method for achieving this is necessarily guided by constitutional considerations in Australia. Australian judicial review is constitutionally entrenched as a consequence of a largely formalist theory of the separation of the judicial branch from the legislative and Executive branches. It would not be constitutionally feasible to conclude that the scope of the entrenched jurisdiction is simply a matter of judicial discretion, although matters of judgment are certainly involved. Constitutional doctrine requires that the criteria for limiting legislative power to restrict access to judicial review be firmer than 'judicial discretion'.

VII. NEW ZEALAND

New Zealand is currently witnessing a lively debate as to the scope for adopting variable standards of review,[78] but whether in the cases[79] or academic commentaries,[80] the debate has not really reached 'error of law'. Rather, it has focused almost entirely on the more substantive grounds (such as *Wednesbury* unreasonableness, and proportionality) or on issues connected to the protection of enacted human rights or fundamental common-law rights.

When it comes to 'error of law', New Zealand's judicial review literature tends to follow the major developments in English cases reasonably closely.[81] As in England, the old distinction between jurisdictional and non-jurisdictional errors of law has gone from the general common-law principles relating to judicial review.[82]

Construction disputes between builders and their contractors are regulated in New Zealand, as elsewhere, by legislation empowering arbitrators to make 'rough justice' interim determinations very speedily, with a view to

[78] In addition to the contributions to the present book, see, especially, the essays in [2010] *New Zealand Law Review* (Part 2).

[79] The Court of Appeal recently endorsed variable 'deference' or 'latitude' in the context of a discrimination complaint brought under the Bill of Rights: see *Ministry of Health v Atkinson* [2012] 3 NZLR 456, [172–79] (CA).

[80] D Knight, 'Mapping the Rainbow of Review: Recognising Variable Intensity' [2010] *New Zealand Law Review* 393.

[81] See Knight (n 80) 414, noting Taggart's argument that New Zealand courts should consider the Canadian cases: Taggart (n 32).

[82] *Bulk Gas Users Group v Attorney General* [1983] NZLR 129 (CA); *Peters v Davison* [1999] 2 NZLR 164 (CA); *R v Refugee Status Appeals Authority* [2012] NZHC 567, [12].

maintaining cash flows to the contractors. Any final determination of the parties' positions is postponed. Judicial review of the interim determinations will rarely be granted, but the Court of Appeal rejected an attempt to spell out the criteria for judicial restraint by reference to any distinction between jurisdictional and non-jurisdictional errors of law, whether 'jurisdiction' be understood narrowly in a pre-*Anisminic* way,[83] or broadly (as in Australia) as a conclusory term representing any and all of the available grounds of judicial review.[84]

In a move that is perhaps unique to New Zealand, however, employment legislation requires the courts to distinguish between the various categories (narrow and broad) of jurisdictional error. A privative clause drawn soon after *Anisminic*, and with obvious reference to Lord Reid's classic list of reviewable errors in that case,[85] precludes judicial review of decisions of the specialist employment court except for bad faith, lack of jurisdiction 'in the narrow and original sense of the term [that the court] has no entitlement to enter upon the inquiry in question',[86] or where the challenge is to an order that the employment court has no power to make under any circumstances. That precludes judicial review for error of law,[87] although it should be added that the Act provides mechanisms for appeals on questions of law arising from most of the specialist court's business.[88]

The Court of Appeal explicitly rejected America's *Chevron* deference, saying that it is 'fundamental and constitutionally important'[89] to the preservation of the rule of law that courts have the last word on questions of law. The courts still adhere, however, to the doctrine of legislative supremacy, (hence its obedience to the employment legislation's privative clause), and to an expanded concept of ultra vires as judicial review's primary legitimacy basis. Aside from the context of privative clauses, therefore, error of law has now become a larger component than previously of ultra vires.[90]

Judicial review remains discretionary, although it will usually be granted where the ground of challenge has been established. In addition to the usual criteria for discretionary restraint, including delay and the availability of alternative remedies, New Zealand's courts emphasise restraint where they see this as appropriate to specific legislative contexts.[91] Indeed, as in Canada, the New Zealand courts frequently emphasise the

[83] *Rees v Firth* [2012] 1 NZLR 408, [18] (CA).
[84] Ibid, [31].
[85] *Anisminic* (n 37) 171.
[86] Employment Relations Act 2000 (NZ), s 193(2)(a).
[87] *Parker v Silver Fern Farms Ltd* [2012] 1 NZLR 256, [53] (CA).
[88] The exception is that court's tort jurisdiction.
[89] *Wool Board Disestablishment Co Ltd v Saxmere Co Ltd* [2011] 2 NZLR 442, [117], [224] (CA).
[90] R Ye, 'The Demise of Ultra Vires in New Zealand: To Be? Not to Be!' (2010) 8 *New Zealand Journal of Public and International Law* 287.
[91] Eg *Rees v Firth* [2012] 1 NZLR 408.

'contextual' factors relevant to particular cases. Building on the work of Mike Taggart,[92] Dean Knight has written of the context/deference couplet, arguing that contextual variance of the intensity of scrutiny in judicial review goes hand-in-hand with 'deference', even though that latter term is anathema to some senior judges.[93] Knight's arguments are that deference is practised covertly, if not overtly, and that what troubles the judges is any attempt to establish a finely defined calibration of *levels* of deference. As in England, there is no need for a separate *doctrine* of deference; rather, it is in any particular case the outcome of the combined effect of interpretive and discretionary considerations.

There is no equivalent as yet to England's functionalist criteria in *Cart*, whereby as a matter of discretion, judicial review was limited by reference to the need to conserve scarce judicial resources, and by reference to the quality and independence of the primary decision-maker. Were the *Cart* issues to arise, however, one might expect the New Zealand courts to be sympathetic to its overall reliance on a structured discretionary approach, as opposed to a rule-based approach. There is a more generally expressed strong antagonism to so-called formalism, which is seen as the antithesis of open-ended judicial discretion.[94]

VIII. OVERVIEW

There appears to be one overriding lesson from this survey. No matter whether the reader is from the United States, Canada, England, Australia or New Zealand—the grass on the other side of your fence might be different from yours, but it is no greener. And if you fancy switching seeds, you will have to consider a lot else as well, including the way you cultivate the grass, plus the fact that your audience, your demographic, has a visceral dislike of the look of your neighbour's crop.

Comparisons are possible, of course, and sometimes useful, but they can also be dangerous, especially between countries whose legal systems use much the same terminology.[95] I have shown, for example, that 'jurisdictional error' and its cognates have borne a range of meanings within the legal systems of England, Canada, Australia and New Zealand. I have noted England's drift to pragmatism in its definition of 'error of law', but limitations of space have prevented me from following that up in any detail

[92] M Taggart, 'Proportionality, Deference, *Wednesbury*' [2008] *New Zealand Law Review* 423.

[93] D Knight, 'Mapping the Rainbow of Review: Recognising Variable Intensity' [2010] *New Zealand Law Review* 393.

[94] *Chamberlains v Lai* [2007] 2 NZLR 7, [207–23] (Tipping J) (SC).

[95] J Boughey, 'Administrative Law: the Next Frontier for Comparative Law' (2013) 62 *International and Comparative Law Quarterly* 55 is more optimistic.

with regard to the other countries in this survey. It must suffice to say that the most important variant is that different countries show different levels of reluctance to treat serious and material fact-finding errors as errors of law. For present purposes, I have focused on mistaken interpretations of the governing statutory law, because every system treats mistakes of that type, at least, as 'errors of law'.

Each country in this survey already has variable standards of review for error of law. Indeed, how could they not? Courts are not the only bodies that need to engage in serious interpretive exercises in statutory interpretation; administrative bodies must also interpret their governing law, as must adjudicative bodies, and the courts cannot possibly be expected to second-guess all such exercises. Each country, however, differs in the way that it varies the intensity of scrutiny.

The United States and Canada seek to impose pre-determined calibrations of deference, whilst England, New Zealand and Australia abjure the 'deference' word in this context and, more importantly, any attempt at fixed calibrations. All countries swear by the rule of law, of course, but for present purposes, that means different things in different countries. England and New Zealand regard it as axiomatic that the judges should always have the last word on questions of law, with the result that any legislative attempt to cut back on that might invite a challenge to their doctrines of legislative supremacy. United States courts also profess to have the last word on questions of law, but their *Chevron* work-around is to rebrand law as policy.[96]

Legislative supremacy is subject to constitutional constraints in America, Canada and Australia, but with radically different results. America's *Chevron* literature is overtly political—imputing congressional delegation to agencies simply from statutory ambiguity would be a workable interpretive rule if it were regularly applied, but it is not, and in any event, its true justification is not congressional intent (which is entirely fictitious) but a different conception of the separation of powers. Viewed as a system of 'checks and balances', the American courts feel less inclined to retain the last word on statutory interpretation where agency interpretations are reasonably democratic (in the sense that they have gone through a process of public consultation and promulgation), because the agencies are accountable to the elected President. The democratic legitimacy of the administrative state has been *the* dominant concern of American administrative law since the New Deal. The net result is that the American conception of the

[96] '"Delegalisation" of the administrative process' was how it was described in *Enfield City Corporation v Development Assessment Commission* (2000) 199 CLR 135 at 152, [42], citing K Werhan, 'Delegalizing Administrative Law' [1996] *University of Illinois Law Review* 423, 457.

separation of powers has conceded more power to agencies on legal questions because they are *not* independent of the President, and because that accountability makes them indirectly accountable electorally.

Legislative intent or meaning seem to rank fairly low in the Canadian scale of factors that bear on that country's standard of review analysis; even a privative clause is taken as merely one of four relevant factors. The actual or supposed expertise of the primary decision-maker became for a while the dominant *motif* in the Canadian cases, but that is no longer credible. Australia's separation of powers doctrine prevents its courts from acknowledging that the Executive branch might ever have greater legal expertise than the judiciary. Nevertheless, the Australian inclination to allow greater latitude to courts *and* some legally qualified tribunals implies a judgement that subjects are entitled access to at least one forum whose legal expertise and independence deserve respect and, therefore, some level of finality. Without any underpinning from a formal separation of powers, but simply as an exercise in common-law development, England's decisions in *Cart* and *Jones* have gone a step further. *Cart* said that it will ration access to judicial review from bodies that are independent of government and legally well-qualified. *Cart* allows the tribunals *and* the courts to tighten or relax the level of scrutiny according to a pragmatic sense of what would be fair and in accordance with the rule of law, and what is needed to maintain the effectiveness and credibility of the decision-making processes and institutions. In contrast to the American position, therefore, English and Australian courts go more lightly on court-like bodies *because* they are like courts, and because they are independent of government.

In terms of the purely doctrinal differences between the countries in this survey, perhaps the most stark differences are between generalist attempts to calibrate the level of judicial scrutiny, and context-dependent approaches that vary between different administrative structures.

11

Deference on Relevance and Purpose? Wrestling with the Law/Discretion Divide

HANNA WILBERG*

I. INTRODUCTION

WHETHER THERE SHOULD be deference on questions of relevance and purpose is an oddly neglected aspect of the broader question to which this part of the book is devoted. This essay explores this question in relation to three jurisdictions: the United Kingdom, New Zealand and Canada.[1]

The broader question concerns deference on questions of law: whether reviewing courts should be prepared to defer to primary decision-makers' interpretation of the relevant statute in appropriate contexts.[2] Deference to primary decision-makers' statutory interpretation means that reviewing courts will uphold some interpretations without asking whether they are, in the courts' view, the best interpretations. They will do this so long as the interpretations are within what the courts consider to be the range of reasonably available interpretations,[3] or so long as the reasons given are

* Senior Lecturer in Law, the University of Auckland. For helpful comments on drafts of this essay, I am very grateful to Mark Aronson, Peter Cane, Paul Daly, Mark Elliott, Andrew Green, Grant Huscroft, Dean Knight, David Mullan and Marcelo Rodriguez Ferrere. Thanks also go to the participants in a Cambridge Centre for Public Law seminar for discussion of a version of this essay, and to my Administrative Law students over the past few years for indulging my initial explorations of this topic (in particular, Matthew Scoltock and Peter Bevan who wrote excellent and thought-provoking essays broadly on this topic). Any errors or infelicities remain mine.

1 I chose the first two of these because they are familiar to me and similar to each other; the third for an instructive contrast.

2 On this, see H Wilberg and M Elliott, 'Deference on Questions of Law: A Survey of Taggart's Contribution and Themes in the Wider Literature' (ch 8 in this volume); and M Taggart, 'The Contribution of Lord Cooke to Scope of Review Doctrine in Administrative Law: A Comparative Common Law Perspective' in P Rishworth (ed), *The Struggle for Simplicity in the Law: Essays in Honour of Lord Cooke of Thorndon* (Wellington, Butterworths, 1997) 189.

3 See *Dunsmuir v New Brunswick* 2008 SCC 9, [2008] 1 SCR 190, [47].

capable of justifying the interpretations.[4] Such deference has traditionally been applied in a very strong form to primary decision-makers' factual determinations and exercises of discretion, but not to statutory interpretation.

The aspect to be explored in this essay concerns the grounds of irrelevant considerations, failure to take account of mandatory considerations, and improper purposes—what I will call for brevity's sake the relevance and purpose grounds. The question is whether courts should ever accord deference to primary decision-makers' views on what is relevant or what are permissible purposes for exercising a statutory power. This aspect has to date received surprisingly little attention. The most notable recent exception is Timothy Endicott's *Administrative Law* book, which considers deference on these grounds in some detail.[5] It was his discussion that drew my attention to this topic.

In this essay, I approach this ultimately normative question via questions about taxonomy: in the scheme of grounds for judicial review, how should these grounds be classified, and what follows from that classification in terms of the availability of deference? There is a great deal of uncertainty on this taxonomical issue in the case law and commentary.

Parts II and III of this essay concern the orthodox UK and New Zealand approach to questions of law, and part IV the alternative deferential approach favoured by some commentators and adopted by the Canadian courts. While I am attracted by the latter approach, in this essay I do not discuss the relative merits of these two approaches. Rather, I ask in relation to each how the relevance and purpose grounds fit into that approach.

II. THE ORTHODOX UK AND NEW ZEALAND APPROACH

A. The Orthodox Approach to Standards of Review Generally

The orthodox approach in the UK and New Zealand is to reject any deference on questions of statutory interpretation. These are questions of law and thus questions for the courts: courts intervene to correct any interpretation which, in their view, is not the best interpretation.[6] In contrast,

[4] D Dyzenhaus, 'The Politics of Deference: Judicial Review and Democracy' in M Taggart (ed), *The Province of Administrative Law* (Oxford, Hart Publishing, 1997) 279, 303–304; adopted in *Baker v Canada* (1999) 174 DLR (4th) 193 (SCC), [65]. The statement in *Dunsmuir* (n 3) [47] combines both versions.

[5] T Endicott, *Administrative Law*, 2nd edn (Oxford, Oxford University Press, 2009) 272–73 and 276–77. For further exceptions, see nn 101–102 and accompanying text.

[6] *Bulk Gas Users Group v Attorney-General* [1983] NZLR 129 (CA); *R v Hull University Visitor, ex p Page* [1993] AC 682 (HL). Adherence to this approach remains firm in New Zealand. In the UK, many see signs of potential erosion in *Jones v First Tier Tribunal* [2013] UKSC 19, [2013] 2 AC 48, [45]–[46]. For the different version of this approach adhered to in Australia, see P Cane, 'Judicial Control of Administrative Interpretation in Australia and the United States' (ch 9 in this volume) and M Aronson 'Should We Have a Variable Error of Law Standard?' (ch 10 in this volume).

questions of fact and the exercise of discretion are merits questions which are entrusted to primary decision-makers.[7]

In theory, the two types of merits questions were long considered not reviewable as such at all. Review was available only where decisions on them were so unreasonable as to compel the inference that there must have been an error of law.[8] That fiction has largely been abandoned in favour of accepting *Wednesbury* unreasonableness or irrationality as a ground in its own right, alongside illegality,[9] and it is generally accepted that irrationality involves some judicial evaluation of the substantive merits of a decision-maker's exercise of a discretion (or of a finding of fact).[10] In other words, while all reviewable errors render a decision ultra vires in the broad sense, unreasonableness or irrationality is not a species of error of law in the narrower sense of the illegality ground of review. However, the old insistence that substantive merits were never for the courts was for long still partly salvaged by emphasising that intervention on the irrationality ground was exceptional.[11]

This approach can be described in terms of standards of review and degrees of deference: the illegality ground concerning questions of law involves review on a 'correctness' standard involving no deference at all, while the irrationality ground concerning questions of fact and exercises of discretion involves review on a highly deferential 'rationality' standard.[12] It is worth noting, however, that the language of standards of review and deference is essentially foreign to the traditional way of thinking described above, in which all questions were quite simply either questions for the court or unreviewable.

More recently, the concept of variable standards of review and varying degrees of deference has been developed, but only as a further qualification to the otherwise highly deferential rationality standard for reviewing exercises of discretion and fact-finding.[13] Deference has also been much debated in the context of the Human Rights Act 1998 (UK) and the New Zealand Bill of Rights Act 1990, especially in relation to the proportionality test.[14]

[7] *Associated Provincial Picture Houses Ltd v Wednesbury Corporation* [1948] 1 KB 223 (CA).

[8] *Edwards (Inspector of Taxes) v Bairstow* [1956] AC 14 (HL).

[9] *Council of Civil Service Unions v Minister for the Civil Service* (*CCSU*) [1985] 1 AC 374 (HL) 410–11.

[10] See, eg A Lester and J Jowell, 'Beyond *Wednesbury*: Substantive Principles of Administrative Law' [1987] *Public Law* 368, 369–70; P Craig, 'The Nature of Reasonableness Review' [2013] *Current Legal Problems* 1, 2, 4–5. D Galligan, *Discretionary Powers: A Legal Study of Official Discretion* (Oxford, Clarendon Press, 1990) 263 still considered this a 'striking statement'.

[11] *CCSU* (n 9) 410.

[12] See, eg M Taggart, 'Proportionality, Deference, *Wednesbury*' [2008] *New Zealand Law Review* 423, 430, 451.

[13] *R v Ministry of Defence, ex p Smith* [1996] QB 517 (CA); *Wolf v Minister of Immigration* [2004] NZAR 414 (HC). See Taggart, 'Proportionality' (n 12).

[14] See H Wade and C Forsyth, *Administrative Law*, 11th edn (Oxford, Oxford University Press, 2014) 308–15.

But aside from that, there is virtually never any explicit variation in the standard of review on questions of law.[15]

In relation to the classification into questions of law, fact or discretion on which the orthodox approach relies, a point of clarification may be helpful. Often it sounds as though these classifications refer to the nature of the impugned decision as a whole. However, that makes no sense: decisions are not normally pure exercises of discretion or findings of fact or interpretations of law—they are a composite.[16] What these classifications really refer to, therefore, is something more particular. This can be put in two different ways: the classifications refer to the *aspect* of the decision that is challenged by a particular ground, and correspondingly to the *basis* for the court's intervention on that ground. The 'discretion' classification is more often put in the first way: it means that a ground challenges the discretionary aspect of a decision. The 'law' classification is more often put the second way: it means that courts invoking this ground intervene on the basis of statutory interpretation.

The justification for the orthodox approach is not often elaborated in detail, but may be stated as involving three main reasons. First, ensuring public decision-makers' compliance with the law is necessary for upholding the rule of law. Secondly, interpreting and applying the law is part of judges' essential constitutional role. Third and finally, respect for Parliament's will requires ensuring that those who are granted power by statute exercise it in accordance with that statute.[17]

B. Conflicting Sources on the Place of the Relevance and Purpose Grounds

The place of the relevance and purpose grounds within this orthodox scheme of grounds and standards of review is rarely addressed explicitly. The *standard* of review on these grounds is almost universally assumed to be correctness. Usually that is tacitly assumed by commentators and tacitly applied by courts, but it has also been confirmed by the courts on the few occasions where they have addressed the question explicitly.[18]

[15] For discussion of avenues for covert deference, see Wilberg and Elliott (n 2); Aronson (n 6).

[16] See, eg Galligan (n 10) 9.

[17] See *Bulk Gas* (n 6) 133; *Anisminic Ltd v Foreign Compensation Commission* [1969] 2 AC 147 (HL) 174 (Lord Reid), 208 (Lord Wilberforce); *Page* (n 6) 701–702. For recent explicit statements of the rule of law rationale, see also *R (Unison) v Monitor* [2009] EWHC 3221 (Admin), [2010] PTSR 1827, [60] (Cranston J); *Wool Board Disestablishment Company Ltd v Saxmere Co Ltd* [2010] NZCA 513, [2011] 2 NZLR 442, [116]–[118] (Hammond J; a dissenting opinion, but the majority did not disagree with this point).

[18] See, eg *Padfield v Minister of Agriculture, Fisheries and Food* [1968] AC 997 (HL) 1030; *Tesco Stores Ltd v Secretary of State for the Environment* [1995] 1 WLR 759 (HL) 764.

When it comes to *taxonomy*, however, there are two apparently conflicting strands in the case law and commentary. On the one hand, the use of the correctness standard implies that these grounds must involve questions of law. Consistently with that, in the few cases where courts have addressed this question they have classified these grounds as illegality grounds,[19] that is, as involving questions of law.[20] *De Smith's Judicial Review* also expressly adopts this classification,[21] while other commentators have noted its use in the cases while reserving their position on it.[22]

On this first approach, the ground of failing to take account of mandatory relevant considerations starkly illustrates the orthodox law/discretion divide. Whether a consideration is mandatory is a question of law which courts will determine on a correctness standard. However, the weight to be assigned to a mandatory consideration is a matter for the decision-maker, and courts will intervene only if the weight assigned is *Wednesbury* unreasonable.[23]

On the other hand, however, many commentators classify the relevance and purpose grounds as concerning abuse of discretion.[24] Often, they draw attention in this context to the fact that the *Wednesbury* decision included these grounds in its broader 'comprehensive'[25] or 'umbrella'[26] sense of unreasonableness.[27] Craig acknowledges that these grounds are more commonly classified as illegality,[28] but has reservations about this. He has pointed out that the line between these grounds and irrationality is an uncertain and malleable one.[29]

[19] *R v Secretary of State for the Environment, ex p Hammersmith and Fulham LBC* [1991] 1 AC 521(HL) 597 expressly rejects a proposed classification as irrationality.

[20] See, eg *Padfield* (n 18) 1030.

[21] H Woolf and others, *De Smith's Judicial Review*, 7th edn (London, Sweet & Maxwell, 2013) ch 5, and see also [11-019].

[22] P Craig, *Administrative Law*, 7th edn (London, Sweet & Maxwell, 2012) [19-001(i)]; Craig, 'Reasonableness' (n 10) 5; DR Knight, 'Mapping the Rainbow of Review: Recognising Variable Intensity' [2010] *New Zealand Law Review* 393, 417.

[23] *New Zealand Fishing Industry Association Inc v Minister of Agriculture and Fisheries* [1988] 1 NZLR 544(CA), 552; *Tesco* (n 18) 764.

[24] Wade and Forsyth (n 14) ch 11; Craig (n 22) ch 19; M Elliott, *Beatson, Matthews and Elliott's Administrative Law: Text and Materials*, 4th edn (Oxford, Oxford University Press, 2011) ch 8; P Cane, *Administrative Law*, 5th edn (Oxford, Clarendon Press, 2011) ch 6.5.

[25] *Wednesbury* (n 7) 229.

[26] Craig (n 22) [19-002]; Craig, 'Reasonableness' (n 10) 5.

[27] Also Wade and Forsyth (n 14) 292–93; Endicott (n 5) 45. C Harlow and R Rawlings, *Law and Administration*, 3rd edn (Cambridge, Cambridge University Press, 2009) 43–44, question whether these were indeed intended to be two separate principles. Their preferred view seems to be that the relevance and purpose grounds represent the entirety of the unreasonableness ground, which would then not involve any element of merits review. *De Smith's Judicial Review* (n 21) [11-019] also notes the broad usage in the case, but says that today we would classify the wider group of grounds as illegality.

[28] Craig, *Administrative Law* (n 22) [19-001(i)]; Craig, 'Reasonableness' (n 10) 5.

[29] P Craig, 'Political Constitutionalism and the Judicial Role: A Reply' (2011) 9 *International Journal of Constitutional Law* 112, 124–27; see also P Hogg, 'The Supreme Court of Canada and Administrative Law, 1949–1971' (1973) 11 *Osgoode Hall Law Journal* 187, 206–207.

It is usually not clear on what basis and for what reason commentators adopt the 'discretion' classification. In particular, they do not mention the standard of review in this context, and do not say that the classification entails a deferential standard of review.[30] Some of them are unlikely to support such an argument.

III. EVALUATING THE CONFLICTING CLASSIFICATIONS

This part of the essay evaluates the conflicting classifications of the relevance and purpose grounds as falling on either side of the law/discretion divide. Throughout this part, I proceed on the assumption that we should maintain the orthodox approach of arranging grounds and standards of review according to the law/discretion divide: illegality grounds attract a correctness standard, while irrationality grounds attract a rationality standard.[31] The sole question in this part is how the relevance and purpose grounds should be classified within this orthodox scheme.

Section A outlines the basic argument for the 'law' classification. Sections B and C examine two possible objections to the 'law' classification that may underlie the 'discretion' classification. Although this alternative classification, and the deferential standard of review that it would entail on the orthodox approach, has some intuitive appeal, my conclusion in relation to both objections is that they must fail. While both objections draw attention to significant features of the relevance and purpose grounds, they are not valid objections to the 'law' classification for the purposes of assigning a standard of review within the orthodox approach. By way of a postscript in section E, however, I suggest a different method for addressing valid concerns about correctness review on these grounds.

A. The Argument in Favour of the Courts' 'Law' Classification

If the alternative classification of the relevance and purpose grounds as falling on the discretion side of the divide was a valid classification for the purposes of assigning grounds and standards of review within the orthodox scheme, that would mean that they fall within the broader umbrella of the irrationality ground, rather than that of the illegality ground. That in turn would mean that they involve judicial evaluation of the merits, as noted earlier.[32]

Very arguably, however, judicial evaluation of the merits is in fact not the basis on which the courts use these grounds. This is the basic argument for classifying these grounds as involving questions of law, as the courts have

[30] Except the sources in n 29.
[31] For discussion of an alternative approach, see part IV.
[32] See above, n 10 and accompanying text.

done. While questions concerning the merits may well arise in the context of deciding what the statute provides (a point to which I will return),[33] courts intervene not on the basis that their view of the merits is better, but on the basis that it is their responsibility to determine what the statute requires or permits.[34] Courts determine the propriety of purposes and the relevance of considerations by a process of statutory interpretation.[35]

Relevance and purpose questions can, of course, be merits questions: what factors *should* be considered and what purposes pursued, in the sense that they are the most appropriate in the circumstances, is at the very heart of deciding what is a good decision. But they become questions of law when and to the extent that the statute expressly or impliedly regulates what considerations or purposes *may or must* be considered or pursued: contravention of such statutory direction is illegal. The argument for the 'law' classification of the relevance and purpose grounds is that when courts intervene on these grounds, they do so on this latter, statutory basis, entailing illegality.

The same line between merits and legality can indeed be seen in relation to other grounds that are clearly illegality grounds. For example, whether a school principal *should* expel or merely suspend a student for a breach of school rules is a merits question, just like the question what are the most appropriate factors to consider and purposes to pursue. But if the relevant statute confers only limited powers on the principal, then whether the principal *may* expel as well as suspend is a question of law: if the principal is empowered only to suspend, then a decision to expel is illegal. In exactly the same way, questions of relevance and purpose are questions of law where the question is what may or must be considered by virtue of the statute.

A qualification to the statutory basis of these grounds may perhaps be found in cases where common-law principles rather than statutory directions are invoked. For instance, public power must be exercised for public purposes—pursuit of private interests (private gain, favour or ill will) is always improper.[36] Whether this is a qualification at all is open to

[33] See section C of this part III.

[34] Correspondingly, if we ask what *aspect* of the *decision* is challenged (as per text following n 16), the answer is that it is the decision-maker's interpretation of the statute as permitting consideration or pursuit of the impugned considerations or purposes—albeit often the decision-maker will not have turned her mind to this, but will have merely tacitly assumed that her reasons were consistent with the statute.

[35] See *Padfield* (n 18) 1030; P Cane and L McDonald, *Principles of Administrative Law: Legal Regulation of Governance*, 2nd edn (Oxford, Oxford University Press, 2012) 139–40; Taggart, 'Proportionality' (n 12) 427; D Dyzenhaus, M Hunt and M Taggart, 'The Principle of Legality in Administrative Law: Internationalisation as Constitutionalisation' (2001) 1 *Oxford University Commonwealth Law Journal* 5, 26; J McLean, P Rishworth and M Taggart, 'The Impact of the New Zealand Bill of Rights on Administative Law' in *The New Zealand Bill of Rights Act 1990* (Auckland, Legal Research Foundation, 1992) 62, 68.

[36] *R (Corner House Research) v Director of the Serious Fraud Office* [2008] UKHL 60, [2009] 1 AC 756, [53].

debate—some may prefer to see such general constraints as implicit in all grants of statutory power, and in that sense having a statutory basis. For present purposes, the short point is that even if such principles are found in the common law rather than statute, invoking them still involves questions of law.

B. First Objection: These Grounds Structure the Exercise of Discretion

By way of objection to the courts' classification of the relevance and purpose grounds as falling on the 'law' side of the divide and hence coming under the broader umbrella of the illegality ground, it may be said that these grounds structure the exercise of discretion, and thus intrude into the discretionary aspect of a decision in a way that other illegality grounds do not. This may be what some of the commentators have in mind in adopting their alternative classification of these grounds as involving abuse of discretion. In this section I argue that this is a valid point about the nature of these grounds, but that it does not provide a convincing reason for the more deferential review that would be entailed by a 'discretion' classification on the orthodox approach.

i. A Valid Point About the Impact on Discretion

KC Davis's framework for control of discretion is helpful in articulating the distinction I am suggesting here, although his account did not focus on judicial review. Illegality grounds can be classified as either *confining* discretion by determining the scope of a power; or *structuring* the exercise of discretion by requiring or prohibiting certain reasons.[37] The relevance and purpose grounds fall into the latter category—they structure discretion by providing standards to guide its exercise.[38]

These grounds thus go beyond merely policing the legal boundaries of the power: they concern not the legal scope of the power, but the exercise of discretion within that scope. Even if the decision-maker has power to do what she did, in the sense of power to achieve the outcome she achieved (such as expelling a student, to return to my earlier example), her reasons will still be scrutinised. Her decision may still be unlawful if her reasons were defective in terms of the considerations taken into account or the purposes pursued. (Indeed, by this route these grounds have the potential for precluding some of the outcomes that otherwise would have been within

[37] KC Davis, *Discretionary Justice: A Preliminary Inquiry* (Urbana, Ill, University of Illinois Press, 1977), helpfully summarised by Cane (n 24) 171.

[38] Cane and McDonald (n 35) 138; also Cane (n 24) 172.

the scope of a power.[39]) Some commentators have therefore suggested that these grounds impact more than other illegality grounds on the exercise of discretion entrusted to the decision-maker.[40]

ii. What About the Improper Purposes Ground?

But is this point valid for the improper purposes ground as well as the relevance grounds? Does purpose not go to the scope of the power rather than to the exercise of discretion within that scope, at least in some cases? There is a degree of uncertainty and even confusion about the nature of the improper purposes ground. Let me show that at least some versions of the ground do involve structuring the exercise of discretion by prohibiting some reasons, rather than confining the scope of the power.

First, we must be careful to note that not every reliance on purposive interpretation amounts to invoking the improper purposes ground. Purposive interpretation can also be used to interpret provisions defining the scope of the power, and indeed can also be used to defend rather than challenge a decision.

The next point to note is that there is a type of purpose-based illegality where the statutory purpose is not served at all by the decision, and as a result the decision is outside the scope of the power. For example, in *Seaton*, a compulsory acquisition notice was quashed because it was not for the purpose of a 'Government work' at all.[41] But that is not the only kind of improper purposes complaint. Indeed, the New Zealand Supreme Court in *Seaton* rejected the label 'improper purposes' for this type of illegality.[42] There is, however, an overlap between this type of illegality and a 'true' improper purposes case: where a purpose pursued by the decision-maker has frustrated the statutory purpose,[43] it is true to say *both* that the purpose pursued was improper *and* that the decision-maker had no power at all to make the decision because the statutory purpose was not served.

The main point, finally, is that there are many other reasons for challenging a purpose pursued by a decision-maker as improper. The challenged purpose may prejudice or compromise pursuit of the statutory purpose without necessarily frustrating it; or it may be specifically prohibited by the statute;

[39] Elliott (n 24) 235, 238; Endicott (n 5) 272, 275–76 (where the point may be slightly overstated).

[40] Endicott (n 5) 267, 272, 275–76; Elliott (n 24) 235.

[41] *Seaton v Minister for Land Information* [2013] NZSC 42, [2013] 3 NZLR 157; discussed in H Wilberg, 'Administrative Law' [2013] *New Zealand Law Review* 715, 719–25.

[42] *Seaton* (n 41) [38]. This may have been partly due to particular wording of the statutory test: the power was available for 'any land required for a Government work'.

[43] This was one of the ways in which the House of Lords described the defect in *Padfield* (n 18) 1033.

or it may be impliedly excluded in some other way, such as by an exhaustive statement of purposes which does not include the challenged purpose.[44]

All of these latter 'true' versions of improper purposes challenges do involve structuring rather than confining the discretion. The classification of the relevance and purpose grounds as not concerning the legal scope of the power but rather controlling the exercise of discretion within that scope is therefore valid for improper purposes as well as relevance grounds.

iii. What are the Implications for the Standard of Review?

The remaining question concerns the implications of this classification: does it mean that these grounds fall on the 'discretion' side of the law/discretion divide for the purposes of the standard of review, and should therefore attract only deferential review? There are at least four reasons to doubt this. The first and basic reason is that even if these grounds intrude further into the exercise of discretion, it may still be true that the *basis* for the courts' intervention is statutory interpretation,[45] which entails correctness review.

Secondly, the three reasons for this orthodox correctness standard on questions of statutory interpretation[46] apply equally to statutory directions concerning relevance and purpose. First, upholding the rule of law requires enforcement of such directions just as much as it requires enforcement of statutory limits to the scope of powers. Secondly, in both cases this is part of the constitutional responsibility of courts to interpret and apply the law. Thirdly, respect for Parliament's will requires enforcement of both types of statutory provision.

The third reason for doubt is this. If the argument for deference on relevance and purpose relies on the notion that, barring irrationality, decision-makers should be free to reach decisions for legally impermissible reasons so long as the outcome is within the legal scope of their power, this may be seen as a partial throwback to the narrow jurisdictional doctrine[47] that was abandoned in *Anisminic*.[48] Even those who favour a move to deference on questions of law do not propose a return to that particular 'blunt … instrument'.[49]

[44] *Attorney-General v Ireland* [2002] 2 NZLR 220 (CA), [42]–[45].

[45] Or to put it the other way round (as per text following n 16), it may still be true that the challenged *aspect* of the *decision* is the decision-maker's (express or tacit) interpretation of the statute as permitting the challenged reasoning.

[46] Text accompanying n 17.

[47] See *Anisminic* (n 17) 182–83 (Lord Morris, dissenting). It would only be a partial throwback because under the old jurisdictional doctrine, errors within jurisdiction (ie within the scope of the power) were not reviewable at all (unless they appeared on the face of the record), not even on a deferential standard.

[48] Ibid, 210 (Lord Wilberforce).

[49] Taggart, 'Scope of Review' (n 2) 213.

Finally, it is debatable whether the relevance and purpose grounds really do intrude further into the exercise of discretion. The precise opposite argument could also be made. These grounds are also often described as reasoning *process* grounds. It is then sometimes said that they do not intrude into the substance of the discretion in the same way as limits on the scope of the power: they merely control the process leading to a decision, rather than the substantive outcomes.[50] I have reservations about the validity of this opposite argument as well, as I will explain.[51] What it demonstrates, however, is that the relative intrusiveness of grounds which structure rather than confine discretion is very much open to debate.

In light of these four reasons for doubt, the best conclusion may well be that this distinction between structuring discretion and confining its scope has no significance for the standard of review. In terms of the law/discretion divide, as seen earlier,[52] both the reasons and the outcome of a decision can be assessed in terms of their merits; yet both of them can be regulated by statutory limits and requirements, and in both cases questions about such statutory limits and requirements are questions of law.

C. Second Objection: There is Discretion in Statutory Interpretation

A further objection to classifying the relevance and purpose grounds as illegality grounds concerning questions of law is that there is always an element of discretion in statutory interpretation generally, and that this is especially so in determining relevance and purpose. While this is true, I argue in this section that it does not entail a 'discretion' classification of these grounds for the purposes of assigning standards of review within the orthodox approach.

That statutory interpretation involves an element of discretion, policy or judgement cannot, I think, be denied. It is partly due to the indeterminacy of language. It is also due to the requirement of contextual and purposive interpretation, which may have an impact even on relatively clear language, and to the fact that the relevant purpose is often open to debate.[53]

Craig and many other commentators have made this point specifically in relation to the relevance and purpose grounds: 'what are relevant considerations or proper purposes will often not be self-evident',[54] and determination of such questions often entails 'judicial value judgment and use of

[50] See further Part IV C i.
[51] Ibid.
[52] Part III A.
[53] See Cane (n 24) 64; Galligan (n 16) 9–11, also 20–21 and 23–24.
[54] Craig (n 22) [19-002].

substantive principles'.[55] 'Moreover, the boundary line between this form of intervention and more direct substitution of opinion by the judiciary may well become blurred.'[56]

Among the often-cited cases that illustrate these points particularly clearly is the 1920s case of *Roberts v Hopwood*.[57] The House of Lords there applied the values of its class and time by holding that a local authority's statutory power to pay salaries and wages 'as it sees fit' could be exercised only so as to pay a fair wage for the work done. 'Socialistic philanthropy' (paying an increase above the rate of inflation) and a 'feminist ambition to secure equality of the sexes' (paying men and women at the same rate) were irrelevant considerations. Even the landmark *Padfield* decision,[58] not usually thought of as controversial, can be seen to reflect some contestable value judgements about the competing interests engaged by a milk marketing scheme.[59]

This room for discretion or judgement in applying the relevance and purpose grounds gives rise to an objection to the 'illegality' classification of these grounds within the orthodox approach. That objection may take one of three forms. I will take these in turn, to show why each of them must be rejected.

i. Doubts About the Law/Discretion Divide? Introducing Two Types of Discretion

In the first version of the objection, some of the commentators who point out the room for discretion in statutory interpretation go on to deny that there is any clear line between law and discretion at all, and to argue that we should not allocate standards of review based on such a blurry or even illusory line.[60]

However, this proposal involves abandoning the orthodox approach to standards of review, rather than merely challenging the courts' classification of the relevance and purpose grounds within that approach. In this part of the essay, as already noted, I am examining the best classification of these grounds on the assumption that the orthodox approach is right

[55] Ibid, [19-001iii]. See also Craig 'Political Constitutionalism' (n 29) 124–27; Cane and McDonald (n 35) 141; Elliott (n 24) 238–39; Hogg, 'Supreme Court' (n 29) 207; Galligan (n 10) 295.

[56] Craig (n 22) [19-002].

[57] *Roberts v Hopwood* [1925] AC 579 (HL).

[58] *Padfield* (n 18).

[59] See Endicott (n 5) 46 and 272–73; also J Beatson, 'The Scope of Judicial Review for Error of Law' (1984) 4 *Oxford Journal of Legal Studies* 22, 27–28; R Austin, 'Judicial Review of Subjective Discretion—At the Rubicon; Whither Now?' (1975) 28 *Current Legal Problems* 150, 167–72. It is worth reading the dissenting opinion of Lord Morris for the competing perspective.

[60] See sources in n 87 and also n 78, and text at nn 140–141.

in maintaining a line between law and discretion, and insisting that courts should apply a correctness standard on one side of the line and a rationality standard on the other side. The alternative approach advocated by these commentators is examined below, in part IV of this essay.

But this objection does raise the question how the orthodox approach with its reliance on the distinction between law and discretion can be maintained once it is recognised, as it must be, that there is scope for discretion or judgement within statutory interpretation. Does that not render the line-drawing impossible, and thus the orthodox approach incoherent?

The answer, I suggest, lies in drawing a line between two different types of discretion or judgement exercised in two different contexts. On one side of the line is the sort of discretion that forms part of determining what a statute provides, expressly or by implication. On the other side is discretion in the sense of evaluation of the merits of a decision. I will call the former type of discretion 'interpretive judgement'. A valid interpretive judgement requires the interpreter to identify an adequate foundation in the text or context of the statute for considering that judgement to represent the statutory policy or purpose.[61] That is what distinguishes it from other types of discretion. While discretion always implies responsibility to decide for valid reasons that correspond to the type of authority,[62] in the case of interpretive judgement those valid reasons are of this particularly limited and specialised kind. Drawing the line between the two types of discretion or judgement will often be difficult and contentious, but I do think it is a conceptually valid line.

For instance, it would have been difficult for the House of Lords in *Roberts v Hopwood* to find a statutory foundation for the social value judgements that it imposed in that case.[63] In contrast, in *Roncarelli v Duplessis* there was a statutory foundation for the Supreme Court of Canada's intervention (as well as a foundation in more general public law principles). The liquor licensing statute in issue did not say that a licencee's habit of standing bail for Jehovah's Witnesses arrested for pamphleteering was irrelevant: it was silent on the criteria for the liquor licensing power. But this consideration was logically irrelevant to the statutory subject matter of liquor licensing, and thus impliedly impermissible as a matter of statutory interpretation.[64]

[61] While this may sound like a positivist approach to statutory interpretation, the approach proposed here is agnostic on theories of statutory interpretation. Those theories essentially determine what counts as relevant context, and the relationship between text and context. All I am saying here is that once the guidance from the text and any relevant context runs out, any further judgement is no longer interpretive judgement.

[62] Endicott (n 5) 234; Galligan (n 10) 6–8, and see also 30 and 140; contrast F Bennion, 'Judgment and Discretion Revisited: Pedantry or Substance?' [2005] *Public Law* 707, 709–10, 715.

[63] See n 57 and accompanying text.

[64] *Roncarelli v Duplessis* [1959] SCR 121 (SCC), 140. For this method of interpretation, see also Galligan (n 10) 308–13.

If it is accepted that this line can be drawn, then the orthodox approach remains available. Even in the face of recognition that statutory interpretation involves judgement or discretion, the orthodox approach can maintain its line between statutory interpretation and discretion, and can persist in allocating standards of review based on that line.

ii. All Relevance and Purpose Challenges Concern Exercises of Discretion?

Even if it is accepted that challenges involving statutory interpretation can fall on the 'law' side of the law/discretion divide despite the room for judgement, a second version of the objection still needs to be considered. It may still be argued that the relevance and purpose grounds as a group must fall on the 'discretion' side because, as we saw, they provide particularly large scope for judgement.

However, there are two answers to this objection. First, that larger scope for judgement in fact only applies to some relevance and purpose challenges—generally those, like *Roberts v Hopwood*, where criteria of relevance or purpose are expressed in broad or vague terms;[65] and those, like *Roncarelli* or *Padfield*, where courts are asked to imply criteria of relevance or purpose.[66] There are other cases where a challenge invokes a narrow and specific criterion of relevance or purpose that is expressly provided in the statute. While in such a case there is still some room for judgement in deciding the meaning of that criterion, that is no different from any other illegality grounds. On the orthodox approach, such a question would clearly be a question of law: the judgement involved can only be what I have called interpretive judgement.

Secondly, if my analysis under the previous heading is accepted, then even the types of challenge that involve greater scope for judgement because criteria are broad, vague or have to be implied will often fall on the 'law' side. Even in such a case, a court's answer to a relevance or purpose question may have its foundation in the statutory text or context—as I suggested was the case in *Roncarelli v Duplessis*.

In conclusion, on the orthodox approach all relevance and purpose challenges that have a statutory foundation fall on the 'law' side of the line.

iii. Relevance and Purpose Grounds May Fall on Either Side of the Line?

The analysis so far suggests that relevance and purpose challenges can fall on either side of the line, depending on whether or not the particular

[65] That is the type of provision which Endicott (n 5) 237 says confers a 'resultant discretion'.

[66] M Aronson and M Groves, *Judicial Review of Administrative Action*, 5th edn (Pyrmont, NSW, Thomson Reuters, 2013) [5.40].

relevance or purpose argument has its foundation in the statutory text or context. That leads to the third and final version of the objection to the 'law' classification: while some challenges on these grounds involve questions of law, others do not and hence should not attract a correctness standard.

This objection does involve a valid point: there are indeed cases where the statutory guidance on relevance and purpose runs out.[67] Such challenges cannot fall on the 'law' side of the line and should not attract a correctness standard.

Once again, however, there are two answers to this. First, where the statutory direction runs out, usually that means that there is no basis for judicial intervention on relevance and purpose grounds at all. The consideration that has been challenged as irrelevant or mandatory is neither of these things: it falls into the intermediate category of permissible but optional considerations.[68] The statute has left the choice to the decision-maker.

But that is not a complete answer. It is conceivable that there may still be some non-statutory[69] basis for judicial intervention on the ground that the challenged consideration was irrelevant or the purpose improper—perhaps because it is illogical in the context of the decision-maker's overall reasoning. In such cases, the type of discretion involved is no longer interpretive judgement but judicial evaluation of the merits. A 'law' classification of such a relevance and purpose challenge is thus inappropriate, and on the orthodox approach such challenges should only attract deferential rationality review.

To this possibility there is, however, the second answer: such (fairly exceptional) cases indeed fall on the discretion side and should attract only rationality review—but they simply do not involve the same ground of review as the usual statute-based relevance and purpose challenges. If we are to adhere to the orthodox approach of arranging grounds and corresponding standards of review according to the law/discretion divide, then we cannot accommodate grounds that straddle this divide. On the orthodox approach, a ground that has no statutory foundation and attracts deferential rationality review is for that very reason a type of irrationality ground that falls on the discretion side of the divide.

[67] Put more precisely, while the guidance may never run out (my thanks to Trevor Allan for raising this), there comes a point where any statutory guidance is so equivocal that it no longer provides a legitimate basis for reviewing judges to substitute their judgement for that of the primary decision-maker.

[68] *CREEDNZ v Governor-General* [1981] 1 NZLR 172 (CA), 183; *Re Findlay* [1985] 1 AC 318 (HL) 333; *Corner House* (n 36) [40].

[69] And more broadly non-legal: ie also not invoking general legal principles concerning permissible purposes for using public powers as discussed at n 36.

D. Conclusion on Classification within Orthodox Approach

In this part I have evaluated the conflicting classifications of the relevance and purpose grounds. On the one hand, it seems fairly clear that these grounds do not involve evaluation of the merits in the sense that the irrationality ground does: they involve statutory interpretation. On the other hand, there are at least two senses in which they do involve or concern discretion. However, neither of these two points leads to the conclusion that these grounds fall on the discretion side of the law/discretion divide, which would entail deferential rationality review on the orthodox approach. First, the fact that these grounds structure rather than confine discretion is of doubtful significance for the standard of review. Secondly, it is true that statutory interpretation to determine relevance and purpose questions involves an element of discretion. However, this type of discretion (which I have called interpretive judgement) is distinguishable from discretion in the sense of evaluation of the merits. To the extent that relevance and purpose arguments are occasionally made without statutory foundation, such arguments are best classified as part of the irrationality ground.

E. A Postscript on Judicial Restraint within Correctness Review

Given that the relevance and purpose grounds fall on the law side of the divide and thus must attract correctness review on the orthodox approach, there remains a valid concern about the scope for judicial discretion. There is a risk that judges will inadvertently cross the line from interpretive judgement into evaluation of the merits, while continuing to apply correctness review. That would amount to usurping the discretion confided by Parliament to the primary decision-maker. This concern may account for the lingering sense that a correctness standard may not be appropriate for these grounds—but in fact the concern applies to all exercises of statutory interpretation, not just to the relevance and purpose grounds.

How to address that concern (other than by moving to the alternative approach discussed in the next part) is a question beyond the scope of this essay, but let me provide a very brief sketch of a solution. I suggest the risk can be minimised if judges err on the side of restraint when asked to read down broadly expressed purposes or criteria, or to imply further restrictive purposes or criteria. Whenever the statutory basis is doubtful, judges would do well to avoid reading in such restrictions on statutory powers. They would do well to accept, for instance, that some broad statements of purpose are meant to leave further choices to the decision-maker,[70]

[70] See *Unison Networks Ltd v Commerce Commission* [2007] NZSC 74, [2008] 1 NZLR 42, [53]–[54] for an instance of this approach.

and to classify any further restrictive criteria urged on them as permissible but optional considerations.[71] Failure to observe this sort of restraint is, I suggest, what makes cases such as *Roberts v Hopwood* controversial.

IV. THE ALTERNATIVE, DEFERENTIAL APPROACH

This part considers an alternative, deferential approach to questions of law and statutory interpretation, focusing on the version that has been proposed by some commentators and adopted in Canada. Section A outlines this approach and the reasons for it. Section B returns to the central question in this essay: it considers the place of the relevance and purpose grounds within this alternative approach, and whether deference is available in relation to them. It starts by outlining why I would expect an affirmative answer to the latter question, and then surveys the unsettled position in the commentary and the Canadian case law. Section C finally explores and evaluates some possible reasons for this unsettled position.

A. The Alternative Approach to Standards of Review Generally

The orthodox approach to questions of law generally has been questioned by several commentators,[72] and abandoned by the courts in Canada and the United States,[73] in favour of an alternative, deferential approach where courts in appropriate contexts defer to administrative interpretations of statutes by applying some form of reasonableness standard. That means upholding interpretations without asking whether they are, in the courts' view, the best interpretations; so long as the interpretations are within what the courts consider to be the range of reasonably available interpretations, or so long as the reasons given are capable of justifying the interpretations.[74]

[71] See n 68 for the cases recognising this category. For proposals that it be used as a means of restraint, see Elliott (n 24) 235, 239; Aronson and Groves (n 66) [5.30]; Endicott (n 5) 274, 276; A Irvine, 'Judges and Decision-Makers: The Theory and Practice of *Wednesbury* Review' [1996] *Public Law* 59, 67.

[72] P Craig, 'Jurisdiction, Judicial Control, and Agency Autonomy' in I Loveland (ed), *A Special Relationship? American Influences on Public Law in the UK* (Oxford, Oxford University Press, 1995) 173; Craig (n 22) ch 16; Taggart, 'Scope of Review' (n 2); P Daly, *A Theory of Deference in Administrative Law: Basis, Application, and Scope* (Cambridge, Cambridge University Press, 2012); Endicott (n 5) 308–28; Knight, 'Mapping' (n 22).

[73] *Canadian Union of Public Employees Local 963 v New Brunswick Liquor Corporation* (*CUPE*) [1979] 2 SCR 227; *Dunsmuir* (n 3); *Chevron USA Inc v NRDC* (1984) 467 US 837; *United States v Mead Corp* (2001) 533 US 218.

[74] See nn 3–4. The choice between these two options is uncertain and unsettled in Canadian law, as are the details of the second option.

In Canada, the jurisdiction on which I focus in this part, until recently this approach took a highly contextual form. Whether and to what extent deference is appropriate in the particular context was determined by applying a range of contextual factors related to the nature of the question; the expertise, specialisation or other qualifications of the decision-maker in relation to that question; and indications of Parliament's intent in conferring the power, such as privative clauses.[75] While Canada's commitment to such contextualism is currently slightly less clear, following the attempt at simplification in *Dunsmuir*,[76] a similarly contextual approach has also been favoured by several of the commentators.[77]

Behind this alternative, deferential approach lies a different understanding of questions of law,[78] which ties in with a more general dissenting tradition of scepticism about the need for and benefits of oversight by the ordinary courts in administrative law.[79] Contrary to assumptions underpinning the orthodox approach (which its critics often associate with Dicey), there is no bright line separating questions of law from questions of fact or from matters of discretion, policy or judgement. Questions of law do not necessarily have uniquely right answers which courts are always best qualified to give. The policy animating a regulatory scheme and its practical context are relevant to determining the best interpretation of a statutory provision within that scheme. Administrative decision-makers are thus sometimes better placed to interpret their empowering statute than reviewing courts, in terms of relative expertise, experience, or other qualifications in relation

[75] These 'pragmatic and functional' factors were developed in *UES, Local 298 v Bibeault* [1988] 2 SCR 1048; *Pushpanathan v Canada (Minister of Citizenship and Immigration)* [1998] 1 SCR 982.

[76] *Dunsmuir* (n 3). The simplified 'standard of review analysis' substituted by this decision (ibid, [63]) partly sidelines the contextual factors in favour of a more categorical approach (ibid, [51]–[61]; but cf [55] and [64]), and abandons the choice between two distinct reasonableness standards in favour of one (ibid, [45]). While the Supreme Court insists on the paradoxical position that the single reasonableness standard is not variable yet still 'governed by the context' (*Alberta (Information and Privacy Commissioner) v Alberta Teachers' Association* 2011 SCC 61, [2011] 3 SCR 654, [47]), the Federal Court of Appeal has forged an approach in which contextual factors determine the breadth of the range of reasonable decisions: see, eg *Canada (Minister of Transport, Infrastructure and Communities) v Farwaha* 2014 FCA 56. For a full account of the Canadian journey, see P Daly, 'The Struggle for Deference in Canada' (ch 12 in this volume).

[77] Eg Taggart, 'Scope of Review' (n 2); Knight, 'Mapping' (n 22).

[78] See *CUPE* (n 73) 235–37, 242; *National Corn Growers Association v Canada (Import Tribunal)* [1990] 2 SCR 1324, 1332–43 (Wilson J); *Baker* (n 4) [54]–[55]. And see Taggart, 'Scope of Review' (n 2) especially 196, 198, 202–205, 212–13; Craig (n 22) ch 16; Daly, *A Theory of Deference* (n 72) especially chs 3 and 6; Endicott (n 5) ch 9; S Wildeman, 'Pas de Deux: Deference and Non-Deference in Action' in CM Flood and L Sossin (eds), *Administrative Law in Context* (Toronto, Edmond Montgomery Publications, 2013) 323, 329–30; Beatson (n 59); Galligan (n 10) 14–20; P Hogg, 'Judicial Review: How Much Do We Need?' (1974) 20 *McGill Law Journal* 157, 161–62; Hogg, 'Supreme Court' (n 29) 188–89.

[79] See Wilberg and Elliott (n 2); MD Walters, 'Respecting Deference as Respect: Rights, Reasonableness and Proportionality in Canadian Administrative Law' (ch 15 in this volume).

to the subject matter. The legislature, moreover, may sometimes be seen to have allocated interpretive authority to the administrative decision-maker rather than to reviewing courts.

B. The Puzzling Uncertainty about the Relevance and Purpose Grounds

My question here is not whether this alternative deferential approach should be adopted or maintained—though I should declare that I do find the approach attractive. Rather, my question concerns the implications for the relevance and purpose grounds: assuming this alternative deferential approach is adopted and accepted, should the possibility of deference extend to the relevance and purpose grounds? This section starts by outlining the answer I would expect, and then surveys the position in the commentary and case law, which is puzzlingly different and uncertain.

i. The Expected Answer

I would have assumed that when the possibility of deference is extended from the control of discretion and fact-finding to questions of law, as it is on the alternative approach, it would obviously be available for the relevance and purpose grounds as well. Four reasons may be noted.

First, the alternative approach rejects fixed standards of review based on the type of question: the availability and extent of deference for all questions rather depends on a range of contextual factors that include but are not limited to the type of question. There seems no reason why the same should not apply to the relevance and purpose grounds. Secondly, the resulting central innovation of the alternative approach is that questions of statutory interpretation can attract deference. I have concluded that these grounds involve statutory interpretation,[80] so this innovation should apply to them. Thirdly, if my conclusion on the type of question involved is doubted, the alternative is to consider these grounds to involve discretion, to a greater or lesser degree. On that basis, deference would be even more obviously appropriate: discretion has always attracted deference, on both the orthodox and the alternative approach. Finally, the reasons for the alternative approach[81] seem to be at least equally applicable to the relevance and purpose grounds: in particular, given that there is at least as much scope for policy and judgement on these grounds as on other issues of statutory interpretation,[82] administrative expertise and experience are at least as relevant on these grounds.

[80] Part III C.
[81] See section A of this part IV.
[82] See part III C.

ii. The Silence of the Leading Commentators

When we turn to the commentators who have argued for the alternative deferential approach, we find only limited positive support for my expected answer that the availability of deference extends to the relevance and purpose grounds.

Craig and Taggart, the leading critics of correctness review on questions of law in the UK and New Zealand respectively, simply do not touch on the relevance and purpose grounds in this context. Their arguments for the alternative approach tend to focus on issues as to the meaning of express words rather than issues as to what criteria might be implied; and on provisions defining the scope of a power rather than on provisions specifying what considerations or purposes are permissible or mandatory.[83] The one exception in Taggart's essay on deference on questions of law is one cryptic footnote, which notes that relevance grounds are usually classified as involving control of discretion, and questions the orthodox sharp divide between law and fact; but does not address what this means in terms of standard of review.[84] Where Craig and Taggart do discuss the relevance and purpose grounds elsewhere in their work, they tend not to focus on the question of deference in that context.

As for the classification of the relevance and purpose grounds, most of the commentators who have argued for an alternative deferential approach to questions of law tend to see these grounds as involving abuse of discretion[85] (as do most Canadian commentators both before and since the introduction of the alternative deferential approach there);[86] but all of them also cast doubt on the law/discretion divide.[87] According to Craig, indeed, the line between these grounds and irrationality is uncertain and manipulable—an observation that appears to concern both classification and the standard of review on these grounds.[88] Taggart, on the other hand, notes the Canadian courts' then frequent classification of these grounds as jurisdictional, but does so without indicating his own position.[89]

[83] Taggart, 'Scope of Review' (n 2); Craig (n 22) ch 16.

[84] Taggart (n 2) 201, fn 69.

[85] Craig (n 22) ch 19; Endicott (n 5) ch 8; also Beatson (n 59) 26–27.

[86] See, eg Hogg, 'How Much Do We Need?' (n 78) 170–72; Hogg, 'Supreme Court' (n 29) 206; D Mullan, 'Deference from *Baker* to *Suresh* and Beyond—Interpreting Conflicting Signals' in D Dyzenhaus (ed), *The Unity of Public Law* (Oxford, Hart Publishing, 2004) 21; G Cartier, 'Administrative Discretion: Between Exercising Power and Conducting Dialogue' in CM Flood and L Sossin (eds), *Administrative Law in Context* (Toronto, Edmond Montgomery Publications, 2013) 381, 391, 399.

[87] Taggart, 'Scope of Review' (n 2) 198, 203–204, 205, fn 69; Daly, *A Theory of Deference* (n 72) 255–57; Endicott (n 5) 347–49; Hogg, 'How Much Do We Need?' (n 78) 161–62; Hogg, 'Supreme Court' (n 29) 188–89.

[88] Craig, 'Political Constitutionalism' (n 29) 124–27.

[89] M Taggart, 'Globalization, "Local" Foreign Policy, and Administrative Law' in G Huscroft and M Taggart (eds), *Inside and Outside Canadian Administrative Law* (Toronto, University of Toronto Press, 2006) 259, 272.

Two commentators who do support my expected answer at least to some extent are Endicott and Knight. Endicott in particular clearly proposes deference in applying the relevance and purpose grounds. Even he does not discuss these grounds in his discussion of deference on error of law, except very briefly in passing near the end.[90] In his chapter on substantive fairness, however, he presents the relevance and purpose grounds as being among the most interventionist,[91] and expressly argues for deference to be available in applying them.[92] A reasonableness standard should be used for them unless relevance and purpose criteria are 'specifically' provided by statute.[93] This reads broadly similar to the American approach to deference.[94]

Knight's work on variable intensity may at first sight appear to concern substantive review only in its narrow sense concerning merits questions. However, he discusses variable intensity and deference according to context as an approach that applies across all grounds of review—and hence as including deference on questions of law.[95] In that context, his survey of overt and covert forms of deference in the New Zealand case law includes discussion of the forms of restraint that are occasionally used in applying the relevance and purpose grounds.[96]

Daly is a further recent exception to the silence on my question. He has indeed acknowledged that deference on statutory interpretation should logically extend to the relevance and purpose grounds.[97] However, he calls instead for the traditional nominate grounds to be abandoned altogether: they should not be used as anything more than 'indicia' of unreasonableness.[98] That is partly because he rejects the law/discretion line on which the distinctions between these grounds are founded.[99] In addition, he is concerned that because of their association with correctness review, the use of traditional grounds such as the relevance and purpose grounds is liable to undermine judicial commitment to deference.[100]

Earlier commentators, writing around the time when the British courts were abandoning the jurisdictional approach and before the Canadian courts introduced the alternative deferential approach, apparently were more likely to include discussion of these grounds and a call for deference in relation to them. Hogg, for instance, noted the room for judgement and disagreement in statutory interpretation as to relevance or purpose, and concluded that

[90] Endicott (n 5) 347 in ch 9.
[91] Ibid, 267, 272 in ch 8.
[92] Ibid, 273, 276–77, 349.
[93] Ibid, 273.
[94] *Chevron* (n 73).
[95] Knight, 'Mapping' (n 22).
[96] Ibid, 417.
[97] Daly, 'Struggle for Deference' (n 76) part IV.
[98] Daly, *A Theory of Deference* (n 72) 262.
[99] Ibid, 256–57.
[100] Ibid, 260–61; also Daly, 'Struggle for Deference' (n 76) part IV.

courts should be ready to defer to decision-maker's answers to these questions in appropriate cases.[101] Beatson noted a tendency under the old jurisdictional approach of justifying jurisdictional review on the relevance and purpose grounds on the basis that they only concerned process. He considered this to represent an undue widening of the scope of review[102]—which must mean that he rejected correctness review on these grounds.

iii. Mixed Record in the Canadian Cases

Canadian courts, of course, cannot simply maintain silence on this question: they have had to fix standards of review for all types of challenge, including those on relevance and purpose grounds. An important qualification is that explicit reliance on specific grounds of review is rare in recent Canadian case law (a point to which I will return).[103] However, among the arguments advanced in support of challenges, arguments concerning relevance and purpose continue to feature. Uncertainty about the standard of review in relation to such arguments arises from a very mixed record:[104] the possibility of deference here took a long time to be introduced at all, and has still not settled in securely.

For some 20 years after deference on questions of law was first introduced,[105] a correctness standard continued to be applied to relevance and purpose arguments.[106] Views on classification were also uncertain and contradictory, as in the UK and New Zealand. The correctness standard was consistent with the commonly adopted view that these grounds were jurisdictional.[107] However, the apparently conflicting classification of these grounds as concerning control of discretion also featured frequently—as it continues to do.[108] L'Heureux-Dubé J, dissenting in *Shell v Vancouver*, criticised courts for applying 'vague doctrinal terms' such as relevance and purpose, in order to assess reasonableness under a 'cloak' of 'vires', allowing them to 'substitute their views'.[109]

[101] Hogg, 'How Much Do We Need?' (n 78) 171–72; Hogg, 'Supreme Court' (n 29) 206–207. See also Galligan (n 10) 294–95, raising the same questions albeit without committing to an answer.

[102] Beatson (n 59) 28–29.

[103] See section C ii of this part IV.

[104] D Mullan, 'Unresolved Issues on Standard of Review in Canadian Judicial Review of Administrative Action—the Top Fifteen!' (2013) 42 *Advocates' Quarterly* 1, 42 says there is a 'perennial issue' about the relationship of the nominate grounds, such as relevance and purpose, with the standards of review.

[105] In *CUPE* (n 73).

[106] G Van Harten, G Heckman and DJ Mullan, *Administrative Law: Cases, Text and Materials*, 6th edn (Toronto, Edmond Montgomery Publications, 2010) 956–57. For a notable example, see *Shell Canada Products Ltd v Vancouver (City)* [1994] 1 SCR 231 (SCC).

[107] As noted in Taggart, 'Globalization' (n 89) 272; Mullan, 'Deference from *Baker* to *Suresh*' (n 86) 24.

[108] *Baker* (n 4) [53]. For commentary adopting this view, see n 86.

[109] *Shell v Vancouver* (n 106) 244, 258. However, her focus was on arguing for deference to municipalities; that deference usually applies to statutory interpretation was mentioned only once: ibid, 246–47.

The Supreme Court finally extended its variable standards of review approach to apply also to relevance and purpose arguments only in *Baker* in 1999.[110] The treatment of the issue there was rather obscure, however, because the Court took the step of extending the alternative deferential approach to these arguments as part of a broader move to extend the approach to review of 'decisions classified as discretionary' generally. In that category the Court included review on grounds of both relevance and purpose and orthodox *Wednesbury* unreasonableness.[111] Accordingly, the extension of the variable standards approach had the potential to result both in greater deference on relevance and purpose arguments[112] and in reduced deference in the field previously covered by the ground of *Wednesbury* unreasonableness.[113]

Moreover, the focus in *Baker* is on this latter aspect: the Court's brief reasons for the extension of the variable standards approach are very much focused on justifying the reduction in deference from the old *Wednesbury* unreasonableness ground.[114] The fact that there is a potential *increase* in deference on relevance and purpose arguments is stated only by way of assuaging concerns about that reduction in deference.[115]

Indeed, it is not at all clear that the move to deference on relevance and purpose arguments was even put into action in *Baker* at all. Despite purporting to apply a reasonableness standard, when it comes to identifying a mandatory relevant consideration—the interests of an illegal immigrant's children must be considered in deciding whether to grant a 'humanitarian and compassionate' exemption from deportation—the Court proceeds on the basis of its own reading of the statute in context.[116] This looks more like correctness review: the Court does not say that it would have been unreasonable for the official not to have considered the children's interests relevant. In contrast, the opposite move to lesser deference in the field previously covered by *Wednesbury* unreasonableness is very clearly applied: the Court reviews the weight accorded to the mandatory consideration on a much more intensive standard than the *Wednesbury* unreasonableness standard that was traditionally used for questions of weight.[117]

Subsequent case law and commentary interpreting *Baker* has tended to continue this focus on the possible reduction in deference from the traditional *Wednesbury* standard, rather than on the introduction of deference

110 *Baker* (n 4).
111 Ibid, [53].
112 That is expressly contemplated ibid, [65].
113 Mullan, 'Deference from *Baker* to *Suresh*' (n 86) discusses these as 'two polarities' and seeks to reconcile what he sees as an apparent contradiction.
114 *Baker* (n 4) [53]–[54].
115 Ibid, [55].
116 *Baker* (n 4) [67]–[74].
117 Ibid, [75]. For the traditional position, see *NZ Fishing Industry Association* (n 23) 552; *Tesco* (n 18) 764.

on relevance and purpose.[118] When commentators do advert to the issue concerning relevance and purpose arguments, they always note the Court's express statement that deference is now available in disposing of these arguments.[119] But they also tend to present this as novel and even radical, and to wonder whether courts will follow it.[120]

More than 15 years after *Baker*, this idea of extending deference to relevance and purpose arguments has still not settled in at all securely. The recent decision of the Federal Court of Appeal in *Forest Ethics* does clearly and expressly affirm that deference is available in relation to relevance arguments.[121] However, it is not difficult to find Supreme Court decisions post-*Baker* that tacitly appear to apply a correctness standard to these arguments, despite having concluded that a reasonableness standard is appropriate for review of the impugned decision.[122] In *Chamberlain*, for instance, a school board's decision not to approve a book depicting same-sex families was struck down for failure to consider relevant considerations and taking account of irrelevant ones. Although a reasonableness standard is selected as appropriate for this case, the relevance issues are discussed almost uniformly in terms implying a correctness standard.[123] The word 'unreasonable' tends to feature throughout as no more than a conclusory label: if the board has erred in law, then its decision must be declared unreasonable.[124]

Similarly, several cases have repeated a formulation of the deferential standard of review according to which reasonable decisions will stand so long as the decision-maker has 'appl[ied] the correct legal test'—and going by the application of that formulation, the 'legal test' that has to be 'correct' appears to include questions of relevance and purpose.[125]

[118] Eg *Suresh v Canada* 2002 SCC 1, [2002] 1 SCR 3; Mullan, 'Deference from *Baker* to *Suresh*' (n 86). See also, more generally, Daly, *A Theory of Deference* (n 72) 255–58; M Taggart, 'The Impact of Apartheid on Commonwealth Adminstrative Law' [2006] *Acta Juridica* 158, 203, but cf 204.

[119] Van Harten, Heckman and Mullan (n 106) 957; Mullan, 'Unresolved Issues' (n 104) 43–44; Cartier, 'Administrative Discretion' (n 91) 399–400. See also *Kane v Canada (Attorney-General)* 2011 FCA 19, 328 DLR (4th) 193, [102] (Stratas JA dissenting).

[120] Mullan, 'Deference from *Baker* to *Suresh*' (n 86) 23–27; Taggart, 'Impact of Apartheid' (n 118) 204; Wildeman, 'Deference' (n 78) 348–49.

[121] *Forest Ethics Advocacy Association v National Energy Board* 2014 FCA 245, [65]–[69].

[122] As noted in Mullan, 'Unresolved Issues' (n 104) 48–50 and 77–78; also Cartier, 'Administrative Discretion' (n 86) 400; Daly, 'Struggle for Deference' (n 76).

[123] *Chamberlain v Surrey School District No 36* 2002 SCC 86, [2002] 4 SCR 710, [58]–[61]; but compare [57]. It will be recalled that *Baker* (n 4) itself is open to similar criticism: text at n 116.

[124] *Chamberlain* (n 123) [15], [56], [71]–[72]. For an arguably similar approach, see also *Kane* (FCA) (n 119) [6], [68]–[81] and the dissenting judgment's criticism of this, especially [124] (reversed on different grounds in *Canada (Attorney-General) v Kane* 2012 SCC 64, [2012] 3 SCR 398).

[125] *Lake v Canada (Minister of Justice)* 2008 SCC 23, [2008] 1 SCR 761, [41]; *Halifax (Regional Municipality) v Canada (Public Works and Government Services)* 2012 SCC 29, [2012] 2 SCR 108, [43] (also [55]).

Several commentators have made similar criticisms of the *Retired Judges* case.[126] In *Chieu*, indeed, the Court expressly assigned a correctness standard to a relevance issue, on the basis that this was a legal and therefore jurisdictional issue.[127]

C. Exploring and Evaluating Some Reasons for the Unsettled Position

In this final section, I explore and evaluate some possible reasons why there is such limited support for the expected position in the Canadian case law and in the commentary favouring the alternative approach.

As we have seen, the mixed record in the case law appears to be at least partly related to confusion. One potential source of confusion lies in the contradictory classifications of the relevance and purpose grounds. Another lies in Canada's retention of the concept of jurisdictional error.[128] Most recently this has been controversially confirmed as one of the exceptional categories of case attracting correctness review.[129] For many years before that, it functioned as no more than a conclusory label for cases attracting correctness review based on the contextual factors, but use of the jurisdictional terminology always presented the risk of slipping back into correctness review *because* a matter was classified as jurisdictional.[130] As we have seen, that was particularly the case for relevance and purpose arguments.

But are there any other reasons for the courts' and commentators' frequent failure to accord or even contemplate deference on relevance and purpose arguments in the context of the alternative deferential approach; and are these good reasons? Let me consider two.

i. No Deference Needed Because these Grounds Involve Only Process?

There is one difference between the relevance and purpose grounds or arguments and some other illegality grounds that may be seen as counting in

[126] *CUPE v Ontario (Minister of Labour)* 2003 SCC 29, [2003] 1 SCR 539. See, eg G Huscroft, 'Judicial Review from *CUPE* to *CUPE*: Less is Not Always More' in G Huscroft and M Taggart (eds), *Inside and Outside Canadian Administrative Law: Essays in Honour of David Mullan* (Toronto, University of Toronto Press, 2006) 296; Daly, 'Struggle for Deference' (n 76).

[127] *Chieu v Minister of Citizenship and Immigration* 2002 SCC 3, [2002] 1 SCR 84, [24].

[128] Criticised, eg by Taggart, 'Scope of Review' (n 2) 206.

[129] *Dunsmuir* (n 3) [59].

[130] For accounts of this, see MD Walters, 'Jurisdiction, Functionalism, and Constitutionalism in Canadian Administrative Law' in C Forsyth and others (eds), *Effective Judicial Review: A Cornerstone of Good Governance* (Oxford, Oxford University Press, 2010) 300, 306–308; A Macklin, 'Standard of Review: Back to the Future?' in CM Flood and L Sossin (eds), *Administrative Law in Context* (Toronto, Edmond Montgomery Publications, 2013) 279, 294, 307; Daly, 'Struggle for Deference' (n 76).

favour of a less deferential standard of review on these grounds. That is that these grounds are often said to be about 'process'. Beatson pointed out that this was often suggested as a reason for correctness review, and that it may mean one of two different things.

First, the 'process' terminology may be confused with 'procedural' in the sense of procedural fairness requirements such as the principles of natural justice, which normally attract correctness review.[131] While this analogy clearly represents confusion,[132] the point does not necessarily go without saying.

Secondly, properly understood, the 'process' label means that these grounds impose limits or requirements on the *reasoning process*, as distinct from the substantive outcome.[133] This is true—it is just a different way of saying that they serve to structure rather than confine discretion, as discussed in part III.[134] Beatson expressed various doubts but appeared to leave open the possibility that this feature might count in favour of correctness review.

But is this classification really significant for the standard of review? Does it mean that these grounds are less intrusive, and hence correctness review is appropriate? In the different context of the choice of mechanisms for giving effect to rights, treating rights as mandatory considerations provides weaker protection than reading the scope of statutory powers subject to a presumption of substantive consistency with the rights.[135] On the former approach, it is lawful to infringe the right, so long as it has been taken into account[136] (and so long as the weight accorded to it is not unreasonable).[137] This might be thought to indicate that reasoning process grounds are generally less intrusive than grounds that concern the substantive outcome.

However, for the purposes of assigning standards of review, it is not at all clear that reasoning process grounds such as relevance and purpose are less intrusive than other illegality grounds in a way that calls for a less deferential standard of review. To the contrary, as we saw in part III, it has also been suggested that relevance and purpose grounds encroach on the exercise of discretion to a greater extent than illegality in the form of

[131] Beatson (n 59) 28–29.

[132] Ibid, 27–29.

[133] Reasoning process is the heading under which they are discussed in Cane and McDonald (n 35) ch 5.3.

[134] Part III B.

[135] *R (SB) v Governors of Denbigh High School* [2006] UKHL 15, [2007] 1 AC 100; *Belfast City Council v Miss Behavin' Ltd* [2007] UKHL 19, [2007] 1 WLR 1420; McLean, Rishworth and Taggart (n 35); C Geiringer, '*Tavita* and All That: Confronting the Confusion Surrounding Unincorporated Treaties and Administrative Law' (2004) 21 *New Zealand Universities Law Review* 66.

[136] McLean, Rishworth and Taggart (n 35); Geiringer (n 135).

[137] *New Zealand Fishing Industry Association* (n 23) 552; *Tesco* (n 18) 759.

exceeding the scope of the power.[138] On that basis, they might give rise to a greater, not lesser, need for deference. As I pointed out there, both claims are open to doubt. In my view, it is best to accept that there is no significant difference between reasoning process grounds and scope of power grounds in terms of the appropriate standard of review.

ii. Does the Alternative Approach Render the Nominate Grounds Redundant?

Secondly, there is a very different possible reason for the commentators' silence on the relevance and purpose grounds and the lack of a settled position in relation to them in the case law. The reason may lie in a view that it is unnecessary and inappropriate to 'segment' a decision under challenge into different aspects that attract different grounds of challenge and different standards of review. The traditional nominate grounds of review, such as the relevance and purpose grounds, served to ensure that some types of errors were addressed on a correctness standard while other types of error were either off limits or reviewable only with extreme deference.[139] There is no need for this when all aspects of the decision are reviewable on the same system of variable standards of review. On this view, the topic of this essay—the categorisation of the relevance and purpose grounds or arguments and the standard of review to be applied to them—ceases to be a question.

Whether this view can be validly adopted depends, however, on the degree to which the law/discretion divide is abandoned. The alternative deferential approach always involves the view that this divide is less clear than traditionally thought and that it should not be determinative of the standard of review.[140] However, the traditional grounds become entirely redundant in the way I have suggested only if the divide is entirely dismissed as both illusory and irrelevant. The position on this is uncertain in both the commentary and the case law.

The commentators who favour the alternative deferential approach all question the law/discretion divide.[141] However, most of them probably would not go so far as to consider the line entirely illusory and irrelevant. And most do not expressly dismiss the traditional nominate grounds. The reason for their silence is thus a matter of speculation. The exceptions are Endicott and Daly. Daly argues against retention of the traditional nominate grounds, while Endicott argues against the overarching grounds of

[138] See part III B.

[139] Knight, 'Mapping' (n 22) 413–15: they 'encapsulate an "off-the-shelf"' calibration of standards.

[140] See text following n 79.

[141] See nn 87–88.

illegality and rationality. Both are concerned that analysis in terms of these grounds is liable to encourage excessive recourse to the old correctness standard.[142] As for the law/discretion divide, Endicott does indeed appear to dismiss this as illusory;[143] while Daly does not seem to go that far.[144]

Canadian courts abandoned the law/discretion divide as determinative of standards of review in *Baker*, as we have seen. But again, the statements in that case do not seem to go further and dismiss the divide as illusory and irrelevant.[145] As to whether decisions under challenge should be 'segmented' into different aspects attracting different grounds of challenge and different standards of review, the position in the cases is unsettled.[146]

On the one hand, whether the point in issue is a question of law (statutory interpretation) or one of fact, policy or discretion is not infrequently still relied on as relevant to the standard of review.[147] Many challenges also continue to turn on discrete issues of statutory interpretation.[148] Critics of 'segmentation' continue to find themselves in the minority.[149] A dictum in *Dr Q* has been cited as abandoning segmentation: the traditional grounds, 'while still useful as familiar landmarks, no longer dictate the journey'.[150] However, in light of its context, this is best read as meaning only that standards of review are no longer summarily determined by invoking these grounds;[151] not that the grounds should no longer be used.[152]

On the other hand, however, we have already noted that explicit reliance on the traditional nominate grounds is rare in recent Canadian case law. There is at least a noticeable trend towards what we might call a 'global'

[142] Daly, *A Theory of Deference* (n 72) 160–62; Daly, 'Struggle for Deference' (n 76) part IV; Endicott (n 5) 348–49. See also Van Harten, Heckman and Mullan (n 106) 787. This is a concern shared by Abella J: see n 149.

[143] Endicott (n 5) 347. This view may also possibly be implicit in passing references to deference on questions of law in Taggart, 'Proportionality': see Wilberg and Elliott (n 2).

[144] Daly, *A Theory of Deference* (n 72) 256–58; but cf Daly, 'Struggle for Deference' (n 76) part IV.

[145] *Baker* (n 4) [54]–[55].

[146] Pointed out in Mullan, 'Unresolved Issues' (n 104) 64–69; also 42–51.

[147] Including in *Dunsmuir* (n 3) [53]. Following *Dunsmuir*'s introduction of the single reasonableness standard, this distinction is now often considered a significant part of the context in *applying* that standard: see, eg *Alberta Teachers' Association* (n 76) [47], [85]–[86]; *First Nations Child and Family Caring Society of Canada v Canada (Attorney-General)* 2013 FCA 75, 444 NR 120, [13]–[14] (Stratas JA).

[148] To name only a few of the many recent instances: *Dunsmuir* (n 3) itself; *McLean v British Columbia (Securities Commission)* 2013 SCC 67, [2013] 3 SCR 895; *Canadian National Railway Co v Canada (Attorney-General)* 2014 SCC 40.

[149] Abella J is the main critic on the current Supreme Court: Mullan, 'Unresolved Issues' (n 104) 64–69, 76–81. See, eg her dissent on the standard of review issue in *Rogers Communications Inc v Society of Composers, Authors and Music Publishers of Canada* 2012 SCC 35, [2012] 2 SCR 283, [74]–[88].

[150] *Dr Q v College of Physicians and Surgeons* 2003 SCC 19, [2003] SCR 226, [24].

[151] See Mullan, 'Unresolved Issues' (n 104) 44.

[152] As claimed in Daly, *A Theory of Deference* (n 72) 262; Daly, 'Struggle for Deference' (n 76) part IV.

approach. This eschews a focus on particular steps in the reasoning process, particularly on points of statutory interpretation, and instead assesses the decision as a whole—the reasoning process together with the substantive outcome—in one single analysis and on one single standard of review.[153]

For instance, in *Baker* the Court formulated the question to be determined as 'whether the decision in this case, and the immigration officer's interpretation of the scope of the discretion conferred upon him, were unreasonable'.[154] Consistently with this, it then proceeded to consider questions of relevance and questions of weight at the same time, rather than as separate questions to be disposed of one after the other.[155] Similarly in *Catalyst Paper*, the reasonableness standard was simply applied to the challenged by-law as such, rather than to any particular step in the authority's reasoning process.[156] The Court noted that the attempt in older cases to maintain a clear distinction between policy and legality, and to confine review to the latter, had not prevailed.[157]

The Supreme Court's explanation of the reasonableness standard in *Dunsmuir*—as concerned with both the reasoning process and whether the decision falls within a range of acceptable outcomes[158]—may also be invoked in support of the global approach.[159] The reading of that passage is, however, contested. In *Newfoundland Nurses' Union*, the entire passage was read as concerning the reasonableness of a decision-maker's answer to a particular question (such as a question of statutory interpretation) that arose in the course of making the impugned decision. It was the reasonableness *of that particular answer* that should be assessed by asking both whether that answer is reasonable and whether the decision-maker's reasons for it are capable of justifying it.[160] On that reading, *Dunsmuir* does not support the global approach.[161]

It is also worth recalling that even cases that purport to apply one uniform reasonableness standard to the challenged decision as a whole often turn out to have applied a correctness standard to questions of legality, such as relevance and purpose questions.[162] *Baker* is one of those cases.[163]

[153] Sometimes, it seems that reasonableness has reverted to being the ground as well as the standard of review.

[154] *Baker* (n 4) [63].

[155] Ibid, [64]–[75].

[156] *Catalyst Paper Corporation v Corporation of the District of North Cowichan* 2012 SCC 2, [2012] 1 SCR 5.

[157] Ibid, [14].

[158] *Dunsmuir* (n 3) [47].

[159] See, eg *Catalyst Paper* (n 156) [16].

[160] *Newfoundland and Labrador Nurses' Union v Newfoundland and Labrador (Treasury Board)* 2011 SCC 62, [2011] 3 SCR 708, [14].

[161] Instead, the passage in question at least partly affirms deference 'as respect', the version of deference proposed in Dyzenhaus, 'Politics of Deference' (n 4).

[162] See nn 123–126 and accompanying text.

[163] See n 114 and accompanying text.

To some extent, as noted, this simply reflects confusion. But it may also reflect a lingering sense that there *is* a relevant difference between legality issues and merits issues after all.

In my view, the global approach is taking variability too far. If indeed this is the approach the Supreme Court in *Baker* meant to introduce, then that was a wrong turning. Segmentation in appropriate contexts is a necessary part of the standards of review analysis. The unsettled nature of Canadian standards of review law generally may be due partly to this trend away from established categories and distinctions.[164]

Among the distinctions that remain significant is the distinction between statutory interpretation and evaluation of the merits. I agree with the proponents of the alternative approach that the orthodox understanding of this distinction required modification, as outlined earlier: questions of statutory interpretation do not always have one right answer which judges are best placed to provide.[165] The great advance of the Canadian alternative deferential approach is this insight that the divide between questions of law, fact and discretion is not as clear-cut as it may seem, and that factors other than the application of this divide are relevant to the standard of review. This divide should therefore not be determinative. However, it does not follow that the divide is illusory and irrelevant. That conclusion would be another instance of throwing out the baby with the bathwater.[166]

My proposal for maintaining the distinction between statutory interpretation and evaluation of the merits was set out in part III.[167] To summarise, while interpretation does involve discretion or judgement, there is a line between interpretive judgement and evaluation of the merits. The line depends on whether an adequate foundation can be found in the words of the statute or in the relevant context for considering a particular judgement to be part of the statute's policy or purpose. Drawing this line itself involves judgement, and reasonable people will often disagree on it. But that does not mean that it is an illusory or invalid line: in order for a particular interpreter's line to be respectable, it needs to be supported by plausible statutory interpretation reasoning.

The upshot of this view on statutory interpretation is an approach to standards of review that sits between the orthodox UK approach and the

[164] On the other hand, the move in *Dunsmuir* (n 3) back to treating some categories as presumptively determinative may be criticised as going too far in the other direction: see P Daly, 'The Unfortunate Triumph of Form over Substance in Canadian Administrative Law' (2012) 50 *Osgoode Hall Law Journal* 317; though cf A Green, 'Can There Be Too Much Context in Administrative Law? Setting the Standard of Review in Canadian Administrative Law' (2014) 47 *University of British Columbia Law Review* 443.

[165] Section A of this part IV.

[166] That is how Taggart, 'Scope of Review' (n 2) 213 criticises the abandonment of pluralism along with its old blunt instrument, the jurisdictional doctrine, in the move to the current orthodoxy: see Wilberg and Elliott (n 2) part II.

[167] Part III C i.

global approach that may be emerging in Canada. Segmentation must remain available: if the distinction between interpretation and evaluation is to be maintained, it can only be applied to *aspects* of the decision, not the decision as a whole. For instance, a relevance challenge raises a question of statutory interpretation, while an inadequate or excessive weight challenge raises a merits question. Both may arise in the same case, but they can only be analysed separately.

The distinction between them should continue to be a highly relevant factor in determining the standard and intensity of review.[168] As a result, within each individual case there should always be a gap between the standard or intensity applied by a court in scrutinising the decision-maker's interpretation of the statute, and the standard or intensity on which the court evaluates the merits of a decision. Though the gap will not be as large as on the orthodox approach, questions of statutory interpretation will always be reviewed on a *less* deferential standard, or more intensively, than merits questions arising in the same case.

For instance, there will always be a gap between the standards or intensity of review on a mandatory relevant consideration argument and on the evaluation of the weight given to that consideration within the same case. In a context where other factors call for close supervision and there are no real reasons for deference, a court will assess on a correctness standard whether the statute, properly interpreted, required the consideration to be taken into account. If so, the weight which the decision-maker in fact accorded to that consideration will then be assessed only on a reasonableness standard, but it will be fairly closely scrutinised.[169] On the other hand, in a context where other factors call for significant deference, the court will assess the interpretation only on a reasonableness standard: was it reasonable to read the statute as permitting the consideration to be ignored? If the consideration was in fact taken into account, the weight accorded to it will then be reviewable only on a very deferential standard.

Within this scheme, it makes sense to retain the various traditional illegality grounds: they continue to serve the useful function of identifying particular types of error in statutory interpretation. Moreover, the illegality grounds as a group usefully mark out challenges where the nature of the question is a factor favouring less deference. The Supreme Court in *Khosa*

[168] In the context of the Federal Court of Appeal's current approach to applying the single reasonableness standard (see n 76 and, eg *Farwaha* (n 76); *First Nations Child and Family Caring Society* (n 147); *Forest Ethics* (n 121)), it should be one of the factors that determine the breadth of the range of reasonable answers.

[169] Recall that this is precisely the approach that was in fact applied in *Baker* (n 4), while purporting to apply reasonableness to the decision as a whole: text at n 114. Contrary to the Court's weighing of the factors for and against deference (ibid, [62]), arguably there were such strong factors in favour of more intensive review in that case (see Mullan, 'Deference from *Baker* to *Suresh*' (n 86) 26) that correctness review on the relevance issue was appropriate.

rightly held that use of nominate grounds of review does not preclude application of the Canadian standards of review analysis: the grounds can be applied in accordance with whatever is the appropriate standard of review in each case.[170] Even Daly, after all, accepts that the grounds can continue to serve as 'indicia' of unreasonableness—that means they identify reviewable types of error.[171]

The concern that reliance on the relevance and purpose grounds tends to compromise judges' commitment to deference is, of course, not unfounded, given the established tradition of correctness review on these grounds.[172] However, there may be better ways of dealing with this risk of confusion. The global approach, far from buttressing the commitment to deference, involves its own significant risk of inadvertent correctness review on legality issues, as we saw earlier.[173] Where a decision as a whole is reviewed on a reasonableness standard, often that standard is actually applied only to aspects of the merits, such as the weight accorded to competing factors. Legality issues are tacitly treated as preliminary issues and reviewed on a correctness standard.[174] Alternatively, the temptation is to apply the conclusion of 'unreasonableness' to an enquiry conducted entirely in terms of correctness.[175]

V. CONCLUSION

In this essay, I have sought to help fill a gap in the case law and commentary on the standard of review on questions of law, by considering in detail how to classify the relevance and purpose grounds, and whether deference may accordingly be appropriate when using these grounds. I considered that question first on the assumption that orthodox correctness review on questions of law is otherwise to be maintained, and then in the context of the alternative deferential approach which involves deference on questions of law.

Perhaps my most significant conclusion is that the relevance and purpose grounds are best categorised as involving and concerning statutory interpretation; and that it is possible and remains desirable for the purposes of

[170] *Canada (Citizenship and Immigration) v Khosa* 2009 SCC 12, [2009] 1 SCR 339, [42]–[44], [35]–[36] and [49]–[51] and see its discussion in Daly, *A Theory of Deference* (n 72) 258–59.

[171] Daly, *A Theory of Deference* (n 72) 162.

[172] While review should always be *more* intensive on these grounds than on merits questions, *automatic* correctness review on these grounds is, of course, entirely inconsistent with the alternative approach.

[173] See discussion above, text to nn 123–126.

[174] Eg *Retired Judges Case* (n 126); *Halifax (Regional Municipality)* (n 125).

[175] Eg *Chamberlain* (n 123).

assigning standards of review to distinguish that type of ground from those involving evaluation of the merits.

On that basis, within the orthodox approach these grounds must continue to attract correctness review (albeit with appropriate restraint). Within the alternative deferential approach, deference should be available on the relevance and purpose grounds just as on other illegality grounds. The divide between grounds involving statutory interpretation and those involving evaluation of the merits should not be abandoned, as appears to be suggested by some commentary and case law: this divide should continue to be used as one relevant factor in determining the appropriate standard of review for each individual question arising in a case.

12

The Struggle for Deference in Canada

PAUL DALY*

I. INTRODUCTION

IN THE COMMON-LAW tradition, courts are at the apex of the interpretive hierarchy. Traditionally, their role has been to answer legal questions authoritatively. When inferior bodies, including administrative decision-makers,[1] commit jurisdictional errors the superior courts will intervene to correct them.

AV Dicey's hugely influential account of English public law identified judges as the 'guardians of the rule of law', on whom it was incumbent 'to ensure that any person or body relying on power delegated by the legislature abide by the terms and conditions on which that power was granted'.[2] Sure enough: 'In debates over the relationship of the courts to the administration, the Rule of Law remains the rallying-cry for those who favour judicial intervention.'[3]

A deferential approach to judicial review requires judges, however, to be satisfied by an answer that is merely reasonable, even on questions of law.[4] It does not need to be the answer the judge would have given after due consideration of the question. Intervention is possible only where an interpretation 'cannot be rationally supported by the relevant legislation'.[5]

* Assistant Professor of Law, University of Montreal. Thanks, with the usual disclaimer, to Mark Aronson, Peter Cane, Mark Elliott, Benjamin Grant and Hanna Wilberg for comments.

[1] By 'administrative decision-makers' I simply mean any body subject to the law of judicial review of administrative action, a purely functional definition which I trust serves the purposes of the present essay.

[2] *National Corn Growers Association v Canada (Import Tribunal)* [1990] 2 SCR 1324, 1333 (Wilson J).

[3] H Arthurs, 'Rethinking Administrative Law: A Slightly Dicey Business' (1979) 17 *Osgoode Hall Law Journal* 1, 4.

[4] '[A] rational basis for a holding of law means that a *reasonableness* test rather than a *rightness* test of administrative determination is applied': H Janisch, 'Towards a More General Theory of Judicial Review in Administrative Law' (1989) 53 *Saskatchewan Law Review* 327, 336.

[5] *Canadian Union of Public Employees Local 963 v New Brunswick Liquor Corporation (CUPE)* [1979] 2 SCR 227, 239.

Deferring to administrative decision-makers' interpretations of law requires judges to pull against the current of tradition.[6] Intervention is justifiable only in extreme cases, not in ordinary ones. Administrative autonomy must be respected, tradition put to one side. Whether judges accord epistemic deference—reserving for themselves the final decision but according significant weight to the conclusions of the front-line decision-maker—or doctrinal deference—carving out a space into which courts will not intrude as long as the impugned decision is reasonable[7]—a deferential approach requires them to no longer think as lawyers traditionally have thought.

Since the 1970s, the Supreme Court of Canada[8] has attempted to chart a deferential course to judicial review of interpretations of law. It has repeatedly been buffeted by traditionalist storms pushing it towards a more interventionist course. The concept of jurisdictional error, with its teaching that on some matters an administrative decision-maker must be correct or face judicial intervention, has usually been at the eye of the storm.[9] This is the story I will tell.

Other jurisdictions may find useful lessons in Canada's deferential journey. The story reveals the reasons why deference ought to be accorded to administrative decision-makers' interpretations of legal provisions; it provides tools to counter interventionism. Yet it also reveals how difficult it is to convince courts to adopt a deferential approach; it warns of the serious commitment that is necessary to maintain deference. In short, the story of deference in Canada is one of an apparently never-ending struggle.

[6] See, eg HW MacLauchlan, 'Judicial Review of Administrative Interpretations of Law: How Much Formalism Can We Reasonably Bear?' (1986) 36 *University of Toronto Law Journal* 343, 367. And perhaps also the current of legal practice which emphasises the primacy of lawyerly tools of analysis in the search for the best answers to legal questions (L Tremblay, 'La norme de retenue judiciaire et les "erreurs de droit" en droit administratif: une erreur de droit? Au-delà du fondationalisme et du scepticisme' (1996) 52 *Revue du Barreau* 141) and the differing perspectives that judges and administrators bring to bear on the task of interpreting statutes (R Macdonald, 'On the Administration of Statutes' (1987) 12 *Queen's Law Journal* 488, 494–504).

[7] See P Daly, *A Theory of Deference in Administrative Law: Basis, Application and Scope* (Cambridge, Cambridge University Press, 2012) ch 1.

[8] I focus on the Supreme Court of Canada because, especially since 1975, when it gained full control over its docket in non-criminal cases, it has assumed the responsibility of setting out general principles which apply across the country.

[9] As has been explained by P Craig, 'Dicey: Unitary, Self-Correcting Democracy and Public Law' (1990) 106 *Law Quarterly Review* 105, 113: 'It is apparent that the execution of the legislative will may require the grant of power to a Minister or administrative agency. Herein lies the modern conceptual justification for non-constitutional review. It was designed to ensure that the sovereign will of Parliament was not transgressed by those to whom such grants of power were made. If authority had been delegated to a Minister to perform certain tasks upon certain conditions, the courts' function was, in the event of challenge, to check that only those tasks were performed and only where the conditions were present. If there were defects on either level, the challenged decision would be declared null.'

The 'conditions' to which Craig refers may include, but are not limited to, errors of law. My focus in this essay will be on errors of law rather than errors of fact, a subject that has exercised the Court much less (though see *Bell v Ontario Human Rights Commission* [1971] SCR 756, overruled in *Halifax (Regional Municipality) v Nova Scotia (Human Rights Commission)* 2012 SCC 10, [2012] 1 SCR 364).

I will proceed in chronological order rather than discussing discrete themes. Doubtless others would choose different time periods: I look at four different periods (1949–1979, 1979–1998, 1998–2008 and 2008–present). While I appreciate the attraction of a thematic approach, the narrative of struggle provides an excellent structure around which to discuss the basis of deference; the means of implementing deference; and the inevitable challenges of implementation.[10] I have set out my own preferred views on these issues at great length[11] and though they doubtless influence my reading of the evolution of Canadian law my goal in this essay is descriptive.

II. DEFERENCE BEFORE THERE WAS DEFERENCE: 1949–1979[12]

One cannot understand the appearance of a distinctively deferential approach to judicial review of administrative action in Canada in the mid-to-late 1970s without appreciating the doctrinal landscape from which it emerged. Yet lessons cannot be drawn too readily from earlier periods. Writing in the early 1970s, Professor Hogg took the view that the Supreme Court of Canada's reasons for judgment were 'often woefully inadequate' and decried the 'lamentable' state of Canadian administrative law.[13] Lord Diplock famously said that: 'Any judicial statements on matters of public law if made before 1950 are likely to be a misleading guide to what the law is today.'[14] This is certainly true of Canada. Reference was made in the early years of that decade to the 'twilight' of judicial review.[15]

Deference can take several forms, one of which is the creation of exclusive spheres of authority.[16] During judicial review's twilight years, administrative decision-makers were free to make errors within jurisdiction.

[10] In keeping with the focus of this collection, I do not discuss procedural review. The standard traditionally applied has been one of correctness, but this position has recently been challenged: *Maritime Broadcasting System Ltd v Canadian Media Guild* 2014 FCA 59; *Re: Sound v Fitness Industry Council of Canada* 2014 FCA 48; *Syndicat des travailleuses et travailleurs de ADF—CSN c Syndicat des employés de Au Dragon forgé inc* 2013 QCCA 793. It is too early to tell whether a deferential approach will win the approval of the Supreme Court of Canada.

[11] Daly (n 7). See also P Daly, 'Unreasonable Interpretations of Law' in J Robertson, P Gall & P Daly, *Judicial Deference to Administrative Tribunals in Canada: Its History and Future* (Toronto, LexisNexis, 2014) 233, reprinted in (2014) 66 *Supreme Court Law Review* (2d) 233.

[12] The Supreme Court of Canada only became the final authority on matters of Canadian law shortly after 1949, when appeals to the Privy Council were abolished with prospective effect.

[13] P Hogg, 'The Supreme Court of Canada and Administrative Law, 1949–1971' (1973) 11 *Osgoode Hall Law Journal* 187, 222.

[14] *R v Inland Revenue Commissioners, ex p National Federation of Self-Employed and Small Businesses* [1982] AC 617, 649 (HL).

[15] G LeDain, 'The Twilight of Judicial Control in the Province of Quebec?' (1952) 1 *McGill Law Journal* 1.

[16] M Hunt, 'Sovereignty's Blight' in N Bamforth and P Leyland (eds), *Public Law in a Multi-Layered Constitution* (Oxford, Hart Publishing, 2003) 337, 346–47.

They had the 'right to be wrong'.[17] Twilight evokes darkness and in cases decided before the modern law of judicial review began to take shape courts were indeed unwilling to shine a light on certain areas of administrative decision-making.

However, jurisdictional limits were policed by the courts, sometimes jealously.[18] This is unsurprising, once one considers how the Canadian 'legal profession' was quick to 'condemn' administrative decision-makers as 'usurpers' of the role of the courts.[19] In *Jarvis v Associated Medical Services Inc*,[20] an employer allegedly dismissed a manager for engaging in union activities. The Ontario Labour Relations Board ordered the employer to reinstate her. Neither the Ontario Court of Appeal nor the majority of the Supreme Court of Canada had great difficulty in striking down the Board's decision. A manager was not an 'employee' and the Board lacked jurisdiction to order her reinstatement.

Yet inside these limits all was dark as far as reviewing courts were concerned: 'so long as an administrative authority has acted within its statutory jurisdiction a court will not interfere with its decision'.[21] A good example is *Commission des relations ouvrières du Québec v Burlington Mills Hosiery Co of Canada*.[22] Here, Quebec's labour relations regulator had excluded employees under the age of 16 from a bargaining unit, with the result that a negotiating group was certified. Abbott J sharply rejected the employer's application for judicial review. Determining who is 'to be included or excluded from a bargaining unit' was one of the Board's 'principal functions'

[17] *R v Nat Bell Liquors* [1922] 2 AC 128 (HL) 151–52 , *per* Lord Sumner.

[18] See, eg *Toronto Newspaper Guild v Globe Printing* [1953] 2 SCR 18 (decision of the Ontario Labour Relations Board quashed for failure to take into account a relevant factor (whether individuals had resigned from a union between the application for certification and the certification hearing)); *Labour Relations Board v Canada Safeway Ltd* [1953] 2 SCR 46, 50 (Kerwin J) (decision of the British Columbia Labour Relations Board upheld because it was correct; compare Rand J (at 54–55) upholding the Board because 'its judgment can be said to be consonant with a rational appreciation of the situation presented'); *The Queen v Leong Ba Chai* [1954] 2 SCR 10 (writ of mandamus issued against a refusal to admit to Canada a child born out of wedlock because the child was in fact legitimate under the law of the child's place of birth). There was also a series of cases in the 1950s in which exercises of discretion were struck down for improperly interfering with individuals' rights of religion and freedom of association. See, eg *Smith and Rhuland Ltd v The Queen* [1953] 2 SCR 95 (refusal to certify a bargaining group because an official was a communist was an invalid exercise of discretion). In another line of cases, however, exercises of discretion which were characterised as 'administrative' were beyond review as long as exercised in accordance with statutory requirements. See, eg *Calgary Power Ltd and Halmrast v Copithorne* [1959] SCR 24; *Moore v Minister of Manpower and Immigration* [1968] SCR 839.

[19] J Willis, 'Administrative Law and the British North America Act' (1939) 53 *Harvard Law Review* 251, 262. There are, of course, echoes here of Lord Hewart, *The New Despotism* (London, Benn, 1929).

[20] *Jarvis v Associated Medical Services Inc* [1964] SCR 497.

[21] LeDain (n 15) 5.

[22] *Commission des relations ouvrières du Québec v Burlington Mills Hosiery Co of Canada* [1964] SCR 342.

and fell within its 'exclusive jurisdiction': 'provided it exercises that discretion in good faith its decision is not subject to judicial review'.[23]

A similar example is *Labour Relations Board v Traders' Service Ltd*.[24] A company complained that some employees had been wrongly included in a bargaining group certified by the British Columbia Labour Relations Board. It was alleged that these employees worked for a different company, albeit one headquartered at the same address and with the same management. On this point, Judson J held, there was no basis for judicial intervention. Determining to which company the employees belonged was the 'very subject-matter' of the Board's adjudication and 'entirely within' its jurisdiction: 'It was for the Board and the Board alone to make the finding on the one issue and this finding is not open to review by the Court.'[25]

Judicial review doctrine in Canada greatly resembled English judicial review doctrine up to and including a large part of the 1970s. Indeed, the landmark decision of the House of Lords in *Anisminic Ltd v Foreign Compensation Commission*,[26] which largely did away with the concept of error of law within jurisdiction, had some Canadian precursors. In *Jarvis v Associated Medical Services Inc*,[27] Cartwright J expressly approved the approach taken by a lower-court judge: 'it is trite to observe that the Board cannot by an erroneous interpretation of any section or sections of the Act confer upon itself a jurisdiction which it otherwise would not have'.[28] He also commented: 'The extent of the Board's jurisdiction is fixed by the statute which creates it and cannot be enlarged by a mistaken view entertained by the Board as to the meaning of that statute.'[29]

Shortly after *Anisminic*, the Supreme Court of Canada decided *Metropolitan Life Insurance v International Union of Operating Engineers*,[30] the 'high water mark' of 'activist' judicial review of administrative action in

[23] Ibid, 346. Absence of good faith relates more to the manner of exercise of a statutory power than to the substantive reasonableness of the exercise of the power. See, eg *Roncarelli v Duplessis* [1959] SCR 121, 140–41, where the decision-maker was liable for damages because his order to cancel the plaintiff's liquor licence was made with malice.

[24] *Labour Relations Board v Traders' Service Ltd* [1958] SCR 672. See also *Labour Relations Board of Saskatchewan v The Queen* [1969] SCR 898, where a privative clause was effective.

[25] Ibid, 679. One should note, however, that in Judson J's view there was 'ample evidence' to support the Board's conclusion and that any other conclusion would have been 'surprising' (at 678). See also *Memorial Gardens Association (Canada) Ltd v Colwood Cemetery Company* [1958] SCR 353, 357 (suggesting that the conclusions of administrative bodies were open to limited review even on factual matters though only to the existence rather than to the sufficiency of evidence).

[26] *Anisminic Ltd v Foreign Compensation Commission* [1969] 2 AC 147 (HL).

[27] *Jarvis v Associated Medical Services Inc* [1964] SCR 497.

[28] Ibid, 502.

[29] Ibid, 502.

[30] *Metropolitan Life Insurance v International Union of Operating Engineers* [1970] SCR 425.

Canada.[31] Review for error of law was copperfastened.[32] The Court held that the Board had committed a reviewable error of law by misconstruing the statutory term 'members of the trade union':[33]

> In proceeding in this manner the Board has failed to deal with the question remitted to it (ie whether the employees in question were members of the union at the relevant date) and instead has decided a question which was not remitted to it (ie whether in regard to those employees there has been fulfilment of the conditions stated above).[34]

In addition to its strong position on errors of law, the Supreme Court of Canada took an aggressive stance against erroneous findings of jurisdictional fact.[35] Although the distinction between jurisdictional and non-jurisdictional error accorded deference within limits, it became clear that those limits would be so strictly policed by reviewing courts that deference was largely illusory. No real space was carved out for administrative decision-makers, whose autonomy ultimately depended on the good grace of the judges. Contemporary commentators were disquieted. In a survey of the Supreme Court of Canada's labour law jurisprudence, a large part of which consisted of judicial review cases, Paul Weiler ventured to suggest 'that the tacit assumption concerning Canadian courts, especially among academic commentators, is that the judiciary as a whole is rather unsympathetic to both unions and administrative agencies in their decision-making'.[36] Underneath the technical language of jurisdiction and error of law ran a current of hostility to administrative bodies.

And that technical language was capable of manipulation to achieve the end of undermining administrative decision-makers. The distinction between jurisdictional and non-jurisdictional errors of law and fact was

[31] J Evans, H Janisch, D Mullan and R Risk, *Administrative Law: Cases, Text and Materials*, 3rd edn (Toronto, Edmond Montgomery, 1989) 565. Another notorious case from the same era is *Port Arthur Shipbuilding Co v Arthurs* [1969] SCR 85, in which the decision of an arbitration board was quashed for error of law on the face of the record.

[32] The existence of s 96 of the Constitution Act 1867 was doubtless influential. This provision requires that judges of the superior courts in the provinces be appointed by the federal government. Despite its technical character, s 96 has been held to guarantee a minimum of judicial review of administrative action: see *Crevier v Attorney General (Québec)* [1981] 2 SCR 220. Though *Crevier* came some time after the Supreme Court of Canada's deferential turn, it followed a relatively consistent line of cases. One commentator celebrated *Metropolitan Life* as being faithful to the principles underlying s 96: J Lyon, 'Comment' (1971) 49 *Canadian Bar Review* 365. The potential influence of the traditionalist *First Report of the Royal Commission Inquiry into Civil Rights (McRuer Report)* (Toronto, 1968) should also not be overlooked.

[33] Labour Relations Act RSO 1960, c 202, s 7(3).

[34] *Metropolitan Life Insurance* (n 30) 435.

[35] *Bell* (above n 9) (order of prohibition granted against a board of inquiry from holding a public hearing into an allegation of racial discrimination by a landlord against a potential tenant on the basis that the premises was not a 'self-contained dwelling unit' as required by the relevant statutory provisions).

[36] P Weiler, 'The "Slippery Slope" of Judicial Intervention: the Supreme Court and Canadian Labour Relations 1950–1970' (1971) 9 *Osgoode Hall Law Journal* 1, 9.

'sufficiently vague—some would say meaningless—to offer a means of review of any erroneous finding of fact or law'.[37] Accordingly, a broad conception of jurisdictional error allowed reviewing courts to reduce the autonomy of administrative decision-makers and keep them within closely confined boundaries. Often, the Court would be 'utterly submerged by a mistaken zeal to "correct" the agency's decision'.[38] Commenting later on *Anisminic* and *Metropolitan Life*, Wilson J suggested that they reflected a failure to appreciate '(1) that [administrative decision-makers'] decisions are crafted by those with specialized knowledge of the subject matter before them; and (2) that there is value in limiting the extent to which their decisions may be frustrated through an expansive judicial review'.[39]

At least one judge had recognised this at a relatively early point. As Rand J put it, in dissent, in *Toronto Newspaper Guild v Globe Printing*: 'It is to no purpose that judicial minds may be outraged by seemingly arbitrary if not irrational treatment of questions raised: these views are irrelevant where there is no *clear departure* from the field of action defined by the statute.'[40] Here, the reference to 'clear departure' suggests that the apparently exclusive spheres of authority might blur around the edges.[41]

But it was not until the mid-to-late 1970s that a distinct Canadian approach began to emerge.[42] In *Service Employees' International Union, Local No 333 v Nipawin District Staff Nurses Association et al*,[43] Dickson J refused to quash a labour relations board's refusal to certify a union on the basis that it was a company-dominated organisation. The domination in question was that of *another union*, not the employer. The Court of Appeal had concluded that the board had committed an error of law by failing to ask whether the union was dominated by the *employer*, an argument

[37] Hogg (n 13) 205. See, similarly, Weiler (n 36) 79.

[38] Hogg (n 13) 205.

[39] *National Corn Growers Association* (n 2) 1335. See P Bryden, 'Justice Wilson's Administrative Law Legacy: The National Corn Growers Decision and Judicial Review of Administrative Decision-Making' (2008) 41 *Supreme Court Law Review* (2d) 225.

[40] *Toronto Newspaper Guild* (n 18) 30 (emphasis added). See also *Labour Relations Board v Canada SafewayLtd* [1953] 2 SCR 46, 54–55 where Rand J upheld the decision of the Board because 'its judgment can be said to be consonant with a *rational appreciation* of the situation presented' (emphasis added). Again, the reference to 'rational appreciation' suggests that the decision-maker might have a margin of appreciation in respect of its interpretation and application of some statutory provisions.

[41] Contradictory tendencies are perhaps to be expected. As Weiler (n 36) 33 noted in his study of the Supreme Court of Canada's labour relations jurisprudence: 'It is impossible to perceive any real pattern in these decisions.'

[42] Nowadays, it can safely be said 'that the worlds of English and Canadian administrative law now exist in parallel universes': M Walters, 'Jurisdiction, Functionalism, and Constitutionalism in Canadian Administrative Law' in C Forsyth, M Elliott, S Jhaveri and others (eds), *Effective Judicial Review: a Cornerstone of Good Governance* (Oxford, Oxford University Press, 2010) 300, 302.

[43] *Service Employees' International Union, Local No 333 v Nipawin District Staff Nurses Association et al* [1975] 1 SCR 382.

that did not appeal to Dickson J. Judicial intervention would sometimes be appropriate, but 'if the Board acts in good faith and its decision can be rationally supported on a construction which the relevant legislation may reasonably be considered to bear, then the Court will not intervene'.[44]

A true landmark decision followed a few years later, with Dickson J again the creator: *Canadian Union of Public Employees Local 963 v New Brunswick Liquor Corporation*.[45] During a lawful strike, management replaced employees with management personnel, an apparent breach of labour relations legislation which provided that 'the employer shall not replace the striking employees or fill their position with any other employee'.[46] This provision was badly drafted: it 'bristles with ambiguities'; one judge considered that there were four possible interpretations.[47] The Board's conclusion was that replacing striking employees with management personnel was not permissible.

The Court of Appeal considered that the ambiguous provision was jurisdictional and that any error would justify judicial intervention:[48]

> Two questions are therefore raised by the complaint,
>
> 1. Does the *Act* prohibit management personnel replacing striking employees? and if so
> 2. Did management personnel replace employees?
>
> It is the latter question which is the subject matter of the complaint and the primary matter for enquiry by the Board. The first question is a condition precedent to and collateral to determining the second.

Dickson J did not reject the premise that jurisdictional error could justify judicial intervention. But he warned courts to be cautious about too lightly concluding that provisions are jurisdictional in nature: 'The question of what is and is not jurisdictional is often very difficult to determine. The courts, in my view, should not be alert to brand as jurisdictional, and therefore subject to broader curial review, that which may be doubtfully so.'[49] In the present case, the matter plainly fell within the broad authority of the Board.

Moreover, there were formal and substantive reasons for deference.[50] A privative clause protected decisions of the Board, 'a specialized tribunal which administers a comprehensive statute regulating labour relations', a task requiring it 'not only to find facts and decide questions of law, but also

[44] Ibid, 388–89.

[45] *Canadian Union of Public Employees Local 963* (n 5).

[46] Public Service Labour Relations Act, RSNB 1973, c P—25, s 19.

[47] *Canadian Union of Public Employees Local 963* (n 5) 230.

[48] *New Brunswick Liquor Corp v Canadian Union of Public Employees, Local 963* (1978) 21 NBR (2d) 441, [20].

[49] *Canadian Union of Public Employees Local 963* (n 5) 233.

[50] D Dyzenhaus, 'The Politics of Deference: Judicial Review and Democracy' in M Taggart (ed), *The Province of Administrative Law* (Hart Publishing, Oxford, 1997) 279, 290.

to exercise its understanding of the body of jurisprudence that has developed around the collective bargaining system, as understood in Canada, and its labour relations sense acquired from accumulated experience in the area'.[51]

Given that the Board was acting within its jurisdiction, a very high threshold had to be surpassed by the applicant for judicial review. The interpretation was not beyond review entirely, but intervention would only be justifiable in extreme cases: 'Put another way, was the Board's interpretation so patently unreasonable that its construction cannot be rationally supported by the relevant legislation and demands intervention by the court upon review?'[52] Dickson J acknowledged that, 'at first glance', the Board's interpretation might seem unreasonable 'if one draws too heavily upon private sector experience', but a 'careful reading' of the pertinent materials revealed a sound basis for the Board's conclusion: 'At a minimum the Board's interpretation would seem at least as reasonable as the alternative interpretations suggested in the Court of Appeal.'[53] This, a commentator wrote shortly after, was a 'clear message' that the 'rules of the game had been radically altered'.[54] Where the legislature had created a specialised, expert tribunal and protected its decisions by way of a privative clause, courts could intervene only in extreme cases:[55]

> The composition and institutional structure of the agencies, together with the expertise and the wide range of procedural tools available to them, apparently persuaded the courts that these bodies had indeed been given the primary statutory responsibility for implementing and elaborating the legislative mandate within their area of regulation.

This was the case in many fields other than labour law, which dominated the Court's development of a deferential approach.

III. A NEW APPROACH: 1979–1998

Despite the eloquence of Dickson J's formulation, the concept of jurisdictional error remained afloat. Dickson J's decision in *CUPE* left the jurisdictional door ajar, though with a warning not to go through it. All Dickson J had done was to urge caution on the part of reviewing courts, an

[51] *Canadian Union of Public Employees Local 963* (n 5) 235–36.

[52] Ibid, 237.

[53] Ibid, 242.

[54] B Langille, 'Judicial Review, Judicial Revisionism and Judicial Responsibility' (1986) 17 *Revue genérale de droit* 169, 193. This message was underscored by a trilogy of labour relations decisions in which the new 'patent unreasonableness' test was applied to the decision under review: *Volvo Canada Ltd v UAW, Local 720* [1980] 1 SCR 178; *Douglas Aircraft Co of Canada v McConnell* [1980] 1 SCR 245; *Alberta Union of Provincial Employees, Branch 63 v Board of Governors of Olds College* [1982] 1 SCR 923.

[55] J Evans, 'Developments in Administrative Law: the 1984–85 Term' (1986) 8 *Supreme Court Law Review* (2d) 1, 27.

attitudinal shift. It remained true that '[n]o satisfactory test has ever been formulated for distinguishing findings which go to jurisdiction from findings which go to the merits'.[56] Where a question could be dressed in jurisdictional garb, intervention by a reviewing court would remain justifiable. And given the hold exerted over the lawyerly mind by traditionalist conceptions of jurisdictional error and the rule of law, the attitudinal shift urged by Dickson J would be insufficient to withstand interventionist tides.[57]

That something more robust was needed was demonstrated by the decision of the Supreme Court of Canada in *Syndicat des employés de production du Québec et de l'Acadie v Canada Labour Relations Board*.[58] The dispute turned on whether a refusal to work overtime amounted to an unlawful strike. The Board concluded that it did. Two parts of the Board's order were challenged: in one part, the Board ordered immediate compliance by workers in two geographic areas, but not a third; and in another part, the Board ordered the parties to submit to arbitration.

The union made an ambitious argument that the existence of a strike was a condition precedent to the Board's jurisdiction. Beetz J turned this argument aside with ease, describing 'the question of the existence of a strike and of its legality' as falling 'within the special expertise of the Board'.[59] Absent a 'manifestly unreasonable' error, the Board's answer to these questions could not be disturbed by a reviewing court.[60]

Yet Beetz J also acknowledged the continued vibrancy of the concept of jurisdictional error: 'Such an error, even if committed in the best possible good faith, will result nonetheless in the decision containing it being set

[56] SA de Smith, H Woolf and J Jowell, *Judicial Review of Administrative Action*, 5th edn (London, Sweet & Maxwell, 1995) 255. See, similarly, L Jaffe, 'Judicial Review: Constitutional and Jurisdictional Fact' (1957) 70 *Harvard Law Review* 953, 959. Indeed, citing Professor Craig, the Supreme Court of Canada recognised this in *Blanchard v Control Data Canada Ltd* [1984] 2 SCR 476, 491: 'It is clear that all the 'X' conditions can to some extent be categorized as prerequisites to the exercise of the 'Y' powers. In my view, there is no logical reason for distinguishing between condition X1 and condition X2 and concluding that one is preliminary and the other is not. Thus, if all the 'X' conditions are said to be preliminary, the administrative tribunal has lost the capacity to err: it can only exercise the power conferred on it by the law if it is right in its interpretation of what is meant by X1, X2 and X3. Ultimately, the distinction between an appeal and judicial review is somewhat fine. This distinction becomes non-existent if we also adopt the theory that the administrative tribunal cannot err as to the content of powers Y1, Y2 and Y3, since it is then exercising a power that the law does not confer on it.'

[57] As was said by one commentator after *CUPE*, 'this doctrinal approach to jurisdiction is inherently incapable of providing rational stopping points on the slippery slope towards judicial over-intervention. What is missing is any coherent theory of deference supporting functional reasons why courts should defer to administrative competence and expertise.' H Janisch, 'Bora Laskin and Administrative Law: An Unfinished Journey' (1985) 35 *University of Toronto Law Journal* 557, 568.

[58] *Syndicat des employés de production du Québec et de l'Acadie v Canada Labour Relations Board* [1984] 2 SCR 412.

[59] Ibid, 422.

[60] Ibid, 425.

aside.'[61] He quashed the second part of the Board's order on the basis that the Board's empowering statute did not vest in it the power to refer disputes to arbitration. Indeed, the Board's order 'infringe[d] the rules of interpretation' and led to a result 'contrary to the intent of the legislator'.[62] With jurisdictional error lurking in the background, more than an attitudinal shift was required.[63] A paradigm shift was necessary.

When it came, interestingly, the paradigm shift was effected by Beetz J in *Union des employés de service, local 298 v Bibeault*,[64] yet another labour relations case. This time, the issue was whether a union's certification survived the award of a public contract to a different enterprise. Both a labour commissioner and the Labour Board found that it had.

Beetz J continued to accept that a decision-maker who commits a jurisdictional error acts outside the powers granted to it and is thus liable to see its decisions struck down on judicial review.[65] But he acknowledged the significant difficulties in applying the concept of jurisdictional error and decried its tendency to lead reviewing courts to ask themselves the wrong questions in judicial review cases. Rather than asking 'Is this a preliminary or collateral question to the exercise of the tribunal's power?' a reviewing court should ask, 'Did the legislator intend the question to be within the jurisdiction conferred on the tribunal?'[66]

It was necessary to formulate a test for determining whether or not a question was jurisdictional in nature. Beetz J found a solution in the Court's growing acceptance of the relative institutional competence of administrative decision-makers. The formal and substantive reasons for deference provided a way to answer the key question of legislative intent: did the legislature intend that the decision-maker, or the reviewing court, should take the decision at issue? To answer this question, Beetz J held, a reviewing court should look at 'the wording of the enactment conferring jurisdiction

[61] Ibid, 421. Beetz J distinguished this from the 'initial jurisdiction' of the administrative decision-maker, established at the outset of the inquiry (at 421); he also referred to jurisdiction-conferring provisions (at 424).

[62] Ibid, 432.

[63] B Langille, 'Judicial Review, Judicial Revisionism and Judicial Responsibility' (1986) 17 *Revue genérale de droit* 169, 198 suggested shortly after this decision that the Supreme Court of Canada was full of 'contempt ... for its own recent pronouncements': 'Thus, by resurrecting the false god of 'jurisdiction' in the form of the new distinction between sections which confer jurisdiction and those which do not, the Court has rewritten history and redrawn the map of judicial review.' Another commentator wrote of the decision as an 'unpleasant surprise': Evans (n 55) 26. It would certainly have been possible for the Court to apply the patent unreasonableness test to all interpretations of law. But it was not required to do so. In *Blanchard v Control Data Canada Ltd* [1984] 2 SCR 476, 491 Beetz J acknowledged the conceptual difficulties with jurisdictional error and that it was liable to 'distort' the role of reviewing courts. But the solution was not to discard the concept, rather to ensure that it would be used only with 'a great deal of caution', limiting its application 'as far as possible'.

[64] *Union des employés de service, local 298 v Bibeault* [1988] 2 SCR 1048.

[65] Ibid, 1086.

[66] Ibid, 1087.

on the administrative tribunal ... the purpose of the statute creating the tribunal, the reason for its existence, the area of expertise of its members and the nature of the problem before the tribunal'.[67] Formal and substantive reasons for deference would be revealed by this analysis.

Applying this new 'pragmatic and functional' analysis[68] Beetz J identified a jurisdictional question. The decision-makers had 'no special expertise' in defining and applying 'the concepts of alienation and operation by another' because these were 'civil law concepts' falling within the judicial domain:[69] 'the legislative context ... and the area of expertise of the labour commissioner clearly indicate that the legislator did not intend the commissioner's decision as to the existence of an alienation or operation by another of an undertaking to be conclusive'.[70] On the facts, the decision-makers' desire to protect the union's certification could not overcome the plain language of the statute.

This opened Beetz J up to the objection that the pragmatic and functional analysis was a wolf in sheep's clothing, simply a more complicated way to reach results which achieved the end of strictly confining the limits of administrative decision-makers' authority.[71] However, requiring judges to apply a pragmatic and functional analysis had the benefit of requiring them to *justify* their decisions to intervene in light of the language of the whole of the statute and the relative competence of the administrative decision-maker in question.[72] Judges could no longer simply incant the magic words 'jurisdictional error' and proceed to quash a decision with which they did not agree.[73] Short of the outright abolition of the concept of jurisdictional error, a pragmatic and functional analysis the application of which focuses judicial attention on the formal and substantive reasons for deference was the best way to secure autonomy for administrative bodies. If nothing else, it served an educational purpose by exposing judges to the workings of public administration.

Another difficulty was soon to emerge, however. Questions of law were said to invite judicial intervention in some circumstances regardless of the merits of the administrative decision-maker's interpretation.[74] Consider

[67] Ibid, 1088.

[68] Ibid, 1088.

[69] Ibid, 1097.

[70] Ibid, 1098.

[71] See, eg S Wildeman, 'Pas de Deux: Deference and Non-Deference in Action' in L Sossin and C Flood (eds), *Administrative Law in Context*, 2nd edn (Toronto, Edmond Montgomery, 2013) 323, 334–35.

[72] See, eg C L'Heureux-Dubé, 'L'arrêt *Bibeault*: une ancre dans une mer agitée' (1994) 28 *Revue juridique Thémis* 731.

[73] As La Forest J made clear in *Canadian Association of Industrial, Mechanical and Allied Workers, Local 14 v Paccar of Canada Ltd* [1989] 2 SCR 983, 1003, the relevant question was the 'legislative intention' whether to vest a decision in the decision-maker or the reviewing court.

[74] Thus in *McLeod v Egan* [1975] 1 SCR 517, 519 Laskin CJ suggested it would be inappropriate to defer to the interpretation by a labour arbitrator of a 'general public enactment'.

Canada (Attorney General) v Mossop.[75] The applicant here sought to take bereavement leave after the death of his partner's father. His request was refused. Both the applicant and his partner were male and the collective agreement in force at the applicant's place of work provided only for bereavement leave for opposite-sex unmarried couples. The applicant complained that the treatment of same-sex couples was discriminatory, a complaint upheld by the Canadian Human Rights Tribunal. The Tribunal's view was that this amounted to discrimination based on 'family status'.[76]

A majority of the Supreme Court of Canada refused to defer to the Tribunal. Writing for the majority on this point, La Forest J justified his position in the following terms:[77]

> The superior expertise of a human rights tribunal relates to fact-finding and adjudication in a human rights context. It does not extend to general questions of law such as the one at issue in this case. These are ultimately matters within the province of the judiciary, and involve concepts of statutory interpretation and general legal reasoning which the courts must be supposed competent to perform. The courts cannot abdicate this duty to the tribunal. They must, therefore, review the tribunal's decisions on questions of this kind on the basis of correctness, not on a standard of reasonability.

There were features which distinguished *Mossop* from other cases: there was no privative clause protecting the Tribunal, it was subject to review where it had 'erred in law',[78] and it operated in an area in which courts had long claimed a specialised expertise. Nonetheless, *Mossop* stood as an endorsement of judicial supremacy. General questions of law were in the judicial domain. On matters involving the 'concepts of statutory interpretation', only a judicial writ would run.

Yet *Mossop*'s potential to knock the Supreme Court of Canada off its deferential course was never fully realised.[79] The pragmatic and functional analysis reached its logical conclusion in *Pushpanathan v Canada (Minister of Citizenship and Immigration)*.[80] Bastarache J outlined a multi-factor test designed to require justification for judicial intervention in terms of

[75] *Canada (Attorney General) v Mossop* [1993] 1 SCR 554.

[76] Canadian Human Rights Act RSC, 1985, c H-6, s 3.

[77] *Mossop* (n 75) 585.

[78] Federal Court Act, RSC, 1985, c F–7, s 28.

[79] Though see similarly *Gould v Yukon Order of Pioneers* [1996] 1 SCR 571 (whether human rights legislation applied to a fraternal organisation which refused to admit women as members); *Quebec (Commission des droits de la personne et des droits de la jeunesse) v Montréal (City)* 2000 SCC 27, [2000] 1 SCR 665 (whether medical conditions could amount to 'handicap[s]' for the purposes of human rights legislation).

[80] *Pushpanathan v Canada (Minister of Citizenship and Immigration)* [1998] 1 SCR 982. In my view, *Pushpanathan* represents the logical conclusion of the pragmatic and functional analysis because it sidelines the concept of jurisdictional error as completely as possible. Two other very significant cases deserve a mention. In *Domtar Inc v Quebec (Commission d'appel en matière de lésions professionnelles)* [1993] 2 SCR 756, the Court stated that a divergence between two tribunals on the appropriate interpretation of a statutory provision is not an

legislative intent, 'a bold judicial venture designed to infuse jurisdiction with meaningful normative content'.[81] Only those questions the legislature intended to reserve to the courts should be treated as 'jurisdictional', to be determined by reference to four factors: the presence or absence of a privative clause or right of appeal;[82] the relative expertise of the decision-maker; the purpose of the statutory framework; and the nature of the question at issue.

Jurisdictional error as a stand-alone concept was gutted.[83] 'Jurisdiction' became 'simply descriptive of a provision for which the proper standard of review is correctness, based upon the outcome of the pragmatic and functional analysis':[84]

> In other words, 'jurisdictional error' is simply an error on an issue with respect to which, according to the outcome of the pragmatic and functional analysis, the tribunal must make a correct interpretation and to which no deference will be shown.

To say that a statutory provision was 'jurisdictional' and required judicial review on a standard of 'correctness' was simply to say that, on an application of the pragmatic and functional analysis, the question was one for the courts, not for the administrative decision-maker. Moreover, the 'nature of the question' was just one factor amongst several. Categorising a question as 'legal', as a majority of the Court had done in *Mossop*, would not be sufficient to justify judicial intervention. Deference on questions of law seemed firmly anchored and sheltered by a multi-factor test from the rip-tide of jurisdictional error.

IV. INTERVENTIONISM PREVAILS ON JURISDICTIONAL AND LEGAL QUESTIONS: 1998–2008

Despite the apparent triumph of the pragmatic and functional analysis, interventionist tides continued to drag judges back towards more familiar

independent basis for judicial review. Both interpretations could co-exist, as long as both were reasonable. Less dramatically, in *British Columbia Telephone Co v Shaw Cable Systems (BC) Ltd* [1995] 2 SCR 739, the Court performed an analysis of the constitutive legislation of two tribunals that had issued contradictory decisions in order to determine which ought to prevail, rather than undertake an independent analysis.

[81] Walters (n 42) 307.

[82] As for privative clauses, it soon became clear that truly privative language was not the only means of indicating a legislative intent to vest power in administrative decision-makers: 'Although their preclusive effect may be less obvious than that of the true privative clause, other forms of clauses purporting to restrict review may also have privative effect.' *United Brotherhood of Carpenters and Joiners of America, Local 579 v Bradco Construction* [1993] 2 SCR 316, 333 (Sopinka J). See also *Pasiechnyk v Saskatchewan (Workers' Compensation Board)* [1997] 2 SCR 890, 905.

[83] It still retained some vitality, in the sense that administrative decision-makers had to operate within boundaries set ultimately by reviewing courts, but these boundaries were largely to be marked out by reasonableness.

[84] *Pushpanathan* (n 80) [28].

shores: 'The temptation for judges to slip into old ways of thinking in which the formal concept of jurisdiction is an active legal norm rather than a passive legal outcome has sometimes been overwhelming.'[85] Questions that would traditionally have been seen as jurisdictional had an almost magical capacity to attract judicial intervention, the multi-factor test notwithstanding; 'jurisdictional error began to resurface but in a shadowy form'.[86]

Chieu v Canada (Minister of Citizenship and Immigration)[87] is a good example. The applicant was an immigrant to Canada who had claimed he was single and had no dependents when in fact he was married and had a son.[88] When the misrepresentation came to light, his removal from Canada was ordered. He appealed to the discretion of the Immigration Appeal Division to overturn a removal order where, 'having regard to all the circumstances of the case, the person should not be removed from Canada'.[89] The Division refused to have regard to the hardship the applicant alleged he would suffer if returned to his home country. Concluding that the relevant domestic considerations did not militate in favour of allowing the applicant to remain in Canada, the Division denied his appeal.

What is striking is how the Supreme Court of Canada characterised the issue. One would have thought that whether foreign hardship could be taken into account by the Division in exercising its discretion was a question best answered by the administrative decision-maker. Yet Iacobucci J considered this question to be jurisdictional in nature. He noted that '[a]dministrative bodies generally must be correct in determining the scope of their delegated mandate' and despite the 'considerable expertise' the Division had in weighing up the relevant factors, 'the *scope* of this discretionary jurisdiction itself is a legal issue ultimately to be supervised by the courts'.[90]

While this alone was not a basis for reviewing the decision on a standard of correctness, it was an important consideration. Applying the traditional tools of statutory construction, Iacobucci J held that foreign hardship could be taken into account by the Division.

Evidently, the concept of jurisdictional error continued to exert a significant influence despite the dominance achieved by the pragmatic and

[85] Walters (n 42) 307.

[86] D Mullan, 'The McLachlin Court and the Public Law Standard of Review: A Major Irritant Soothed or a Significant Ongoing Problem?' in D Wright and A Dodek (eds), *Public Law at the McLachlin Court: The First Decade* (Toronto, Irwin Law, 2011) 97.

[87] *Chieu v Canada (Minister of Citizenship and Immigration)* 2002 SCC 3, [2002] 1 SCR 84.

[88] The effect of ss 27(1)(e) and 32(2) of the Immigration Act RSC 1985, c I-2 was to provide for the removal from Canada of permanent residents who had gained that status by misrepresenting material facts.

[89] Immigration Act RSC 1985, c I-2, s 70(1)(b).

[90] *Chieu* (n 87) [24] (emphasis added).

functional analysis.[91] Indeed, when the Court revised the judicial review framework in *Dunsmuir v New Brunswick*, 'true' jurisdictional questions were said to attract a standard of review of correctness,[92] a tacit admission of the persistence of the concept of jurisdictional error standing alone.[93]

In the early days of the pragmatic and functional analysis jurisdictional error persisted to some extent where the relevant statutory provisions provided for an appeal from an administrative decision-maker to the courts.[94] Deference was to be predicated on the existence of a privative clause or a clause providing that the administrative decision-maker's decision was 'final and binding'.[95] However, the Court also made reference to the need to account for 'the principle of specialization of duties',[96] which later became the springboard for the application of the pragmatic and functional analysis to clauses providing for appeals.[97] Appeals were no longer automatically *de novo*, even on questions of law. The reader will not be surprised to learn, however, that appeals often attracted the application of the correctness standard of review, at least for 'pure questions of law',[98] especially where these had 'significant precedential value'.[99] Thus in *Pushpanathan v Canada (Minister of Citizenship and Immigration)*, which would otherwise represent the apotheosis of the pragmatic and functional

[91] Another example of jurisdictional error's continuing influence is *ATCO Gas & Pipelines Ltd v Alberta (Energy & Utilities Board)* 2006 SCC 4, [2006] 1 SCR 140. Here, a utility company applied to dispose of an asset which was no longer used or useful for the provision of services. The regulator asserted the authority to allocate some of the net gain from the sale to the company's rate-paying customers. The Court held (at [31]) that the regulator had to be correct in determining whether it had the authority to make an order relating to the allocation of the proceeds of the sale: 'The interpretation of general concepts such as "public interest" and "conditions" ... is not foreign to courts and is not derived from an area where the tribunal has been held to have greater expertise than the courts.' Deference was owed only to the Board's exercises of its rate-setting power, not its interpretations of the scope of its regulatory authority (at [27]).

[92] *Dunsmuir v New Brunswick* 2008 SCC 9, [2008] 1 SCR 190, [59]: 'Administrative bodies must also be correct in their determinations of true questions of jurisdiction or *vires*.' Courts were warned to take a 'robust view' of jurisdiction and Dickson J's admonition not to treat as jurisdictional questions which may be doubtfully so was recalled (ibid).

[93] The Court has since suggested that it will cast the category off altogether (see *Alberta (Information and Privacy Commissioner) v Alberta Teachers' Association* 2011 SCC 61, [2011] 3 SCR 654, [34]; *McLean v British Columbia (Securities Commission)* 2013 SCC 67, [25]) but has not yet undone *Dunsmuir's* jurisprudential knot.

[94] *Bell Canada v Canada (Canadian Radio-Television and Telecommunications Commission)* [1989] 1 SCR 1722, 1747

[95] Ibid, 1745.

[96] Ibid, 1746.

[97] *Pezim v British Columbia (Superintendent of Brokers)* [1994] 2 SCR 557; *Canada (Director of Investigations and Research) v Southam* [1997] 1 SCR 748.

[98] *Canada (Deputy Minister of National Revenue) v Mattel Canada Inc* 2001 SCC 36, [2001] 2 SCR 100, [33]. See also *Harvard College v Canada (Commissioner of Patents)* 2002 SCC 76, [2002] 4 SCR 45, [150]; *Canada (Commissioner of Competition) v Superior Propane Inc* 2001 FCA 104, [2001] 3 FC 185, [169]; *Monsanto Canada Inc v Ontario (Superintendent of Financial Services)* 2004 SCC 54, [2004] 3 SCR 152, [10].

[99] *Harvard College* (n 98) [140].

analysis, a question of international law was held to require the application of a standard of correctness.[100] Unsurprisingly, in *Dunsmuir*, the Court retained a category of questions of general law of central importance to the legal system which were to be answered by courts.[101]

Moreover, questions deemed to be legal and jurisdictional were sometimes 'segmented'. In *ATCO Gas & Pipelines Ltd v Alberta (Energy & Utilities Board)*, the jurisdictional aspect of the regulator's decision was hived off and subjected to more intense scrutiny.[102] Something similar occurred in *Lévis (City) v Fraternité des policiers de Lévis Inc.*[103] A police officer was dismissed by the municipality after pleading guilty to serious criminal offences. But there were two provisions which potentially applied, one of which provided for automatic dismissal,[104] the other of which provided that in limited circumstances another sanction could be substituted for dismissal.[105] An arbitrator ordered that the officer be reinstated. This decision was ultimately quashed by the Supreme Court of Canada. Of interest for present purposes is that the determination of which statutory provision applied was subject to a separate, more intrusive, standard of review than was the exercise of the arbitrator's authority to impose an appropriate sanction: 'Multiple standards of review should be adopted when there are clearly defined questions that engage different concerns under the pragmatic and functional approach.'[106]

Abella J concurred in the result, sounding a note of caution about the appropriateness of segmentation: 'legal issues ought not to be declared readily extricable when they are legitimately and necessarily intertwined with the adjudicator's mandate and expertise'.[107] Writing for a majority of the Court, she gave a strong warning about this practice in *Council of Canadians with Disabilities v VIA Rail Canada Inc.*[108] Federal transportation legislation vested in the Canadian Transportation Agency the power to determine the existence of 'undue obstacle[s]' to the mobility of people with disabilities.[109] The Agency concluded that VIA Rail's

[100] *Pushpanathan* (n 80).

[101] *Dunsmuir* (n 92) [55].

[102] 'To determine the Board's power to allocate proceeds from a sale of utility assets suggests a standard of review of correctness ... [but] [t]he second question regarding the Board's actual method used for the allocation of proceeds likely attracts a more deferential standard': *ATCO Gas & Pipelines Ltd* (n 91) [32–33].

[103] *Lévis (City) v Fraternité des policiers de Lévis Inc* 2007 SCC 14, [2007] 1 SCR 591.

[104] Cities and Towns Act RSQ c C-19, s 116(6).

[105] Police Act RSQ, c P-13.1, s 119(2).

[106] *Lévis* (n 103) [20]. See also *Moreau-Bérubé v New Brunswick (Judicial Council)* 2002 SCC 11, [2002] 1 SCR 249; *United Taxi Drivers' Fellowship of Southern Alberta v Calgary (City)* 2004 SCC 19, [2004] 1 SCR 485.

[107] *Lévis* (n 103) [112].

[108] *Council of Canadians with Disabilities v VIA Rail Canada Inc* 2007 SCC 15, [2007] 1 SCR 650.

[109] *Canada Transportation Act* SC 1996, c 10, s 5(g)(ii) and 172.

redesign of its train cars imposed an 'undue obstacle' and made an order to that effect, an order that was vigorously contested by the company.

Abella J disagreed with the Federal Court of Appeal that the Agency had no special expertise with regard to human rights such that its decision to proceed with the complaint was subject to review on a standard of correctness. For Abella J this approach had 'the capacity to unravel the essence of the decision and undermine the very characteristic of the Agency which entitles it to the highest level of deference from a court—its specialized expertise'.[110] For: 'If every provision of a tribunal's enabling legislation were treated as if it had jurisdictional consequences that permitted a court to substitute its own view of the correct interpretation, a tribunal's role would be effectively reduced to fact-finding.'[111] Segmentation is a siren call to the Diceyan ear.[112] While it is possible that a segmented 'legal' or 'jurisdictional' component would be subjected to a less intensive standard of review, the cases are not encouraging.

The segmentation phenomenon and its potentially deleterious consequences are best appreciated by reference to cases dealing with the review of the exercise of discretion. In theory, the distinction between 'law' and 'discretion' has been abolished for the purposes of judicial review in Canada.[113] Reasonableness is what counts: 'The nominate grounds, language of jurisdiction, and ossified interpretations of statutory formulae, while still useful as familiar landmarks, no longer dictate the journey.'[114] Nonetheless, there has been a marked tendency for courts to employ the

110 *VIA Rail Canada* (n 108) [88].

111 ibid, [89].

112 At least when it occurs within a statute, as in *Canadian Broadcasting Corp v Canada (Labour Relations Board)* [1995] 1 SCR 157. Here, Iacobucci J took the view (at [48]) that segmentation could *protect* the autonomy of an administrative decision-maker, decrying the proposition that 'every time an administrative tribunal encounters an external statute in the course of its determination, the decision as a whole becomes open to review on a standard of correctness' because this 'would substantially expand the scope of reviewability of administrative decisions, and unjustifiably so'. In this case, however, Iacobucci J was addressing a situation in which the decision-maker, charged with determining if an unfair labour practice had occurred, had regard to broadcasting legislation, which was not the decision-maker's constitutive statute. This situation did not require Iacobucci J to effect a segmentation *within* the decision-maker's constitutive statute. Moreover, a better way for reviewing courts to protect administrative autonomy would be to defer on interpretive questions closely related to the decision-maker's mandate.

113 See *Baker v Canada (Minister of Citizenship and Immigration)* [1999] 2 SCR 817, [54] (noting that there is 'no easy distinction to be made between interpretation and the exercise of discretion').

114 *Dr Q v College of Physicians and Surgeons of British Columbia* 2003 SCC 19, [2003] 1 SCR 226, [24]. See also *Kane v Canada (Attorney General)* 2011 FCA 19 (reversed 2012 SCC 64, [2012] 3 SCR 398), [107] (Stratas JA, dissenting): 'We interfere because the tribunal has reached an outcome based on an indefensible interpretation, application or exercise of Parliament's law. We do not interfere simply because the tribunal has failed to consider something that we happen to think is relevant.'

traditional grounds for review of abuse of discretion, in the traditional way, to assess the reasonableness of a decision.[115]

The difficulty is the following. Quashing a decision on judicial review for use of a power for an improper purpose or based on irrelevant considerations requires the reviewing court to have regard to statutory purpose and text. Yet determinations of statutory purpose and relevancy are questions of interpretation.[116] Accordingly, deference to administrative decision-makers' interpretations of law implies deference to administrative decision-makers' interpretations of statutory purpose. However, these legal aspects of exercises of discretion have consistently been treated as falling within the judicial domain.[117]

Consider the *Retired Judges Case*: *CUPE v Ontario (Minister of Labour)*.[118] In the Canadian province of Ontario, some workers in the healthcare sector are obliged to resolve differences with their employers concerning the terms of collective agreements by submitting to compulsory arbitration. Arbitral panels were to be composed of one member, if the parties agreed whom to appoint, or three members in case of disagreement. Union and management could each nominate one member of a three-member panel; the Minister nominated the other.[119] At issue was the Minister's decision to nominate retired judges to complete the three-member panels. The challenge was brought by a trade union, concerned that retired judges would not be sufficiently alive to employee interests.

For a majority of the Court, Binnie J employed the traditional tools of statutory interpretation to determine the purpose of the legislation,[120] concluding that the intention of the legislature was for the Minister to have

[115] Indeed, British Columbia's Administrative Tribunals Act SBC 2004, c 45 defines as patently unreasonable an administrative decision that:

(a) is exercised arbitrarily or in bad faith,
(b) is exercised for an improper purpose,
(c) is based entirely or predominantly on irrelevant factors, or
(d) fails to take statutory requirements into account.

This restatement of the traditional grounds of review for abuse of discretion has survived the *Dunsmuir* reformulation of the standards of review, because of its statutory status. See *British Columbia (Workers' Compensation Board) v Figliola* 2011 SCC 52, [2011] 3 SCR 422, [20].

[116] P Craig, 'The Nature of Reasonableness Review' [2013] *Current Legal Problems* 1, 5.

[117] This concern is not new: 'There is a danger that the doctrines of improper purpose or irrelevant considerations will be used by a court as a device to substitute its opinion on the contested matter for that of the statutory agency': Hogg (n 13) 207. There is thus some basis for Lorne Sossin's suspicion that the expansion of the pragmatic and functional analysis to exercises of discretion 'extended its reach if not its grasp': 'Developments in Administrative Law: the 1997–1998 and 1998–1999 Terms' (2000) 11 *Supreme Court Law Review* (2d) 37, 57.

[118] *Retired Judges Case*: *CUPE v Ontario (Minister of Labour)* 2003 SCC 29, [2003] 1 SCR 539.

[119] Hospital Labour Disputes Arbitration Act RSO 1990, c H.14, ss 4, 5 and 6.

[120] '[T]he words of an Act are to be read in their entire context and in their grammatical and ordinary sense harmoniously with the scheme of the Act, the object of the Act, and the intention of Parliament': E Driedger, *Construction of Statutes*, 2nd edn (Toronto, Butterworths, 1983) 87. See, eg *Rizzo & Rizzo Shoes Ltd (Re)* [1998] 1 SCR 27.

regard in exercising his power to nominate arbitrators 'to relevant labour relations expertise as well as independence, impartiality and general acceptability within the labour relations community'.[121] Accordingly, while the Minister's decision to nominate retired judges as arbitrators was reviewable on a standard of patent unreasonableness,[122] the 'limited nature' of his mandate—as defined by the Court—was an 'important factor'.[123]

Here, the Minister had rejected 'expertise and broad acceptability as qualifications'.[124] Appointing 'an inexpert and inexperienced chairperson who is not seen as broadly acceptable in the labour relations community' caused the Minister to frustrate the state's purpose which was 'industrial peace in hospitals and nursing homes'.[125] Binnie J summed up his conclusions tellingly: 'In my view, with respect, *having regard to what I believe to be the legislative intent* manifested in the [statute], the Minister's approach to the s. 6(5) appointments was patently unreasonable.'[126]

This is to impose 'fetters that are jurisdictional in nature' and to render 'the concept of deference practically irrelevant'[127] by leaving 'little room for deference or respect for the decision-maker's appreciation of those factors or considerations that were relevant to the interpretation of a particular statutory provision or the exercise of a particular statutory power'.[128]

V. THE BATTLE FOR REASONABLENESS: 2008–PRESENT

Implementing deference proved very difficult. The failure to do so satisfactorily led to the reformulation of judicial review doctrine in *Dunsmuir v New Brunswick*,[129] which in turn set the scene for the modern equivalent of previous battles for deference. Today the question is whether a revised conception of reasonableness will withstand the traditional interventionist forces of jurisdictional error and error of law.

To place the current struggle in its proper context, some background is necessary. The multi-factor test was eventually accompanied by multiple 'standards of review'. Applying the pragmatic and functional analysis would indicate to a reviewing court whether to subject the impugned

[121] *Retired Judges Case* (n 118) [111].

[122] Ibid, [154].

[123] Ibid, [156].

[124] Ibid, [182].

[125] Ibid, [184].

[126] Ibid, [184] (emphasis added). See, similarly, *Halifax (Regional Municipality) v Canada (Public Works and Government Services)* 2012 SCC 29, [2012] 2 SCR 108.

[127] G Huscroft, 'Judicial Review from *CUPE* to *CUPE*: Less is Not Always More' in M Taggart and G Huscroft (eds), *Inside and Outside Canadian Administrative Law: Essays in Honour of David Mullan* (Toronto, University of Toronto Press, 2006) 307.

[128] D Mullan, 'Deference from *Baker* to *Suresh* and Beyond—Interpreting Conflicting Signals' in D Dyzenhaus (ed), *The Unity of Public Law* (Oxford, Hart Publishing, 2004) 24.

[129] *Dunsmuir* (n 92).

decision to a correctness, reasonableness *simpliciter* or patent unreasonableness standard. Correctness was always easy to define: it allowed the reviewing court to substitute its judgment for that of the administrative decision-maker.

Maintaining two distinct standards of reasonableness was a greater challenge.[130] Patent unreasonableness was said to be a 'very strict test' met only by a decision that was 'clearly irrational, that is to say evidently not in accordance with reason'.[131] A decision would have to be 'so flawed that no amount of curial deference can justify letting it stand', in which case, however, the defect 'once identified, can be explained simply and easily, leaving no real possibility of doubting that the decision is defective'.[132] Applying the standard of reasonableness *simpliciter* required a reviewing court to ask whether the decision-maker had produced 'reasons that can stand up to a somewhat probing examination'.[133] Application of this standard was said to require 'deferential self-discipline'.[134] Intervention would be justifiable 'only if there is no line of analysis within the given reasons that could reasonably lead the tribunal from the evidence before it to the conclusion at which it arrived'.[135]

In a devastating set of concurring reasons in *Toronto (City) v Canadian Union of Public Employees, Local 79*[136] LeBel J identified 'significant practical problems inherent in distinguishing meaningfully between the two standards'.[137] It had been suggested that the magnitude of the error was the defining characteristic of a patently unreasonable decision. Yet, LeBel J recalled, one judge queried 'how helpful it is to substitute one adjectival phrase for another and define patent unreasonableness in terms of rational indefensibility. It seems to me that this simply injects one more opportunity for ambiguity into a test which is already fraught with ambiguity'.[138] A purely linguistic test was thus liable to invite impressionistic conclusions from reviewing courts. It had also been suggested that patent unreasonableness depended on the obviousness of the error.[139] The suggestion would have to be that hidden, or hard-to-find, but very serious errors would not render a decision unreasonable. But, LeBel J concluded, this would presumably require recourse to a minimally-searching form of judicial review,

[130] The following paragraphs draw on Daly (n 7) 174–77.

[131] *Canada (Attorney General) v Public Service Alliance of Canada* [1993] 1 SCR 941, 963–64.

[132] *Law Society of New Brunswick v Ryan*, 2003 SCC 20, [2003] 1 SCR 247, [52].

[133] *Canada (Director of Investigation and Research) v Southam Inc* [1997] 1 SCR 748, [56].

[134] *Law Society of New Brunswick* (n 132) [46].

[135] Ibid, [55].

[136] *Toronto (City) v CUP, Local 79* 2003 SCC 63, [2003] 3 SCR 77.

[137] Ibid, 137.

[138] *Canadian Association of Industrial, Mechanical and Allied Workers Local 14* (n 73) 1022.

[139] See, eg *National Corn Growers Association* (n 2) 1370: 'In some cases, the unreasonableness of a decision may be apparent without detailed examination of the record.'

which would in turn raise 'a more theoretical quandary: the difficulty of articulating why a defect that is obvious on the face of a decision should present more of an imperative for court intervention than a latent defect'.[140] Rule of law considerations counted against judicial laxity in respect of illogical or irrational decisions, however deep the illogicalities or irrationalities were hidden. As a trial judge put it,[141]

> attempting to follow the [Supreme] Court's distinctions between 'patently unreasonable', 'reasonable' and 'correct', one feels at times as though one is watching a juggler juggle three transparent objects. Depending on the way the light falls, sometimes one thinks one can see the objects. Other times one cannot and, indeed, wonders whether there are really three distinct objects at all.

Confusion about the multiple standards of review provided the impetus for reform. Bastarache and LeBel JJ announced in the opening paragraph of their joint majority reasons in *Dunsmuir v New Brunswick*,[142] that it was time for a 'reassessment' of the 'troubling question' of judicial review of administrative action, for the Court had failed to identify 'solutions that provide real guidance for litigants, counsel, administrative decision makers or judicial review judges'.[143]

The three standards were reduced to two, correctness and reasonableness. Reasonableness was described in elegant terms as requiring a reviewing court to inquire into 'the existence of justification, transparency and intelligibility within the decision-making process' and with 'whether the decision falls within a range of possible, acceptable outcomes which are defensible in respect of the facts and law'.[144]

The multi-factor 'pragmatic and functional' analysis was also sidelined, in favour of a categorical 'standard of review' analysis.[145] For example: 'Deference will usually result where a tribunal is interpreting its own statute or statutes closely connected to its function, with which it will have particular familiarity.'[146] As Fish J subsequently explained, correctness applies to (1) constitutional issues; (2) a questions of general law both of central importance to the legal system as a whole and outside the adjudicator's specialised area of expertise; (3) the drawing of jurisdictional lines between two or more competing specialised tribunals; and (4) true questions of

[140] *Toronto (City) v CUPE, Local 79* (n 136) 143. See also *Voice Construction Ltd v Construction & General Workers' Union, Local 92*, 2004 SCC 23, [2004] 1 SCR 609, [40–42]; L LeBel, 'Some Properly Deferential Thoughts on Deference' (2008) 21 *Canadian Journal of Administrative Law and Practice* 1.

[141] *Miller v Workers' Compensation Commission (Newfoundland)* (1997) 154 Nfld and PEIR 52, 57–58 (LD Barry J).

[142] *Dunsmuir* (n 92).

[143] Ibid, [1].

[144] Ibid, [47].

[145] For a critique, see P Daly, 'The Unfortunate Triumph of Form over Substance in Canadian Administrative Law' (2012) 50 *Osgoode Hall Law Journal* 317.

[146] *Dunsmuir* (n 92) [54].

jurisdiction or *vires*. Reasonableness is normally the governing standard where the question at issue: (1) relates to the interpretation of the tribunal's home statute or statutes closely connected to its function, with which it will have particular familiarity; (2) raises issues of fact, discretion or policy; or (3) involves inextricably intertwined legal and factual issues.[147]

This later hardened into an outright presumption that reasonableness will apply when a decision-maker is interpreting its constitutive statute.[148] Post-*Dunsmuir*, on each occasion that it has granted leave to appeal a provincial court of appeal decision that has identified a question which attracts the correctness standard of review, the Supreme Court of Canada has refused to apply the standard of correctness.[149] Even the tantalising category of 'true' jurisdictional error has been kept shut. Reasonableness is now the dominant standard.[150] But as was said shortly after *Dunsmuir*, the effect was to 'simply postpone the complexity [of the multi-factor test] to a second stage, that of identifying where, on a spectrum of reasonableness, the reviewing court should locate itself in assessing the decision under attack'.[151] Indeed, it is precisely at this stage of the analysis that interventionist winds have blown the Court off its nominally deferential course. One storm has now abated. Another is just beginning.

The first storm involved the Court's reference in *Dunsmuir* to 'justification, intelligibility and transparency' as hallmarks of reasonableness. Lower courts began to pick apart fully reasoned decisions on the basis that the reasons given were lacked rigour and coherence. Interventionism was embraced.[152] However, in *Newfoundland and Labrador Nurses' Union v Newfoundland and Labrador (Treasury Board)*,[153] and a series

[147] *Smith v Alliance Pipeline* 2011 SCC 7, [2011] 1 SCR 160, [26].

[148] *Alberta (Information and Privacy Commissioner)* (n 93) [34]; *Rogers Communications Inc v Society of Composers, Authors and Music Publishers of Canada* 2012 SCC 35, [2012] 2 SCR 283, [15].

[149] *Nolan v Kerry (Canada) Inc* 2009 SCC 39, [2009] 2 SCR 678 (claim of jurisdictional error); *Nor-Man Regional Health Authority Inc v Manitoba Association of Health Care Professionals* 2011 SCC 59, [2011] 3 SCR 616 (question of general law); *Alberta (Information and Privacy Commissioner)* (n 93) (jurisdictional error); *Communications, Energy and Paperworkers Union of Canada, Local 30 v Irving Pulp & Paper, Ltd* 2013 SCC 34 (question of general law); *McLean* (n 93) (question of general law). A correctness standard was applied to a jurisdictional issue in *Northrop Grumman Overseas Services Corp v Canada (Attorney General)* 2009 SCC 50, [2009] 3 SCR 309 but only because previous case law had satisfactorily identified the appropriate standard (at [10]).

[150] See, eg J Evans, 'Triumph of Reasonableness: But How Much Does It Really Matter?' (2014) 27 *Canadian Journal of Administrative Law and Practice* 101.

[151] D Mullan, '*Dunsmuir v New Brunswick*: Standard of Review and Procedural Fairness for Public Servants: Let's Try Again!' (2008) 21 *Canadian Journal of Administrative Law and Practice* 117, 125.

[152] See, eg *Public Service Alliance of Canada v Canada Post Corp* 2010 FCA 56.

[153] *Newfoundland and Labrador Nurses' Union v Newfoundland and Labrador (Treasury Board)* 2011 SCC 62, [2011] 3 SCR 708.

of other decisions,[154] the Court clamped down. It noted how in *Dunsmuir* it had also counselled courts to have regard to reasons 'which could be offered in support of a decision'.[155] Accordingly, *Dunsmuir's* reference to 'justification, intelligibility and transparency' was not an invitation to reviewing courts to conduct a 'line-by-line treasure hunt for error' in which it would pick apart the reasons offered to support a decision.[156] Subsequently, the Court specified that the question for the reviewing court, when examining the reasoning of an administrative decision-maker, was simply whether the court could 'clearly understand' the reasons given.[157] That what the Court doubtless intended as a fresh breeze turned into perilously strong winds is further evidence of the power of interventionism.[158]

The second storm is potentially much more damaging. It involves the second prong of the reasonableness standard in *Dunsmuir*: that decisions must fall within a 'range of possible, acceptable outcomes'. In determining the outer limits of the 'range' it appears that the reasonableness of administrative interpretations of law is adjudged by reference to judicial principles of statutory interpretation, such that little separates modern reasonableness review from prior interventionist approaches.

The most prominent example of reasonableness review relying on the strict application of the principles of statutory interpretation is *Canada (Canadian Human Rights Commission) v Canada (Attorney General)*.[159] The Canadian Human Rights Tribunal had the power to award 'expenses' incurred by the victim of discrimination[160] and sought to defray the legal costs of a partially successful claimant. Writing for a unanimous Court, LeBel and Cromwell JJ described the question as one of statutory interpretation, requiring the application of judicially developed principles.

[154] See, eg *Public Service Alliance of Canada v Canada Post Corp* 2011 SCC 57, [2011] 3 SCR 572 (adopting the dissenting reasons of Evans JA: 2010 FCA 56); *Communications, Energy and Paperworkers Union of Canada, Local 30* (n 149).

[155] *Dunsmuir* (n 92) [48], citing Dyzenhaus (n 50) 286.

[156] *Communications, Energy and Paperworkers Union of Canada, Local 30* (n 149) [54].

[157] *Agraira v Canada (Public Safety and Emergency Preparedness)* 2013 SCC 36, [89].

[158] A similar, though less momentous, debate occurred in *National Corn Growers Association* (n 2). Gonthier J, for a majority of the Court, took the view that a determination of whether the decision-maker's conclusions were reasonable required reference to the reasons given by the decision-maker (at 1383). Gonthier J's conclusion was that reference to these provisions might *influence* the reviewing court's determination of the reasonableness of a decision, rather than resolve it conclusively, and thus did not undermine deference. He did not, contrary to Wilson J's charge, 'engage in the very kind of meticulous analysis of the Tribunal's reasoning that *CUPE* made clear courts should not conduct' (at 1349). An interpretation of law is not a brute fact; it can only be understood in context, which, when the impugned interpretation has been produced by an administrative decision-maker, is one provided by the reasons given for the interpretation.

[159] *Canada (Canadian Human Rights Commission) v Canada (Attorney General)* 2011 SCC 53, [2011] 3 SCR 471. The discussion here draws on P Daly, '*Dunsmuir's* Flaws Exposed' (2012) 58 *McGill Law Journal* 483. See also Wildeman (n 71).

[160] Canadian Human Rights Act RSC 1985, c H-6, s 53(2).

On reviewing the text, context, legislative history, purposes and parallel provisions in other jurisdictions they concluded: 'the text, context and purpose of the legislation clearly show that there is no authority in the Tribunal to award legal costs and that there is no other reasonable interpretation of the relevant provisions'.[161] Indeed, LeBel and Cromwell JJ rebuked the Tribunal for not having employed legal principles: its decision to adopt a dictionary meaning of 'expenses' and articulate a beneficial policy outcome 'led the Tribunal to adopt an unreasonable interpretation of the provisions in issue'.[162]

Or, put another way, the Tribunal's decision was unreasonable because it was incorrect. A revealing contrast is provided by *Agraira v Canada (Public Safety and Emergency Preparedness)*, where the Minister's interpretation was 'eminently reasonable' *because* it was 'consistent' with the interpretation reached by the Court applying the principles of statutory interpretation.[163]

It has been said that this was not reasonableness masquerading as correctness, rather a reflection that the 'range' of reasonable outcomes referred to in *Dunsmuir* is simply narrower on questions of law: 'In the case of matters involving statutory interpretation, the Supreme Court has often articulated the range of possible, acceptable outcomes open to the administrative decision-maker in a narrow way, likely because of the specificity of the particular statutory provisions in issue.'[164] Indeed[165]

> if a reviewing court concludes that one interpretation is 'right', after conducting a textual, contextual, and purposive interpretative analysis of the legislation, and giving careful and respectful consideration to the tribunal's reasons ... the court may intervene to ensure administrative compliance with the legislature's clearly expressed intention. The rule of law requires nothing less.

Writing for a unanimous Court on this point, Moldaver J effectively adopted this approach in *McLean v British Columbia (Securities Commission)*, commenting that where 'the ordinary tools of statutory interpretation lead to a single reasonable interpretation' the range of reasonable outcomes 'will necessarily be limited to a single reasonable interpretation—and the

[161] *Canada (Canadian Human Rights Commission)* (n 159) [64].

[162] Ibid, [64]. See, similarly, *British Columbia (Workers' Compensation Board) v Figliola*, 2011 SCC 52, [2011] 3 SCR 422; *Canada (Canadian Human Rights Commission)* (n 159); *Alberta (Education) v Canadian Copyright Licensing Agency (Access Copyright)* 2012 SCC 37; *Saskatchewan (Human Rights Commission) v Whatcott* 2013 SCC 11.

[163] *Agraira* (n 157) [86–88].

[164] *Canada (Attorney General) v Abraham*, 2012 FCA 266, [48] (Stratas JA).

[165] *Qin v Canada (Citizenship and Immigration)* 2013 FCA 263, [33] (Evans JA). This reflects a position expressed many years ago by then-Professor Evans: 'Developments in Administrative Law: the 1988–1989 Term' (1990) 12 *Supreme Court Law Review* (2d) 1, 57–58.

administrative decision maker must adopt it'.[166] Ambiguity has apparently become the gateway to deference.[167]

The tendency for reasonableness to shade into correctness is hardly a new phenomenon. In defining the patent unreasonableness standard in *Fraser v Public Service Staff Relations Board*[168] Dickson CJ held that a decision could be quashed if 'the statutory decision maker makes a mistake of law, such as addressing his or her mind to the wrong question, applying the wrong principle, failing to apply a principle he or she would have applied, or incorrectly applying a legal principle'.[169] This 'repeats the list of "nullifying" errors' set out by Lord Reid in *Anisminic*, a list traditionally associated with correctness review.[170] There was an ever-present danger that review for patent unreasonableness would slip into review for correctness.[171]

Yet a willingness to assert judicial supremacy by using the principles of statutory interpretation to set the limits of the 'range' of acceptable interpretive outcomes, or by identifying 'clear' statutory provisions further underlines the power of traditionalist thinking. The very purpose of the principles of statutory interpretation is to help judges to find the best answers to legal questions. They are not designed to identify ambiguity; they are designed to resolve it. This approach requires courts to insist on the application of *judicially* crafted principles of interpretation to circumscribe the authority of *administrative* decision-makers, holding non-lawyers to legal standards and moving them to adopt an interpretive mindset that is not necessarily their own. Administrative decision-makers are taught by reviewing courts that it is better to think like lawyers, even if the legislature's goal of empowering administrative decision-makers in the first place was to avoid having decisions made by people who think like lawyers.[172]

In addition, declaring that 'clear' provisions must be enforced by reviewing courts is very much like saying that 'jurisdictional' provisions must be enforced by reviewing courts. The distinction between 'clear' and 'unclear'

[166] *McLean* (n 93) [38]. Citations omitted.

[167] On one reading, ambiguity has always been a pre-requisite for deference: Evans (n 150) 108. There is some evidence in the historical record to support this position, but the question was never broached in clear terms.

[168] *Fraser v Public Service Staff Relations Board* [1985] 2 SCR 455.

[169] Ibid, 465. This case involved a federal decision-maker and an application of the 'erred in law' provision of the Federal Court Act, RSC, 1985, c F–7, s 28. Nonetheless, Dickson CJ conflated review under this provision with the 'common law principles of judicial review' (ibid), a stance that has consistently been maintained. See, generally, *Canada (Citizenship and Immigration) v Khosa*, 2009 SCC 12, [2009] 1 SCR 339.

[170] D Mullan, *Administrative Law*, 2nd edn (Toronto, Irwin Law, 2001) 69.

[171] See, eg I Holloway, '"A Sacred Right": Judicial Review of Administrative Action as a Cultural Phenomenon' (1993) 22 *Manitoba Law Journal* 28, 64–65.

[172] See also Arthurs (n 3) 20: 'It is through the use of [common law] presumptions and interpretative rules, some of which are explicitly hostile to Parliament's intention, that judicial revision of legislation takes place.'

statutory provisions threatens to prove just as tenuous and malleable as the distinction between jurisdictional and non-jurisdictional error.[173] Both distinctions have their origins deep in traditionalist waters.

This recalls a revealing dispute which occurred in *Canadian Association of Industrial, Mechanical and Allied Workers v Paccar of Canada*.[174] In a set of concurring reasons, Sopinka J suggested that because reasonableness 'is not a quality that exists in isolation' and requires a reviewing court to make a 'relative statement' about 'the logical relationship between the grounds of the decision and premises thought by the court to be true', it would be necessary for the reviewing court to evaluate the merits of the impugned decision.[175]

It is of course true that assessing reasonableness 'must involve an evaluation of the merits'. But it does not follow that the reviewing court must assess the correctness of the decision under review and then ask itself whether the decision-maker departed too far from the court's preferred result. Such an approach is traditionalist. It puts the courts at the top of the interpretive hierarchy. And it makes intervention easier to justify, on the basis that a benchmark established by the reviewing court has not been met. A court which determines that the decision-maker has not arrived at the best answer is (all things being equal) more likely to intervene than a court which limits itself to asking whether the decision was reasonable.

The approach suggested in opposition by La Forest J is preferable. For him, it was 'sufficient to say that the result arrived at by the Board is not patently unreasonable'; it was 'not necessary to go beyond' saying 'that the result reached by the Board is as reasonable as the alternative'.[176]

Reference to reasonableness is not 'superfluous', as Sopinka J suggested; it ensures that reviewing courts are appropriately deferential. But the fact that Sopinka J would make the suggestion at all is evidence of the hold that interventionism has on the judicial mind and demonstrates the difficulty of inculcating a deferential attitude. And, of course, the dispute demonstrates how too interventionist an approach to the reasonableness of interpretations of law could undermine deference: 'starting from a finding that the adjudicator's decision is incorrect may colour the reviewing court's subsequent assessment of the reasonableness of competing interpretations'.[177] La Forest J's pungent observation that '[c]urial deference is more than just a fiction courts resort to when they are in agreement with the decisions of the tribunal'[178] rings as true today as when it was first made. It is further

[173] P Daly, 'Deference on Questions of Law' (2011) 74 *Modern Law Review* 694.

[174] *Canadian Association of Industrial, Mechanical and Allied Workers* (n 138).

[175] Ibid, 1018.

[176] Ibid, 1005.

[177] *Toronto (City) v CUPE, Local 79* (n 136) [91].

[178] *Canadian Association of Industrial, Mechanical and Allied Workers, Local 14* (n 73) 1004. See, similarly, *Canadian Union of Public Employees, Local 301 v Montreal (City)* [1997] 1 SCR 793, [53].

evidence of the strength of interventionist currents that those that dragged Sopinka J away from a deferential approach two decades ago now threaten to do the same to a new generation of judges.

VI. CONCLUSION

The emergence of deference in Canadian administrative law was contingent on several factors. First, a long period of judicial meddling in the work of labour relations tribunals provoked a strong reaction from some of the country's most prominent legal scholars.[179] John Willis had waged a long battle against perceived judicial excess,[180] but in the 1970s, Paul Weiler (later a professor at Harvard),[181] Peter Hogg (later English-speaking-Canada's pre-eminent scholar of constitutional law)[182] and Harry Arthurs (later the Dean at Osgoode Hall Law School)[183] joined the fray. Second, this scholarly criticism coincided with the ascension to the Supreme Court bench of Bora Laskin, a ferocious critique of the doctrines of judicial review:[184] 'Laskin believed that courts should be kept out so as to allow for positive administrative creativity, not that courts should have a positive role in prodding administrative agencies towards the attainments of the social objectives of empowering legislation.'[185] Significantly, Laskin was on the bench at the same time as his successor as Chief Justice, Brian Dickson, who, 'influenced by his colleague ... thought that law's meaning in relation to complex regulatory matters may often be better expressed by expert and experienced administrators than ordinary judges'.[186] Thus, '[t]aking its inspiration from the advocacy of writers such as Willis and its leadership from Justices Laskin (a former academic colleague of Willis) and Dickson, the Supreme Court of Canada entered an era of deference to the administrative process that persists, by and large, to this day'.[187]

That the emergence of deference may well have been an accident of history would explain much of the doctrinal 'ebb and flow' that Canadian

[179] It has been said that Canada's judicial review jurisprudence has been 'inextricably linked to the labour law field'. D Mullan, 'Developments in Administrative Law: the 1983–84 Term' (1985) 7 *Supreme Court Law Review* (2d) 1, 8.

[180] See, eg 'Foreword' in J Willis (ed), *Canadian Boards at Work* (Toronto, Macmillan, 1941) 71; J Willis, 'The McRuer Report: Lawyers' Values and Civil Servants' Values' (1968) 18 *University of Toronto Law Journal* 351.

[181] Weiler (n 36).

[182] Hogg (n 13).

[183] Arthurs (n 3).

[184] B Laskin, 'Certiorari to Labour Boards: The Apparent Futility of Privative Clauses' (1952) 30 *Canadian Bar Review* 986.

[185] Janisch (n 57) 559.

[186] Walters (n 42) 304.

[187] D Mullan, '*Willis v McRuer*: A Long-Overdue Replay with the Possibility of a Penalty Shoot-out' (2005) 55 *University of Toronto Law Journal* 535, 557.

administrative law has experienced over the past 40 years.[188] An attitude championed by a cadre of true believers in deference must inevitably struggle for dominance with traditionalist common-law thinking. It remains necessary 'to provide antidotes to the propensity of courts to see themselves as experts on many issues of regulatory law and to downplay the capacities of tribunals in relation to those same questions'.[189] It is questionable whether the emerging presumption of reasonableness review will provide the necessary antidotes. For interventionist judges will more readily find clear answers to questions of statutory interpretation or narrowly confine the range of permissible decisions and they will no longer have to couch these conclusions in terms of 'the general context and operation of a statute before applying it'.[190] Requiring a cursory nod to the presumption of reasonableness review, unaccompanied by an appreciation of the relative institutional competence of the decision-maker, is unlikely to cause judges to go against the common law's traditional flow.[191]

The problem may well be what David Dyzenhaus termed the 'paradox of the recognition of rationality': 'To recognise rationality is at the same time to claim a judicial role in supervising the administrative process to ensure that it meets standards of rationality, even if a sincere attempt is made to conceive those differently.'[192] There is no doubting the sincerity of Canadian judges, past and present. But there is no doubting either that they have struggled to swim against the current. Given deference's apparently unending struggle against tides of tradition and interventionism the closing words of F Scott Fitzgerald's *The Great Gatsby* seem apt: 'So we beat on, boats against the current, borne back ceaselessly into the past.'

[188] C L'Heureux-Dubé, 'The "Ebb" and "Flow" of Administrative Law on the "General Question of Law"' in Taggart (n 50) 308.

[189] D Mullan, 'Establishing the Standard of Review: The Struggle for Complexity?' (2004) 17 *Canadian Journal of Administrative Law and Practice* 59, 72. As has been said by Evans (n 55) 41: 'Judicial attitudes are likely to prove more important than words in shaping this area of the law, although when the legal principles that courts are to apply do not reflect their substantive concerns, confusion is always likely to arise.'

[190] Arthurs (n 3) 18.

[191] I have argued that the categorical approach in fact requires reviewing courts to have regard to multiple factors in order to determine into which category a decision falls: Daly (n 145). But a thoroughgoing presumption of reasonableness would render this initial step unnecessary. Reviewing courts would instead dive straight into the application of reasonableness without any appreciation of the waters into which they are venturing.

[192] Dyzenhaus (n 50) 289. A modest attempt to address the paradox is made in Daly, 'Unreasonable Interpretations of Law' (n 11).

Part C

Rights-Based Review

13

Process and Outcome in Judicial Review of Public Authority Compatibility with Human Rights: A Comparative Perspective

CLAUDIA GEIRINGER*

I. INTRODUCTION

DISCUSSIONS OF THE scope and intensity of substantive review at common law often use as a counterpoint the judicial approach to assessing public authority compliance with domestic human rights instruments such as the Human Rights Act 1998 (UK) ('UK Human Rights Act') and the New Zealand Bill of Rights Act 1990 (NZ) ('NZ Bill of Rights').[1] Accounts of this kind generally build on two assumptions: first, that the statutory (or constitutional) obligation of public authority compatibility with human rights is policed (in relation to some or all rights) through the application of a proportionality test; secondly, that this inquiry into proportionality is a results-based inquiry that focuses on the ultimate decision reached or action taken by the public authority. Building on these premises, the focus of interest for the administrative lawyer is on the influence of this human rights paradigm on the development of the substantive ground of review at common law—whether there is (or should be) cross-fertilisation and if so, how much and in what form.

The terms of this comparison, however, belie the complex and vexed questions that continue to surround the proper approach to reviewing public authority compatibility with human rights instruments. The preoccupation

* Professor of Public Law, Victoria University of Wellington; Director, New Zealand Centre for Public Law. My thanks for helpful comments to Matthew Groves, David Mullan, Sir Philip Sales and the two editors of this volume.

[1] Eg M Taggart, 'Proportionality, Deference, *Wednesbury*' [2008] *New Zealand Law Review* 423; P Craig, 'Proportionality, Rationality, and Review' [2010] *New Zealand Law Review* 265. See also J Varuhas, 'Against Unification' (ch 5 in this volume).

of this essay is with one aspect of that complexity: the difficulties that have confronted judges throughout the Commonwealth in sustaining a purely results-based account of their role in reviewing public authority compatibility with human rights. Ultimately, in each of the jurisdictions to have adopted the so-called Commonwealth model of human rights protection,[2] process-based considerations have insinuated themselves into the judicial supervision of administrative decision-making—albeit in strikingly different ways.

The discussion begins with the United Kingdom—the jurisdiction to have come closest to sustaining a purely results-based account of the courts' role in assessing public authority compatibility with human rights. The essay uses the academic debate that this approach has generated to tease out some key policy considerations that militate both for and against allowing process-based inquiry into the compatibility assessment. It then examines developments in the Australian state of Victoria, in Canada and (briefly) in New Zealand, in each of which courts and legislatures have deployed different strategies to inject a degree of process-based inquiry into the judicial supervision of administrative decision-making under the respective human rights instruments.

Ultimately, the essay seeks to establish four key propositions. The first is that judges and legislatures in each of these jurisdictions are confronted, at least in part, by a common set of competing policy considerations—considerations that, on the one hand, militate against a purely results-based approach to assessing public authority compatibility with human rights but that, on the other, also tell against excessive juridification of public authority decision-making processes.

The second is that, despite that common starting point, the strategies adopted in each jurisdiction also respond to a range of contextual factors that are unique to that jurisdiction—factors that lend particular salience to one or more of these policy considerations and/or that constrain the options available to courts and legislatures in seeking to negotiate their way through the competing concerns.

The third (and related) proposition is that, ultimately, each of the jurisdictions has adopted a strikingly different strategy for accommodating a degree of process-based inquiry in the assessment of public authority compatibility with human rights. It would be overambitious in a broad comparative piece of this kind to seek to evaluate comprehensively the suitability of these distinctive local responses to the process/outcome dilemma. This essay does, though, seek to develop a more modest point. It is that a challenge common to all four jurisdictions is the myriad of contexts

[2] See S Gardbaum, *The New Commonwealth Model of Constitutionalism: Theory and Practice* (Cambridge, Cambridge University Press, 2013).

in which public authority decision-making occurs. The final proposition developed in this essay is thus that one-size-fits-all approaches to the process/outcome question may prove difficult to sustain; that a framework is needed that is sufficiently flexible to respond to variations in the rights that are at issue, the type of decision-maker, and the nature of the particular decision.

II. THE UNITED KINGDOM: PROCESS AS A PRECURSOR TO DEFERENCE

The key provision relating to public authority compatibility in the UK Human Rights Act is section 6, which provides that (subject to override by primary legislation) it is unlawful for a public authority to act in a way which is incompatible with the rights and freedoms protected by the European Convention on Human Rights. By virtue of the Convention itself (as interpreted by the Strasbourg Court) this obligation of compatibility corresponds, in the case of many (but not all) rights, to an obligation on public authorities not to place disproportionate limits on protected rights.

As noted above, the preoccupation of this essay is with the approach taken by the courts to supervising this obligation of public authority compatibility and, in particular, with the role of outcome-focused versus process-focused inquiry in that assessment. As a preliminary matter, it may be helpful to clarify the concept of 'process' being invoked here. The contrast that we are concerned with is between an approach that involves independent outcome-focused judicial evaluation of the ultimate decision reached or action taken by a public authority, and an approach that, instead (or as well), involves judicial evaluation of the contemporaneous process of rationalising the decision engaged in at first instance by the administrative body. This concept of process is far broader than the traditional common-law ground of review for procedural fairness and overlaps more directly with common-law doctrines such as relevant/irrelevant considerations, retention and fettering of discretion, and the duty to supply adequate reasons.[3]

The starting point under the UK Human Rights Act is that the obligation of compatibility placed on public authorities themselves by section 6 is ordinarily one of result or outcome. But neither the language of section 6, nor the text of the European Convention, obviously dictate the proper role of the UK courts when reviewing the discharge of that obligation. Nor

[3] See T Hickman, *Public Law after the Human Rights Act* (Oxford, Hart Publishing, 2010) 224. Aileen Kavanagh has recently rejected a distinction between 'process' in this sense, and the 'substance' of a decision, but her analysis does not disturb the distinction between 'process' and 'outcome': A Kavanagh, 'Reasoning about Proportionality under the Human Rights Act 1998: Outcomes, Substance and Process' (2014) 130 *Law Quarterly Review* 235, 246–48.

does the fact that the courts are themselves public authorities, required to act compatibly with Convention rights—what acting 'compatibly' demands of the courts when reviewing the actions of first instance decision-makers depends not on the text but on the view that is taken of the relative powers and responsibilities of the different branches of government within the UK constitution.

Nevertheless, as is well known, in the leading UK decision of *R (Begum) v Denbigh High School Governors*, the House of Lords held that the ultimate question for the courts when supervising the discharge of the section 6 obligation is one of result. The question for the court is not whether the public authority relied on a defective process of reasoning, but whether the actions of the public authority were (substantively) incompatible with Convention rights.[4] In so finding, their Lordships reversed the decision of the Court of Appeal, which had focused on procedural inadequacies in the defendants' decision-making processes and had criticised the defendants (the head teacher and board of governors of a high school) for failing to engage in a structured proportionality assessment.[5]

The House of Lords and, more recently, the Supreme Court have affirmed the *Denbigh High* approach on a number of subsequent occasions.[6] Through this line of cases, the UK comes closer than any other jurisdiction in this survey to eliminating process-based considerations from the judicial assessment of public authority compatibility with human rights. Nevertheless, it does not exclude them entirely. It is well established that, in considering whether or not a public authority has met its obligations under section 6, UK courts may accord a degree of weight or latitude to the judgement of the primary decision-maker.[7] The extent of that latitude varies with context, and the process followed by the public authority is clearly relevant to that contextual assessment. So, in *Denbigh High* itself, Lord Hoffmann accepted that 'the way in which the [decision-maker] approached the problem may help to persuade a judge that its answer fell within the area of judgment accorded

[4] *R (Begum) v Denbigh High School Governors* [2006] UKHL 15, [2007] 1 AC 100, [29–31] (Lord Bingham), [68] (Lord Hoffmann).

[5] *R (SB) v Denbigh High School* [2005] EWCA Civ 199, [2005] 1 WLR 3372, [75–78] (Brooke LJ), [92] (Scott Baker LJ).

[6] Eg *Belfast City Council v Miss Behavin' Ltd* [2007] UKHL 19, [2007] 1 WLR 1420; *In the matter of B (a Child)* [2013] UKSC 33, [2013] 1 WLR 1911, [84] (Lord Neuberger) (though a majority of three distinguished the situation where the first instance decision-maker is a court).

[7] Eg *R v Director of Public Prosecutions, ex p Kebilene* [2000] 2 AC 326, 381 (Lord Hope); *Secretary of State for the Home Department v Rehman* [2001] UKHL 47, [2003] 1 AC 153, [31] (Lord Steyn); *Huang v Secretary of State for the Home Department* [2007] UKHL 11, [2007] 2 AC 167, [16].

to it by the law'.[8] And subsequently, in *Belfast City Council v Miss Behavin' Ltd*, Lord Rodger (affirming the *Denbigh High* approach) noted that:[9]

> [W]here the public authority has carefully weighed the various competing considerations and concluded that interference with a Convention right is justified, a court will attribute due weight to that conclusion in deciding whether the action in question was proportionate and lawful.

The ratio of *Denbigh High* is thus that a failure of process or reasoning does not provide an *independent* basis for concluding that a public authority's actions are incompatible with human rights. The quality of the decision-making process may, however, be relevant to the adjectival question of how much weight or latitude to accord to the judgement of the public authority when making that ultimate assessment.

Their Lordships rationalised their decision to reject a more central role for process-based inquiry in part on the basis of text and precedent.[10] But of particular interest for this essay are the broader policy reasons underlying the decision. Their Lordships drew in particular on Thomas Poole's searing critique of the Court of Appeal's decision in *Denbigh High*.[11] To recapitulate, the Court of Appeal had criticised the head teacher and board of governors for failing to engage in their own assessment of the proportionality of their intended actions. In disapproving that approach, Poole argued that proportionality is a legal test, developed in the specific context of adjudication and without any obvious relevance outside the context of judicial decision-making. There are, he said, 'obvious dangers in assuming that such a test can be translated easily into the "crowded universe" of public administration, where decision-makers work in a variety of contexts and decision-making settings and where there are various time and resource constraints'.[12] The Court of Appeal's insistence that public authorities themselves apply the proportionality test was 'a recipe for judicialisation on an unprecedented scale'[13] which threatened to make 'a fetish of procedure'[14] and to 'impose a stifling culture of formalism on public administrators that is quite at odds with the substantive objectives of the Act itself'.[15]

[8] *Denbigh High* (n 4) [68] (Lord Hoffmann); see also [31] (Lord Bingham).

[9] *Miss Behavin'* (n 6) [26] (Lord Rodger); see also [91] (Lord Neuberger).

[10] *Denbigh High* (n 4) [29–30] (Lord Bingham), [68] (Lord Hoffmann).

[11] T Poole, 'Of Headscarves and Heresies: The *Denbigh High School* Case and Public Authority Decision-Making under the Human Rights Act' [2005] *Public Law* 685, cited in *Denbigh High* (n 4) [31] (Lord Bingham). See also *Miss Behavin'* (n 6) [13] (Lord Hoffmann), [28] (Lord Rodger), [92] (Lord Neuberger).

[12] Poole (n 11) 692, citing DJ Galligan, *Due Process and Fair Procedures: A Study of Administrative Procedures* (Oxford, Oxford University Press, 1996) 346–47.

[13] Poole (n 11) 698.

[14] Ibid, 691.

[15] Ibid, 695. See also T Poole, 'Between the Devil and the Deep Blue Sea: Administrative Law in an Age of Rights' in L Pearson, C Harlow and M Taggart (eds), *Administrative Law in a Changing State: Essays in Honour of Mark Aronson* (Oxford, Hart Publishing, 2008) 40–41.

This concern about the juridification of administrative procedure is a weighty one, and underscores the important point that process-focused modes of review are not always less intrusive than results-focused ones—particularly when the inquiry amounts to a searching critique of a public authority's reasoning process.[16] It also underscores the diversity of contexts governed by section 6, and the difficulty in articulating process-based requirements that apply uniformly across all of them.

On the other hand, academic critiques of the *Denbigh High* approach also disclose a set of competing policy concerns that may arise from the marginalisation of process-based inquiry.[17] For the purposes of this essay, I wish to highlight four.

The first is that a judicial focus on outcomes rather than process may do little to advance the project of developing a 'human rights culture' in government. Some commentators argue, to the contrary, that by bringing process-based considerations into the calculation of deference, the *Denbigh High* approach offers an incentive (albeit an indirect one) to public authorities to institute robust decision-making processes.[18] However, others argue that this incentive is weak or even absent.[19] Further, on the *Denbigh High* approach, public authorities receive no direct guidance from the courts as to *how* to go about discharging their obligations under section 6. It is for public authorities themselves to translate the proportionality test (an inapposite legal test) into workable processes and procedures that will discharge their statutory responsibilities at first instance. This is a compartmentalised view of the discharge of human rights obligations that is based in scepticism about the modelling effect of administrative law.[20] A more coordinated approach might see the courts as having a direct role in supporting the development of a 'human rights culture' by insisting that administrative decisions are made 'in the right way'.[21]

A second (and related) concern is that an exclusive focus on outcomes sits uncomfortably with the expectation sometimes expressed by advocates of proportionality review that the 'constitutionalisation' of administrative law (through, amongst other things, the impact of human rights-derived

[16] See Kavanagh (n 3) 247–48.

[17] Eg J Beatson and others, *Human Rights: Judicial Protection in the United Kingdom* (London, Sweet & Maxwell, 2008) [3-114–3-126]; Hickman (n 3) ch 8; J McLean, 'The Impact of the Bill of Rights on Administrative Law Revisited: Rights, Utility, and Administration' [2008] *New Zealand Law Review* 377; D Mead, 'Outcomes Aren't All: Defending Process-Based Review of Public Authority Decisions under the Human Rights Act' [2012] *Public Law* 61; H Wilberg, 'The Bill of Rights in Administrative Law Cases: Taking Stock and Suggesting some Reassessment' (2013) 25 *New Zealand Universities Law Review* 866.

[18] See P Sales, 'Law and Democracy in a Human Rights Framework' in D Feldman (ed), *Law in Politics, Politics in Law* (Oxford, Hart Publishing, 2013) 229–30.

[19] Hickman (n 3) 238–39; Mead (n 17) 68, 77.

[20] See, eg Poole (n 11) 693–94.

[21] Beatson and others (n 17) [3-122]. See also Hickman (n 3) 236–39; Mead (n 17) 76–79; Wilberg (n 17) 891.

methodologies) will foster a 'culture of justification' in which administrative decision-makers must give (good) reasons for their decisions.[22] This idea of a culture of justification is sometimes said to undermine any hard-and-fast process/substance distinction because it requires rights to be weighed 'against the reasons offered in defence of governmental action'.[23] If there is a 'culture of justification' at work in the *Denbigh High* paradigm, it is a somewhat insipid one that is focused on ex post facto justification in the context of a judicial challenge.

The third policy concern identified in the literature relates to the desirability of equipping the courts with flexibility to manage their delicate institutional relationship with the elected branches of government. As noted above, the *Denbigh High* approach enables the courts, in appropriate circumstances, to give credit for a good process by according significant weight to the judgement of the public authority. But this does not assist the courts in cases where the process followed was poor but where there are nevertheless strong institutional reasons to accord a high degree of deference to the primary decision-maker. In such cases, the *Denbigh High* approach leaves the court with two (arguably unsatisfactory) options. If (despite the poor process) the court accords a high degree of latitude to the judgement of the public authority, the Convention rights may '[fall] between two stools',[24] with neither the first instance decision-maker nor the court closely engaging with them. On the other hand, if the court refuses to accord significant weight to the judgement of the public authority, this may leave the court both institutionally exposed and, potentially, ill-equipped to make the decision before it. Arguably, therefore, it is desirable for courts to have available to them the option, in an appropriate case, of resting a decision solely on process considerations, and remitting the decision to the primary decision-maker for a fresh determination.[25]

The fourth policy concern that I wish to highlight relates to the bifurcated relationship between human rights law and administrative law reflected in the *Denbigh High* decision.[26] My interest here is not so much with bifurcation within the substantive ground of review (the issue that preoccupied Professor Taggart in his final piece),[27] but in the relationship between

[22] Eg E Mureinik, 'Beyond a Charter of Luxuries: Economic Rights in the Constitution' (1992) 8 *South African Journal of Human Rights* 464; D Dyzenhaus, M Hunt and M Taggart, 'The Principle of Legality in Administrative Law: Internationalisation as Constitutionalisation' (2001) 1 *Oxford University Commonwealth Law Journal* 5; J McLean, P Rishworth and M Taggart, 'The Impact of the Bill of Rights on Administrative Law' in Legal Research Foundation, *The New Zealand Bill of Rights Act 1990* (August 1992) 62.

[23] See Poole (n 15) 18.

[24] Beatson and others (n 17) [3–123].

[25] See, eg Beatson and others (n 17) [3–123]; R Gordon, 'Structures or Mantras? Some New Puzzles in HRA Decision-Making' [2006] *Judicial Review* 136, [13–16]; Hickman (n 3) 225–26, 241; Mead, (n 17) 79; Wilberg (n 17) 891.

[26] Eg *Denbigh High* (n 4) [68] (Lord Hoffmann).

[27] Taggart (n 1).

human rights law and administrative law more generally. Prior to the entry into force of human rights instruments such as the UK Human Rights Act, the courts throughout the Commonwealth were in the process of evolving an eclectic range of techniques (such as irrationality, the principle of legality, the requirement to take into account mandatory relevant considerations, and a right to reasons) in order to offer protection to human rights interests within the framework of administrative law. The concern expressed by some commentators is that a *Denbigh High*-type approach may arrest this development by artificially confining the impact of Convention rights to proportionality review. This, it is sometimes suggested, is undesirable both because it limits the type of challenges available to victims of Convention breaches, and also because it may stultify the organic development of administrative law.[28]

In sum, the question of how (if at all) to interweave process considerations into the judicial evaluation of public authority compatibility with statutory human rights requirements implicates a range of competing policy concerns, underlying which are more general intuitions about the proper distribution of responsibility between courts and administrative bodies, and the degree and type of judicial control that it is appropriate to project over administrative decision-making. The *Denbigh High* decision can be seen as one attempt to navigate through this complex terrain. It would be overly ambitious in a broad comparative piece of this kind to seek to add my voice to the extensive literature either censuring or defending the decision.[29] Instead, this essay seeks to de-naturalise the decision by locating it in a comparative context and by characterising it as one of a range of solutions developed by judges and legislators throughout the Commonwealth to address a common set of policy challenges.

At the same time, one should not underestimate the extent to which matters of local context and culture may have influenced and constrained (if not necessarily dictated) the unique solutions that have been adopted in each of the jurisdictions being considered.[30] In the case of the UK, a key factor is,

[28] Beatson and others (n 17) [3-122]; Hickman (n 3) 231; Mead (n 17) 72, 80. For similar concerns expressed in the Canadian context, see G Cartier, 'The *Baker* Effect: A New Interface between the Canadian Charter of Rights and Freedoms and Administrative Law—The Case of Discretion' in D Dyzenhaus (ed), *The Unity of Public Law* (Oxford, Hart Publishing, 2004) 75–77; JM Evans, 'The Principles of Fundamental Justice: The Constitution and the Common Law' (1991) 29 *Osgoode Hall Law Journal* 51, 73. Against, Varuhas (n 1), arguing for a conceptual separation between Convention law and administrative law.

[29] For three recent contributions, see TRS Allan, 'Judicial Deference and Judicial Review: Legal Doctrine and Legal Theory' (2011) 127 *Law Quarterly Review* 96, 105–107; Kavanagh (n 3); Mead, (n 17).

[30] See C Geiringer, 'Source of Resistance to Proportionality Review of Administrative Power under the New Zealand Bill of Rights Act' (2013) 11 *New Zealand Journal of Public and International Law* 123.

of course, the relationship between the UK Human Rights Act and the European Convention. Critics of the *Denbigh High* approach have argued, to the contrary, that a results-focused approach is dictated neither by the text of the European Convention nor the jurisprudence of the Strasbourg Court.[31] That is undoubtedly correct as far as it goes. Even accepting that the Strasbourg case law tends on the whole to focus on outcomes rather than process,[32] there is no reason in principle why this should flow through into decisions of the domestic courts. International treaties (the European Convention being no exception) impose obligations on the state as a unified entity, and so international institutions are relatively blind to internal constitutional divisions of responsibility, such as between the courts and the executive.[33] In contrast, the domestic courts must decide 'how the area of judgment allowed [to the state by the Strasbourg Court] should be distributed between the legislative, executive and judicial branches of government'.[34] For that reason, as Thomas Poole has put it, tethering the analysis of the UK courts to Strasbourg jurisprudence is 'rather like tying the peso to the dollar'.[35]

But even accepting that this is so, the relationship between the UK Human Rights Act and the European Convention has obvious explanatory power. First, the fact that the protected rights are sourced directly in an international treaty rather than a domestic statute or constitution may mean that the fourth policy concern articulated above—about promoting unity and avoiding compartmentalisation in public law—has rather less salience in the UK than in some other jurisdictions (or at least it may provide support for the contrary argument).[36] Secondly, the key object of the UK legislation—to 'bring rights home' from Strasbourg by providing domestic judicial remedies for breaches of the Convention—undoubtedly

[31] Eg Beatson and others (n 17) [3-125]; Gordon (n 25); Hickman (n 4) 243–44; Mead (n 17) 69–70.

[32] Against, see the discussions of the Strasbourg case law in the authorities listed at n 31.

[33] J McLean, 'Problems of Translation—The State in Domestic and International Public Law and Beyond' in H Charlesworth and others (eds), *The Fluid State: International Law and National Legal Systems* (Sydney, Federation Press, 2005) 210. See also *R (S and KF) v Secretary of State for Justice* [2012] EWHC 1810 (Admin) [72–73], pointing out that the results-oriented tradition of proportionality analysis at Strasbourg is in part a product of the fact that Convention rights were applied to the UK for decades before the UK Human Rights Act came into effect, in circumstances in which public authorities were not themselves addressing the rights in any kind of structured way.

[34] *Denbigh High* (n 4) [63] (Lord Hoffmann). See also Beatson and others (n 17) [3-115]; *R (ProLife Alliance) v BBC* [2003] UKHL 23, [2004] 1 AC 185, [75–76] (Lord Hoffmann).

[35] Poole (n 15) 41.

[36] See Varuhas (n 1). But see Hickman (n 3) 230–31, usefully contrasting two different ways of characterising the UK Human Rights Act: as a source of domestic rights or as a remedy for breach of Convention law. For recent UK case law evincing a desire for greater integration of Convention and administrative law, see *Osborn v Parole Board* [2013] UKSC 61, [2013] 3 WLR 1020; *Kennedy v The Charity Commission* [2014] UKSC 20, [2014] 2 WLR 808.

creates an incentive on the UK courts to develop judicial solutions that mirror those available at Strasbourg. Tying the peso to the dollar may not be required as a matter of Convention law, but it is nevertheless the most efficient method for risk-averse judges to pre-empt recourse by residents of the UK to the right of individual petition to Strasbourg.

These factors have undoubtedly influenced (though not dictated) the approach of the UK courts. But for that reason, even supporters of the *Denbigh High* approach would acknowledge that the rule is likely to come under pressure at least to the extent that the Strasbourg Court itself imposes process-based obligations on public authorities in some circumstances.[37] More generally, both supporters and detractors of the decision agree on the need for flexibility in formulating approaches to review of public authority compatibility that are sensitive to context. For critics of the *Denbigh High* decision, its real failing is its attempt to articulate a one-size-fits-all approach. Thus, Tom Hickman suggests:[38]

> The considerations to which decision-makers would have to advert, the degree of investigation and inquiry that they ought to undertake, and the extent to which they ought to address Convention rights and legal tests explicitly (if at all) would depend on the type of decision and the context in which it was taken. What would be required of a school would not be the same as what would be required of a planning committee, and neither could be equated with decision-making by immigration officials. [This] ... is how administrative law has always worked.

Along similar lines, one of the key reasons Aileen Kavanagh is inclined to be *less* critical of the decision is because she sees it as the product of a particular context, and as a reaction to the peculiarly formalistic approach imposed on the head teacher and school board by the Court of Appeal in the case below. She does not think we should read into it a blanket exclusion of process considerations that is inattentive to particular decision-making contexts.[39]

The area of apparent common ground, therefore, is the need to move beyond the parameters of *Denbigh High* itself and to develop context-specific approaches that acknowledge the myriad of situations in which public authority decision-making occurs.[40]

[37] See, eg Sales (n 18) 232.

[38] Hickman (n 3) 247.

[39] Kavanagh (n 3) 243–45, 255–56. See also T Poole, 'The Reformation of English Administrative Law' (2009) 68 *Cambridge Law Journal* 142, 150–51.

[40] This requires an extension of the project of 'institutional sensitivity' usefully advanced by Alan Brady in his recent monograph on deference and proportionality under the UK Human Rights Act: ADP Brady, *Proportionality and Deference under the UK Human Rights Act: An Institutionally Sensitive Approach* (Cambridge, Cambridge University Press, 2012).

III. THE STATE OF VICTORIA: BUILDING A HUMAN RIGHTS CULTURE

Although Australia has not adopted a federal bill of rights, two Australian jurisdictions—Victoria and the Australian Capital Territory—have enacted bills of rights at the local level. As these two instruments are structurally similar, discussion here will focus on Victoria, which is the larger of the two jurisdictions.

Like the UK Human Rights Act, the Charter of Human Rights and Responsibilities Act 2006 (Vic) ('Victorian Charter') is a statutory bill of rights which seeks to enhance the role of the courts and other constitutional actors in human rights protection while preserving the ultimate sovereignty of Parliament. The UK instrument was a significant influence on the drafting of the Victorian Charter,[41] and the two instruments share a number of operational features. For the purposes of the present discussion, the most relevant point of similarity is that section 38(1) of the Victorian Charter draws directly on section 6 of the UK Human Rights Act in providing that it is 'unlawful' for a public authority to 'act in a way that is incompatible with a [Charter] right'.[42]

There are two respects, however, in which the Victorian Charter departs self-consciously from the UK model in the obligations that it imposes on public authorities. Each of these departures can be seen, at least in part, as a response to the process/substance conundrum explored above.

The first departure concerns the wording of section 7(2) of the Charter—the limitation clause. Unlike the European Convention (which incorporates relevant limits on rights into the scope of individual guarantees), the Victorian Charter contains a freestanding clause, specifying in general terms the circumstances in which Charter rights can be limited. Section 7(2) begins by stipulating that the rights set out in the Charter 'may be subject under law only to such reasonable limits as can be demonstrably justified in a free and democratic society based on human dignity, equality and freedom'. This wording evokes section 1 of the Canadian Charter of Rights and Freedoms ('Canadian Charter')—a provision that itself drew on limiting language found in individual guarantees in the European Convention. As is well known, both the Canadian and European formulae have been held to generate a proportionality inquiry, in which the court is directed to assess the offending measure against four criteria (sometimes paraphrased in the literature as proper purpose, suitability, necessity and overall proportionality), with a failure to meet any one of these criteria rendering the measure incompatible.[43]

[41] See the numerous references to the UK experience in Human Rights Consultation Committee, *Rights, Responsibilities and Respect: The Report of the Human Rights Consultation Committee* (2005).

[42] Ibid, 63.

[43] Eg *R v Oakes* [1986] 1 SCR 103; *Huang* (n 7) [19].

Significantly, though, section 7(2) of the Victorian Charter invites a somewhat different approach. That is because it goes on to state an open-ended list of 'factors' that must be 'taken into account' in deciding whether a limit is demonstrably justified. Although the list of factors appears to invite a similar set of inquiries to those generated by the Canadian/European test,[44] it incorporates these inquiries into an overarching and open-ended weighing process rather than treating them as a series of knockout blows. Thus, case law on section 36 of the South African bill of rights[45] (on which section 7(2) of the Victorian Charter was modelled) stresses that section 36 necessitates an 'overall assessment' in which 'the Court must engage in a balancing exercise and arrive at a global judgment on proportionality and not adhere mechanically to a sequential check-list'.[46] In this way, the Victorian/South African formulation also appears to eliminate the need for the complex exercises in line drawing (such as into what precisely qualifies as a less restrictive means for the purposes of the necessity test) that have sometimes beset the proportionality literature.[47]

It is instructive to examine the reason given in the Report of the Victorian Human Rights Consultation Committee (which gave rise to the Charter initiative) for proposing to follow the South African precedent. The Committee noted that they had received feedback from New Zealand practitioners that the New Zealand limitation clause (which is modelled on the Canadian one) 'can be difficult to interpret and apply on a day-to-day basis'.[48] The Committee went on to say that it wanted 'to make sure that the Charter, *which will more often be interpreted within government than by the courts*, is as easy as possible to apply'.[49] In short, then, the members of the Victorian Consultation Committee conceived of the section 7(2) criteria as factors that would directly guide administrative decision-making, and recommended for that reason that the South African model be preferred.

The second legislative response to the process/substance conundrum is found in section 38(1) itself. The injunction to act 'compatibly' with human rights is only one prong of a dual obligation imposed on public authorities

[44] The factors expressly listed in s 7(2) are: the nature of the right; the importance of the purpose of the limitation; the nature and extent of the limitation; the relationship between the limitation and its purpose; and any less restrictive means reasonably available to achieve the purpose the limitation seeks to achieve.

[45] Constitution of the Republic of South Africa Act 1996, ch 2.

[46] *S v Manamela* 2000 (5) BCLR 491, [32] (SACC).

[47] See, eg A Barak, *Proportionality: Constitutional Rights and their Limitations* (Cambridge, Cambridge University Press, 2012) ch 11.

[48] Human Rights Consultation Committee (n 41) 47.

[49] Ibid (emphasis added). See also G Williams, 'The Victorian Charter of Human Rights and Responsibilities: Origins and Scope' (2006) 30 *Melbourne University Law Review* 880, 898–99.

by section 38(1). The section goes on to specify that it is also 'unlawful' for a public authority 'in making a decision, to *fail to give proper consideration* to a relevant human right'.[50] When enacted, this 'proper consideration' requirement was unique amongst the Commonwealth human rights instruments.[51]

The novel nature of the section 38(1) obligation of 'proper consideration', and the reasons for its inclusion, were addressed only obliquely in the Report of the Victorian Consultation Committee. One possible (though unstated) motivation for its inclusion may relate to uncertainty as to the relief that would be available for a failure by a public authority to act compatibly with a Charter right. The Victorian Government's *Statement of Intent* (which functioned as the terms of reference for the Consultation Committee) stated that 'the Government does not wish to create new individual causes of action based on human rights breaches'.[52] Against that background, a draft remedies provision proposed by the Consultation Committee affirmed the availability of judicial review to the extent that it 'would have been available had the act or decision been unlawful apart from the Charter'.[53] What this would mean for judicial review remedies under the Charter was not, however, self-evident. One difficulty stemmed from the fact that in Australia, a number of administrative law remedies only lie when there has been a 'jurisdictional' error, and it was unclear whether the Australian courts would ultimately regard section 38(1) unlawfulness as going to 'jurisdiction'. This might (potentially) be more likely to the extent the obligation was framed as one to *consider* human rights, as Australian administrative law already recognised a failure to consider mandatory relevant considerations as a form of jurisdictional error.[54]

Whether or not this provided one motivation for the inclusion of the 'proper consideration' requirement, an additional source of motivation can be found in the corollary of the Victorian Government's reticence in respect of the provision of judicial remedies, which was its enthusiastic embrace of the notion that a charter would foster the development of a 'human rights culture' in government decision-making. The Government's

[50] Emphasis added.

[51] A similar provision has since been added to the Australian Capital Territory's legislation: Human Rights Act 2004 (ACT), s 40B, introduced by the Human Rights Amendment Act 2008 (ACT).

[52] Department of Justice (Vic), *Human Rights in Victoria: Statement of Intent* (2005), appended to Human Rights Consultation Committee (n 41) 161, 163.

[53] Draft Charter of Human Rights and Responsibilities, cl 40, appended to Human Rights Consultation Committee (n 41). As ultimately adopted, s 39 of the Charter is even more elliptical. It provides: 'If, otherwise than because of this Charter, a person may seek any relief or remedy in respect of an act or decision of a public authority on the ground that the act or decision was unlawful, that person may seek that relief or remedy on a ground of unlawfulness arising because of this Charter.'

[54] See *Minister for Aboriginal Affairs v Peko-Wallsend Ltd* [1986] HCA 40, (1986) 162 CLR 24.

Statement of Intent announced a focus 'on prevention and dispute mediation rather than litigation by ensuring that [the Government's] policies and programmes reflect good human rights practice and are therefore not likely to be challenged as breaching human rights standards'. Though accepting that the courts had a role to play, the Government stressed that its approach was 'to address human rights issues through mechanisms that promote dialogue, education, discussion and good practice rather than litigation'.[55] This emphasis on the development of a human rights culture was further reflected throughout the Consultation Committee's report,[56] in the structure of the instrument,[57] and in broader changes made to law and practice in conjunction with the Charter.[58]

A useful comparison might be drawn in this regard with the origins of the UK Human Rights Act. As noted above, it was born out of a desire to 'bring rights home', that is, to provide domestic judicial remedies for human rights breach and thus pre-empt recourse to Strasbourg. This focus on the provision of judicial remedies pervaded the White Paper that accompanied the UK legislation. Even the chapter on public authority obligation focused on the role of the courts in remedying breaches rather than on the role of public authorities in discharging the obligation at first instance.[59]

The word 'culture' does not appear in the UK White Paper. It appears over 50 times in the report of the Victorian Consultation Committee. An overriding focus in the report was on improving the quality of government decision-making and embedding human considerations into the day-to-day work of government.[60] This was to be achieved not just through the imposition and enforcement of obligations on public authorities, but through a programme of training and education spearheaded by specialist agencies—a dedicated human rights unit in the Department of Justice and a revamped Equal Opportunity and Human Rights Commission with specific oversight and education functions.[61]

None of this is to oversimplify the complex motivations that accompanied the conception of both instruments, nor to downplay the important work that was done in the UK in association with the enactment of the

[55] *Statement of Intent* (n 52) 162.

[56] Especially ch 5.

[57] Eg Charter of Human Rights and Responsibilities Act 2006 (Vic), pt 4, extending the responsibilities of the Victorian Equal Opportunity and Human Rights Commission.

[58] Eg the Charter also added a new 'public sector value' to the Public Administration Act 2004 (Vic), s 7(1)(g), creating non-enforceable requirements for all public sector employees to provide advice and make decisions consistently with human rights and to actively implement and promote human rights.

[59] Secretary of State for the Home Department, *Rights Brought Home: The Human Rights Bill* (1997) especially ch 2.

[60] Eg Human Rights Consultation Committee (n 41) iii, 10–11, 62–63 and 108–10.

[61] Ibid, 66–67, 92, 97–98 and 101–10.

UK Human Rights Act to transform government practice.[62] The point is simply that the notion of building a human rights culture in government was central to the entire conception of the Victorian Charter in the same way that 'bringing rights home' was central to the conception of the UK Human Rights Act.

Against that background, it is perhaps not surprising that the process/substance dichotomy reflected in cases such as *Denbigh High* would be rejected by the drafters of the Victorian Charter. In discussing the scope of the duties that should be placed on public authorities, the Consultation Committee noted strong support in the submissions it had received for 'human rights standards being incorporated into the development and delivery of government policy' and also for 'an obligation to be placed on all public authorities, including government departments, agencies and enterprises, to consider the Charter generally in their practices and procedures'.[63] Ultimately, the Committee considered that 'the first step in cultivating a culture of human rights in government is to make human rights one of the considerations that officials must consider in their day to day decision making'.[64]

In sum, then, the first of the four policy considerations identified above—the concern about the role of human rights obligations in promoting the development of a human rights culture in government—appears to have had special salience in the Victorian context. For that reason, amongst others, the drafters of the Victorian Charter explicitly rejected a model of public authority liability that was limited to obligations of result rather than process. They did this most explicitly by twinning a result-based obligation on public authorities to act 'compatibly' with human rights with a process-based obligation to give 'proper consideration' to human rights. But additionally, they sought to structure the obligation of compatibly in a way that would speak directly to public authorities (by adopting the South African, rather than the Canadian, formulation of reasonable limits).

There is still only limited case law on section 38(1) of the Charter from which to assess how this regime of public authority obligation is working in practice.[65] Two judgments of the Supreme Court of Victoria are, however,

[62] See, eg Hickman (n 3) 23–24; Mead (n 17) 77–78.

[63] Human Rights Consultation Committee (n 41) 62.

[64] Ibid, 124. See also ibid, 63, noting the desirability of being 'as explicit as possible regarding the duties imposed on public authorities', so as to 'provide clear direction to public authorities, assist senior public servants in their efforts to promote a human rights culture within their departments and give life to human rights standards for everyone engaged in public service in Victoria'.

[65] Reasons for this probably include the broad merits jurisdiction of the Victorian Civil and Administrative Tribunal, the comparatively narrow definition of 'public authority' in s 4(1)(j) of the Victorian Charter (which excludes courts and tribunals except when they are acting in an administrative capacity), and the narrow and opaque remedies provision (s 39). On the latter, see J Gans, 'The Charter's Irremediable Remedies Provision' (2009) 33 *Melbourne University*

worthy of mention. *PJB v Melbourne Health* concerned the 'compatibility' prong of the section 38(1) obligation. Bell J held that the Victorian Civil and Administrative Tribunal had breached its section 38(1) duty to act compatibly with Charter rights in appointing an administrator to take over the financial affairs of a psychiatrically disabled man because, in the Court's assessment, the resulting interference with the applicant's Charter rights was disproportionate.[66]

Bell J considered that the 'compatibility' limb of section 38(1) of the Charter, read together with section 7(2), imposed an obligation on public authorities not to limit Charter rights disproportionality. His Honour drew heavily on the UK case law, including *Denbigh High*, in holding that this requirement of proportionality was an obligation of result on which the court must form 'an independent and objective judgment', although the quality of the decision-making process might affect the degree of weight accorded to the reasoning of the primary decision-maker.[67]

It is perhaps worth noting in passing that the nexus identified by Bell J between section 38(1) incompatibility and section 7(2) proportionality is potentially unstable. That is because early case law on section 32(1) of the Victorian Charter (the duty to interpret legislation 'compatibly' with human rights) has raised (but not yet resolved) the possibility that 'compatibility' with Charter rights may mean compatibility with the rights in their undiluted or prima facie form (that is, before section 7(2) has been brought into play).[68] However, it is hard to see how section 38(1) could function effectively if *not* given content by section 7(2) and, for that reason (amongst others), I put the debate aside for the purposes of the present discussion.[69]

The second case, *Castles v Secretary to the Department of Justice*, concerned a decision to refuse the plaintiff, a prisoner, necessary approvals to travel from prison to receive *in vitro* fertilisation treatment.[70] Emerton J held that the Secretary of Justice's refusal amounted to a denial of the plaintiff's Charter right to be treated with dignity and humanity.[71] She held that in the particular circumstances (and using the Charter as one of

Law Review 105; M Groves, 'Tribunals, Judicial Review and the Victorian Charter' (2012) 23 *Public Law Review* 3; *Director of Housing v Sudi* [2011] VSCA 266, 33 VR 559, [214] (Weinberg JA).

[66] *PJB v Melbourne Health* [2011] VSC 327. The Tribunal was acting in an administrative capacity and was therefore a 'public authority' for the relevant purposes.

[67] Ibid, [310], [312].

[68] See *R v Momcilovic* [2010] VSCA 50, 25 VR 436; *Momcilović v The Queen* [2011] HCA 34, (2011) 245 CLR 1.

[69] A nexus between sections 38(1) and 7(2) was also patently intended by those involved in drafting the instrument: see Geiringer (n 30) 145–46.

[70] *Castles v Secretary of the Department of Justice* [2010] VSC 310, [2010] 28 VR 141.

[71] Victorian Charter, s 22(1).

the available tools of statutory interpretation), the decision not to facilitate Ms Castles' IVF treatment breached a statutory duty to provide access to 'reasonable medical care and treatment necessary for the preservation of health'.[72]

No claim was pursued in *Castles* of breach of the section 38(1) duty to act 'compatibly' with Charter rights but the plaintiff did allege breach of the duty to give the Charter rights 'proper consideration'. In rejecting this part of the claim, Emerton J elucidated the meaning of 'proper consideration' in the following manner:[73]

> The Charter is intended to apply to the plethora of decisions made by public authorities of all kinds. The consideration of human rights is intended to become part of decision-making processes at all levels of government. It is therefore intended to become a 'common or garden' activity for persons working in the public sector, both senior and junior. In these circumstances, proper consideration of human rights should not be a sophisticated legal exercise. Proper consideration need not involve formally identifying the 'correct' rights or explaining their content by reference to legal principles or jurisprudence. Rather, proper consideration will involve understanding in general terms which of the rights of the person affected by the decision may be relevant and whether, and if so how, those rights will be interfered with by the decision that is made. As part of the exercise of justification, proper consideration will involve balancing competing private and public interests. There is no formula for such an exercise, and it should not be scrutinised over-zealously by the courts.

Justice Emerton accepted that it would be insufficient merely to 'invoke the Charter like a mantra', but held that it would be:[74]

> [S]ufficient in most circumstances that there is some evidence that shows the decision-maker seriously turned his or her mind to the possible impact of the decision on a person's human rights and the implications thereof for the affected person, and that the countervailing interests or obligations were identified.

In the context of the particular claim, Emerton J considered it sufficient that the Secretary of Justice had received briefings from officials, including legal advice on the human rights issues (though the content of the legal advice had been redacted at trial) and that the Secretary had provided brief written reasons to the plaintiff for her decision to refuse the necessary permits in which she asserted (without elucidating) that she had considered and weighed the Charter rights.[75]

What is particularly notable about Emerton J's attempt to give content to the 'proper consideration' requirement is the (presumably deliberate)

[72] Corrections Act 1986 (Vic), s 47(1)(f).
[73] *Castles* (n 70) [185].
[74] Ibid, [186].
[75] Ibid, [187].

absence of any reference to the section 7(2) proportionality criteria. In rejecting an approach to 'proper consideration' that involves formalistic application of the section 7(2) factors, Emerton J's decision in *Castles* is highly attentive to the dangers of undue formalism articulated by Thomas Poole and others in the UK context—and rightly so. Her minimalist approach to the requirements of 'proper consideration' may also have the unstated advantage of maximising the likelihood of section 38(1) unlawfulness ultimately being recognised as a form of jurisdictional error.[76]

It is worth reflecting, though, on whether it can really have been the drafters' intention to divorce the content of the 'proper consideration' requirement so completely from the 'compatibility' obligation. The essence of the compatibility/proportionality requirement is not just that Charter rights must be considered, but that public authorities must give effect to them in the absence of an overriding policy objective to the contrary that cannot be achieved by any other means. Might the specific legislative meaning of 'proper' consideration not derive at least *some* colour from that context? For example, might it require, at least in some cases, some appreciation from the decision-maker of the priority that the right deserves and of the need for weighty considerations to overcome it; or some attempt, where appropriate, to evaluate other potential policy solutions?

It is worth recalling in this respect the express efforts (discussed above) to draft section 7(2) in language that could be utilised directly by administrative decision-makers. Further, since the Charter was enacted, a number of public authorities have indeed imbedded some proportionality-derived concepts (such as minimal impairment) into their policy and delivery frameworks, suggesting that the section 7(2) factors have been of utility to public authorities in at least some policy settings.[77] The *Castles* approach to 'proper consideration' is somewhat at odds with these developments.

Importantly, though, what amounts to 'proper' consideration of a Charter right must surely vary with context. In some situations, the 'proper' level of consideration would surely be none at all—for example, because no rights are adequately implicated, because the inconsistency with Charter rights was not (and could not have been) apparent to the public authority,[78] or because the human rights considerations had been addressed at the prior stage of setting a rule and, in the particular circumstances, nothing is to be achieved by further individualised consideration. On the other hand, one

[76] See the discussion at n 54 and associated text. The Supreme Court has now held that section 38(1) unlawfulness is not a form of jurisdictional error, and the decision is under appeal: *Bare v Small* [2013] VSC 129, *Bare v Small* [2013] VSCA 204.

[77] See, eg Victorian Equal Opportunity and Human Rights Commission, *Talking Rights: Compilation Report* (May 2011). But see Scrutiny of Acts and Regulations Committee, *Review of the Charter of Human Rights and Responsibiliteis Act 2006* (2011), recommendation 13 and [400–03], complaining about the 'inaccessibility' of s 7(2) and calling for its reform.

[78] See *R v Forsyth* [2013] ACTSC 179 [198].

might question whether the minimal process requirements articulated by Emerton J are sufficient to capture the level and type of consideration that one might expect from a more expert and specialised decision-maker, or where very significant rights are at stake. The challenge for the Victorian courts, just as in the UK, is to move beyond a one-size-fits-all approach and to articulate context-specific guidance that maps out the institutional factors than can affect the type and level of human rights consideration that is appropriate in different decision-making contexts.

As neither Bell nor Emerton JJ had before them both prongs of the section 38(1) obligation, a number of broader questions remain unanswered as to the relationship between them. For example, what remedies should attach if a decision-maker has not given human rights 'proper consideration' but has reached a result which the court deems to be substantively 'compatible'? At first glance, to send the decision back for reconsideration in such circumstances would seem to be futile. On the other hand, what if a conclusion of results-based 'compatibility' could be reached only after a difficult exercise in line-drawing and/or after attaching a degree of weight to the assessment of the primary decision-maker? As suggested above, might it not sometimes be better in such a case for a court to leave the question of compatibility unanswered and to provide the decision-maker with an opportunity to reconsider the matter adopting a proper process?

A number of aspects of the relationship between 'compatibility' and 'proper consideration' thus remain uncertain—as does the manner in which these concepts intersect with other aspects of Australia's distinctive constitutional and administrative law framework.[79] What is clear, though, is that the Victorian 'proper consideration' obligation is an additional and independent requirement which does not displace the results-based assessment of 'compatibility' with human rights.[80] In other words, the Victorian response to the outcome/process conundrum posed by *Denbigh High* is to retain the result-based obligation and to supplement it with an autonomous process-based requirement. The Victorian approach thus operates on either side of the process/outcome boundary but the boundary itself remains intact. This provides an interesting point of contrast for the new Canadian approach which, instead, merges process and outcome considerations into a composite proportionality assessment.

[79] Eg, is the prescription of judicial abstinence made in the preceding paragraph even available in the Victorian context bearing in mind, on the one hand, Australian constitutional conceptions of the nature of judicial power and, on the other, ongoing uncertainty as to whether s 38(1) unlawfulness amounts to jurisdictional error?

[80] Bell J did suggest that there could never be a finding of 'proper' consideration if the substantive result reached was incompatible with the Charter: *PJB v Melbourne Health* (n 66) [312]. However, read in context and in the light of the *Castles* decision (which Bell J affirms), this observation was probably meant simply to underline the point that discharge of the obligation of 'proper consideration' does not amount to discharge of the companion requirement of 'compatibility'.

IV. CANADA: THE UNITY OF PUBLIC LAW

The Canadian Charter contains no direct textual equivalent to the Victorian/UK obligation of public authority 'compatibility' with (nor to the process-based Victorian requirement of 'proper consideration' of) human rights. Rather, the obligation on administrative officials derives from section 32 of the Canadian Charter, which states simply that the Charter 'applies' to the legislatures and governments of all the provinces and territories of Canada, as well as to the federal Parliament and government.

As noted above, the engine room of proportionality in the Canadian Charter is section 1, which stipulates that the Charter 'guarantees the rights and freedoms set out in it subject only to such reasonable limits prescribed by law as can be demonstrably justified in a free and democratic society'. Judicial consideration of section 1 has occurred primarily in the context of challenges to the constitutionality of legislation, and it is in that context that the Supreme Court of Canada developed and refined the well-known *Oakes* test.[81] According to that test, the party seeking to justify the intrusion on a Charter right must establish four criteria: that the objective underlying the offending measure is sufficiently important to justify overriding a constitutional right, that the measure is rationally connected to that objective, that the measure impairs the right as little as reasonably possible, and that there is overall proportionality between the beneficial and deleterious effects of the measure.[82]

The *Oakes* test thus demands a predominantly results-based inquiry into the consistency of legislation with Charter rights. The question for our purposes is whether this results-based approach also governs Charter review of administrative decision-making. In its 1989 decision in *Slaight Communications v Davidson*, the Supreme Court of Canada answered that question in the affirmative.[83] Lamer J (partly dissenting but reflecting the views of the majority on this point) took as his starting point the fact that, as the Charter has supreme law status, any legislation that is inconsistent with it is of no force or effect. Accordingly, he reasoned, an exercise of administrative discretion that is inconsistent with section 1 of the Canadian Charter is beyond power. The courts should therefore use the *Oakes* methodology to test whether exercises of administrative discretion are compatible with the Charter and, thus, lawful.[84]

[81] *Oakes* (n 43); as developed in later cases such as *RJR-MacDonald Inc v Attorney-General of Canada* [1995] 3 SCR 199.

[82] This is similar to recent articulations of proportionality in the UK context: see *Huang* (n 7) [19].

[83] *Slaight Communications v Davidson* [1989] 1 SCR 1038. See also *Ross v New Brunswick School District No 15* [1996] 1 SCR 825; *Multani v Commission scolaire Marguerite-Bourgeoys* 2006 SCC 6, [2006] 1 SCR 256.

[84] *Slaight Communications* (n 83) 1077–78 (Lamer J).

Though consistent with the *Denbigh High* approach, this line of reasoning proved unstable in the Canadian context. Not only was it applied inconsistently[85] but, when applied, it engendered both fierce academic critiques,[86] and strongly worded judicial dissents.[87] Ultimately, in 2012, the Supreme Court of Canada (in a unanimous decision) resiled from the approach—at least as far as Charter challenges to 'adjudicated administrative decisions' are concerned. In *Doré v Barreau du Québec*, the Court formulated an alternative approach that, it asserted, sits more squarely within the mainstream framework of Canadian administrative law.[88] According to that framework, which sets Canadian administrative law somewhat apart from other common-law jurisdictions, the first task for a reviewing court is to determine which of the two standards of review—correctness or reasonableness—is appropriate to apply to the particular decision. This is, in effect, an inquiry into how much deference is due to the body being reviewed, bearing in mind matters such as the nature of the decision and the expertise of the administrative body.[89] The (more deferential) reasonableness standard operates as the default standard in the vast majority of cases, applying not just to judicial review of the merits of the decision but, as well, to questions of law within the specialised expertise of the decision-maker.

In *Doré*, the Supreme Court held that this same framework should apply in Charter cases involving adjudicated administrative decisions.[90] It also said that, even in Charter cases, the more deferential reasonableness standard would generally be the appropriate one. That is because: 'Even where *Charter* values are involved, the administrative decision-maker will generally be in the best position to consider the impact of the relevant *Charter* values *on the specific facts of the case*.'[91] This means that, in the majority of cases, the question for the reviewing court is now not whether the *Oakes* test applies but whether the decision was a reasonable one in the circumstances. What precisely that reasonableness inquiry might require is explored further below.

[85] Eg *Lake v Canada (Minister of Justice)* [2008] 1 SCR 761. For a useful discussion on this point, see D Mullan, 'Section 7 and Administrative Law Deference—No Room at the Inn?' (2006) 34 *Supreme Court Law Review* (2d) 227.

[86] Eg Cartier (n 28).

[87] Especially *Multani* (n 83).

[88] *Doré v Barreau du Québec* 2012 SCC 12, [2012] 1 SCR 395.

[89] *Dunsmuir v New Brunswick* 2008 SCC 9, [2008] 1 SCR 190, superseding the earlier framework, which utilised three standards of review—correctness, reasonableness *simpliciter* and patent unreasonableness.

[90] It is not yet clear whether the new approach will extend beyond 'adjudicated' administrative decisions.

[91] *Doré* (n 88) [54].

A number of questions remain outstanding as to the broader implications of the *Doré* decision.[92] For the specific purposes of this discussion, however, there are three aspects of the decision that I wish to highlight.

The first relates to the Canadian Supreme Court's motivations for abandoning the *Slaight Communications* approach to Charter review. It will be remembered that the policy concern that most directly drove the inclusion of an express process-based obligation in the Victorian Charter was the concern to provide clear standards of conduct for government officials and, thus, to foreground the role of the Charter in supporting the emergence of a human rights culture. As will be seen below, the *Doré* decision speaks implicitly to that issue too (by elaborating specific guidance on the process that should be followed by administrative decision-makers). But the policy concern that had special salience in the Canadian context was a different one: the concern about bifurcation of constitutional and administrative law.[93] Critics of *Slaight Communications* had expressed concern about the emergence of a two-track approach, in which Charter values were estranged from the evolution of mainstream administrative law.[94] They worried that this would freeze the natural evolution of the common law and that, as a result, 'a rich source of thought and experience about law and government will be overlooked or lost altogether, and will eventually atrophy'.[95]

The resonance of this argument needs to be understood by reference to modern developments in Canadian law, which had arguably opened the way for the assimilation of Charter principles into the mainstream body of administrative law.[96] At the time of *Slaight Communications*, the Canadian courts restricted the review of the exercise of discretion to something akin to *Wednesbury* unreasonableness. In 1999, in *Baker v Canada (Minister of Citizenship and Immigration)*, the Supreme Court moved instead to its present approach (albeit initially adopting three, rather than the current two, standards of review).[97] Despite being grounded in a policy of deference to administrative decision-makers, this 'standards of review' approach (or 'pragmatic and functional' approach, as it was initially called) also underlined the existence of judicially-enforced limits on administrative discretion.

[92] See M Walters, 'Respecting Deference as Respect: Rights, Reasonableness and Proportionality in Canadian Administrative Law' (ch 15 in this volume); D Mullan, 'Unresolved Issues on Standard of Review in Canadian Judicial Review of Administrative Action—the Top Fifteen!' (2013) 42 *The Advocates' Quarterly* 1.

[93] An additional concern for the *Doré* Court was the practical difficulty in applying the *Oakes* methodology to individualised administrative decision-making: *Doré* (n 88) [38–42].

[94] Eg Cartier (n 28) 75–77; Evans (n 28) 73 (advocating for a 'mixed approach' in which administrative law principles are consulted *prior* to consideration under the Charter framework); *Blencoe v British Columbia (Human Rights Commission)* [2000] 2 SCR 307, [189] (LeBel J). See, also, the discussion in Walters (n 92).

[95] Evans (n 28) 73.

[96] For fuller discussion of this point, see Cartier (n 28); Geiringer, 'Sources of Resistance to Proportionality Review' (n 30); Walters (n 92).

[97] *Baker v Canada (Minister of Citizenship and Immigration)* [1999] 2 SCR 817.

Importantly for our purposes, the *Baker* Court stressed that the sources of those limits included 'the fundamental values of Canadian society, and the principles of the *Charter*'.[98] Relevantly, *Baker* also introduced a general obligation on public authorities to give reasons when important individual interests are at stake. It was this new values-based (and justification-based) paradigm that critics of *Slaight Communications* suggested had opened up possibilities for the Charter to 'nurture' administrative law rather than develop down a separate track through the application of *Oakes*-style proportionality review.[99]

This line of reasoning was embraced by the Supreme Court of Canada in *Doré*.[100] The Court contrasted 'the values-based approach in *Baker*' with 'the more formalistic template in *Slaight*'[101] and embraced the former as a 'richer conception of administrative law, under which discretion is exercised "in light of constitutional guarantees and the values they reflect"'.[102]

The second aspect of *Doré* that I wish to highlight is the competing readings of the decision that are available in relation to the role of section 1 of the Charter (the reasonable limitations clause) in cases involving administrative discretion. The first is that, although Charter 'values' (as opposed, perhaps, to concrete rights) must inform administrative discretion, section 1 itself is inapplicable. This reading draws on the use throughout the *Doré* decision of the indeterminate phrase 'Charter values'.[103] It also draws on the suggestion made by a number of critics of *Slaight Communications* that an exercise of discretion is not 'prescribed by law' in the sense that term is deployed in section 1 of the Charter.[104] That argument is only touched on in passing (though with apparent approval) in *Doré* itself.[105] However, Abella J, who delivered the judgment of the Court, was party to an earlier joint concurring judgment in *Multani v Commission scolaire Marguerite-Bourgeoys*, in which the argument was embraced with enthusiasm.[106]

I confess to finding this 'prescribed by law' argument puzzling. Section 1 of the Charter constitutionally guarantees the rights in the Charter subject *only* to limits that are reasonable and prescribed by law. This means that if administrative discretions are not either 'prescribed by law', or authorised

[98] Ibid, [56].

[99] Eg Cartier (n 28) 75–76.

[100] *Doré* (n 88) [26–35].

[101] Ibid, [31].

[102] Ibid, [35], citing *Multani* (n 83) at [152] (LeBel J).

[103] It appears 29 times. For discussion of the significance of this language, see Mullan (n 92) 54 fn 241; Walters (n 92); V MacDonnell, 'Developments in Constitutional Law: The 2011–2012 Term' (2012) 59 *Supreme Court Law Review* (2d) 51, 96.

[104] See, eg *Multani* (n 83) [112–25] (Deschamps and Abella JJ) and the sources cited there. The argument focuses in part on the difference between the English phrase 'prescribed by law' and the equivalent in the French text, 'une règle de droit'.

[105] *Doré* (n 88) [37].

[106] *Multani* (n 83) [112–25] (Deschamps and Abella JJ).

(and therefore constrained) by a rule that *is* prescribed by law, administrators are constitutionally prohibited from using their discretionary powers to place *any limits at all* on Charter rights. Even if that were a plausible reading of the text of section 1, it is a reading that would render the Charter unworkable. And it does not, in any event, support the conclusion in *Doré* that administrative decisions may limit Charter rights so long as they operate within the boundaries set by administrative law.

The second (and more coherent) reading of *Doré* is that administrative decision-makers *are* bound by section 1 of the Charter but that the *Oakes* test is nevertheless inapposite to review of administrative decision-making.[107] This line of reasoning relies on the creation of conceptual space between *Oakes*—a legal test to be applied by judges in supervising the legislatures' discharge of section 1 of the Charter—and the underlying obligation contained in section 1 itself. The underlying obligation inheres across a range of contexts; the particular approach to be taken to its discharge varies.[108]

This reading of *Doré* is supported by a number of passages in the Court's judgment. Abella J for the Court noted that although the 'traditional section 1 analysis' is an 'awkward fit' in administrative law challenges (because some of the questions posed by the *Oakes* test seem inapposite to individualised administrative decision-making), 'the protection of *Charter* guarantees is a fundamental and pervasive obligation, no matter which adjudicative forum is applying it'.[109] The Court rejected 'a formulaic application of the *Oakes* test' but contended that its essence could be distilled into an approach that sat within the framework of ordinary administrative law and that 'works the same justificatory muscles: balance and proportionality'.[110] Importantly, the Court signalled that the notion of 'proportionality' was to remain at the heart of the inquiry. In administrative law cases, the question for the Court was 'whether, in assessing the impact of the relevant *Charter* protection and given the nature of the decision and the statutory and factual contexts, the decision reflects a proportionate balancing of the *Charter* protections at play'.[111]

Thus, despite shedding the formal justificatory structure of the *Oakes* test, the Supreme Court in *Doré* signalled that the section 1 touchstone of 'proportionality' remains the yardstick for determining the reasonableness of administrative decisions that limit Charter rights. This line of reasoning might be thought to build on three propositions. First, what is required to

[107] See J Boughey, 'Rights, Review and Reasonableness: The Implications of Canada's New Approach to Administrative Decision-Making and Human Rights for Australia' (2013) 35 *Sydney Law Review* 283, 296.

[108] See, eg *Multani* (n 83) [150], [155] (LeBel J).

[109] *Doré* (n 88) [4].

[110] Ibid, [5].

[111] Ibid, [57]. See also ibid, [6].

achieve proportionality takes its colour from the context and, in particular, is not the same for administrators as for legislators.[112] Secondly, what is meant by 'reasonableness' also takes its colour from the context and, specifically, from the underlying obligation of proportionality in section 1 of the Charter.[113] Thirdly (and as suggested earlier with reference to the UK), the precise nature of the supervisory role of the courts depends not just on the text of the Charter, but on the view that is taken of the relative powers and responsibilities of the different branches of government within Canada's constitutional system. The *Doré* Court's assessment is that the mainstream administrative law framework (grounded, as it is, in a policy of judicial deference to administrative decision-making) speaks to this question of relative powers and responsibilities just as much in the Charter context as in any other. In the Court's opinion, deference is justified 'on the basis of legislative intent, respect for the specialized expertise of administrative decision-makers, and recognition that courts do not have a monopoly on adjudication in the administrative state'.[114]

The *Doré* approach thus relocates Charter cases within the mainstream Canadian administrative law framework but does so in a way that preserves the basic character of the section 1 obligation. As well as importing from section 1 the language and basic technique of proportionality, the Court also appears to import the section 1 onus of proof, noting that the decision-maker (a disciplinary body) 'must ... demonstrate that they have given due regard to the importance of the expressive rights at issue'.[115] David Mullan had commented on this reversal of burden in pre-*Doré* administrative law cases implicating Charter values.[116] Mullan pointed out, though, that the content of the reverse burden related not to the 'correctness' of the decision but rather to 'the extent to which the government gave reasons that genuinely addressed the position of the [applicant] and provided a rational basis for departing from it, and one that was sustainable on a reasonable view of the facts'.[117] Mullan presciently saw this approach as a useful starting point in developing a methodology that accords appropriate deference to primary decision-makers without devaluing Charter rights.[118]

[112] See ibid, [36–38].

[113] See ibid, [54]. This proposition had a foundation in pre-*Doré* case law in which the Supreme Court, though resisting any further formal refinement of the two administrative law standards of review (correctness and reasonableness), emphasised that reasonableness is a flexible standard that 'varies with the context and the nature of the impugned administrative act': *Catalyst Paper Corporation v North Cowichan (District)* 2012 SCC 2, [2012] 1 SCR 5, [23], relied on in *Doré* (n 88) [54]. See also *Canada (Citizenship and Immigration) v Khosa* 2009 SCC 12, [2009] 1 SCR 339, [59] (Binnie J); Mullan (n 92) 74–81.

[114] *Doré* (n 88) [30] citing *Dunsmuir* (n 89).

[115] *Doré* (n 88) [66]. It would ordinarily fall on the applicant in an administrative law case to prove that the decision had fallen foul of the relevant administrative law standard.

[116] Mullan (n 85) 246–47.

[117] Ibid, 246.

[118] Ibid, 248.

This links to the third and final aspect of the *Doré* case that I wish to highlight: the way in which the decision subverts the process/outcome distinction on which the *Denbigh High* case rests. It will be remembered that the innovation of the Victorian Charter was to stipulate an autonomous process-based obligation that functions as an add-on to a results-based compatibility/proportionality assessment. That approach leaves in place the underlying conceptual distinction between the two modes of review.

The *Doré* approach, by contrast, subverts the process/outcome distinction by merging process and outcome into one inquiry. This was already an emerging feature of Canadian 'reasonableness' review. So, for example, in *Dunsmuir*—the case in which the Supreme Court established the 'reasonableness' standard of review in its present form[119]—the Court noted that a judge conducting a reasonableness inquiry would need to refer 'both to the process of articulating the reasons and to outcomes'. It continued:[120]

> In judicial review, reasonableness is concerned mostly with the existence of justification, transparency and intelligibility within the decision-making process. But it is also concerned with whether the decision falls within a range of possible, acceptable outcomes which are defensible in respect of the facts and law.

What *Doré* adds is that this merged process/outcome inquiry provides the foundation not only for an assessment of 'reasonableness' but also, in Charter cases, of proportionality. The *Doré* Court began its explanation of how to apply the reasonableness standard in the specific context of Charter rights with the injunction that 'both decision-makers and reviewing courts must remain conscious of the fundamental importance of *Charter* values in the analysis'.[121] The Court then proceeded to address the question: 'How then does an administrative decision-maker apply *Charter* values in the exercise of statutory discretion?'[122] The answer: the decision-maker must ascertain the statutory objectives that are at stake, and then ask how the *Charter* value at issue will best be protected in the light of them.[123] Noting more than once the alignment between this inquiry and the *Oakes* test,[124] the Court stressed that: 'This is at the core of the proportionality exercise, and requires the decision-maker to balance the severity of the interference of the *Charter* protection with the statutory objectives.'[125]

[119] See n 89 and associated text.

[120] *Dunsmuir* (n 89) [47]. See also D Dyzenhaus and E Fox-Decent, 'Rethinking the Process/Substance Distinction: *Baker v Canada*' (2001) 51 *University of Toronto Law Journal* 193; E Fox-Decent, 'The Internal Morality of Administration: The Form and Structure of Reasonableness' in Dyzenhaus (n 28) 143; Boughey (n 107) 311–13; M Lewans, 'Deference and Reasonableness Since *Dunsmuir*' (2013) 38 *Queens Law Journal* 59, 93–97.

[121] *Doré* (n 88) [54].

[122] Ibid, [55].

[123] Ibid, [55–56].

[124] Ibid, [56], [57].

[125] Ibid, [56].

In contradistinction to the decision of the House of Lords in *Denbigh High*, the *Doré* Court thus viewed the notion of proportionality in section 1 as a standard to be considered by administrative decision-makers themselves, albeit in a less formulaic manner than would be dictated by the *Oakes* test. It was only after this extended exploration of the implications of section 1 for the decision-making process that the Court finally turned to the obligations of the reviewing court. It noted that:[126]

> On judicial review, the question becomes whether, in assessing the impact of the relevant *Charter* protection and given the nature of the decision and the statutory and factual contexts, the decision reflects a proportionate balancing of the *Charter* protections at play. As LeBel J. noted in *Multani*, when a court is faced with reviewing an administrative decision that implicates *Charter* rights, '[t]he issue becomes one of proportionality' … and calls for integrating the spirit of s. 1 into judicial review. Though this judicial review is conducted within the administrative framework, there is nonetheless conceptual harmony between a reasonableness review and the *Oakes* framework, since both contemplate giving a 'margin of appreciation', or deference, to administrative and legislative bodies on balancing *Charter* values against broader objectives.
>
> If, in exercising its statutory discretion, the decision-maker has properly balanced the relevant *Charter* value with the statutory objectives, the decision will be found to be reasonable.

Turning to apply this approach to the facts of the particular case (involving a decision by a disciplinary council to reprimand a lawyer for making immoderate remarks about a judge), the Court noted that the disciplinary body was required to demonstrate that they had given 'due regard to the importance of the expressive rights at issue'—a balancing exercise that was fact-dependent and discretionary.[127] The Court then observed:[128]

> All we have been asked to determine is whether the Disciplinary Council's conclusion that a reprimand was warranted … was a reasonable one. To make that assessment, we must consider whether this result reflects a proportionate application of the statutory mandate with Mr. Doré's expressive rights.

The precise relationship between considerations of process and outcome in this inquiry could doubtless be better explicated. What is clear from the above, however, is that the judicial duty to ensure the 'proportionality' and thus 'reasonableness' of the decision-making process combines both process and outcome dimensions. The approach is grounded in the policy of deference that characterises Canada's contemporary administrative law framework and thus places a primary emphasis on 'the existence

[126] Ibid, [57–58].
[127] Ibid, [66].
[128] Ibid, [67].

of justification, transparency and intelligibility within the decision-making process'. But it does not abnegate the Court's ultimate responsibility to ensure that decisions fall within a range of 'acceptable' and 'defensible' outcomes.

This merged process/outcome inquiry offers a response of sorts to each of the four policy concerns identified above.[129] In response to the first concern—the need for guidance to administrative decision-makers in order to advance the project of building a human rights culture—the *Doré* decision brings together the obligations of decision-makers and courts in a way that speaks equally to each. In response to the second concern—the impoverished conception of the 'culture of justification'—the *Doré* decision exemplifies an approach that places special (but not exclusive) significance on contemporaneous justification, given as part of the decision-making process. In response to the third concern—the desirability of equipping the courts with the flexibility to manage their delicate institutional relationship with the elected branches of government—by combining process and outcome considerations into a single inquiry, the *Doré* approach will presumably allow the courts to emphasise or de-emphasise process and/or outcome considerations in particular cases in order to formulate a response that is protective of the institutional position of both administrators and courts. In response to the fourth concern—the bifurcated approach to constitutional and administrative law—addressing that bifurcation is self-evidently at the heart of the *Doré* decision.

But is the *Doré* approach sufficiently attentive to the concern about administrative formalism that had so much sway in the UK context? Does the decision make a 'fetish of procedure' and will it contribute to a 'stifling culture of formalism on public administrators'?[130] These questions are certainly worth posing as the procedural stipulations laid down for the first instance decision-maker in *Doré*, though expressed in a less formalised manner, were not substantially different from those so roundly rejected by the House of Lords in *Denbigh High*.[131] However, it is important to bear in mind that the *Doré* Court had before it not the governors of a high school but a lawyers' disciplinary council, and the Court confined its remarks to 'adjudicated administrative decisions'. The procedural stipulations articulated by the Court do not seem inappropriate when placed in that context. The key to avoiding the trap of undue formalism identified in *Denbigh High* may lie not so much in a rejection of *Doré* itself, but in the manner in which the approach is expanded into other decision-making contexts. As in Victoria, what amounts to 'proper' consideration must

[129] See nn 18–29 and associated text.

[130] Poole (n 11) 691, 695, discussed in nn 11–16 and associated text.

[131] See *Denbigh High* (CA) (n 5) [75] (Brooke LJ).

surely vary enormously with context. There seems no reason in principle, however, why the Canadian 'reasonableness' framework cannot prove itself sufficiently flexible to accommodate this sort of institutional sensitivity.

V. NEW ZEALAND: FALLING BETWEEN TWO STOOLS

I have written elsewhere about the reluctance of the New Zealand courts to engage in results-based proportionality review of administrative decision-making.[132] In short, the New Zealand courts' response to the process/outcome conundrum posited above has been one of near paralysis. The jurisprudence in this area is uncoordinated and contradictory, and there has been an absence of leadership from the appellate courts. Rare examples can be found of judges conducting some form of results-based justifiability/proportionality inquiry.[133] More often, though, judges either refuse to engage at all with the impact of the NZ Bill of Rights on administrative discretion, or default to a process-based inquiry that sits more comfortably with orthodox understandings of the role of the courts in supervising administrative action.[134] But the jurisprudence falls well short of articulating a clear alternative process-based account of the courts' role in supervising exercises of administrative discretion to ensure consistency with the NZ Bill of Rights Act. Some judges have adopted an orthodox mandatory considerations approach (in which consideration is not given to the weight the decision-maker attaches to the relevant factor);[135] others have adopted a hybrid approach in which the adequacy or intensity of the consideration given to bill of rights issues by the first instance decision-maker is, in some way, assessed.[136] This latter category of cases contains the seeds within it of a mixed process/outcome approach perhaps not dissimilar to that formulated by the Canadian Supreme Court in *Doré*, but the approach (if it can even be called that) is uncoordinated and poorly articulated, and has not received the clear imprimatur of the appellate courts.

I have suggested elsewhere a range of textual and contextual reasons for the reluctance of the New Zealand courts to engaging in results-based proportionality review of administrative decision-making.[137] Ironically, one of these is the distinct preference of New Zealand judges, especially

[132] Geiringer (n 30). See also Wilberg (n 17).

[133] But examples above the level of the High Court almost entirely concern rights that are considered to be absolute, in other words, rights that do not attract a proportionality balancing exercise. It is engagement with proportionality in the administrative law context to which the New Zealand courts are particularly averse: see Geiringer (n 30) 132–33.

[134] Ibid, 131–38.

[135] Eg *Television New Zealand Ltd v Viewers for Television Excellence Inc* [2005] NZAR 1 (HC).

[136] Eg *Television New Zealand Ltd v West* [2011] 3 NZLR 825 (HC).

[137] Geiringer (n 30) 143–58.

those at appellate level, for contextualism over formalism in administrative law.[138] This trend no doubt stems from Lord Cooke's simplicity project. In his seminal essay 'The Struggle for Simplicity in Administrative Law', for example, Sir Robin warned against adding to the difficulties of administrative law through 'superfluous complications of principle'.[139] But unlike the UK, this hostility to formalism has led New Zealand judges to reject rather than adopt results-based proportionality review. The formalism of *Oakes*-style proportionality reasoning has been rejected as inapposite not just to the work of administrative decision-makers themselves (as in the UK) but, as well, to judicial review of administrative action. The problem is that no convincing alternative methodology has been substituted in its place.

VI. CONCLUSION

The foregoing analysis serves the following purposes. The first is to undermine the beguiling simplicity of the *Denbigh High* proposition that public authority 'compatibility' with human rights is a question of result. The statement is true as far as it goes, but does not negate the possibility that the obligation to act compatibly with human rights may generate subsidiary procedural duties for administrative decision-makers. Whether that is so, and what form of review courts should engage in when supervising the discharge of these (substantive and procedural) obligations, is a question that can only be answered by the administrative law of the particular country, and in the light of the view that is taken of the relative powers and responsibilities of the different branches of government within that country's constitution.

Secondly, the analysis suggests that despite their distinctiveness, the approaches developed across the Commonwealth can, at least in part, be seen as attempts to navigate a common set of competing policy concerns. On the one hand, there is the fear about juridifying administrative decision-making and placing unrealistic and inappropriate procedural burdens on officials. On the other hand, there are the four competing policy concerns identified in part II[140] which have at their heart unease about the aridity of a top-down approach to human rights compatibility that takes, as its

[138] See DR Knight, 'A Murky Methodology: Standards of Review in Administrative Law' (2008) 6 *New Zealand Journal of Public and International Law* 117; DR Knight, 'Mapping the Rainbow of Review: Recognising Variable Intensity' [2010] *New Zealand Law Review* 393. See also S Elias, 'Administrative Law For "Living People"' (2009) 68 *Cambridge Law Journal* 47, 65–66.

[139] R Cooke, 'The Struggle for Simplicity in Administrative Law' in M Taggart (ed), *Judicial Review of Administrative Action in the 1980s: Problems and Prospects* (Auckland, Oxford University Press, 1986) 5, 14.

[140] See text to nn 17–28.

starting point, the ex post facto justification of public authority actions in the course of judicial proceedings.

The salience of this latter group of concerns is reflected in the fact that all the jurisdictions to have adopted the Commonwealth model presently deploy some form of process-based inquiry when scrutinising public authority compatibility with human rights. Even the UK approach is founded on an uneasy ambivalence towards process-based assessment—*Denbigh High* holds simultaneously that process considerations play no part in the nature of the legal obligation imposed on public authorities by the UK Human Rights Act; and that process considerations are important (in some cases, it seems, even decisive) to the way the Court approaches its supervisory role.

On the other hand (and thirdly), this analysis also serves to highlight the uniqueness of each of the four jurisdictions canvassed here. Not only has one or more policy consideration sometimes had special resonance within a particular jurisdiction; but other more unique factors have also come into play—such as, for example, the impulse in the UK to 'bring rights home' (that is, to provide domestic judicial remedies that prevent recourse to Strasbourg). Additionally, in evolving an approach to this question of judicial supervision of human rights compatibility, the courts have been restricted by the constitutional context and by the particular set of public law tools available in the respective jurisdiction.

This aspect of the analysis highlights the danger of constitutional borrowing.[141] For that reason, I confine my reform prescriptions to the jurisdiction I know best. The incoherent state of New Zealand law on this question is wholly unsatisfactory and further development of the law is much to be desired. But the deep-set suspicion of formalism in administrative law held by New Zealand judges makes it unlikely, I would suggest, that the UK or Victorian approaches will have much resonance in New Zealand. On the other hand, one cannot help wondering whether some aspects of the new Canadian approach might provide inspiration to the New Zealand courts in formulating a way forward. Such a process of constitutional borrowing would need to be treated with care. Obviously, the Canadian approach cannot be directly transplanted as not all of the tools of Canadian administrative law that paved the way for *Doré* are available to New Zealand judges. Most obviously, the Canadian deference-based 'standards of review' approach, in which *Doré* is located, is unique to that jurisdiction. Nevertheless, there is ample recognition in New Zealand administrative law that reasonableness is a flexible standard, the application of which varies with context.[142] There seems no reason in principle

[141] Poole (n 15) 19–22; Geiringer (n 30) 124–25, 144.

[142] See Knight, 'A Murky Methodology' (n 138); Knight, 'Mapping the Rainbow of Review' (n 138).

why the New Zealand courts should not be able to develop a mixed process/outcome approach to reasonableness review in NZ Bill of Rights cases that draws on the basic concept of proportionality and that focuses the inquiry on the decision-makers' own obligations to ensure that its actions do not disproportionately limit protected rights.

The final point developed in this essay, however, is that any approach that contains a process dimension must be sensitive to the range of decision-making contexts in which human rights apply. There are a number of factors potentially at play here, including the nature and expertise of the decision-maker, the centrality of human rights issues to their mandate, the nature of the decision (for example, policy-making versus policy delivery), the nature of the right that is at stake, the time frame in which the decision needs to be made or the action taken, the resources available to the decision-maker when doing so, and the extent to which reasons could generally be expected to be given by them. The challenge for the courts in all these jurisdictions is to move beyond one-size-fits-all approaches and to begin to map out the institutional factors that can affect the type and level of human rights consideration that is appropriate in different decision-making contexts.

14

Crown Powers, the Royal Prerogative and Fundamental Rights

PHILIP SALES*

I. INTRODUCTION

THE CROWN HAS a range of powers recognised by the common law, entirely apart from those conferred by statute. They derive from three sources: the residue of executive power which the king possessed historically, the residue of powers attached to the king as the feudal chief of the country and (as it is put by Anson) 'attributes with which the Crown is invested by legal theory ... from practical convenience, including the attribution of perpetuity'.[1] They can be divided into powers existing under the royal prerogative, which are enjoyed by the Crown alone by virtue of its special position as guardian of the public interest, and those which the Crown enjoys in the same way as every other person, simply by virtue of it having legal personality. I will refer to these as prerogative powers and common-law powers, respectively.[2] Clarity is promoted by bearing this conceptual distinction in mind when analysing the basis on which their exercise may be controlled by the courts.

* Lord Justice of Appeal, Court of Appeal in England and Wales.

[1] A Berriedale Keith, *Anson's Law and Custom of the Constitution*, 4th edn (Oxford, Clarendon Press, 1935) 18–19.

[2] The term 'Crown's common law powers' was used in *R (Hooper) v Secretary of State for Work and Pensions* [2005] UKHL 29, [2005] 1 WLR 1681, *R (Association of British Civilian Internees Far East Region) v Secretary of State for Defence* (*ABCIFER*) [2003] EWCA Civ 473, [2003] QB 1397, [39] and in House of Lords Select Committee on the Constitution, *The Pre-emption of Parliament* (2013). The Crown's common-law powers are called 'third source' powers by Professor BV Harris in a series of articles, to distinguish them from statutory and prerogative powers: 'The "third source" of authority for government action' (1992) 108 *Law Quarterly Review* 626; 'The "third source" of authority for Government action revisited' (2007) 123 *Law Quarterly Review* 225; 'Government "third source" action and common law constitutionalism' (2010) 126 *Law Quarterly Review* 373.

Recognition of the distinction between prerogative powers and the Crown's common-law powers makes the well-known definition of the prerogative given by Blackstone[3] more helpful for present purposes than that proposed by Dicey,[4] which conflates them. Dicey's definition has tended to be cited more frequently.[5] However, leading judges have also said, in line with Blackstone, that rights common to the Crown and everyone else are not aspects of the prerogative. This appears now to be accepted at the highest level.[6]

In this essay, I examine legal control of the exercise of the prerogative and common-law powers of the Crown through judicial review. I discuss the extent to which judicial review of the Crown's prerogative and common-law powers can be assimilated with conventional judicial review of the exercise of statutory powers. This lays the foundation for a discussion on how legal analysis based on what are sometimes called 'fundamental rights', or common-law constitutionalism, has a bearing on the exercise of the Crown's powers. I argue that this is through their impact on application of the rationality standard of review, rather than by being treated as free-standing positive rights recognised in public or private law. In this way, I suggest, an appropriate balance is struck between the increasing judicialisation of the constitution and the residue of governmental discretion inherent in those powers.

II. THE CONCEPT OF THE CROWN

The notion of the Crown is famously opaque, yet of potentially major significance for legal and constitutional purposes.[7] In some contexts, the term is used to refer generally to the national executive government. This is legally imprecise, because members of the government are individuals who exercise the legal powers conferred on their ministerial offices by statute

[3] W Blackstone, *Commentaries on the Laws of England* 1st edn (Oxford, Clarendon Press, 1765–79) bk I, ch 7, p 232: 'those rights and capacities which the King enjoys alone'; and see Ministry of Justice, *The Governance of Britain: Review of the Executive Royal Prerogative Powers: Final Report* (2009) [29].

[4] AV Dicey, *Introduction to the Study of the Law of the Constitution*, 10th edn (London, Macmillan, 1959) 424: 'The residue of discretionary or arbitrary authority, which at any given time is legally left in the hands of the Crown.'

[5] *Attorney-General v De Keyser's Royal Hotel* [1920] AC 508, 526 (HL); *Burmah Oil Co Ltd v Lord Advocate* [1965] AC 75, 99, 137, 165 (HL); *Council of Civil Service Unions v Minister for the Civil Service (GCHQ)* [1985] AC 374, 398, 416 (HL); *R (Bancoult) v Secretary of State for Foreign and Commonwealth Affairs (No 2)* [2008] UKHL 61, [2009] 1 AC 453, [69].

[6] Eg *De Keyser's Royal Hotel* (n 5) 571; *Burmah Oil* (n 5) 164, 165; *Hooper* (n 2); *R (New London College Ltd) v Secretary of State for the Home Department* [2013] UKSC 51, [2013] 1 WLR 2358, [28].

[7] M Sunkin and S Payne (eds), *The Nature of the Crown: A Legal and Political Analysis* (Oxford, Oxford University Press, 1999).

and who advise the monarch on the exercise of her legal powers and are authorised to exercise them on her behalf. On the other hand, the Crown is a concept distinct from the person of the monarch. The powers attached to the Crown survive the passing of individual monarchs. Since those powers are exercised today by ministers or by the monarch bound by convention to act directly on their advice, they could be exercised in case of need in most if not all cases by ministers on behalf of a monarch who was a minor or incapacitated in some way.

Since at least the start of the seventeenth century and the use of the concept by Sir Edward Coke, the Crown has been regarded as a corporation sole, an immortal artificial person on the model of the parson in church property law. As Maitland summarises Coke's view, 'Kings and parsons are artificial persons, corporations sole, created not by God but by the policy of man: Co. Lit. 2 a, 250 a; *Sutton's Hospital* case, 10 Rep. 26 b.'[8]

In *Calvin's Case* the judges recognised that the king had two capacities, one as a natural person 'subject to death, infirmity and such like' and the other as 'a politic body or capacity so called, because it is framed by the policy of man ... and in this capacity the King is deemed to be immortal, invisible, not subject to death, infirmity, infancy, noneage &c'.[9] The move by Coke to model the King in his public capacity on a priest in his can be seen in the context of a European notion of the secular state drawn from ideas of the Church as a *corpus mysticum* or corporation,[10] but given a distinctive English twist.

Maitland was bitingly critical of this conceptual move. It was not carried through in logical fashion and anomalies had to be corrected by statute. But the worst of it, in his view, was that, as a result of what he regarded as an unhelpful legal development,

[8] FW Maitland, 'The Crown as Corporation' (1901) 17 *Law Quarterly Review* 131.

[9] *Calvin's Case* (1607) 7 Co Rep 1a, 10a. See EH Kantorowicz, *The King's Two Bodies: A Study in Mediaevel Political Theology* (Princeton, Princeton University Press, 1957); J McLean, *Searching for the State in British Legal Thought: Competing Conceptions of the Public Sphere* (Cambridge, Cambridge University Press, 2012). Some offices of Secretary of State have been granted legal personality as corporations sole in their own right, under transfer of functions orders made under the Ministers of the Crown (Transfer of Functions) Act 1946 and the Ministers of the Crown Act 1975, and so these Ministers do not need to rely on the corporate status of the Crown for capacity to act: see, eg article 3 of the Business, Innovation and Skills Order 2009/2748. As a matter of statutory interpretation, it is easy infer that the same limits upon exercise of this legal capacity should apply as in the case of the Crown's corporate personality, as discussed below. A similar legislative technique has been adopted to confer wide general powers on local authorities, to allow them to do anything an individual may do, under s 1 of the Localism Act 2011.

[10] A Ryan, *On Politics: A History of Political Thought from Herodotus to the Present* (London, Allen Lane, 2012) ch 8 and 403–404; C Thornhill, *A Sociology of Constitutions: Constitutions and State Legitimacy in Historical-Sociological Perspective* (Cambridge, Cambridge University Press, 2011) 25–39.

> we are compelled to introduce into our legal thinking a person whose personality our law does not formally or explicitly recognise. We cannot get on without the State, or the Nation, or the Commonwealth, or the Public, or some similar entity, and yet that is what we are professing to do.

In other words, the conception of the king or Crown as a corporation sole has stifled the development of a more natural and useful conception, of the State as a form of corporation (a corporation aggregate, as Maitland put it) in its own right.

There is not much doubt that classification of the Crown as a corporation sole is the correct legal view, albeit one that is sometimes lost sight of.[11] This view has the considerable authority of Coke, Blackstone, Maitland and, in modern times, Sir William Wade behind it,[12] as well as explicit recognition in authority.[13] It is deeply rooted in the common law.

Although not spelled out by Maitland, perhaps the most damaging effect of using this particular conception of the Crown as identified with the monarch, rather than a legal concept of the State, was to inhibit the extension of judicial review of government decisions. For decisions taken under the Crown's prerogative or common-law powers, it was thought for much of the twentieth century that they were not reviewable. How could the King's courts judge the King's own actions?[14] It was not obvious that the classic response to circumvent any such doctrine, that any immunity of the monarch/Crown from suit did not apply to actions of ministers of the monarch,[15] would apply in cases where, as a matter of legal theory, it was the monarch/Crown which acted in person.

The conception of the Crown as a corporation sole rather than a corporation aggregate (the State) masks the requirement that rules authorising the making of decisions within particular parameters are required to give the

[11] The relevant authorities are sometimes not cited, which can cause confusion. In *Town Investments Ltd v Department of the Environment* [1978] AC 359, 400 (HL) Lord Simon of Glaisdale described the Crown as a corporation aggregate, whereas at 384 Lord Diplock described it as a corporation sole. Lord Woolf in *M v Home Office* [1994] 1 AC 377 (HL) attempted to combine both views, saying that the Crown 'can be appropriately described as a corporation sole or a corporation aggregate'—criticised by HWR Wade, 'The Crown, Ministers and Officials' in Sunkin and Payne (n 7) 24.

[12] Wade (n 11) 23–24: 'The Crown's legal personality is obvious from the fact that it can convey land and make contracts without statutory assistance.' Although in theory this might be explained in terms of the monarch's legal personality as an individual, this is not a realistic analysis in modern constitutional terms: P Hogg and P Monahan, *Liability of the Crown*, 3rd edn (Scarborough, Carswell, 2000) 13–14, 219.

[13] Including *Attorney-General v Kohler* (1861) 9 HLC 654, 670; *Re Mason* [1928] Ch 385, 401 (ChD).

[14] *M v Home Office* (n 11) 395, 407–408. The formula that the 'king can do no wrong' has been given over-extensive application: HWR Wade and CF Forsyth, *Administrative Law*, 10th edn (Oxford, Oxford University Press, 2009) 696: '[The king's] legal position, the powers and prerogatives which distinguish him from an ordinary subject, is given to him by the law, and the law gives him no authority to transgress.'

[15] See the discussion in *M v Home Office* (n 11).

State form and coherence and to make it properly accountable for its actions. If the Crown had been conceptualised as a corporation aggregate, the need for authorisation rules to determine whose actions, made under what conditions, would count as the actions of the State would have been clear.

There is much force in Maitland's criticism, yet in many decades after Maitland wrote the conceptual transformation for which he called did not occur. The use of legislation as the main form of governance and the continuing growth in the creation of statutory regimes and powers from the late nineteenth century meant that there was little real need to focus in depth on the concept of the State as such. The tools at hand (statutory interpretation, office-holders with statutory powers and, on the rare occasions when it was necessary, the notion of the Crown as corporation sole) were adequate for the purposes to which the courts wished to put them. The political nature of the British constitution suppressed the need to develop a clearer legal conception of the State. The political convention that the Crown's powers should be exercised on advice from ministers, politically accountable in Parliament, reduced the pressure for development of alternative legal controls. Moreover, as described below, the areas in which the Crown's prerogative powers fell to be exercised tended to be those which called for highly particularistic judgments in relation to which the courts naturally hesitated to lay down clear binding rules. And in light of the advances achieved by the interventionist state and the need for strong collective government during two world wars, in the period of the sleep of administrative law before its awakening in the early 1960s, the courts were not strongly motivated to press for explicit justification of government action, and did not seek to explore weaknesses in the conceptual basis for such action.

Conversely, a reduction of faith in political and non-legal administrative processes in the period after World War II[16] has tended to encourage and legitimise legal controls in relation to the exercise of political power and has underpinned development of judicial review in relation to statutory powers, which in turn has generated an extension of judicial review to other forms of public power.[17] With the heightened importance given to legal forms of control, legal analysis and the legal concepts on which it depends attract new attention.

[16] JM Jacob, *The Republican Crown: Lawyers and the Making of the State in Twentieth Century Britain* (Aldershot, Dartmouth, 1996). The breakdown in political consensus and Keynesian welfarist economics from the early 1970s also resulted in an emphasis on putting faith in law and markets rather than politics for social ordering: DT Rodgers, *Age of Fracture* (London, Belknap, 2011); C Crouch, *The Strange Non-Death of Neo-Liberalism* (Cambridge, Polity Press, 2011) ch 1; McLean (n 9) ch 8.

[17] *R v Panel on Take-over and Mergers, ex p Datafin plc* [1987] QB 815 (CA); cf *R v Criminal Injuries Compensation Board, ex p Lain* [1967] 2 QB 864 (QBD).

Maitland's criticism of the concept of the Crown as a corporation sole is also somewhat overstated. It tends to overlook aspects of the idea which are capable of being developed to approach more closely a residual conception of the State which is suitable—or at least serviceable—in the modern world. It is possible to marry up the idea of the Crown as a corporation sole with the principle that '[i]n order that an act of the Crown may be recognised as an expression of the Royal will and have any legal effect whatever, it must in general be done with the assent of, or through some Minister or Ministers who will be held responsible for it',[18] so as to produce a focus on the conditions according to which the action of some Minister will produce the legal effect that some valid act has been done by the Crown, so reducing the practical difference from the concept of a corporation aggregate.

Further, if the King or Crown is an artificial person 'framed by the policy of man' and through the means of the common law, there is scope for aspects of the basic concept of the corporation sole to be spelled out with increasing refinement and adjusted to modern circumstances. The common law is capable of conceptual development and adaptation over time to maintain internal balance and coherence and to meet identified social needs. The possibility of judicial legislation within the common law has come to be explicitly recognised in modern times.[19] Judges have the ability, within the parameters set by the common-law tradition and using concepts furnished by that tradition, to adjust the concept of the Crown as corporation sole. The contours of the common-law concept of the Crown as corporation sole can be made to correspond more closely to the need for judicial control which has come to be felt in a modern constitutional state.

Judicial review of the exercise of statutory power has developed and its principles have come to be reflected onto the more hidden areas of exercise of the Crown's prerogative and common-law powers. Thus, judicial review principles taken from statutory contexts were extended to cover prerogative powers in the *GCHQ* case in 1985.[20] They have been applied to exercise of the Crown's common-law powers.[21] Whereas the convention that the Crown exercises its powers on the basis of advice from ministers was a factor which previously tended to diminish the need for a searching legal

[18] Dicey (n 4) 325.

[19] Lord Reid, 'The Judge as Law Maker' [1972] *Journal of the Society of the Public Teachers of Law* 22; P Sales, 'Judges and Legislature: Values into Law' (2012) 71 *Cambridge Law Journal* 287.

[20] *GCHQ* (n 5).

[21] Eg *R v Ministry of Defence, ex p Walker* [2000] 1 WLR 806 (HL); *R (Mullen) v Secretary of State for the Home Department* [2004] UKHL 18, [2005] 1 AC 1; *ABCIFER* (n 2). The Crown regularly accepts in litigation that ordinary judicial review principles apply, albeit without spelling out the theoretical underpinning for such a view: see, eg *Shrewsbury and Atcham BC v Secretary of State for Communities and Local Government* [2008] EWCA Civ 148, [2008] 3 All ER 548, [22].

analysis of the powers of the Crown,[22] in the more legalised constitution which now exists it has come to operate as a factor to justify extension of judicial review of the exercise of such powers.[23] The development of judicial review to supplement political controls in respect of decision-making by ministers in the standard case of use of statutory powers has made it appear natural to use similar standards of judicial review in respect of decision-making by ministers using Crown powers.

III. THE POWERS ENJOYED BY THE CROWN

At a basic conceptual level the powers of the Crown can be divided between three distinct sources: statute, royal prerogative and common law.

First, most importantly, statutory powers are regularly conferred upon the central executive government, which represents the Crown in the broad, non-technical sense of the term when it is used as a synonym for such government. Typically, statutory powers are conferred upon a Secretary of State or Minister. Statutory powers are not in practice conferred distinctly on the Crown as monarch or corporation sole. Ministers are taken to represent the government departments which they head. They act with the assistance of and often through the whole machinery of those departments.[24] Judicial review of the exercise of such powers is the standard case of judicial review of central government decision-making. I put this type of case to one side.

Secondly, there are powers which arise under the royal prerogative (powers which are unique to the Crown). Prerogative powers are powers historically recognised as inhering in the Crown to enable it to pursue the good of the realm (for example, in relation to defence, the conduct of international relations and the maintenance of public order)[25] or as relics of feudal authority (for example the power to confer honours).[26] Prerogative powers may be divided into legislative powers and executive powers, but these are categories which run into each other.

The Crown's main legislative powers relate to the government of overseas territories, where it acquired legislative rights by conquest or cession of territory. There is an elaborate law governing the extent of these legislative

[22] Cf BS Markesinis, 'The Royal Prerogative Re-visited' (1973) 32 *Cambridge Law Journal* 287.

[23] Thus Lord Roskill in *GCHQ* (n 5) 417 explained that there is no logical reason why the fact that the source of executive power is the prerogative and not statute should today deprive the citizen of a similar right of challenge to the manner of its exercise.

[24] *Carltona Ltd v Commissioners of Works* [1943] 2 All ER 560 (CA); *Bushell v Secretary of State for the Environment* [1981] AC 75, 95 (HL).

[25] *R v Secretary of State for the Home Department, ex p Northumbria Police Authority* [1989] QB 26 (CA).

[26] See *The Governance of Britain* (n 3).

rights and the ways in which they might be limited or lost.[27] But with the loss of all but a tiny rump of the former Empire, this law has diminished greatly in importance and is seldom deployed in the courts.[28] The Crown's former domestic powers of legislation have likewise shrunk to a tiny rump, to the point where they are now best characterised as a set of residual executive powers.

The Crown's common-law or 'third source' powers are conventionally regarded as the ordinary legal powers attached to persons with legal personality. Executive action based on these powers includes ordinary matters such as making contracts, conveying and holding property and so on, as well as effecting telephone interception for police and national security purposes (before this came to be regulated by statute),[29] maintaining a register of sex offenders[30] and payment of money for various purposes, including to operate an *ex gratia* payment scheme[31] or to take steps to prepare for proposed changes in the law but in advance of legislation.[32]

Ministers who exercise prerogative and common-law powers on behalf of the Crown are always accountable to Parliament for their actions. Where the exercise of the powers involves the expenditure of money, particularly direct political control is exerted by Parliament.[33] There is pressure from Parliament to extend and strengthen its oversight and control of the executive government using Crown powers,[34] and government itself seeks to legitimise its exercise of such powers by recourse to votes in Parliament—most importantly in relation to the taking of military action in Iraq in 2003, in Libya in 2011 and in Syria in 2013.

The boundary between the Crown's legislative and executive prerogative powers and common-law powers is not always clear. For example, *GCHQ* was treated as a prerogative case, but it could equally be analysed as a

[27] K Roberts-Wray, *Commonwealth and Colonial Law* (London, Stevens, 1966); Anson (n 1).

[28] Roberts-Wray's book has not been replaced as the leading commentary.

[29] *Malone v Commissioner v Metropolitan Police Commissioner* [1979] Ch 344, 369–70 (Ch D).

[30] *R v Secretary of State for Health, ex p C* [2000] 1 FLR 627 (CA).

[31] Eg compensation schemes for miscarriages of justice (*Mullen* (n 21)) and victims of crime (*Lain* (n 17) and *Walker* (n 21)) or scheme to pay legal expenses of British citizens facing trial abroad (*R (Sandiford) v Secretary of State for Foreign and Commonwealth Affairs* [2013] EWCA Civ 581, [2013] 1 WLR 2938, [55]–[60]; [2014] UKSC 44).

[32] *Shrewsbury and Atcham BC* (n 21); *The Pre-emption of Parliament* (n 2).

[33] Requirement for funds to be voted by primary legislation in Supply and Appropriation Acts. It is a fundamental constitutional principle that there be full Parliamentary control over taxation and expenditure: Dicey (n 4) 315–18; *Lain* (n 17) 881, 886–87, 888; *Hooper* (n 2) [46]. There is also extensive administrative control exercised by the Treasury over use of money voted by Parliament: T Daintith and A Page, *The Executive in the Constitution: Structure, Autonomy and Internal Control* (New York, Oxford University Press, 1999); HM Treasury, *Managing Public Money* (2013); HM Treasury, *Government Financial Reporting Manual* (2013).

[34] *The Pre-emption of Parliament* (n 2).

case involving exercise of the Crown's common-law powers as employer, whereby it could operate its right to terminate employment in the civil service at will and offer re-engagement on different terms, specifying as a term of employment that workers at GCHQ could not belong to a trade union. As Lord Diplock said, the possibility of this alternative analysis was not a matter of practical significance.[35] The various *ex gratia* schemes under the Crown's common-law powers in substance have the character of legislation conferring rights on individuals to receive money according to the rules of the scheme. The distinction between the Crown's legislative prerogative powers and its common-law powers is, in practical terms, more illusory than real in the case of use of common-law powers to deploy public funds and resources to create whole legislative codes for important areas of governmental action, such as instituting compensation schemes, registers of information affecting citizens or systems for authorisation of interception of communications.

Similarly, in *Bancoult (No 2)*[36] it was noted that the practical outcome achieved by legislation under the prerogative (expulsion and exclusion of the Chagos Islanders) might have been achieved by the Crown exercising its rights as landowner to exclude them.[37]

This tendency of the different forms of Crown powers to run into each other and overlap in their operation and effect is significant. It makes it difficult to sustain an argument that there should be any radically different approach to the standards of control to be applied by the courts in relation to the different powers. The various powers of the Crown are increasingly clearly seen as different aspects of public power wielded by the Crown as a cipher for the State.[38]

IV. HISTORICAL AND JURISPRUDENTIAL PERSPECTIVES

The prerogative and common-law powers of the Crown have a long history, dating back to the medieval period. English constitutional history can be given narrative coherence as the story of the gradually increasing subjection of the Crown and its powers to processes of control.[39] In medieval times, the prerogative powers of the king were linked with his feudal rights in

[35] *GCHQ* (n 5) 412.

[36] *Bancoult (No 2)* (n 5).

[37] Ibid, [160] (Lord Mance).

[38] Understood as a juristic person. cf M Loughlin, 'The State, the Crown and the Law' in Sunkin and Payne (n 7).

[39] FW Maitland, *The Constitutional History of England* (Cambridge, Cambridge University Press, 1908); Thornhill (n 10) 139–53.

various respects,[40] including his rights in relation to mobilising the defence of the realm.

In the early modern period, the Tudors made increased appeals to Parliament and used statutes to implement policy and buttress royal power. Parliament's authority was enhanced. This led to a new focus on the intention of Parliament, rather than the king, as the institution which made law in the form of statute.[41] In parallel with this development, the conception of the Crown's prerogative powers also began to change, to be thought of less as purely personal feudal entitlements of the monarch and more as powers to act in the public interest.[42]

Attempts by successive monarchs to govern with only limited recourse to an increasingly assertive Parliament for tax revenue meant that greater emphasis was placed on the Crown's feudal prerogative rights, as a means of raising revenue by other means. The *Ship Money* case in the reign of Charles I arose out of one such initiative.[43] These initiatives were resisted with vigour. Early in Charles's reign, Parliament registered its concern about the use of prerogative power in the Petition of Right (1628). Charles responded by dissolving Parliament and seeking to rule without it. When, under the financial pressure of war in Scotland, Charles was forced to summon the Long Parliament, the resistance to royal prerogative power was brought into focus with the Grand Remonstrance (1641). Parliament sought to control a range of prerogative powers of the Crown, including revenue raising powers which might be abused and powers to raise an armed militia or to disapply statutory provisions in individual cases. Civil war followed.

Despite the Restoration, resistance to rule by prerogative continued, culminating in the Glorious Revolution of 1688.[44] A new constitutional settlement was put in place, based on the Bill of Rights of 1689 and the Act of Settlement 1701. The fundamental principle that revenue should be voted to the executive by Parliament was established. The king's power to raise money by means other than taxes voted by Parliament was treated as circumscribed.[45] Control of the purse strings by Parliament is a major part of the foundation of political control of the executive by Parliament. The new political settlement was accepted and constitutional stability returned.

[40] M McGlynn, *The Royal Prerogative and the Learning of the Inns of Court* (Cambridge, Cambridge University Press, 2003).

[41] A Cromartie, *The Constitutionalist Revolution: An Essay on the History of England 1450–1642* (Cambridge, Cambridge University Press, 2006); Thornhill (n 10) 97–98; N Duxbury, *Elements of Legislation* (Cambridge, Cambridge University Press, 2013) 20–25.

[42] McGlynn (n 40) 235–36, 258–59.

[43] *R v Hampden* (1637) 3 St Tr 826; Thornhill (n 10) 139–41.

[44] T Harris, *Revolution: The Great Crisis of the British Monarchy, 1685–1720* (London, Allen Lane, 2006).

[45] Eg *Attorney-General v Wilts United Dairies* (1922) 91 LJ (KB) 897 (HL), 37 TLR 884 (CA).

The doctrine of the sovereignty of Parliament was treated as established.[46] Significant government policies had to be implemented through legislation made in Parliament. The Crown's prerogative powers were further reduced over time, against a background of continuing distrust of prerogative power which deepened 'as the idea of the British polity as a parliamentary democracy has solidified'.[47] It is now well established, again at the level of fundamental principle, that the Crown has no general prerogative power to commit a wrong actionable by an individual as a matter of private law.[48]

From this historical perspective, those areas where the Crown's prerogative powers continue to exist are comparatively minor. As Lord Reid put it in *Burmah Oil*, 'The prerogative is really a relic of a past age, not lost by disuse, but only available for a case not covered by statute.'[49] The priority of legislative provision over the remnants of royal prerogative is clear, and is reflected in the comparative ease with which prerogative powers may be found to be abrogated by implication when Parliament passes legislation which occupies the same field of application.[50]

The prerogative powers which were once important for governing the Empire have similarly declined in significance with the creation of representative legislatures in the territories which made it up and with the reduction in the Empire since World War II.

The Crown's common-law powers were historically less controversial, because they did not create any special rights for the monarch. A king who could raise revenues from his own estates (or from feudal dues) could spend them like any other landowner. The king had a defence if sued personally in his own courts, but the procedure of the petition of right was developed as a substitute process for justice to be done if someone had contracted with or been wronged by the monarch. Remedies in court regarding wrongs committed by the Crown were opened up by the Crown Proceedings Act 1947.[51] There was practical political control through Parliament's control of public funds.

Although the Crown's powers operate as a residual category of legal authority, of far less importance than powers conferred on the executive by statute, they remain a significant source of governmental power, particularly for dealing with situations which arise outside what may have been foreseen or contemplated by Parliament when it has legislated.

[46] J Goldsworthy, *The Sovereignty of Parliament: History and Philosophy* (Oxford, Clarendon Press, 1999); Thornhill (n 10) 147.

[47] T Poole, 'The royal prerogative: case comment on *R (Bancoult) v Secretary of State for Foreign and Commonwealth Affairs* [2008] UKHL 61; [2009] 1 AC 453' (2010) 8 *International Journal of Constitutional Law* 146, 147.

[48] *Entick v Carrington* (1765) 19 State Tr 1030; *Bancoult (No 2)* (n 5) [69].

[49] *Burmah Oil* (n 5) 101.

[50] *De Keyser's Royal Hotel* (n 5).

[51] Wade and Forsyth (n 14) ch 21.

It is a familiar feature of general rules laid down in advance that they may fail to make suitable provision for every situation which may later arise.[52] That is particularly so across the wide range of areas requiring action by Government. There was a strand of argument up to and during the Civil War which sought to justify the extent of the king's prerogatives on these grounds, by reference to Aristotle's concept of *epieikeia*.[53]

However, from a modern constitutionalist perspective, the Crown's powers, perceived as operating outside the scope of legal rules, appear to suffer from a want of legitimacy. This is both because they appear to allow for the exercise of power unbounded by such rules and because of the absence of their direct endorsement by the democratic legislature. As David Beetham observes:[54]

> If legitimate power is, as I have argued, power that is valid according to rules, and where the rules themselves are justifiable by and in conformity with underlying norms and beliefs, then the main way in which the powerful will maintain their legitimacy is by respecting the intrinsic limits set to their power by the rules and underlying principles on which they are grounded. Legitimate power, that is to say, is limited power ... A feature of the modern world is the increasingly precise legal specification of the respective powers, or 'sphere of competence', of each powerholder.

Nonetheless, both objections can be overstated. There is a place for modern recognition of the old idea of the (desirable, or at any rate inevitable) incompleteness of legal rules discussed by Aristotle.

In a discussion which emphasises the importance in a democracy of government by rules, Tom Campbell still points out that 'the impressive range of rationales' for such government[55]

> cannot and do not establish that all state power must be exercised in this way. Patently, some political decisions, such as in the conduct of war, the adoption of treaties and the location of capital cities, require decisions which are highly

[52] Aristotle's *epieikeia* or equity, *Nichomachean Ethics*, Book V, 1137b 12–29: law addresses the usual case, while equity allows for a 'correction of law where it is defective owing to its universality ... about some things it is impossible to lay down a law in advance, so that a decree is needed'. See RA Wasserstrom, *The Judicial Decision: Toward a Theory of Legal Justification* (Oxford, Oxford University Press, 1961) ch 10. Wasserstrom highlights an ambiguity in the concept, as referring to classes of case which ought not to be governed by rules or to the need for rules which govern a class of case to be modified at the point of application in situations of hardship (107–108).

[53] Cromartie (n 41); Aristotle, *Politics* (Oxford, Oxford University Press, 1995) 123–31.

[54] D Beetham, *The Legitimation of Power* (Macmillan, Basingstoke, 1991) 35; also Poole (n 47) 147; Thornhill (n 10) 7; MJ Braddick, *State Formation in Early Modern Englandc 1550–1700* (Cambridge, Cambridge University Press, 2000).

[55] TD Campbell, *The Legal Theory of Ethical Positivism* (Aldershot, Dartmouth, 1996) 61. Cf Aristotle, *Politics* (n 53) 129, s 1287b19: '"Is the rule of the best law preferable to that of the best man?" Matters which belong to the sphere of deliberation are obviously ones on which it is not possible to lay down a law...'

particularistic, although they can all be taken in accordance with rule-based authority assignation.

Raymond Geuss makes a similar point:[56]

> [T]o attempt in a thoroughgoing and comprehensive way [in a *Rechtsstaat*] to oppose a discretionary power which is to some extent unpredictable is not a coherent project, because such discretionary power is of the essence of politics. First of all, one might wonder whether it is in principle ever possible to make the exercise of power completely predictable by setting down absolutely unambiguous guidelines for its use ... They need to be applied and this requires a constructive activity on the part of the person doing the application. Finally, one must simply exercise one's faculty of judgment. In addition ... politics is in part about dealing with the unexpected, and one of the points of having public officials and a government at all is to allow them to respond quickly and flexibly to urgent matters that have not been anticipated.

It is notable that where general governmental power is conferred on the executive by statute to replace areas of residual prerogative power, it is often done in very wide terms which leave wide discretion with the executive about how to react to situations, much as did the prerogative or common-law powers which the statute replaces.[57] In view of the width of the discretion conferred, there is in fact little gain in terms of concrete legal control over the exercise of power by the executive. If Parliament simply abolished the Crown's prerogative and common-law powers, the probability is that it would have to re-invent them or something very like them in the form of reserve governmental powers of great width conferred by statute.

This feature of the royal prerogative, that it tends to apply in areas which are not well suited to rule-based forms of governance, is one reason why the courts are reluctant to impose significant substantive restraints on the exercise of prerogative power.[58] The great importance of the decision in *GCHQ* is that it requires a focus on the substantive issue of the justiciability of the particular powers being exercised—that is, on their amenability and suitability to judicial control by application of legal rules or standards. It thereby disallows the operation of broad assumptions about the non-reviewability of prerogative powers. It is a decision which prohibits the over-inclusive application of the concept of *epieikeia*, while still allowing for it to operate in appropriate cases. The government is required to explain the cases where rule-based governance is not appropriate.

[56] R Geuss, *History and Illusion in Politics* (Cambridge, Cambridge University Press, 2001) 107–108.

[57] Eg the Civil Contingencies Act 2004 and s 1 Localism Act 2011.

[58] See Lord Roskill's list in *GCHQ* (n 5) 418 of areas likely to be non-justiciable: prerogative powers 'relating to the making of treaties, the defence of the realm, the prerogative of mercy, the grant of honours, the dissolution of Parliament and the appointment of ministers'.

Another reason why the courts are reluctant to intervene is that the absence of a statutory context makes it more difficult to identify clear and legitimate standards by reference to which the courts can say that the exercise of the Crown's prerogative or common-law powers is unlawful. Important basic techniques employed by the courts when conducting judicial review of the exercise of statutory powers, in particular referring to the proper purpose for which a statutory power may be used (to be inferred from the statute itself)[59] or identifying mandatory relevant or mandatory irrelevant factors bearing on the decision (again, to be inferred by a process of construction of the statute)[60] are not readily available. See, for example, this observation by Dyson LJ in *ABCIFER* in discussing a challenge to the criteria adopted for operation of an *ex gratia* compensation scheme:[61]

> It is important to bear in mind that … this was a non-statutory scheme introduced by the Government exercising its common-law powers. In setting up the scheme the Government was painting on a clean canvas. In such a case there are obvious difficulties in determining what factors are relevant. These difficulties were recognised by Lord Donaldson of Lymington MR in *R v Panel on Take-overs and Mergers, ex p Guinness plc* [1990] 1 QB 146, 159:
>
> Irrationality, at least in the sense of failing to take account of relevant factors or taking account of irrelevant factors, is a difficult concept in the context of a body which is itself charged with the duty of making a judgment on what is and what is not relevant.

It is possible to conceive of legal challenges to the exercise of Crown powers based on improper purpose, error of law or irrationality. Examples of improper purpose would be exercise of powers because the relevant Minister was motivated by personal spite or had been bribed. Error of law may occur where a Minister fails to understand the true scope of some prerogative power and therefore fails properly to address the question whether it should be exercised.[62] The courts will enforce rationality standards in the exercise of the Crown's common-law[63] and prerogative[64] powers. However, these are egregious cases where there is a clear failure to comply with generally accepted standards of behaviour for public authorities. It remains harder to identify unlawfulness in the exercise of these powers once one moves away from these clear instances. Similarly, the absence of a statutory framework which confers discretion but also requires

[59] *Padfield v Minister of Agriculture, Fisheries and Food* [1968] AC 997 (HL).

[60] Eg *Associated Provincial Picture Houses v Wednesbury Corporation* [1948] 1 KB 223 (CA).

[61] *ABCIFER* (n 2) [39].

[62] *R v Secretary of State for the Home Department, ex p Bentley* [1994] QB 349 (DC).

[63] *ABCIFER* (n 2); *Secretary of State for Defence v Elias* [2006] EWCA Civ 1293, [2006] 1 WLR 3213; *Sandiford* (n 31) [2014] UKSC 44, [65–66].

[64] *Bancoult (No 2)* (n 5).

that a public authority maintain the ability to exercise it without unduly fettering its discretion[65] leaves the Crown able to exercise its prerogative or common-law powers by means of imposing clear bright-line rules without reservation of discretion.[66] Thus, the absence of a statutory framework tends to mean that review of the Crown's prerogative and common-law powers is primarily focused on concepts of procedural fairness and the back-stop category of rationality.

The Crown's prerogative and common-law powers are pre-supposed by the form of legislation and by gaps left untouched by legislative provision, where some power of action is required. Parliamentary draftsmen have been alert to and have drafted legislation having regard to the basic principle that the Crown does not need to have powers conferred upon it by statute in order to be able to have power or capacity to act. Within government circles, this is sometimes referred to as the 'Ram doctrine'.[67] It is a doctrine which simply reflects the underlying conceptual position described above.[68]

There has been criticism of the Ram doctrine, most recently in the Constitution Committee report, *The Pre-emption of Parliament*.[69] Lord Brown of Eaton-under-Heywood said that in his time as First Treasury Counsel he had never heard of the Ram doctrine; but he confirmed his understanding of the basic legal position that, entirely outside statute, the Crown has the legal capacity of an ordinary person.[70] In the event, though critical of the expression given to the relevant legal principle in the form of Ram's note of advice, the Committee's report agrees that the Crown has common-law powers. The Committee recommended greater parliamentary scrutiny of the exercise of such powers, and was critical of what it took to be Ram's suggestion that ordinary judicial review could not apply in relation to the exercise of those powers. It is, in fact, very doubtful that Ram intended to make any such claim (his advice was directed to other issues); and Government has not maintained any such position in the courts (at any rate, in recent times).

In view of the basic constitutional divide between the powers of the Crown (recognised by the common law, as a feature of the Crown's legal personality) and the powers of statutory corporations (which are themselves defined and delimited by statute in the process of creation of the corporate

[65] *British Oxygen Co Ltd v Minister of Technology* [1971] AC 610 (HL).

[66] *Sandiford* (n 31) [2013] EWCA Civ 581, [53–54]; [2014] UKSC 44, [54–64], [78–85]; *Elias* (n 63).

[67] After the exposition in a Memorandum dated 2 November 1945 by Granville Ram, First Parliamentary Counsel.

[68] Contra A Lester and M Weait, 'The Use of Ministerial Powers without Parliamentary Authority: the Ram Doctrine' [2003] *Public Law* 413.

[69] *Pre-emption of Parliament* (n 2).

[70] Ibid, question 56.

personality established by it—the idea underlying the *ultra vires* doctrine),[71] for centuries parliamentary drafters have not included full expression of Crown powers of action in legislation because it has not been necessary to do so. In this indirect way, the position and powers of the Crown have been recognised and further woven into the constitutional fabric by Parliament. There are, for example, no general statutory provisions empowering the Crown to pay money for public purposes. It has been unnecessary to introduce them, because the Crown has that power by virtue of its legal personality recognised in the common law. This is, for example, the legal basis on which a minister of the Crown (such as the Foreign Secretary) can pay a sum of money to meet an award of just satisfaction made by an international court such as the European Court of Human Rights.[72] There is no statute which empowers him to do this.

There has been a recent suggestion by Carnwath LJ, obiter, in *Shrewsbury & Atcham BC*,[73] to the effect that the Crown does not have the legal capacity which attaches to an individual, but should be regarded simply as having a more limited range of powers which could be described as incidental to governmental functions. In this, Carnwath LJ was following a proposal made in the sixth edition of *De Smith's Judicial Review*.[74] However, the actual analysis in *Shrewsbury & Atcham BC* proceeded on the footing that the conventional view regarding the capacity of the Crown as a corporation sole is correct. Carnwath LJ accepted that the Court was bound by previous authority of the Court of Appeal on that point (*R v Secretary of State for Health, ex p C*).[75] Richards LJ gave a judgment disagreeing with Carnwath LJ's suggestion, and re-affirming the conventional view of the Crown's common-law powers.[76]

The authority for attributing capacity to the Crown as a corporation sole goes deeper and wider than simply *ex p C*, as explained above. It is, for example, difficult to regard the many and various *ex gratia* compensation schemes which have been set up over many years using the Crown's common-law powers as something which could be lawful under the limited view of the Crown's common-law powers proposed by *De Smith*. Such schemes have been reviewed by the House of Lords on several occasions (and by other courts still more frequently) without it being suggested that they are unlawful. In particular, in *Hooper*[77] all members of the Appellate

[71] Eg *R v Somerset CC, ex p Fewings* [1995] 1 All ER 513 (Laws J) (QB).

[72] The exercise of which in individual cases was part of the background in *Hooper* (n 2).

[73] Above (n 21) [43]–[49].

[74] H Woolf, J Jowell and A Le Sueur, *De Smith's Judicial Review*, 6th edn (London, Sweet & Maxwell, 2007) [5-022–5-025].

[75] Above (n 30).

[76] Ibid, [72]–[74].

[77] Above (n 2).

Committee of the House of Lords proceeded on the footing that the government could make *ex gratia* payments or set up an *ex gratia* compensation scheme using the Crown's common-law powers, subject only to the question whether those powers had been abrogated in the particular context by statutory intervention. The setting up of such a scheme (or a sex offenders register or a system for interception of communications) is not incidental to some other government function, it is the exercise of a primary government function in its own right.

In Richards LJ's view, the complex process of government includes a vast amount of work which is not based on statutory powers,[78] but which has to have a legal basis, 'and the simple and satisfactory explanation is that it depends heavily on the "third source" of powers, ie powers that have not been conferred by statute and are not prerogative powers in the narrow sense but are the normal powers (or capacities and freedoms) of a corporation with legal personality'.[79] He accepted that the exercise of such powers is subject to judicial review on ordinary public law grounds, but went on:[80]

> But I think it unnecessary and unwise to introduce qualifications along the lines of those suggested by Carnwath LJ ... to the effect that they can only be exercised 'for the public benefit' or for 'identifiably "governmental" purposes'. It seems to me that any limiting principle would have to be so wide as to be of no practical utility or would risk imposing an artificial and inappropriate restriction upon the work of government.

It is respectfully suggested that Richards LJ's view accords best with principle and authority. Historically, the recognition of the Crown's public capacity as a corporation sole was to overcome problems which otherwise arose if public power was simply taken to reside in the individual person of the monarch (death, incapacity and so on). It was a move to extend the capacities of the Crown beyond what they would have been if the Crown were simply identified with a mortal individual, not to limit them. It is clear that the basic legal capacities of the monarch/Crown were still taken to be those of an ordinary individual. In *The Bankers Case*, for example, the reasoning of Holt CJ specifically included reference to the idea that upon accession to the throne the king could not be regarded as having less power (that is to say, to alienate property or rights as security for borrowing) than

[78] He was speaking of the work required to prepare for legislation, but the point has general application.

[79] *Shrewsbury & Atcham BC* (n 21) [73]. As Professor Harris observes, 'The limiting of acceptable third-source action, to that for the public benefit and governmental purposes, as suggested by Carnwath LJ and supported by Waller LJ, is a compromise which would be difficult for the courts to supervise, given the vagueness of the respective concepts': 'Government "Third-Source" Action and Common Law Constitutionalism' (2010) 126 *Law Quarterly Review* 373, 376.

[80] *Shrewsbury & Atcham BC* (n 21) [74].

any subject would have: the contrary suggestion was 'absurd, because by this he would have less power than any of his subjects, or than he himself had, when he was a subject'.[81]

The Crown's common-law powers have always been treated as a reserve of governmental power, which is, in principle, available to meet any exigencies which may arise outside the scope of legislative foresight. In terms of the discussion above, it is a reserve power which allows for recognition of the need for *epieikeia* or capacity to adapt flexibly to unforeseen or highly particularised circumstances in the exercise of governmental functions. As Richards LJ observed, it is unclear to what extent these powers would be reduced if the formulation proposed by *De Smith* and Carnwath LJ were adopted; and if they were reduced—so disabling the state from action unless time could be found for legislation to be passed—that could well prove to be an inappropriate and unwise impediment to governmental action. Governing has always been a complex and difficult activity, and complexity of governance has increased, not decreased, in modern societies.[82] It seems inappropriate for the courts at this juncture to be seeking to re-interpret established concepts to reduce residual governmental powers and capacities, at any rate without a clear view where that might take us and what problems it might give rise to. The courts should be wary about undermining an important foundation of flexibility in modern statecraft without very good reason.[83] This is not the type of change in the law which is authorised under the understanding of the common-law tradition. Common-law concepts are not infinitely malleable, according to the policy views of particular judges. There is no general consensus that this development would be beneficial, and the courts cannot see with confidence where the change might lead.[84]

Moreover, the change is unnecessary. There is no serious suggestion that the general ordinary principles of judicial review do not apply, as appropriate, to the exercise of the Crown's common-law powers (albeit it is fair to say that the theoretical basis for this has, perhaps, not been spelled out). Therefore, the courts already have available the usual tools appropriate to

[81] *The Bankers Case* (1700) Skin 601, 603.

[82] See, eg D Coyle, *The Economics of Enough: How to Run the Economy as if the Future Matters* (Princeton, Princeton University Press, 2011); D Runciman, *The Confidence Trap: A History of Democracy in Crisis from World War I to the Present* (Princeton, Princeton University Press, 2013) 265 (in 'the fissile, complex, frighteningly interconnected world of the twenty-first century').

[83] M Oakeshott, *Rationalism in Politics and Other Essays* (Indianapolis, Liberty Press, 1991) emphasising the importance of practical knowledge based on experience rather than formal rules; JC Scott, *Seeing Like a State: How Certain Schemes to Improve the Human Condition Have Failed* (New Haven, Yale University Press, 1998) ch 9.

[84] Cf P Sales, 'Rationality, Proportionality and the Development of the Law' (2013) 129 *Law Quarterly Review* 223, 232–34.

ensure that use of these powers is kept within proper bounds appropriate to a modern constitutional democratic state. In fact, on an expansive view of the interpretation offered by *De Smith*, it is by no means clear what additional protection beyond this might in practice be achieved by introducing the new proposed test. On the other hand, on a narrow view, the courts would be intervening to deprive the Crown of powers which until now it has been assumed to have, in areas where it would be highly questionable that this would constitute a legitimate development of the law by the courts.

Nonetheless, there are dicta in the recent decision of the Supreme Court in *New London College*[85] which indicate that Carnwath LJ's call for a review of the extent of the Crown's common-law powers is likely to be taken up at that level. Lord Carnwath called attention to his dicta in *Shrewsbury & Atcham BC* and re-affirmed them.[86] Lord Sumption described the basis of the Crown's non-statutory powers as 'controversial' and indicated that the question would need to be examined on another occasion.[87] This essay is, in part, an attempt to address that controversy.

V. JUDICIAL CONTROL OF THE CROWN'S PREROGATIVE AND COMMON-LAW POWERS

The most basic level of control of the Crown's prerogative powers is through the doctrine that the Crown only has such powers as are recognised by the courts, that is, the courts police the boundaries of prerogative power.[88] The Crown's claims of constitutional authority are thus filtered through common-law doctrine, much as the distinct claims of constitutional authority by another locus of constitutional power, namely claims of parliamentary privilege by Parliament, are scrutinised.[89] Whilst the common law is not exactly the source of prerogative power and parliamentary privilege, it is only to the extent that they are recognised by the common law and permitted to have operation that the authority claims which they embody are effective in law. This involves an examination of historical claims and practices over time.[90]

85 *New London College* (n 6).

86 Ibid, [34].

87 Ibid, [28].

88 *Burmah Oil* (n 5) 101; *Bancoult (No 2)* (n 5) [69]. The courts' claim to be entitled to do this is long-standing: *Prohibitions del Roy* (1607) 12 Co Rep 63; *The Case of Proclamations* (1611) 12 Co Rep 74, 76 ('The King hath no prerogative, but that which the law of the land allows him'); *GCHQ* (n 5) 398.

89 *Stockdale v Hansard* (1839) 9 Ad & E 1. In both cases—as noted by Markesinis (n 22) 293—the claim of the holder of a power is not conclusive; the courts will decide on its existence and true extent.

90 *Burmah Oil* (n 5) 101; *Bancoult (No 2)* (n 5) [69].

By a familiar process, prerogative powers may readily be lost by implication from legislative intervention covering the same field in a particular area of governmental activity.[91] This is the main reason why, with the expansion of statutory regulation over time, the extent of the royal prerogative has been so greatly diminished.

The Crown's common-law powers can also be impliedly abrogated where Parliament has legislated. In *R v Secretary of State for the Home Department, ex p Fire Brigades Union*[92] the House of Lords held that the Crown's power to set up a revised criminal injuries compensation scheme had been impliedly abrogated by primary legislation covering the same field, laying down criteria of entitlement different from those proposed by the Crown, even though the legislative scheme had not yet been commenced. Parliament did not legislate in vain. It did not intend the Minister to have an unconstrained choice to implement its scheme or a different scheme of his own devising.

However, despite the similarity of the approach, by contrast with abrogation of prerogative powers it may be more difficult to find that Parliament intended to achieve implied abrogation of the Crown's common-law powers, which are simply powers the Crown enjoys as a legal person like any other and which are in many ways fundamental to its ordinary mode of functioning.[93] This suggestion was discussed, but without being resolved, in *Hooper*.[94] As noted by Lord Hoffmann, the Crown submitted that it was more difficult to find an implied intention in a statute under the principle in *De Keyser's Royal Hotel* to abrogate the Crown's common-law powers:

> The right to spend money is not a power which the Crown enjoys as executive but simply by virtue of being a legal person like any other. A statute would have to be a good deal more explicit before it could be interpreted as extinguishing such a commonplace power.

Lord Hoffmann considered that there was a good deal of force in this suggestion.[95]

In *New London College*, Lord Sumption referred to Lord Hoffmann's comments about this, to call them in question in the context of the debate whether the Crown has the same power or capacity as an ordinary legal person.[96] But as regards the question whether the theory of implied

[91] *De Keyser's Royal Hotel* (n 5); *Burmah Oil* (n 5); *R (Alvi) v Secretary of State for the Home Department* [2012] 1 WLR 2208; cf *New London College* (n 6).

[92] *R v Secretary of State for the Home Department, ex p Fire Brigades Union* [1995] 2 AC 513 (HL).

[93] Particularly in light of the principle that statutes are not taken to affect the Crown unless there is express provision to that effect or by necessary implication: *Lord Advocate v Dumbarton DC* [1990] 2 AC 580 (HL).

[94] *Hooper* (n 2). See Lord Hoffmann at [46–47] (receptive to the suggestion) and Lord Brown at [122–24] (who applied *Fire Brigades Union* (n 92)).

[95] *Hooper* (n 2) [46–47]; also [75]–[83] (Lord Hope).

[96] *New London College* (n 6) [28].

abrogation taken from *De Keyser's Royal Hotel* applies with equal force in the context of the Crown's common-law powers as in the context of the prerogative powers, it might be thought that the narrower the basic residual powers and capacities of the Crown are taken to be, in line with the view taken in *De Smith*, the stronger the proposed point of distinction would be. This remains an area to be explored in future.

In *Hooper*, Lord Brown considered that the Social Security Contributions and Benefits Act 1992 (which provided for payments to be made to widows, but not to widowers) impliedly excluded the Crown's common-law power to introduce 'a scheme to make matching extra-statutory payments to widowers'.[97] However, it may be that his judgment was a reaction to the suggestion by the claimants in that case that the Crown should use its powers to introduce a scheme to make payments to an entire class of persons. He did not address a narrower class of case, regarding the continued existence of the Crown's common-law powers to make payments to settle claims brought in Strasbourg by individual widowers. He did not suggest that such payments as had been made had been unlawful. It is possible that a distinction between the two types of situation might be spelled out, but it is not straightforward to see how a clear dividing line could be articulated.

Turning to review of the exercise of the Crown's powers which are untouched by or survive legislative intervention, the distinction which has previously been drawn between the court's control via examination of the existence and extent of a prerogative power and the proposition that the court 'cannot inquire into the propriety of its exercise'[98] is not a particularly stable one. One can easily conceive of the 'extent' of a prerogative power as qualified by conditions as to the way in which it is exercised, much as one can conceive of the extent of a statutory power as qualified by such conditions (for example, that it should be exercised having regard to relevant considerations, in a fair manner, respecting legitimate expectations and so on).

For prerogative powers, therefore, it is possible to say that the courts can find inherent limits in the powers themselves, reflecting their nature as powers recognised by the common law as conferred uniquely on the Crown for the public benefit. There are many aspects of the public good, and the obligation to act fairly and properly respecting procedural safeguards can be regarded as one dimension of it. As Lord Pearce said in *Burmah Oil*,[99] the Crown is subject to the rule of law. It is not difficult to see that this can be taken to import a procedural dimension. In *Burmah Oil* the House of Lords held that demolition of property in the face of the Japanese advance

[97] *Hooper* (n 2) [122]–[124].
[98] As proposed in *GCHQ* (n 5) at 398.
[99] *Burmah Oil* (n 5) 147.

in Burma in World War II was lawful in exercise of the royal prerogative, but that such a general prerogative power, going beyond taking action which was necessary on the battlefield itself, could not be exercised without making payment of compensation. Lord Reid observed that 'the wider the scope of the prerogative [that is, beyond cases of pure battlefield necessity] the stronger is the case for compensation';[100] in other words, the proper exercise of prerogative was taken to be conditional upon acceptance of an obligation to pay compensation. As Markesinis notes, the strong impression from this is that the courts were clearly, albeit indirectly, attempting to regulate the way in which prerogative rights were exercised.[101] It might equally be said that the wider the scope of prerogative powers, the stronger the case that they should be exercised fairly and on rational grounds. The tendency noted by Markesinis has strengthened and widened.

The conception of prerogative power as conferred on the Crown for the public benefit has allowed the courts to identify or interpret the powers as subject to qualification as to the manner of their exercise, in much the same way as basic qualifications are read into statutory powers—that they be exercised within the bounds of the power in question, without procedural impropriety and on a rational basis. For executive prerogative powers, this step was taken decisively in *GCHQ*; for legislative prerogative powers, in *Bancoult (No 2)*.

This framework of reasoning does not seem apposite in relation to control of the Crown's common-law powers (for example, to make contracts, to hold and spend money or to own property). The private law rights the Crown has (for example as owner of property, as a party to a contract, as a person with a cause of action in restitution or tort and so on) are the same as those which a natural person has. It is, I think, difficult to say that the ordinary private law rights the Crown possesses are somehow, unlike private law rights of anyone else, subject to implicit limitations *qua* rights. The private law rights the Crown has should be regarded as tools in the hands of the Crown (acting by its executive agents). The critical question is to examine limitations to which the person wielding those tools might be subject.

I therefore suggest that the basis for judicial control of the exercise of those rights lies not in implied limits in the rights themselves, but in implied limits to the extent of the Crown's powers as a corporation sole, as recognised by the common law. The Crown enjoys the private law rights it holds as tools which may only be employed by it for the purposes for which the common law recognises it as having special legal personality as a corporation sole, that is, for the public good. This suggested model is one of a sort of common-law ultra vires doctrine, where certain attempts at action by the Crown would be found to be unlawful and ineffective (for example,

100 Ibid, 106.

101 Markesinis (n 22) 296.

where acting for improper purposes—such as if bribed—or in a capricious or arbitrary manner); or where the Crown's power to act as corporation sole is regarded as conditional on ministerial advice being given, and that advice is itself open to legal challenge on such grounds. The analysis also allows for incorporation of standards of fairness to be applied and enforced in respect of action by the Crown to utilise its powers. It simply tracks in that regard the way that fairness standards are found to be implied into the powers of statutory corporations wielding public authority, as implied conditions for the lawful exercise by them of their powers, including private law powers.[102] The recent observation by Lord Sumption in the *New London College* case that 'it is open to question whether the analogy with a natural person is really apt in the case of public or governmental action' perhaps opens the way to the sort of more explicit and searching analysis which I have attempted in this essay.[103]

This analysis indicates that Maitland's lament that the common law used the concept of corporation sole rather than the State has in practice been addressed over time. The Crown as corporation sole is regarded as the repository for certain forms of state power, and is subject to legal control.

VI. THE SIGNIFICANCE OF "FUNDAMENTAL RIGHTS" IN JUDICIAL REVIEW OF EXERCISE OF CROWN POWERS

A. Review on Grounds of Violation of Fundamental Rights: Professor Harris's Position

Professor Harris has suggested that the doctrine of the principle of legality applied to statutory construction, using the idea of fundamental rights, can also be applied to control exercise of the Crown's common-law powers.[104] He says that fundamental rights are rights in positive law, and that they can only be compromised if the principle of proportionality is satisfied.[105] He maintains:[106]

> It would be inconsistent and arbitrary for the Government to be constrained by fundamental common law rights when exercising a statutory or prerogative power of decision-making, and yet able to compromise such rights when exercising its residuary freedom to do that which is not legally prohibited. To uphold such rights in respect of Government statutory and prerogative decision-making is to recognise their status in positive law, so it follows that such positive law rights

[102] Cf *Wandsworth LBC v Winder* [1985] AC 461 (HL).
[103] *New London College* (n 6) [28].
[104] Harris (n 79).
[105] Ibid, 385–89.
[106] Ibid, 394.

> will be available to impose judicially enforceable limits on the Government's purported exercise of its residuary third-source freedom.
>
> If this were not so, the Government would be free to do under the third source that which the court would not be willing to recognise the Government as capable of doing under a vague statutory authorisation. Also, should Government third-source action not be so constrained, employment of the principle of legality in statutory interpretation would not achieve its objective.

On the basis of this reasoning, he advances a justification for a particularly strong form of judicial control of exercise of the Crown's common-law powers:[107]

> When the Government is acting under the third source, there is no positive law specifically authorising the Government action and therefore no positive law empowerment to weigh against the competing common law fundamental right. Rather, the reviewing court in the course of making a proportionality decision, has to weigh its own assessment of the Government's argued justification for its decision, independent of any positive law right, against a contextual appreciation of the competing common law fundamental right.

There are a number of difficulties with this analysis. The most fundamental is that Professor Harris goes too far in trying to characterise the rights in question as having the status of positive law rights of individuals. The fundamental or constitutional rights to which he refers are properly to be analysed as strong constitutional presumptions in the interpretation of statutes, particularly employed to justify reading down statutory provisions drafted in wide general language. They are not positive law rights in the sense suggested by Professor Harris.[108] They do not constitute private law rights in the sense of enforceable rights such as those enjoyed by individuals under the law of contract or the law of tort. It is questionable whether fundamental or constitutional rights exist in the common law as a dimension of common-law constitutionalism. There is much to be said for the recent assessment by Brice Dickson, who gives the answer 'no' to the question whether the House of Lords or the Supreme Court has recognised the concept of 'constitutional rights' within the common law.[109]

Moreover, Professor Harris's argument proves too much. If the fundamental rights referred to in the interpretation of statutes under the principle

[107] Ibid, 395–96.

[108] Eg *Watkins v Secretary of State for the Home Office* [2006] UKHL 17, [2006] 2 AC 395, [26], [58–64] (inappropriate to use concept of 'constitutional right' to develop the law of tort); *R (Youssef) v Secretary of State for Foreign and Commonwealth Affairs* [2012] EWHC 2091 (Admin), [2013] 2 WLR 904. cf P Sales, 'A Comparison of the Principle of Legality and Section 3 of the Human Rights Act 1998' (2009) 125 *Law Quarterly Review* 598.

[109] B Dickson, *Human Rights and the United Kingdom Supreme Court* (Oxford, Oxford University Press, 2013) ch 2.

of legality have the status of positive legal rights, it is difficult to see how the Crown would have *any* legal power to infringe them by exercise of its common-law or prerogative powers.[110] That would be contrary to basic constitutional law.[111] As he himself notes, the Crown has 'no positive law empowerment to weigh against the competing common law fundamental right'. Yet at the same time he says that the Crown may infringe such a right, subject to review by the courts. It is obscure, on his analysis, how the Crown could do this. Perhaps he might say that a common-law fundamental right has defeasibility built into it: it is to be interpreted as a right not to be affected in a particular way unless there is a sufficient countervailing public interest. But this is a formulation of a right which is not used in any of the cases, and is at a level of complexity which one might think it is difficult for the courts simply to state as a positive law right at this stage of development of the law. It is not a right of the simple form typically recognised by the common law, such as a contractual right or a right to protection of the law of tort.

More particularly, it is not a right with the formulation used by the courts when operating the principle of legality in the field of statutory interpretation. In that context, simple so-called fundamental rights are identified,[112] and the question is whether there are sufficient indications in the text or scheme of the statute being interpreted to show that Parliament intended to disapply that right or override that interest when conferring statutory power upon some person. The defeasibility in relation to that right or interest is not built into the formulation of the fundamental right, but rather is a function of the interpretation of the statute. This discussion brings out the inappropriateness of the analogy with the principle of legality proposed by Professor Harris.

An attempt to rely on fundamental rights of this kind outside the context of statutory interpretation would be inappropriate and would give them excessive force.[113] In the context of statutory interpretation, the fundamental rights are defeasible, in the sense that they are always capable of being overridden by the language or scheme of the statute, read in light of all applicable aids to interpretation. But outside that context, there is no framework in which they can be balanced against other public goods or

[110] At any rate, in the case of prerogative powers, absent some exceptional special authorisation supplied by the power itself, as in *Burmah Oil* (n 5). The Crown has no such authorisation in relation to exercise of its common-law powers.

[111] See the authorities at n 48.

[112] Although the language of 'rights' is used in the cases, that is really a way to indicate a particular intensity of recognised interest sufficient to trigger the principle of legality approach to interpretation of statutes. The list of fundamental rights, understood in this sense, is not entirely stable or closed: D Feldman, 'The Nature and Significance of "Constitutional" Legislation' (2013) 129 *Law Quarterly Review* 343, 345–46.

[113] As the House of Lords found in the context of the law of tort in *Watkins* (n 108).

interests, and potentially overridden where appropriate in the overall public interest. Professor Harris's approach gives the notion of constitutional rights excessive force as a constraint upon governmental action.

The context in which fundamental rights are deployed under the principle of legality is also very different for a further reason. Where the principle of legality is applied, constitutional or fundamental rights are used to read down what would otherwise be *new* wide powers for a public authority created by the legislature. The principle operates as an aid to interpretation of legislative powers to safeguard against the courts construing wide statutory formulations of new powers too readily according to the literal language used. The principle makes clear it is wrong to interpret legislation in this way, without due regard for the background of constitutional principles and expectations against which the legislation was passed. It operates as a check that Parliament really did intend to qualify or override those rights.[114] But Professor Harris seeks to treat such rights, even though they are not positive law rights, as cutting down or limiting *existing* rights or capacities of the Crown. These are not 'rights' which have ever been used in this sense.

This also undercuts Professor Harris's contention, in the passage quoted above, that unless the courts limit the exercise of the Crown's common-law powers by reference to fundamental rights, the principle of legality would be by-passed in an illogical way and would not achieve its objective. This is not correct.[115] The principle of legality operates as a safeguard against over-broad interpretation of new statutory powers. It is not undermined if it is not applied in relation to the Crown's existing common-law powers. In relation to exercise of those powers, the ordinary principles of judicial review provide an appropriate degree of judicial control against misuse. Issues of fundamental rights do have a place in the application of those principles, as a feature of the rationality test as explained below; but they do not give rise to the sort of intensive decision-making by the courts in place of judgments made by the executive which Professor Harris advocates.

Finally, recent authorities on the Crown's prerogative and common-law powers either do not support, or are positively inconsistent with, Professor Harris's proposed approach. In *ABCIFER* there was reference to a test that like cases should be treated alike unless there is a valid reason for treating them differently.[116] But this is readily assimilated as an aspect of rationality

[114] *R v Secretary of State for the Home Department, ex p Simms* [2000] 2 AC 115, 131–32 (HL); Sales (n 108).

[115] See *Bancoult (No 2)* (n 5) [45], where Lord Hoffmann refers to the principle of legality as set out in *Simms* and makes it clear it does not imply that application of ordinary judicial review standards to exercise of prerogative powers is inappropriate.

[116] Above (n 2) [83–86]; Harris (n 79) 377.

analysis, and has been so assimilated.[117] In *Bancoult (No 2)*, there was unanimity of approach by both the Law Lords in the majority[118] and those in the minority[119] as to the appropriate analytical pathway where fundamental rights are potentially affected by exercise of prerogative powers, namely that those rights are taken into account as an aspect of rationality review, leading to a requirement of heightened or anxious scrutiny on the model set out in *R v Ministry of Defence, ex p Smith*.[120] This, surely, is very strong authority against the approach proposed by Professor Harris: it is difficult to see why there should be a more intrusive approach to judicial review in the case of exercise of the Crown's common-law powers (which can produce no change in the rights or status of citizens) than in respect of the Crown's legislative prerogative powers (which can).

Still more recent authority has rejected an attempt to rely on fundamental rights and the principle of legality as a constraint on government action outside the context of interpretation of statutory powers. In *R (Youssef) v Secretary of State for Foreign and Commonwealth Affairs*,[121] the Divisional Court (Toulson LJ and Silber J) held that the principle of legality is a principle of statutory interpretation which has no application in a case involving exercise of the Crown's powers at common law to make representations in support of or against including the claimant on international lists of persons subject to sanction or control on grounds of suspicion of involvement in terrorism. The decision was upheld on appeal.[122] The Court of Appeal characterised the powers being exercised as prerogative powers and confirmed that a conventional rationality test was applicable.

B. Fundamental Rights and Rationality Review

By contrast with the approach proposed by Professor Harris, it is suggested that the proper role of 'fundamental rights' in the context of judicial control of the Crown's prerogative and common-law powers is as a factor relevant to application of the rationality test, in the flexible way in which that test is applied with due sensitivity to context under the approach set out in *ex p Smith*.[123] The courts have not swung from a position in which exercise of the Crown's prerogative and common-law rights was thought to be

[117] *Matadeen v Pointu* [1999] 1 AC 98, 109 (PC).
[118] *Bancoult (No 2)* (n 5) [45] and [52–58] (Lord Hoffmann); [111–14] (Lord Rodger); [120], [123] and [131–32] (Lord Carswell).
[119] Ibid, [71–72] (Lord Bingham); [162–86] (Lord Mance). This was also the approach of the Divisional Court and the Court of Appeal: see the summary by Lord Mance at [162].
[120] *R v Ministry of Defence, ex p Smith* [1996] QB 517 (CA).
[121] *Youssef* (n 108).
[122] *Youssef* [2013] EWCA Civ 1302, [2014] 2 WLR 1082, [36–43].
[123] *R v Ministry of Defence, ex p Smith* (n 120).

beyond review to a position in which the courts are taken to be the primary judge of the circumstances in which they may be exercised; rather, they have adopted a nuanced middle ground, in which the executive remains the primary decision-maker but subject to ordinary established judicial review standards.

The practical outcome is that executive action in reliance on the Crown's prerogative and common-law powers is subject to constitutional legal controls; but if, notwithstanding those controls, it is thought to require greater regulation by way of statutory underpinning, that is a matter left to Parliament. By contrast, the approach proposed by Professor Harris would involve greater initial direct control by the courts which, if found to be unduly restrictive, would need to be corrected by intervention by Parliament. The position to which the authorities seem to point at the moment is more consistent with the way in which control of the Crown's prerogative and common-law powers has developed up till now, by gradual piecemeal intervention by Parliament legislating to supersede those powers. It also involves the implicit recognition that legislative time is itself a scarce resource and that the courts should generally leave it to government and Parliament to decide how it should be used.

In the context of the *ex p Smith* approach, 'fundamental rights' are a way of describing powerful factors or interests which tend to reduce the scope of discretion under the rationality standard, but which fall to be balanced against other factors which may tend to widen it.[124] That in turn gives rise to questions about how the variable rationality test operates in this context, or indeed in any context.

The flexible nature of the concept of rationality in English public law is well recognised, but perhaps not always well theorised. How can there be a spectrum of different levels of rationality, reflecting different intensities of judicial scrutiny? Is not an appeal to the idea of 'rationality' an appeal to a single, non-flexible standard? Or, as is sometimes said in relation to one formulation which reflects a more intensive form of rationality review—the 'anxious scrutiny' test[125]—every judge always gives anxious scrutiny to every administrative decision which he or she is called on to review; so the test does not appear to offer clear criteria to differentiate it in its application from ordinary rationality review.

I suggest that the answer to the conundrum of a flexible rationality standard lies in the density, or otherwise, of common background understandings which form the context in which the administrative decision in question falls to be considered.[126] As Alastair MacIntyre explains, invoking

124 See, eg *Bancoult (No 2)* (n 5) [58] and [114].

125 *Bugdaycay v Secretary of State for the Home Department* [1987] AC 514 (HL).

126 Cf A MacIntyre, *Whose Justice ? Which Rationality?* (London, Duckworth, 1988); Sales (n 19).

Aristotle and Hume, 'practical rationality with a determinate structure is always informed by … the practices of some distinctive form of social order and … it is *qua* member of such a form of social order and not merely *qua* individual that someone exercises determinate practical rationality'.[127] Rationality can only be assessed in a social context which presupposes and reflects common values and understandings. There is no neutral, free-standing form of rationality. Practical rationality is an aspect of a tradition, a 'systematically embodied form of human life' with its own evaluative practices.[128]

The idea can be illustrated by two cases. In *R v Secretary of State for the Environment, ex p Hammersmith and Fulham LBC* the House of Lords considered a designation by the Minister of local authorities as having engaged in excessive expenditure.[129] Since his power of designation involved the exercise of political judgement, in relation to which our constitutional traditions allow for a wide divergence of views and resolution of differences in the political arena, only a very attenuated form of rationality review was applicable.[130] In *Kennedy v The Charity Commission*, on the other hand, the Supreme Court referred to the duty of the Commission to consider whether to release information to journalists about inquiries it had conducted into charities subject to its jurisdiction and made it clear that the exercise of its discretion would be highly conditioned by a presumption in favour of openness, having regard to the role of the Commission to report on charities and maintain public confidence in them and the relevance of basic principles of open justice. The standard of rationality review would be more intensive, given the context of the background understandings regarding what was to be expected of the Commission against which it would take place.[131]

The case of review of exercise of the Crown's prerogative and common-law powers provides a good test ground to examine this approach, because of the absence of a statutory framework to inform the rationality context. By contrast, where it is the exercise of a statutory power which is in issue, the primary source of the relevant background understandings will be the statutory scheme in which that power is embedded. However, even in that situation, there will be scope for argument by reference to other background understandings, not set out or directly reflected in the statute itself,

[127] MacIntyre (n 126) 320–21.

[128] Ibid, 391.

[129] *R v Secretary of State for the Environment, ex p Hammersmith and Fulham LBC* [1991] 1 AC 521 (HL).

[130] Ibid, 597.

[131] *Kennedy v The Charity Commission* [2014] UKSC 20, [45]–[56], [106]–[132], cf [234]–[247]. See also *Sandiford* (n 31) [2014] UKSC 44, [65]–[66]; *R (Ingenious Media Holdings plc) v HMRC* [2013] EWHC 3258 (Admin), [50].

but nonetheless capable of informing the rationality context in respect of that power: 'fundamental rights', criteria of rational, non-capricious behaviour such as like treatment of like cases, general political principles and expectations and so on (the list is not closed).

A rationality approach based on referring to the density of common background understandings offers the advantages that, first, it could allow the courts to spell out and articulate the underlying factors which drive the ebb and flow of intensity of review under the rationality heading, thereby promoting greater transparency and predictability of response; and, secondly, flowing from that, it would allow scope for integrating in a more coherent and satisfactory way the judicial review standards to be applied in highly varied statutory contexts and also in relation to the Crown's prerogative and common-law powers. There should be a common focus on identifying the criteria according to which rationality of a measure may be assessed.

A further attraction is the scope for integrating this approach, with width or narrowness of administrative discretion driven by identified and articulated factors, with the important focus in administrative law in recent years on the principle of legality in the context of statutory interpretation.[132] It is in the context of identifying what is to count as a 'fundamental right' or interest sufficient to trigger a more intensive standard of rationality review that the case law on the principle of legality *is* capable of providing assistance. This is because the question asked for the purposes of that principle (what background understandings are sufficiently strong to lead to an expectation that Parliament did not intend to qualify them by mere general words in a statute?) is very similar to the question asked on intensified rationality review (what background understandings are sufficiently strong to lead to an expectation that the decision-maker ought rationally to have particularly good reasons to override them?). The operation of the principle of legality draws upon common background understandings which are taken to inform the meaning which Parliament intended a statutory provision to have. There is a sort of partnership between the courts, Parliament and Government in identifying those common background understandings. In order to use the principle of legality to produce a plausible interpretation of Parliament's intended meaning in promulgating legislation (and one which can be regarded as legitimate in light of Parliament's democratic authority as the body entitled to frame and make law and to have its intention in doing so respected and given effect), the courts have to identify background understandings which not only they would subscribe to but

[132] Sales (n 108).

which it can reasonably be said other constitutional actors, in particular parliamentarians, also share.[133]

Of course, there is scope for judges to seek to impose their views when interpreting what Parliament has done, on the basis that they imagine that the only reasonable or plausible view of background understandings is their own.[134] That is why the principle of legality as a principle of statutory interpretation is potentially dangerous from a constitutional point of view, since if applied without caution it may be used by judges to re-write a statute without having sufficient warrant for overriding the intention of Parliament, the institution which is charged with promulgating laws and has the democratic legitimacy to do so.[135] Respect for democratic legitimacy imposes an obligation on the courts to try to be clear-eyed about what background understandings really are so commonly and powerfully held as to inform statutory interpretation in this way, by application of the principle of legality; otherwise they may put their own legitimacy as decision-makers in jeopardy in the eyes of the public. This discipline has forced the courts to engage in reasoning drawing on our common political and constitutional traditions to identify the interests or so-called fundamental or constitutional rights which require special recognition and protection in this way, using those traditions as a source of legitimate objective standards of judgment to which the courts can make appeal when justifying their decisions.

This style of reasoning lends itself to being adapted to inform the flexible approach to identifying relevant standards for rationality review. *Bancoult (No 2)* provides a good example. The courts can seek to identify then draw upon common background understandings of what is generally right and proper in order to impose stricter standards of rationality (that is, a narrower area of discretion for the decision-maker). This mode of inquiry is capable of being more determinate as a guide to the practical content of the flexible rationality standard, since it appears to offer practical criteria to which the courts can refer both for guidance and to legitimise the decisions they make. The cases on the principle of legality can furnish determinate source material to which the courts can refer to assist in identifying such background understandings.

Law and legal doctrine are addressed to a range of audiences. We live in a constitutional culture which generates background understandings,

[133] Sales (n 84) 228. There is an important difference between the principle of legality and the application of the rationality standard as regards the relevant time to address the question of background understandings: for the former, for reasons of democratic and constitutional principle, it is the time at which Parliament enacts the law in question; for the latter, it is the time at which a public official acts, since the rationality of his actions will depend upon the background understandings in place at that time.

[134] See, eg J Sumption, 'Judicial and Political Decision-Making: the Uncertain Boundary' [2011] *Judicial Review* 301.

[135] *R v Lord Chancellor, ex p Lightfoot* [2000] QB 597, 609 (Laws J).

which may be more or less commonly held and which may change over time. Observations by Jack M Balkin about the interpretation of the US constitution are equally or still more apposite in the current discussion:[136]

> Constitutional argument relies on professional judgment, but professional judgment relies on assumptions about what both professionals and nonprofessionals think is reasonable at any point in history. The self-image of professionals is that of reasonable people who proceed through reasoned arguments; therefore professionals often care deeply about what others think is reasonable or beyond the pale. That is, they care about reasonableness as a social product. But what is reasonable in this sense of the word depends on the practice of persuasion in public life, the institutions of public thought and expression, and the gradual development of public values and public opinions. Hence legal professionals' sense of reasonableness depends indirectly on the success or failure of the mobilisations and countermobilisations that shape and influence public values and public opinion.

There is a range of sources which inform judicial and public opinion and which together are capable of generating background understandings which may come to be widely shared so as to have strong normative force within what Balkin calls a 'spectrum of plausibility' about constitutional legal claims.[137] 'Reasonableness is not a single set of correct views; rather it is a distribution of possible positions about which reasonable people might differ, bounded by other views that are off-the-wall. The boundaries of the reasonable and the unreasonable, which people use to judge legitimacy, are produced in social life, including through politics.'[138] However, if the courts wish to use these understandings to inform rationality review, there is an onus on them to spell out what they are and the evidence for them.[139]

The form of the reasoning on rationality where a special interest or 'right' of this kind is identified becomes this: given that this identified, generally recognised important interest or 'right' is to be interfered with, is it rational for the decision-maker to take the measure in question? In the manner explained by MacIntyre and Balkin, our common social life and our political and constitutional traditions inform the standards of rationality to be applied.

It is important to recognise that incorporation of this sort of analysis into the rationality standard provides a more limited basis for intervention by the courts in executive decision-making than the distinct cross-use of the principle of legality proposed by Professor Harris. Rationality is a limited

[136] JM Balkin, *Constitutional Redemption: Political Faith in an Unjust World* (Cambridge, Mass, Harvard University Press, 2011) 12.

[137] Ibid, 180.

[138] Ibid, 61. On the concept of public opinion, see also BN Cardozo, *The Paradoxes of Legal Science* (New York, Columbia University Press, 1928) 47–56; J Thompson, *British Political Culture and the Idea of 'Public Opinion', 1867–1914* (Cambridge, Cambridge University Press, 2013).

[139] Cf Sales (n 84) 230.

basis for intervention for two important reasons. First, our pluralist society is characterised by deeply contested individual, social and political outlooks and standards of judgement. It may be difficult to identify with clarity an understanding or expectation which is sufficiently widely held or recognised as to allow the conclusion that the general standard of rationality has been affected by it to the degree that would justify application of a more intensive standard of judicial review. Secondly, it is highly significant that under even an intensified rationality approach, the public authority charged with making the decision remains the primary decision-maker, whose evaluative judgement regarding how to proceed is not to be second-guessed by the courts, but only checked to see that it falls within the rationality parameters of judgement allowed to it.[140]

VII. THE CROWN AND THE HUMAN RIGHTS ACT 1998

Ministers of the Crown, when acting as such, are public authorities. When they act in exercise of the Crown's common-law or prerogative powers, or in exercise of their own legal capacities for public purposes, the usual duty to act compatibly with Convention rights under section 6(1) of the Human Rights Act 1998 (HRA) will apply in relation to them in the same way as to any other public authority. It is the HRA which now creates for Ministers, as for other public authorities, the most direct and powerful obligation to act in compliance with human rights. This is done straightforwardly as a matter of statutory obligation.

However, there is a way in which exercise of the Crown's prerogative or common-law powers may be immunised against this statutory obligation. The Crown can exercise its powers by means of promulgating an Order in Council. An Order in Council is designated a form of primary legislation for the purposes of the HRA.[141] This means that it takes effect according to its terms, even if it is incompatible with Convention rights. The only remedy in such a case is a declaration of incompatibility under section 4. Where an Order in Council requires action to be taken or provides that action may be taken notwithstanding possible incompatibility with Convention rights, the statutory obligation under section 6(1) of the HRA is displaced by virtue of section 6(2), in the same way as it may be by primary legislation in the form of a statute. But this does not mean that the Order in Council is immune from review on ordinary judicial review principles, including in particular on rationality grounds.[142] In important respects, those rationality grounds may be conditioned by Convention rights operating as part of

[140] Cf *Matadeen* (n 117) 609.
[141] HRA, s 21(1)(f)(i).
[142] *Bancoult (No 2)* (n 5).

the background of relevant constitutional understandings, just as they may inform the content of the principle of legality.[143]

VIII. CONCLUSION

We are playing 'catch up' with notions of the State, slowly adjusting the medieval concepts of kingship and rule which have survived, tempered by the fires of the Civil War and the Glorious Revolution, into our times.[144] Those concepts now encounter the dominant conceptions of democracy and rule of law in a modern constitutional state which, in the second decade of the twenty-first century, frame our attitudes to constitutional and public law. Maitland's prediction at the end of his essay that the State as a concept would come to assert itself in our legal thinking is coming true.

The growth of judicial review in relation to the Crown's prerogative and common-law powers also bears out another of Maitland's observations. Maitland wrote to Dicey: 'The only direct utility of legal history … lies in the lesson that each generation has an enormous power of shaping its own law.'[145] We have the legal conceptual resources inherent in our common-law tradition to move on, and the case law shows we are moving on, from excessively medieval conceptions of the Crown.

[143] *R (Osborn) v Parole Board* [2013] UKSC 61, [2013] 3 WLR 1020; *Kennedy v The Charity Commission* (n 131) [45]–[47]; *R v Lord Chancellor, ex p Witham* [1998] QB 575 (QBD); *R (Faulkner) v Secretary of State for Justice* [2013] UKSC 23, [2013] 2 AC 254, [29] (referring to the naturalisation of human rights standards into domestic law).

[144] For a general review, see McLean (n 9). Developments in the law also address the relationship of the state understood as a juristic person and the state understood as a legal system: ibid, chs 7–9.

[145] Quoted in *GCHQ* (n 5) 417. cf M Krygier, 'Law as Tradition' (1986) 5 *Law and Philosophy* 237–62.

15

Respecting Deference as Respect: Rights, Reasonableness and Proportionality in Canadian Administrative Law

MARK D WALTERS*

I. INTRODUCTION

The idea of proportionality in law is both new and old. Let me begin this essay with a brief story about its oldness.

Once upon a time, the judges of an island kingdom gathered to decide a case involving the question of whether the king could, without the consent of the legislative assembly for the kingdom, impose a charge upon his people for the purpose of building ships to protect the realm from a threatened invasion. Normally the king needed an enactment of the legislature to take property from his subjects. But some years earlier, the king's lawyers had argued that there was a special law of state separate from the ordinary law of the land that clothed the king with the absolute power to act for the public good in all matters of state. On that occasion, an old but wise jurist had voiced his objections to this argument. There was only one law of the land, he said, and although this law respected executive power it also bounded and admeasured or apportioned executive power. In the course of deciding the case on the ship tax, the judges now appeared to accept this proposition. Although they said that the king had the power to appropriate the property of individuals for the public good in times of emergency, they also concluded that this power came from the ordinary, general or common law of the land.

The result of this acknowledgment was profound. It had been said before, at least by those who thought there was a separate law of state,

* Faculty of Law, Queen's University, Ontario. My thanks to Stephanie Lalonde for her research assistance in preparing this essay. I also wish to acknowledge the funding assistance provided by the Social Sciences and Humanities Research Council of Canada.

that ordinary lawyers and judges could not examine the king's acts of state because those acts were based upon a kind of reasoning that was alien to their ways of thinking. But having accepted that the king's power in matters of state derived from the ordinary law, the lawyers and judges present that day began to examine this power in the ordinary legal way. They began to articulate reasons for why statesmen were better placed than judges to make decisions about how to respond to certain kinds of problems. They started to discuss the possibility that, even so, the king's special power might be conditioned by certain principles. As one lawyer argued by analogy, a ship's master may be justified in throwing goods overboard in order to save the ship from a storm, but not simply because he sees a distant cloud on the horizon. The power was an awesome one and its exercise was justified only in cases of necessity. Another lawyer went further and said that the power could not be used arbitrarily but had to honour the ideal of equality, and so the king could not impose burdens upon some people and not others without reason. The judges were unsure about some of these points. In the past they had said that the king could do no wrong and that he was the sole judge of what the exigencies of state demanded. But now at least one of the judges ventured the claim that an unreasonable use of the king's power without cause would not be warranted by their judgment in the case that they decided that day.

By upholding the king's power, it appeared at first as though the judges had simply affirmed the absolute discretion of the sovereign to act for the public good as he thought best. Yet those who listened carefully to the debates of the lawyers and judges in this case detected signs of a change. They could see something that even the judges themselves did not fully appreciate: that the discretionary power of the king, having been enveloped by ordinary law, was now a subject for ordinary legal discourse, and as a result there emerged the possibility of examining acts of the sovereign in light of principles of equality, necessity, coherence and reasonableness that are inherent within that kind of discourse. They could see now what the old jurist meant when he said that the ordinary law respected and admeasured power at the same time. They could see that respect or deference should be extended to the executive only insofar as executive power is admeasured or apportioned, or, in other words, only insofar as the use of power is justified as proportionate. Those who observed saw the possibility for a new legal culture in which the sovereign would have to show not just that he had the formal authority to act but also that his acts were substantively justified. In this new legal culture, the awesome power of sovereignty would be reserved for real storms not distant clouds.

The story I have just told is not entirely fanciful. It is based upon the famous *Case of Ship Money* decided in 1637.[1] I have, of course, taken some

[1] *R v Hampden* (*Case of Ship Money*) (1637) 3 St Tr 825.

liberties with historical truth. I have imagined that there were observers who heard in the speeches delivered in the *Case of Ship Money* evidence of an emerging legal culture, a culture of justification, in which proportionality structures the legal exercise of executive discretion. This part of the story is imagined, but it has some foundation in fact. It has been said that the early seventeenth century in England was a time of 'cultural transformation' which saw older ideas of the common law as a set of customs peculiar to particular courts give way to a newer idea of the common law as a comprehensive normative framework within which governance generally was to be understood.[2]

But was English legal culture transformed into a culture of justification? Was proportionality adopted as a principle governing the justification of governmental power? The old and wise jurist in my story is Sir Edward Coke—and in fact Coke *did* insist both that there was no separate 'law of state' and that the king's prerogative was 'highly tendered and respected' but also 'bound[ed]' and 'admeasured', that is apportioned, by the common law.[3] Furthermore, the speeches in the *Ship Money* case *did* contain the arguments about 'equality', 'necessity' and 'reasonableness' (and distant clouds) that were described in my story.[4] Something like proportionality *is* evident in these lines of thought. However, it must be said, the idea that the common law would only respect acts of executive discretion if they met a test of proportionality was at best inchoate in the legal narratives of the day—indeed, for that matter, it is an idea that is not fully accepted in common-law jurisdictions in relation to the exercise of statutory discretion, let alone prerogative discretion, even now. After more than three centuries, we are still learning what it means to live in a culture of justification.

In this essay, I will focus upon the place of justification and proportionality within the public law of one common-law jurisdiction—Canada. Proportionality has a firm foothold in Canada: it governs the judicial review of legislative acts and governmental decisions that limit rights that are guaranteed by written constitutional law, which means, for the most part, rights guaranteed by the Canadian Charter of Rights and Freedoms.[5] Proportionality is assumed to arise from, and to be confined by, the field of constitutional law and constitutional rights. I will argue, however, that this understanding of proportionality is too narrow and that the 'cleavage'[6]

[2] A Cromartie, 'The Constitutionalist Revolution: The Transformation of Political Culture in Early Stuart England' (1999) 163 *Past and Present* 76, 81–82, 107.

[3] 'Proceedings in Parliament Relating to the Liberty of the Subject' (1628) 3 St Tr 59–234, at 68, 78, 81–82, 153. Crown lawyers had pushed the idea of a 'law of state' separate from the common law in *Darnel's Case* or *Case of the Five Knights* (1627) 3 St Tr 1.

[4] *Ship Money* (n 1) 926, 927, 989, 1010, 1231.

[5] Canadian Charter of Rights and Freedoms, Part I of the Constitution Act, 1982, being Schedule B to the Canada Act 1982 (UK), 1982, c 11.

[6] M Taggart, 'The Tub of Public Law' in D Dyzenhaus (ed), *The Unity of Public Law* (Oxford, Hart Publishing, 2004) 455, 467 ('The cleavage of [Canadian] public law in Charter rights on the one side and everything non-Charter on the other is not attractive').

between review based on the Charter and review based on common-law principles is unjustified. Proportionality is properly understood as a principle closely associated with the rule of law that is engaged whenever the exercise of legislative, executive or administrative discretion affects any important rights, interests, values, or expectations, including (but not limited to) the category of rights that Mike Taggart in his influential argument on proportionality and reasonableness described as 'fundamental common law rights'.[7] Proportionality is, we may say, a general principle of common law.

That I have begun my argument about proportionality in Canada with a story based on an ancient case from English legal history may seem strange—but there is method to my madness. Of course my story is full of anachronistic references. I have alluded to ideas like Etienne Mureinik's 'culture of justification' and David Dyzenhaus's 'deference as respect' that have been developed only recently.[8] I have drawn inspiration from a body of literature that is only now emerging that links justification and proportionality to a general theory of authority, legality and legitimacy.[9] And of course the very idea of 'proportionality' that is central to my story is one that really only emerged from its late-nineteenth-century origins in Prussian administrative law to take shape within German public law in the mid-twentieth century, and its migration through the decisions of the European Court of Human Rights to Canada and then to other common-law jurisdictions and other legal systems is very much a late-twentieth/early-twenty-first century phenomenon.[10] Still, I think anachronism has some value on this occasion. Thinking about the old common law in light of modern ideas of justification, deference and proportionality may help us to understand things about the common law that we might otherwise have overlooked. The idea of proportionality, despite its modern and continental genesis, may capture well the implicit logic and aspirations of the common law in its formative moments—and perhaps too in its present-day manifestations.

Reorienting our thoughts about proportionality in this way may be particularly helpful in a common-law jurisdiction like Canada, where proportionality is considered to have been imported from continental Europe

[7] M Taggart, 'Proportionality, Deference, *Wednesbury*' [2008] *New Zealand Law Review* 423, 465–69.

[8] E Mureinik, 'A Bridge to Where? Introducing the Interim Bill of Rights' (1994) 10 *South African Journal of Human Rights* 31; D Dyzenhaus, 'The Politics of Deference: Judicial Review and Democracy' in M Taggart (ed), *The Province of Administrative Law* (Oxford, Hart Publishing, 1997) 279. On the connection between the 'culture of justification' and 'deference as respect', see D Dyzenhaus, 'Law as Justification: Etienne Muireinik's Conception of Legal Culture' (1998) 14 *South African Journal of Human Rights* 11.

[9] M Cohen-Eliya and I Porat, *Proportionality and Constitutional Culture* (Cambridge, Cambridge University Press, 2013).

[10] A Barak, *Proportionality: Constitutional Rights and their Limitations* (Cambridge, Cambridge University Press, 2012) 182.

through the written text of a human rights instrument. This positivist understanding of proportionality leaves it isolated from other areas of public law—in particular from administrative law. Proportionality, from this perspective, is part of a special law of the constitution that is separate and above administrative law. To reimagine proportionality as part of the common law, then, is to return to an older common-law tradition that I hope my story about ship money brings to mind, namely, the idea of a singular *ordinary* law of the land that shapes the exercise of governmental power by virtue of principle not pedigree. My argument will be that proportionality is a common-law principle that forms part of a body of unwritten constitutional principles expounded through ordinary styles of legal interpretation, and that as such it contributes to the coherence and unity of public law. It is a principle, to put it simply, that protects important rights and interests whether these rights and interests happen to find shelter under written constitutional law or not.

The topic of proportionality and its reach is broad and complex, and I will not attempt to address all of its dimensions in this essay. I will instead focus upon the debate that has emerged in Canada about whether cases involving administrative discretion and the Charter belong to constitutional law or administrative law. The latest case on this point, *Doré v Barreau du Québec*, may offer some support for the idea that proportionality is a common-law principle with the potential to extend past Charter cases.[11] After looking at this debate, I will then return to the broader themes of justification, proportionality, and the unity and ordinariness of public law. I will conclude by saying that the extension of proportionality in Canada beyond the world of written constitutional rights will ultimately depend upon the full acceptance by judges of the idea of 'deference as respect' that Professor Dyzenhaus develops, and in particular the culture of justification and the unity of public law that this idea implies. I will seek to resurrect the old idea that there is just one law of the land, and even if that law has special administrative and constitutional law dimensions, those dimensions are integrated through the common cause of legality.

II. JUDICIAL REVIEW AND THE BORDER BETWEEN ADMINISTRATIVE AND CONSTITUTIONAL LAW

There was a time, long before the advent of the Canadian Charter of Rights and Freedoms, when constitutional values could be woven seamlessly into judicial narratives on administrative discretion—a time when there was a kind of unity of public law in Canada. In a few short paragraphs in the

[11] *Doré v Barreau du Québec* 2012 SCC 12, [2012] 1 SCR 395.

seminal 1959 case of *Roncarelli v Duplessis*, which concerned the decision by a provincial premier to revoke a restaurant owner's liquor licence on grounds of his religious beliefs, Justice Ivan Rand moved from explicit statutory provisions to implied statutory conditions to underlying constitutional values, and back again, with efficient and almost simple assertions of reason, to reach the conclusion that the premier had acted unlawfully.[12] Rand J's reasoning honoured no legal boundaries. The case was a case about non-contractual liability under Quebec's Civil Code, but it was also a case with a distinctively common-law flavour that addressed administrative law concerns about statutory discretion and constitutional law concerns about freedom of religion and the rule of law. It was a private law case about compensation for wrongful conduct and a public law case exemplary of the so-called 'implied bill of rights' that emerged in the days before the adoption of human rights instruments in Canada. If *Roncarelli v Duplessis* was an extraordinary case, it was largely because it manifested so well the unity and ordinariness of public law.[13]

The enactment of the Constitution Act 1982, and with it the Canadian Charter of Rights and Freedoms, served to harden law's internal boundaries and thus to complicate the relationship between constitutional law and administrative law in Canada.[14]

> One problem faced by public lawyers when a human rights instrument is injected into the legal system—whether it be entrenched (as in Canada and South Africa) or by way of an 'ordinary' statute (as in the UK and New Zealand)—is to know how to fit it in with existing administrative laws.

A decade has passed since Mike Taggart made this observation and the problem that he identified still remains unresolved—at least in Canada.

The adoption of human rights instruments in common-law jurisdictions gives rise to two basic questions for administrative law. The first question concerns the adequacy of existing mechanisms of judicial review. Are the general principles governing the judicial review of administrative action sufficient, either as they stand or with modification, to address cases in which it is claimed that administrative discretion infringes a right that the instrument protects; or is an entirely new approach necessary if rights secured by the new instrument are to get the added protection that the instrument contemplates? The second question concerns the broader implications—the ripple effects—of the human rights instrument for other areas of public law. If the instrument does prompt a re-assessment of the law of judicial review, what effect, if any, will these changes have within

[12] *Roncarelli v Duplessis* [1959] SCR 121.

[13] See essays in 'The Legacy of *Roncarelli v Duplessis*, 1959–2009' (2010) 55 *McGill Law Journal* (special issue).

[14] Taggart, 'Tub of Public Law' (n 6) 465–66.

surrounding bodies of law? In particular, might they reinforce developments in the law governing judicial review in cases involving rights and interests falling beyond the protective reach of the new human rights instrument? Will the human rights instrument promote division or unity within public law?

Answering these questions involves addressing the tension between traditional forms of reasonableness review in administrative law and newer forms of proportionality review that are often associated with constitutional law. Under traditional approaches to reasonableness, exemplified by the classic *Wednesbury* formulation, officials who act in good faith and who take into consideration factors relevant to the discretionary power that they have been allocated have the freedom to balance those factors, including any fundamental rights that may be at stake, in any way they wish when exercising their discretionary power, so long as the decision they reach is not so unreasonable that no reasonable decision-maker could have made it.[15] In contrast, proportionality review assumes that human rights have a presumptive weight that will generally prevail over competing policy objectives unless those objectives can be shown to be pressing and substantial in a democratic society and the means adopted to secure them are rationally connected to the objective, impair rights as little as possible, and produce salutary results that are not outweighed by deleterious effects.

In Canada, this four-part proportionality test is primarily associated with the judicial task of testing the constitutionality of *legislation* rather than *administrative* acts. It was borrowed from European sources in the 1986 case of *R v Oakes* in order to determine whether legislation that limits a right protected by the Canadian Charter of Rights and Freedoms may be saved under section 1 of the Charter—which provides (echoing phrases found in the European Convention on Human Rights) that Charter rights are guaranteed 'subject only to such reasonable limits prescribed by law as can be demonstrably justified in a free and democratic society'.[16] The derivation of proportionality in *Oakes* from section 1 of the Charter therefore gives proportionality a textual foothold within written Canadian constitutional law.

However, it would be wrong to assume that proportionality is therefore textually imprisoned as a result. In this respect, it is helpful to recall that just a few years after *Oakes* the Supreme Court of Canada ruled in *R v Sparrow* that legislative limitations on 'existing aboriginal and treaty rights', the rights that are recognised and affirmed for the aboriginal

[15] *Associated Provincial Picture Houses Ltd v Wednesbury Corporation* [1948] 1 KB 223 (CA).

[16] *R v Oakes* [1986] 1 SCR 103. The European influence, though important, was not explicit in the Court's judgment. See D Grimm, 'Proportionality in Canadian and German Constitutional Jurisprudence' (2007) 57 *University of Toronto Law Journal* 383.

peoples of Canada by section 35 of the Constitution Act 1982, must be justified under a proportionality test analogous to *Oakes* (as supplemented by additional requirements, such as a duty of consultation, arising from the special fiduciary relationship existing between the Crown and aboriginal peoples). This despite the fact that the aboriginal and treaty rights secured by section 35 are not subject to section 1 of the Charter and there is no other 'explicit language' mandating a justification test for these rights within the Constitution.[17] *Sparrow* suggests, then, that proportionality transcends *Oakes* and section 1 of the Charter and that it draws its normative force from the architecture of principle that defines Canadian constitutionalism broadly conceived.

This general point is perhaps illustrated by a case that is now largely forgotten in Canada. In the 1985 case of *Fraser v Public Service Staff Relations Board*, a case which involved the judicial review of an administrative decision made before the Charter came into force that restricted freedom of political expression, the Court reasoned that the freedom in question, as 'a principle of our common law constitution', could not be limited unless the decision could be justified as meeting standards that look (in retrospect at least) roughly like what the Court would describe a year later in *Oakes* as proportionality.[18] As Justice Jean Beetz would observe in 1987, the 'balancing of conflicting values' on judicial review in order to ensure that rights are not inappropriately limited may take place 'under s 1 of the *Charter*, or in a common law or administrative law context such as the *Fraser* case'.[19] For a brief moment, then, proportionality *was* acknowledged as a general common-law principle—but that moment passed and proportionality's common-law manifestation was forgotten as the attention of public lawyers turned to the interpretive challenges presented by the written provisions of the new Charter.

Although proportionality subsequently gained notoriety in Canadian law in relation to the review of the constitutionality of legislation, the analytical framework adopted for proportionality in *Oakes* mandates a form of structured and intensive scrutiny of governmental action that is arguably superior to traditional or even modified forms of reasonableness review in cases where the exercise of administrative discretion is alleged to infringe human rights. Although a 'crude distinction' between reasonableness and proportionality must be avoided, given the variable intensities with which both can be applied,[20] the more exacting form of justification

[17] *R v Sparrow* [1990] 1 SCR 1075, 1108–109, 1114–19. See D Newman, 'The Limitation of Rights: A Comparative Evolution and Ideology of the *Oakes* and *Sparrow* Tests' (1999) 62 *Saskatchewan Law Review* 543.

[18] *Fraser v Public Service Staff Relations Board* [1985] 2 SCR 455, [20].

[19] *Ontario (Attorney General) v OPSEU* [1987] 2 SCR 2, [148].

[20] M Elliott, 'From Bifurcation to Calibration: Twin-Track Deference and the Culture of Justification' (ch 4 in this volume) part V.

for governmental acts demanded by proportionality has led to its adoption, or at least calls for its adoption, by judges reviewing administrative action affecting human rights secured by written human rights instruments. Writing in 2004, Taggart assumed that the 'famous Canadian *Oakes* test' (or some version of proportionality like it) would govern the law of judicial review of administrative discretion involving human rights in both the United Kingdom, under the Human Rights Act 1998, and New Zealand, under the New Zealand Bill of Rights Act 1990.[21]

For scholars like Taggart who see a victory of proportionality over traditional reasonableness review in cases arising under written human rights instruments, the next question is whether proportionality might extend beyond the scope of human rights instruments as a principle of common law.[22] However, in Canada, despite the initial possibilities for such an argument presented by the *Fraser* case, the debate has taken a different trajectory. Little attention has been given to the possibility that proportionality might structure reasonableness review in non-Charter cases.[23] But more puzzling, perhaps, is the fact that in recent years judges have rejected the use of *Oakes* proportionality even when reviewing administrative discretion involving Charter rights—though they appear to have replaced it with an administrative law reasonableness test based on the *spirit* of *Oakes*.[24] Common lawyers from other jurisdictions may rightly ask: what is going on in Canada?

What is going on in Canada, I think, is a tendency by judges to emphasise the divided and exceptional nature of public law rather than its unity and ordinariness. To make this point, however, it will be necessary to sketch the debates on proportionality and Charter rights in Canada over the past 25 years or so.

The initial position of the Supreme Court of Canada articulated in the 1989 case of *Slaight Communications* was that when the exercise of a statutory discretion limited a Charter right the decision would be held invalid unless it could be justified under the *Oakes* proportionality test mandated by section 1 of the Charter.[25] The only point of debate at that time was whether judges needed to perform the proportionality analysis mandated by constitutional law if the decision under review was obviously

[21] Taggart, 'Tub of Public Law' (n 6) 476. This view proved correct in relation to the UK, but has not been fully realised in New Zealand: C Geiringer, 'Sources of Resistance to Proportionality Review of Administrative Power under the New Zealand Bill of Rights Act' (2013) 11 *New Zealand Journal of Public and International Law* 123; H Wilberg, 'The Bill of Rights in Administrative Law Cases: Taking Stock and Suggesting Some Reassessment' (2013) 25 *New Zealand Universities Law Review* 866.

[22] Taggart, 'Proportionality, Deference, *Wednesbury*' (n 7) 470.

[23] A rare exception is G Régimbald, 'Correctness, Reasonableness and Proportionality: A New Standard of Judicial Review' (2005) 31 *Manitoba Law Journal* 239.

[24] *Doré* (n 11).

[25] *Slaight Communications Inc v Davidson* [1989] 1 SCR 1038.

unreasonable in the administrative law sense and would be quashed for that reason anyway. Writing for the majority, Chief Justice Brian Dickson concluded that because reasonableness review in administrative law is based on 'unarticulated and undeveloped values' and lacks the same degree of 'structure and sophistication' as proportionality review, the application of the reasonableness standard might produce misleading results in value-laden Charter cases.[26] It thus made sense to bypass the less onerous administrative law analysis and go straight to the more rigorous constitutional law analysis in cases where it is claimed that administrative discretion infringes Charter rights.

There were two closely-related criticisms of *Slaight Communications*. First, it was said that judges were wrong to assume that the common law governing reasonableness review in administrative law was necessarily unstructured and unsophisticated in human rights cases. If given the chance, the common law might develop structure and sophistication in such cases; but if deprived of this opportunity to evolve, administrative law might 'atrophy' instead with negative consequences for non-Charter cases.[27] (We may pause to note that the *Fraser* case,[28] apparently already forgotten, supported this argument about the common law's potential.) Second, it was argued that if the administrative law analysis is skipped and judges go straight to the constitutional analysis, 'a rich source of thought and experience about law and government will be overlooked or lost altogether'.[29] It was better for judges to consider the reasonableness of a decision in the administrative law sense first, so that they could gain an appreciation for the particular values of public administration implicated by the case which would then enrich the subsequent *Oakes* proportionality analysis that would be required if the decision survived the initial administrative law analysis.

The critique of *Slaight Communications* was strengthened considerably by the 1999 decision of the Supreme Court of Canada in *Baker*, which involved the judicial review of an exercise of ministerial discretion denying humanitarian and compassionate relief to a Jamaican woman facing deportation in circumstances that affected the interests of her Canadian-born children.[30] In the judgment quashing the decision on non-Charter grounds, Justice Claire L'Heureux-Dubé restated the basic lesson from *Roncarelli v Duplessis*, that discretionary power must always be exercised consistently with implied statutory limits and underlying constitutional values. She affirmed that discretion might in certain cases be reviewed on a standard

[26] Ibid, 1049.

[27] JM Evans, 'The Principles of Fundamental Justice: The Constitution and the Common Law' (1991) 29 *Osgoode Hall Law Journal* 51, 73.

[28] *Fraser* (n 18).

[29] Evans (n 27) 73.

[30] *Baker v Canada (Minister of Citizenship and Immigration)* [1999] 2 SCR 817.

more intensive than the (*Wednesbury*-like) patent unreasonableness standard that then prevailed in Canada, and, finally, she invoked the idea of 'deference as respect' developed by David Dyzenhaus and so arguably advanced a new approach to justification in Canadian administrative law. This was a clear break with the traditional approach to reasonableness review.[31] Clearly administrative law reasonableness was not so unstructured and unsophisticated as the judges in *Slaight Communications* thought it was.[32] It has been argued that the common law of judicial review is concerned only with the public interest in good administration rather than individual rights and interests, and thus administrative law and constitutional law are rightly bifurcated.[33] As a matter of principle, however, no sharp distinction can be made between upholding the public interest in good administration and respecting individual rights and interests—and the decision in *Baker*, a case that inspired a book of essays entitled *The Unity of Public Law*,[34] is a good reminder of this basic point.

Still, not just the judges in *Slaight Communications* but their critics too, even those relying upon *Baker*, assumed that administrative law and constitutional law offered different perspectives on the justifiability of administrative decisions in Charter cases (though of course the critics thought there would be convergence over time). Was there an alternative view? In his dissent in *Slaight Communications*, Beetz J concluded that the decision under review in that case was an 'absurdity' and 'disproportionate and unreasonable from a practical point of view' and therefore 'unreasonable from an administrative law point of view', and so he found 'difficulty in conceiving how it could be reasonable within the meaning of s 1 of the *Charter*'.[35] Where others saw difference, Beetz J seemed to see common ground between the approaches to review—a view consistent with his earlier statement about the *Fraser* case mentioned above. Though his sketchy comments can be interpreted in a number of ways, one possible interpretation is that the common law of administrative review in human rights cases simply matches proportionality review in constitutional law. But this possibility seems not to have been taken seriously, and it is worth pausing to consider why.

The answer lies in the fact that in the early 1980s the Supreme Court of Canada had entered upon what may be seen as two separate public law

[31] M Liston, '"Alert, alive and sensitive": *Baker*, the Duty to Give Reasons, and the Ethos of Justification in Canadian Public Law' in D Dyzenhaus (ed), *The Unity of Public Law* (Oxford, Hart Publishing, 2004) 113.

[32] G Cartier, 'The *Baker* Effect: A New Interface Between the *Canadian Charter of Rights and Freedoms* and Administrative Law—The Case of Discretion' in D Dyzenhaus (ed), *The Unity of Public Law* (Oxford, Hart Publishing, 2004) 61.

[33] J Varuhas, 'Against Unification' (ch 5 in this volume).

[34] D Dyzenhaus (ed), *The Unity of Public Law* (Oxford, Hart Publishing, 2004).

[35] *Slaight Communications* (n 25) 1063–64.

projects that continue to this day: a constitutional law project of building a body of rules and principles capable of giving powerful normative force to the Charter based upon intensive judicial concern for the fundamental rights that it guarantees, and an administrative law project of constructing a pragmatic and functional law of judicial review centred upon judicial deference to specialist administrative and executive decision-makers.[36] The decisions of Justice Bertha Wilson in two cases illustrate nicely the distinctive interpretive attitudes judges adopted with respect to each project. In the 1985 *Singh* case, refugee claimants argued that they ought to have been given a hearing before their fate was decided. Wilson J agreed. But confronted with the choice between securing fair hearing rights by reading the relevant provisions of the immigration statute in light of common-law principles of procedural fairness and striking the legislation down for violating the claimants' Charter right not to be deprived of life or liberty without fundamental justice, Wilson J sprang almost instinctively for the Charter argument, emphasising the need for judges to uphold the 'supreme law' of the land.[37] We may contrast this attitude with the one that Wilson J adopted in the 1990 case of *National Corn Growers*, a non-Charter judicial review case.[38] Here Wilson J sketched out a theoretical explanation for the functionalist turn in Canadian administrative law. We thus find the denunciation of the Diceyan 'rule of law' view that there is a singular conception of 'ordinary law' that judges must uphold, and we find a corresponding celebration of the 'specialist perspective' of the administrator and the 'pragmatic and functional' values of 'efficiency', 'expertise' and 'experience' that judges must learn to respect. When she exchanged her constitutional law hat for an administrative law hat, so to speak, Wilson J—like many of her colleagues on the bench in similar circumstances—seemed like a different judge.

This is not to say that the two projects are inconsistent. On the contrary, it will be argued in part III of this essay that they are integrated and complementary interpretive enterprises—that no change of hats is necessary at all. The difficulty, however, is that there seems to be an assumption that the two projects *are* separate and theoretically distinct. The classic American image of constitutional rights captured by Ronald Dworkin, that rights are 'trumps' that judges enforce over public policy goals,[39] was never really an accurate depiction of rights enforcement under the Charter, given the Canadian commitment to the European proportionality model. But, as Taggart observed, even within the '(constitutional) methodology

[36] The development of the administrative law project has not been, it should be noted, entirely smooth. See P Daly, 'The Struggle for Deference in Canada' (ch 12 in this volume).

[37] *Singh v Minister of Employment and Immigration* [1985] 1 SCR 177, [32], [33], [69].

[38] *National Corn Growers Assn v Canada (Import Tribunal)* [1990] 2 SCR 1324, 1332–43.

[39] R Dworkin, *Taking Rights Seriously* (Cambridge, MA, Harvard University Press, 1977) 184–200.

of proportionality' one must start the analysis 'with the right', and when the government action cannot be justified 'then the right operates as a (constitutional) *trump* that cannot lawfully be interfered with by the decision maker'.[40] The image of rights as trumps—indeed the post-war rise of a distinctive rights-discourse in general—has exerted an implicit but powerful hold over the judicial mind and helps to explain why judges see constitutional law and administrative law as distinctive enterprises.[41]

This assumption is reinforced by the judicial understanding of the administrative law project. The pragmatic and functional turn in Canadian administrative law is at least partly an acceptance of what Martin Loughlin describes as the functionalist 'style' in public law thought, and so it is informed by a scepticism about judicial forms and concepts (especially those associated with rights and the rule of law), as well as a faith in the possibility that norms of good governance appropriate for the modern welfare state will emerge through the practices and experience of specialist administrators.[42] It is significant, for example, that in *National Corn Growers* Wilson J cited the article in which Harry Arthurs famously denounced Dicey's rule of ordinary law as a myth that hides the reality of a 'highly pluralistic legal system' in which broad domains of specialist law developed by non-judges proliferate and flourish.[43]

The judicial concession of control over the various spheres of specialist law to expert administrators is perhaps a distinctly Canadian development.[44] The 'pragmatic and functional' approach was initially used to explain the use of a deferential standard in the judicial review of administrative interpretations of law.[45] But the approach was later extended to the review of discretion in *Baker* and came to be seen as an 'overarching or universal theory' for judicial review of all kinds of administrative decisions[46]—a theory that has retained its normative pull even though the 'pragmatic and functional' label is now eschewed.[47] As a result of the functionalist turn, the very adjective 'ordinary' when applied to 'law' has, in Canada, attracted

[40] Taggart, 'Proportionality, Deference, *Wednesbury*' (n 7) 440.

[41] For a recent defence of administrative-constitutional law bifurcation, see P Daly, *A Theory of Deference in Administrative Law: Basis, Application and Scope* (Cambridge, Cambridge University Press, 2012) ch 5.

[42] M Loughlin, 'The Functionalist Style in Public Law' (2005) 55 *University of Toronto Law Journal* 361. See, in general, MD Walters, 'Jurisdiction, Functionalism and Constitutionalism in Canadian Administrative Law' in C Forsyth and others (eds), *Effective Judicial Review: A Cornerstone of Good Governance* (Oxford, Oxford University Press, 2010) 300–16.

[43] HW Arthurs, 'Rethinking Administrative Law: A Slightly Dicey Business' (1979) 17 *Osgoode Hall Law Journal* 1, 8.

[44] H Wilberg, 'Administrative Law' [2010] *New Zealand Law Review* 177, 192.

[45] *UES, Local 298 v Bibeault* [1988] 2 SCR 1048.

[46] DJ Mullan, 'Establishing the Standard of Review: The Struggle for Complexity?' (2004) 17 *Canadian Journal of Administrative Law and Practice* 59, 62.

[47] *Dunsmuir v New Brunswick* 2008 SCC 9, [2008] 1 SCR 190.

derision from the highest places.[48] Canadian judges have accepted the view, heretical from Dicey's perspective, and from Dworkin's, that the rule of law 'can speak in several voices'.[49] Of course, this pluralistic understanding of the rule of law sits uneasily with a commitment to fundamental rights and values. If such rights and values are to be regarded as reviewable limits on discretion, then, as David Mullan has observed, it is 'simply difficult to see how they fit within the pragmatic and functional approach'.[50]

There is, in short, a sense in which public law in Canada has become divided into special or extraordinary bodies of law each with its own value system or ethic—a functionalist ethic for administrative law and a rights ethic for constitutional law—and these two ethics are not just different from but incommensurable with each other. In those cases where the two normative worlds collide, as they do whenever administrative discretion is exercised in a way that limits Charter rights, this doctrinal and theoretical bifurcation has made it difficult for judges to adopt coherent responses. The initial debate prompted by *Slaight Communications* centred upon the order of analysis. Should the administrative law analysis precede the constitutional law analysis or not? In recent years, however, the territorial claims staked on behalf of the two domains of law have hardened. An unseemly turf war for exclusive possession of cases involving administrative discretion and the Charter has emerged.

The struggle began in earnest in the 2006 case of *Multani v Commission Scolaire Marguerite-Bourgeoys*, a case which addressed whether a school board had infringed a student's Charter right to freedom of religion when it prohibited him from carrying a Sikh religious knife, or kirpan, to school.[51] Writing for the majority of the Court, Justice Louise Charron insisted that 'to rely solely on the principles of administrative law to decide the substantive issue rather than applying the principles of constitutional justification … could well reduce the fundamental rights and freedoms guaranteed by the *Canadian Charter* to mere administrative law principles or, at the very least, cause confusion between the two'.[52] We may say, then, that Charron J saw this case as part of the Court's constitutional law project and thus governed by the rights ethic. She applied *Oakes* proportionality and held the board's decision invalid because the goal of school safety could have

[48] C L'Heureux-Dubé, 'The "Ebb" and "Flow" of Administrative Law on the "General Question of Law"' in M Taggart (ed), *The Province of Administrative Law* (Oxford, Hart Publishing, 1997) 308, especially 310–11.

[49] *Toronto (City) v CUPE Local 79* 2003 SCC 63, [2003] 3 SCR 77, [131] (LeBel J), quoting B McLachlin, 'The Roles of Administrative Tribunals and Courts in Maintaining the Rule of Law' (1998–1999) 12 *Canadian Journal of Administrative Law and Practice* 171, 175.

[50] Mullan, 'Struggle for Complexity' (n 46) 67.

[51] *Multani v Commission Scolaire Marguerite-Bourgeoys* 2006 SCC 6, [2006] 1 SCR 256.

[52] Ibid, [15], [16].

been secured by less stringent measures (by requiring the student to stitch a sheathed kirpan into his clothing rather than banning it outright).

In their concurring reasons, however, Justices Rosalie Abella and Marie Deschamps argued that cases of this kind are 'more appropriately decided by recourse to an administrative law review than to a constitutional law justification'.[53] For Deschamps and Abella JJ, then, the case was part of the Court's administrative law project and so governed by the functionalist ethic. In the end, however, their application of administrative law principles amounted to little more than a kind of implicit and pale version of proportionality: in an analysis that was much less structured than Charron J's, they concluded, as she had, that the school board had failed to consider ways of pursuing school safety without banning the kirpan outright.

The difference in approaches in *Multani* arose in part from different responses to the simple fact that judging the proportionality of a specific administrative decision involves scrutinising particular individuals and facts in a way that judging the proportionality of legislation may not. For Charron J, this simply meant fine-tuning the application of the *Oakes* proportionality test. When *Oakes* is applied to a specific administrative decision rather than a general legislative rule, she observed, the inquiry is not unlike the 'reasonable accommodation' analysis applied under the various provincial and federal human rights statutes in Canada that prohibit discrimination in employment and other private sector relationships.[54] Reasonable accommodation in this sense means that the distinctive needs or attributes of people must be accommodated by adjusting regular practices unless doing so would cause undue hardship to the enterprise in question.[55] This sounds like proportionality—and indeed the Court had by this time already acknowledged that *Oakes* proportionality and reasonable accommodation are 'generally equivalent'.[56]

Deschamps and Abella JJ disagreed. In their view, *Oakes* proportionality is 'conceptually' limited to the task of assessing general rules in light of societal interests, and therefore administrative decisions concerning localised or specialised matters should be left to administrative law reasonableness review.[57] Reasonable accommodation and *Oakes* proportionality are, they thought, in 'two different analytical categories', for one requires dialogue and reconciliation between individuals and the other a measuring of broad societal aims against rights abstractly conceived.[58] 'An administrative law analysis is microcosmic,' they said, 'whereas a constitutional

[53] Ibid, [85].
[54] Ibid, [52]–[53].
[55] *Ontario Human Rights Commission and O'Malley v Simpsons-Sears Ltd* [1985] 2 SCR 536.
[56] *Eldridge v British Columbia (Attorney General)* [1997] 3 SCR 624, [79].
[57] *Multani* (n 51) [119].
[58] Ibid, [29], [131]–[132].

law analysis is generally macrocosmic' and the 'separate streams—public versus individual—should be kept distinct'.[59] They expressed concern about 'blurring the distinction between the principles of constitutional justification and the principles of administrative law' thereby 'impair[ing] ... the analytical tools developed specifically for each of these fields'.[60] Administrative law is a special body of law and '[i]ts integrity should be preserved'.[61] Implicit within these comments was a forceful defence of the distinctive functionalist ethic found in administrative law from the perceived threats presented by the rights ethic of constitutional law.

The battle over the terrain occupied by administrative discretion and Charter rights was waged again in *Doré v Barreau du Québec*, and this time the forces for administrative law won—though not without some compromises.[62] *Doré* involved a decision by a disciplinary tribunal suspending a lawyer from practice for 21 days for writing an inflammatory letter to a judge, a decision that was argued to violate the lawyer's Charter right to freedom of expression. The Supreme Court of Canada upheld the lower courts in rejecting this claim, but in the process it also rejected the position adopted by the majority in *Multani*. Writing for a unanimous Court, Abella J held that the judicial review of an exercise of administrative discretion that limits a Charter right, at least in the adjudicative context, is not subject to the justificatory *Oakes* proportionality test found in constitutional law but rather is to be reviewed using an administrative law reasonableness test—albeit one that is informed by the *spirit* of *Oakes*. The decision therefore contains a curious mix of doctrinal bifurcation and interpretive synthesis.

Abella J's arguments in *Doré* track those she and Deschamps J made in *Multani*. She continued to maintain that *Oakes* is 'conceptually difficult' to apply when reviewing individuated decisions rather than general norms.[63] Her deeper concern, however, was that the constitutional law rights ethic is fundamentally different from the administrative law functionalist ethic, and in these kinds of cases the administrative law ethic should prevail. To apply *Oakes* proportionality in relation to administrative decisions, Abella J candidly stated, 'undoubtedly protects *Charter* rights, but it does so at the risk of undermining a more robust conception of administrative law'.[64] Here Abella J invoked the assistance of the critics of *Slaight Communications* who had argued that by skipping the administrative law analysis in these cases and going straight to the constitutional law analysis, judges lost the

[59] Ibid, [132].
[60] Ibid, [85].
[61] Ibid, [137].
[62] *Doré* (n 11).
[63] Ibid, [3], [4], [36]–[38].
[64] Ibid, [34].

rich learning on law and government embodied by administrative law.[65] However, as we have seen, those critics argued merely that administrative law not be skipped before turning to constitutional law. Now, however, Abella J concluded that administrative law must displace constitutional law as the sole source of governing principle. Only then will the 'expertise and specialization' of the administrator control the task of 'weighing *Charter* values'.[66]

Abella J's reference to Charter 'values' rather than Charter rights is significant, and confusing. In this respect, she turned to a line of cases that establish that although the Charter is not directly applicable in litigation involving private parties who rely upon the common law, the 'values' underlying the Charter must guide judges in the way that they interpret the common law. Given the absence of any claim that a governmental act infringes a Charter right, these cases hold a flexible balancing of competing values rather than the *Oakes* proportionality analysis to be appropriate when considering whether a common-law rule should be modified so that it conforms with Charter values.[67] Abella J concluded that the same kind of balancing should govern cases involving administrative discretion and the Charter—but how far she intended to take this analogy is unclear given that in the case of an administrative decision there *is* a governmental act challenged and there *are* Charter rights at stake.

Abella J persisted with the idea that the Charter is manifested as a set of values within administrative law, putting particular weight on the 1999 *Baker* case. Administrative law may have been unstructured and unsophisticated when *Slaight Communications* was decided, but in her view *Baker* 'altered' that situation and deprived *Slaight Communications* of its foundations.[68] In *Baker*, she said, 'L'Heureux-Dubé J. concluded that administrative decision-makers are required to take into account fundamental Canadian values, including those in the *Charter*, when exercising their discretion'.[69] Administrative law *is* value-based contrary to what Dickson CJ said in *Slaight Communications*.

The use of *Baker* to support the Charter values argument in *Doré* has some difficulties. First, did L'Heureux-Dubé J actually mean to alter the law on this particular point? Perhaps not. Her reference to the classic case of *Roncarelli v Duplessis* suggests that she was merely reminding us that statutory powers must always be exercised consistently with implied statutory limits and general constitutional values like the rule of law. Second, it

[65] Ibid, [27], citing Evans (n 27) and Cartier (n 32).
[66] Ibid, [47], [54].
[67] Ibid, [39]–[41], citing (among other cases) *Hill v Church of Scientology of Toronto* [1995] 2 SCR 1130.
[68] Ibid, [28].
[69] Ibid, [28], citing *Baker* (n 30) [53]–[56].

is important to note that L'Heureux-Dubé J did not actually say (as Abella J said she did) that administrative decision-makers are required to take into account 'fundamental Canadian values, including those in the *Charter*' when exercising their discretion. Rather, L'Heureux-Dubé J said that administrative discretion must be exercised 'consistent with the *Canadian Charter of Rights and Freedoms*' (citing *Slaight Communications* as authority), and she later said that discretion must be exercised consistently with 'the fundamental values of Canadian society, and the principles of the *Charter*'.[70] So while she meant to say that 'values' define the legal contours of discretion,[71] she did not actually refer to 'Charter values'.

It is important to recall that by this time 'Charter values' had become a term-of-art in common-law cases involving private parties where the Charter has no direct application. In these cases, Charter *values* are what judges turn to when Charter *rights* are not available. As Justice Peter Cory had explained in one of the Charter values cases—in a statement with which L'Heureux-Dubé J concurred—'[i]t is very important to draw th[e] distinction between Charter rights and Charter values'.[72] It can therefore be assumed that in *Baker* L'Heureux-Dubé J chose her words carefully. She meant to say that every exercise of administrative discretion must be shaped by Canadian values and Charter principles—not because Charter rights are not directly applicable in such cases but, quite the reverse, because they are.

Whatever L'Heureux-Dubé J may have intended to do in *Baker*, there is little doubt about what Abella J intended to do in *Doré*. By conceptualising Charter rights as Charter values, Abella J was able to advance her claim that the common-law principles governing reasonableness review in administrative law can provide the appropriate mechanism for testing administrative decisions that affect Charter rights. Abella J seemed to think that the Charter is built into the very essence of common-law administrative reasonableness as a set of values that shapes the legal contours of administrative power. From her perspective, the great advantage of applying the Charter indirectly through a set of values incorporated by the common law into the doctrine of administrative reasonableness rather than directly through a source of written, positive constitutional law is that the Charter's meaning will, as a result, be shaped by the rich body of learning on law and government that is supposedly embedded within administrative law. In this way, the Charter is incorporated into the administrative law project and defined by the administrative law ethic.

But if Charter values are incorporated into administrative law, so too are Charter conceptions of proportionality—and this is another dimension of

[70] *Baker* (n 30) [53], [56].

[71] M Moran, 'Authority, Influence and Persuasion: *Baker*, Charter Values and the Puzzle of Method' in D Dyzenhaus (ed), *The Unity of Public Law* (Oxford, Hart Publishing, 2004) 389.

[72] *Hill* (n 67) [95].

interpretive synthesis that marks the *Doré* decision. *Oakes* proportionality may be unsuited for the review of administrative discretion affecting Charter values, but its 'essence', once articulated in the context of administrative reasonableness review, 'works the same justificatory muscles'.[73] Although review of discretion in Charter cases will exhibit meaningful deference to administrators and will be sensitive to individual concerns and localised facts, 'at the core of the proportionality exercise' will be the need 'to balance the severity of the interference of the *Charter* protection with the statutory objectives' that inform the grant of discretion.[74] The result is that 'the role of judicial review for reasonableness aligns with the one applied in the *Oakes* context'—the 'spirit' of the constitutional law proportionality exercise will be replicated in a suitably modified form within the administrative law context leading to 'conceptual harmony' between the two.[75]

How the result differs from Charron J's application of *Oakes* proportionality in *Multani* is unclear. One difference, however, may be that *Doré* assumes that administrative decision-makers themselves will, or should, engage in at least an informal proportionality analysis before making their decisions. The reasonableness of any act of discretion that limits a Charter right will thus be contingent upon an integrated understanding of the reasoning process undertaken by the decision-maker and the application of proportionality to the resulting decision by the reviewing judge—an approach that, as Claudia Geiringer argues, separates Canadian from United Kingdom law on this point and arguably enhances a human rights culture within the executive and administrative branches of government.[76]

In *Doré*, we are taken down a long and difficult road across the borderlands dividing domains of law, from the dangerous land of constitutional law to the promised land of administrative law, only to find upon our arrival that, looking back across the frontier, we miss what we have left behind and we seek to reinvent the old ways in our new home. The insight that values and principles can be transported across doctrinal borders betrays judicial brilliance—but in the end one is left wondering whether a lot of intellectual energy was spent in order to overcome a frontier that is purely imaginary. Perhaps Beetz J was, in his dissent in *Slaight Communications*, right all along: there is no difference between administrative law and constitutional law in cases involving administrative discretion and constitutional rights.

To summarise, then, the travails of the Supreme Court of Canada as it has tried to understand the relationship between administrative law and constitutional law suggest two basic propositions. First, there remains

[73] *Doré* (n 11) [5].
[74] Ibid, [56].
[75] Ibid, [56], [57].
[76] C Geiringer, 'Process and Outcome in Judicial Review of Public Authority Compatibility with Human Rights: A Comparative Perspective' (ch 13 in this volume).

today a very powerful judicial commitment to the idea that administrative law represents a distinctive body of law, the integrity of which must be preserved. Even in cases where administrative discretion affects a constitutional right, the administrative law ethic—one that seems to be informed by functionalism and pluralism—must govern. Second, the Court also appreciates that in these kinds of cases constitutional values must exert some normative force too. The solution, then, has been to reconceive reasonableness review within administrative law as embracing the essence of proportionality review in constitutional law, at least where administrative discretion affects the Charter.

The question that now arises is whether proportionality, having been reborn as an element of administrative law reasonableness, may be extended to protect important rights or interests that fall outside the realm of 'Charter values'.

III. PROPORTIONALITY AS A COMMON-LAW PRINCIPLE

The Supreme Court of Canada has ruled that proportionality forms part of the common law of reasonableness within Canadian administrative law—but only because Charter values have also been held to form part of that law. In this respect we confront a paradox. On the one hand, the incorporation of proportionality into administrative law suggests a healthy kind of interpretive synthesis. On the other hand, however, it seems that this synthesis is a concession judges have made so that they can maintain doctrinal bifurcation between areas of law. The Charter has been given effect in cases involving administrative discretion through values that form part of administrative law rather than as rights guaranteed directly by written constitutional law, precisely because of a judicial desire to maintain a firm doctrinal line between the domains of administrative law and constitutional law. This doctrinal line is thought to exist because the two bodies of law are each assumed to have their own normative orientation or ethic. Charter values have been allowed into administrative law so that they can become redefined as part of *its* ethic as a way of protecting the integrity of administrative law from what are perceived to be imperial threats that the rights discourse found within constitutional law would otherwise present.

Given the reasons for why proportionality has been acknowledged to form part of administrative law in Canada, its extension by judges to protect non-Charter rights or interests seems unlikely, since that would result in the very thing that its incorporation into administrative law was designed to prevent—the constitutionalisation of administrative law. The observation by Dyzenhaus, Hunt and Taggart—'[p]aradoxically, the stronger the protection given to values in the constitutional document, the more traditionalist judges might be inclined to maintain seals on the spheres'

between administrative law and constitutional law—seems applicable in Canada.[77] To take a recent example, in the post-*Doré* case of *Agraira v Canada* the Court upheld the exercise of ministerial discretion to remove from Canada a Libyan national for national security reasons because the man had many years earlier been connected with an anti-Gadhafi group that had on occasion used violence—but neither counsel nor judges thought to consider whether the salutary effects of the decision on national security might have been tenuous and speculative and outweighed by the immediate and profoundly deleterious effects on the man and his family. No Charter rights or values were at stake and proportionality was thus forgotten.[78] As David Mullan noted in 2010, 'it is a case of going from one extreme to the other once the Charter's application is triggered'[79]—and nothing in *Doré* seems to have changed that.

In this final part of this essay, I will argue that in cases like *Agraira*, where the 'values' that are affected by administrative or executive discretion are important values but not 'Charter' values, judicial review should be governed by the same general proportionality principle that governs when Charter values are at stake. This argument follows from two related points. First, proportionality is not an alien idea imported into administrative law, but rather it is a common-law principle that is an integral part of administrative law and exists independently of Charter values. Second, constitutional law and administrative law are not separate domains of law that must be kept apart but complementary parts of a unified system of public law supported by a common and coherent set of fundamental principles of political morality.

These two points are perhaps best explored and explained by revisiting the idea of 'deference as respect' that the Court purported to adopt in *Baker*. In the course of this analysis, however, it will also help to remember the story about the case of ship money that I related at the beginning of this essay. If the idea of a separate law of state is rejected in favour of a singular ordinary law of the land, then proportionality must be considered to be one important way of ensuring that executive discretion is never left outside the law but is always (as Coke said) both respected and admeasured by law.

It is appropriate to begin by recalling the intimate connection between proportionality and justice. Ideas of symmetry, elegance, harmony, and proportion were all linked in classical thought, and the rhetorical value of

[77] D Dyzenhaus, M Hunt and M Taggart, 'The Principle of Legality in Administrative Law: Internationalisation as Constitutionalisation' (2001) 1 *Oxford University Commonwealth Law Journal* 5, 16.

[78] *Agraira v Canada (Minister of Public Safety and Emergency Preparedness)* 2013 SCC 36, [2013] 2 SCR 559, [88], [91].

[79] D Mullan, 'Proportionality—A Proportionate Response to an Emerging Crisis in Canadian Judicial Review Law?' [2010] *New Zealand Law Review* 233, 239.

these ideals was closely related to substantive conceptions of distributive and corrective justice.[80] The assumption that law should exhibit qualities of unity and coherence, both in terms of logical or formal consistency but also in terms of substantive consistency between its various departments and sub-departments and the underlying principles of moral or political thought that they presuppose, was part of a 'humanist' movement in early common-law discourse—and it is this idea of common-law humanism that was reflected much later in the modern ideal of 'law as integrity' that Ronald Dworkin made famous.[81]

The ideal of integrity that Dworkin expounded—the political value of unity and consistency in our moral and legal commitments to each other based on the equal concern and respect owed to all—thus resonates with ideas that inform the ordinary interpretive enterprise in the common-law tradition, and it suggests that the idea of proportionality fits naturally within that interpretive enterprise. However, elements of Dworkin's work have obscured the value of this ideal for the modern administrative state. His talk of right answers, his distinction between principle and policy, and his assertion of rights as trumps are difficult to reconcile with judicial respect for the legal worlds created and inhabited by specialist administrators and the people they regulate.[82] Dworkin's understanding of discretion—as the space left within the hole in the doughnut[83]—leaves the impression, much as *Wednesbury* does, that law stops at the boundaries of discretion. This understanding of discretion permits judicial deference of a sort. Law offers right answers right up to the edge of the discretionary power, ensuring that legal authority exists for the exercise of that power, but within the space left for discretion law has nothing really to say—in this space virtually anything goes, short of 'lunacy'.[84]

On this account, the deference extended to decision-makers is what David Dyzenhaus calls 'submissive deference', a kind of deference found within a culture of authority.[85] Once a government minister qualifies himself or herself for the exercise of authority in a case like *Agraira* for example, the law has no preference as to which decision selected from a range of possible decisions they may make. Indeed, the functionalist ethic that seems to underlie Canadian administrative law may even encourage

[80] T Poole, 'Proportionality in Perspective' [2010] *New Zealand Law Review* 369.

[81] R Dworkin, *Law's Empire* (Cambridge, MA, Harvard University Press, 1986); MD Walters, 'Legal Humanism and Law as Integrity' (2008) 67 *Cambridge Law Journal* 352.

[82] M Allars, 'On Deference to Tribunals, With Deference to Dworkin' (1994) 20 *Queen's Law Journal* 163.

[83] R Dworkin, 'The Model of Rules' (1967) 35 *University of Chicago Law Review* 14, 32.

[84] M Aronson, 'Process, Quality, and Variable Standards: Responding to an *Agent Provocateur*' in D Dyzenhaus, M Hunt and G Huscroft (eds), *A Simple Common Lawyer: Essays in Honour of Michael Taggart* (Oxford, Hart Publishing, 2009) 5, 6 (referring to '*Wednesbury*'s lunacy standard').

[85] Dyzenhaus, 'Politics of Deference' (n 8) 286.

submissive deference, since it says that plural understandings of law and government are to flourish within spheres of administrative discretion—that the rule of law 'speaks in several voices'.[86]

Dyzenhaus offers a different understanding of deference—*deference as respect*—or deference earned through reasoned justification of governmental decisions. Although the Supreme Court of Canada claims to have adopted the Dyzenhausian idea of deference as respect—indeed Justice Louis LeBel has stated that the idea 'captures both the spirit and letter of what courts should be doing when reviewing administrative action'[87]—in fact judges have not yet fully appreciated what 'deference as respect' really implies. Mark Elliott has argued that the amorphous idea of deference in administrative law can only really be understood by reference to an account of what *justification* of governmental decisions is in different contexts, which in turn depends upon normative constitutional theory.[88] This is also Dyzenhaus's position. A closer look at Dyzenhaus's argument reveals that 'deference as respect' arises from a theory about the rule of law which in turn flows from a general theory of law and democracy. Without respecting the theory of law underlying deference as respect, one cannot respect deference as respect—and there is reason to doubt whether the Supreme Court of Canada fully respects that theory. To understand this argument, it is necessary to return to Dyzenhaus's essay on deference as respect.

In his essay, Dyzenhaus explains how judges in common-law jurisdictions have generally tried to embrace two opposing ideals at once, the ideal of 'democratic positivism' (associated with Bentham) that directs judges to obey legislatures and/or those whom the legislature has delegated administrative or executive power, and 'liberal antipositivism' (associated with Blackstone) that directs judges to uphold the innate wisdom of the common law and the value that it places on the rights and liberties of the individual.[89] Dyzenhaus argues that most common-law judges are 'Diceyan' judges in that they are, in effect, torn between honouring the two principles

[86] *CUPE Local 79* (n 49).

[87] L LeBel, 'Some Properly Deferential Thoughts on Deference' (2008) 21 *Canadian Journal of Administrative Law and Practice* 1, 5–6. The essay in which Dyzenhaus explains his idea has now been cited in *10* Supreme Court of Canada judgments: *Canada Safeway Ltd v Retail, Wholesale and Department Store Union, Local 454* [1998] 1 SCR 1079, [29]; *Baker* (n 30) [65]; *Trinity Western University v British Columbia College of Teachers* [2001] 1 SCR 772, [61]; *Law Society of New Brunswick v Ryan* [2003] 1 SCR 247, [49]; *Canadian Union of Public Employees (CUPE) v Ontario (Minister of Labour)* 2003 SCC 29, [2003] 1 SCR 539, [17]; *Barrie Public Utilities v Canadian Cable Television Assn* [2003] 1 SCR 476, [85]; *Toronto (City) v CUPE* (n 49), [122]; *Dunsmuir* (n 47) [48]; *Alberta (Information and Privacy Commissioner) v Alberta Teachers' Association* 2011 SCC 61, [2011] 3 SCR 654, [52]; *Newfoundland and Labrador Nurses' Union v Newfoundland and Labrador (Treasury Board)* 2011 SCC 62, [2011] 3 SCR 708, [11]–[12].

[88] Elliott (n 20).

[89] Dyzenhaus, 'Politics of Deference' (n 8) 280.

of constitutional law that Dicey identified, parliamentary sovereignty and the rule of law, and thus they have come to embody the inconsistent attitudes of democratic positivism and liberal antipositivism.[90] The result is a compromise that produces submissive deference: judges insist upon their monopoly over law up to the point where the legislature carves out a space for administrators, after which they relinquish control and submit to administrative choices made in that space about which of many possible outcomes should be selected. Law on this account is positive law: it is fixed as a matter of fact by legislators, judges, or administrators depending upon where authority is fixed on any given point.

The idea of deference as respect, however, is premised upon a very different theory of law. Dyzenhaus insists that law is not a matter of fact but rather it is an interpretive enterprise that is premised upon reciprocity between state and citizen and upon a commitment to a unity between legality, morality and democratic legitimacy that is achieved through the constant and all-pervasive requirement that power be justified to those in relation to which it is exerted. Dyzenhaus writes:[91]

> My thesis is that the substance of the rule of law is the equality of all citizens before the law and that the form of the rule of law is the procedures whereby public officials demonstrate that they have lived up to—are accountable to—that substance.
>
> It is an anti-positivist thesis in that it claims a distinct moral content to the rule of law. But it is also a democratic thesis, in that it requires that the content be developed through the institutions of government and not determined by abstract philosophising.
>
> ...
>
> [D]eference as respect ... is inherently democratic. It adopts the assumption that what justifies all public power is the ability of its incumbents to offer adequate reasons for the decisions which affect those subject to them. The difference between mere legal subjects and citizens is the democratic right of the latter to require an accounting for acts of public power.
>
> The legislature, the administration and the courts are then just strands in a web of public justification. The courts' special role is as an ultimate enforcement mechanism for such justification.

Dyzenhaus thus imagines law in the same way that the observers in my story about the case of ship money, related at the outset of this essay, imagined law. Law is a 'web' that extends across the range of governance leaving *no* matters of state, no matter how sensitive the issue or how strong the arguments for executive discretion, outside its purview. This law, to be meaningful as *law*, must be in a very basic sense just *ordinary* law,

[90] Ibid, 280–81.
[91] Ibid, 305, 307.

the kind of law that an ordinary lawyer—a simple common lawyer (to borrow an expression)—could reason through on the basis of the commitment to integrity and equality that defines the ordinary legal interpretive method. Of course, just as the judges in the story about ship money did, Dyzenhaus acknowledges that statecraft involves special skills or knowledge that judges do not have, and so the extension of law across the affairs of state will invariably mean that law's perspective on the exercise of power will not always involve a full reconsideration of the decision made but rather will on many occasions be limited to ensuring that power is appropriately justified. Ordinary law will respect but also admeasure power. Or, we may say, law will respect power when it is admeasured or apportioned—or proportionate.

Once law is seen in this way the idea that legislative sovereignty and the rule of law are two constitutional principles that pull in different directions no longer makes sense.[92] The judge's only job is to see if power is justified as law, and this job is not accomplished by *first* defining what law requires and *then* testing governmental decisions against that standard; rather, it means that judges must examine the reasons that justify decisions to ensure that they can be law. Law does not exist *out there*, but rather it is a product of an interpretive discourse that respects the ideas, knowledge, experience and expertise of those who are closest to the challenges of state at issue.

From the Dyzenhausian perspective, then, the idea that judges should defer to administrative selections from a range of reasonable alternative decisions is nonsensical—and so too is the idea that the rule of law can speak in several different voices. The only focus of attention is the actual decision under review and its justifiability, and in this respect legality has a *singular* identity that is revealed through *ordinary* interpretive techniques that take seriously the special knowledge and expertise of legislatures and administrators who made the decision.[93] The Dyzenhausian theory of law is informed by Fuller's idea that law is a reciprocal enterprise between state

[92] Dyzenhaus's views thus share common ground with those of Trevor Allan, whose version of '[c]ommon law constitutionalism … denies that we have to choose between democracy and fundamental rights, or between parliamentary sovereignty and the rule of law': TRS Allan, *The Sovereignty of Law: Freedom, Constitution, and Common Law* (Oxford, Oxford University Press, 2013) 15.

[93] As Trevor Allan has argued, '[m]atters relevant to deference are *internal* to ordinary legal analysis' rather than being invoked after a legal conclusion is reached in order to displace that conclusion: TRS Allan, 'Judicial Deference and Judicial Review: Legal Doctrine and Legal Theory' (2011) 127 *Law Quarterly Review* 96, 116. Allan's objection to the idea of a separate doctrine of deference is not, in other words, inconsistent with Dyzenhaus's 'deference as respect' (see TRS Allan, 'Deference, Defiance, and Doctrine: Defining the Limits of Judicial Review' (2010) 60 *University of Toronto Law Journal* 41, 47), but rather is a response to a view about deference that separates judicial understandings of what the law is from the reasons for why judges should respect the understandings reached by other institutional actors about what the law is. For a critique of Allan's arguments see A Kavanagh, 'Defending Deference in Public Law and Constitutional Theory' (2010) 126 *Law Quarterly Review* 222.

and citizen. But Dworkin's influence is also clear—a debt that Dyzenhaus acknowledges.[94] Like Dworkin, Dyzenhaus believes that the goal of interpretation is always to find the *single* answer that shows the legal order in its best light given its underlying moral and political values. But unlike Dworkin, Dyzenhaus acknowledges expressly the primary role that administrators must play within the modern state for the discovery of that answer in specific cases—subject of course to the critical requirement of justification. Although in his essay on deference as respect Dyzenhaus did not equate justification with proportionality, the connection seems implicit.[95]

The Supreme Court of Canada may have picked up the phrase 'deference as respect', but has it taken on board the theory of law that gives it meaning? In the now-leading case of *Dunsmuir v New Brunswick*, LeBel J, writing with Justice Michel Bastarache, began with a worryingly Diceyan (in Dyzenhaus's sense) discussion of the 'tension' between the rule of law and legislative sovereignty.[96] Later, they stated that they 'agree with David Dyzenhaus' as to the nature of 'deference as respect', but they proceeded to define reasonableness review as follows:[97]

> Reasonableness is a deferential standard animated by the principle ... [that] certain questions that come before administrative tribunals do not lend themselves to one specific, particular result. Instead, they may give rise to a number of possible, reasonable conclusions ... In judicial review, reasonableness is concerned mostly with the existence of justification, transparency and intelligibility within the decision-making process. But it is also concerned with whether the decision falls within a range of possible, acceptable outcomes which are defensible in respect of the facts and law.

This statement suggests that the judges are still unsure about their commitment to deference as respect in its proper sense. The justification branch of reasonableness review embodies deference as respect, but the reasonable-range-of-outcomes branch harkens back to deference as submission. The Court may still be trapped by the functionalist ethic that celebrates pluralist over interpretivist conceptions of legality. And here we confront the real obstacle to deference as respect: it seems inconsistent with the theory of administrative law that judges seem to think defines public law in Canada today. Judges have assumed that they must either impose their view of law and government or they must withdraw altogether and let multiple views

[94] Dyzenhaus, 'Politics of Deference' (n 8) 307 fn 66.

[95] See in this respect, D Dyzenhaus, 'Proportionality and Deference in a Culture of Justification' in G Huscroft, BW Miller and G Webber (eds), *Proportionality and the Rule of Law: Rights, Justification, Reasoning* (New York, Cambridge University Press, 2014).

[96] *Dunsmuir* (n 47) [27]–[33]. See also M Bastarache, 'Modernizing Judicial Review' (2009) 22 *Canadian Journal of Administrative Law and Practice* 227: discussing *Dunsmuir*, he indicated that he and LeBel J 'chose at the outset to provide a foundational overview of the underpinnings of judicial review' which sought '[i]n a nutshell' to explain that 'judicial review seeks to address an underlying tension between the rule of law and legislative intent'.

[97] *Dunsmuir* (n 47) [47].

of law and government emerge among specialist regulators. Dyzenhaus rejects the dichotomy because he adopts an intepretivist theory of law that integrates legality and discretion through a principle of justification.

We are now in a position to return to the case law on administrative discretion and the Charter examined above. The entire line of cases, from *Slaight Communications* to *Doré*, is a dramatic contest between what I called the constitutional law rights ethic and the administrative law functionalist ethic. This is, I think, essentially the same contest that Dyzenhaus describes between liberal anti-positivism and democratic positivism. If we respect deference as respect in a genuine manner, however, it should be clear that these kinds of distinctions no longer exist. Deference as respect is premised upon a distinctive attitude toward law and democracy which denies the possibility of any real divisions between our concern for governmental function and our concern for rights, or between our respect for legislative will and our commitment to the rule of law, or, for that matter, between the body of law known as administrative law and the body of law known as constitutional law. Thinking back to the early common law, the idea advanced by Coke that power is both respected and admeasured suggests that no gaps in law exist where discretion is untrammelled, for there will always be a particular legal perspective—the ordinary legal perspective—available to ask whether respect should be extended to power because it is admeasured or proportionate. Proportionality is the missing link between the ideal of integrity in law and the reality of official discretion in law. Deference as respect implies a culture of justification and a unity of legal reason.

Proportionality is closely linked with integrity in law, and as such it is an aspect of ordinary legal interpretive method within the common-law tradition. Proportionality can thus be said to be a common-law principle. However, in Canada it may also be possible to think of proportionality as taking its place, along with federalism, respect for minorities, democracy, the rule of law, judicial independence and aboriginal self-determination, as an 'unwritten constitutional principle'.[98] Like all unwritten constitutional principles, proportionality should inform legal and constitutional interpretation generally. When administrative discretion affects Charter rights in Canada, administrative law and constitutional law converge and yield the same answers based upon a proportionality analysis, and when administrative discretion affects important rights, interests, values or expectations that have been left outside the protective shelter of written constitutional law, the very same conclusion will obtain.

[98] On unwritten constitutional principles in Canada, see MD Walters, 'Written Constitutions and Unwritten Constitutionalism' in G Huscroft (ed), *Expounding the Constitution: Essays in Constitutional Theory* (Cambridge, Cambridge University Press, 2008) 245.

If *Doré v Barreau du Québec* marked a kind of victory for administrative law in a struggle with constitutional law for ownership over disputed legal terrain, that victory may prove to be short-lived. As this book was going to press, the Supreme Court of Canada rendered its decision in *Loyola High School v Québec (Attorney General)*—the first case to reach the Court since *Doré* to address the judicial review of a discretionary administrative decision affecting fundamental rights protected by the Canadian Charter of Rights and Freedoms.[99] In this case, a decision by the Quebec minister of education refusing to grant an exemption to a private Catholic school from the requirement of teaching a secular course on world religions was held on judicial review to be an unjustified limitation on the Charter right to freedom of religion. This decision was then reversed by the Quebec Court of Appeal. On appeal to the Supreme Court of Canada, Abella J, writing for herself and three other judges, applied *Doré*. She held that rather than apply section 1 of the Charter to see if an administrative decision affecting Charter 'values' was justified, 'a *robust* proportionality analysis consistent with administrative law principles', one that 'respects the expertise' of the decision-maker, was required[100]—and she concluded that the minister's decision in this case did *not* (for the most part) meet that standard. McLachlin CJ and Moldaver J, joined by Rothstein J, wrote separate reasons. Although they were largely in agreement with Abella J's conclusion, they referred neither to *Doré* nor to administrative law principles, but instead framed the question as whether the minister's decision breached the 'constitutional right' to religious freedom, and, if so, whether that breach was 'justified under s. 1' of the Charter.[101] It would seem, then, that three of Canada's highest judges have now retreated back across the frontier into the field of constitutional law in cases dealing with administrative discretion and fundamental rights, for reasons that they have, so far, kept to themselves. And so the unfortunate and unnecessary struggle between administrative and constitutional law in Canada continues.

[99] *Loyola High School v Québec (Attorney General)* 2015 SCC 12.
[100] Ibid, [3], [42].
[101] Ibid, [88].

Index

www.ingramcontent.com/pod-product-compliance
Lightning Source LLC
LaVergne TN
LVHW052218200926
848481LV00001B/147
* 9 7 8 1 5 0 9 9 1 7 0 4 4 *